# GAME CHANGERS

## The Greatest Plays in
## Dallas Cowboys
## Football History

Ed Housewright

TRIUMPH
BOOKS

*To Connor, the best son ever. You're the joy of my life.*

Triumph Books and colophon are registered trademarks of Random House, Inc.

Library of Congress Cataloging-in-Publication Data

Housewright, Ed.
 Game changers : the greatest plays in Dallas Cowboys football history / Ed Housewright.
   p. cm.
 Includes bibliographical references.
 ISBN-13: 978-1-60078-220-6
 ISBN-10: 1-60078-220-5
 1. Dallas Cowboys (Football team)—History I. Title.
 GV956.D3H674 2009
 796.332'94097642812—dc22

                    2009021899

This book is available in quantity at special discounts for your group or organization. For further information, contact:
   **Triumph Books**
   542 South Dearborn Street
   Suite 750
   Chicago, Illinois 60605
   (312) 939-3330
   Fax (312) 663-3557
   www.triumphbooks.com

Printed in China
ISBN: 978-1-60078-220-6
Design by Sue Knopf/Patricia Frey
Page production by Patricia Frey
Photos courtesy of Getty Images unless otherwise indicated

# Contents

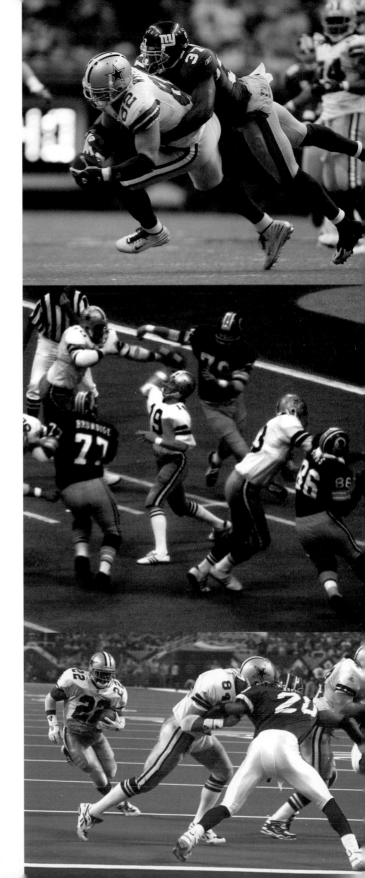

# Foreword

Playing for the Dallas Cowboys was a dream come true for me. In high school I was a quarterback and wore No. 12—Roger Staubach's number. I could never imagine that someday I would be catching touchdown passes from my idol.

I spent a wonderful decade with the Cowboys, from 1977 to 1986. Early in my career I had the good fortune of being paired with Drew Pearson, one of the greatest Cowboys receivers of all time. I'm proud to say that Drew and I terrorized opposing secondaries. Defenses couldn't focus on one of us or the other would burn them.

When I was a rookie, we beat the Denver Broncos 27–10 in Super Bowl XII. How's that for a start to your career? The following season, 1978, I earned a starting position and made the Pro Bowl. I caught 46 passes, averaged almost 18 yards per reception, and scored six touchdowns.

More important, the Cowboys returned to the Super Bowl. Unfortunately, we lost 35–31 to the Pittsburgh Steelers. I had a 39-yard touchdown pass that tied the game 7–7. Regrettably, I never played in another Super Bowl. I came close, particularly in 1979, Staubach's last season. We had a great team but lost to the Los Angeles Rams 21–19 in the divisional playoffs.

The 1979 season was special because I made the most memorable reception of my career. In the regular-season finale I caught an eight-yard touchdown pass that gave us a heart-stopping, 35–34 comeback victory over the Washington Redskins. That play is included in this book.

I have many, many fond memories of my playing days. Equally important, I made life-long friends. I still keep in touch with many of my former teammates, such as Tony Dorsett, Robert Newhouse, Ed "Too Tall" Jones, and, of course, Roger Staubach.

At his retirement ceremony, Roger joked that I constantly said I could get open. But, hey, it was the truth. I didn't believe there was a cornerback in the league who could cover me. And, thanks to Roger, I was able to catch many passes.

As you read *Game Changers: The Greatest Plays in Dallas Cowboys Football History*, I hope you'll feel the excitement we did as players. I'll always consider myself blessed to wear the Silver and Blue and be part of America's Team.

—Tony Hill

Tony Hill

# Great Passes and Catches

Drew Pearson (No. 88) near the end zone after catching the game-winning 50-yard Hail Mary pass. *Photo courtesy of AP Images.*

**December 28, 1975**

# A Play that Defined a Team

## Pearson's 50-yard Hail Mary Catch from Staubach Makes Both into Legends

Drew Pearson and Roger Staubach teamed up for many big plays during the 1970s, but none was bigger than the famous Hail Mary catch. It occurred in a divisional playoff game against the heavily favored Minnesota Vikings in 1975.

The play gave birth to the "Hail Mary" phrase, now commonly used to describe desperate, last-second plays. It also became the signature play of Pearson's outstanding 11-year career, and it cemented Staubach's reputation as a master of the dramatic comeback.

"The game changed Dallas Cowboys history," Staubach said. "We went to three Super Bowls within a span of four years from '75 to '78. A free-agent receiver who made that play helped us to become America's Team. And he got me into the Hall of Fame."

During the 1975 season the Vikings had tied for the league's best record at 12–2, easily winning the Central Division title. They scored the most points in the NFC, averaging almost 27 points a game, while giving up the second-fewest.

The Cowboys, meanwhile, stumbled into the playoffs as a wild-card team with a 10–4 record. Dallas, which had a dozen rookies on its roster, won four games by a total of six points or less. The Vikings, on the other hand, trounced opponents by scores of 38–0, 42–10, and 28–3. Minnesota, coming off two straight Super Bowl losses, seemed to have its best team yet.

# Game Details

## Dallas Cowboys 17 • Minnesota Vikings 14

| | | | | | |
|---|---|---|---|---|---|
| Cowboys | 0 | 0 | 7 | 10 | **17** |
| Vikings | 0 | 7 | 0 | 7 | **14** |

**Date:** December 28, 1975
**Team Records:** Minnesota 12–2, Dallas 10–4
**Scoring Plays:**
MN—Foreman one-yard run (Cox PAT)
DAL—Dennison four-yard run (Fritsch PAT)
DAL—Fritsch 24-yard FG
MN—McClanahan one-yard run (Cox PAT)
DAL—D. Pearson 50-yard pass from Staubach (Fritsch PAT)

The first-round playoff game was played in Metropolitan Stadium in Bloomington, Minnesota, with temperatures in the mid-20s. Snow surrounded the field. Fans huddled in the stands, their breath visible in the icy air. Both teams played sluggishly in the first quarter, which ended without a score. In the second quarter, Minnesota's All-Pro back Chuck Foreman had a one-yard touchdown run to give the Vikes a 7–0 lead.

Dallas tied the game in the third quarter on a four-yard run by Doug Dennison. The score remained 7–7 heading into the fourth quarter. The Cowboys took a three-point lead on a 24-yard field goal by Toni Fritsch. But the Vikings counterpunched with a 70-yard drive, capped by Brent McClanahan's one-yard touchdown run. Minnesota pulled ahead 14–10.

With less than two minutes to play, Dallas got the ball at its own 15-yard line. Staubach already had a reputation for pulling off late-comeback wins, but the odds seemed particularly long this time. The Cowboys faced one of the league's best defenses, the famed Purple People Eaters, led by All-Pro linemen Carl Eller and Alan Page.

The final completion was the most dramatic and kept Dallas in the game. On a fourth down that could have been the Cowboys' last gasp, Staubach connected with Pearson for 22 yards and a first down at the 50-yard line.

Now only 32 seconds remained. Staubach lined up five yards behind center in the shotgun formation. Pearson spread out to the right. He sped down the sideline, and Staubach lofted a long pass that came up short, forcing Pearson to stop and turn around at the 5-yard line. As he did, he collided with Vikings cornerback Nate Wright. Wright fell down, and Pearson caught the ball awkwardly against his right hip.

He ran into the end zone to give Dallas the win, 17–14. Pearson tossed the ball into the stands in celebration, while Minnesota fans sat in stunned silence. The Vikings complained that Pearson illegally pushed Wright to make the catch, but officials let the play stand.

"I have never had a more eerie sensation on the football field than during the aftermath of our touchdown," Staubach said. "The crowd was so shocked there wasn't a sound from the stands. It was as though all of a sudden we were playing in an empty stadium."

After the score, irate fans threw debris onto the field in protest. A whiskey bottle hit field judge Armen Terzian, knocking him unconscious and opening a gash on his forehead that required 11 stitches to close.

In a postgame interview, Staubach uttered the infamous "Hail Mary" statement. In describing the long touchdown pass to Pearson, he said he closed his eyes and threw the ball as far as he could.

"It was just a Hail Mary pass—a very, very lucky play," Staubach said.

**It's over, it's done. There'll be no grieving for me. I have a life to live.**
**—MINNESOTA QUARTERBACK FRAN TARKENTON**

# Drew Pearson

Drew Pearson didn't have great size or speed.

He didn't even have an impressive collegiate résumé when he arrived as a free agent at the Cowboys' training camp in 1973. But Pearson had an unwavering, perhaps inexplicable confidence that he could play in the NFL. He wound up being one of the greatest receivers in Cowboys history during a stellar 11-year career.

Pearson quickly won the trust of quarterback Roger Staubach, the team's inspirational leader. The two began working out regularly in the weeks leading up to the 1973 training camp.

"It didn't take long to realize he caught everything I threw," Staubach said.

Pearson arrived at a fortuitous time. Bob Hayes was entering his final season as a Cowboys starter. The other starter was Otto Stowe, an unproven receiver just acquired in a trade. When Stowe broke his ankle at mid-season, Pearson became a starter and never relinquished the job.

He finished the 1973 season with 22 receptions, a 17.6-yards-per-catch average, and two touchdowns. The next year Pearson caught 62 passes for conference-leading 1,087 yards. He was named All-Pro, an honor he would receive twice more. Pearson provided the Cowboys with a gutsy, dependable receiver who knew how to get open and didn't shy away from taking a hit.

Pearson retired after the 1983 season with statistics that many think should earn him a spot in the Pro Football Hall of Fame. He had 489 receptions for 7,822 yards and 48 touchdowns.

"I lived the American Dream because of a little bit of athletic ability, hard work, and a desire not to disappoint my family and friends," Pearson said.

> You get guys like Drew and Roger, and they just believe they can do it. They've done it before and expect it to happen.
>
> —DALLAS COACH TOM LANDRY

Pearson, pictured here in 1975, became one of the best receivers in Cowboys history and was Roger Staubach's go-to guy.
*Photo courtesy of AP Images.*

January 31, 1993

# A Clutch Catch

### Novacek's 23-Yard Touchdown Powers Dallas to Super Bowl XXVII Blowout

The Dallas Cowboys looked invincible as they rolled into Super Bowl XXVII. They had compiled a 13–3 record, best in team history, and beaten opponents by scores of 27–0, 37–3, and 30–3.

The Cowboys' Super Bowl opponent, the Buffalo Bills, had finished 11–5 and qualified for the playoffs only as a wild-card team. They were making their third straight Super Bowl appearance but still looking for their first victory.

The Cowboys, under brash fourth-year coach Jimmy Johnson, exuded confidence as the game approached. Buffalo, however, got on the scoreboard first. The Bills blocked a Mike Saxon punt, then Pro Bowl back Thurman Thomas scored on a two-yard run to give Buffalo a 7–0 lead early in the first quarter.

Some Cowboys fans panicked. Dallas, one of the league's best teams in the 1960s and 1970s, hadn't been to a Super Bowl in 15 years. Now, with a prime chance to win its third world championship, the Cowboys had committed a costly early blunder.

However, one of Dallas' best players quickly evened the score. All-Pro tight end Jay Novacek caught a 23-yard touchdown pass from Troy Aikman late in the first quarter. His touchdown gave the Cowboys momentum, and they proceeded to trounce the Bills. Only 15 seconds after Novacek's catch, Dallas scored a go-ahead touchdown. At halftime Dallas had a commanding 28–10 lead and extended it to 52–17 by game's end.

Novacek starred throughout the game. He led the Cowboys with seven catches totaling 72 yards. Novacek had been a remarkable find for Dallas. The

Jay Novacek runs for the touchdown after catching a 23-yard pass from Troy Aikman in Super Bowl XXVII on January 31, 1993.

> **W**e caught them in two-deep coverage, and Novacek split the middle of the field, between the safeties, on a 23-yard catch and run for a touchdown. The game was tied and beginning to unfold inevitably in our direction.
>
> —COWBOYS COACH JIMMY JOHNSON ON NOVACEK'S FIRST-QUARTER TOUCHDOWN

# Game Details

## Dallas Cowboys 52 • Buffalo Bills 17

| | | | | | |
|---|---|---|---|---|---|
| **Bills** | 7 | 3 | 7 | 0 | **17** |
| **Cowboys** | 14 | 14 | 3 | 21 | **52** |

**Date:** January 31, 1993

**Team Records:** Dallas 13–3, Buffalo 11–5

**Scoring Plays:**

BUF—Thomas two-yard run (Christie PAT)

DAL—Novacek 23-yard pass from Aikman (Elliott PAT)

DAL—Jones two-yard fumble return (Elliott PAT)

BUF—Christie 21-yard FG

DAL—Irvin 19-yard pass from Aikman (Elliott PAT)

DAL—Irvin 18-yard pass from Aikman (Elliott PAT)

DAL—Elliott 20-yard FG

BUF—Beebe 40-yard pass from Reich (Christie PAT)

DAL—Harper 45-yard pass from Aikman (Elliott PAT)

DAL—Smith 10-yard run (Elliott PAT)

DAL—Norton nine-yard fumble return (Elliott PAT)

Cowboys signed him as a free agent in 1990, expecting him to be a role player, not a starter. Instead, he immediately became a starter and blossomed into one of the league's best tight ends. In his first season, Novacek caught 59 passes. The next year, 1991, he also had 59 receptions. Novacek turned in his best season in 1992. As the Cowboys marched toward the Super Bowl, Novacek grabbed 68 passes and scored six touchdowns, earning Pro Bowl honors for the second straight year.

Dallas back Emmitt Smith called Novacek "sure-handed" and "deceptively quick" in his autobiography, *The Emmitt Zone.*

"With that unorthodox running style of his, he lulls people to sleep, then beats them badly," Smith wrote. "We call Jay 'Paycheck' because he's so clutch."

Novacek played three more seasons for the Cowboys, helping them win two more Super Bowls. In Super Bowl XXVIII, another blowout of the Bills, Novacek caught five passes to tie Michael Irvin for the team lead. In Super Bowl XXX, the Cowboys' final championship of the 1990s, Novacek came through again.

He had five receptions and caught a three-yard touchdown pass in the first quarter to give Dallas a 10–0 lead. Like Novacek's score in Super Bowl XXVII, this one gave the Cowboys a surge that powered them to victory. Dallas defeated the Pittsburgh Steelers 27–17.

Novacek finished his 11-year NFL career with 422 receptions and 30 touchdowns—not bad for a mere sixth-round draft choice by the St. Louis Cardinals. In five seasons with the Cardinals, Novacek had given no indication of the player he would become for Dallas. He started only six games and never had more than 38 receptions in a season.

When he put on the Silver and Blue, he became one of the Cowboys' key contributors in their three Super Bowl wins. No player exceeded expectations more than Novacek.

# Dallas' Stellar Tight Ends

Jay Novacek became the latest in a string of great tight ends for the Cowboys. The list started with Frank Clarke and Pettis Norman in the 1960s and continued with the fiery Mike Ditka and reliable Billy Joe DuPree in the 1970s. Doug Cosbie took over for DuPree in 1982 and broke his receiving records.

Cosbie seemed like the consummate pass-catching tight end—until Novacek arrived as a free agent in 1990. Like Cosbie, Novacek was tall, rangy, and fast. He, too, played more like a wide receiver than a tight end. Novacek surpassed Cosbie's receiving marks in the mid-1990s.

His record, however, lasted only a decade until Jason Witten became the Cowboys' latest tight-end sensation. In his fifth season, in 2007, Witten broke Novacek's reception record of 339. Through 2008 Witten had 429 catches and 25 touchdowns, three more than Novacek scored as a Cowboy.

"Jason has a combination of Doug Cosbie, Billy Joe DuPree, and Jay Novacek," DuPree said. "He's a little faster, a little quicker, than they anticipate."

**Jay always finds a way to get open.**
**—DALLAS BACK EMMITT SMITH**

Jason Witten, perhaps the best receiving tight end in Cowboys history, stiff-arms Antonio Pierce of the Giants in a game on December 14, 2008.

October 23, 2006

# Romo Takes Over

## 53-yard Touchdown Pass Helps Him Lock Up Starting Role

The Tony Romo era began at halftime of the sixth game of the 2006 season.

Drew Bledsoe, the 14-year veteran who started for the Cowboys, had been ineffective in the first half against the Giants. Dallas trailed 12–7, and Bledsoe had completed only seven of 12 passes for 111 yards. He'd also thrown an interception.

Coach Bill Parcells, who brought Bledsoe to Dallas in 2005, made a decision that would change the franchise. He turned over the offense to Romo, and he did well enough to keep the job the rest of 2006—and beyond. Romo threw two touchdown passes against the Giants, the last a 53-yarder to Patrick Crayton. That pass validated Parcells' decision and gave teammates confidence in Romo as the new leader.

Dallas lost the game 36–22, and Romo threw three interceptions. So his debut wasn't flawless. But he gained Parcells' trust and clearly demonstrated the moxie to be a top-notch NFL quarterback. The succession of second-rate quarterbacks the Cowboys had endured since Troy Aikman retired in 2000 finally came to an end.

Romo, who completed 14 of 25 passes for 227 yards, said he was disappointed with his second-half performance against the Giants.

"You go in, and you've got to perform," he said. "That's my job—to help this team win—and I didn't do that."

Parcells gave Romo a qualified endorsement, but that's about all he gives any player.

"Some good, some bad," Parcells said of Romo's play.

Romo's emergence was phenomenal considering how he had begun: as an undrafted free agent from little Eastern Illinois in 2003. He started as the third-string quarterback before working his way up the depth chart.

If Bledsoe had performed as expected, Romo might have waited several more seasons for his chance. Parcells had coached Bledsoe at New England, where he played from 1993 to 2001. Bledsoe had three Pro Bowl seasons but lost his job to Tom Brady, who would develop into an all-time great, leading the Patriots to three Super Bowl wins.

After three so-so seasons with the Buffalo Bills, Bledsoe came to Dallas in 2005. He had a decent season, completing 60 percent of his passes and throwing 23 touchdowns. He was a definite upgrade over the grab bag of predecessors: Vinny Testaverde, Quincy Carter, Anthony Wright, Drew Henson, Chad Hutchinson, Ryan Leaf, and Clint Stoerner. As the 2006 season began,

Tony Romo prepares to throw a 53-yard touchdown pass to Patrick Crayton on October 23, 2006. *Photo courtesy of AP Images.*

# Game Details

## New York Giants 36 • Dallas Cowboys 22

| | | | | | |
|---|---|---|---|---|---|
| Giants | 9 | 3 | 14 | 10 | **36** |
| Cowboys | 0 | 7 | 0 | 15 | **22** |

**Date:** October 23, 2006
**Team Records:** Dallas 3–2, New York 3–2
**Scoring Plays:**
NY—Burress 50-yard pass from Manning (Feely PAT)
NY—Safety, Arrington sacked Bledsoe in end zone
NY—Feely 31-yard FG
DAL—Bledsoe one-yard run (Vanderjagt PAT)
NY—Shockey 13-yard pass from Manning (Feely PAT)
NY—Jacobs three-yard run (Feely PAT)
DAL—Owens eight-yard pass from Romo (Romo run)
NY—Feely 32-yard FG
NY—Dockery 96-yard interception return (Feely PAT)
DAL—Crayton 53-yard pass from Romo (Vanderjagt PAT)

Bledsoe still was relatively young, 34, and seemed to have a lock on the Dallas job.

But he struggled in the first five games, barely completing 50 percent of his passes and throwing seven touchdowns and seven interceptions. His eighth interception cost him his job. It happened in the first half of the Giants game when the Cowboys had marched inside the New York 5-yard line.

"Too many mistakes," Parcells said of his decision to bench Bledsoe.

Enter Romo. He threw an eight-yard touchdown pass to Terrell Owens in the third quarter before connecting with Crayton for the 53-yard score in the fourth. Romo progressed tremendously the remaining 10 games of the 2006 season. He wound up completing 65 percent of his passes and throwing 19 touchdowns—good enough for a Pro Bowl selection. He provided a spark at quarterback the Cowboys hadn't seen since the Aikman era.

In 2007 Romo turned in another Pro Bowl season. He completed 64 percent of his passes and threw an astonishing 36 touchdowns as the Cowboys rolled to a 13–3 record, their best since 1992, easily winning the NFC East. In Romo's first playoff game, the Cowboys again faced the Giants, a wild-card team. The Giants pulled off a shocking 21–17 upset, and Romo's mediocre game didn't help the cause. He was 18 of 36 for 201 yards, with a touchdown and an interception.

But Romo's confidence never wavers. He shook off the Giants game and started the 2008 season in typical fashion. The Cowboys jumped to a 3–0 start as Romo completed 67 percent of his passes and averaged almost 300 yards per game.

The Cowboys clearly have Super Bowl talent after a decade of ups and downs. Most important, they have a strong leader who can match up with any quarterback in the league.

# The Giants' Improbable Championship

The Cowboys had no business losing to the Giants in the 2007 divisional playoff game. That was certainly the consensus of Cowboys players and fans, and they'd had every reason to be confident heading into the game.

Dallas posted a 13–3 regular-season record, easily winning the NFC East. New York finished second at 10–6 and earned a wild-card playoff spot. The Cowboys led the NFC in scoring, averaging more than 28 points per game. They won several lopsided games, such as a 35–7 victory over the St. Louis Rams and a 34–3 drubbing of the New York Jets. The Giants, meanwhile, lost their first two games and had several narrow wins as they chased a playoff spot.

But in the playoffs, regular-season records don't matter. The Giants came into Texas Stadium refusing to be intimidated by the Cowboys. New York struck first on a 52-yard touchdown pass from Eli Manning to Amani Toomer. Dallas went ahead on a five-yard touchdown reception by Terrell Owens and a one-yard

Tight end Jason Witten (No. 82) is tackled by Giants safety James Butler during the 2007 NFC Divisional Playoff Game.

run by Marion Barber. New York tied the score 14–14 with a four-yard touchdown reception by Toomer.

The back-and-forth scoring continued, with Dallas kicking a 34-yard field goal to take a 17–14 lead. But the Giants scored last on a one-yard touchdown run by Brandon Jacobs for the shocking 21–17 win.

Many Cowboys players and fans attributed the loss more to Dallas' poor performance than to New York's good one. But as the playoffs unfolded, the Giants showed they were no fluke. They pulled off another huge upset in the NFC Championship Game, downing the Green Bay Packers 23–20 in overtime.

New York took a 6–0 second-quarter lead on field goals of 29 and 37 yards. Green Bay then countered with a 90-yard touchdown pass from Brett Favre to Donald Driver. A 36-yard field goal gave the Packers a 10–6 halftime lead. The lead flip-flopped several times in the second half. Green Bay kicked a 37-yard field goal in the fourth quarter to tie the game 20–20 and send it to overtime. Just 2:35 into the extra period, Lawrence Tynes kicked a 47-yard field goal to win the game at Lambeau Field. Tynes was an unlikely hero, having already missed two field goals.

In Super Bowl XLII the Giants seemed to face an impossible task: defeating the seemingly invincible New England Patriots. The Pats had compiled a perfect 16–0 regular season, then easily took care of the Jacksonville Jaguars and San Diego Chargers in the playoffs.

The Patriots and the entire country were in for a surprise in the Super Bowl. The Giants scored first on a 32-yard field goal that ended a 63-yard drive. The Patriots responded with a one-yard touchdown run by Laurence Maroney. They held a slim 7–3 lead going into the fourth quarter.

The Giants, however, scored two touchdowns to win 17–14 and pull off one of the greatest upsets in NFL history. The winning play was a 13-yard pass from Manning to Plaxico Burress with only 35 seconds remaining. It capped an impressive 12-play, 83-yard drive that took only 2:07.

"The guys on this team and the run we've made, it's hard to believe—it really is," Manning said.

Patrick Crayton hurdles Giants defensive back Will Demps on his way to a touchdown on October 23, 2006.

Quincy Carter prepares to throw what would become a 36-yard touchdown pass to Jason Witten to secure a 19–3 win over the New York Giants.

January 3, 2004

# Parcells Works His Magic

Carter's Touchdown Pass Seals 19–3 Win Over Giants, Playoff Appearance in Coach's First Year

Jerry Jones hired Bill Parcells in 2003 to work miracles. At the end of his first season it appeared he had. Parcells, who had won two Super Bowls, rebuilt the Cowboys from a 5–11 laughingstock to a playoff team.

Dallas clinched its first playoff appearance since 1999 with a 19–3 win over the New York Giants. A 36-yard touchdown pass from Quincy Carter to tight end Jason Witten put the Cowboys ahead 10–3 and on their way to their most significant win in years.

"This franchise is on its way to getting back on the top," Carter said.

The win gave the Cowboys a 10–5 record. They lost their final game 13–7 to the New Orleans Saints, but the playoff mission had been accomplished. Dallas fans, swooning over Parcells, had visions of a Super Bowl. But the magic ended with a 29–10 loss to the Carolina Panthers in the wild-card playoff game.

Dallas never contended in the game, falling behind 16–3 at halftime. The Panthers extended the lead to 26–3 before Carter rushed for a meaningless nine-yard touchdown in the fourth quarter.

"I'm here to try to win every game as coach," Parcells said. "We had an opportunity to advance, and I'm disappointed that we didn't."

Still, the loss didn't diminish Parcells' status as a miracle worker. He broke new ground in Dallas. In Parcells' three previous coaching stops—the Giants, the Jets, and the Patriots—his team didn't advance to the playoffs in his first year. In Dallas they did.

Parcells had basically taken the same team that had been 5–11 three straight years under Dave Campo. He developed Carter, the third-year quarterback, much more than Campo had. In 2003, under Parcells, Carter completed almost 58 percent of his passes and threw 17 touchdowns—a huge improvement over his two previous seasons.

The Cowboys had taken Carter in the second round of the 2001 draft from Georgia. Jones, in particular, liked Carter's mobility and saw great potential. Most NFL scouts, however, thought the Cowboys took Carter much too high in the draft because of his questionable passing ability. In Carter's first two seasons he did little to win over skeptics. Because of his lackluster history, Carter's 2003 performance was even more encouraging. If Parcells could transform Carter into a top quarterback, the Cowboys' upside would be enormous.

The Parcells touch became evident early in the 2003 season. After dropping the opener 27–13 to the Atlanta Falcons, the Cowboys raced to a 6–2 record at the season's midpoint. The wins included a 38–7 shellacking of the Detroit Lions in which Carter threw three touchdown passes.

In the season's second half, however, the Cowboys played only .500 to finish 10–6. They were maddeningly inconsistent. For instance, they shut out the Washington Redskins 27–0 but played pitifully in a 36–10 loss to the Philadelphia Eagles. The Cowboys' marginal talent became obvious.

However, several players besides Carter emerged as potential stars. Most notable was Witten, a rookie tight end. He caught 35 passes for 347 yards and also proved to be an excellent blocker. The Cowboys' playoff appearance in 2003 created only greater enthusiasm for Parcells' second season in 2004. To almost every-

one's surprise, however, the Cowboys regressed. They dropped to 6–10. The disappointing season included a 49–21 loss to the Eagles.

Maybe the Parcells touch would reemerge in 2005, people thought. His third season was an improvement, as the Cowboys finished 9–7, but they missed the playoffs. After Parcells had taken the Cowboys to the playoffs in his first year, fans expected much more by the third season.

People began to wonder if Parcells was overrated and overpaid. The 2006 season shaped up as a pivotal one. Again the Cowboys finished 9–7, but they snuck into the playoffs as a wild-card team. If the Cowboys advanced, fans would regain trust in Parcells.

But Dallas suffered a heartbreaking, last-second loss to the Seattle Seahawks. The Cowboys trailed 21–20 but had moved to the Seahawks' 2-yard line with 1:19 remaining. They were in prime position for a game-winning field goal.

But the chip-shot kick never came about. Quarterback Tony Romo, also the holder on field goals, let a perfect snap slip through his fingers. He grabbed the loose ball and scampered around the left side for the end zone. But he was tackled two yards short. Seattle won 21–20 ending Super Bowl dreams for another year.

That agonizing play was the last under Parcells' watch. He resigned after the season, issuing a vague news release that gave little indication of his reason. The much-anticipated Parcells miracle never happened.

# Game Details

## Dallas Cowboys 19 • New York Giants 3

| | | | | | |
|---|---|---|---|---|---|
| Giants | 3 | 0 | 0 | 0 | 3 |
| Cowboys | 10 | 3 | 3 | 3 | 19 |

**Date:** December 21, 2003

**Team Records:** Dallas 9–5, New York 4–10

**Scoring Plays:**

DAL—Cundiff 24-yard FG

NY—Bryant 45-yard FG

DAL—Witten 36-yard pass from Carter (Cundiff PAT)

DAL—Cundiff 42-yard FG

DAL—Cundiff 21-yard FG

DAL—Cundiff 49-yard FG

This is a perfect example of how great a coach Bill Parcells really is. Right away he told us we could win, and we believed him. Look at us now.

—TIGHT END DAN CAMPBELL

Quincy Carter throws during a game against the Carolina Panthers at Texas Stadium on November 23, 2003, in Irving, Texas.

# The Strange Career of Quincy Carter

The Cowboys made a huge mistake in drafting Quincy Carter. There's no other conclusion to draw. They took him in the second round of the 2001 draft out of Georgia. Owner Jerry Jones pushed for his selection, intrigued by Carter's running ability and speed.

Most scouts, however, questioned his passing ability and didn't see him as a second-round pick. Carter started eight games as a rookie, and the Cowboys finished 5–11 in 2001. Carter directed three of those victories, but his statistics weren't impressive. Still, he performed better than the other quarterbacks who took the remaining eight starts: Anthony Wright, Ryan Leaf, and Clint Stoerner.

In 2002 Carter split time with a different quarterback, Chad Hutchinson. The Cowboys again finished 5–11, and Carter again produced three victories.

The closest Carter came to a breakout season was 2003, his final with the Cowboys. Under new coach Bill Parcells, Carter started all 16 games, and the Cowboys won 10. Carter completed almost 58 percent of his passes and threw 17 touchdowns.

The Cowboys cut him shortly before the start of the 2004 season amid rumors that he failed a drug test. Carter landed with the New York Jets. They signed him as a backup but released him at the end of the 2004 season.

Carter never played another NFL down. He got a tryout with the Montreal Alouettes of the CFL but was promptly cut. Then he sank to the Arena Football League 2. He first played for the Bossier-Shreveport Battle Wings, then was signed by the new Rio Grande Valley Dorados in late 2008.

November 18, 2007

# T.O.'s Record Day

## Owens' First Four-Touchdown Game Highlights Illustrious Career

Terrell Owens carries a lot of baggage wherever he goes. His me-first attitude at receiver eventually wears thin, no matter how many great catches and touchdowns he makes.

Owens wore out his welcome after eight years with the San Francisco 49ers. Then the Philadelphia Eagles excitedly signed him in 2004. Owens performed on the field, earning Pro Bowl honors with 77 catches and 14 touchdowns. But his sparring with teammates, particularly quarterback Donovan McNabb, caused coach Andy Reid to take a drastic step: he cut Owens after the 2005 season.

Owens, a 10-year veteran at that point, had become a pariah to many in the NFL. But Cowboys owner Jerry Jones is willing to take risks many other owners won't. Jones signed Owens, nicknamed T.O., to a three-year, $25 million contract in 2006.

He proved his worth. Owens caught 85 passes and scored 13 touchdowns. However, he had a maddening tendency to drop passes. More than a dozen catchable balls slipped through his hands. Fans grew so weary that they started keeping a tally and flashing it at games. Jones, however, didn't complain.

In 2007 Owens had one of the best seasons of his glittering career. He had 81 receptions, 15 touchdowns, and a 16.7-yards-per-catch average. He made the Pro Bowl for the sixth time and the first

time since 2004. Owens helped Dallas race to a 13–3 record, tied for best in franchise history.

He had his best game late in the year against the Washington Redskins. Owens caught four touchdowns in a 28–23 win. His final touchdown, covering 52 yards, was the longest and most spectacular. It came midway through the fourth quarter and sealed the victory for Dallas.

"I pride myself in trying to make plays for the team," Owens said. "When my number's called and opportunities are there for us to make plays, I know that's my job."

In 2008 Owens got off to another fast start. In a 28–10 opening-day win against the Cleveland Browns, Owens caught five passes for 87 yards, including a 35-yard touchdown. In the second game, a 41–37 victory

## Game Details

### Dallas Cowboys 28 • Washington Redskins 23

| | | | | | |
|---|---|---|---|---|---|
| Redskins | 7 | 3 | 3 | 10 | **23** |
| Cowboys | 0 | 7 | 7 | 14 | **28** |

**Date:** November 18, 2007

**Team Records:** Dallas 8–1, Washington 5–4

**Scoring Plays:**

WAS—Cooley 19-yard pass from Campbell (Suisham PAT)

DAL—Owens four-yard pass from Romo (Folk PAT)

WAS—Suisham 45-yard FG

DAL—Owens 31-yard pass from Romo (Folk PAT)

WAS—Suisham 39-yard FG

DAL—Owens 46-yard pass from Romo (Folk PAT)

WAS—Suisham 44-yard FG

DAL—Owens 52-yard pass from Romo (Folk PAT)

WAS—Moss five-yard pass from Campbell (Suisham PAT)

# T.O. In His Own Words

From *T.O.*, by Terrell Owens and Jason Rosenhaus, 2006

**On his childhood:** Scrawny and quiet—that's what I was like growing up in Alexander ("Alex") City, Alabama. Alex City is a small country town where there's nothing to do but get into trouble. As a teenager, I was the perfect target for the big bully on the block: I was skinny, awkward-looking, and kept to myself. The one thing I could do well was run, and believe me, I needed to do a lot of that. In my neighborhood, there was always a group of bad teens hanging out, waiting to pounce on a kid like me.

**On why he has excelled:** I am as good as I am because God has blessed me with talent and because I have worked as hard as any person on the planet to get here. Unlike so many other professional athletes, I eat with extreme discipline, rarely drink alcohol, don't smoke, and don't use illegal drugs of any kind. I sleep properly, lift weights, run until I drop, practice intensely, and do everything humanly possible to be the best that I can be.

**When he stood on the Cowboys star at Texas Stadium while playing for the 49ers:** I scored a touchdown in the second quarter, and then I ran from the end zone over toward the middle of the field and stood on the famous blue Dallas star, the symbol of "America's Team." I raised my arms and looked up to the sky. My teammates loved it—and the Cowboys hated it.... The Cowboys players, not surprisingly, responded. Dallas running back Emmitt Smith scored a touchdown later and emulated me, scolding the 49ers sideline.

> **T**his is one of the greatest games, really, that I feel like I've played in, just me coming through in the clutch.
>
> —TERRELL OWENS

**On his greeting in Philadelphia after signing with the Eagles:** I arrived in style: the Eagles flew me in on a private jet and sent a limousine to the airport to bring me to the team's facility. The fans were waiting for me to show up and greeted me like a big shot. I knew how hungry the fans were for a Super Bowl win after losing in the NFC Championship Game three years in a row. It was an exciting time.

**On signing with the Cowboys:** When Jerry Jones flew into Atlanta and picked me up in his private jet, I was holding back tears.... The jet had a big Cowboys star emblem on it, and was the nicest jet I had ever been in. It was decorated with pictures of the three Super Bowl trophies the team won in the 1990s, as well as pictures of the great players on those teams such as Troy Aikman, Michael Irvin, and Emmitt Smith.

**On why he wrote the book:** I'm not asking you to love me, and I certainly don't want you to hate me. I'm just asking you to take into account what I have to say with an open mind. I want you to judge for yourself, not based on what the media says, but based on what I have written.

over Philadelphia, Owens scored two touchdowns, one covering 72 yards.

Near the end of the season, with Dallas at a disappointing 8–5, Owens started doing what he always does: complaining about not getting the ball. He charged that quarterback Tony Romo threw too often to Pro Bowl tight end Jason Witten, a friend.

Ever since Owens entered the league as a third-round pick of San Francisco in 1996, he has been a combustible mix of extraordinary talent and massive ego. From time to time one becomes more dominant than the other. As a rookie Owens started 10 games, catching 35 passes and scoring four touchdowns. He gave indications of his future greatness.

From 1997 through his final season with the 49ers in 2003, Owens was a full-time starter. He made the Pro Bowl four times. His best season came in 2002 when he caught 100 passes and scored 13 touchdowns. In eight seasons with San Francisco, Owens had almost 600 receptions and scored 81 touchdowns, matching his uniform number.

No wonder Philadelphia signed him to a seven-year, $49 million contract before the 2004 season. The next year, however, Owens asked for a new contract, saying he needed to "feed his family." That marked the beginning of the end for Owens with the Eagles. He later criticized the franchise, saying it showed a "lack of class" for not recognizing his 100th career touchdown.

Jones has largely taken a hands-off approach with Owens, tolerating his outbursts while savoring his big plays. At the end of 2007, which ended with a disappointing loss to the New York Giants in the first round, Jones signed Owens to a new four-year, $34 million contract.

Six games into the 2008 season, the Cowboys acquired another Pro Bowl receiver, Roy Williams, from the Detroit Lions. People immediately wondered how Owens would react. Would he pop off, worried that Williams would steal the limelight from him?

Owens was unusually subdued.

"He's a great player," he said. "He gives us another playmaker."

54 CHUCK HOWLEY 1961-1973

17 DON MEREDITH 1960-1968

OWENS
81

Terrell Owens celebrates his fourth-quarter touchdown against the Washington Redskins at Texas Stadium on November 18, 2007.

December 31, 1967

# 50-Yard Option Play Surprises Packers

## Rentzel's Touchdown Catch Gives Dallas Temporary Lead in Ice Bowl

Dallas receiver Lance Rentzel, not Green Bay quarterback Bart Starr, could have been the hero of the Ice Bowl. Rentzel caught a 50-yard touchdown pass early in the fourth quarter that gave the Cowboys a 17–14 lead. The throw came on an option play from running back Dan Reeves.

At kickoff the temperature at Lambeau Field was 13 degrees below zero with a strong wind. As the game progressed, the temperature dropped further. The frozen field more closely resembled an ice rink than a football field. Players on both teams had trouble keeping their footing long enough to make a good gain.

Given the circumstances, Rentzel's catch was even more amazing, and it jolted the mighty Packers.

"When that happened, it seemed to get colder over on our sideline," Green Bay running back Chuck Mercein said.

Rentzel's touchdown gave Dallas its first lead. Green Bay had taken a 14–0 advantage on two touchdown passes from Starr to receiver Boyd Dowler. The Cowboys, however, got back in the game when defensive end Willie Townes hit Starr and caused a fumble. George Andrie, another defensive end, picked up the loose ball and shuffled seven yards for a touchdown.

A 21-yard field goal shortly before halftime pulled Dallas to within 14–10. Neither team could conquer the brutal weather and score in the third quarter. In the fourth Green Bay simply had to keep Dallas from moving the ball to win. The Packers seemed up to the task.

But on the first play of the final period, Dallas quarterback Don Meredith pitched the ball to Reeves. Packers safety Willie Wood and cornerback Bob Jeter bit and moved up to make a play. Reeves then stopped and heaved a long throw to Rentzel, who had broken past both defenders.

"I was slow mentally on that play," Jeter said. "We all knew about Reeves' option pass, but I didn't react."

The Cowboys might have felt confident. But the Packers, playing under legendary coach Vince Lombardi,

Lance Rentzel runs for a touchdown after catching a 50-yard pass from Dan Reeves. His touchdown put the Cowboys ahead in the fourth quarter of the Ice Bowl. *Photo courtesy of AP Images.*

It was going to be a touchdown. I really knew it, and it was the most marvelous feeling in the world.

—LANCE RENTZEL

certainly wouldn't give up. With 4:50 left in the game, the Packers began a drive at their own 32-yard line. Unlike Dallas, Green Bay didn't try to make a big play. Instead, Starr threw a series of short passes to his running backs, who slid to one first down after another. Nine plays later, the Packers had a first down at the Cowboys' 1-yard line.

The disheartened Dallas defensive linemen tried to dig their cleats into the ice to mount a stop. On first and second downs, they succeeded. Each time, they kept running back Donny Anderson out of the end zone. Now

> **I** saw Reeves cock his arm. I tried to get back, but when the ball was in the air, I knew it was gone.
>
> **—PACKERS CORNERBACK BOB JETER**

# Game Details

## Green Bay Packers 21 • Dallas Cowboys 17

| | | | | | |
|---|---|---|---|---|---|
| Cowboys | 0 | 10 | 0 | 7 | **17** |
| Packers | 7 | 7 | 0 | 7 | **21** |

**Date:** December 31, 1967

**Team Records:** Green Bay 9–4–1, Dallas 9–5

**Scoring Plays:**

GB—Dowler eight-yard pass from Starr (Chandler PAT)

GB—Dowler 46-yard pass from Starr (Chandler PAT)

DAL—Andrie seven-yard fumble return (Villanueva PAT)

DAL—Villanueva 21-yard FG

DAL—Rentzel 50-yard pass from Reeves (Villanueva PAT)

GB—Starr one-yard run (Chandler PAT)

Green Bay faced third down with only 16 seconds left. After calling a timeout to confer with Lombardi, Starr brought his team to the line. Instead of handing off again or attempting a pass, he kept the ball. Behind a block by guard Jerry Kramer, Starr squeezed into the end zone, giving Green Bay a 21–17 victory.

"We were so close," Rentzel said.

The 1967 season marked Rentzel's first with the Cowboys. They acquired him in a trade from the Minnesota Vikings, who had drafted him two years earlier from Oklahoma. Rentzel had an outstanding initial year with the Cowboys, catching 58 passes for almost 1,000 yards. He scored eight touchdowns and had an excellent 17.2-yards-per-catch average. Rentzel followed up with two more stellar seasons in 1968 and 1969. He caught 97 passes and scored 18 touchdowns.

Only 26 years old, Rentzel's future seemed limitless. But in 1970 his Dallas career abruptly ended, and his life took an irrevocable turn. Rentzel was arrested in Highland Park, an affluent Dallas suburb, for exposing himself to a young girl. He immediately quit the Cowboys, pled guilty to the crime, and was given five years of probation.

Rentzel later wrote a poignant book about the arrest, called *When All the Laughter Died in Sorrow*. In it he apologized to his wife, glamorous actress Joey Heatherton.

"The humiliation crushed me," Rentzel wrote. "I had ruined my reputation and my career. I had destroyed my marriage and driven away the only woman I'd ever really loved."

In 1971 the Cowboys traded Rentzel to the Los Angeles Rams. He had three moderately successful seasons, but his statistics didn't compare to those he had with Dallas. He regretted that he couldn't complete his career as a Cowboy.

"You can never get away from something like that," Rentzel wrote of his arrest. "What you can do is become a better person, treat people right, and own up to your mistakes. You don't make them again, and I haven't."

# Legal Problems

Lance Rentzel was the first Cowboy to have a high-profile run-in with the law. His arrest for indecent exposure in 1970 shocked players and team officials. It spelled an end to his Dallas career.

But other Cowboys subsequently had legal problems that embarrassed them and others. In 1973 John Niland, a Pro Bowl guard, was arrested late at night in a Dallas neighborhood after running down a street in a crazed state. Seven police officers finally subdued the burly Niland and took him to a hospital for psychiatric evaluation.

While being arrested, Niland injured his elbow and suffered nerve damage in his hand. He played for Dallas through the 1974 season and then was traded to the Philadelphia Eagles in 1975. Niland played one year for the Eagles before retiring.

In 1987 another star's career ended after an arrest. Kicker Rafael Septien, the most productive kicker in team history, was indicted for sexually assaulting a 10-year-old girl, the daughter of a friend. Septien maintained his innocence, but the Cowboys released him.

In the 1990s the legal problems of the Cowboys seemed to escalate. Pro Bowl receiver Michael Irvin was arrested for cocaine possession in 1996. The NFL suspended him for five games. Defensive tackle Leon Lett also served a suspension for drug possession.

In 2003 defensive back Dwayne Goodrich was convicted of criminally negligent homicide. After leaving a strip club late at night, Goodrich struck and killed two men who had stopped to help a motorist on a freeway. He injured a third man before leaving the scene in his BMW.

"I don't hate him," the injured man said at Goodrich's trial. "I feel sorry for him."

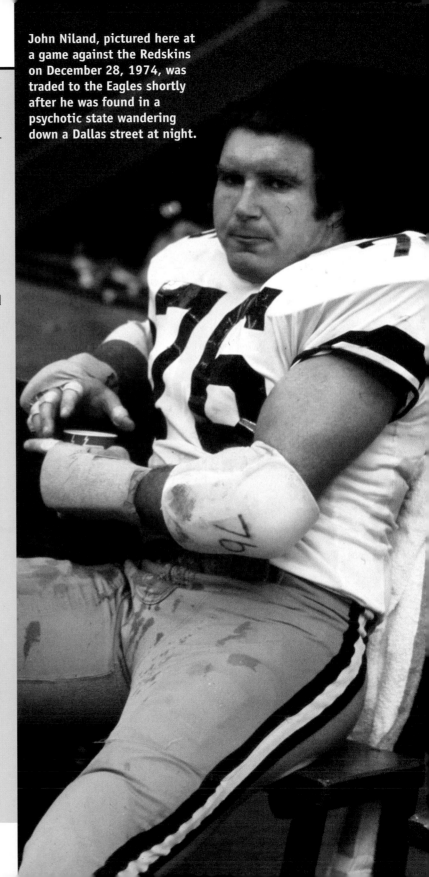

John Niland, pictured here at a game against the Redskins on December 28, 1974, was traded to the Eagles shortly after he was found in a psychotic state wandering down a Dallas street at night.

## A Forgotten Player, a Successful Author

When Lance Rentzel joined the Cowboys in 1967, he replaced Pete Gent in the starting lineup. Gent, who never played college football, signed as a free agent in 1964. After learning the receiver position, he gradually logged more playing time.

In 1966, Gent's best season, he caught 27 passes for 474 yards. But the next year, Rentzel arrived and became an instant star. He caught 58 passes and scored eight touchdowns, including a 74-yarder. Gent, meanwhile, rarely saw action, catching only nine passes.

After another unproductive year, Gent was traded to the New York Giants. But the Giants waived him before the 1968 season. After he left football, Gent struck gold as a writer. His first novel, *North Dallas Forty*, came out in 1973 and painted an unflattering picture of professional football. In the book coaches urge injured players to take painkillers, even though playing may jeopardize their careers.

Players are portrayed as wild drinkers and womanizers. *North Dallas Forty* is a thinly veiled reference to the Cowboys, and team officials hated it. The book's authoritarian coach, B.A. Strothers, clearly was patterned after Cowboys coach Tom Landry.

The film version of *North Dallas Forty* came out in 1979 and starred Nick Nolte as Phil Elliott, a star receiver. He's a conflicted character. He realizes pro football is strictly a business and that players are pawns of management. But Elliott also loves the game and can't leave it, even though his body is falling apart.

"What's important is the moment of the catch," Elliott says in the film. "That feeling, that high. Hell, I can take the crap. I can take the manipulation. I can take the pain. As long as I get that chance every Sunday."

Lance Rentzel catches the 50-yard touchdown pass from running back Dan Reeves in the fourth quarter of the Cowboys' 21-17 loss to the Green Bay Packers in the Ice Bowl on December 31, 1967.

Cowboys wide receiver Butch Johnson dives to make a fingertip catch in the end zone for a 45-yard touchdown reception during the third quarter of the Cowboys' 27–10 victory over the Denver Broncos in Super Bowl XII on January 15, 1978.

January 15, 1978

# Stretching for a Catch

Butch Johnson's 45-Yard Fingertip Grab for Touchdown Lifts Dallas to 27–10
Win in Super Bowl XII

The Cowboys had a pair of great receivers in the late 1970s and early 1980s: Drew Pearson and Tony Hill. A third receiver, Butch Johnson, also made some big plays in a part-time role.

None was bigger than a diving fingertip grab Johnson made in Super Bowl XII. Dallas had taken a 13–0 halftime lead over the Denver Broncos. But early in the second half the Broncos kicked a 47-yard field goal and showed signs of rallying.

Midway through the third period, Dallas faced a third-and-10 at the Denver 45-yard line. Coach Tom Landry decided to gamble. Quarterback Roger Staubach dropped back and heaved a bomb that Johnson dove for, barely grabbing it as he crossed the goal line parallel to the turf. When Johnson hit the ground, the ball popped loose, but officials ruled he had possession and awarded Dallas a touchdown. The Cowboys had a commanding 20–3 lead, and the game was essentially over.

"I actually thought I threw it too far, and Butch Johnson made a sensational catch," Staubach said. "Butch had a flair for making those kind of catches."

Later in the third quarter, Denver's Rob Lytle scored on a one-yard touchdown run to make the score 20–10. Dallas put the game away midway through the fourth quarter when receiver Golden Richards hauled in a 29-yard touchdown pass. Staubach, however, didn't throw the ball. Running back Robert Newhouse, on an option play, made the unlikely pass to put Dallas in front 27–10. Newhouse was filling in for starter Tony Dorsett, who had sprained a knee in the first half and was sidelined.

"Newhouse was the consummate team player," Pearson said. "Whatever role Landry wanted him to play, Newhouse was willing to play it and not just play it, but play it well."

Dallas and Denver came into the game with identical 12–2 regular-season records, the best in their conferences. The Cowboys led the NFC in scoring, averaging almost 25 points per game. The Broncos, meanwhile, were known for their suffocating Orange Crush defense. Denver gave up the fewest points in the AFC, an average of only 10 per game.

The Cowboys scored first on a three-yard touchdown run by Dorsett late in the first quarter. Efren Herrera added

# The Other Receivers

The Cowboys have a tradition of outstanding receivers. Bob Hayes, with his blistering speed, was the first to make a mark in the 1960s. He starred from 1965 to 1974, catching 365 passes and scoring 71 touchdowns, many on bombs. He was voted into the Pro Football Hall of Fame in 2009.

As Hayes left, Drew Pearson rose to prominence. He played from 1973 to 1983, making the Pro Bowl three times. Tony Hill was next. His career lasted from 1977 to 1986 and also included three Pro Bowl appearances. Just two years later Michael Irvin arrived as a No. 1 draft pick. His 12-year career culminated with induction into the Pro Football Hall of Fame. This decade, flashy Terrell Owens continued the succession of greatness at wide receiver.

Over the decades, however, Dallas has had many lesser-known receivers. Some, like Butch Johnson, had moments in the spotlight. Johnson's terrific fingertip touchdown grab in Super Bowl XII helped Dallas defeat the Denver Broncos 27–10. His Cowboys

Cowboys wide receiver Drew Pearson makes a dramatic catch over a New York Giants defender in the Cowboys' 24–3 victory at Texas Stadium on October 8, 1978.

field goals of 35 and 43 yards to give Dallas a 13–0 half-time lead. Throughout the game the Cowboys' defense turned back the Broncos' offense. Denver had only 156 yards of total offense, compared with 325 for Dallas. Only 35 of Denver's yards came through passing.

Broncos quarterback Craig Morton, a former Cowboy, performed miserably. He completed only four of 15 passes and threw four interceptions before being yanked. Morton's replacement, Norris Weese, didn't do much better, hitting only four of 10 passes.

Dallas defensive linemen Randy White and Harvey Martin harassed Denver quarterbacks all game. Their pressure contributed to the four interceptions. For their work, White and Martin were named co-MVPs—the first time players shared the award.

The win gave Dallas two Super Bowl triumphs in the 1970s. The Cowboys also won Super Bowl VI 24–3 over the Miami Dolphins. Sandwiched between that game and the Denver win, Dallas lost to the Pittsburgh Steelers in Super Bowl X 21–17. The Cowboys made a fourth Super Bowl appearance in the 1970s, losing to Pittsburgh again, 35–31, in Super Bowl XIII.

Pittsburgh emerged as the team of the decade with four Super Bowl wins. Besides beating Dallas twice, the Steelers also downed the Minnesota Vikings 16–6 in Super Bowl IX and the Los Angeles Rams 31–19 in Super Bowl XIV.

The 1980s wouldn't be as kind to the Dallas Cowboys. Their leader, Staubach, retired at the end of the 1979 season. His successor, Danny White, performed adequately, but Dallas lost three straight NFC Championships from 1980 to 1982. Afterward Dallas began a steady decline. In 1984 the Cowboys finished 9-7 to miss the playoffs for the first time in a decade. In 1986 the Cowboys dipped to 7-9, their first losing season since 1964.

However, Johnson's highlight-reel touchdown in Super Bowl XII provided one of the most memorable moments in the 1970s, a decade of excellence.

> **T**hat really put the game away. We led 20–3.
> —ROGER STAUBACH

# Game Details

## Dallas Cowboys 27 • Denver Broncos 10

| | | | | | |
|---|---|---|---|---|---|
| Cowboys | 10 | 3 | 7 | 7 | 27 |
| Broncos | 0 | 0 | 10 | 0 | 10 |

**Date:** January 15, 1978

**Team Records:** Dallas 12–2, Denver 12–2

**Scoring Plays:**

DAL—Dorsett three-yard run (Herrera PAT)

DAL—Herrera 35-yard FG

DAL—Herrera 43-yard FG

DEN—Turner 47-yard FG

DAL—Johnson 45-yard pass from Staubach (Herrera PAT)

DEN—Lytle one-yard run (Turner PAT)

DAL—Richards 29-yard pass from Newhouse (Herrera PAT)

career lasted from 1976 to 1983, overlapping with both Pearson and Hill. Johnson never was a full-time starter, but he played regularly. His best seasons came in 1980 and 1981. In 1980 Johnson caught 19 passes and scored four touchdowns. In 1981 he had 25 receptions and five touchdowns.

Golden Richards slightly predated Johnson, and he was a starter. He beat out Hayes in 1974 and remained a starter through 1977. During that period, Richards caught a respectable 83 passes and scored 15 touchdowns. Early in 1978, after Hill became a starter, Richards was traded to the Chicago Bears.

The Cowboys had high hopes for Doug Donley, whom they drafted in the second round in 1981. He had blazing speed not seen since Hayes. Injuries, however, cut short his career. Donley started only 10 games during his four-year stint, all but one in 1984, his final season. He caught 32 passes, more than he had in the combined prior three seasons. But shoulder problems spelled the end of his career.

Mike Renfro joined the Cowboys in 1984 from the Houston Oilers and played four years in Dallas. Renfro was slow compared to Donley, but he ran good routes and made clutch catches. His best season was 1985, when he caught 60 passes and scored eight touchdowns.

In the 1990s Alvin Harper had a few good seasons as the starter opposite Irvin. Harper started five games as a rookie in 1991, then became a full-time starter from 1992 to 1994. During that time the Cowboys won back-to-back Super Bowls. He always played in Irvin's shadow, but Harper was remarkably consistent. He caught 35 passes in 1992, 36 in 1993, and 33 in 1994.

This decade, the Cowboys have had a string of receivers who started but never achieved stardom. They include Rocket Ismail in 2000 and 2001, Joey Galloway from 2001 through 2003, Terry Glenn from 2003 to 2006, and Keyshawn Johnson in 2004 and 2005. Finally, a big-name receiver, Terrell Owens, joined Dallas in 2006 and stayed until 2008.

Butch Johnson falls over the goal line after his spectacular touchdown catch of Roger Staubach's 45-yard pass during the third quarter of Super Bowl XII against the Denver Broncos on January 15, 1978.

As a pass-catcher, Butch has better concentration than any receiver I've ever seen.

—OFFENSIVE COORDINATOR DAN REEVES

November 28, 1974

# Rousing Game for a Rookie

### Longley Leads Cowboys to Three Late Touchdowns, Upset of Redskins

The Cowboys have had a string of marquee quarterbacks: Don Meredith, Roger Staubach, Troy Aikman, and now Tony Romo. Clint Longley doesn't qualify as one of the all-time greats, but he turned in a performance for the ages in 1974.

Longley, a rookie who hadn't played all year, rallied the Cowboys to three late touchdowns in a dramatic 24–23 victory over the Washington Redskins on Thanksgiving Day. The winning touchdown came with only 35 seconds left. The Redskins had put seven defensive backs in to guard against a long completion, but it didn't matter.

With the ball at midfield, Longley spotted All-Pro receiver Drew Pearson streaking down the right sideline. Under pressure, Longley threw a perfect strike. Pearson caught it at the 4-yard line and sped in for the go-ahead touchdown. The Dallas crowd erupted, and teammates mobbed the boyish Longley.

"A triumph of the uncluttered mind," veteran offensive guard Blaine Nye called his performance.

The final touchdown alone would have made Longley a Cowboys legend. But he preceded it with two other touch-down drives to put Dallas in a position to win. Longley came into the game midway through the third quarter after starter Roger Staubach suffered a concussion. Dallas trailed 16–3, and the game seemed out of reach—especially with a no-name quarterback at the helm.

In his first possession, however, Longley methodically moved the Cowboys down the field and hit tight end Billy Joe DuPree on a 35-yard touchdown. A fluke? Apparently not. In the fourth quarter Longley led another drive that ended with a one-yard touchdown run. Dallas now led 17–16. Longley had already put on a magnificent performance, but he wasn't finished.

The Redskins' Duane Thomas, a former Cowboy, scored on a 19-yard run to put Washington back on top, 23–17. With less than a minute remaining, Longley started the team's final drive. After reaching midfield with 35 seconds left, he performed his miracle. After his headline-grabbing game, Longley returned to backing up Staubach. The next year, 1975, Longley saw little action. He played in only four games, completing a dismal seven of 23 passes.

In 1976 Longley's career unraveled in an incident almost as famous as his Washington performance. Only

Clint Longley throws one of several touchdown passes against the Redskins on November 28, 1974. The Cowboys were behind 16–3 when Longley came into the game in the third quarter and rallied his team to a 24–23 victory.

days before the start of the season, Longley was throwing passes to Pearson. Pearson dropped one, and Longley chided the veteran.

Staubach, who considered Pearson his No. 1 target, took offense at Longley's remark. Words ensued between Staubach, the future Hall of Famer, and Longley, the one-hit wonder. Staubach, known as a clean-living family man, hardly seemed the type to fight with a teammate.

But that's what he did. After practice he and Longley met on an empty field. Longley threw the first punch, grazing Staubach's head. Staubach then tackled the smaller Longley and pinned him to the ground. Assistant coach Dan Reeves, a former Dallas running back, intervened and separated the two. Reeves worried what the temperamental Longley might do next.

"If I were you, I'd be careful," Reeves warned Staubach. "I wouldn't turn my back on him."

# Game Details

## Dallas Cowboys 24 • Washington Redskins 23

| Redskins | 3 | 6 | 7 | 7 | 23 |
|----------|---|---|----|---|----|
| Cowboys  | 3 | 0 | 14 | 7 | 24 |

**Date:** November 28, 1974
**Team Records:** Washington 8–3, Dallas 6–5
**Scoring Plays:**
DAL—Herrera 24-yard FG
WAS—Moseley 45-yard FG
WAS—Moseley 34-yard FG
WAS—Moseley 39-yard FG
WAS—Thomas nine-yard pass from Kilmer (Moseley PAT)
DAL—DuPree 35-yard pass from Longley (Herrera PAT)
DAL—Garrison one-yard run (Herrera PAT)
WAS—Thomas 19-yard run (Moseley PAT)
DAL—Pearson 50-yard pass from Longley (Herrera PAT)

Those were wise words that Staubach should have heeded. A few days later Longley approached Staubach as he was putting on his shoulder pads. Without a word Longley punched Staubach in the face, knocking him into some equipment and opening a cut over his left eye.

Immediately Longley fled the locker room, went to the airport and caught a flight, and never rejoined the team. The Longley saga had ended in the same unlikely, dramatic fashion it started. Longley and Staubach never spoke again.

"I'd prefer to keep it that way," Staubach wrote in his autobiography.

Longley kept a low profile after the run-in and rarely talked about it. Once, however, he gave an uncharacteristic interview and discussed it.

"What happened between Roger and me is something I don't think about," Longley said. "That was a long time ago."

Longley's career sputtered after his ill-advised punch at Staubach. The Cowboys traded him to the San Diego Chargers, where he again served as a backup. He completed 12 of 24 passes, with two touchdowns and three interceptions, in 1976.

He then had brief flings with the Toronto Argonauts of the Canadian Football League and the minor-league Shreveport Steamer. Afterward Longley worked as a sportswriter for a Dallas-area weekly newspaper. Later he moved to South Texas and lived on the beach, keeping largely to himself.

He may have disappeared, but he hasn't been forgotten.

> **I** think he [Longley] could have been a very good quarterback in the National Football League if he had done everything right.
>
> **—RECEIVER DREW PEARSON**

# Duane Thomas

At 6'2" and 220 pounds, Duane Thomas was a remarkable combination of size, speed, and power. As a rookie he became a regular in the sixth game because of an injury to starter Calvin Hill. He finished the season with 803 yards and an average of 5.3 yards per carry. Thomas was named Rookie of the Year.

He started in Super Bowl V against the Baltimore Colts but had his poorest game of the year, rushing for only 35 yards. Worse, he had a goal-line fumble that may have cost Dallas the game.

After his sensational rookie year, Thomas held out for a new contract. The Cowboys traded Thomas to the New England Patriots, but the Patriots voided the trade because Thomas wouldn't take a physical exam or follow orders in practice. He was shipped back to the Cowboys, but he continued his contract holdout.

Finally, in the second game of the 1971 season, Thomas announced he'd play—but under protest. He played, but he didn't talk. Thomas wouldn't exchange a word with the press or his teammates.

"It was amazing," defensive tackle Jethro Pugh said. "We were best friends, but you could ask him something and he was just silent."

On the field, however, Thomas continued to impress. He led the team in rushing with 793 yards, and the Cowboys advanced to the Super Bowl for the second straight year.

The next training camp, Thomas continued his silent treatment and skipped practices. Finally the Cowboys sent Thomas to the San Diego Chargers. He held out the entire year in a contract dispute. In 1973 he was traded to the Redskins and had two so-so seasons. He had one last go-round with the Cowboys in 1976.

This time his attitude wasn't a problem, but his skills had deteriorated with his layoffs. The Cowboys cut Thomas in training camp.

**Though Duane Thomas (pictured here in 1970) was playing for the Redskins in the November 28, 1974, game, he made his debut with the Cowboys as their No. 1 draft pick in 1970.**

# The
# Carries

Emmitt Smith immediately after breaking the all-time rushing record in the Cowboys' game against the Seahawks on October 27, 2002. *Photo courtesy of AP Images.*

October 27, 2002

# Emmitt's Big Day

## Smith Sets All-Time Rushing Mark With 11-Yard Carry

Few Cowboys fans cared that their team lost to the Seattle Seahawks 17–14 midway through the 2002 season. They watched the game in hopes that Emmitt Smith would break Walter Payton's NFL mark. They weren't disappointed.

With Dallas trailing by seven points in the fourth quarter, Smith broke through the Seattle defense for 11 yards, eclipsing Payton's seemingly unreachable record of 16,726 yards. Officials stopped the game and presented Smith the game ball for his historic achievement. The 63,854 fans in Texas Stadium stood and gave No. 22 a long, loud ovation. A banner dropped from the roof, proclaiming Smith the new rushing king.

"Today was a special day," Smith said.

He finished the game with 109 yards rushing and the season with 975 yards. It would be his 13th and final year as a Cowboy. Owner Jerry Jones, always looking at the bottom line, decided not to re-sign the aging Smith. He wanted to shed his hefty salary and develop younger players.

Instead of retiring, Smith signed with the Arizona Cardinals. In 2003, his first year with Arizona, Smith had his poorest year, rushing for only 256 yards. But Smith returned to form in 2004, his final year. At age 35, Smith rushed for 937 yards, averaging 3.5 yards per carry and scoring nine touchdowns. Coincidentally, his rushing total exactly matched his rookie mark back in 1990.

Amazingly, Smith never suffered a serious injury throughout his 15-year career. His durability helped him finish his career with 18,355 yards rushing—a total that may never be broken.

Smith probably could have played a few more seasons, most likely in a backup role. Instead he chose to retire—not as a Cardinal but as a Cowboy. Jones signed Smith to a ceremonial contract to allow him to do so.

"It's been a tremendous ride," Smith said in a tearful retirement speech. "It's one that I'm proud of."

Many fellow players from the Super Bowl–winning teams of the early 1990s paid tribute to Smith.

"I'm going to be biased when you ask who's the greatest running back of all time," said former fullback Daryl

# Daryl Johnston

Emmitt Smith wouldn't be the NFL's all-time leading rusher without Daryl "Moose" Johnston, the fullback whose bruising blocks opened holes for No. 22. Smith is the first to give Moose credit.

"Nobody's tougher than Moose, nobody works harder, and no one appreciates him more than I do," Smith wrote in his 1994 autobiography, *The Emmitt Zone*.

Fans watched Smith plow through defenses, score touchdowns, and rack up rushing titles with regularity. But only astute observers noticed that Johnston, 6'2" and 238 pounds, usually led the way for his more celebrated teammate.

Some blocking fullbacks resent the attention running backs receive. Not Johnston. He basked in the anonymity and cheered Smith on as he approached Walter Payton's rushing record of 16,726 yards.

Johnston also was an underappreciated receiver coming out of the backfield. In 1993, the season the Cowboys won Super Bowl XXVIII, he caught 50 passes. The next year he had 44 catches. For his career, he scored 14 touchdowns receiving, compared with only eight rushing.

In his first eight seasons, Johnston didn't miss a single game because of injury. However, in 1997 he suffered a neck injury and had to have two vertebrae fused. Johnston played for two more seasons, but his effectiveness waned.

When Johnston retired in 1999, Smith trailed Payton's rushing record by only 2,763 yards. Johnston had to watch Smith surpass the mark without him. At Smith's retirement press conference in 2005, he thanked Moose for his contributions.

"Daryl, I love you to death," Smith said, crying. "You've been there through thick and thin. I don't know why, but every time I think of you, I always break down."

Daryl "Moose" Johnston, pictured here in a game against the Redskins on October 10, 1998, facilitated Emmitt Smith's all-time rushing record by opening holes with his skillful blocks.

Johnston, who opened holes for Smith. "It's always been Emmitt."

Smith defied the odds throughout his career. He wasn't big or fast by NFL standards. In fact, 16 teams passed on Smith in the first round of the 1990 draft because of questions about his potential.

But one man could see Smith's future greatness: Jimmy Johnson, who joined the Cowboys as head coach in 1989. He had recruited Smith to play for him at the University of Miami. But Smith, who played high school football in Pensacola, Florida, chose the University of Florida instead.

There he quickly made his mark, starting as a freshman and rushing for 1,341 yards to lead the Southeastern Conference. In three seasons Smith logged 3,928 yards—second on the Gators' all-time rushing list. Smith skipped his senior year to declare for the NFL draft.

Johnson persuaded Jones to trade spots in the draft to nab Smith. He became the Cowboys' most heralded rookie running back since Tony Dorsett in 1977.

"Emmitt Smith brings star quality to us," Johnson said.

Smith, however, angered some fans and team officials by missing his first training camp in a contract dispute. Days before the 1990 season, Smith signed a three-year, $3 million contract. But after four games he hadn't produced a 100-yard day. His best game total was only 63 yards.

Could Johnson have been wrong about Smith? No. In the season's fifth game, Smith exploded for 121 yards. He finished his rookie year only 63 yards short of his 1,000-yard goal.

"I had a decent year, but it didn't satisfy me," Smith said.

Soon after, he met his expectations—and exceeded those of most fans. In Smith's second year, he led the league with 1,563 yards rushing, the first Cowboy to achieve the honor. In 1992, his third year, Smith set a Cowboys record with 1,713 yards, again leading the NFL. He played a critical role in the Cowboys' stellar 13–3 record and their 52–17 blowout of the Buffalo Bills in Super Bowl XXVII. It would be the first of three Super Bowl wins during the Smith era.

He won four NFL rushing titles and made the Pro Bowl eight times as a Cowboy. The next milestone for Smith: induction into the Pro Football Hall of Fame. His first year of eligibility is 2010. No player has ever been more deserving of football's highest honor.

# Game Details

## Seattle Seahawks 17 • Dallas Cowboys 14

| | | | | | |
|---|---|---|---|---|---|
| Seahawks | 0 | 7 | 0 | 10 | **17** |
| Cowboys | 0 | 0 | 7 | 7 | **14** |

**Date:** October 27, 2002

**Team Records:** Dallas 3–4, Seattle 1–5

**Scoring Plays:**

SEA—Alexander two-yard run (Lindell PAT)

DAL—Galloway 39-yard pass from Hutchinson (Cundiff PAT)

SEA—Alexander five-yard run (Lindell PAT)

DAL—Smith one-yard run (Cundiff PAT)

SEA—Lindell 20-yard FG

> **Y**ou don't know how much this star really means to me.
>
> —EMMITT SMITH, WHILE PATTING A COWBOYS HELMET DURING HIS RETIREMENT SPEECH

January 3, 1983

# Dorsett Dashes for Touchdown

His 99-yard Romp Sets Unbreakable Record

Before Emmitt Smith achieved greatness with the Cowboys, Tony Dorsett slashed through opposing defenses. He ranked among the league's top backs in the late 1970s and 1980s, just as Smith did in the 1990s.

Without question, Smith and Dorsett stand out as the greatest backs in Cowboys history. Yet their running styles varied greatly. Smith, at 5'9" and 215 pounds, could punish defenders and drag them toward the first-down marker. Dorsett, 5'11" but only 192 pounds, relied on lightning speed instead of power. No one has ever hit the hole quicker than Dorsett or been faster in the open field.

Dorsett demonstrated his breakaway ability in a Monday-night game near the end of the 1982 season. The Cowboys, facing the Minnesota Vikings, were backed up to their own 1-yard line in the fourth quarter. Dallas trailed 24–13. On first down, quarterback Danny White handed the ball to Dorsett and, as usual, he hit the hole almost before the defensive linemen got out of their stances.

See ya.

Dorsett juked a linebacker, stiff-armed a defensive back, and sprinted down the sideline for a touchdown.

The 99-yard run set an NFL record for a rushing play that can never be broken.

"It was only after I finally got back to the bench that I realized what I had accomplished," said Dorsett, who was in his sixth season.

Dorsett even made the great play without his reliable blocking mate, Ron Springs. Springs, because of a mix-up, remained on the sideline as Dorsett sped for a touchdown. All Springs could do was cheer.

Minnesota held on to win 31–27. The Cowboys finished the strike-shortened season at 6–3, while the Vikings were 5–4. Dallas advanced to the NFC Championship Game but lost to the Washington Redskins 31–17. Dorsett earned his third Pro Bowl selection.

The Cowboys had made Dorsett their top pick in the 1977 draft. The Seattle Seahawks, entering their second year in the NFL, had the right to take Dorsett. But Dorsett, a Heisman Trophy winner and four-year All-American at Pittsburgh, made it clear he didn't want to play for the Seahawks. They had posted a dismal 2–12 record in their inaugural season. The Cowboys desperately needed a top running back, so they pulled off a blockbuster trade,

We're Real Radio
WCCO
8·3·0

**FJ 76**

Cowboys running back Tony
Dorsett drops the ball after
he completed a record-
setting 99-yard run from
scrimmage against the
Vikings on January 3, 1983.
*Photo courtesy of AP Images.*

swapping their first-round pick and three second-round choices to Seattle for Dorsett. It became one of the all-time draft steals.

When the 1977 season began, veteran Preston Pearson was the Cowboys' starting running back. Coach Tom Landry liked to bring rookies along slowly, even heralded ones like Dorsett. Dorsett played early on but didn't start until the 11th game. Still, he rushed for 1,007 yards and 12 touchdowns, including an 84-yard run.

# Game Details

## Minnesota Vikings 31 • Dallas Cowboys 27

| Cowboys | 3 | 7 | 3 | 14 | 27 |
|---------|---|---|---|----|----|
| Vikings | 0 | 10 | 7 | 14 | 31 |

**Date:** January 3, 1983

**Team Records:** Dallas 6–2, Minnesota 4–4

**Scoring Plays:**

DAL—Septien 42-yard FG

DAL—Thurman 60-yard interception return (Septien PAT)

MIN—Danmeier 28-yard FG

MIN—Brown one-yard run (Danmeier PAT)

MIN—Brown 13-yard pass from Kramer (Danmeier PAT)

DAL—Septien 22-yard FG

MIN—Turner 33-yard interception return (Danmeier PAT)

DAL—Dorsett 99-yard run (Septien PAT)

DAL—Springs two-yard run (Septien PAT)

MIN—Young 14-yard pass from Kramer (Danmeier PAT)

> **I**t was just a fortunate time and a fortunate play for me.
>
> **—TONY DORSETT**

Dorsett's stats improved every year. He had his best year in 1981, gaining 1,646 yards and averaging almost five yards per carry. Dorsett's role in Dallas changed dramatically when the Cowboys acquired Herschel Walker in 1986. Walker, a Heisman Trophy winner like Dorsett, played in the USFL for three years after leaving the University of Georgia. When the upstart league folded, Walker signed with the Cowboys.

The press and fans loved Walker's presence. People envisioned a dream backfield with him and Dorsett. Walker, 6'1" and 225 pounds, relied on brute power and straight-ahead speed to gain yardage. He wasn't shifty and elusive like Dorsett. Walker was more like a rocket shot from a launching pad.

The Cowboys experimented with playing both backs at the same time, but neither had any interest in blocking. Both saw themselves as featured backs who should follow the blocks of someone else. So coaches began alternating Dorsett and Walker in 1986. They were a nice one-two punch that kept defenses guessing. Dorsett carried 184 times for 748 yards. Walker had similar stats: 151 carries for 737 yards. Walker scored 12 rushing touchdowns, while Dorsett had five.

In 1987, Walker's second season, he got more work than Dorsett. Walker carried 209 times for 891 yards, whereas Dorsett had only 130 carries for 456 yards. Dorsett, then 33 years old, saw he was being phased out. He asked for, and received, a trade to the Denver Broncos in 1988. Dorsett played one season, gaining 703 yards, before retiring.

Dorsett rushed for 12,036 yards and scored 72 touchdowns in 11 seasons as a Cowboy. He held the rushing record until Smith arrived in 1990. Smith obliterated Dorsett's stats, gaining 17,162 yards and scoring 153 touchdowns during his 13-year Cowboys career.

No back, however, has ever matched Dorsett's silky smoothness and pure speed. If you need proof, watch a replay of his 99-yard touchdown burst against the Vikings.

# Players Go On Strike

Tony Dorsett's record-setting 99-yard touchdown run came in one of the NFL's most unusual seasons. Teams played only nine regular-season games, instead of 16, because of a players' strike. The shortened season mandated a different playoff format. After the regular season, the top eight teams from each conference made the playoffs. They were seeded 1–8 based on their records. Dallas, which finished 6–3, was seeded second in the NFC behind the Washington Redskins, who had an 8–1 record.

In the first round of the playoffs, Dallas defeated the Tampa Bay Buccaneers 30–17. In the second round, the Cowboys defeated the Green Bay Packers 37–26.

Dallas then faced Washington in the NFC Championship Game, losing 31–17 to the Redskins.

**Cowboys place-kicker Rafael Septien, right, pats teammate Tony Dorsett on the head after his record-setting 99-yard touchdown run in the fourth quarter against the Vikings on January 3, 1983.**
*Photo courtesy of AP Images.*

That was all we needed. We could feel their coffin nailing shut.
—GUARD NATE NEWTON ON SMITH'S
THIRD-QUARTER TOUCHDOWN

Emmitt Smith follows his Cowboys teammates as they lead him into the Buffalo Bills end zone in Super Bowl XXVIII. This 15-yard touchdown run secured the 30–13 win for the Cowboys.

January 30, 1994

# Touchdown Seals Super Bowl Repeat

## Smith's 15-Yard Touchdown Run Breaks Tie, Powers Cowboys to 30–13 Super Bowl XXVIII Win

Emmitt Smith not only gained 18,355 yards rushing during his 15-year career, but he consistently played best when it mattered most. Case in point: Super Bowl XXVIII.

The Cowboys were tied 13–13 with the Buffalo Bills midway through the third quarter. Dallas was trying for its second straight Super Bowl win over Buffalo and was having more difficulty than many expected. In fact the Bills had had a surprising 13–6 halftime lead. But less than a minute into the third quarter, Dallas safety James Washington had a 48-yard fumble return for a touchdown to tie the game.

The Cowboys needed another score to keep the momentum. Emmitt Smith stepped up. Still early in the third quarter, Dallas began a drive at its own 36-yard line and fed the ball to Smith seven times while marching down the field. On Smith's final carry, he ran 15 yards for a touchdown to give Dallas a 20–13 lead and the surge needed to win the game.

"I still love watching that drive when I see it today," Smith said. "I'll never forget it as long as I live."

Now Dallas had control of the game. Early in the fourth quarter, Smith played a key role in another touchdown drive. The Cowboys started from the Buffalo 39-yard line after an interception. Smith quickly gained 10 yards on two rushes and caught a nine-yard pass to move Dallas close to the goal line. On fourth-and-goal from the 1-yard line, coach Jimmy Johnson decided against a chip-shot field goal. Again he turned to Smith, who ran in for a touchdown to give the Cowboys a commanding 27–13 edge.

Eddie Murray added a 20-yard field goal to make the final 30–13 and let the Cowboys accomplish the rare feat of back-to-back world championships.

Smith not only scored two touchdowns, he powered for 132 yards rushing on 30 carries—with 92 coming in the crucial second half. He also caught four passes for 26 yards. Not surprisingly, he won the game's Most Valuable Player award, and Smith presented more evidence of why he's one of the greatest running backs of all time.

Without his contributions, the Cowboys probably wouldn't have dominated the NFL in the early 1990s. After winning Super Bowl XXVIII, the Cowboys failed in their bid for a three-peat. But they roared back in 1995 and captured Super Bowl XXX 27–17 over the Pittsburgh Steelers.

During those four seasons when the Cowboys won three Super Bowls, Smith made the Pro Bowl each year and put up awesome numbers. He gained a total of 6,456 yards rushing and scored 73 touchdowns on the ground. Showing his versatility, Smith also caught 228 passes for 1,465 yards.

The Cowboys' first championship of the 1990s, Super Bowl XXVII, was a 52–17 rout. After Dallas took a 14–7 first-quarter lead, the outcome was never in doubt. Many expected the Cowboys to have the same ease in their rematch with Buffalo in Super Bowl XXVIII. But it took Smith's 15-yard touchdown run in the third quarter to irrevocably turn the game in their favor.

After the third Super Bowl win in 1995, Dallas' fortunes changed dramatically. In 1996 the Cowboys won the NFC East but lost in the second round. In 1998 they lost in the first round of the playoffs. Then things turned ugly. From 2000 to 2002, the Cowboys posted miserable 5–11 records each year, never contending for the playoffs.

From 1996 to 2002, however, Smith chugged along in his quest to overtake Walter Payton as the NFL's all-time leading rusher. He accomplished the feat with an 11-yard run against the Seattle Seahawks on October 27, 2002.

# Game Details

## Dallas Cowboys 30 • Buffalo Bills 13

|          |   |    |    |    |        |
|----------|---|----|----|----|--------|
| Cowboys  | 6 | 0  | 14 | 10 | **30** |
| Bills    | 3 | 10 | 0  | 0  | **13** |

**Date:** January 30, 1994
**Team Records:** Dallas 12–4, Buffalo 12–4
**Scoring Plays:**
DAL—Murray 41-yard FG
BUF—Christie 54-yard FG
DAL—Murray 24-yard FG
BUF—Thomas four-yard run (Christie PAT)
BUF—Christie 28-yard FG
DAL—Washington 48-yard fumble return (Murray PAT)
DAL—Smith 15-yard run (Murray PAT)
DAL—Smith one-yard run (Murray PAT)
DAL—Murray 20-yard FG

The 2002 season turned out to be his last in Dallas. Owner Jerry Jones, sensing Smith was near the end and looking to shed his hefty salary, released him. Smith signed with the Arizona Cardinals and played two seasons, padding his career rushing totals. He retired after the 2004 season with 18,355 yards rushing—a record as safe as any in the NFL.

At his retirement speech Smith made it clear his loyalties remained with Dallas.

"You don't know how much this star means to me," he said, touching a Cowboys helmet.

Smith set so many records and produced so many lasting memories that it's hard to rank them. Die-hard Dallas fans could argue endlessly over the list. But don't forget the 15-yard touchdown run in Super Bowl XXVIII. Without it, conceivably, the Cowboys could have lost the game and never established their 1990s dynasty.

# Emmitt's Roller-Coaster Season

The Cowboys began the 1993 season without Emmitt Smith, and the season began miserably. Dallas lost its first two games as Smith and owner Jerry Jones waged a bitter contract dispute. Smith had already established himself as the league's top back. After being the Cowboys' No. 1 draft pick in 1990, Smith wasted no time in making his mark.

He rushed for 937 yards as a rookie, followed by 1,563 in 1991 and 1,713 in 1992. So Smith felt he deserved a substantial raise over his $465,000 salary. As he and Jones bickered, the Cowboys collapsed. They suffered a 35–16 blowout to the Washington Redskins in the 1993 opener. The next week, the Buffalo Bills, the team Dallas pummeled in Super Bowl XXVII, beat the Cowboys 13–10.

Emmitt Smith (No. 22) cuts around teammate Daryl Johnston (No. 48) in a game against the Green Bay Packers on October 3, 1993. Because of a contract dispute between Smith and Jerry Jones, the Cowboys actually started the 1993 season without him on the field.

Fans and players clamored for Smith's return. Jones, however, was defiant.

"Emmitt Smith is a luxury, not a necessity, for the Cowboys," he said in one interview.

But after Dallas lost its first two games, Jones wised up. He opened his wallet wide and gave Smith a four-year, $54 million contract.

"When he signs his contract for four years, then the Cowboys are big winners," Jones said when announcing the deal.

He was right. With Smith back on the field, the Cowboys reeled off seven straight wins and regained their Super Bowl form. During the rest of the season Dallas lost just two games, finishing 12–4 and winning the NFC East. Smith won his third straight rushing title, compiling 1,486 yards, despite missing the first two games. He also was named the league's Most Valuable Player.

Along the way, Smith had some huge games. In a 23–10 win over the Philadelphia Eagles, Smith gained 237 yards—the highest single-game total in 16 years. But Smith's most impressive performance came in the season's final game against the New York Giants. Both teams had 11–4 records and were playing for the divisional title.

Dallas took a 13–0 lead in the first half, but Smith severely separated his shoulder. "I could barely move my arm," he said. Many players would have sat out the second half. Not Smith.

"He said, 'Let me play until I can't play,'" coach Jimmy Johnson said.

Smith's resolve became greater when the Giants narrowed the Cowboys' lead to 13–7 early in the third quarter. Even with Smith back in the game, the Giants dominated. They kicked a field goal to tie the game at the end of regulation.

In overtime the Cowboys relied on Smith, despite his injury. He ran or caught passes on nine plays in a 10-play drive. It ended with a 41-yard field goal that gave Dallas a 16–13 win and a huge boost heading into the playoffs. Smith and the Cowboys then continued to roll. The season culminated with a 30–13 shellacking of Buffalo in Super Bowl XXVIII.

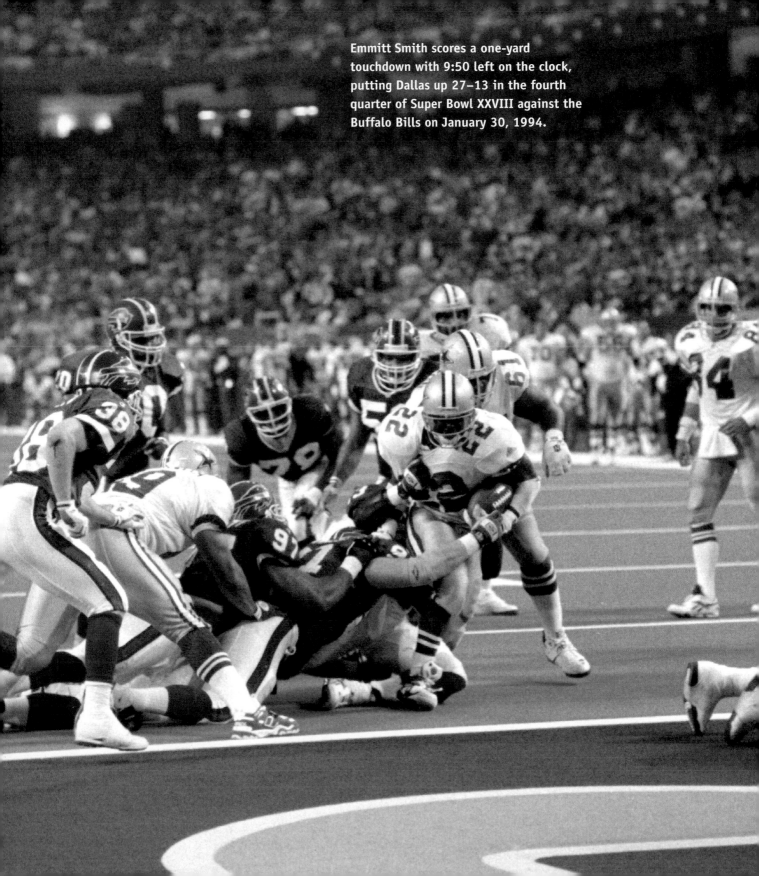

Emmitt Smith scores a one-yard touchdown with 9:50 left on the clock, putting Dallas up 27–13 in the fourth quarter of Super Bowl XXVIII against the Buffalo Bills on January 30, 1994.

January 2, 1994

# Emmitt Gets Three-Peat

## Smith's 46-yard Run Against Giants Gives Him Third Straight Rushing Title

Emmitt Smith wasted little time in becoming a superstar. In only his second year in 1991, he led the league in rushing with 1,563 yards. Was it a fluke? Not hardly. Smith repeated as rushing champ the next season with 1,713 yards.

Smith then gained 1,486 yards in 1993 to win a third straight rushing title—a feat accomplished only three other times in NFL history. Not surprisingly, the Cowboys dominated the league during those years. In 1992 they won Super Bowl XXVII, pounding the Buffalo Bills 52–17. In 1993 they repeated as champs, downing Buffalo again in Super Bowl XXVIII 30–13.

Smith locked up his third straight rushing title in 1993 with 1,486 yards. He narrowly won the title in a dramatic 16–13 overtime win against the New York Giants in the season's final game. Smith's 46-yard run just before halftime provided the margin to edge rookie Jerome Bettis of the Los Angeles Rams.

On the play, Smith suffered a separated shoulder. But he still played in the second half and finished with 168 yards rushing.

"I came in with the intention of doing whatever it took to win," Smith said. "At halftime the injury was pretty tough. I had to make a decision. I wanted to keep playing."

In 1994 Smith gained 1,484 yards but finished 399 yards behind the rushing leader, Barry Sanders. The Cowboys failed in their bid for a Super Bowl three-peat. The next season, however, Smith stormed back with a career-high 1,773 yards rushing to take his fourth and final title. Not coincidentally, the Cowboys returned to the top, defeating the Pittsburgh Steelers 27–17 in Super Bowl XXX.

The Cowboys wouldn't win another Super Bowl during Smith's career, but he kept on racking up yardage. He had his eye set on Walter Payton's all-time rushing record of 16,726 yards. By 2000 the Cowboys hardly resembled the dynasty of the early 1990s. Their record sank to 5–11, and Smith

Emmitt Smith runs 46 yards against the Giants on January 2, 1994, giving him his third straight rushing title.

# Players Drafted Before Emmitt

Emmitt Smith fooled many NFL experts. They thought he was too small and slow to succeed. How wrong they were. All Smith did was become the league's all-time leading rusher with 18,355 yards over 15 seasons.

Of the 16 players drafted before Smith, only one was a running back: Blair Thomas, the No. 2 pick of the New York Jets.

The No. 1 overall pick was quarterback Jeff George out of Illinois. The Indianapolis Colts drafted George, expecting him to be a perennial Pro Bowler. George, however, became an NFL journeyman, playing for five teams over 12 seasons without making the Pro Bowl once.

Here are picks 3 through 16, with their college and team that drafted them.

3. Cortez Kennedy, defensive tackle, Miami, Seahawks.
4. Keith McCants, defensive end, Alabama, Buccaneers.
5. Junior Seau, linebacker, USC, Chargers.
6. Mark Carrier, safety, USC, Bears.
7. Andre Ware, quarterback, Houston, Lions.
8. Chris Singleton, linebacker, Arizona, Patriots.
9. Richmond Webb, tackle, Texas A&M, Miami Dolphins.
10. Ray Agnew, defensive tackle, North Carolina State, New England Patriots.
11. Anthony Smith, defensive end, Arizona, Los Angeles Raiders.
12. James Francis, linebacker, Baylor, Bengals.
13. Percy Snow, linebacker, Michigan State, Chiefs.
14. Renaldo Turnbull, linebacker, West Virginia, Saints.
15. Lamar Lathon, linebacker, Houston, Oilers.
16. James Williams, cornerback, Fresno State, Bills.

Jeff George, pictured here playing for the Colts in 1992, was the No. 1 pick in the 1990 draft.

was the only remaining "Triplet." The other two, Troy Aikman and Michael Irvin, had recently retired because of injuries.

In 2000 Smith gained 1,203 yards, followed by 1,021 in 2001. He broke Payton's record in the eighth game of the 2002 season on an 11-yard run. He finished the year, his 13th, with 17,162 yards. Afterward Cowboys owner Jerry Jones chose not to re-sign Smith. He then signed with the Arizona Cardinals and played two more seasons, gaining a total of 1,193 more yards. He pushed his career total to 18,355.

The NFL may never see another back as productive as Smith. He rarely missed games with injuries and rarely had a bad outing. In 1991, the year of his first rushing title, Smith averaged 4.3 yards per carry and scored 12 touchdowns. In 1992, when he repeated as rushing champ, Smith improved his average carry to 4.6 yards and his touchdown total to 18. The next season he averaged an incredible 5.3 yards per carry.

Smith, at 5'9" and 210 pounds, wasn't big by NFL standards, and he wasn't particularly fast. In fact he was the 17th pick in the 1990 draft because of concerns about his speed. But he had incredible vision that allowed him to see tiny holes, and he had the ability to bounce off tacklers like a pinball.

Of course Smith had some help in amassing his prodigious yardage. In his retirement speech, he credited fullback Daryl "Moose" Johnston, who opened gaping holes for Smith.

"Nobody's tougher than Moose, nobody works any harder, and no one appreciates him more than I do," Smith said.

Smith made his mark as a rusher, but he was a complete player. His receiving ability made him doubly dangerous. He caught 486 passes during his Dallas career, making him the club's third all-time leading receiver. Since Smith left the Cowboys in 2002, they haven't had another back win a rushing title. In fact, until Smith arrived, the Cowboys had never had a player lead the league in rushing. Even the great Tony Dorsett, who played from 1977 to 1987, didn't accomplish the feat. His career-high of 1,646 yards in 1981 left him 28 yards behind the rushing winner, George Rogers of the New Orleans Saints.

Cowboys fans may have taken Smith's rushing titles for granted during the 1990s dynasty. Now that he's gone, the titles carry even greater significance.

> **E**mmitt's like a mule. As long as he's standing, he'll work.
>
> —GUARD NATE NEWTON

# Game Details

## Dallas Cowboys 16 • New York Giants 13 (OT)

| | | | | | | |
|---|---|---|---|---|---|---|
| Cowboys | 3 | 10 | 0 | 0 | 3 | **16** |
| Giants | 0 | 0 | 10 | 3 | 0 | **13** |

**Date:** January 2, 1994

**Team Records:** Dallas 11–4, New York 11–4

**Scoring Plays:**

DAL—Murray 32-yard FG

DAL—Smith five-yard pass from Aikman (Murray PAT)

DAL—Murray 38-yard FG

NY—Bunch one-yard run (Treadwell PAT)

NY—Treadwell 29-yard FG

NY—Treadwell 32-yard FG

DAL—Murray 41-yard FG

December 27, 1992

# Emmitt's Run Enables Record Season

## Smith's 31-Yard Touchdown Helps Cowboys Achieve Best-Ever 13–3 Mark

The Cowboys dominated the NFL in 1992 as few teams ever had. They sprinted to a 13–3 record to easily win the NFC East. They posted a 27–0 shutout and had routs of 37–3 and 30–3 en route to a manhandling of the Buffalo Bills in Super Bowl XXVII.

The Cowboys won their final regular-season game 27–14 over the Chicago Bears to ensure the 13–3 record, the best in franchise history. The game serves as a micro-cosm of the entire season, demonstrating the Cowboys' many offensive and defensive weapons.

Emmitt Smith, the Pro Bowl back in his third year, put the game away with a 31-yard touchdown run in the third quarter. He took a handoff from Troy Aikman, veered to the right, then cut back across the grain.

"Fullback Daryl Johnston wiped out Bears defensive end Richard Dent as left tackle Mark Tuinei sealed off the pursuit with a block on outside linebacker Ron Cox," the *Dallas Morning News* wrote. "Smith sped through the hole, then split safety Mark Carrier and corner-back Richard Fain with interference from wide receiver Michael Irvin."

The score gave the Cowboys a 10–0 lead, and they extended it to 27–0 before the Bears scored two late, meaningless touchdowns.

Smith finished the game with 20 carries for 131 yards. His season total of 1,713 yards gave him his second straight rushing title and broke the Cowboys' all-time mark of 1,646 yards set by Tony Dorsett in 1981. Aikman, another Pro Bowler, completed 10 of 20 passes for 78 yards, while backup Steve Beuerlein completed eight of 11 for 99 yards. Dallas was equally deadly running or passing the ball throughout 1992. The team averaged almost 26 points per game, second-highest in the league.

The Chicago game also illustrated Dallas' defensive domination. The Cowboys held the Bears scoreless until the fourth quarter. The Bears had only 28 yards rushing and 64 yards passing. During the season the Cowboys held opponents to an average of only 15 points per game, fifth-best among the 28 teams.

Emmitt Smith's 31-yard touchdown run against the Chicago Bears on December 27, 1992, helped secure the Cowboys'
13–3 record for the season, the best in franchise history.

# Bill Bates

More than any player on the roster, Bill Bates deserved to enjoy the unprecedented 13–3 season in 1992 and the ensuing Super Bowl victory. Yet he missed most of the year with a knee injury. He had made the team in 1983 as an undrafted free-agent safety out of Tennessee. His kamikaze-style of play on special teams won him a spot.

Bates routinely made bone-crushing hits in the open field. In his first two seasons Bates was named the league's Special Teams Player of the Year.

Bates, 6'1" and 200 pounds, gradually logged more time in regular-game situations. In 1986, his fourth season, Bates earned a starting spot at strong safety. His best season was 1988, his last as a starter. Bates had an interception and made 124 tackles.

When Jimmy Johnson took over as coach in 1989, many people expected Bates to join the list of veterans Johnson cut. But Johnson saw Bates' value to the team and kept him.

In the fifth game of 1992 Bates suffered a torn anterior cruciate ligament (ACL), one of the most serious knee injuries. He had a season-ending surgery.

Some players never return from an ACL injury, but Bates did. In 1993 he led the special teams with 25 tackles and helped Dallas return to the top. Bates played on passing downs in the Cowboys' 30–13 defeat of the Buffalo Bills in Super Bowl XXVIII.

Two years later he was part of another championship team. The Cowboys defeated the Pittsburgh Steelers 27–17 in Super Bowl XXX. After the 1997 season Bates reluctantly retired at the urging of team officials and became an assistant coach.

**Cowboys safety Bill Bates during the NFC divisional playoff, a 35–9 victory over the Green Bay Packers on January 8, 1995, at Texas Stadium.**

The 1992 season marked the culmination of the rebuilding process that Cowboys owner Jerry Jones and coach Jimmy Johnson began in 1989. That season the Cowboys compiled the league's worst record, 1–15. Four years later they had climbed to the top. It had been a steady climb. The Cowboys improved to 7–9 in 1990, 11–5 in 1991, and then 13–3 in 1992.

Regular-season records, no matter how impressive, can become irrelevant in the playoffs if a team stumbles. The Cowboys did not. They easily dispatched the Philadelphia Eagles 34–10 in the divisional game and the San Francisco 49ers 30–20 in the NFC Championship Game.

Both games again highlighted Dallas' overall excellence. In the Eagles game, Smith rushed for 114 yards and a touchdown. Aikman threw for 200 yards and two touchdowns, with no interceptions. The Dallas defense allowed only 63 yards rushing and 115 yards passing.

## Game Details

### Dallas Cowboys 27 • Chicago Bears 14

| | | | | | |
|---|---|---|---|---|---|
| **Bears** | 0 | 0 | 0 | 14 | **14** |
| **Cowboys** | 0 | 3 | 24 | 0 | **27** |

**Date:** December 27, 1992

**Team Records:** Dallas 12–3, Chicago 5–10

**Scoring Plays:**

DAL—Elliott 21-yard FG
DAL—Smith 31-yard run (Elliott PAT)
DAL—Maryland 26-yard fumble return (Elliott PAT)
DAL—Richards three-yard run (Elliott PAT)
DAL—Elliott 34-yard FG
CHI—Green six-yard run (Butler PAT)
CHI—Zorich 42-yard fumble return (Butler PAT)

The Cowboys faced a big test the next week in the NFC Championship Game. Dallas played the 49ers, who, at 14–2, had the only record better than the Cowboys'. San Francisco scored more points than Dallas during the regular season and allowed fewer. The Cowboys, however, didn't lack confidence. Before the game Johnson surprised people by predicting victory.

"We will win the ballgame," he proclaimed on a Dallas radio talk show. "You can put that in three-inch headlines."

The Cowboys backed up Johnson's words on the field. They took a 10–7 second-quarter lead on a five-yard rushing touchdown by Smith and never trailed. The Cowboys scored 13 fourth-quarter points to pull away from the 49ers. Smith got his second touchdown of the game on a 16-yard pass from Aikman.

Smith finished with 114 yards rushing, compared with 69 for Ricky Watters, the 49ers' leading gainer. Aikman outclassed San Francisco quarterback Steve Young and completed 24 of 34 passes for 322 yards, with two touchdowns and no interceptions. Young, meanwhile, connected on 25 of 35 for 313 yards. He threw one touchdown but two interceptions.

The Cowboys played even better in Super Bowl XXVII. They annihilated the Bills 52–17 to crown a magnificent season. And the Cowboys' brilliance was only beginning. They repeated as champs the next year, blowing out Buffalo again 30–13 in Super Bowl XXVIII. A 27–17 win over the Pittsburgh Steelers in Super Bowl XXX gave Dallas an unprecedented three Super Bowl wins in four seasons.

But the Dallas dynasty first emerged during the historic 1992 regular season.

> **I** knew what I needed. It was nice to get it all in one shot. The touchdown. The rushing title.
>
> —EMMITT SMITH

September 16, 2007

# Barber Makes a Statement

Marion the Barbarian Has 40-Yard Touchdown Run to Stake Claim as Team's Top Back

In 2003 the Cowboys faced an enormous challenge: replacing Emmitt Smith. Of course, you don't replace the NFL's all-time leading rusher, whom owner Jerry Jones chose not to re-sign. You simply hope to find a back who can be moderately successful and reliable.

The Cowboys failed. They started Troy Hambrick at running back in 2003. He gained 972 yards but averaged only 3.5 yards per carry. The 2004 season saw nine-year veteran Eddie George and rookie Julius Jones share the duties. Jones showed some flash, gaining 819 yards. He improved in 2005 with 993 yards rushing. Jones stepped it up more in 2006, gaining 1,084 yards.

Still, team officials still weren't entirely sold on Jones, who could be inconsistent. In 2007 coaches decided to give more playing time to Marion Barber, an intriguing third-year player. He didn't start a single game in 2007, but he logged more carries and gained more yardage than Jones while coming off the bench.

Barber made a lasting impression on a 40-yard touchdown run in the second game. His fourth-quarter score helped the Cowboys beat the Miami Dolphins 37–20 and improve to 2–0. Star receiver Terrell Owens dubbed him "Marion the Barbarian" after the game.

Marion Barber completes a 40-yard touchdown run to defeat the Miami Dolphins on September 16, 2007.

Earlier Barber had a one-yard touchdown run to give Dallas a 10–3 lead. In the Miami game Barber showed why he's so valuable. He's an excellent short-yardage back, especially around the goal line, and he can break long runs.

Barber finished the Miami game with 14 carries for 89 yards. Jones, by comparison, had 15 carries for only 32 yards. Barber began to prove he was the better back. His worth increased as the 2007 season progressed. In the third game, Barber rushed 15 times for 102 yards and a touchdown. The Cowboys routed the Chicago Bears 34–10. Jones, meanwhile, was a nonfactor with seven carries for 26 yards.

# Game Details

## Dallas Cowboys 37 • Miami Dolphins 20

| | | | | | |
|---|---|---|---|---|---|
| Cowboys | 3 | 7 | 10 | 17 | **37** |
| Dolphins | 3 | 3 | 7 | 7 | **20** |

**Date:** September 16, 2007

**Team Records:** Dallas 1–0, Miami 0–1

**Scoring Plays:**

MIA—Feely 37-yard FG

DAL—Folk 26-yard FG

DAL—Barber one-yard run (Folk PAT)

MIA—Feely 45-yard FG

MIA—Booker 18-yard pass from Green (Feely PAT)

DAL—Curtis two-yard pass from Romo (Folk PAT)

DAL—Folk 28-yard FG

DAL—Folk 47-yard FG

DAL—Owens 34-yard pass from Romo (Folk PAT)

MIA—Hagan 21-yard pass from Green (Feely PAT)

DAL—Barber 40-yard run (Folk PAT)

By the season's midpoint Barber had clearly distanced himself from Jones. Barber had 535 yards rushing and five touchdowns, versus 353 yards and two touchdowns for Jones. The Cowboys were flying high at 7–1, so coaches avoided disrupting the rotation and starting Barber. In the season's second half Barber further outclassed Jones. He wound up with 975 yards rushing and 10 touchdowns, compared with 588 yards and only two touchdowns for Jones. Barber earned a trip to the Pro Bowl, an extremely rare honor for a nonstarter.

After finishing 13–3 the Cowboys had Super Bowl dreams. But their hopes came crashing down with a 21–17 divisional playoff loss to the New York Giants, whom the Cowboys had already beaten twice in the regular season.

Dallas coach Wade Phillips rewarded Barber with a start, but the change backfired. Barber started out strong, gaining 101 yards and a touchdown in the first half. But in the second, the Giants' defense stiffened. Barber gained only 28 yards and didn't get in the end zone.

Jones once again contributed little. He picked up only eight yards on three carries in his last game as a Cowboy. Jerry Jones, not surprisingly, chose not to re-sign Julius Jones after the 2007 season. Barber entered the 2008 season as the undisputed starter.

Unfortunately, he suffered a dislocated toe late in 2008, and his production suffered. He gained 885 yards, down from 975 in 2007. Still, Barber has proven he's the real deal. He'll never be Emmitt Smith—no one will—but he's developed into one of the league's top backs.

> **B**arber thinks he's a tough guy sometimes. He likes to get into the secondary and lower his shoulder and try to run people over.
>
> —MIAMI LINEBACKER JOEY PORTER

# NFC East Hard to Beat

Year in and year out the Cowboys play in one of football's toughest divisions. The NFC East's four teams—the Cowboys, New York Giants, Philadelphia Eagles, and Washington Redskins—can usually stack up against any team in the league.

For example, look at 2008. Each team finished at least .500. The Giants won the division with a 12–4 record, followed by the Eagles at 9–6–1, the Cowboys at 9–7, and the Redskins at 8–8. Of the NFL's eight divisions, only one other—the NFC South—had every team finish at least .500.

Some other divisions epitomize mediocrity. In the final game of the 2008 season, the Denver Broncos (8–7) played the San Diego Chargers (7–8) for the AFC West title. If either had been in the NFC East, the team would have been fighting to stay out of the cellar. The NFC West wasn't much better. The Arizona Cardinals won the division with a 9–7 record. The second-place finisher, the San Francisco 49ers, came in at 7–9. The Seattle Seahawks placed third at 4–12, while the St. Louis Rams came in last at 2–14.

Marion Barber runs against the Redskins in a game on November 16, 2008. The Cowboys, Redskins, and other teams in the NFC East are usually the best teams in the league.

The NFC East's dominance also was seen in 2007. Again all four teams finished at least .500. The Cowboys compiled a 13–3 record, with the Giants second at 10–6. The Redskins were third at 9–7, and the Eagles were last at 8–8. Only the AFC South had every team compile at least a .500 record.

The NFC East has some of the best rivalries in football. The Cowboys and Redskins routinely play close games, regardless of either team's record. The rivalry intensified in the early 1970s when George Allen became the Redskins' coach. Both teams had outrageous characters, such as Diron Talbert of the Redskins, who liked to antagonize opposing players.

In the mid-1980s the Cowboys' main rival became the Eagles. The loudmouthed Buddy Ryan became coach in 1986, and he transformed the Eagles from losers to winners. Ryan managed to incense two Cowboys coaches, Tom Landry and Jimmy Johnson, by running up scores in blowout wins.

The Giants could emerge as the Cowboys' next top rival in the NFC East. The Giants stunned the Cowboys 21–17 in the 2007 divisional playoff game. Most people expected the Cowboys, who had already beaten the Giants twice in the regular season, to roll over New York again. Dallas had a 13–3 record, compared with New York's record of 10–6. But the regular-season records turned out to be meaningless. After defeating Dallas, New York went on to win Super Bowl XLII 17–14 over the New England Patriots.

In 2008 the Giants again showed their strength. The Cowboys were the preseason favorite to win the division, despite the Giants' Super Bowl victory. But the Cowboys, beset by key injuries, finished a disappointing 9–7. The Giants, meanwhile, won the division with a 12–4 record.

Both the Cowboys and Giants have deep, talented rosters. Expect many more shootouts in the coming years.

Marion Barber runs through a hole in the Miami Dolphins' defense at Dolphin Stadium on September 16, 2007.

Cowboys tight end Jason Witten continues to run with the ball despite losing his helmet during this 38–17 victory over the Philadelphia Eagles on November 4, 2007, at Lincoln Financial Field.

November 4, 2007

# Headstrong

## Tight End Jason Witten Proves Intensity in Long Run without Helmet

Jason Witten personifies old-school toughness. The best example occurred in a game against the Philadelphia Eagles midway through the 2007 season. Witten caught a pass 20 yards downfield and immediately took a huge hit. His helmet flew off. Fans gasped and expected him to drop to the turf.

But Witten didn't hesitate for even a split second. He continued running down the field and picked up another 30 yards after the hit, his hair flapping in the wind, blood dripping from his nose. Witten downplayed the incident. "I'm a tight end," he said. "I can't go down right away."

Announcers and teammates, however, marveled at Witten's toughness. "He's Superman right now; what can you say?" guard Leonard Davis said.

In the 2008 season Witten played several games with broken ribs—one of the most painful injuries. He took several hits on the sore ribs but never came out of the game.

"Injuries happen to a lot of different people," offensive coordinator Jason Garrett said. "But he's not going to get slowed down by anything minor. He's going to be out there playing."

Witten has emerged as the greatest pass-catching tight end in Cowboys history. That's quite an accomplishment, considering the team's

legacy of top-notch tight ends. The list most recently includes Pro Bowl tight end Jay Novacek in the 1990s. He was preceded by Doug Cosbie in the 1980s and Billy Joe DuPree in the 1970s—both also Pro Bowlers.

In the 1990s Novacek helped the Cowboys win three Super Bowls with his excellent route-running and key catches. He played for the Cowboys from 1990 to 1995. When he retired, Novacek held the team reception record for tight ends with 339 catches for 3,576 yards and 22 touchdowns. The record seemed secure.

But Witten soon began chipping away at the record. The Cowboys had taken Witten in the third round of the 2003 draft from Tennessee. There he began his collegiate career as a defensive end before switching to offense. He set a school record for catches and receiving yards in a season by a tight end.

The Cowboys expected Witten to be a solid player, but

> **H**e's the best because he blocks. He's not one-dimensional. Some of these tight ends are the types you put in the slot or outside, and you try to keep them away from the line of scrimmage.
>
> **—ANNOUNCER JOHN MADDEN**

they had no idea he would develop into a superstar. In his second season he became a full-time player and made 87 receptions for almost 1,000 yards and scored six touchdowns. It was the first of five straight Pro Bowl seasons.

He had his best season in 2007, the year of the helmetless run. Witten caught 96 passes, only six shy of the NFL record for tight ends. He also scored a career-high seven touchdowns. His best game occurred late in the year against the Detroit Lions. He had an amazing 15 catches, breaking a 40-year-old Cowboys record for receptions in a game.

In 2008 Witten started strong. In each of the first three games, all victories, Witten led the team in receiving. In the opener, a 28–10 win over the Cleveland Browns, he had six catches for 96 yards. He followed up with seven receptions for 110 yards and then seven catches for 67 yards in the third game.

At 6'5" and 260 pounds, Witten is a punishing blocker as well as a prolific receiver. He's also a nice guy. In 2007 he was a finalist for the NFL Man of the Year Award for his community involvement. He has formed the Jason Witten S.C.O.R.E. Foundation to help families affected by domestic violence.

Owner Jerry Jones recognized Witten's value as a player and team leader by giving him a six-year, $28 million contract extension after the 2006 season. Barring serious injury, Witten should have many more excellent seasons. At the end of 2008 he was only 26 years old. He could set records that no future Cowboys tight end could touch.

# Game Details

## Dallas Cowboys 38 • Philadelphia Eagles 17

| | | | | | |
|---|---|---|---|---|---|
| Cowboys | 14 | 7 | 14 | 3 | **38** |
| Eagles | 7 | 0 | 3 | 7 | **17** |

**Date:** November 4, 2007

**Team Records:** Dallas 6–1, Philadelphia 3–4

**Scoring Plays:**

DAL—Jones two-yard run (Folk PAT)

PHI—Westbrook three-yard run (Akers PAT)

DAL—Curtis one-yard pass from Romo (Folk PAT)

DAL—Barber five-yard run (Folk PAT)

DAL—Owens 45-yard pass from Romo (Folk PAT)

PHI—Akers 36-yard FG

DAL—Witten 20-yard pass from Romo (Folk PAT)

DAL—Folk 22-yard FG

PHI—Baskett 10-yard pass from McNabb (Akers PAT)

# Philadelphia Rivalry

The Cowboys have several longtime rivals in the NFC East. The Washington Redskins most often come to mind. But the Cowboys-Eagles rivalry often approaches the intensity level of the Cowboys and Redskins. The Cowboys' dislike of Philadelphia, and vice versa, grew in the mid-1980s when the feisty Buddy Ryan took over as Eagles coach.

Ryan brought swagger and attitude to the lowly Eagles, who had endured four straight losing seasons. By his third season, 1988, the Eagles won the NFC East, an amazing turnaround.

From 1986 to 1990, the Buddy Ryan era, the Eagles routinely thrashed the Cowboys. The two teams met 10 times, and the Eagles won eight. One of the most notorious games occurred on October 25, 1987. Philadelphia led 30–20 with only seconds left in the game. Ryan shocked the Cowboys by calling a bomb to try to get another touchdown. Dallas was flagged for pass interference, and Philadelphia got a first down at the Cowboys' 1-yard line. On the game's last play, instead of having quarterback Randall Cunningham take a knee, Ryan called a run. The Eagles scored, extending the final score to 37–20 and worsening the Cowboys' humiliation.

Landry, known as a gentleman who was slow to anger, was steaming. He refused to shake hands with Ryan afterward, as coaches customarily do.

Two seasons later, Jimmy Johnson replaced Landry as Cowboys coach. Johnson charged that Ryan had put a bounty on quarterback Troy Aikman and kicker Luis Zendejas for an upcoming Thanksgiving Day game. Ryan denied the talk of a bounty. However, during the game, Philadelphia linebacker Jessie Small injured Zendejas on a kickoff, fueling rumors. The Eagles pounded the Cowboys 27–0. Johnson blew up after the game.

"I would have said something to Buddy, but he wouldn't stand on the field long enough," Johnson said. "He put his big fat rear into the dressing room."

Ryan cackled in response. "I've been on a diet, lost a couple of pounds," he said. "I thought I was looking good."

**Former Cowboys coach Jimmy Johnson charged that Eagles coach Buddy Ryan, pictured here, had put a bounty on the heads of Cowboys Troy Aikman and Luis Zendejas.**

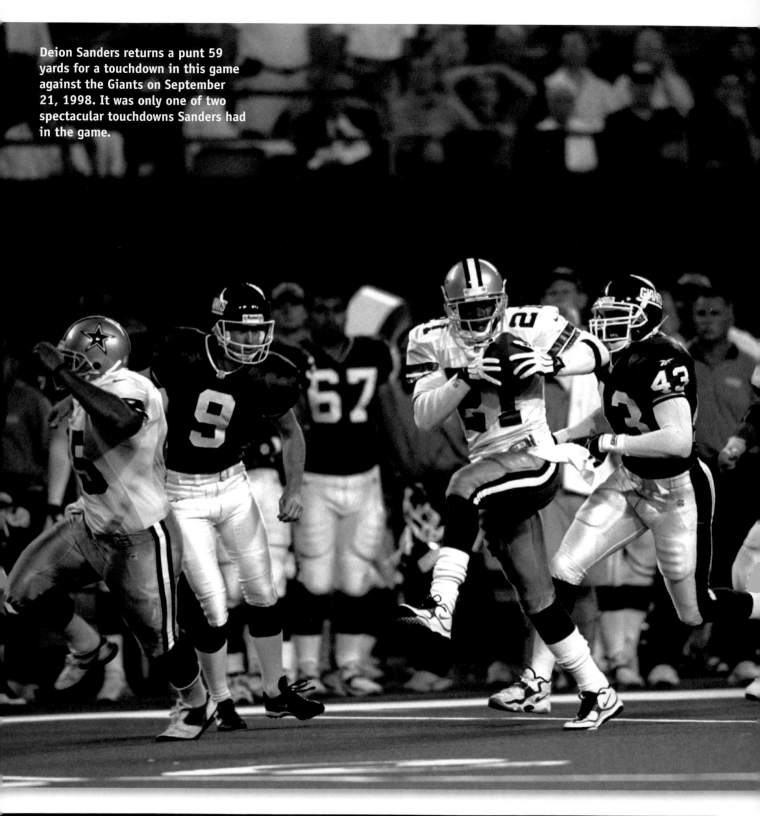

Deion Sanders returns a punt 59 yards for a touchdown in this game against the Giants on September 21, 1998. It was only one of two spectacular touchdowns Sanders had in the game.

## September 21, 1998

# Showtime

### Deion Sanders Returns Interception 71 Yards for Touchdown, Follows 59-Yard Punt-Return Touchdown

Deion Sanders was an easy player to love. And hate. He was phenomenally talented, perhaps the best cornerback to ever play pro football. But he had an ego to match and a propensity for showboating that irritated opponents and fans.

Still, Sanders was difficult not to admire. At his peak Prime Time essentially shut down half the field for the opposing offense. Quarterbacks wouldn't even throw in his direction, knowing he had receivers blanketed and was ready to snatch an interception and turn it into six points.

One of Sanders' greatest plays occurred in 1998. In a Monday-night game against the New York Giants, he returned a punt 59 yards for a touchdown in the second quarter to give Dallas a 7–0 edge. It was the fourth punt-return touchdown of his career. But Sanders made an even more spectacular play in the fourth quarter. He returned an interception 71 yards for a touchdown to seal a 31–7 Dallas blowout. It marked his eighth touchdown off an interception.

"That was an unbelievable performance," Dallas special teams coach Joe Avezzano said.

Sanders struck a humble tone after one of the most memorable games of his career, which began in 1989.

"Today, I was blessed," Sanders said after the game. "But I couldn't do it by myself. The guys out there with me were blocking their butts off."

Sanders had more dramatics five games later. He returned a punt 69 yards for a touchdown in a 34–0 shutout of the Philadelphia Eagles.

# A Two-Sport Star

Deion Sanders didn't just excel in football. He was a fine professional baseball player for nine years too. Sanders was drafted as a baseball player first. The New York Yankees took him in the 30th round of the 1988 amateur draft. Sanders signed and made it to the major leagues in 1989, the same year the Atlanta Falcons took him as their No. 1 pick in football.

In 1989 and 1990 Sanders played 71 games for the Yankees. He batted .234 his first season, then slumped to a paltry .158 in 1990. After the season the Yankees released Sanders, but the Atlanta Braves came calling. Sanders played for the Braves from 1991 through 1994—the first three years he was also earning Pro Bowl honors for the Falcons in football.

In 1994 Sanders split the baseball season between Atlanta and the Cincinnati Reds. Sanders hit .288 for Atlanta and .277 for Cincinnati in 1994. He began the 1995 season with Cincinnati, then was traded to the San Francisco Giants, where he spent the bulk of the year. He batted .285 for the Giants with an outstanding .346 on-base percentage.

The 1995 season was also Sanders' first with the Cowboys. Owner Jerry Jones seemed miffed that Sanders still wanted to play baseball, despite signing a $35 million football contract. But Jones didn't try to stop Sanders from taking to the baseball diamond.

Sanders didn't play baseball in 1996 but returned to the Reds in 1997, signing as a free agent. Sanders then retired from baseball. But in 2001, after being out of baseball for three seasons, he signed again with the Reds. However, he played in only 32 games and hit .173. He then left baseball for good.

By that time Sanders had also retired from football, but he returned in 2004 and 2005 to play for the Baltimore Ravens. Now, apparently, his athletic career is over. Sanders has turned to broadcasting and works as a football commentator.

In addition to his football greatness, Deion Sanders also played Major League Baseball for the Yankees, the Braves, and the Reds. Here he slides into third base while playing for the Reds.

Sanders played for the Cowboys from 1995 through 1999. He had some of his best years in Big D. He made the Pro Bowl three times and helped the Cowboys win Super Bowl XXX at the end of his first season. Sanders again demonstrated his versatility in the 27–17 victory over the Pittsburgh Steelers. Playing on offense, he caught a 47-yard pass to set up a touchdown that gave Dallas a 10–0 lead.

Cowboys owner Jerry Jones signed Sanders to a $35 million contract, including a $12.9 million signing bonus, after the 1994 season. Sanders had helped the San Francisco 49ers defeat Dallas 38–28 in the previous NFC Championship Game. The loss ended the Cowboys' hope of a Super Bowl three-peat. Jones wanted the electrifying Sanders on his side as he pursued another championship. The signing worked. In Sanders' first season in the Silver and Blue, the Cowboys returned to the NFL pinnacle.

From 1997 through 1999 Dallas began a steady decline from its Super Bowl–winning years. The Cowboys made the playoffs twice during that period but lost in the first round both years. Sanders performed well, though. In 1998, his best season, he had five interceptions and returned 24 punts for an average of 15.6 yards per return, a career high.

After the 1999 season Jones chose not to re-sign Sanders, who was 32 years old. The Washington Redskins inked him, and he started 15 games, intercepting four passes. Sanders then retired—at least temporarily. After being out of football for three seasons, Sanders then signed with the Baltimore Ravens in 2004. He played two years, retiring after the 2005 season at age 38. He was a part-time player in Baltimore but still had five interceptions.

The Ravens were Sanders' fifth team during his 14-year career. The Atlanta Falcons had drafted Sanders in the first round in 1989. He played five years in Atlanta, intercepting an astounding 24 passes and returning three for touchdowns, the longest of which was 82 yards. After

**H**e's a special, special athlete. I don't think people realize there are some great football players on the other team trying to stop him. But he goes around and through them. I don't know how he does it, but he does.

—DALLAS QUARTERBACK JASON GARRETT

# Game Details

## Dallas Cowboys 31 • New York Giants 7

| | | | | | |
|---|---|---|---|---|---|
| **Cowboys** | 0 | 17 | 7 | 7 | **31** |
| **Giants** | 0 | 7 | 0 | 0 | **7** |

**Date:** September 21, 1998
**Team Records:** Dallas 1–1, New York 1–1
**Scoring Plays:**
DAL—Sanders 59-yard punt return (Cunningham PAT)
NY—Toomer 36-yard pass from Kanell (Daluiso PAT)
DAL—Davis 80-yard pass from Garrett (Cunningham PAT)
DAL—Cunningham 40-yard FG
DAL—Williams 18-yard run (Cunningham PAT)
DAL—Sanders 71-yard interception return (Cunningham PAT)

leaving the Falcons in 1993 Sanders signed with the 49ers for a season before coming to Dallas.

Throughout his career, Sanders had moments of humility, but he couldn't hide his cockiness for long.

"I was never good," Sanders said. "I was always great."

# Opposition Plays

Dwight Clark of the San Francisco 49ers leaps to receive a six-yard catch from quarterback Joe Montana in the end zone with 51 seconds left, facilitating the 49ers' 28–27 win and sending them to their first Super Bowl.

January 10, 1982

# A Play That Haunted the Cowboys

## The Catch Keeps Dallas from Super Bowl, Elevates 49ers

The San Francisco 49ers became the dominant team of the 1980s, in large part because of the Catch. Dwight Clark's late touchdown pass from Joe Montana gave the 49ers a narrow 28–27 win in the 1981 NFC Championship and propelled them to the first of four Super Bowl wins of the decade. Before the Catch, and the win, the 49ers had been mostly mediocre.

Montana, a third-round pick out of Notre Dame in 1979, was just becoming a star. But for most of the 1981 championship game, he didn't play like one. He threw three interceptions as the Cowboys took a 27–21 lead late in the game. But careers are often made on late-game rallies, and Montana pulled off one of the greatest. With less than five minutes left in the game, Montana started a drive at his own 11-yard line.

Ten plays later, the 49ers had marched to the Dallas 6-yard line with less than a minute to play. On third-and-3, Montana rolled to his right, avoiding a ferocious rush by Dallas defensive linemen Ed "Too Tall" Jones and Larry Bethea. Montana lofted the ball high to get it over the outstretched arms of Jones, who stood 6'9".

Many players and fans thought Montana was throwing the ball away to avoid a sack. But Clark, standing inches from the back of the end zone, made a leap for the ages and snagged the ball in his fingertips, then came down with both feet in bounds for a touchdown.

The San Francisco crowd erupted, while Dallas players stood in shocked silence. The Cowboys took over with 51 seconds left. On first down, quarterback Danny White threw a perfect strike across the middle to receiver Drew Pearson. He broke free and seemed to have a chance to score. But San Francisco cornerback Eric Wright grabbed Pearson's jersey and brought him down at the Dallas 44. On the next play, White fumbled as he dropped to pass. The 49ers recovered and ran out the final seconds.

"I was stunned," Pearson said. "We never expected the 49ers to be able to drive it like they did and win the game."

# Game Details

## San Franciso 49ers 28 • Dallas Cowboys 27

| | | | | | |
|---|---|---|---|---|---|
| 49ers | 7 | 7 | 7 | 7 | **28** |
| Cowboys | 10 | 7 | 0 | 10 | **27** |

**Date:** January 10, 1982

**Team Records:** San Francisco 13–3, Dallas 12–4

**Scoring Plays:**

SF—Solomon eight-yard pass from Montana (Wersching PAT)

DAL—Septien 44-yard FG

DAL—Hill 26-yard pass from White (Septien PAT)

SF—Clark 20-yard pass from Montana (Wersching PAT)

DAL—Dorsett five-yard run (Septien PAT)

SF—Davis two-yard run (Wersching PAT)

DAL—Septien 22-yard FG

DAL—Cosbie 21-yard pass from White (Septien PAT)

SF—Clark six-yard pass from Montana (Wersching PAT)

> **At the time, I didn't have any idea what it would come to mean. Nobody did.**
>
> —DWIGHT CLARK

The 49ers beat the Cincinnati Bengals 26–21 two weeks later in Super Bowl XVI. For the Cowboys, the 1981 San Francisco game marked their second straight NFC Championship loss. They would suffer a third the next year, falling to the Washington Redskins 31–17.

White had four outstanding seasons after taking over for the legendary Roger Staubach, who retired in 1979. But, fair or unfair, his inability to get the Cowboys to the Super Bowl tarnished his legacy and damaged the team's confidence throughout the 1980s. After losing a third straight NFC Championship in 1982, the Cowboys didn't win another playoff game the rest of the decade.

They sank to unthinkable depths, finishing with losing records from 1986 to 1989.

Would their fate have been different if Clark hadn't made the Catch? Many would say yes.

# Dwight Clark

Mention Dwight Clark, and people think of the Catch. His legacy is inextricably tied to the dramatic game-winning catch he made in the 1981 NFC Championship Game.

But he had many other big plays during a solid nine-year career. Clark started three games as a rookie and made 18 receptions. The next year, he started 12 games and made 82 receptions, including eight for touchdowns.

In 1981 Clark had a breakout year. Before making the Catch he had 85 regular-season receptions. He earned a Pro Bowl spot in 1981 and again in 1982.

Of course Clark is frequently asked about the Catch. After scoring the touchdown, his mind raced.

"I was so excited I didn't realize we had to kick the extra point to win the game," Clark said. "I just figured, we scored and it's over."

Kicker Ray Wersching added the extra point to give the 49ers the exciting 28–27 win.

Clark wasn't even the No. 1 receiver on the touchdown play. Quarterback Joe Montana's first target was Freddie Solomon. But when Montana rolled out and saw Solomon covered, he locked in on Clark.

"When people say he was trying to throw the ball away, I just say, 'No, it was a spectacular throw, made under duress,'" Clark said. "It was thrown exactly where it needed to be thrown."

Cowboys cornerback Everson Walls in action during the NFC's 45–3 victory over the AFC in the 1984 NFL Pro Bowl, played on January 29, 1984, at Aloha Stadium.

# Everson Walls

The Catch could have ruined Everson Walls' career. After all, he was an undrafted rookie who gave up the game-winning touchdown in an NFC Championship Game. The next week, he graced the cover of *Sports Illustrated*—trailing Dwight Clark as he made the memorable catch.

But Walls rebounded from the debacle and built a stellar 13-year career. Walls had played college football at Grambling, and despite leading the nation in interceptions as a senior, he went undrafted.

But Walls attended the Cowboys' 1981 training camp, confident of making the team. He had been a lifelong Cowboys fan. Walls lived walking distance from the practice facilities and used to watch the team work out. Walls immediately impressed coaches with his big-play ability.

As a rookie he led the NFL in interceptions—the first rookie to do so in 14 years. From 1982 to 1985 he had a total of 23 interceptions and made the Pro Bowl three times.

He has always felt he received too much criticism for the 1981 NFC Championship loss to the 49ers. People remember that Clark beat him for the game-winning touchdown. But most don't remember Walls' two interceptions and recovered fumble. "My thoughts of that game have always been mixed because I was on my way to an MVP game," Walls said.

In 1990 second-year head coach Jimmy Johnson cut Walls as he looked for younger, faster players. He finished his Dallas career with 44 interceptions—second only to Mel Renfro's 52.

After being released, Walls became a starter for the rival New York Giants and played a big role in the Giants' 20–19 win over the Buffalo Bills in Super Bowl XXV. In 1992 Walls was traded to the Cleveland Browns. He retired after the 1993 season.

January 17, 1971

# A Bitter Loss

O'Brien's 32-Yard Field Goal Gives Colts
Stunning 16–13 Super Bowl V Win

The Cowboys should have won Super Bowl V. Ask anyone who watched the game. Dallas had several chances to put away the Baltimore Colts, but costly mistakes kept the game close.

With only five seconds remaining and the score tied 13–13, Baltimore's Jim O'Brien hit a 32-yard field goal to give the Colts an astounding 16–13 win. Dallas' legendary defensive tackle, Bob Lilly, reflected the team's utter frustration when he hurled his helmet 40 yards downfield at the final gun.

"To lose that game like we did was the lowest point of my career," said the Hall of Famer.

O'Brien seemed like an unlikely savior for the Colts. He was a rookie and had made only 19 of 34 field-goal attempts during the season. He had also missed two extra points. In Super Bowl V O'Brien had missed a field goal and an extra point before lining up for the game-winner. The kick was never in question. It sailed straight and true, like a dagger in the Cowboys' collective heart. "We beat ourselves," Tom Landry said. "The fumbles and interceptions killed us."

To understand the Cowboys' ire, consider their recent past in championship games. In the 1966 and 1967 title games, Dallas narrowly lost to Green Bay in the final seconds. In the first, Dallas fell 34–27 when Don Meredith threw an end-zone interception on fourth down. In the second, the famous Ice Bowl, Green Bay's Bart Starr snuck into the end zone from one yard out with 13 seconds left. The Packers won 21–17.

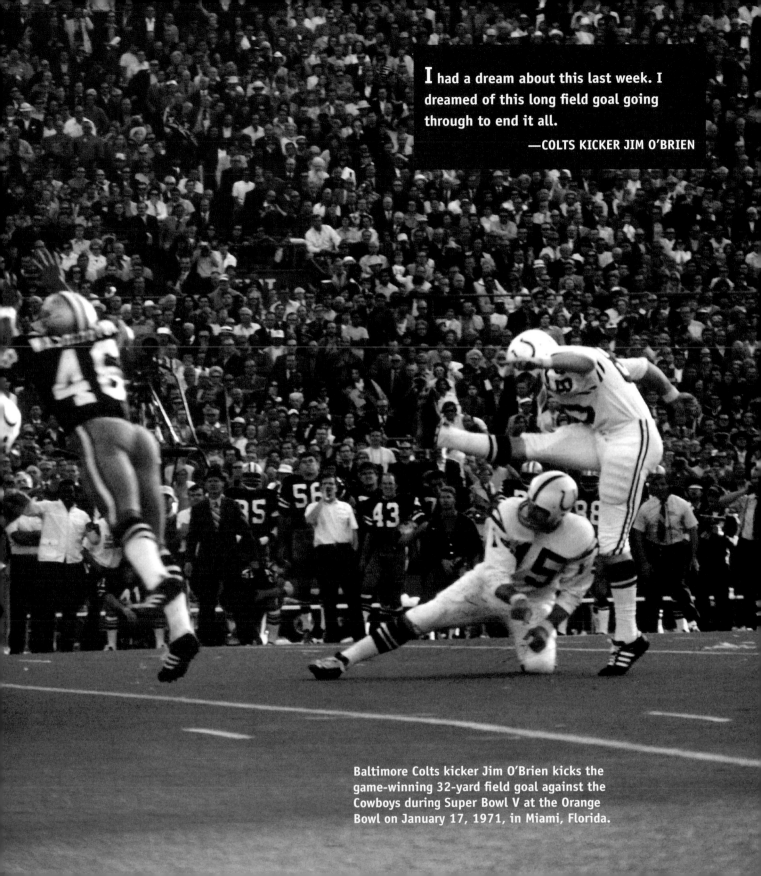

Baltimore Colts kicker Jim O'Brien kicks the game-winning 32-yard field goal against the Cowboys during Super Bowl V at the Orange Bowl on January 17, 1971, in Miami, Florida.

In Super Bowl V, following the 1970 season, Dallas wanted to finally shed its growing reputation as a big-game loser. The Cowboys took a 6–0 lead early in the second quarter on Mike Clark's second field goal. But less than a minute later Baltimore scored a touchdown on a bizarre play.

The Colts' Johnny Unitas dropped back and fired a pass across the middle to receiver Eddie Hinton. The ball sailed high and deflected toward Dallas cornerback Mel Renfro. It skimmed off his fingers into the arms of Baltimore's big tight end John Mackey. He rumbled 75 yards for a touchdown, but the Cowboys protested mightily.

Renfro insisted he didn't touch the ball. If true, the play should have been called back. The rules prevent an offensive player from tipping a ball to a teammate unless a defender touched it in between. The officials, however, let the touchdown stand. Dallas gained a little redemption by blocking the extra point to keep the game tied 6–6.

Fired up, the defense clamped down on the Colts. Dallas linebacker Lee Roy Jordan blasted Unitas, causing him to fumble, and Dallas recovered. The Cowboys quickly moved toward the goal line, and rookie sensation Duane Thomas scored on a seven-yard pass from Craig Morton to put Dallas up 13–6 at halftime.

The Cowboys caught another huge break on the second-half kickoff. Baltimore fumbled, and Dallas recovered at the Colts' 31-yard line. Five plays later Dallas had marched to the 2-yard line. Thomas took a handoff but fumbled inches from the goal line. After a mad struggle for the ball, Dallas center Dave Manders emerged from the pile holding it high. Incredibly the referees awarded the ball to the Colts. Baltimore lineman Bubba Smith had yelled "Our ball! Our ball!" amid the confusion and apparently swayed the officials.

For the second time, the Cowboys felt robbed by the refs. The third quarter ended with Dallas clinging to a seven-point lead. Midway through the fourth period, Dallas committed a costly turnover. Morton tossed a short pass to fullback Walt Garrison, but it was high and deflected off his fingers. Colts safety Rick Volk intercepted and returned the ball to the Dallas 3-yard line. Tom Nowatzke scored on a two-yard run to tie the game at 13.

The Cowboys regrouped and moved to the Baltimore 48-yard line with only two minutes remaining. They were closing in on a game-winning field goal. Or so they thought. But Morton threw his third interception, coming off a wobbly pass in the flat to halfback Dan Reeves. The ball skimmed off his fingers, and Baltimore linebacker Mike Curtis intercepted. He returned it to the Dallas 28-yard line with just over a minute remaining. The Colts ran the ball twice to get in position for a field goal. Then O'Brien ran onto the field. He said he had dreamed he would kick the game-winning field goal. To the Cowboys' dismay, he was right.

## Game Details

### Baltimore Colts 16 • Dallas Cowboys 13

| | | | | | |
|---|---|---|---|---|---|
| Colts | 0 | 6 | 0 | 10 | **16** |
| Cowboys | 3 | 10 | 0 | 0 | **13** |

**Date:** January 17, 1971

**Team Records:** Baltimore 11–2–1, Dallas 10–4

**Scoring Plays:**

DAL—Clark 14-yard FG

DAL—Clark 30-yard FG

BAL—Mackey 75-yard pass from Unitas (PAT blocked)

DAL—Thomas seven-yard pass from Morton (Clark PAT)

BAL—Nowatzke two-yard run (O'Brien PAT)

BAL—O'Brien 32-yard FG

**I** don't take anything away from the Colts. But we should have won.

**—DALLAS LINEMAN BOB LILLY**

# Chuck Howley

Players are normally ecstatic when they receive the Super Bowl's Most Valuable Player award. Not Dallas linebacker Chuck Howley. He was named the top player of Super Bowl V in a losing effort. "It was hard to rejoice," Howley said. "We had just lost the biggest game of the season." He remains the only player on a losing team to be named Super Bowl MVP.

Howley and his teammates got redemption the next year, pounding the Miami Dolphins 24–3 in Super Bowl VI. Early in the fourth quarter Howley intercepted a pass near midfield and seemed headed for a touchdown. But he tripped and fell at the 9-yard line. The play didn't hurt the Cowboys, but it made Howley wince.

"Nobody around me, blockers everywhere, and I just crash," Howley said. "Needless to say, it was a little embarrassing."

Howley's 15-year career contained many more highlights than lowlights. He had been a first-round draft pick of the Chicago Bears in 1958 but suffered a serious knee injury in his second year and was released. He thought his career was over, and he returned to his native West Virginia and bought a gas station.

The Cowboys came calling a year later, and Howley joined them for their second season in 1961. He became a starter and made an immediate impact. By 1965, his fifth Dallas season, Howley was named All-Pro. He received the honor five more times.

Throughout the late 1960s and early '70s Howley was an integral part of the Doomsday Defense. He retired after the 1973 season with glittering statistics and was inducted into the Cowboys' Ring of Honor in 1976, only the fourth player to receive the recognition.

Howley had a remarkable combination of size, speed, and big-play ability. Many believe he should be in the Pro Football Hall of Fame. Howley, however, has never complained. He let his play speak for itself.

"I gave what I could," Howley said. "You look back on life and think, *Was there more I could have done?* I don't know that I could have."

Cowboys linebacker Chuck Howley earned MVP honors in Super Bowl V, becoming the first player on a losing team to do so. The Cowboys lost Super Bowl V 16–13 to the Baltimore Colts on January 17, 1971.

Green Bay Packers Hall of Fame quarterback Bart Starr turns to hand off to running back Donny Anderson in a 21–17 victory over the Dallas Cowboys in the 1967 NFL Championship Game on December 31, 1967, at Lambeau Field. Starr's quarterback sneak sealed the victory for his team in the game that has come to be known as the Ice Bowl.

December 31, 1967

# Icy Agony

## Starr's Late Quarterback Sneak Sinks Cowboys in Ice Bowl

On a single play, Bart Starr became a Green Bay Packers immortal and a Dallas Cowboys nemesis. Starr's dramatic one-yard quarterback sneak with 16 seconds left gave the Packers a 21–17 win over the Cowboys in the 1967 NFL Championship Game.

The game will always be remembered as much for the bone-chilling weather as for this play. The temperature at Green Bay's Lambeau Field stood at 13 degrees below zero at kickoff, and winds gusted at 15 miles per hour. The temperature and wind chill dropped further as the game progressed.

But few, if any, of the more than 50,000 die-hard Packers fans left the stadium. After all, Green Bay, Wisconsin, was Title Town, USA. The Packers had beaten the Cowboys 34–27 in the previous year's championship, and fans wanted to see their players repeat and earn their fifth title of the 1960s.

The Packers and Cowboys presented a classic matchup. Green Bay, under legendary disciplinarian coach Vince Lombardi, had a grind-it-out style of offense and a smothering defense. Dallas, led by the cerebral Tom Landry, had a speedy offense prone to big plays and an intimidating defense known as "Doomsday."

The Packers, slight favorites, took a 14–0 lead in the second quarter after Starr threw his second touchdown pass to Boyd Dowler, this one covering 46 yards. But the Cowboys fought back. Dallas' Willie Townes unloaded on Starr as he dropped to pass, forcing a fumble. Fellow lineman George Andrie scooped up the ball and rumbled seven yards for a touchdown. The Cowboys then recovered a fumbled Packers punt and kicked a 21-yard field goal to pull to within 14–10 at halftime.

# Bart Starr

Starr had an outstanding 16-year career that culminated in his induction into the Pro Football Hall of Fame. But in his first few seasons Starr seemed destined for mediocrity.

He was a mere 17th-round pick out of Alabama and played little as a rookie in 1956. Although he saw more action in his second and third seasons, Starr threw twice as many interceptions as touchdowns. But in his fourth year, 1959, Vince Lombardi took over as coach of the hapless Packers. Lombardi, a keen judge of talent, saw untapped potential in Starr.

Lombardi's confidence in Starr quickly paid off. In 1960 Starr developed into one of the NFL's top quarterbacks, completing 57 percent of his passes and earning a spot in the Pro Bowl. He led the Packers to an 8–4 record and the Western Division title. The season ended, however, with a 17–13 loss to the Philadelphia Eagles in the NFL title game.

In 1961 Starr had an even better season, completing 58 percent of his passes and throwing 16 touchdowns. He was named All-Pro, and Green Bay won the first of five NFL championships in the 1960s. From 1960 to 1967 Starr compiled an astounding 73–18–4 record.

In 1967 Starr had his most memorable performance in the 21–17 Ice Bowl victory over the Dallas Cowboys. His one-yard quarterback sneak in the closing seconds gave the Packers their fifth title.

After the win Starr led Green Bay to the second of back-to-back Super Bowl wins. The Packers had crushed the AFL's Kansas City Chiefs 35–10 in Super Bowl I. They followed up the Ice Bowl victory with a 33–14 hammering of the Oakland Raiders in Super Bowl II. In both title games Starr was named MVP.

In his later years Starr's performance trailed off and the Packers declined. In his final season, 1971, Starr played in only four games, throwing three interceptions and no touchdowns. The Packers finished 4–8–2, last in the NFC Central Division.

But Starr's legacy was secure. Only two years after he retired, the Packers retired his No. 15 jersey. Despite his extraordinary success, Starr remained humble. He took pride in team accomplishments more than individual glory.

**Bart Starr throws a pass during Super Bowl I against the Kansas City Chiefs at Memorial Coliseum on October 15, 1967, in Los Angeles.**

In the third quarter neither team scored. The frozen field made footing treacherous and eliminated Dallas' speed advantage. Early in the fourth quarter the Cowboys stunned the Packers and their huddled fans. Halfback Dan Reeves hit receiver Lance Rentzel on a 50-yard touchdown pass—a remarkable play under the difficult conditions. Dallas had its first lead, 17–14. But Green Bay, despite giving up 17 straight points, didn't lose its composure. Lombardi wouldn't allow that.

With 4:50 left in the game, Starr began a drive at his own 32-yard line. He completed a series of short passes to his running backs, who skated to one first down after another. After nine plays the Packers had a first down at the Dallas 1-yard line. Less than a minute remained. The weary, disheartened Cowboys now had to stage a defensive stand for the ages.

They almost pulled it off. The Dallas linemen, their breath visible in the icy air, turned back Green Bay's Donny Anderson on first and second downs. The Packers faced third down with only 16 seconds remaining. Starr called his team's last timeout to confer with Lombardi. The coach quickly ruled out kicking a tying field goal, deciding to gamble and go for the win.

Many Dallas players and coaches expected a pass. After all, Green Bay had tried two unsuccessful rushes. If the Packers ran the ball again and didn't score, time would run out. Instead Lombardi called a quarterback sneak, putting the team's fortunes in the hands of Starr. He took the snap, lowered his head, churned his legs, and found a sliver of an opening to squeeze in for the game-winning touchdown.

Dallas took the kickoff and lined up with 13 seconds remaining. But two desperation passes by quarterback Don Meredith fell incomplete, and the game ended. The Cowboys, after mounting a valiant comeback, suffered a devastating defeat—one that would haunt the franchise for years.

"We were so close," Rentzel said.

> **A**s bad as the cold was for us, it had to be worse for them. They were all hunched over, rubbing their hands, moving their legs up and down, trying to persuade themselves that they weren't insane to be playing football in this ridiculous weather.
>
> —PACKERS OFFENSIVE LINEMAN JERRY KRAMER

# Game Details

## Green Bay Packers 21 • Dallas Cowboys 17

|         |   |    |   |   |    |
|---------|---|----|---|---|----|
| Cowboys | 0 | 10 | 0 | 7 | **17** |
| Packers | 7 | 7  | 0 | 7 | **21** |

**Date:** December 31, 1967

**Team Records:** Green Bay 9–4–1, Dallas 9–5

**Scoring Plays:**

GB—Dowler eight-yard pass from Starr (Chandler PAT)

GB—Dowler 46-yard pass from Starr (Chandler PAT)

DAL—Andrie seven-yard fumble return (Villanueva PAT)

DAL—Villanueva 21-yard FG

DAL—Rentzel 50-yard pass from Reeves (Villanueva PAT)

GB—Starr one-yard run (Chandler PAT)

January 15, 1995

# Short Run, Huge Impact

## Rookie Fullback's One-Yard Touchdown Plunge Kills Cowboys' Chance of Super Bowl Three-Peat

Talk about a horrendous start to a big game. The Cowboys had a major meltdown at the start of the 1994 NFC Championship Game against the San Francisco 49ers. They couldn't have picked a worse time to collapse.

The Cowboys were trying to become the first team to win three straight Super Bowls. They had demolished the Buffalo Bills twice—52–17 in Super Bowl XXVII and 30–13 in Super Bowl XXVIII. If the Cowboys could get past the 49ers, they would be in prime position to accomplish the historic feat. The Cowboys had already beaten San Francisco in the two previous NFC Championships to advance to the Super Bowl, so they didn't lack confidence.

"We had San Francisco's number, and they weren't going to beat us," Dallas safety Darren Woodson said.

No one could have imagined how the game would start. On the Cowboys' third play, quarterback Troy Aikman threw a short pass that was intercepted and returned 44 yards for a touchdown. On the next drive, receiver Michael Irvin caught an Aikman pass but fumbled as he stretched for a first down. The 49ers quickly scored on a 29-yard touchdown pass. San Francisco now led 14–0, and only 4:19 had elapsed.

It was close to panic time, and the game had just begun. Yet Dallas' situation became even more desperate. On the ensuing kickoff, the Cowboys fumbled. Seven plays later the 49ers lit up the scoreboard again. Rookie fullback William Floyd, a bruising 242 pounds, scored on a one-yard run.

For the rest of the game Floyd wasn't a factor. He carried only six times for 19 yards. San Francisco's Pro Bowl running back Ricky Watters bore the brunt of the work. But Floyd's short touchdown run essentially sealed a 49ers victory. Even with the Cowboys' star-studded roster,

they couldn't overcome a three-touchdown hole against a team as strong as the 49ers.

Floyd's name may be forgotten in the history books. He had a mediocre seven-year career with San Francisco and Carolina, gaining a total of only 1,141 yards. But that one-yard plunge dealt a lethal blow to the Cowboys midway through the first quarter of the all-important NFC Championship Game.

"It was like a horror movie," first-year coach Barry Switzer said. "I couldn't believe it."

Dallas' pregame swagger, born of back-to-back championships, had disappeared. All eyes focused on Switzer, who had replaced Jimmy Johnson. Would Switzer chew out his players after falling behind 21 points? Would he kick their rears? Instead, he used humor to motivate them.

"I turned to them and said, 'Guys, you know what's great about being down 21–0 after seven minutes?'" Switzer recalled. "They all looked at me like I'm crazy. I said, 'Because we got 53 minutes to get back in this SOB.'"

# Game Details

## San Francisco 49ers 38 • Dallas Cowboys 28

| | | | | | |
|---|---|---|---|---|---|
| Cowboys | 7 | 7 | 7 | 7 | **28** |
| 49ers | 21 | 10 | 7 | 0 | **38** |

**Date:** January 15, 1995

**Team Records:** San Francisco 13–3, Dallas 12–4

**Scoring Plays:**

SF—Davis 44-yard interception return (Brien PAT)

SF—Watters 29-yard pass from Young (Brien PAT)

SF—Floyd one-yard run (Brien PAT)

DAL—Irvin 44-yard pass from Aikman (Boniol PAT)

SF—Brien 34-yard FG

DAL—Smith four-yard run (Boniol PAT)

SF—Rice 28-yard pass from Young (Brien PAT)

DAL—Smith one-yard run (Boniol PAT)

SF—Young three-yard run (Brien PAT)

DAL—Irvin 10-yard pass from Aikman (Boniol PAT)

Maybe he used the best approach. The Cowboys did start playing like themselves. Late in the first quarter Aikman threw a 44-yard touchdown pass to get Dallas' first points. In the second quarter Emmitt Smith had a four-yard touchdown run to close the gap to 24–14. Dallas had momentum and confidence. But just before halftime 49ers receiver Jerry Rice caught a 28-yard touchdown pass to extend their lead to 31–14.

Still, Dallas had awoken. Could they pull off an incredible comeback in the second half? In the third quarter the Cowboys and 49ers traded touchdowns, making the score 38–21. Midway through the fourth, Aikman led the Cowboys on an 89-yard drive that ended with a 10-yard touchdown pass to Irvin. Now the score stood at 38–28.

The dream of victory and a Super Bowl three-peat then died. The 49ers' defense stiffened and kept the Cowboys out of the end zone. Fittingly, the 49ers sacked Aikman on the game's final play.

"This is very tough," Aikman said. "I've never lost a playoff game before."

Players and coaches still were trying to grasp how the Cowboys, a team that made few mistakes, could commit three costly turnovers in the first seven minutes.

"I have racked my brain, and I don't think I've fumbled in two or three years," Irvin said. "I can't believe that happened here."

Switzer chose to focus on how the Cowboys had fought their way back into the game after the disastrous start.

"This team didn't quit on either side of the ball," he said. "It was a gutsy performance by the two-time defending world-championship football team."

> **Y**ou make the kind of mistakes we made in the first part of the ballgame, and you say, "How in the world will we have a chance to win the ballgame?" But we did.
>
> —BARRY SWITZER

# Steve Young

Steve Young watched from the sideline as Joe Montana led the San Francisco 49ers to two Super Bowl wins in the late 1980s. Young had great talent, but people wondered if he would get a chance to win his own Super Bowl.

He did in 1994, his fourth year as a starter. Young had replaced Montana and had played well, earning Pro Bowl honors in 1992, 1993, and 1994. But he didn't win a Super Bowl title, as Montana had done routinely.

Young had his finest season in 1994, completing 70 percent of his passes and throwing 35 touchdowns. The 49ers finished the regular season 13–3, rolling over teams by scores of 50–14, 44–14, and 42–3.

But 49ers fans still had doubts about Young. Sure, he had led the 49ers to the playoffs in 1992 and 1993, but they'd lost the NFC Championship both times to the Cowboys. However, the third straight title game against Dallas proved to be Young's redemption. He completed just 13 of 29 passes for 155 yards, but he threw for two touchdowns and ran for a third. Most important, he shed the title of the best NFL quarterback never to play in a Super Bowl. In the 1994 championship game, the 49ers bolted to a 21–0 first-quarter lead over Dallas. Young's 29-yard touchdown pass to Ricky Watters aided the cause.

In Super Bowl XXIX, Young again excelled. The 49ers rolled over the San Diego Chargers 49–26 and Young was named Most Valuable Player. Young had four more Pro Bowl seasons before retiring in 1999.

Young's statistics earned him entry into the Pro Football Hall of Fame in 2005. In his acceptance speech, he talked about the difficulty of being a backup in San Francisco before getting his shot.

"It was tough to live with during some of those years," Young said. "But as I look back I am thankful for the struggles and trials that I had and for the opportunities that were given to me."

San Francisco 49ers quarterback Steve Young throws a pass against the Dallas Cowboys at Texas Stadium in the 1993 NFC Championship Game on January 23, 1994. The Cowboys defeated the 49ers 38–21.

January 18, 1976

# Swann Song

Receiver's 64-Yard Touchdown Catch Beats Cowboys 21–17 in Super Bowl X

Lynn Swann killed the Cowboys in Super Bowl X. His four receptions for 161 yards helped the Pittsburgh Steelers topple the Cowboys 21–17 and earned him the Most Valuable Player award.

Swann's 64-yard touchdown catch late in the fourth quarter iced the game, giving Pittsburgh a 21–10 lead.

"Far downfield, Swann had a half-step on cornerback Mark Washington," the *Dallas Morning News* reported. "He grabbed the ball inside the Dallas 5-yard line and raced into the end zone, tossing the ball jubilantly back over his head to celebrate the score. Swann and the Steelers seemed to think the contest was settled."

In the first half Swann made two phenomenal, acrobatic catches. The most impressive was a 53-yard grab down the middle of the field. Swann made the juggling catch while falling, despite good coverage by Washington.

"It always makes me feel good when the passing game plays such a big role in a victory," Swann said. "We're a running team. We're known as a grind-it-out club, and we win with that. But the passing game was clicking today."

Swann, Pittsburgh's No. 1 draft choice in 1974 out of USC, had a Pro Bowl year in 1975. He caught 49 passes for 781 yards and scored 11 touchdowns. Swann played nine seasons, retiring in 1982 at age 30. In 2001 he was inducted into the Pro Football Hall of Fame. His four catches in Super Bowl X helped put him there.

The Steelers' victory over the Cowboys was their second straight Super Bowl win. Pittsburgh had won Super Bowl IX 16–6 over the Minnesota Vikings. The Steelers won two more championships in the 1970s, clearly establishing themselves as the team of the decade. Pittsburgh defeated Dallas again 35–31 in Super Bowl XIII. In that game, the Steelers' other star receiver, John Stallworth, burned the Cowboys. He had two touchdowns, one covering 28 yards and the other 75. The next year the Steelers beat the Los Angeles Rams 31–19 in Super Bowl XIV.

The Cowboys' two Super Bowl losses to the Steelers still haunt players. In both games Dallas had chances to win. In Super Bowl XIII Cowboys tight end Jackie Smith dropped a sure touchdown in the end zone that could have won the game.

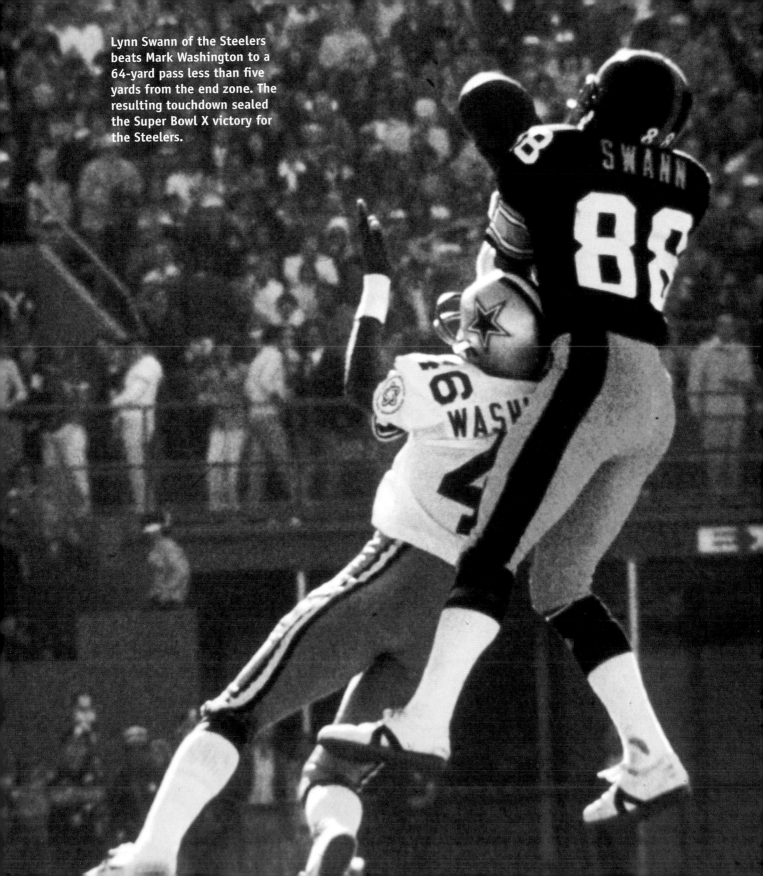

Lynn Swann of the Steelers beats Mark Washington to a 64-yard pass less than five yards from the end zone. The resulting touchdown sealed the Super Bowl X victory for the Steelers.

# Terry Bradshaw

Terry Bradshaw padded his Hall of Fame résumé with two Super Bowl victories over the Cowboys. He had a combined 527 yards passing and six touchdowns in Super Bowl X and Super Bowl XIII. In each, he made clutch plays to ensure victory for the Pittsburgh Steelers.

In the second win, Bradshaw got revenge on cocky Dallas linebacker Thomas "Hollywood" Henderson. Leading up to the game Henderson had said Bradshaw was so dumb, he "couldn't spell *cat* if you spotted him *T* and *C*." Bradshaw responded with an MVP performance, completing 17 of 30 passes for 318 yards and four touchdowns. "Ask Henderson if I was dumb today," Bradshaw said after the game.

Bradshaw had a rocky beginning in the NFL. In his first two seasons, he started 21 games and compiled an 8–13 record. He threw 46 interceptions, compared with only 19 touchdowns.

He had a breakout season in 1972. He started every game and led Pittsburgh to an 11–3 record to top the AFC Central. In the divisional playoff game, the Steelers beat the Oakland Raiders 13–7. In the AFC Championship, however, the Steelers fell 21–17 to the Miami Dolphins.

Two seasons later Bradshaw led the Steelers to a 16–6 victory over the Minnesota Vikings in Super Bowl IX. He completed nine of 14 passes for 96 yards and one touchdown.

In 1975 Bradshaw made the Pro Bowl for the first of three times. He completed almost 58 percent of his passes in directing the Steelers to a 12–2 record. In Super Bowl X he passed for 209 yards and two touchdowns to beat Dallas 21–17.

In 1978 Bradshaw had his finest year. The Steelers finished 14–2, and he threw 28 touchdown passes. In the two playoff games leading up to Super Bowl XIII, Bradshaw performed magnificently. The Steelers' 35–31 Super Bowl win over the Cowboys gave Bradshaw three rings and established him as an all-time great.

Bradshaw got a fourth the next year, as the Steelers downed the Los Angeles Rams 31–19 in Super Bowl XIV. He had another strong performance, passing for 309 yards and two touchdowns. He was chosen MVP for the second time.

His stats, plus his 4–0 record in Super Bowls, made him an easy Hall of Fame choice in 1989.

**Pittsburgh Steelers Hall of Fame quarterback Terry Bradshaw fires a pass during the AFC divisional playoff, a 28–10 victory over the Baltimore Colts on December 27, 1975.**

The 1975 version of the Steelers could have been their best. They sent 11 players to the Pro Bowl—three on offense and eight on defense. Besides Swann, the others included quarterback Terry Bradshaw, running back Franco Harris, and defensive linemen Joe Greene and L.C. Greenwood.

The Steelers finished 12–2 to win the AFC Central with the conference's best record. Their famed Steel Curtain defense allowed only 162 points—an average of only 11.6 per game, tops in the NFL. The Steelers swept through the playoffs, defeating the Baltimore Colts 28–10 and the Oakland Raiders 16–10 to reach Super Bowl X.

Dallas surprised many people by advancing to the Super Bowl. The Cowboys finished 10–4, earning a wild-card spot with a team that included 12 rookies. In the opening round of the playoffs Dallas defeated the favored Minnesota Vikings 17–14 on Drew Pearson's famed Hail

> **Cliff Harris came over one time after a play and told me I was lucky because he just missed me with a good shot.**
>
> **—LYNN SWANN**

Mary touchdown catch. The next week the Cowboys pounded the Rams 37–7.

The Steelers were favored over the Cowboys, but Dallas struck first with a 29-yard touchdown pass from Roger Staubach to Drew Pearson. Pittsburgh responded with a seven-yard touchdown pass, then Dallas kicked a 36-yard field goal to take a surprising 10–7 halftime lead.

Neither team scored in the third quarter. In the fourth, Pittsburgh blocked a punt, and the ball rolled out of the end zone for a safety. Then field goals of 36 and 18 yards gave the Steelers a 15–10 lead. After Swann's long touchdown catch, the Cowboys responded with a 34-yard touchdown reception by rookie Percy Howard to make the score 21–17. Dallas got the ball back once more, but the game ended with a Staubach interception.

Swann had several more outstanding seasons after Super Bowl X. Two years later, in 1977, he caught 50 passes for 789 yards and seven touchdowns. Swann's best season came in 1978, the year the Steelers beat the Cowboys in Super Bowl XIII. That year Swann had a career-high 61 receptions for 880 yards and 11 touchdowns.

In Super Bowl XIV, the Steelers' last championship of the 1970s, Swann led the Steelers with five catches for 79 yards, including a 47-yard touchdown. But he made his career with his MVP performance in Super Bowl X. The Cowboys unwittingly helped punch Swann's ticket to the Hall of Fame.

> **Nobody can properly cover Lynn Swann by himself.**
>
> **—MARK WASHINGTON**

# Game Details

## Pittsburgh Steelers 21 • Dallas Cowboys 17

| | | | | | |
|---|---|---|---|---|---|
| Cowboys | 7 | 3 | 0 | 7 | **17** |
| Steelers | 7 | 0 | 0 | 14 | **21** |

**Date:** January 18, 1976

**Team Records:** Pittsburgh 12–2, Dallas 10–4

**Scoring Plays:**

DAL—D. Pearson 29-yard pass from Staubach (Fritsch PAT)

PIT—Grossman seven-yard pass from Bradshaw (Gerela PAT)

DAL—Fritsch 36-yard FG

PIT—Safety, Harrison blocked Hoopes' punt our of end zone

PIT—Gerela 36-yard FG

PIT—Gerela 18-yard FG

PIT—Swann 64-yard pass from Bradshaw (kick failed)

DAL—Howard 34-yard pass from Staubach (Fritsch PAT)

**Johnny Roland returns a punt 74 yards for a touchdown to begin a thorough embarrassment of the Cowboys in the first game of** *Monday Night Football* **in 1970.**
*Photo courtesy of AP Images.*

November 16, 1970

# Monday Night Massacre

**Roland's 74-Yard Punt Return Touchdown Begins Cards' 38–0 Rout**

In 1970 the Cowboys made their debut on *Monday Night Football*. It was a memorable game—for all the wrong reasons. The Cowboys embarrassed themselves, losing 38–0 to the St. Louis Cardinals at home. Dallas got off to a horrendous start and never recovered. St. Louis' Johnny Roland returned a punt 74 yards for a touchdown in the first quarter to start the slaughter.

"I had fielded the same type of punt earlier on a fair catch," Roland said. "But I had made up my mind that if I got another one like that, I was going to see what I could do with it."

The big plays continued. John Gilliam had a 48-yard end-around for a touchdown in the second quarter, and Jim Bakken kicked a 31-yard field goal to give St. Louis a 17–0 halftime lead. In the second half the game really got out of hand. Roland scored two more touchdowns on runs of three and 10 yards. Roy Shivers ended the scoring with a 29-yard touchdown run to make the final score 38–0.

The Cotton Bowl crowd booed heartily. Quarterback Craig Morton played pitifully, completing only eight of 26 passes and throwing three interceptions. Some fans turned to the announcers' booth, where former Dallas quarterback Don Meredith was helping to call the game.

"We want Meredith!" they shouted. "We want Meredith!"

Meredith, who had retired after the 1968 season, wanted no part of the debacle.

"Not a chance," he told viewers.

Ironically, the Monday-night meltdown might have helped the Cowboys. Afterward their record stood at 5–4. The Cowboys then won five straight games to finish the season at 10–4 and win the NFC East. The Cardinals were 7–2 after beating Dallas, but they collapsed down the stretch and finished 8–5–1, out of the playoffs.

After the humiliating loss, coach Tom Landry had an interesting response. Instead of cracking the whip on players, he loosened up. The unexpected strategy worked, and players motivated themselves to salvage the season, defensive tackle Bob Lilly said.

"Landry realized that everyone was pushing too hard, so he relaxed everything," Lilly said. "For the only time in my career with the Cowboys, I heard him tell everyone to just have fun. Shoot, we even started playing volleyball and touch football once a week instead of running wind sprints and sitting in the meeting room."

The Cowboys stormed back the week after the St. Louis blowout. They soundly defeated the Washington Redskins 45–21. Rookie running sensation Duane Thomas scored three touchdowns. A 16–3 win over the Green Bay Packers followed. Then the Cowboys manhandled the Redskins again, this time 34–0. The 1970 season ended with a 52–10 pounding of the Houston Oilers. The incomparable Bob Hayes caught four touchdown passes, the last covering 59 yards.

In the playoffs the Cowboys kept their momentum. They won an ugly 5–0 contest over the Detroit Lions in the divisional game. In the NFC Championship Game the Cowboys downed the San Francisco 49ers 17–10 to advance to their first Super Bowl.

The Cowboys, however, had a disheartening end to the season. In an error-filled game, they lost 16–13 to the Baltimore Colts. Colts rookie kicker Jim O'Brien had a 32-yard field goal in the final seconds for the win. Dallas had

# Game Details

## St. Louis Cardinals 38 • Dallas Cowboys 0

| | | | | | |
|---|---|---|---|---|---|
| Cardinals | 7 | 10 | 0 | 21 | **38** |
| Cowboys | 0 | 0 | 0 | 0 | **0** |

**Date:** November 16, 1970
**Team Records:** St. Louis 6–2, Dallas 5–3
**Scoring Plays:**
STL—Roland 74-yard punt return (Bakken PAT)
STL—Gilliam 48-yard run (Bakken PAT)
STL—Bakken 31-yard FG
STL—Roland 10-yard run (Bakken PAT)
STL—Roland three-yard run (Bakken PAT)
STL—Shivers 29-yard run (Bakken PAT)

multiple chances to win the game, but a goal-line fumble by Thomas and three costly interceptions by Morton gift-wrapped the game for the Colts.

Still, the Cowboys could be proud of their remarkable recovery after the 38–0 shellacking. Some teams would have folded up and quit. Not the Cowboys.

Their resolve paid dividends the next season. In 1971 the Cowboys improved to 11–3, again winning the NFC East. In the playoffs Dallas beat the Minnesota Vikings 20–12 and then toppled the 49ers 14–3 in the NFC Championship Game. Dallas then played an almost flawless game in dominating the Miami Dolphins 24–3 in Super Bowl VI.

The drive that fueled the championship run had its roots in the 38–0 nightmare of 1970.

# Monday Night Redemption

It's impossible to erase the memory of the 38–0 loss the Cowboys suffered in the opening season of *Monday Night Football*. But since then they've been on the winning end of several Monday-night blowouts.

Here are the Cowboys' five most lopsided wins:
- 38–0 over Baltimore Colts, September 4, 1978.
- 40–3 over New Orleans Saints, September 24, 1973.
- 35–0 over New York Giants, September 4, 1995.
- 34–0 over Philadelphia Eagles, November 2, 1998.
- 37–7 over Houston Oilers, December 13, 1982, and 44–14 over Washington Redskins, September 9, 1985, are tied.

Emmitt Smith breaks the tackle of the New York Giants' Vencie Glenn and runs for a 60-yard touchdown in the first quarter of a 35–0 drubbing of the Giants at Giants Stadium on September 4, 1995.

# Fumbles
## and
# Blunders

January 6, 2007

# A Playoff Victory Slips Away

Romo's Mishandling of Snap on Easy Field Goal Leads to 21–20 Seattle Win

Tony Romo has developed into the next great Cowboys quarterback, following the likes of Roger Staubach and Troy Aikman. He beat incredible odds, starting as an undrafted free agent and sitting on the bench for four years before getting his shot.

The Romo fairytale reached its pinnacle in the 2006 season. He had a Pro Bowl year after taking over as starter in the seventh game. Romo completed 65 percent of his passes and threw 19 touchdowns. Dallas finished 9–7 and earned a wild-card playoff slot. The team drew a manageable playoff opponent, the Seattle Seahawks, who also finished 9–7. Dallas took a 10–6 halftime lead, in part because of a 13-yard touchdown pass from Romo to Patrick Crayton. But the Seahawks went ahead 21–20 late in the fourth quarter on a 37-yard touchdown pass.

> **I**t looked like a good snap. I can't tell you what happened after that.
>
> **—BILL PARCELLS**

The stage was set for Romo to pull off his first dramatic playoff comeback. The Cowboys started at their own 28-yard line with 4:24 left. Romo moved the team to the Seattle 2-yard line with 1:19 left. The fiery Bill Parcells, in his fourth season as Cowboys coach, anticipated getting the franchise's first playoff win since 1996. So did everyone else watching the game. All the Cowboys had to do was make a 19-yard field goal—shorter than an extra point.

But Romo, an experienced holder, flubbed a perfect snap in dry conditions. Dallas fans shrieked. Romo tried to salvage the play. He picked up the ball, stumbled, then sprinted toward the left side of the end zone. He came up two yards short, tackled from behind by defensive back Jordan Babineaux.

After being tackled, Romo laid on the ground for a few seconds, face down on the turf, absorbing the enormity of the miscue. In the locker room the boyish Romo cried openly. Admirably he faced the bright TV lights of a news conference to apologize to fans and teammates.

"I don't know that I've ever felt this low at any point," he said.

Coaches and teammates tried to soothe Romo. They said all the clichés: football is a team game, we win and

Tony Romo, left, bungles the snap as kicker Martin Gramatica steps in for the kick with 1:19 left in this game against the Seattle Seahawks on January 6, 2007. It cost the Cowboys a spot in the playoffs. *Photo courtesy of AP Images.*

Quarterback Troy Aikman rolls out to his right during Super Bowl XXVIII against the Buffalo Bills on January 30, 1994.

# Life after Troy Aikman

The Cowboys were spoiled at the quarterback position for more than a decade. Aikman, the team's No. 1 draft choice in 1989, immediately became the starter and held the job until he retired after the 2000 season. His accomplishments earned him quick induction into the Pro Football Hall of Fame. But when he retired, the Cowboys hadn't done an adequate job of planning for his replacement. As a result, they ran through seven quarterbacks from 2001 until 2006, when Tony Romo emerged as the starter.

In 2001 the Cowboys played musical chairs at quarterback. Quincy Carter, the team's No. 2 draft that year, started eight games. Ryan Leaf, a No. 1 pick of the San Diego Chargers who had failed miserably, started three games. Anthony Wright, a free agent, got three starts. Clint Stoerner, another free agent, started twice. None played well enough to hold on to the job.

In 2002 the Cowboys played only two quarterbacks: Carter and Chad Hutchinson, a 25-year-old rookie who had played professional baseball after college.

Just before the 2004 season, the Cowboys released Carter. There were rumors of a failed drug test, but the team never confirmed the reports. The Cowboys then turned to a proven, albeit ancient, quarterback: Vinny Testaverde. He had had an excellent 17-year career with four teams. But when he came to Dallas he was 41 years old. Still, he played better than the 20-somethings he replaced. But the Cowboys disappointed again, finishing 6–10.

For 2005 the Cowboys signed another proven veteran: Drew Bledsoe. He started every game and proved to be the best quarterback since Aikman. But early in 2006 Bledsoe's performance dipped dramatically. At halftime of the sixth game, Parcells made Romo the starter. The Cowboys lost the game, but Romo threw two touchdowns and showed flashes of brilliance.

In the games to come, the free-agent find would surpass everyone's expectations.

lose together, no one player costs the team a game. But the words seemed hollow to Romo.

Some thought the Cowboys could advance to the Super Bowl. It was a lofty prediction, but Romo had pulled off the improbable many times before. Instead the Cowboys could only wonder *What if?* The Seahawks lost the next week to the Chicago Bears, who won the NFC Championship Game and advanced to Super Bowl XLI. That could have been the Cowboys.

Some people worried if the botched snap would haunt Romo and the Cowboys. Would it destroy his confidence? Would the fairytale end and Romo return to an anonymous life as a backup?

No. Romo had overcome adversity before, and he wasn't going to let one bad play crush his spirit. In 2007

Romo showed the same star quality he had the previous year. He completed 64 percent of his passes, tossing 36 touchdowns. The Cowboys finished 13–3, their best record since the Super Bowl–winning year of 1992. They scored the most points in the NFC and won lopsided games by scores of 35–7, 34–3, and 34–10.

They made the playoffs but once again suffered a painful loss. The Cowboys fell 21–17 to the wild-card New York Giants, the eventual Super Bowl champs. But the loss was much more of a team effort. No one could point the finger directly at Romo.

Again in 2008 Romo showed no ill effects from the mishandled snap against the Seahawks. He played with swagger, leading the Cowboys to an easy 28–10 opening win and a 3–0 start. Then he broke his finger in the sixth game, and the Cowboys struggled with backups Brad Johnson and Brooks Bollinger. They suffered blowouts of 34–14 and 35–14.

Romo's importance to the team became obvious in his absence. When he returned in the season's 10th game, the Cowboys resumed their winning ways. They won a hard-fought game 14–10 over the Washington Redskins, then rolled over San Francisco and Seattle.

Few people ask Romo about the playoff nightmare against the Seahawks in 2006. He's had many big games since, proving his mental toughness. Owner Jerry Jones rewarded Romo with a six-year, $67.5 million contract during the 2007 season.

With Romo's talent and big-play ability, he'll surely have playoff success. And he no longer has to hold for field goals. He's much too valuable for that.

# Game Details

## Seattle Seahawks 21 • Dallas Cowboys 20

| | | | | | |
|---|---|---|---|---|---|
| Cowboys | 3 | 7 | 7 | 3 | **20** |
| Seahawks | 3 | 3 | 7 | 8 | **21** |

**Date:** January 6, 2007

**Team Records:** Dallas 9–7, Seattle 9–7

**Scoring Plays:**

SEA—Brown 23-yard FG

DAL—Gramatica 50-yard FG

SEA—Brown 30-yard FG

DAL—Crayton 13-yard pass from Romo (Gramatica PAT)

SEA—Stevens 15-yard pass from Hasselbeck (Brown PAT)

DAL—Austin 93-yard kickoff return (Gramatica PAT)

DAL—Gramatica 29-yard FG

SEA—Safety, Glenn fumbles, ball rolls out of end zone

SEA—Stevens 37-yard pass from Hasselbeck (pass failed)

> **Y**ou coach long enough, you end up seeing about everything.
>
> —SEATTLE COACH MIKE HOLMGREN

January 21, 1979

# A Devastating Drop

## Jackie Smith's Mishandling of Easy Touchdown Pass Helps Steelers Win Super Bowl XIII

Jackie Smith had a magnificent Hall of Fame career. He caught 480 passes for nearly 8,000 yards and scored 40 touchdowns. He retired in 1978 with more receptions than any tight end in NFL history.

Yet most fans remember just one of Smith's plays, and it wasn't a game-winning touchdown or an open-field run. It was a dropped pass in the end zone of Super Bowl XIII. In the third quarter, with the Cowboys trailing the Pittsburgh Steelers 21–14, Smith worked free in the end zone. Dallas quarterback Roger Staubach spotted Smith and tossed a soft, 10-yard pass to him.

The ball, however, was slightly behind the wide-open Smith. He turned his shoulders to grab the ball and slipped. As he fell to the ground, the ball bounced off his hands onto the turf. A classic photo shows Smith prone on the ground, an agonizing grimace on his face. Dallas went on to lose the game 35–31. Staubach always blamed himself for not making a better throw.

"I've gone over that pass to Smith time and time again," he said.

Cowboys tight end Jackie Smith drops a pass in the end zone during Super Bowl XIII against the Pittsburgh Steelers at the Rose Bowl on January 21, 1979. The dropped pass cost the Cowboys the Super Bowl win.

A photographer also caught coach Tom Landry after the drop. The normally emotionless coach threw his head back and gritted his teeth as if in great pain. Afterward he said he felt nothing but sympathy for Smith.

"I never saw a more despondent player than Jackie Smith in the locker room following Super Bowl XIII," Landry said. "Jackie felt absolutely sick. And I felt for him."

Smith, a 6'4", 235-pound bear of a man, had no comment about the drop. In the years afterward, he patiently answered questions about the play. But before Super Bowl XXX, as a new generation of Cowboys and Steelers faced off, reporters wanted to revisit the famous play.

Smith didn't cooperate.

# Game Details

## Pittsburgh Steelers 35 • Dallas Cowboys 31

| | | | | | |
|---|---|---|---|---|---|
| Steelers | 7 | 14 | 0 | 14 | **35** |
| Cowboys | 7 | 7 | 3 | 14 | **31** |

**Date:** January 21, 1979

**Team Records:** Pittsburgh 14–2, Dallas 12–4

**Scoring Plays:**

PIT—Stallworth 28-yard pass from Bradshaw (Gerela PAT)

DAL—Hill 39-yard pass from Staubach (Septien PAT)

DAL—Hegman 37-yard fumble return (Septien PAT)

PIT—Stallworth 75-yard pass from Bradshaw (Gerela PAT)

PIT—Bleier seven-yard pass from Bradshaw (Gerela PAT)

DAL—Septien 27-yard FG

PIT—Harris 22-yard run (Gerela PAT)

PIT—Swann 18-yard pass from Bradshaw (Gerela PAT)

DAL—DuPree seven-yard pass from Staubach (Septien PAT)

DAL—Johnson four-yard pass from Staubach (Septien PAT)

> **A**ll Jackie wanted was to win a Super Bowl. Roger tried to throw the ball a little too easily. Jackie was expecting a stronger throw.
>
> **—COACH TOM LANDRY**

"I think 17 years is enough to be nice, and I don't want to be nice about it anymore," he said.

Smith played only one season for the Cowboys. He had retired after a stellar, 15-year Pro Bowl career with the St. Louis Cardinals. There he had been a model of consistency for a struggling team. His best season came in 1967 when he caught 56 passes and scored nine touchdowns, including an 76-yarder.

Smith played with abandon, often flattening would-be tacklers, yet he was incredibly durable. He appeared in 121 straight games from his rookie year in 1963 to 1971 before missing time with an injury. He also had 45 consecutive games in which he caught at least one pass.

Yet for all Smith's exploits, the Cardinals team made the playoffs only twice during his tenure and never advanced beyond the divisional round. The Cowboys, knowing they had Super Bowl potential heading into the 1978 season, signed the 38-year-old, battle-tested veteran to back up Pro Bowl tight end Billy Joe DuPree.

Smith proved his worth in the Cowboys' narrow 27–20 divisional playoff win over the Atlanta Falcons. He caught three passes, including a two-yard touchdown pass to tie the game.

After the gut-wrenching Super Bowl loss, Smith retired. In 1994 he was inducted into the Pro Football Hall of Fame. It's a mystery why voters waited so long to give Smith football's highest honor.

> **I**t's hell to lose.
>
> **—COWBOYS GENERAL MANAGER TEX SCHRAMM**

# The Pittsburgh Problem

Dallas' 35–31 loss to Pittsburgh in Super Bowl XIII came only three years after Super Bowl X, where the Cowboys fell 21–17 to the Steelers. In both games, Dallas could have won. In the first quarter of Super Bowl X the Cowboys held a 10–7 halftime lead. Dallas held on to the precarious lead through the third quarter.

But in the fourth quarter the Steelers put up 14 unanswered points. They scored on a 64-yard touchdown reception by Lynn Swann, who had given the Cowboys fits all day. He made four highlight-reel catches, setting a Super Bowl record with 161 yards receiving.

Late in the fourth quarter, Staubach threw a 34-yard touchdown to bring the Cowboys to within four points. They stopped the Steelers and got the ball back with 1:22 remaining. Staubach, king of the dramatic comeback, seemed poised to pull off another miracle.

He moved Dallas to the Pittsburgh 38-yard line with less than a minute to play. But he threw two incompletions followed by an interception in the end zone. Pittsburgh held on to win.

In Super Bowl XIII Pittsburgh took an early 7–0 lead on a touchdown pass from Terry Bradshaw to John Stallworth. But Dallas answered with two touchdowns to take a 14–7 lead but then trailed 21–14 at halftime. In the third quarter Dallas held Pittsburgh scoreless and kicked a field goal to close the gap to 21–17.

In the final period, Franco Harris had a 22-yard touchdown run, which was followed by an 18-yard touchdown catch by Lynn Swann. Under Staubach, the Cowboys mounted a furious comeback. He threw two touchdown passes to make the score 35–31. But Pittsburgh then ate up the remaining time, and Dallas never got the ball back.

Cowboys who played in both Super Bowls still sting from the losses.

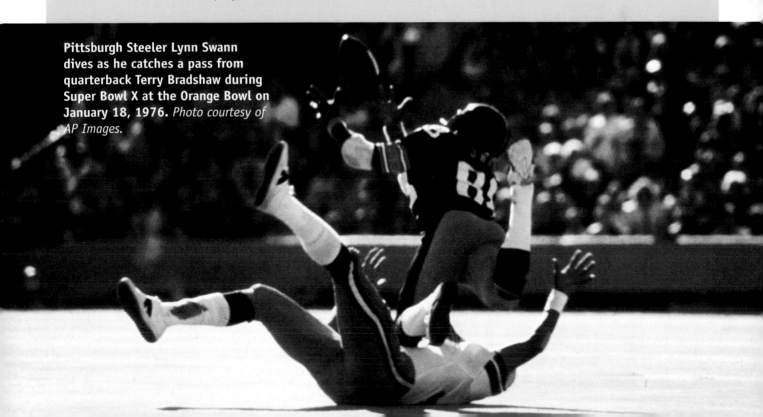

**Pittsburgh Steeler Lynn Swann dives as he catches a pass from quarterback Terry Bradshaw during Super Bowl X at the Orange Bowl on January 18, 1976.** *Photo courtesy of AP Images.*

# Super Bowl Dry Spell Awaits

By the late 1970s, the Cowboys were making regular Super Bowl appearances. The 35–31 loss to the Steelers in Super Bowl XIII marked the Cowboys' fifth trip to the summit. No team had more visits.

Few could have imagined the wasteland that would lie ahead. Dallas wouldn't return to the Super Bowl for 15 years. During that decade and a half, the Cowboys had several opportunities to reach the big game but fell short each time.

The most painful period occurred between 1980 and 1982 immediately after quarterback Roger Staubach retired. For three straight years the Cowboys advanced to the NFC Championship Game, shouting distance from the Super Bowl.

But each time, under quarterback Danny White, they couldn't get the job done. In 1980, White's first season as a starter, the Cowboys fell 20–7 to division rival Philadelphia in the NFC Championship Game. The next season ended with a painful 28–27 loss to San Francisco—the game that featured the Catch, Joe Montana's last-second touchdown to Dwight Clark. In strike-shortened 1982, the Cowboys got drubbed by Washington 31–17 in the final game before Super Bowl XVII.

Those three seasons were agonizing for Cowboys fans and players. But they were nothing compared to the misery to come. During the rest of the 1980s, the Cowboys' combined regular-season record was a lowly 49–62. In 1984 Dallas missed the playoffs for the first time in a decade. In 1986 the Cowboys posted their first losing season in 22 years.

The decline only accelerated. In 1988, after the Cowboys finished with a dismal 3–13 record, the unthinkable occurred: Tom Landry, the only coach in the club's 29-year history, was fired by new owner Jerry Jones. But in the first year under new head coach Jimmy Johnson, the team sank to new depths with a 1–13 record. By 1990 fans wondered if the Cowboys would ever return to glory.

Quarterback Danny White looks to hand off during the Cowboys' 38–0 victory over the Tampa Bay Buccaneers in the 1981 NFC Divisional Playoff Game on January 2, 1982, at Texas Stadium. Between 1980 and 1982, the Cowboys were unable to advance to the Super Bowl under quarterback White.

Tony Romo is sacked by Kawika Mitchell (No. 55) for a 14-yard loss in the fourth quarter of the NFC divisional playoff game against the New York Giants on January 13, 2008. *Photo courtesy of AP Images.*

January 13, 2008

# Romo Magic Fails

## Quarterback Can't Throw Late touchdown, Cowboys Upset by Giants in Playoffs

Tony Romo has made a career out of doing the improbable. Few expected the free agent to even make the Cowboys' roster. When he did, few expected him to be anything but a backup. After he became a starter midway through 2006, few could foresee he would become a Pro Bowl player with an incredible knack for the big play.

However, by the time the Cowboys met the New York Giants in the 2007 playoffs, Romo had proven himself beyond any doubts. Romo and the Cowboys, runaway winners of the NFC East, were expected to easily handle the wild-card Giants. But the game didn't follow the script.

The scrappy Giants, behind two touchdown passes by Eli Manning, tied the game at 14 shortly before halftime. In the second half the New York defense stiffened, and Dallas could manage only a 34-yard field goal. In the fourth quarter, the Giants pulled ahead 21–17 on a one-yard run by Brandon Jacobs.

Still, with less than two minutes remaining, the Cowboys began a final drive with a chance to win. All they needed was another Romo touchdown pass. On third down Romo overthrew receiver Patrick Crayton in the end zone. On fourth down, with only 15 seconds left, Romo's pass to Terry Glenn was intercepted in the end zone.

The promising season had come to a screeching halt.

"It hurts," Romo said after the game. "It's tough right now."

Romo had thrown a team-record 36 touchdown passes during the season. But when the Cowboys needed a touchdown the most, Romo didn't produce. Fans couldn't believe the Cowboys lost. They couldn't believe Romo hadn't saved the day one more time. Romo had a mediocre game by his standards: 18 of 36 with one touchdown and one interception. But he doesn't deserve all the blame for the loss.

The Cowboys committed 11 penalties, several that killed drives. Receivers dropped passes. The defense couldn't stop the Giants' running game.

"It's a shame on our part, because we have the talent on this team," star receiver Terrell Owens said.

The Cowboys rolled through the regular season, compiling a 13–3 record, tied for best in the NFC. They averaged more than 28 points per game, second in the NFL to the 16–0 New England Patriots. Dallas, which sent 11 players to the Pro Bowl, seemed to have few, if any, weaknesses. Because the Cowboys won their division, they had a week off during the wild-card playoff round.

Romo received some criticism for taking off to Mexico with Jessica Simpson, his glamorous singer/actress girlfriend. Maybe the trip sent the wrong message. Maybe he should have led his teammates in daily workouts at home. But his jaunt seems an unlikely reason for the Cowboys' overall lackluster performance against the Giants.

The Giants began strong. On the game's first possession they drove 77 yards in six plays, culminating in a 52-yard touchdown pass to Amani Toomer. The Cowboys' first drive, by contrast, ended in a punt.

The Cowboys held the Giants on the subsequent drives and began a possession on their own 4-yard line. Romo directed a masterful, nine-play scoring drive that ended in a five-yard touchdown pass to Owens. On their next possession, the Cowboys scored again. A one-yard touchdown run by Marion Barber capped a 20-play, 90-yard drive.

Dallas, which had begun the game sluggishly, now seemed to be hitting its stride. However, with only seven seconds left in the first half, Toomer caught his second touchdown pass, this one covering four yards. The score blunted the momentum Dallas had gained with its long touchdown drive.

In the third quarter Dallas had another long drive, this one covering 62 yards. But instead of a touchdown, the Cowboys managed only a 34-yard field goal. Still, they had a 17–14 lead. Early in the fourth quarter the Giants began a drive at the Cowboys' 37-yard line. Six plays later,

> **W**e had a good position going into the playoffs, and it's just so disappointing because you put in so much time.
>
> **—TONY ROMO**

# Game Details

## New York Giants 21 • Dallas Cowboys 17

| | | | | | |
|---|---|---|---|---|---|
| Giants | 7 | 7 | 0 | 7 | **21** |
| Cowboys | 0 | 14 | 3 | 0 | **17** |

**Date:** January 13, 2008

**Team Records:** Dallas 13–3, New York 10–6

**Scoring Plays:**

NY—Toomer 52-yard pass from Manning (Tynes PAT)

DAL—Owens five-yard pass from Romo (Folk PAT)

DAL—Barber one-yard run (Folk PAT)

NY—Toomer four-yard pass from Manning (Tynes PAT)

DAL—Folk 34-yard FG

NY—Jacobs one-yard run (Tynes PAT)

Jacobs had a one-yard touchdown run that proved to be the game-winner.

Romo still had a chance to work his magic. With 1:50 left in the game, Dallas began a drive at its own 48-yard line. Five plays later the Cowboys had moved to the Giants' 23-yard line, striking distance from the goal line. But two incompletions, followed by an interception, ended the Cowboys' hopes of a dream season.

"I'm dying," said owner Jerry Jones, who had signed Romo to a six-year, $67 million contract earlier in the season. "I'm absolutely dying."

# Marion Barber

Marion Barber pulled off a rare feat in 2007: he made the Pro Bowl despite not starting a game all season. He didn't complain that Julius Jones started each week. Barber quickly entered the game and went to work. He wound up getting more carries than Jones, 204 to 164. And Jones rushed for only 588 yards, almost 400 fewer than Barber.

For the playoff game against the New York Giants, Dallas coach Wade Phillips gave Barber his first start. In the first half of the New York game, Phillips looked like a genius. Barber gained 101 yards on 16 carries, scoring a one-yard touchdown to give Dallas a 14–7 lead. In the second half Barber was much less effective, rushing 11 times for only 28 yards. The playoff loss, however, didn't hurt Barber's stock with owner Jerry Jones.

He didn't try to re-sign Julius Jones during the off-season. Instead the owner gave Barber a seven-year, $45 million contract. He was now the man. Early in the 2008 season, Barber broke loose for 142 yards in a 27–16 win over the Green Bay Packers. Dallas improved to 3–0.

The Cowboys had taken Barber in the fourth round of the 2005 draft. His career began slowly. He rushed for 538 yards as a rookie and 654 his second year. During those same two seasons, Jones totaled 2,077 yards. But in 2007 Barber emerged as the leading rusher.

Barber constantly improvises. If the intended hole isn't open, he'll bounce one direction or the other until he finds daylight. At 5'11" and 221 pounds, he's stockier and more powerful than Jones. He'll punish defenders as he gains yardage.

Barber is notoriously quiet. He doesn't grant interviews, and reporters have stopped asking him for comments. He lets his actions do the talking.

Marion Barber runs the ball against the Philadelphia Eagles on December 28, 2008, at Lincoln Financial Field.

December 10, 1995

# Questionable Play Call

## Switzer's Fourth-and-1 Decision Backfires, Gives Eagles Win

Cowboys owner Jerry Jones surprised everyone when he named Barry Switzer coach in 1994. Even Switzer. He said he was getting out of the shower in his Norman, Oklahoma, home when the phone rang and Jones made the offer.

"I said, 'Who wouldn't want to coach the best team with the best coaching staff and the best players?'" Switzer said.

Switzer seemed like an unlikely choice for a couple of reasons. One, he had been out of football for five years since resigning under pressure at Oklahoma. Two, Switzer had no professional coaching experience. His potent wishbone offense helped him win three collegiate national championships, but it wouldn't translate to the pros. Still, Jones was convinced he had the right man to succeed the enormously successful Jimmy Johnson, who had won two Super Bowls in five years.

"Barry is recognized as a motivator, and he's loyal to his players to a fault," Jones said. "Those were the traits I wanted in my head coach."

Anticipation mounted for the 1994 season. In the opener the Cowboys easily defeated the Pittsburgh Steelers 26–9. They also won the second week 20–17 over the Houston Oilers. The Cowboys finished 12–4 and won the NFC East. In the opening round of the playoffs Dallas whipped the Green Bay Packers 35–9. But in the NFC Championship Game the Cowboys fell to the San Francisco 49ers 38–28. The Cowboys had committed three early turnovers that allowed the 49ers to build a 21–0 first-quarter lead.

Criticism of Switzer increased in his second year when he made a coaching decision that baffled many fans and commentators. The Cowboys were playing the Philadelphia Eagles late in the season, and the Cowboys faced a fourth-and-1 at their own 29-yard

Running back Emmitt
Smith leaps high atop
a pile of linemen and
is stopped short of the
first down by Eagles
linebacker Kurt Gouveia
(No. 54).

line. The game was tied 17–17 late in the fourth quarter. Everyone assumed the Cowboys would punt, because they were deep in their own territory.

Instead, Switzer called a running play called Load Left, and the Eagles stopped Emmitt Smith short of the first down. The ball went over on downs. Three plays later the Eagles kicked a 42-yard field goal to win with 1:30 remaining.

"It surprised us," Philadelphia coach Ray Rhodes said of Switzer's decision. "I think I would have punted in that situation."

The Cowboys rebounded and won the last two games to finish 12–4 for the second straight year. In the first playoff game the Cowboys met the Eagles again. Switzer and the Cowboys got revenge with a 30–11 pasting. In the NFC Championship Game the Cowboys beat the Green Bay Packers 38–27 to earn a trip to Super Bowl XXX.

## Game Details

### Philadelphia Eagles 20 • Dallas Cowboys 17

| | | | | | |
|---|---|---|---|---|---|
| Cowboys | 7 | 10 | 0 | 0 | **17** |
| Eagles | 3 | 3 | 8 | 6 | **20** |

**Date:** December 10, 1995
**Team Records:** Dallas 10–3, Philadelphia 8–5
**Scoring Plays:**
PHI—Anderson 42-yard FG
DAL—Smith 10-yard run (Boniol PAT)
DAL—Boniol 21-yard FG
DAL—Brown 65-yard interception return (Boniol PAT)
PHI—Anderson 27-yard FG
PHI—Watters one-yard run (Barnett pass from Peete)
PHI—Anderson 38-yard FG
PHI—Anderson 42-yard FG

> **I** was a little surprised. But when they lined up in the same blocking scheme the second time, I knew it was coming, and I knew where I had to be to stop it.
> —EAGLES DEFENSIVE TACKLE ANDY HARMON

There the Cowboys dominated the Pittsburgh Steelers 27–17. Switzer had won redemption.

"We did it our way, baby!" Switzer screamed to Jones in the postgame celebration.

The jubilation wouldn't last long. The next season, 1996, the Cowboys dipped to 10–6 and, after beating the Minnesota Vikings 40–15 in the first playoff game, lost 26–17 the next week to the Carolina Panthers. The 1997 season was even worse. The Cowboys finished an almost unthinkable 6–10 and missed the playoffs. Jones fired Switzer.

Some players said Switzer had been a good fit initially. His laid-back style was a welcome change from the authoritarian approach of Johnson. But after four seasons of loose reins, the Cowboys had become undisciplined and unfocused.

Jones made another surprising hire to replace Switzer. He picked Chan Gailey, offensive coordinator of the Pittsburgh Steelers. Gailey lasted only two seasons. In his first, 1998, the Cowboys finished 10–6 and made the playoffs but lost in the first round. In 1999 the Cowboys were 8–8 and made the playoffs. Again they exited in the first round.

Jones then fired Gailey and made another unexpected hire. He tapped the team's defensive coordinator, Dave Campo, who had never been a head coach at any level. Players liked and respected Campo, but they never feared him as they had Johnson. The Cowboys had three straight 5–11 seasons under Campo. He doesn't deserve all the blame. The team's talent had deteriorated dramatically since the last Super Bowl win in 1995. Many stars had

If we kick into the wind, they're going to come back and kick a field goal. We just needed to do something with the ball.

—BARRY SWITZER

Barry Switzer, pictured here at an October 2, 1994, game against the Redskins, may have cost the Cowboys a victory over the Eagles with his dubious play-calling.

signed lucrative free-agent contracts with other teams, and the Cowboys hadn't drafted well.

After the 2002 season Jones fired Campo and named the first big-name coach since Switzer. Jones turned to Bill Parcells, who had won two Super Bowls with the New York Giants. His four-year tenure, however, didn't produce a single playoff win.

In hindsight, Switzer's stint looks more successful. He may not have had more talent than Campo, Gailey, or Parcells, but at least he produced. During Switzer's four years, the Cowboys were 40–24—a .625 winning percentage. Not even Parcells approached that. Maybe Jones made the right decision after all.

# A Messy Divorce

Cowboys fans will always wonder *What if?* What if owner Jerry Jones hadn't fired coach Jimmy Johnson shortly after he directed the Cowboys to a second Super Bowl win in five years?

Johnson seemed like a miracle worker, and the two seemed like the perfect owner-coach tandem. Jones had deep pockets and didn't mind spending millions to win championships. Johnson knew the X's and O's and was an excellent motivator.

After defeating the Buffalo Bills 30–13 in Super Bowl XXVIII, the Cowboys still had a deep roster—probably the best talent in the league. Wouldn't Jones want Johnson back for a chance to win an unprecedented three straight Super Bowls? Wouldn't Johnson want to be part of the ride?

No and no. Their relationship had grown strained even as the Cowboys' success increased. Both Jones and Johnson had massive egos, and each believed he deserved more credit for the team's amazing turnaround. In their first year together, 1989, the Cowboys finished a woeful 1–15. Three years later they were world champions.

The timing of the Jones-Johnson breakup seemed almost unbelievable. Less than two months after celebrating the Super Bowl XXVIII win, both men were at an NFL meeting in Florida. Jones walked over to a table where Johnson and some friends were gathered. They were talking about the recent Super Bowl win, and Jones proposed a toast.

"Here's to the Dallas Cowboys, and here's to the people who made it possible to win two Super Bowls!" he said proudly.

No one at the table, including Johnson, responded. Jones offered the same toast again, with the same result.

"Go on with your f*cking party," Jones fumed, walking away.

A few hours later Jones was sitting in a hotel bar with some Dallas sportswriters and dropped a bomb: he planned to fire Johnson. Jones told the writers Johnson was disloyal and added, "I think there are 500 coaches who could have coached this team to the Super Bowl."

Word got back to Johnson, and he exploded. He packed his bags and left the Orlando meeting.

"I know I'm arrogant," Johnson later told reporters. "I know I'm self-serving. But somebody please tell me what I've done...so wrong to be ripped the way I have?"

The harsh words between Jones and Johnson floored players, many siding with the coach.

"I think Jerry is trying to stir up controversy because the man can't live straight unless there is a controversy in his life," running back Emmitt Smith said.

After trashing each other in public, Jones and Johnson held several private meetings to see if they could patch up the relationship. They couldn't. On March 29, 1994, six days after Jones fired the first verbal shot, the two held a news conference to announce their split. Both hid any animosity and spoke highly of the other.

"It's fantastic what we were able to do," Johnson said.

In the years since the divorce, both men have admitted mistakes and said they regretted their comments. But the question will always remain, "What if?"

Cowboys owner Jerry Jones (left) and former coach Jimmy Johnson both had massive egos, which led to acrimony and Johnson's eventual firing, though he had led the Cowboys to two Super Bowls in five years.

The
# Sacks

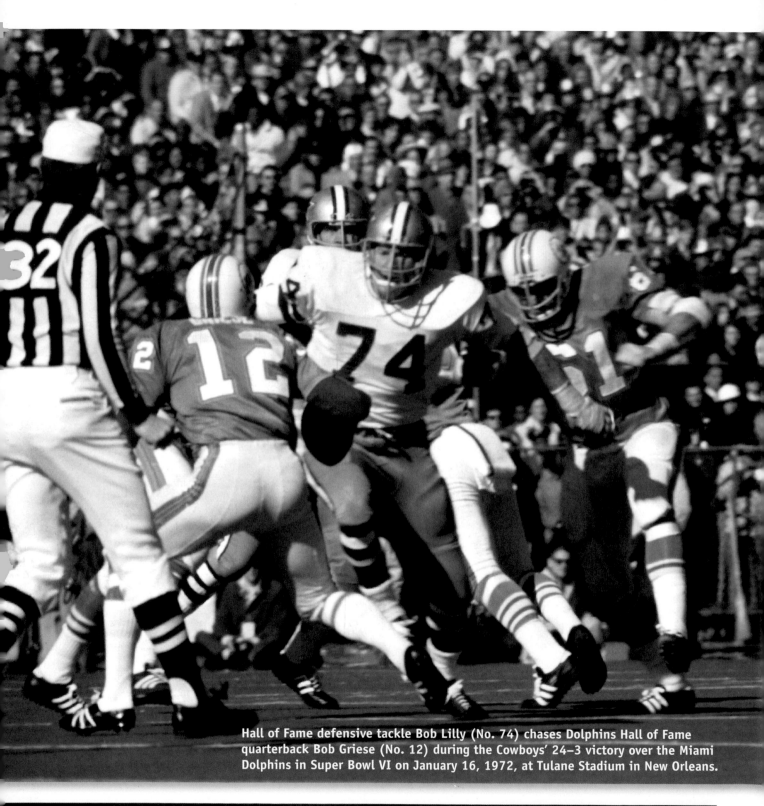

Hall of Fame defensive tackle Bob Lilly (No. 74) chases Dolphins Hall of Fame quarterback Bob Griese (No. 12) during the Cowboys' 24–3 victory over the Miami Dolphins in Super Bowl VI on January 16, 1972, at Tulane Stadium in New Orleans.

# Lilly's Revenge

## All-Pro's 29-Yard Sack Seals Super Bowl VI Win

Bob Lilly made so many great defensive plays during his storied 14-year career that it's difficult to pick one play that defined him. But the most memorable would have to be his 29-yard sack of Miami quarterback Bob Griese in Super Bowl VI. It paved the way for the Cowboys' 24–3 blowout win and their first championship.

Lilly, already a nine-time Pro Bowler, closed in on Griese as he dropped to pass in the first quarter. Griese retreated, spun around, and retreated some more to try to avoid the cat-quick Lilly. He couldn't. The relentless Lilly grabbed Griese deep in Miami territory and flung him to the turf.

"It was a big play because it made a statement," Lilly said. "They were going to lose."

The dramatic sack was even sweeter for Lilly, considering the Cowboys' gut-wrenching loss the previous year in Super Bowl V. Dallas had fallen 16–13 to the Baltimore Colts on a last-second field goal. Lilly, angry and frustrated, ripped off his helmet and threw it 40 yards down the field as the final gun sounded.

"To lose that game like we did was the lowest point of my career," he said.

The loss solidified Dallas' reputation as a team that couldn't win the big game. The Cowboys had also lost two heartbreaking

NFL Championship Games to the Green Bay Packers in 1966 and 1967. Then they suffered back-to-back upset losses to the Cleveland Browns in divisional playoffs before falling to the Colts in Super Bowl V. Because of the losses, the Cowboys had gained an unwanted nickname: Next Year's Champion.

During the 1971 season the Cowboys were on a mission to return to the Super Bowl and win. They finished 11–3, tied for best in the NFL, and easily defeated the San Francisco 49ers and Minnesota Vikings in the playoffs to meet the Dolphins.

Coach Tom Landry later said he felt confident as his team prepared for Super Bowl VI.

"You could see it in the players' eyes," he said. "We were determined no one was going to stop us."

He was right. Dallas dominated Miami early, taking a 10–0 lead in the second quarter. The Dolphins got a field goal before halftime to close within a touchdown. But then the Cowboys scored two second-half touchdowns to cruise to victory.

"My biggest disappointment was that we never challenged," Miami coach Don Shula said.

Quarterback Roger Staubach was the game's Most Valuable Player. He completed 12 of 19 passes and threw two touchdowns. During the 1971 season he had emerged as the team's starting quarterback. He shared the job with Craig Morton the first seven games of the season. But at the midpoint the Cowboys stood 4–3, and Landry entrusted the team to Staubach.

With Staubach as the undisputed leader, the Cowboys won seven straight games to close the regular season. Although Dallas was favored to beat Miami in Super Bowl VI, the Dolphins posed offensive problems. Griese had a trio of outstanding running backs: bruising fullback Larry Csonka, fleet tailback Mercury Morris, and dependable all-purpose back Jim Kiick. In addition, Griese could throw to All-Pro receiver Paul Warfield. But the Dallas defense, led by Lilly, never allowed Miami to make sustained drives.

No one deserved a Super Bowl title more than Lilly. He was the Cowboys' No. 1 draft pick in 1961, a year after the team began play, and he endured the lean years. The Cowboys didn't post their first winning season until 1966.

By then Lilly had become one of the league's elite defensive tackles. And he had earned the nickname "Mr. Cowboy" for his stellar play and dependability. Throughout his career, he missed only one game because of injury.

Not only did Lilly make routine plays, he had a penchant for the dramatic. He scored four touchdowns, remarkable for a defensive lineman. One came on an interception, and three were on fumble returns.

"He is the greatest football player I ever coached," Landry once said.

When the Cowboys desperately needed their first Super Bowl win, Lilly rose to the occasion.

> **H**e's that once-in-a-lifetime player.
>
> **—COACH TOM LANDRY**

# Game Details

## Dallas Cowboys 24 • Miami Dolphins 3

| | | | | | |
|---|---|---|---|---|---|
| **Cowboys** | 3 | 7 | 7 | 7 | **24** |
| **Dolphins** | 0 | 3 | 0 | 0 | **3** |

**Date:** January 16, 1972

**Team Records:** Dallas 11–3, Miami 10–3–1

**Scoring Plays:**

DAL—Clark nine-yard field goal

DAL—Alworth seven-yard pass from Staubach (Clark PAT)

MIA—Yepremian 31-yard FG

DAL—Thomas three-yard run (Clark PAT)

DAL—Ditka seven-yard pass from Staubach (Clark PAT)

# Jethro Pugh

Bob Lilly anchored the Doomsday Defense for more than a decade. But he wasn't alone in making the unit great. His fellow tackle, Jethro Pugh, quietly made plays for years in Lilly's shadow. Lilly was sometimes called a gentle giant because of his unassuming ways. But Pugh shied away from the limelight even more. All he did was show up every Sunday and go about his business, shutting down the opposing offense.

Famed sportswriter Jim Murray of the *Los Angeles Times* once called Pugh the greatest defensive lineman never selected to the Pro Bowl. Pugh represented one of the Cowboys' finest small-college draft choices. He was an 11th-round pick out of tiny Elizabeth City State College in North Carolina in 1965.

When Pugh joined the Cowboys, Lilly already was entrenched at right defensive tackle. Pugh moved into the left-tackle spot and complemented Lilly perfectly. He started from 1967 to 1978, retiring four years after Lilly.

Pugh, who stood 6'6" and weighed 260 pounds, was nicknamed "Buzzard" by his teammates. Unfortunately, he received the most notoriety for his play in the Ice Bowl, the 1967 NFL Championship.

Green Bay's Bart Starr scored a touchdown on a one-yard quarterback sneak with only 16 seconds left to give the Packers a 21–17 win. Offensive guard Jerry Kramer made a block on Pugh that allowed Starr to score. A famous picture shows Pugh on the ground in the end zone, with Kramer lying between him and Starr.

Pugh said it was impossible to get any traction on the frozen field.

"I said to Bob Lilly, 'We've got to call timeout to get an ice pick," he said. "We had to dig holes for our feet. I tried scraping the ice, but I couldn't feel my feet."

Pugh rebounded from the traumatic loss and excelled for another decade. He said coach Tom Landry helped him cope with the unwanted attention of the Ice Bowl.

"He said, 'Jethro, you might as well get used to it because that play is going to be part of pro football history. Nothing can be done about it now,'" Pugh said. "It was better than saying, 'Jethro, you screwed up.'"

Cowboys defensive lineman Jethro Pugh fights through the blocks by the Eagles' Wade Key (No. 72) and Mark Nordquist (No. 68) during a game on October 28, 1973, at Veterans Stadium.

Lee Roy Jordan makes an interception in front of San Francisco 49ers running back Ken Williard in a 20–17 win on August 17, 1969, at Kezar Stadium.

# Lee Roy Jordan

Lee Roy Jordan was the emotional leader of the Dallas defense for 14 years. As middle linebacker, he called the defensive plays and barked orders to his teammates. He didn't mind chewing out someone for a bad play.

"Lee Roy was a holler guy, always full of fire, tough as steel," defensive end Harvey Martin said. "Lee Roy never gave up, and he was a terrific hitter. He could break a leg and still come limping after you on the other."

Jordan made one of his biggest plays against the Miami Dolphins in Super Bowl VI. On Miami's second possession, Jordan crashed into burly fullback Larry Csonka, forcing a fumble that Dallas recovered near midfield.

From the turnover, the Cowboys grabbed a 3–0 lead and proceeded to trounce the Dolphins 24–3 for their first Super Bowl win. Jordan and the rest of the Dallas defense held the potent Miami attack to only 80 yards rushing.

Jordan had been the Cowboys' No. 1 draft pick in 1963 out of Alabama. There he played under legendary coach Paul "Bear" Bryant and earned All American honors as a senior. The Crimson Tide won the national championship his junior year and lost only two games during his career.

"He would have made every tackle on every play if they had stayed in bounds," Bryant wrote in his autobiography. "I never had another one like Lee Roy Jordan."

With the Cowboys, Jordan became a starter in his second year and didn't relinquish the job until he retired in 1976 at age 35. He was named to five Pro Bowls and had 32 interceptions and 18 fumble recoveries.

He was small for a middle linebacker, standing 6'1" and weighing only 215 pounds. By contrast, the Chicago Bears' monster middle linebacker, Dick Butkus, was 6'3" and weighed 245 pounds.

"If Jordan weighed as much as Dick Butkus," Cowboys' defensive coach Ernie Stautner once said, "they'd have to outlaw him from football."

December 14, 2008

# Ware Manhandles Manning

## Defensive End's Three Sacks Lead Cowboys to 20–8 Win Over Super Bowl Champs

The New York Giants spoiled the Cowboys' season in 2007, upsetting them in the divisional playoffs. In 2008 the Giants threatened to leave the Cowboys behind before the playoffs even began.

Late in the season New York had a sparkling 11–2 mark and a comfortable lead in the NFC East. Dallas, meanwhile, was a disappointing 8–5 and still fighting for a playoff spot. In the teams' second meeting of the season, however, the Cowboys made a big statement in pounding the Giants 20–8.

The Dallas defense played its best game in years, sacking New York quarterback Eli Manning eight times. The final sack, by Pro Bowl defensive end DeMarcus Ware, sealed the victory. It came late in the fourth quarter. Manning dropped back to pass, and Ware powered past the offensive line to smother him for a seven-yard loss that helped stall the drive. It was Ware's third sack of the game.

"We're bringing pressure from a lot of areas on the field," he said. "We've got a lot of guys that are playing well."

After the sack, the Giants punted, and the Cowboys took over with about four minutes left. They hoped to pick up a few first downs

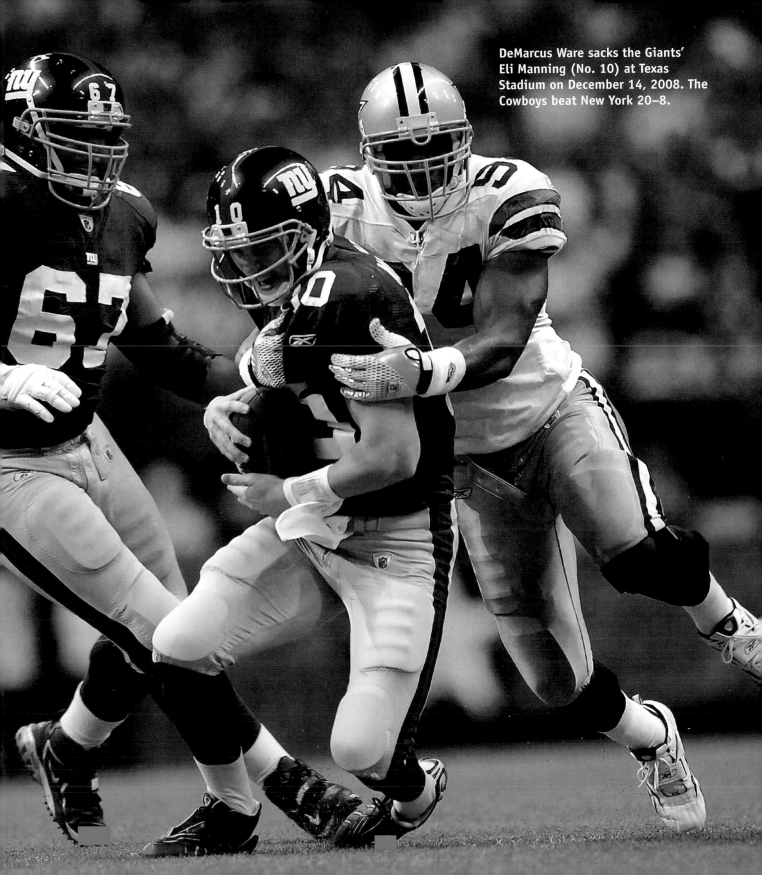

DeMarcus Ware sacks the Giants' Eli Manning (No. 10) at Texas Stadium on December 14, 2008. The Cowboys beat New York 20–8.

and run out the clock. Instead, the Cowboys widened their lead with a 38-yard touchdown run by seldom-used rookie Tashard Choice. He broke through the middle of the line and had clear sailing for a touchdown to ice the game 20–8.

The Giants, the defending Super Bowl champs, had one last drive. But it ended when cornerback Terence Newman intercepted a Manning pass. The win elevated the Cowboys to 9–5, two games behind the Giants with two remaining. Dallas bolted to the top of the wild-card contenders, while serving notice that the Cowboys still had Super Bowl potential.

The Cowboys' offense played well throughout the game. Quarterback Tony Romo completed 20 of 30 passes for 244 yards. He threw two touchdowns and no interceptions. Star running back Marion Barber, who missed the previous game with a sore toe, struggled in his return, gaining only two yards on eight carries. Rookie Tashard

Choice picked up the slack with nine carries for 91 yards and the clinching touchdown.

The Dallas defense, however, stole the show. Besides Ware, four other players had sacks: Greg Ellis, Bradie James, Chris Canty, and Anthony Spencer. With his three sacks, Ware became the league's sack leader at 19. He finished the season with a league-leading 20.

The victory helped nullify the infighting on the Cowboys. The previous week, star receiver Terrell Owens had allegedly complained that Romo was throwing too often to tight end Jason Witten, a friend. Offensive coordinator Jason Garrett met with several players to try to calm the storm.

After the win everyone downplayed the conflict.

"It's just part of playing football," Romo said. "We have a lot of highly competitive individuals who want to win."

Owens said simply, "Winning cures everything."

Dallas still needed to win the remaining two games against the Baltimore Ravens and Philadelphia Eagles to be assured of a playoff spot, but they fell short, dropping both.

# Game Details

## Dallas Cowboys 20 • New York Giants 8

| | | | | | |
|---|---|---|---|---|---|
| Giants | 0 | 3 | 0 | 5 | **8** |
| Cowboys | 0 | 7 | 0 | 13 | **20** |

**Date:** December 14, 2008

**Team Records:** New York 11–2, Dallas 8–5

**Scoring Plays:**

DAL—Crayton 34-yard pass from Romo (Folk PAT)

NY—Carney 34-yard FG

DAL—Anderson one-yard pass from Romo (Folk PAT)

NY—Safety, Romo sacked by Kiwanuka in end zone

NY—Carney 47-yard FG

DAL—Choice 38-yard run (pass failed)

# Decades of Dominant Defense

Many of the most famous names in Cowboys history played on offense: Emmitt Smith, Troy Aikman, Michael Irvin, Roger Staubach, Tony Dorsett—the list goes on and on.

But the defense sometimes gets overlooked. More seasons than not, Dallas fields a strong defense. The tradition began with the Doomsday Defense of the late 1960s and 1970s. It was anchored by tackle Bob Lilly, an 11-time Pro Bowl player later inducted into the Pro Football Hall of Fame. It also included some outstanding lesser-known players, such as linebackers Chuck Howley and Lee Roy Jordan. Between them they played in 11 Pro Bowls.

In the late 1970s, a new generation of top-notch defenders emerged. They included Randy White, a ferociously intense tackle known as "the Manster." The defensive ends of that generation were Harvey White, a lightning-quick pass rusher, and Ed "Too Tall" Jones, an intimidating 6'9" pass-blocking presence. White and

Cowboys defensive tackle Bob Lilly, here holding back offensive center Bob DeMarco in Super Bowl VI on January 16, 1972, was the centerpiece of the Cowboys' famed Doomsday Defense.

Martin were named co-MVPs of Super Bowl XII as the Cowboys throttled the Denver Broncos 27–10.

In each of the Cowboys' five Super Bowl wins, defense played a huge role. In Super Bowl VI, the Cowboys' first championship, the Dallas defense held the potent Miami Dolphins offense to only three points. The Cowboys' 24–3 domination remains the only Super Bowl in which a team didn't score a touchdown.

The Cowboys' three Super Bowl–winning teams of the 1990s also were built on strong defenses. Charles Haley, a speedy, powerful defensive end, routinely made big plays. In Super Bowl XXVII, the first '90s win, Haley crashed into Buffalo Bills quarterback Jim Kelly in the first quarter. Kelly fumbled, and defensive lineman Jimmie Jones picked up the ball and ran in for a touchdown to give Dallas a 14–7 lead. The Cowboys were on their way to a 52–17 blowout.

In Super Bowl XXVIII Haley and gang were back. The result: another rout of the Bills, this time 30–13. In Super Bowl XXX, the final championship of the 1990s, Dallas defeated the Pittsburgh Steelers 27–17. In the Cowboys' five Super Bowl wins they gave up an average of only 15 points. That's stout defense.

Tom Landry, who coached the Cowboys for the first 29 years, brought a defensive mind-set to the team that remained after he left. He had played defensive back for the New York Giants in the 1950s and later served as the team's defensive coordinator. His influence helped develop some outstanding secondary players. In the 1960s and 1970s safety Mel Renfro and cornerback Cornell Green made multiple Pro Bowl appearances. In the late 1970s safeties Cliff Harris and Charlie Waters also routinely earned Pro Bowl honors. In the 1980s Everson Walls became the NFL's top cornerback. He led the league in interceptions three times.

In the 1990s Darren Woodson continued the tradition of hard-hitting Pro Bowl safeties. Today the Cowboys have top defensive personnel from the line to the secondary. Defense, they say, wins championships. The Cowboys have proven that saying true.

DeMarcus Ware's first sack of Giants quarterback Eli Manning in the December 14, 2008, game at Texas Stadium.

# W. C. FIELDS

# W. C. FIELDS

*A Biography*

# James Curtis

Alfred A. Knopf     New York 2003

This Is a Borzoi Book
Published by Alfred A. Knopf

 Published in the United States by Alfred A. Knopf, a division of Random House, Inc., New York, and simultaneously in Canada by Random House of Canada Limited, Toronto.
Distributed by Random House, Inc., New York.
www.aaknopf.com



Library of Congress Cataloging-in-Publication Data
Curtis, James.
W. C. Fields : a biography / James Curtis.
p. cm.
Includes bibliographical references and index.
ISBN 0-375-40217-9
1. Fields, W. C., 1879–1946. 2. Comedians—United States—Biography.
3. Motion picture actors and actresses—United States—Biography. I. Title

PN2287.F45 C87 2003
791.43'028'092—dc21
[B]
2002027450

Manufactured in the United States of America
First Edition

*For my father, Richard Borah Curtis,*
*who first introduced me to the comedy of W. C. Fields*

I've studied men from my topsy-turvy

Close, and, I reckon, rather true.

Some are fine fellows; some right scurvy;

Most, a dash between the two.

—GEORGE MEREDITH, "Juggling Jerry"

# Contents

## *Part One*: THE SILENT HUMORIST

## *Part Two*: THE GREAT MAN

# List of Illustrations

# *Acknowledgments*

This book came into being through a chance meeting with Everett F. Fields, one of the five children of Claude and Ann Ruth Fields. Everett and I had mutual friends in historian and author Anthony Slide and archivist Robert Gitt, and through their good offices we got to know each other socially over the space of several years. Everett was always gracious in answering my nosey questions about his grandfather, who had fascinated me from childhood. When I began searching for a new subject following the completion of my 1998 biography of James Whale, I casually asked if he and his siblings would cooperate on a new biography of W. C. Fields. I had the sense that Fields had always gotten a raw deal from biographers who embraced the legend at the expense of the man behind it.

Happily, Everett was open to the idea, and over the next few months, I made the acquaintance of his brothers and sister. William C. Fields III, then president of W. C. Fields Productions and the eldest, had done extensive research into the history of the Felton and Dukenfield families during his time in Philadelphia with the FBI in the 1970s, and his notes formed the basis for my understanding of his grandfather's early life. Ronald J. Fields, who had already published two highly regarded books with material drawn from the family's extraordinary collection of papers and scrapbooks, generously gave his approbation and was a valuable source of counsel throughout the research and writing of this book. Dr. Harriet A. Fields shared vivid memories of her parents and grandmother, and Allen Fields, current president of W. C. Fields Productions, granted permission to quote from his grandfather's unpublished letters and manuscripts, as well as to print selected photographs from the Fields family archive. I am profoundly grateful to all of them for their help, hospitality, and friendship.

As extensive as the family collection is, there are unfortunate gaps created, in large part, by Fields' decision to convey important materials to his friend Gene Fowler for the purpose of researching and writing an authorized biography. Over the years, these documents have found their way into private collections, the most significant of which are held by Tim Walker and John McLaughlin. Tim, who acquired much of his collection directly from Will Fowler, Gene Fowler's younger son, was unfailingly helpful in giving me access to every Fields document he owned. John was equally happy to let me study Fields' annotated stories and "sides" from his own amazing collection. George J. Houle, a prominent Los Angeles book and autograph dealer, acquired a number of letters from the late Carlotta Monti and allowed me to read them all.

Donald Deschner, author of *The Films of W. C. Fields,* was extraordinarily generous in making his files available to me, which included hundreds of stills as well as an unpublished remembrance of Fields by director George Marshall. In helping me understand the state of juggling at the turn of the century, as well as the basics of that most ancient of skills, Andrew Conway was a godsend, ever ready to give a reasoned and thoroughly authoritative response to the most rudimentary of questions. In Philadelphia, Milton Kenin made years of research on the Feltons and the Dukenfields available to me, and selflessly acted as a wonderful and learned resource when new questions presented themselves.

Perhaps the most extraordinary of all resources was a cache of material held by the family of Magda Michael, Fields' devoted secretary. I was able to make contact with Magda's daughter, Ginger McFarlane, with the kind help of her own daughter, Susan Nash. Ginger was gracious and forthcoming in her memories of Fields and then, when our visit was at an end, asked if I'd be interested in seeing a few things she had in storage. Several weeks later, we met at Susan's home, where a footlocker held such treasures as a ventriloquist's dummy in Fields' own likeness from 1938, Magda's copy of *Fields for President* inscribed to her from "The Great Man," manuscript pages from a book Magda had started to write in the 1970s, and notes for Fields' own autobiography, dictated in 1946. I cannot adequately express my appreciation to Ginger for sharing this material and allowing me to use it.

From London, Kevin Brownlow sent excerpts of his interview with Alfred Lunt. Mark Cosden, of the Performing Arts Department at Colby College, discussed his work on the Hanlon Brothers and their American counterparts, the Byrne Brothers; Wolfgang Dietzel shared his knowledge of the Althouse family of Soboba Hot Springs; and John Dunning drew from his extensive library of vintage radio magazines in offering rare accounts of Fields' broadcasts. Charles L. Egleston offered the use of his guest room during my time at the University of Colorado; Richard Feiner shared memories of his uncle Matty

Fox. In Darby, Harold Finigan pointed to the site of the Arlington House and remembered how he used to play in the fire lookout when he was a kid. I drew on the collective knowledge of John and Larry Gassman in researching Fields' radio work, and Sam Gill's encyclopedic knowledge of silent film comedy in ferreting out information on the Casino Star Comedies. Tony Slide was kind enough to interview Doris Nolan in Berwick-Upon-Tweed, Karl Thiede allowed me to consult one of the most remarkable private research libraries I have ever seen, and Warren R. Huber, at the age of ninety-nine, shared his childhood memories of Plymouth Park. For knowledge of Kate Dukenfield, W. C. Felton, and the Felton family, I am grateful to Dorothy Schade, her son Art Searfoss, and W. C. Felton III, who shared childhood memories of his grandfather. Elsie May Cunningham (née Dukenfield) was brought into sharper focus through conversations with John Ashcraft and his mother, Mrs. John K. Ashcraft, as well as with John Woodruff and his wife, Dorothy. In San Francisco, Elizabeth Spence gave me a vivid portrait of her grandfather, Bill Dailey. I am also grateful to Judy Sanger for her knowledge of her grandfather, Philip Goodman.

For various courtesies and nudges, I am also indebted to Joe Adamson, Brian Anthony, Frank Bresee, Don Cannon, John Cannon, Joseph Dembo, Tom DiFilippo, Marjorie Fowler, Will Fowler, Amber Geary, Ronnie Gillingham, Herbert Goldman, Betty Goodwin, Howard Green, Muriel Harrison, Charles Higham, Ronnie James, Bill Jennings, Linda Jones, Andrew Kelly, Sandy Krinski, Dr. William Labov, Betty Lasky, Emmet Lavery Jr., Jack Lemmon, Peter Levinson, Linda Gross Lukas, Bill Marx, Scott MacQueen, Roger Montandon, Mike Murnane, Martin Nuetzel, Marvin Paige, James Pepper, Fred Santon, James Smart, Candice Smith, John Towsen, Alan R. Wambold, Delmar Watson, Bob Weide, Ian Whitcomb, Woody Wise, Jordan Young, and Walter the Seltzer Man.

A number of libraries and institutions held parts of the Fields legacy, often through related collections, and I am grateful to the librarians and administrators who made that aspect of my work so enjoyable and rewarding.

Margaret Harrick Library, Academy of Motion Picture Arts and Sciences, Los Angeles: Stacey Behlmer, Scott Curtis, Barbara Hall, and Howard Prouty. American Heritage Center, University of Wyoming: Matt Sprinkle. American Museum of the Moving Image, New York: Eleanor Mish. British Music Hall Society: Howard Lee.

Center for the Preservation of Variety Arts, Los Angeles: Milt Larsen. Darby Free Library: Betty Schell. J. Walter Thompson Collection, Center for Advertising Study, Duke University: Claire Locke. Theatre Collection, Free

Library of Philadelphia: Geraldine Duclow. Fullerton Public Library: Deven McReynolds.

Golden Legend, Los Angeles: Gordon Hollis. Greenwood Cemetary, Philadelphia: David DeLong. Institute of the American Musical, Los Angeles: Miles Kreuger. Juggling Information Service (www.juggling.org): Barry Bakalor. Las Encinas Hospital, Pasadena: Shirley Leopold and Gordon Van Cleve.

Film Study Center, Museum of Modern Art, New York: Charles Silver. New Amsterdam Theatre, New York: Dana Amendola. Pacific Pioneer Broadcasters, Los Angeles: Ken Greenwald and Ron Wolf. Records Center, Philadelphia School District: Bob Edelman. Riverside County Library System, San Jacinto Branch: Chuck Gentry.

St. Louis Municipal Opera: Laura Peters. Salem County Historical Society: Alice Boggs. State Historical Society of Wisconsin: Harry Miller. Stuyvesant High School, New York: Ellen Johnson. UCLA Film and Television Archive: Robert Gitt and Laura Keiser. Twentieth Century–Fox Archive, Arts Library, University of California, Los Angeles: Brigitte J. Kueppers. Sadakichi Hartmann Collection, University of California, Riverside: Sidney E. Berger.

Gene Fowler Collection, University of Colorado at Boulder: Kris McCusker. Keith/Albee Collection, University of Iowa: Ethel Bloesch. David O. Selznick Collection, University of Texas: Steve Wilson. Cinema-Television Library, University of Southern California: Ned Comstock and Steve Hanson. Warner Bros. Archives: Noelle Carter.

Waiting for Godot Books, Hadley, Mass.: Frannie Ness and Gary Oleson. Will Rogers Memorial and Birthplace, Clarmore, Oklahoma: Joe Carter. Wisconsin Center for Film and Theater Research: Ruta Abolins and Ben Brewster. Ziegfeld Club, New York: Nils Hanson.

The core of this book was formed from interviews conducted with those who knew and worked with W. C. Fields and were gracious enough to share their memories. My heartfelt thanks go to Suzanne (Menzies) Antles, Julie Bishop Bergin (Jacqueline Wells), Grace Bradley Boyd, Mary Brian, Louise Currie, Rosita Del Mar, Charlie Eaton, Doris Eaton, Steve Fairfield, Edith Fellows, Gene Fowler Jr., Nona Otero Friedman, Ruth Goodman Goetz, Barbara Hunter (Billee Blanchard), Gloria Jean, Carmencita Johnson, Hal Kanter, Paul Landres, Lucille Layton, Naomi Lewis, A. C. Lyles, Ed Montagne, William Montijo, Constance Moore, Edward Muhl, Joseph Newman, Doris Nolan, Les Paul, Anthony Quinn, Jim Rogers, Jean Rouverol, Sidney Salkow, Artie Shaw, Dr. Raymond Stevens, Gloria Stuart, A. Edward Sutherland,

Philip Trent (Clifford Jones), Harry Watson, Jane Withers, and Patricia Ziegfeld.

Victoria Wilson, senior editor and associate publisher, was wonderfully supportive during the four years it took to research and write this book, and I am deeply grateful for all her help and guidance. Scott Eyman was a tremendous source of advice and encouragement during the course of this project, and it was Scott who elicited Anthony Quinn's memories of Fields after decades of refusing to discuss the subject of the death of his first son. My deepest gratitude goes to my wife, Kim Geary, who was with me throughout it all, clambering through cemeteries and libraries without complaint, and reminding me from time to time why both history and laughter matter.

James Curtis
Los Angeles
October 2002

*Part One*

# THE SILENT
# HUMORIST

*One*

# *Foolish Juggling Notion*

Comedy, Bill Fields would say, is truth—a bit of artful reality, expressed in action or words, carefully exaggerated and brought to a surprise finish. Fields didn't think the mechanics of a gag counted for half as much as the soul behind it. You might coax a laugh from a willing audience over most anything, but a gag wouldn't be memorable without the delight of human recognition.

The comedy Fields propounded reached its apogee with a modest sixty-seven-minute film called *It's a Gift.* In it, he plays an everyman—hardworking, beset by life's frustrations, caring and respectful of a family that no longer appreciates him. He dreams his dreams in private. He is not brilliant, lovable, or even admirable, but his dignity never leaves him, and, in the end, he triumphs as much through luck as perseverance. When it was released, in November 1934, *It's a Gift* was a minor event, bound for a quick playoff in what *Variety* referred to as "the nabes." But the critics took notice, and a groundswell of enthusiasm for the fifty-four-year-old Fields and his work, which had been building for eighteen months, suddenly erupted. Andre Sennwald, writing in the *New York Times,* referred to Fields' growing legion of fans as "idolaters," and, although not necessarily one himself, he concluded his notice by sweeping away all doubt that one of the great comedies of the sound era had arrived. "The fact is that Mr. Fields has come back to us again, and *It's a Gift* automatically becomes the best screen comedy on Broadway."

As Fields pointed out, the appeal of his character was rooted in the characteristics audiences saw in themselves. "You've heard the old legend that it's the little put-upon guy who gets the laughs, but I'm the most belligerent guy on the screen. I'm going to kill everybody. But, at the same time, I'm afraid of everybody—just a great big frightened bully. There's a lot of that in human nature. When people laugh at me, they're laughing at themselves. Or, at least, the next fellow."

Like Mark Twain, Fields believed humor sprang naturally from tragedy, and that it was normal and therefore acceptable to behave badly when things went wrong. One of the key sequences in *It's a Gift* shows an elderly blind man laying waste to Fields' general store with his cane. Afterward, Fields sends him out into a busy street, where he is almost run down in traffic. "I never saw anything funny that wasn't terrible," Fields said. "If it causes pain, it's funny; if it doesn't, it isn't."

"I was the first comic in world history, so they told me, to pick fights with children. I booted Baby LeRoy. The No-men—they're even worse than the Yes-men—shook their heads and said it would never go; people wouldn't stand for it . . . then, in another picture, I kicked a little dog. . . . The No-men said I couldn't do that either. But I got sympathy both times. People didn't know what the unmanageable baby might do to get even, and they thought the dog might bite me."\*

The conniving and bibulous character Fields developed caught the public imagination at a time when the nation was deep in the throes of the Great Depression and the sale of liquor was still prohibited by law. He appeared on the scene as the embodiment of public misbehavior, a man not so much at odds with authority as completely oblivious to it. He drank because he enjoyed it and cheated at cards because he was good at it. Fields wasn't a bad sort, but rather a throwback to a time when such behaviors were perfectly innocuous and government wasn't quite so paternalistic. Harold Lloyd called him "the foremost American comedian," and Buster Keaton considered him, along with Charlie Chaplin and Harry Langdon, the greatest of all film comics. "His comedy is unique, original, and side-splitting."

Fields had the courage to cast himself in the decidedly unfavorable light of a bully and a con man. He not only summed up the frustrations of the common man—he did something about them. Unlike most comedians, he never asked to be loved; he was short-tempered, a coward, an outright faker at times. Chaplin was better known, Keaton more technically ambitious, and Laurel and Hardy were certainly more beloved, but Fields resonated with audiences in ways other comics did not. He wasn't a clown; he didn't dress like a tramp or live in the distant world of the London ghetto. Indeed, for most audiences he lived just down the street or around the corner. He was everyone's disagreeable uncle, or the tippling neighbor who warned off the local kids with a golf club. People responded to the honesty of Fields' character because, like Archie Bunker of a later generation, everyone knew somebody just like him. They admired him in

---

\*Fields saw the importance of investing his character with an element of sympathy, although he bridled at the word itself. "Maybe you wouldn't call it sympathy," he hedged. "Maybe you'd call it forbearance."

a grudging sort of way, and saw the humanity beneath his thick crust of contempt for the world.

"The first thing I remember figuring out for myself was that I wanted to be a definite personality," he said. "I had heard a man say he liked a certain fellow because he was always the same dirty damn so and so. You know, like Larsen in Jack London's *Sea Wolf.* He was detestable, yet you admired him because he remained true to type. Well, I thought that was a swell idea, so I developed a philosophy of my own: *Be your type!* I determined that whatever I was, I'd *be* that, I wouldn't teeter on the fence."

The childhood Fields exaggerated for interviewers was vividly Dickensian, and his run-ins with his father had the brutal energy of Sennett slapstick. Yet the humanity he always strived for in his film treatments failed him when dredging up details of his own early life. He invariably described his father as an abusive scoundrel, his mother as ineffectual and sottish, and his younger self as a Philadelphian version of Huck Finn. He sprang from immigrant stock— his father was British—and however American Fields seemed, there was always an element of the outsider in the characters he played. He embraced the nomadic spirit of his grandfather, whom he never met, and although he was married to the same woman for the entirety of his adult life, he was always at odds with both her and the world, embattled and solitary.

Fields moved through a career that lasted nearly half a century, acquiring slowly the elements of the character by which he is known today. Onstage, he perfected what can best be described as the comedy of frustration, building one of his most popular routines on the petty distractions a golfer encounters while attempting to tee off. His seminal pool act was similarly constructed, leading him to conclude that "the funniest thing a comedian can do is not to do it." In films, he found his voice after an abortive career in silents and became, in the words of James Agee, "the toughest and most warmly human of all screen comedians."

His time as one of Hollywood's top draws was brief—barely six years— and by 1941 his audience had largely abandoned him. Radio, where he could still find work, drained him of any subtlety, due, in large part, to his boozy exchanges with Edgar Bergen's sarcastic dummy, Charlie McCarthy. In spite of his own best efforts, he was constantly at pains to justify a character that had become so fixed in the public mind that he was widely presumed to be the same man he portrayed onscreen. The day he died, Bob Hope made a joke about him on NBC. Hope implied he had seen Fields drunk: "I saw W. C. Fields on the street and waved, and he weaved back." The audience laughed; Fields was by then the most famous drunk in the world. It no longer mattered that he had never played a drunk in his life.

———

In 1880, travelers approaching Philadelphia from Delaware County and points south would generally pass through the tiny borough of Darby on their way to the Quaker City. Less than a mile square, Darby was a mill town and a transportation hub, home to 1,779 permanent residents and a cluster of paper and textile factories that fairly dominated the landscape. Every day, fifteen thousand workers flooded the town, making the central business district, which ran four blocks along Main Street between Tenth and Mill, second only to Chester in terms of size and importance. There were taprooms and cafés, a funeral parlor, a dozen churches, an Odd Fellows lodge, and one of the oldest free libraries in the nation. Both the B&O and Pennsylvania Railroads passed through Darby, and trolleys connected the Philadelphia line with Wilmington and Chester. Just beyond town were cattle and horse ranches and a vast blanket of farmland that stretched toward Media. Wealthy buyers in search of prime racing stock would put up at the Buttonwood Hotel, at the terminus of the Chester Traction Co. line, or sometimes at the Bluebell Tavern, up near Grays Ferry, where George Washington was said to have stopped on his way to Philadelphia for the second inaugural. Of Darby's several inns, however, only one actually catered to the horse trade—a simple stone building at the southeast corner of Main and Mill Streets known as the Arlington House.

Older than the Buttonwood and less historic than the Bluebell, the Arlington stood directly in front of Griswold's Worsted, the largest and most modern of Darby's numerous textile mills, and a block and a half west of the town dock, the central receiving point for freight and supplies brought up the Delaware River and inland via Cobbs Creek. At the noisiest and dustiest intersection in town, the Arlington was a stopping point for dockhands, mill workers, clerks, tradesmen, and tourists on their way to or from Philadelphia. Atop its three modest stories was a fire lookout, a box-like room with windows on all sides that afforded a panoramic view of the mills along the two tidewater streams, Cobbs Creek on the east and Darby Creek on the west, and the main arteries leading off into Lansdowne, to the north, and Sharon Hill, to the south.

Locals and guests pausing at the bar on the ground floor were likely to be served by James Lydon Dukenfield, a robust Brit in his late thirties who ran the hotel with his wife, Kate, and a cousin from New York named Jim Lester. A short, stocky man with intense blue eyes, a thick moustache, and light hair he carefully parted down the middle, Jim Dukenfield broke Arabian horses for a living and obviously saw an opportunity when the little hotel, built on the site of an old flour mill, came up for lease. He was known for his flash temper, his extemporaneous bursts into song (the more sentimental the better), and the two fingers missing from his left hand. He had a ready smile that made him a

congenial host, and an explosive contempt for authority that made him a difficult employee.

Jim had been a volunteer fireman in the days when such companies were
like roaming bands of hooligans that would cut the hoses of rival companies
for the privilege of knocking down a fire. He enlisted with the Philadelphia Fire
Zouaves when the call came for three-year volunteers in August 1861. He
deserted for five months—not responding any better to military authority than
he had to any other kind—and was mustered out after "accidentally" getting
his fingers blown off while on picket duty near Fair Oaks. Four of his nine
brothers also answered the call, and all survived with the exception of George,
two years younger than Jim, who fell at Gettysburg on July 2, 1863. Jim liked to
say he had been wounded at the Battle of Lookout Mountain; his eldest son
said he had more likely been caught picking pockets.

Jim Dukenfield was one of thirteen children, most of whom followed their
father, John Dukinfield, to the United States in the mid-1850s. John was the
second son of George Dukinfield, who in turn was the third son of Lord Dukinfield of Cheshire. John Dukinfield and his elder brother George were born
patricians, but the estate passed in line to a grandson who was a clergyman and
vicar of the county. When he subsequently died without issue, the estate
reverted to the chancery and became property of the kingdom. John moved to
Sheffield—not to work in the mines but to distinguish himself as a comb
maker, carving premium designs from animal horns. He married an Irish
Catholic girl named Ann Lyden and began her career in wholesale motherhood
with the birth of their first son, Walter, in 1835. The business grew steadily, and
by 1837 John had taken George on as a partner. They established a little factory
in Rockingham Street, where they made buttons, spectacle frames, and pocket
knives, and installed their families in adjacent housing nearby.

John was a restless spirit, impulsive and autocratic. He had a big nose that
would later inspire his niece Emily to remark that his grandson, the film comedian he never met, resembled him "especially above the mouth." In 1854, John
was seized with the notion of moving to the United States, where there would
be fresh supplies and a ready market for his imitation pearl buttons and tor-
toiseshell glasses. He packed a trunkful of supplies, enlisted his twelve-year-old
son Jim for the trip, and left Ann, pregnant as usual, in George's care. The voyage was arduous, plagued by bad weather, and they were shipwrecked off the
coast of Glen Cove, Long Island. John and his son made their way to Dudley,
New Jersey, north of Camden, then crossed the Delaware River into Philadelphia, where they opened a dry goods store in the Kensington district, known
because of its concentration of British textile workers as "Little England." Ann
followed with most of the other kids; Godfrey, the youngest, made the crossing
from England in his mother's arms.

The family had largely reassembled by November, when John filed a declaration of intent to become an American citizen. He also began spelling his name "Dukenfield" (with an "en" in place of the "in"), apparently considering this to be an appropriate Americanization of the name. The Dukenfield boys were all fiercely independent—not unlike the old man—and no two spelled the family name alike. According to one source, it derived from "Dug-in-field," meaning "bird-in-field," and there was (and still is) a township in Stockport Parish, near Manchester, called Dukinfield. Jim spelled it with an "en," and other variations included Duckinfield (favored by George as a child), Duckenfield, and even Dutenfield.

The older boys took jobs in and around Philadelphia. Jim, who was good with horses, became a driver. His brother John became a bricklayer, and another brother, George, became a potter. Walter, the eldest, worked as a bartender at the Union Hotel. The family business moved to Girard Avenue, west of Second, and eventually north to 625 Cumberland, where it remained into the 1890s. John Dukenfield opened a tavern on East Norris Street, and it was there that he increasingly spent his time. He managed to drink the business into a downturn, and, in 1859, with six children under the age of ten still living at home, he abandoned his wife and family. Ann struggled mightily with the business, eventually passing it to her brother-in-law George. In 1863, she signed a Mother's Army Pension Petition, claiming her late son George as her sole support and fixing his earning capacity, prior to enlistment, at a dollar a day. In an accompanying affidavit, an acquaintance described John Dukenfield as "a man of intemperate habits" who earned "a very scanty livelihood" and was undependable for support. "Legal compulsion would be useless, owing to his age, habits, and poverty." His whereabouts, added a witness, were unknown.

At the age of sixty, John Dukenfield took off for California to prospect for gold. He made it by rail as far as St. Joseph, Missouri, then completed the journey by wagon train. He surfaced in San Francisco in 1871, where he was operating a wholesale notions business on Larkin Street and stocking it with corsets, diapers, laces, and buttons shipped in from Philadelphia by his niece and nephew. It was through them that he kept in touch with the family and, in 1879, learned of the death of his brother George.

That same year, he also learned of the marriage of one of his sons. On May 18, 1879, Jim Dukenfield married Kate Spangler Felton at the Methodist Memorial Church at Eighth and Cumberland Streets. The eldest daughter of a municipal lamplighter, Kate was a homely young woman with a potato face and a bulbous nose. Her people were British by heritage, not German like most of the Pennsylvania Feltons, and she had known her husband since the 1860s, when her father had a butcher shop in Kensington and Jim worked the streets as a huckster. Kate was easygoing where Jim was eruptive, dry and funny with a sideways delivery. She could handle Jim Dukenfield, bear his children, help run his hotel, and do the reading and writing he had never learned to do for himself. She was twenty-four years of age at the time of their marriage; Jim gave his own age as forty.

Kate got pregnant almost immediately, but was so heavy her condition was never terribly apparent. The Dukenfields took a small brick house near the Lesters at 6320 Woodland Avenue (which turned into Main Street as it crossed Cobbs Creek and veered west into Darby). It was a neighborhood of shoemakers, carpenters, blacksmiths, and millwrights. Every morning, Jim and Kate would catch the horsecar at Sixty-fourth Street and ride the three-mile distance to the steps of the Arlington House. Jim usually had work as a trainer and Kate handled the hotel, relying on her husband's cousin for much of the physical work. She wasn't due for another month when she unexpectedly went into labor during a spell of unseasonably warm weather. By the end of the day on Thursday, January 29, 1880, the Dukenfields had a son.

A colored woman named Kitty put a gold spoon in the baby's mouth and said he was going to "get someplace." He was named for his uncle, William Claude Felton, a twenty-year-old clerk at the time, but the baby was soon being referred to as "Claude," and the name stuck. In fact, the first public record of his name, made at the age of four months, identifies him as "Claude W." instead of "William C." The boy could remember his father once telling him that he had been named for a famous Frenchman, Claude Duval. "It wasn't until years later that I decided to read up on Claude Duval. To my chagrin I found out that the gentleman was certainly famous but infamous as well, for he was a notorious highwayman and feared throughout France."*

Kate gladly abandoned her duties at the hotel, embracing motherhood as a well-earned respite from years of early rising. Jim eventually surrendered the lease and found steady work as a bartender, but he was never far from the horses he loved. "My first memory is that my father took me out of bed at midnight and stood me by the window so that I might see a heavy rain, thunder, and lightning storm," said Claude. "There was a great field across the way where hundreds of horses were put out in pasture. The storm caused the horses to stampede and there were several men in the field trying to quiet [them]."

By 1882, the Dukenfields had relocated to the township of North Penn, where a second son was born on July 26. Named for his uncle Walter, the boy grew to idolize his older brother, who was smaller, less animated, but smarter

---

*Claude Duval (1643–1670) was born in France, but came to England with the Duke of Richmond about 1660. One of the most famous—and romanticized—of all highwaymen, his legend was celebrated in dime novels, serials, and an 1881 comic opera by Edward Solomon.

and more ambitious. Claude had his father's natural disdain for authority and his mother's sense of "low cunning." He addressed them as Jim and Katie— never as Dad and Mom—and was at loggerheads with his temperamental father almost from the time he could walk.

Though anything could set him off, Jim's violent outbursts were short-lived and subject to distraction. One of his pet vanities was his remarkable ability to predict rain by sticking a finger in his mouth and then extending it skyward. Kate learned that she could always diffuse a Dukenfield rage by interrupting him to say that one of the neighbor ladies was planning a picnic and wanted to know what the next day's weather would be. Jim immediately would forget all else, hie himself to the porch, poke one of his remaining fingers in his mouth, and send it aloft to gauge the air currents. After a moment's contemplation, he'd return and calmly announce that Mrs. Fuchswanz could plan her picnic with absolute certitude it would be dry the next day.

Jim Dukenfield's volatility would have cowed most youngsters, but Claude reacted with steely defiance, a trait that would stay with him for the rest of his life. It usually fell to Kate to separate the two, sending Claude off to the room he shared with his baby brother and ushering her husband outside for another weather report. Jim stuck to bartending for the most part, but found work at the Lomax Stables on Marshall Street as well. With his Civil War pension of $15 a month, he was able to move the family into a two-story Philadelphia rowhouse on Somerset Street, one block east of Germantown Avenue, in 1884.

Claude started at the nearby Oakdale School in the fall of 1885. He was a bright kid, but he was easily bored with schoolwork and was a behavior problem. When his teacher, Miss Bertha, applied the usual remedy—a quarter hour's stand in the cloakroom—he busied himself by going through the pockets of his classmates' coats. It got so he enjoyed being sent to the cloakroom so much that Miss Bertha was forced to alter the punishment to a series of strokes administered across the hand by the school principal.

Each morning, Kate would send him off with a lick and a promise, spitting on the corner of her apron and roughly digging the dirt out of his ears with her finger. In the time it would take him to walk the five blocks to school, he would concoct excuses for Miss Bertha on why he had failed to return a properly signed report card. In class, he would jam the rolling doors between rooms by shoving knives, sticks, and other such implements in the tracks and then watch the ensuing commotion with a serene smile. He stuttered when asked to make recitations and lacked the confidence to do consistently well in school. "I was always a lazy boy," he later admitted. "I hated to have to get up and go to school." Timid around girls, he was awkward in the ill-fitting clothes his parents bought for him at secondhand stores; in his entire childhood he could remember only one new suit of clothes.

Whatever affection the boy had for school was instilled in him by his maternal grandmother, Anna Elizabeth Felton, whose two eldest children had both worked as teachers. Unlike her daughter Kate, who took after her compliant father and spent her life quelling trouble rather than causing it, Annie was a feather-hatted steamroller of a woman. Her husband, Tom, was a butcher by trade who, through some political pull, managed to land himself a job as a lamplighter. When he was too sick (i.e., drunk) to work, Annie would hoist the ladder onto her back and make the rounds herself, igniting the arc lamps along Germantown Avenue while enduring the taunts of boys who would tug at her long skirts. Tom died of cirrhosis at the age of fifty-five, and Annie was left to focus her considerable energies on her son Grant, who at age fifteen was still living at home, and her grandson Claude, who was, in the prophecy of the woman at the Arlington House, going to get someplace.

By the spring of 1886, Kate was pregnant with a third child, and Annie moved herself into the house on Somerset to help her daughter cope with the boys. Claude was six at the time, and under his grandmother's stern supervision his schoolwork improved. A daughter, Elsie May Dukenfield, was born in November. Two years later, when Claude was eight, his father was fired from his job at a local saloon when the proprietress found a stash of coins Jim had secreted in a barrel. Annie promptly took charge, moving the family to a three-story house she owned at the corner of Somerset and Germantown. She forced Jim to give up tending bar for a living, and soon he had a new job as a streetcar conductor for the Philadelphia Traction Company.

Claude made his first money selling pansies, but avoided getting a real job until the old man lost his. Then, for a brief time, he worked in a tobacconist's shop to supplement the family income. "My duties often kept me at the counter until midnight," he reminisced. Once, toward the end of a long day, he fell asleep at the counter, knocked over a kerosene lamp, and carried a scar on his hand for the rest of his life. He didn't burn the store down that night, but he was discharged shortly thereafter for innocently "cleaning up" the place by emptying a lot of half-filled cigar boxes into other boxes and unwittingly mixing the brands.

Over the spring and summer of 1889, the spacious new Cambria School was built on Thirteenth Street, a handsome brick building with stone trimmings, steam heat, and attached toilets. Claude entered the fourth grade there in the fall of 1889 and quickly earned a certificate ranking him among the "distinguished scholars of the week," affirming that he "has been punctual in attendance every session, has recited lessons faultlessly, and behaved with the utmost propriety." Dated November 21, 1889, the award marked the academic pinnacle of his young life, for neither Claude nor Walter would go on to high school.

A second daughter, Adele, was born to the Dukenfields in September 1889. The family prospered, but after a fifth child was stillborn in the fall of 1891, Kate's commitment to housekeeping declined precipitously. Late in life, Claude told a friend that his mother would lie in bed all morning "besotted with gin." She'd crawl out at the sound of the noon whistle, tie on an apron, splash her face with water, and appear on the front steps of the house, mopping her brow and loudly declaring that she had been "working all morning over a hot stove."

Food was bought from commission merchants who noisily wheeled their carts down the cobblestone street, sometimes by horse, often by hand. The entire commerce of the city seemed to pass by the house—fishmongers, flower vendors, scissor and knife grinders, women who sold shoelaces and collar buttons, umbrella menders, boys with newspapers and primitive shoe-shine boxes, even glassblowers selling ornamental birds and delicately colored pipes. Kate would sit on the front steps, watch the hucksters make their afternoon rounds, and greet the neighbors as they passed. "Good day to ye, Mrs. Muldoon," she would call out, smiling cordially. Then, as Mrs. Muldoon passed out of earshot, she would shake her head and add, sotto voce, "Terrible gossip, Mrs. Muldoon." To another: "Oh, and how are you today, Mrs. Frankel?" and then, as Mrs. Frankel moved along, "Nasty old bitch, Mrs. Frankel."

The house on Germantown was a jumble of rowdy kids, old clothes, and dirty dishes. "Mother was an old-fashioned homebody," said the youngest of the Dukenfield boys, Leroy. "She would put on a wrapper and leave that on for a couple of days and never go out of the house." The social highlight of Kate's week was a Friday klatch at the home of Jim's cousin Mary, who, with her husband, John Stevenson, ran a dry goods business. Winters were spent in the kitchen, the only room in the house with any warmth to it. "We used to make snowballs," Claude remembered, "dip them in some kind of flavoring, and have a party." Summers were for the big parks—Willow Grove, where John Philip Sousa led the band, Washington, Chestnut Hill, and Fairmont, where one could pack a picnic lunch and watch boat races from the banks of the Schuylkill.

Jim progressed to a driver's position with the Traction Company, but the era of the old two-horse streetcar was rapidly drawing to a close. Cable cars and electric trolleys were beginning to replace them, and men of Jim Dukenfield's age and limited tenure were among the first to be sacked. Jim decided it was time to go back out on his own, and like Kate's industrious brother Billy, who had worked Germantown Avenue above Tioga Street as a "victualer" since the time he was twenty-one, he rented a horse and wagon and, at the age of fifty-two, went back to being a huckster.

That spring, twelve-year-old Claude was pressed into service, helping the old man in his daily rounds. Six times a week, rising before dawn, they would make the four-mile journey to the vast public market near Penn's Landing and collect their day's provisions: oranges, fresh fruits, and vegetables brought up by rail from Jacksonville, peaches and watermelon from Maryland, Delaware, and New Jersey, and apples from western New York and Michigan. Jim would buy his produce at Detweiler's on Callowhill Street, the Newmarket on Second at Pine, and straight off the docks. Wagon loaded, he and his son would then make their way back to the Northern Liberties, where they would trundle the narrow streets and alleys, calling their wares, until late in the day.

Before long, Jim had established routes and regular customers, running the entire business off the cuff. He purchased the horse, an elderly nag called White Swan, and the wagon that went with her, but he was never quite as prosperous as he might otherwise have been, for while he was out vending fruits and vegetables and charging twice what he paid, Kate was selling the same produce out the back door of their house at half his cost and keeping all the proceeds for herself.* At night, Jim would sit in the kitchen, stew about the day's receipts—he was always sure life would be better in England—and balefully regard the children as if they belonged to the neighbors. "Dad, to me, he was a foreigner," Leroy Dukenfield said. "He never seemed to take much interest."

Claude handled the produce with a natural dexterity that could only have served to irritate his eight-fingered father. "It was while pulling door bells and waiting for an answer that he began to juggle potatoes or tomatoes or whatever vegetables he had in his hands at that particular time," his boyhood friend Charlie Van Tagen recalled. The irritability and sudden violence with which Jim Dukenfield ruled the house inspired a similarly combative nature in his son Claude. He'd mock the old man's accent, calling out fruits and vegetables just because he liked the sounds of their names and not because they happened to be on the wagon that day.

Jim's flash temper got the better of him, and with the long hours he and his son spent together, Claude's contempt for his father blossomed into a full-blown hatred. One day, as Claude later told it, "My father patted me on the spine with a spade for a reason I cannot recall. I, in turn, called him a name that reflected on his ancestors and made a bad noise with my mouth at him. I took it on the lam pronto. That night I reposed *al fresco.*"

Claude would later speak of braining his father with a lug box, but in the last year of his life he told his secretary, Magda Michael, that Jim had actually tripped over a garden spade and then hurled it at him in a fit of temper when

---

*Kate Dukenfield was always cagey about money, a trait her eldest son inherited. Everyone thought she was enormously big-busted, but in reality she kept her money up there. When she died, in 1925, her daughter Elsie May took her first-ever look into her accordion wallet and found nearly $40,000 in cash.

the boy impulsively laughed. Claude retaliated by bouncing a bushel basket off his father's head and then, realizing in horror what he had done, broke out in a dead run. The old man, white-hot with fury, chased his son down the street, warning of grave consequences should he ever return. "I felt bad at first on account of the old man hitting me and me hitting him," Claude said, "but before long I was in high spirits."

By most accounts, Claude Dukenfield began running away from home at the age of nine. He loathed the winter cold and getting out of bed when the house was dark and frigid. "That was one of the things that made me run away from home," he said. "My mother would make me get up and go to school." Annie Felton, who mitigated Jim's corrosive fits, relocated to the Kensington district in 1892 and left her twelve-year-old grandson to fend for himself. Claude began ditching class and rebelling against the crowded confines of yet another home, this one in the village of Rising Sun, where the family occupied the southern half of a large-frame twin house.

At nine, Claude escaped to the relative comfort of his uncle Will's house on Germantown Avenue. As his departures grew more frequent, however, he took to sleeping at the Lomax Stables. Finally, at the age of twelve, with his father in no state of forgiveness, he decided to live in an open field. "Some of the fellows had a bunk—you know: you dig a hole in the ground and cover it over with boards and dirt—and I lived in that." The weather was mild ("I'm no chump, I don't run away from home in the winter"), and milk, eggs, bread, and butter could be found "on back door steps and porches at unearthly hours." As a shelter, the dugout had its drawbacks: "It was so short, I couldn't stretch out full length, and when it rained, the water came through the cracks overhead." On particularly muddy nights, Claude took to sleeping in privies, or in freight cars overrun with tramps. The yard bulls who worked for the railroads were brutal: "I got some bad beatings, but once in a while we'd manage to beat them up. Not very often, though, because most bums are yellow cowards." The experience would have broken a lot of kids, but Claude's grandmother had invested him with an unshakable sense of value and self-worth. "No one ever read books or tried to improve themselves in our neighborhood," he said. "If you were not working, you stood on the street corner and the large or older boys made factitious remarks at girls who passed. . . . When they couldn't fight with somebody else, they would fight among themselves."

Fighting was something Claude Dukenfield learned a lot about. He ran with older boys and was beaten in much the same casual manner as he was by his own father. "Every kid in Philadelphia must have taken a whack at my beezer at some time or other." Blessed with Jim Dukenfield's hair-trigger temper, he started as many fights as others picked with him, and was always ready to meet a verbal or physical challenge with a swift, if ofttimes inept, response.

He considered his first street fight his "most vivid childhood memory" and learned to absorb physical punishment with dignity. Because of his almost colorless blond hair, he was awarded the nickname of "Whitey." Best of all, he gained the respect of the others for living the independent life of a runaway. "Any kid who wants to be a hero to the neighborhood gang—all he has to do is stop sleeping in a bed. None of those boys were pretty-willies. Lots of them were bigger and older than I was and could've pushed my face in without half trying. But there always was a time at night, late maybe, when the biggest and toughest of them had to run home to mama."

The chronology, as laid forth in later years, gets a bit murky here. After a few days—or weeks, or months, depending on the account—Claude was invited indoors by some of the older boys who admired his stubbornness and grit. They had rooms over a wheelwright's shop at Marsh's Court called, for reasons obscure even then, "the Orlando Social Club." It was furnished with castoff chairs, a rickety table, and an old piano that refused to play after one of the boys attempted to clean it with water. At the urgings of one Tommy Hunt, they elected Whitey Dukenfield their janitor without dues and allowed him to remain there at night. "I slept in the back room," he remembered, "on an improvised bed made by removing one of the doors and using several bags of hay to pinch-hit for a box-springs mattress." He was also allowed to participate in the petty thefts that passed for recreation. "He had the most wonderful ideas," said his friend Jack Norworth. After considerable study, he decided that laundries and bakeries were the easiest businesses to rob because the proprietors worked in the backs of their stores and used little spring-mounted bells to alert them to entries. So he'd get his pal Charlie Probischer to toss a hat onto the trolley tracks and then dash out after it. The approaching motorman would furiously pound his heel on the bell until the clanging got so loud that it drowned out all other noises. Then Whitey would dart through the door and expertly clean the till, or snatch a pie from under its fly-proof gauze.

"We'd sneak into the chink laundries and grab tickets out of the bundles on the shelves and run like old Nick himself was after us with a pitchfork. Then we'd sell the tickets for ten cents to anyone we could nail. What the hell . . . anyone who sent anything at all to the laundry would send more than ten cents' worth, so whoever bought the tickets couldn't get stuck." Though often ill with what became a chronic cough, he loved his days with the Orlando kids. "I wouldn't have changed places with the richest boy in the finest house in Philadelphia. I didn't even have to mind the cops because I could run faster. You remember cops in those days—big fat slobs they were."

He must have been away from home through the fall of 1892, for he could vividly remember his mother's reluctance to have him over for Thanksgiving dinner. In a sterling example of low cunning, Kate told her son that his grand-

*Whitey Dukenfield, circa 1892*

mother wanted him instead. "She's having goose," she said brightly. And so, on the day of the event, Claude cleaned himself up and made the two-mile walk to Grandma Felton's house on Sterner Street, only to find that her place was under lock and key. A neighbor told him she was off having dinner with friends. "It was only then that I realized that Kate had sent me on this 'wild goose' chase only to forestall my coming home and arousing Jim's ire. I think I snatched some apples from a fruit store to allay my hunger." He was back on Goodman Street by Christmas, but the Yuletide commemoration was no different than it had been for previous years. The children would hang their stockings on Christmas Eve, then awaken the next morning to find that Santa had left each of them a single gift—an orange.

In 1893, with his grandmother urging him toward a respectable career in retailing, he applied for a job as a cash boy at the venerable Market Street department store of Strawbridge and Clothier. He found a queue of boys eager to fill the position, but when a gust of wind blew the Help Wanted sign over, it was Claude who took the initiative to retrieve it. Marching the sign back into the personnel office, he was rewarded with the job, which paid the princely sum of $2 a week. After a couple of weeks of shuttling change between counters, however, he grew disenchanted. "I realized I was not getting anywhere," he said with considerable understatement, and after three months he quit.

He returned to school in the fall, but his father, like most British immigrants, thought it unconscionable that a thirteen-year-old boy wasn't working and contributing to the support of the family. Claude found sanctuary at his sixty-two-year-old grandmother's house, where her devoted son Grant was like an older brother. Domineering as she was, Annie Felton was also forthright and principled and had his best interests at heart. "I think he always tried to emulate her in later life," said Magda Michael. "She was a sturdy character of the Marjorie Main type, and he said up to the time of her death she imagined that any younger man who offered her such an ordinary courtesy as holding a door open for her, or offering her his seat on the trolley car, was making a pass at her."

Jim couldn't do much about his son's living arrangement because the old woman wouldn't let him near the house. On the rare occasions when, after visiting her daughter, she permitted him to drive her home, she demanded that he let her off a couple of blocks away so the neighbors wouldn't see him. Claude may have gone on to classes at Philadelphia's Central High for, unlike his brother Walter, he could read and write fairly well, but he never claimed anything more than a spotty grade school education, and by the fall of 1895, Annie knew the battle had been lost.


Vaudeville was born at approximately the same time as W. C. Fields and in approximately the same place. An outgrowth of the British music hall tradition, variety performances were initially used to draw customers into American beer halls in the 1870s. The first vaudeville theater, Tony Pastor's, was opened in New York in 1881, and the trend to clean shows that could play to "double audiences" (meaning men and women) spread to other cities. By 1885, there were more than twenty such houses in Philadelphia, which was to become known as the "Cradle of Vaudeville" for all the important acts that got their starts there.

Philadelphia was the country's first theater town, beginning when Quaker performance laws were rescinded in the 1780s. The great stage comedian Joseph Jefferson was born in Philadelphia, where three generations of his family ran the Chestnut Street Theatre. Louisa Lane Drew, the definitive Mrs. Malaprop, managed the Arch Street Theatre, served as mother to actor John Drew and his promising sister Georgiana, and, after Georgiana's untimely death, in 1892, as grandmother to Georgiana's three children—Lionel, Ethel, and John Barrymore.

Enoch's Varieties, an important theater during the childhood of Claude Dukenfield, was established in an old church and featured a variegated program of entertainment exclusively for men. In the early 1890s, the Amusements section in the Sunday *Inquirer* was crammed with options. The onus of the stag show, ubiquitous in the 1880s, gave way to "family" entertainment in the 1890s. Forepaugh's Family Theatre, on Eighth Street below Vine, was a repertory house with its own stock company. (In 1939, Fields remembered working a "sideshow" there, perhaps the first performance he ever gave.) Also on Eighth, a veritable rialto of popular theaters, were the Lyceum, the Star, and B. F. Keith's Bijou, an ornate little auditorium that billed itself as "the home of model high-class drawing room vaudeville, filled to overflowing with excellent novelty and comedy features."

A teenage boy looking for entertainment in September 1895 would have passed on Belasco's *La Belle Russe* at People's Theatre, *Little Christopher* at the Chestnut Street Opera House, and Sutton Vane's *Humanity* at the National, preferring instead the broad delights of Donnelly and Girard at the Park, the Russell Brothers (who played Irish servant girls) at Gilmore's Auditorium, or Bradenburgh's Dime Museum at Ninth and Arch, "devoted to the entertainment of young and old, and particularly adapted to the instruction of juvenile minds," whose principal attraction was Eight Female Barbers, an octet of buxom incompetents who shaved and shampooed male volunteers in an instructive mix of sex and bloodletting.

All such venues cost money, however, and it was rare that Claude Dukenfield had the dime admission that most theaters charged for a ticket to the gallery, where long wooden benches took the place of individual seats. A useful acquaintance during this period was the boy whose father owned the cigar shop at which Claude had briefly worked the late shift. The son usually inherited the tickets his father was given for permitting the display of show cards in the window, and one night the comps were for *Eight Bells,* a nautical farce playing a week's stand at the historic Walnut Street Theatre.

Claude, by this time, had a fairly stable job, one that actually met with his grandmother's approval. He was working for a man named Andy Donaldson, earning $4 a week on a Germantown ice wagon. "I had to be up by 3 a.m., but I was through by nine or ten in the morning. Then the driver and I would go to a saloon where they were getting the free lunches ready for the day's business. He would buy me a bottle of ginger ale and I'd have a free sandwich out of the wire cage where the food was kept. At noon, I would go back to the saloon, buy myself another bottle of ginger ale, and have a free bowl of soup. Although for a long time I got most of my food in saloons, I drank nothing but ginger ale."

The hours conflicted with his natural sleeping patterns, and he was always on the lookout for another line of work. In a place like Philadelphia, where early hours were a tradition and homes were usually shuttered by eight, a job that would permit him to sleep late into the day was difficult to find. At home, the situation was exacerbated when Kate unexpectedly gave birth to another son, Leroy Russell Dukenfield. ("Mother thought it was a tumor," Leroy said, "and it was me.") The baby's caterwauling made it nearly impossible for Claude to get a proper night's sleep. Meanwhile, the September heat and "trolley parties" (a new version of the old-fashioned hayride) had cleared out the city's theaters and rendered them hospitable to a late-evening snooze.

*Eight Bells* was a lift of the Hanlon Brothers' *Le Voyage en Suisse,* a landmark conflation of trickery, pantomime, and spectacular scenic effects that had been touring Europe since the late 1870s. The Hanlons' American counterparts, the acrobatic Byrne Brothers, devised their own version in 1891, and were playing a revised edition of it when they made their Philadelphia stopover. It wasn't the crowd-pleasing mechanical effects—which included an elaborate storm at sea—that held Claude Dukenfield's attention that night, however, but rather a brief interlude of comedic juggling at the top of the third act. The setting, according to the script, was the interior of a French mansion, where a servant entered and, after looking around, began juggling the various things he found in the room. Specifically, the routine involved a hat, a cane, and a cigar, although what exactly James A. Byrne did with them is not indicated. In the original Hanlon show, the part of the waiter was played by the great French juggler Henri Agoust, who, to comically divert the attention of the guests at a garden party, frantically began grabbing things off a nearby table— plates, utensils, food, chairs—and juggling them. The specialty built to hilarious, show-stopping proportions, and Claude, who would have been consumed, as usual, with dread over the start of another workday, suddenly forgot his fatigue and was instantly captivated.

He had seen professional jugglers before, but most followed the example of Paul Cinquevalli, a colorful Prussian who worked in tights and leotards and whose stunts were tremendous feats of strength and balance. (One of his signature tricks was to toss a sixty-pound cannonball in the air and catch it on the back of his neck.) Toss juggling was regarded as somewhat passé by the mid-1890s and generally reserved to circus clowns and teams of acrobats who passed Indian clubs. What was different and almost unique about the juggling in *Eight Bells* was the way in which it was integrated into the plot of the show and performed with nontraditional objects to outlandish effect. The impact on a sleepy fifteen-year-old was to make it look as if anyone could do it.

Claude had juggled fruits and vegetables, but at no time had he thought of juggling as the basis of a livelihood. He couldn't imagine himself in pink tights and spangled britches, and the thought of actually speaking onstage filled him with terror. Moreover, his grandmother would never approve of such an absurd vocation. Yet, before him was a juggler who was clearly making a good living working afternoons and evenings and wearing real trousers. "With pleasure," he later said, "I discovered that [Byrne] was not doing anything more than I could do. Leaving the theatre, I walked around the city determined to change the whole scheme of my life."

The next day, he appropriated some Seckel pears from his father's inventory and tried juggling them in earnest. When he could adequately run three pears in what jugglers call a "cascade," he took on a fourth, then progressed to other fruit. "I began taking tomatoes and, in the proper season, Rocky Ford cantaloupes. I juggled all of them." Though he could manipulate fruit with relative ease, he found himself stymied by a lack of material. He decided to start paying attention to what other jugglers did as they came through town, and within days a man known as Harrigan, an "eccentric comedian and juggler," had joined the bill at Keith's Bijou. Claude studied his act, sitting through several performances, and, as with Byrne, he admired the man's use of everyday props over the formal paraphernalia usually favored by jugglers. Harrigan was also quite funny—a clever monologist and singer of song parodies.

At the clubhouse, Claude began amassing a collection of junkyard props with the help of his pals. "Like a lot of youngsters, we played theatre and all had a certain leaning toward the stage," said Charlie Van Tagen. One of the Orlando boys, who worked in a stove foundry, brought him three steel balls. Another, who was a tinsmith, made a funnel so that he could perfect a trick in which he juggled the balls through the funnel. Others contributed old billiard balls, a copper cylinder, broomsticks onto which he nailed cups taken from oil burners ("catching small balls in the cups and continuing to juggle"), and cigar boxes in which the corners had been reinforced. He spent most of his free time practicing, and his family saw very little of him. "I wasn't running wild," he said, "even though it sounds like it. I had a purpose in view all the time, and I was plugging away at it so hard that it kept me out of mischief." With his new-found zeal for performing, he tried expanding his repertoire to some of the other circus skills displayed by the Brothers Byrne. The boys twisted some discarded telegraph wire together and strung it from the chimney of the shop to a nearby tree. Two clothes props, filched from a backyard and weighted with stones, became a balance pole for wire walking.

*James Edward Harrigan,*
*"The Original Tramp Juggler"*

On Thanksgiving, one of the boys' mothers sent over a whole roasted turkey (at least her boy said so), but the bird was unaccompanied by eating utensils and the membership had a free-for-all tearing it apart. Noting Claude's absence from the holiday table, Annie Felton went looking for him and found him precariously balanced on the wire above the wheelwright's shop. Convinced he had fallen in with bad company and was in danger of breaking his fool neck, she got a copper, stormed the clubhouse when he wasn't there, and had every one of his juggling implements confiscated and destroyed. That, she later told him angrily, should put an end to his "foolish juggling notion." And, for a while, at least, it did.

# Two

# Ten and Cakes

To the end of his days, Claude could remember the sense of outrage he felt at his grandmother's laying waste to his juggling gear. Yet, he forgave the old woman "because she thought she was doing it for my own good." He stayed with his job on the ice wagon, but maintained his routine of practice as well, slowly rebuilding his store of props. Over time, his dedication to practice attracted attention in the neighborhood. At the saloon where he ate lunch every day, a Dutch waiter began referring to him as "Whitey the Playactor" because he would buy a ginger ale and not just steal crackers and bologna. Another who took notice was a dapper twenty-eight-year-old Irishman named Bill Dailey, whose particular skill was in the manipulation of three walnut shells and a wad of dough he called the "pea."

Dailey was known around town as "the Professor" for his encyclopedic knowledge of con games and his ability to teach card tricks to practically anyone. In the dexterous Dukenfield boy, the Professor could see the makings of a valuable confederate. He befriended the kid, trained him as a shill, and, on one of their first outings, took him to the Trenton Fair in New Jersey. The two hopped a freight before daybreak at Wayne Junction, got drenched when it took on water while crossing the Delaware, and jumped clear just as the train pulled into the station. Dripping wet, they ran frantically to dry their clothes and stole breakfast from a nearby porch. Making their way to the fairgrounds and clambering over the fence, Dailey improvised a small table on a couple of boxes and began shouting, "It's the old army game! One will get you two; two will get you four; four will get you eight. Find the little pea. It's the old army game!" To prime the crowd, it was Whitey's job to step forward, throw a smacker on the box, guess which shell the pea was under, and walk off with double his money. Others were prompted to come forward, and the hustle was on.

For the fifteen-year-old boy who would become W. C. Fields, the quintessential con man, the Professor's scam lent meaning to the old adage "You can't

*William T. Dailey, circa 1900*

cheat an honest man." Joe Mankiewicz, a screenwriter who later worked with
him, once asked Fields what the expression meant and was shown how the old
army game, like most confidence tricks, "was based upon the fact that you let
the chump believe that he had seen which walnut the pea was under. An honest
man would say, 'Oh, I think I saw it that time. Better do it again.' But if he had
a little larceny in him, you had him hooked—if he thought he could gain something for nothing."

According to Fields, who recalled the experience in a 1942 magazine article,
their time at the Trenton Fair didn't last very long. "An unharnessed gildersleeve
arrived on the scene with the stealth of a Brahma bull. He grabbed the Professor
by the coat, which was still wet, and, with a well-aimed No. 12, E-width, double-
soled boot, came flesh upon my fundament. He almost raised me over the
fence."

Dailey wound up in the jug, and his young assistant didn't make it back to
Philadelphia until nightfall. Their friendship, however, was sealed. It was Bill
Dailey who pushed the Dukenfield boy into show business, becoming his first
manager and arranging his first appearances as a performer. What form these
jobs took is a matter of conjecture, for there seems to be no record of them. In
1939, while compiling a resume of his early career, Fields himself indicated that

he had played medicine shows, but he offered no details. Dailey's daughter, in a 1971 interview, recalled her father doing dances that he and Fields had performed when they were first starting out. Dailey later became an accomplished sand dancer in vaudeville and could sing in a pleasing Irish tenor. He also did a mentalist act in which Fields may have assisted him.

Fields usually dated his first performances from 1897, when he was seventeen years old and living with his family on Rising Sun Lane. His grandmother's house in Kensington was no longer the safe haven it once had been because she disapproved so thoroughly of his performing ambitions and was convinced that Dailey was up to no good. His father was of no help either, and this, he later decided, was actually a good thing. "If he had given me money to learn and buy tricks, I would have purchased a whole act and would have had nothing original. He would not give me a cent, so I had to invent my own act and devise my own tricks."

He didn't quite "invent" his own act, however, and there was nothing original about it—at least at first. The challenge of becoming proficient in the art of juggling was daunting enough; framing these skills in the form of an act was clearly beyond him. According to his sister Adele, he didn't even seem particularly suited to the task of making people laugh. "We never thought Claude was particularly funny off stage," she said. "It was Walter who was funny." The practical option was to steal an act, but the act that initially sparked Claude's interest in juggling was virtually unstealable. The Byrne Brothers performed as a team in a scripted show, and there was little a single juggler could imitate. On the other hand, Jim Harrigan did a twelve-minute solo routine that seemed as if he made it up as he went. Were one to steal an act, Harrigan's would be the one to take. Jugglers who worked by themselves weren't common at the time, as much of the juggling that got performed in vaudeville was done by teams of acrobats or equilibrists. Harrigan was decidedly a different sort, having started out as a gentleman juggler who, one night, found himself unable to get his dress suit out of hock for a performance. "I hastily borrowed odd garments from other performers," he said, "mussed my smooth hair into a tangle, put on a half-inch beard with a handful of burnt paper, and rushed onto the stage as a tramp."

Harrigan built an act around the costume and passed through Philadelphia at least once a year. He'd shuffle out onstage and regard the audience with mock surprise. "Hallo, fellows! Well, I blowed my job again!" He'd strike a match on his whiskers, light a cigarette, and throw his plug hat in the air, catching it on a stick. "Oh, pretty fair!" he'd say. Then he'd throw a box and a bottle in the air so that the lid of the box opened as the bottle passed through it. He'd balance a strip of paper on his nose, juggle three balls, and pass the balls through a flap in his hat. "You've all heard of people talking through their hat," he'd say, "but you've never seen anyone that could juggle through his hat!" Lastly, he'd take twelve cigar boxes and form them into a herringbone pattern, knocking them off one at a time. Juggling the final three, he'd rebuild the boxes in a tall stack with lighted kerosene lamps, knocking off the boxes again and catching each lamp on the back of his hand. "What's the use of working when you can do this for a living? Well, so long, fellows!"

Harrigan was no headliner, but he had been working steadily in burlesque and vaudeville since the late 1880s. As far as anyone knows, he invented the idea of the tramp juggler. Seeing the Byrne Brothers at the Walnut Street Theatre may have sparked Claude Dukenfield's ambition to be a juggler, but it was Harrigan's act at the Bijou that made it seem achievable. Claude was quick with his hands—a talent that served him well as a shoplifter—and had a natural aptitude for the manipulation of balls and sticks.* He also had plenty of time to devote to practice—an absolute necessity. "If a juggler had spent as many hours practicing a musical instrument as he had to spend mastering his tricks," wrote comedian Fred Allen, who also started as a juggler, "he would have been a concert artist."

His life became a diligent rotation of work, sleep, and practice. "I meant to keep it up for a year, every day, but at the end of the year I was only fair, not good, so I took another year. . . . I kept at it, trying new tricks, and kept my mind on it all the time, and found that there was nothing impossible in the juggling line so long as one is determined to succeed." He once told a studio publicist of the scars he carried on his legs from practice: "I'd balance a stick on my toe, toss it into the air, and try to catch it again on my toe. Hour by hour, the damn thing would bang against my shinbones. I'd work until tears were streaming down my face. But I kept on practicing, and bleeding, until I perfected the trick."

Another juggling enthusiast in the neighborhood was Horace Lorette, who would later become known as H. M. Lorette, "the Original Dancing Juggler." Lorette would remember the Dukenfield boy as "a nondescript character" who joined him for some practice sessions at his home at Fifteenth and Cumberland. The boys compared notes on Harrigan's technique and his use of a tramp costume and makeup. "We were both able to do about all that Harrigan did with cigar boxes," Lorette remembered, "and we both had good routines with tennis balls and high hats. We had lots of ideas of our own, too. He did not care anything about club juggling. I had some heavy clubs in the room, but he wouldn't even touch them. He said, 'A single juggler can't get any comedy out of clubs and I'm not interested.' I also tried to teach him a little tap dancing,

---

*A knack for juggling seems to run in the family. W. Claude Fields Jr. could juggle, as can all five of his children. None of them ever had a formal lesson.

but his sense of rhythm was very inadequate. I finally got him into doing a comedy break fairly well."

Paying engagements were hard to come by. "He was only playing little concert halls and church buffets for ice cream and cake," said his brother Walter. Philadelphia's romance with vaudeville had progressed to the point where promoters would hire neighborhood halls and assemble semiprofessional bills of "select" vaudeville to compete with the downtown theaters. Usually the performers were unpaid and did their turns for sandwiches and coffee. The first entry in the first scrapbook Claude Dukenfield assembled is the playbill for one such performance at Asher's Natatorium Hall on January 13, 1898. The seventh slot in this display of local talent was given over to a comic juggling turn by one William C. Felton. The evening also featured a recitation by Miss Helen Bennett, a piano duet by Misses Reba Johnson and Anna Harvey, and a vocal selection from Miss Bessie Friel. It ended with a drawing for a gold watch.

The Natatorium performance was a disaster; the piano player started up in the middle of the act, distracting the audience and killing the momentum. By evidence of the scrapbook, the next engagement did not come until two months later, when Claude played a grand concert and hop at Peabody Hall. The program was more varied this time—a harmonica selection vied with his juggling for novelty—but late performances (he was on second to last) played hell with his early shift on the ice wagon, and, after missing a few mornings, he was fired.

At first, Claude resisted stealing Harrigan's act outright, but such admirable resolve didn't last very long. "I could juggle all right," he explained, "but it was hard to get an engagement because I had no wardrobe, and performers were supposed to have extensive wardrobes then, as now. After I had been jobless long enough, good old necessity became a mother, once more, of invention and I decided to become a tramp juggler." Appearing in tramp makeup intensified the problem of a proper stage name. "Felton" was short and practical and had cachet in Philadelphia, where a section of Bristol township was known as "Feltonville," but his uncle Will was becoming active in the Republican politics of the twenty-fifth ward, and when, in the spring of 1898, he was made a deputy sheriff, it suddenly became wildly inappropriate to stride out onstage in an old tramp's outfit and use the name. So Claude reverted to Dukenfield and, as he later put it, "clipped the head and the torso off the name and just kept the tail." The appearance at Peabody Hall on March 11, 1898, marked the first time he specifically billed himself as a tramp juggler and the first time he appeared under a new and completely original name—W. C. Fields.

Fields' career as a tramp juggler got off to a slow start. There are only four documented performances for the first half of the year 1898, two of which were benefit concerts for the superpatriotic Brotherhood of the Union. Fields could remember appearing at the Republican Club on Somerset Street with the singing Cassidy Brothers, and at a Methodist church function where, after getting stiffed for his fee on a rainy weeknight, he had his assistant, an amiable halfwit known as "Troubles," clear all the umbrellas out of the adjoining cloakroom. "We waited until the pawnshop opened at Germantown and Oakdale. Then we went to Broad and Cambria Streets and disgorged ourselves with steak, potatoes, coffee, and bread with the swank the pawnbroker allowed us for said umbrellas . . . never have I enjoyed food so much as I did that early morning at the motormen and conductors' lunchroom."

Fields' self-appointed manager, Bill Dailey, tried valiantly to arouse interest in his client, but found the commercial venues effectively closed to local talent. The Bijou, still the top vaudeville house in Philadelphia, was booked out of the Keith office in Boston. Gilmore's Auditorium was usually rented to touring companies and rarely assembled its own bills. And the eight acts of vaudeville at the Ninth and Arch Dime Museum were now secondary to the attraction of Lubin's Cineograph, "the greatest of moving picture machines." Burlesque, a form of variety built around a chorus of busty young women, was more hospitable to new talent and gaining in popularity. The 11th Street Opera House, the home of Dumont's Minstrels, added burlesque to its bill in 1896, and the former Arch Street Opera House became the city's newest burlesque theater, the Trocadero, in 1897. Since the girls and their playlet, called a "burletta," were the main attractions of a burlesque show, the surrounding acts didn't have to be good, just cheap. Unfortunately, most burlesque troupes were assembled and booked out of New York City.

The theaters in Philadelphia were closing for the summer when Fields met Dailey in a saloon on Germantown Avenue. The work was obviously in New York, not Philadelphia, and they had to figure out a way to get him there. Benefit concerts were in vogue, and, after a few beers, Dailey suggested they stage one for Fields. They could charge an admission of fifteen cents, pay off the musicians, and keep the rest for themselves. Fields had recently played a concert for the Manhattan Athletic Club at Batley Hall, and Dailey managed to book the place for a benefit performance on June 13, 1898. The bill was comprised of pals like Harry Antrim, Charlie Van Tagen, and monologist Harry S. Fern. A local outfit known as Gray's Orchestra was engaged to furnish the dance music. "Everyone worked feverishly at the idea of my leaving the city," he said. Advertising space on the cards announcing the show was sold to local merchants. "We had some tickets and window cards and even some letterheads all printed on the pay-if-you-can-catch-us plan."

Annie Felton was apoplectic when she learned of the scheme. "I remember my old grandmother was going to have you arrested," Fields reminisced in a

1925 letter to Dailey. "The poor old lady was going to have everyone arrested. She blamed you for me having lost my job on the ice wagon with Andy Donaldson, and in all probability she was right. I might still have that job, or a better one, or even my own wagon and route by this time." More than six hundred people turned out to help Fields meet his medical expenses, but as soon as they were in their seats, the subject of their concern, who was supposedly near death at Samaritan Hospital, emerged from hiding and confiscated the receipts. "I ducked out, I remember, with a cigar box full of money, forgetting to pay the orchestra, or the rent of the hall after twelve." He later described the event as "my start in show business," although he didn't perform that night, and the take (about $90) as "my first real money." On his way back to the family house on the outskirts of Nicetown, he stopped to buy a pair of checkered pants, a blue serge coat, a three-inch piccadilly collar, a pair of pointed-toe shoes, and a straw hat. His mother fixed sandwiches and a thermos of coffee and walked him to the trolley stop. With eight-year-old Adele looking on, Kate tearfully asked if she'd ever see him again. He answered that she would—but only if he made good. He then boarded the trolley to Wayne Junction, where he caught a blind baggage to New York at 4:00 a.m.

The colossal city Fields discovered that summer was still in the throes of coming together. At the first of the year, Brooklyn, Staten Island, Queens, and the Bronx had merged with Manhattan to form the five boroughs of Greater New York. A heat wave was driving temperatures into the eighties, and an aggressive recruitment campaign was on to replenish the armories whose men were off fighting Spanish troops in Cuba and the Philippines. Koster and Bial's Music Hall was featuring Marie Dressler, Josephine Hull, and Harry Kelly in *Cook's Tour,* Maude Adams was closing in *The Little Minister,* and the Edem Musee, a wax museum, was projecting moving pictures of the war, filmed in Manila and Havana Harbor by Edison personnel, for twenty-five cents a seat.

The offices of bookers and agents were concentrated in the area surrounding Union Square, at the grimy lower tip of the theatrical district that extended north along Broadway to Thirty-fourth Street. Fields intended to treat himself to a private room, but was dismayed at the surroundings. "Union Square was a dirty, filthy old tramp place," he said, "and I found a nicer place in Madison Square, where the bums were more refined." The dominant trade papers of the day were the *New York Dramatic Mirror,* which mainly covered the legitimate stage, and the *New York Clipper,* a tabloid-sized summary of the week in vaudeville, burlesque, and sports. As voracious as the appetite for entertainment was, there was also a vast supply of seasoned performers looking for work. The back pages of the *Clipper* were crammed with ads—acts of all stripes announced their availability, and producers seeking musicians, specialties, burlesque girls, and minstrels invited applicants to quote their lowest rates.

Fields began receiving mail at the Twenty-eighth Street offices of the *Clipper*, conveniently wedged between music publishers on Tin Pan Alley, but for an eighteen-year-old whose few performances had been confined to dance halls and auditoriums in the quaint townships and districts of Philadelphia, New York was a sobering blast of cold water. Gamely, he donned his new clothes and made the rounds, but the process of getting work came down to notices, references, experience—none of which he had. It is not known precisely how long he remained in New York, working at odd jobs and depleting his precious funds, or if, once he returned to Philadelphia, he held true to his promise not to see his mother again until he had "made good," but he did come back a sophisticate with a fresh contempt for the city of his youth. Nothing in Philadelphia, which was essentially a conglomeration of villages, could have prepared him for the color and sheer vastness of New York. He disparaged the City of Friends for its dull conservatism—what Henry James referred to as its "Quaker drab"—and for its rigid adherence to the Sunday Concert or "blue" laws that were largely ignored in Manhattan. Saloons in Philadelphia were required to close at midnight on Saturday nights and not to reopen again until one minute past twelve on the following night. Baseball was not permitted on Sundays, and all forms of entertainment, apart from songs and recitations and the bands that played in Fairmont Park, were banned. No longer would becoming a performer merely allow him to sleep "knee deep into the day." It would also be his one-way ticket out of the greatest cemetery in the world, a place he would come to regard as "the jerk city of the east."

Bill Dailey had fled the city himself in the wake of the Batley Hall debacle, but managed to land a booking for his client near Lansdale, where he was spending time with his family. Amusement parks, such as Willow Grove and Washington Park on the Delaware, opened each year at the end of May, just as the uncooled theaters were shutting their doors. Most offered band concerts, picnic grounds, firework displays, scenic waterways, and performances in the gaily painted casinos that doubled as dance halls. The parks were in cahoots with the traction companies, which often sponsored variety bills to boost their off-hours ridership. Chestnut Hill Park, at the terminus of the Germantown line, advertised "the longest 5¢ trolley ride in the world."

One of the smallest such properties, some eighteen miles northwest of town on the Roxborough, Chestnut Hill, and Norristown Railway, was a glorified picnic spot in the Schuylkill Valley known as Plymouth Park. Its weekly casino bills were assembled with vaudeville and burlesque performers at liberty for the summer. ("You either had to go to Europe during the summer, or lay off, or play the parks," said Fields.) Dailey managed to convince impresario

Tony Baker, who booked the Plymouth casino, that W. C. Fields, currently working in New York, would be an outstanding addition to the show. Baker offered the renowned tramp juggler $5 a week "and found" (meaning whatever food he could filch from the park's concessionaires). Fields eagerly accepted the engagement, thereby beginning his professional career.

The first performance took place on August 1, 1898, a hot and humid Monday, at 8:15 in the evening. "I was nervous," Fields later admitted to a friend. "I wasn't sure Norristown was ready for me." The show began with a noisy exchange between Dutch character comics Harry Price and "Sliding" Billy Watson, whose nickname derived from his habit of sliding across the stage as he made an entrance. Price and Watson were followed by Flora Parker, who at fifteen was billed as "America's Youngest and Most Charming Soubrette." Fields took the stage at approximately 8:40, performing, in the words of the *Plymouth Park Gazette,* "original, intricate, and difficult feats." An intense young man onstage, he lacked the casual air of Jim Harrigan's lazy tramp. And, being sensitive about his stuttering, he didn't speak a word. The centerpiece of his act was a cigar box routine, stolen outright from Harrigan and varied only to the extent of dispensing with the kerosene lamps. Sweat pouring down his face, Fields was on and off in eight minutes and was received, as he later remembered it, with "small approval."

His week's stand at Plymouth Park was hardly remunerative. Dailey took 20 percent off the top as a commission, leaving Fields with just $4 to cover his trolley fare from Philadelphia and back. When he calculated that his week's efforts would net him exactly $1, he took to sleeping in the men's dressing room to save money. After two nights, the management threw him out, and he slept in a barn at the edge of town for the remainder of the engagement. Despite the thin reception he received at Norristown, Fields managed to ingratiate himself with Sliding Billy, who billed himself as "America's Favorite Hebrew Impersonator." Watson was a classic—baggy pants and coat, beard, tie askew, a cigar burning, ashes falling everywhere. When he and his partner Price moved on to Atlantic City, Fields tendered the address of the wheelwright's shop over which he slept and asked if Watson could keep an eye out for a job. To his amazement, a collect telegram arrived just a few days later.

The wire was either from Billy Watson, as Fields always maintained, or Fields' juggling chum H. M. Lorette, who told his own version of the story in 1957: "I was booked at the Fortescue Pavilion in Atlantic City. I recommended Fields to the manager, and he gave him two weeks following me. Fields wrote me asking where he could board. I told him to come to the Biscayne Hotel on Arkansas Avenue, near the beach.* Performers got a rate of $7 per week for a

---

*Actually, the Biscayne was on Kentucky Avenue.

nice room and three swell meals." Atlantic City, sixty miles east of town on the New Jersey coast, drew the bulk of its visitors from Philadelphia, where one could board a ferry at the Vine Street wharf, catch the Atlantic Express in Camden, and be checking into the Garden, the Brighton, or the Hotel Rudolf in less than two hours. Since the engagement at Fortescue paid "ten and cakes" (meaning $10 and ordering privileges), Fields would net a healthy $3 a week— a considerable improvement on his Norristown gig. He dug an old trunk out of a nearby junkyard, packed his clothes and equipment, and reluctantly borrowed the train fare from his pals. "It broke my heart to pay a dollar for a train ride and sit in a stuffy coach," he said. "Trains were free. I'd have hopped a freight, but I had to have a ticket on account of my trunk. Later on, when some actor was going to the same next town I was, I'd get him to check my trunk on his ticket and take a freight, but this time there was no way out. I was disgusted at having everything legitimate."

He arrived in Atlantic City convinced somebody was out to steal his battered trunk and its contents. "It never occurred to me that the trunk and the stuff in it were absolutely useless to everybody in the world except me." He made his way to the Biscayne and met up with his friend Lorette. "I was finishing my two weeks when he came in on Sunday," Lorette recounted, "and we sat on the porch and talked things over. He was a little nervous, which wasn't characteristic for him because he had plenty of guts. I stayed over Monday since he wanted me to start applause for certain moves and give him my opinion on the whole arrangement. He did fairly well and I left."

Fortescue's was an open pavilion on two levels that extended out over the sand on wooden pilings with a railed staircase running down to the beach. Established in 1878 by Mrs. Jane Fortescue, it survived the gradual expansion of the Boardwalk and was one of the few businesses permitted to operate on the ocean side. Forty feet of Georgia pine separated the pavilion from a panorama of competing attractions—shell bazaars, merry-go-rounds, toboggan rides, saloons, bathhouses, palm readers, swimming pools, shooting galleries, a haunted forest, bric-a-brac stores, mineral water fountains, an opera house, phonograph parlors, and eateries of every imaginable kind. There were also two massive piers jutting out over the water that carried their own bills of amusement. Couples were pushed along the six-mile Boardwalk in rolling chairs of wicker and steel. Bands, Ferris wheels, minstrel companies, and specialty acts from vaudeville and burlesque vied for the attention of strollers in boater hats and white flannel trousers, ladies in long skirts of organdy and silk.

The pavilion sold sandwiches and beer and had continuous performances to attract the customers. (Frank Tinney, later a famous blackface comedian, played cornet in the pavilion's four-piece band.) "You could get a big glass of beer for a

*Fortescue Pavilion, Atlantic City*

nickel," Fields remembered, "and sit and watch the show while you quaffed your beer." When business was good, Fields performed his juggling act as many as twenty times a day. When business was slack, he donned a two-piece bathing suit, waded out into the water, and pretended to get caught in the undertow.

> I would swim out in the ocean, and when I got out some distance, I'd holler "Help," go under, come up after a moment, spitting a lot of water. Then two or three men, all plants, waiting on the shore, would swim out to me, battle around me while everyone would run up to see what the excitement was. "Someone's drowning!" they'd all begin shouting, and start a ballyhoo. Then, when the crowd was big enough, the men would drag me in. I'd be spitting water here and there, and sometimes one of the bystanders would get a face full. Three or four fellows would carry me then right into the pavilion with the crowd following after us to see what was going to happen. Next, they'd throw me across a table and begin working on me. But, by this time, the band would be playing and the funny Irishman would walk out on stage. So they'd all begin to look at him and forget about me. Finally, I'd get up weakly and slouch away.

Minutes later he would be up onstage, wearing his tramp getup to conceal his identity. Staff at the pavilion were drowned as well. "If it was a woman we rescued, the crowd was particularly large." He found the ploy "a great racket" and, after a few drownings, went to the manager for an advance on his second week's salary. "What the hell?" came the response. "If I had a dollar, I'd have two of you guys swimmin' out there!" As Fields slunk away, the man added for emphasis, "You must think I'm made of money!" The comedy team of Bryant and Richmond was on the bill at the pavilion, and Fields became friendly with William T. Bryant, who was about to split with his partner to go with a New York burlesque company called *The Monte Carlo Girls.* "When he got there," said Fields, "he commended me to the manager. So I came on too."

Burlesque—even the bare-bones "turkey" variety—was a fertile breeding ground for the future stars of vaudeville. Al Jolson, Will Rogers, Leon Errol, Mack Sennett, Charlotte Greenwood, Fannie Brice, Sophie Tucker, and George Sidney all got their starts in touring shows with names like *The Night Owls, The Knickerbockers,* and *The Merry Maidens.* "Burlesque was at one time the swellest entertainment you could find," declared comedian Joe Cook. "It was a mixture, at a lower price, of most of the good qualities of musical comedy, plus the good qualities of vaudeville." Getting into burlesque was a break for Fields; he was offered $25 a week and was eventually onstage for the burletta as well as the olio. "I juggled, played a dozen bits, and got a chance to develop a line of humor." *The Monte Carlo Girls* was no turkey show, but a respectable pageant of plump beauties in silk tights, supported by an assortment of bargain-basement variety acts. It cleaved to the classical structure of burlesque—two pieces and an olio. Specialty turns were performed before the first scenic drop—the "olio drop"—while stagehands struck the set for the first piece and set the stage for the second. Professor T. A. Metz, who wrote the popular tune "There'll Be a Hot Time in the Old Town Tonight," was the musical director, and the proprietor was a man named Jim Fulton, who performed a knockabout comedy act with his brother Jack. Fulton was married to the show's lead singer and nominal star, the buxom Eva Swinburne.

"*The Monte Carlo Girls* will open their season on September 19 and prospects point to a successful tour," announced an item in the *Clipper.* "Manager James C. Fulton has engaged W. T. Bryant (late of Bryant and Richmond), who will be assisted by Ida Barrows, presenting his latest comedy effort, 'The Saving Woman.' Among the others who will appear in the olio are The Orion Trio, Eva Swinburne, Marie Rogers, the Fulton Brothers, and Harry S. Marion. The burlesque 'Thirty Minutes at Monte Carlo' promises to be a happy surprise, being replete with new ideas."

Fulton, like most burlesque managers, was perpetually hard up and financed his tours through the common and widely accepted practice of "leg pulling." Rolling into a town, a few of the girls would latch onto a likely sucker at a local saloon and charm him into "investing" in the show. "Sometimes a manager would pass on his girl to some fellow in the town who had three hundred dollars or enough money to take us to the next town," said Fields. "All that bothered Jim was that every time he interested an angel in the show to pay the bills, the angel got stuck on his wife. He said it seemed odd to him that with 20 other girls in the show, every backer that came along couldn't find anybody else but Mrs. Fulton to be smitten with."

The tour got underway with a three-day engagement at the Star Theatre in Troy, New York, then the show jumped to Albany for another three at the Gaiety. Business was reported as "fair," but gradually improved as the company moved on to Lawrence, Holyoke, and then an entire week's stand in Brooklyn. The original opener, "Thirty Minutes in Monte Carlo," was jettisoned in favor of an armistice-themed celebration called "On the Picnic Grounds at Camp Wikoff." The Monte Carlo Girls, appearing as "military maids," sang and cavorted with naval cadets while the band held forth with a selection of rousing marches. The olio was next with Fields in the No. 2 position (the "deuce" spot) followed by Eva Swinburne, who sang "coon" songs, Bill Bryant, aerialist Rose Lewis, Harry S. Marion, whose songs were illustrated with stereopticon effects, and a pair of European contortion artists called Kluteldi and Lareni. The finale was the burlesque "Ki-Ki," written by Bryant and "enlisting the services of a score of handsome women in the sensational Ki-Ki dance."

When he wasn't onstage, Fields shifted scenery and did other menial jobs. He described his act, largely pinched from Harrigan, as a "rough affair," lacking in style and consistency. "I had no routine except as to the tricks. My comedy business was all dragged in as it occurred to me. I did whatever I thought would appear funny. If I remembered what had gone well at the last performance, I worked it in, but generally I didn't remember." After the Brooklyn date, the tour reverted to split weeks in Easton, Scranton, and Altoona, then disintegrated into a grueling string of one-nighters. The calls were early, the theaters cold, and it was practically impossible to get a square meal or a good night's sleep. "Getting your laundry back on a one-night stand is quite a proposition," Fields once observed. "You can't carry enough in your handbag to last you more than a week, and a change of suits is almost impossible. So, once about every week, the advance agent would make some arrangements in the town whereby the laundry was gathered up and our dirty linen was rushed off to the laundry on our arrival so that it would get back to the theatre before the matinee had finished. On these occasions, our trunks were sent to the basement of the theatre, where we could go down and rummage through them, and take out and put back whatever we saw fit."

There was barely enough money to pay for anything. Jim Fulton was always in arrears on salaries and doled out spending money as if proffering a child's allowance. Fields said,

The first week we didn't get any money, nor the second or the third. In fact, the whole time I was with this show we didn't get any salaries. But we were on the lookout for the money just the same. We used to stand watch in the hotel all night long in front of the manager's door to find out if he was going to duck. We had heard a rumor—there were always such rumors—that he was going to skip with the twenty-five dollars, or whatever it was, and go to New York and leave us flat. I can remember one night, it was my turn to stand guard. Being a kid, I was so sleepy that I thought if I could get one hour's sleep, I wouldn't care if the whole world came to an end. For hours, I sat in the dark narrow corridor of that old hotel staring at the manager's door, under the faint little gas jet, and trying to keep awake.

Fulton didn't skip on Fields' watch, but skip he did. It was in Kent, Ohio, after a Friday-night performance at the local Opera House. He and Swinburne ran out, salaries unpaid, leaving no money for hotel bills, eats, or train fare back to New York. One of the young bloods in town offered to pay $4 for Fields' overcoat on the condition that he arrange an introduction to a particular girl in the chorus. Fields timidly approached the woman, who readily consented to help a pal. "It is strange but true," he later said, "that the people of small towns are sometimes rather cruel to us stage folks; at least to members of cheap companies like that one. This young fellow, for instance, was so obnoxious that I punched his face—and kept my overcoat." Fields managed to sell the coat to another customer for $2—no conditions attached—but was still $6 short on an $18 fare. He strapped his trunk, containing his precious props and wardrobe, to a hand sled and dragged it down a steep hill, sprinting most of the way to keep from being run over by it. At the station, he morosely laid his money before a ticket agent for the B&O Railroad, who told him he had witnessed his performance, spoke glowingly of his skills, and then slammed the window in his face.

Fields parked himself on a bench in the waiting area and settled in for a spell. A few minutes later, the agent reappeared and sheepishly approached him. "I'm going to give you a chance to do some juggling," he said, telling the astonished boy that he was covering the $6 for the ticket and loaning him an additional two for incidentals. "He put two silver dollars in my hand," said Fields, "and laid the ticket across my arm." Fields was back in New York the next day—dejectedly shoveling snow off the Manhattan sidewalks. He thought seriously of returning to Philadelphia, his tail between his legs. "It didn't seem then as though I was ever going to get back in the theatrical business again," he said.

# Three

# A Noble and Superb Girl

Harriet Veronica Hughes was born into a theatrical family and encouraged to embrace show business just as vigorously as it was discouraged for Claude Dukenfield. Hattie's mother, Elizabeth Hughes, was bright and pretty and a good singer, too. She toured vaudeville in the 1880s and appeared with Lillian Russell in *Pepita* when Hattie was just seven. All five of Lizzie's children were performers: Mary, her eldest daughter, was an actress, and her sons, Johnnie and James, both enjoyed respectable careers on the stage. Hattie and her sister Kitty were drilled in song, recitation, and dance, and did a sister act in high school. On her own, Kitty Hughes played Little Eva in *Uncle Tom's Cabin* and appeared onstage with the great Sarah Bernhardt. Hattie lacked her sister's ambition, but was no less theatrical. A strict Catholic, she confined her work to "clubs and church entertainments and schools."

Hattie's father, John Hughes, was an Irish immigrant who taught school in Dublin and worked as a coffee merchant in New York City. Hattie attended Normal College (now Hunter) with the intention of becoming a teacher, but when her father died of a heart attack in July 1897, she quit school and, at the age of nineteen, went to work at the only livelihood she knew—singing and dancing. She must have been looking for a job when an ad appeared in the *Clipper* on September 3, 1898:

BIG BURLESQUE BOOM
25 PRETTY PARISIAN PETS
NATIONS'S NEWEST NOVELTIES
SEASON'S SUREST SUCCESS

*The Monte Carlo Girls*
WANTED: A few more chorus girls, a first-class Sister Act,
A-1 Leader that arranges, and strong German team.

Special and Attractive Printing by
Russell Morgan Litho. Co., Cincinnati, O.
Magnificent Costumes by Mme. Sylvia-Reaves.
Beautiful scenery by Physis Studio, Broadway, N.Y.

ENTIRE NEW BURLESQUE
A strong reputable company of recognized
high-class Vaudeville and Burlesque performers.
I HAVE A FEW WEEKS OPEN.

Address JAMES C. FULTON, 1280 Third Ave., N.Y. City.

Fulton received more than two hundred replies to his ad and was able to assemble a company of forty. Hattie was at a party in Brooklyn when she was introduced to the new juggler, a thin, clean-shaven boy known as "Bill." Five feet eight, with pale blue eyes and a shy, almost diffident manner, he spoke slowly, respectfully, carefully measuring his words. He seemed as if he didn't know quite what to do in a woman's presence, other than to stand bolt upright whenever one entered the room. "He was young and green and so was I," she said.

Small and unfashionably thin for a burlesque girl, Hattie Hughes had thick brown hair and flawless white skin, stark against her long black dress. "I was in crape mourning for my father," she explained. "My mother had the clothes and we continued wearing them." Wary of the stigma of having been in burlesque, Hattie never used the word and was always defensive when asked about it. "It was like a little musical comedy," she said of the final piece, "Ki-Ki," in which she appeared as "Miss Holdout." She employed a stage name—"Flossie"—and kept to herself as much as she could.

There were stern rules of personal conduct in burlesque, and the girls didn't show as much as a bare arm onstage. The practice of doubling up among the men and women of the company, known as "sketching," was prohibited. "Yet," said Fields, "the show wouldn't be running two weeks before girls and boys would be paired off according to their liking, though sometimes ill assorted—a stage hand with a prima donna, and the veteran comic with the youngest chorus girl." Fields soon fell passionately in love with Hattie, and was no doubt impressed with her reciprocal interest in him. One of the best-looking girls in the chorus, she was two years his senior and infinitely better educated. She may well have been his first serious girlfriend.* When the show folded in

*Fields never mentioned an earlier infatuation, but displayed an intimate knowledge of the so-called "notch" joints along Middle Alley, Philadelphia's "low-ceiling price bazaar of sexual relief," where the top price, as he remembered it, was twenty-five cents. "A fellow

Kent, they went their separate ways, but not for long. Over the holidays, he brought her to Philadelphia to meet his family, and soon Hattie was corresponding with Fields' twelve-year-old sister, Elsie May. "Elsie received a letter from Hattie," Kate advised her son, "and I didn't know whether she should answer or not. If you say so, Elsie will be pleased to do so. She said she never met anybody she liked so much with such little acquaintance."

At the time, Fields was rooming in New York with a diminutive young actor ("we all called ourselves actors") and was desperate for work. Having sold his overcoat, he had only a blue serge suit to ward off the cold. The roommate, considerably more affluent, owned a raincoat as well as an overcoat, and he offered the former to his friend Bill, who, being a considerably larger man, could use it only as a prop. "I used to go around in my thin serge suit, with the raincoat hanging jauntily over my arm, hoping to be considered merely eccentric instead of dead broke. Under the circumstances, I had to take the only job I could get."

He began working the twenty-four-hour dime museums—the Globe in the Bowery and Huber's on Fourteenth Street—where the tiny stages were hospitable only to jugglers, magicians, crayon sketch artists, and the like. "It seemed that I did my act every five minutes, all through the day and half the night. But at least I was paid, even though it was only a few dollars a week. I was gaining plenty of practice, too. And there was an advantage in performing twenty times a day, for that gave me twenty different audiences." Free time was spent with Hattie, taking long walks in the park and going to plays, and performing at private functions. "He was playing clubs and entertainments and little smokers," she remembered. He even went to church with her, an experience he regarded more with curiosity than reverence. "It was something new to him. He would make little comments when the priest would speak at High Mass, with his hands up to his mouth." Due to his antipathy for the Catholic faith— he was an avowed atheist and regarded all religions with the suspicion of a seasoned con man—she couldn't take him seriously as a suitor and refused to introduce him to her mother.

It was in New York that Fields met up again with Jim Fulton and was asked to rejoin the show. Fulton was profoundly apologetic over the hasty exit he and his wife had made in Ohio and, as usual, was full of big plans. On January 23, 1899, a newly reconstituted *Monte Carlo Girls* opened a week's stand at Miner's Bowery Theatre. Fred Stone, who was doing a blackface act at the time, remembered Miner's as a smoky beer hall, mostly stag, an institution later renowned for its use of a hook to remove amateur acts from its stage. "Boys

---

was afraid to whistle for his dog after nine o'clock," he said, "for fear of being hit on the sconce with a heavy door key."

went around hawking popcorn, peanuts, cigars, chewing gum, and the latest song hits, while in the top gallery there was always a mob of kids, whistling, yelling to one another, raising a terrific uproar. Just as the curtain was about to go up, a man hit the edge of the gallery railing twice with a big cane, and after that you could have heard a pin drop."

The cast of *The Monte Carlo Girls* was essentially the same as before, with Ramza and Arno, horizontal-bar performers, replacing the original set of contortionists. Fields drew an expanded role in the show, appearing as "Si Flappum, a regular playactor" in the "Picnic Grounds" burlesque. "William C. Fields proved a fairly pleasing tramp juggler," a reviewer for the *New York Dramatic Mirror* affirmed, although the show itself discouraged praise: "The brace of burlesques were of indifferent merit, being hardly up to the standard set by other companies." Fields tried masking his silence with the headline "First Time in America" and celebrated his nineteenth birthday en route with the company to Troy. *The Monte Carlo Girls* played full weeks in Boston, Albany, Newark, and split weeks in Lowell, Massachusetts, and Portland, Maine. "We are all well, and our business has been phenomenal," the company's advance man, R. D. Jenkins, advised the editors of the *Clipper* in February. "We are booked solid until June 10, playing week stands only, and our business manager, Mr. Phillips, is booking the show for next season. It is Mr. Fulton's intention next season to introduce a new burlesque, and he will carry all special scenery and electrical effects, new costumes, and fifty people for producing same."

Jenkins' dispatch was an empty boast, though, for Fulton again deserted the troupe—and his wife this time as well—in Reading, Pennsylvania. The cast elected to continue, with proprietorship conferred upon singer Byron G. Harlan and his assistant, Tom Garrick. A new manager, James F. Woods, signed on in Portland, where *The Monte Carlo Girls* broke all records for a three-night stand and played to five capacity houses. Emboldened, they trumpeted their success in an ad for the *Clipper* under the headline "Turned Them Away," but when the company moved on to Albany, the reception was decidedly less cordial, and Woods disappeared. They picked up an investor—a man named La Forte—and, with a brief interlude of funding, induced Charles E. Taylor, the former business manager of Fred Irwin's *Majestic Burlesquers,* to come and revitalize the show. Taylor added new acts to the olio and announced that he had written a new burlesque for the troupe, but within a fortnight he, too, was gone.

Fulton made an unwelcome reappearance in Philadelphia, where *The Monte Carlo Girls* had a late booking at the Trocadero. A beaming Kate Dukenfield and her family were out front for the first performance on May 22, 1899, and the *Inquirer* may have been influenced by the noisy Dukenfield claque when it reported the next day that Fields had "made a great big hit in his hobo juggling act." Good business inspired Fulton, who still owned the show, to renege on a profit-sharing agreement he had earlier made to keep the company together. Incensed, twelve members of the troupe obtained an attachment on the week's receipts. *The Monte Carlo Girls* came to an abrupt end on May 29 when the company failed to appear for a week's stand at Kernan's Lyceum in the District of Columbia. Hattie returned to New York, but Fields remained in Philadelphia, where he was able to land another week at Plymouth Park. There, in the tiny casino, he shared the bill with the Spencer Brothers, Alva Lenoria, and Dick Leggett, a grotesque character comedian who appeared to grow as he danced a wooden shoe routine. The following week, Fields removed himself to Atlantic City—and the Biscayne—for the balance of the summer.

At the new Steel Pier, Fields found work with *Murphy and Gibson's American Minstrels,* playing bones, telling jokes, dancing, and performing his juggling act. He was engaged for twelve weeks, beginning June 26, but disliked working in blackface and had little aptitude for the musical aspects of the show. Hattie came to Atlantic City, teaming with another girl, Lillian Hern-

*With Harriet Hughes on the Atlantic City Boardwalk, 1899*

don, to play the Boardwalk. Fields stuck with the Murphy and Gibson troupe for a month, finally working out a deal to join *Irwin's Burlesquers* in early August. Hattie and Lillian went with *Miaco's City Club,* a true turkey burlesque show, but not before Fields had written to her mother, Elizabeth Hughes, asking the hand of her daughter in marriage.

Fields always referred to Fred Irwin as the "Ziegfeld of burlesque," and, considering his rocky times with Jim Fulton, the analogy was apt. Fulton had a sizable company, but his material was third-rate and his management inept. Irwin, by contrast, was a man of impeccable taste and showmanship. His companies were clean, tight, and profitable. He treated his people well, and managed several shows from a tidy office on Thirty-third Street. *Irwin's Majestic Burlesquers* had been touring for several seasons when he assembled *Irwin's Burlesquers* to follow the first company in two-week blocks. The economies of touring multiple companies in rotation was, in part, the impetus for the famed "wheel" of the Columbia Amusement Company, a circuit of logical jumps between theaters that brought order to the world of burlesque and diminished the frantic pace of travel. Fred Irwin became one of the founders of the Columbia Wheel in 1900.

A former circus manager, Irwin was originally the star of the *Irwin Bros. Comedy and Vaudeville Company,* which, coincidentally, also featured "A Good Bum Juggler—Harrigan." Irwin liked circus acts—jugglers and acrobats—and packed his olios with crowd-pleasing action. Having caught Fields' act in Atlantic City, where a lot of producers and agents went scouting, Irwin offered him a salary of $25 a week. By this point, Fields was leery of all burlesque people and, figuring he'd never collect it anyway, held out for $35. "Irwin was so amazed at my nerve that he almost had apoplexy. I knew I wouldn't get thirty-five. It would only be the name of my salary. But it would sound well, at any rate, so I held out for it, and he finally agreed."

Irwin told Fields he wanted him to open the show. Being the first on the bill was the worst possible spot—half the audience would still be seating itself and no one would get a clear view of the stage. "To make me open the show was Irwin's way of punishing me," Fields said. "I kicked for a good spot on the bill, claiming I wanted the chance to earn the money." The *Burlesquers* opened their season on August 12, 1899, at the People's Theatre in Cincinnati. Despite a record heat wave, every seat in the house was filled and the crowd was a turnaway. "The newspaper critics must have had a good but early meal, for they were there when the curtain went up and they evidently were feeling fine and friendly." The notices were uniformly good, and the critic for the *Post* actually invoked the word "great" in describing Fields' act. It was an adjective never before applied to him, and he regarded it pragmatically: "I took his notice and called on Irwin for more money. He increased me to fifty dollars a week." Later, Fields learned the critic had never even seen the show.

In Milwaukee, *Irwin's Burlesquers* opened the new 1,200-seat Star Theatre, an ornate shrine to jiggling thighs that was decorated in fashionable shades of gold and olive green. The troupe moved on to Chicago, then stopped in Cleveland, some twenty-five miles from Kent, where Fields, by his later account, looked up the ticket agent who had once staked him to a loan. "His pride in my success could have been no greater had I been his son. Different members of the troupe entertained him, and made him feel glad that he had once been kind to a member of this wandering fraternity." Though he could ill afford it, Fields also gave the man $100.*

When the *Burlesquers* played Miner's Eighth Avenue Theatre in New York, even standing room was sold out. Fields remained at the head of the bill, followed by Bailey and Madison, "acrobatic grotesques," the Baroness Viola von Waldenburg, the musical team of Sliver and Sparks, and Mlle. Marie, who, clad in a one-piece union suit, struck poses for the crowd. The closing burletta, "A Hot Wave," was described by the *Clipper* as "one of the best skits seen here in some time. The costumes and scenery were handsome and highly appropriate to the piece."

Fields diligently rehearsed every day and, according to H. M. Lorette, "improved his act wonderfully." But as he grew more successful by constantly raising the stakes, he grew more anxious as well. "Juggling is difficult," he said,

> and the first five, six, or seven years, you don't know your tricks well enough to do them with your eyes shut. . . . Occasionally, in those days, I'd miss a trick, and so I began to worry. Supposing I go out tonight and do twenty tricks of juggling and miss most of them? Suppose I miss every trick? It was just torture. One day I met an old legit showman named Fletcher. He began talking to me about Shakespeare. I did not know anything about Shakespeare then. Who the hell was he? I guess I was doing some terrible things to get laughs in the first part, because the showman told me once, "Shakespeare said play to the

---

*Fields told this part of the story to Jim Tully in 1933 on the condition he not repeat it. Tully, the bestselling author of *Beggars of Life,* not only wrote it, but spun the material Fields gave him into at least four articles. Fields' irritation with Tully was evident in a 1934 interview with John Moffitt of the *Kansas City Star:* "This incident [meaning the business with the ticket agent] has been used by my neighbor Jim Tully for so many of those articles of his that it is now much more of a Tully possession than it is mine. . . . If there is a light burning [in his window], you may be sure that Mr. Tully is up writing another version of my life, which subsequently will appear in the fan magazines."

select few, then you please yourself" or something like that. That gave me an idea, helped me. I said, Gee whiz, that's good. I must have believed him, young though I was. A real artist pleases himself first, and then hopes he will please the audience.

Fields learned to cover the tricks he missed by purposely fumbling others, thereby getting the audience to pull for him. Wordlessly, he developed a distinct personality for his tramp. "To conceal my youth, I added whiskers to my makeup and, to keep my nerves steady and my eye alert, I refrained from late hours and dissipation." He tried saving at least half his salary, sending as much as $10 a week to his adoring mother. "I hope you will continue to be a good boy to me," she responded in one letter, "as I feel your goodness very much and it goes to my very heart."

After an extended run in New York—which included successful weeks at Miner's Bowery and both the Star and the Empire in Brooklyn—Fields threatened to walk if Irwin didn't bump his salary to $75 a week. "We had no contract," he reasoned. "If I had been a failure, I would have been fired without a moment's hesitation. I wasn't a failure, but the outstanding success of the show. And, as it is a poor rule that doesn't work both ways, I had a right to the increased pay." Irwin upped his pay but made him continue to open the show, and Fields concluded there was nothing he could do to change the man's mind.*

The *Burlesquers* continued with split weeks in Albany and Troy, and full weeks in Cincinnati, Marion, Louisville, and Indianapolis. Fields' introduction to St. Louis, their next stop, was a $5 room at the Rillings Hotel and a Sunday matinee at the Standard Theatre, reputed to be the toughest stop on the Empire Circuit. The hard-boiled audiences at the Standard were legendary, and Frank James, brother of the late outlaw Jesse James, was the gallery doorkeeper. James impressed Fields as "a slight, quiet sort of man who looked as though he had just recently come in from the country, and whose drooping moustache suggested the small-town sheriff of the period. Nothing big, nothing boisterous about him." Fields even thought him kindly, though the "cold, steely glitter" in his gray eyes kept him at a distance. "I didn't try to fool with Frank James," he said.

Fields remained with *Irwin's Burlesquers* until impresario Martin Beck caught his act in Chicago and offered him time on the coveted Orpheum circuit. Figuring he was worth more in vaudeville than he could get in burlesque, Fields surveyed some of the other performers he knew before naming a price. "The artists I approached told me it was like my hide to ask what salary they

---

*It was traditional to open a show with a "dumb" act (i.e., one that did not speak) so that a singer or monologist wouldn't be drowned out by the commotion of people taking their seats.

got, but when I explained that I thought I was worth about a third of their salary, they told me they had been getting $250 a week. They were wonderful liars. I reckoned I was $50 a week better than they, and went back to the agent and told him I would tour the Orpheum for $300 a week. He threw several kinds of fits and finally signed me up for $125 a week." Fields gave Irwin a month's notice and left the show in Buffalo on March 12, 1900. Lizzie Hughes, who had replied to his courtly note of proposal by assuring him that her daughter Hattie was "a noble and superb girl, well worthy to be a wife, qualified with every amiable trait of character," staked him to the train fare to San Francisco, where he would open at the Orpheum on March 18. If successful, he told Hattie, he would send for her and they would be married.

The trip west took three days, the overland pulling into Oakland in the early evening. The tradition for most acts was to visit the Orpheum the next morning and touch the box office, but Fields resisted taking an advance on his salary because he had been robbed while on tour with the *Burlesquers* and was fearful of carrying too much. The theater itself was a rattletrap barn, an old beer hall sadly in need of repair, but it was much too popular to be closed for even a brief period of time. (Many of the better seats, at a top price of fifty cents, were held on a subscription basis.) The city was full of attractions for a visiting easterner—the famous Cliff House, the adjacent Sutro Baths (the largest natatorium in the country), the city's legendary Chinatown—and there was an inexhaustible supply of good restaurants. Epes Sargent, who covered the circuits for forty years, said, "It was possible to play four weeks at the house, never repeat an eating place, and never get a poorly cooked meal, either." The city even boasted what was reputed to be the dirtiest burlesque show in America, but not even the toughest houses permitted bare legs. Fields shared the bill at the Orpheum with Howard Thurston, the great magician, and Mr. and Mrs. Sidney Drew, who performed the domestic comedy sketches they would eventually adapt to film. The theater was "packed to the doors" for the first show of the week, and the *Chronicle* assured its readers that Fields' act was "far above the average." Instantly, he wired Hattie to come join him.

"My, how I clung to that money," he said of his first $125 payday. "I felt sure there must be sharks wanting to steal it from me. So, before I drew it, I arranged with a jeweler to come to the theatre with a $100 ring. I drew my salary, gave him the hundred, and put the ring on my finger. But that ring kept me awake nights for fear it would be stolen or lost. Finally, I sewed it in the pocket of my pajamas. Next week, I sunk my salary into a stock of photographs. I invested every dollar of it every week until I got used to the idea of holding real money—in gold, too, for it was Frisco—of my own."

He spent three weeks at the Orpheum, gradually working his way down the bill as new acts were brought in. Hattie arrived in time for his closing performance on Saturday, April 7, 1900, and the same day, they went to the county clerk's office for a license. Under California law, the twenty-year-old Fields was still a minor and could not be married without parental consent. Hattie, on the other hand, was about to turn twenty-two and was nearly four years past the age of majority for a female. Both fudged their birthdates accordingly. Hattie shaved a year off her age, declaring she had been born on June 7, 1879, a falsehood she maintained for the rest of her life. Fields gently nudged his birthday back to April 9, 1879—the absolute minimum necessary under the law—and publicly held to that date for a number of years.

He reserved a room for Hattie in a fine home "in case things didn't work out" but was unfailingly attentive and never even went back to reclaim the deposit. The next morning, Palm Sunday, William C. Dukenfield and Hattie V. Hughes were married by the Rev. Dr. John A. B. Wilson at the Methodist church on Howard Street.


There was little in Los Angeles at the turn of the century to match the excitement of San Francisco. One could put up at the Van Nuys, the city's only modern hotel, and dine on squab (known locally as dove) after the show, but a week was about all most acts could sustain at the downtown Orpheum. A deal to play the West Coast generally meant three weeks in San Francisco—to compensate the act for losing two weeks in "jumps"—followed by single weeks in L.A., Denver, Kansas City, and Omaha. The eight acts on the bill in Los Angeles included Keno, Welch & Melrose, an acrobatic trio, the singing Neilson Sisters, and a twenty-eight-inch tall impressionist known as Major Mite. The headliner, Charles Sweet, billed himself as a "tramp pianist." Unlike Fields, who worked "in one" (meaning against a drop or curtain at the first entrance to the stage), Sweet traveled with a full set that resembled the living room of an elegant home. Entering through a window, lantern aloft, he'd explain he was examining the property at night because his day job was so demanding. Surveying the valuables, he'd notice a piano, seat himself, and play a series of clever song parodies.

Tramp acts had become so commonplace in vaudeville it wasn't unusual to find more than one on a single bill. To fend off imitators, Jim Harrigan copyrighted his own act and started billing himself as "the *original* tramp juggler." There was Paul Barnes (whose act was similar to Sweet's); William Ritchie, "the original tramp cyclist"; O. K. Sato, another juggler; Nat Wills, "the happy tramp"; Herbert Lloyd; Harry La Toy; the philosophical Lew Bloom; Dave Wellington; and, of course, H. M. Lorette.

Faced with such a pestilence of competing acts, Fields dropped the word "tramp" from his own billing and, abandoning the full beard he wore in burlesque, began calling himself an "eccentric juggler." Incorporating a silk bald cap and an unruly mane of crepe hair that tapered to stubble as it approached the chin, his costume had the exaggerated quality of a Dutch character comedian and suggested not so much a tramp as a maniacal bookkeeper. Indeed, the reviewer for the *Los Angeles Times* described his new look as "Hebraic" and praised his "pawnbroker attitudes." But Fields didn't want to be known as an ethnic comic any more than he wanted to be known as a tramp, and he continued to refine his makeup and mannerisms in search of a proper identity.

Both Hattie and Fields loved the arid climate of southern California, where the daytime temperature hovered in the low seventies while Denver— their next stop on the Orpheum tour—was still buried in snow. They hired a buggy and took a leisurely ride out to Pasadena, ten miles northeast of Los Angeles, to see the elaborate mansions along Orange Grove Avenue (which had become known in the 1890s as "Millionaires' Row"). Dreading the trip east and a return to cold weather, Fields told his wife he was weary of show business and would like to give up juggling altogether and live in Pasadena, where he could manage a theater or go into the grocery business. "From then on," said Hattie, "we had it in mind to settle down there."

When they got back to town, Fields went to First National Bank of Los Angeles and opened an account, the first of dozens he would establish in major cities along the vaudeville circuits. Then, dutifully, he and Hattie took the Santa Fe back along the Orpheum trail to Denver, Kansas City, and, finally, Omaha, stopping to dine at the Fred Harvey restaurants that dotted the plains. In Philadelphia, he took his bride to the family house on Marshall Street, at the very edge of town, where Jim could keep horses and Kate could sit on the front stoop at nightfall and watch, past cornfields and farmland, the trolleys running north along the Old York Road into Montgomery County.

Hattie was extravagantly welcomed into the family, and she could barely recognize Jim Dukenfield from her husband's hair-raising tales of drunkenness and abuse. "Actually," she said, "his father was a nice, rather sporting gentleman who drank very seldom." According to Hattie, Jim confined himself to a few celebratory snorts on the days he went to collect his Civil War pension. Though he was still an excitable man, age had mellowed him considerably. "W.C. and Walter used to needle him mercilessly to get his goat," Adele Dukenfield recalled, "but it was all for fun."

In New York, William Morris booked Fields into Koster and Bial's Roof Garden, soon to close but still fashionable and frequented by the likes of Stanford White, Diamond Jim Brady, and Colonel Jacob Ruppert. It was one of the few venues in the country to make a business of importing European or "Continental" acts. "Dinner was served to the audience in boxes," Fields recalled, "so Morris got me on before they got hungry." He was held three weeks and, being a dumb act, was signed by a German agent at $150 a week. With just two years' experience, Fields now faced the greatest test of an American performer—acceptance by the demanding and ofttimes xenophobic audiences of western Europe.

It was difficult to know the kind of act that would go overseas. Dancing acts were so common that there was virtually no demand for them. Talking and singing acts did better, but only when they took the trouble to adapt their slang and patter to the ears of the locals. Germany was populated with acrobats, and the man on the street could do better tricks than most Americans. Character routines were preferable, so long as they could not be construed as insulting. Those with "gagging" did best when they learned a few lines in the language of their audience, so they at least could get laughs with their mangled attempts at speech. "Fields," said Jim Harkins, a fellow vaudevillian, "could take the simplest juggling trick and just follow it with his face. If a ball that bounced off the floor was supposed to land in his hand, and it went back up in the air and landed in his hand cupped backwards, his registering of surprise in finding this thing in his hand would send the audience into gales and, for that reason, he was the kind of act that could play the world."

With Europe in the offing, Fields decided to work Hattie into the act. He revamped his makeup, reclaiming the wire-mounted whiskers that made him look like Harrigan but adding a heavy accent of brown liner around the eyes and nose to distinguish him from Harrigan's more refined bum. Hattie, dressed in black tights, white tie, and a form-fitting tux, was given the job of handing him his props and absorbing the blame when he missed a trick. He took bookings over the summer in Chicago, playing the parks and the roof garden at the Masonic Temple and working the various circuits—Keith's, Moore's, Kohl and Castle—and a few stray houses along the way. ("You had to pick up your vaudeville dates wherever you could find them," he said.) His fee varied from city to city, but his asking price was always a yard and a quarter—$125 a week.

While fulfilling commitments for the Western Managers' Association, he espied an old sealskin coat hanging backstage (where another player had abandoned it) and gave the doorman $2 for it. Thereafter, he would regally make his entrance wearing the coat and a battered top hat and carrying a cane, all of which he would ceremoniously unload onto Hattie. Slowly, bits of business evolved for her, and she became a bright, effective foil for her husband's indolent tramp. She always disparaged her contribution to the act, saying she was just "background atmosphere," but together Fields and Hattie made a stronger act than a mere single, and Fields pronounced himself pleased with the little

*Blaming Hattie for a missed trick*

playlet they crafted from his former juggling turn. "If you can act out a good trick," he told Hattie, "it can't be stolen."

Hattie formally joined the act in November, when they played the Orpheum time as "Mr. & Mrs. W. C. Fields." They sailed for Europe on December 12 aboard the White Star liner *Ivernia,* Fields practicing as much as the choppy seas would allow, and Hattie reading aloud to him from a trunkful of books. His favorite author was Mark Twain and his favorite character Huck

Finn (whose stormy relationship with his drunken, illiterate "pap" must have had particular resonance), but he liked everything—even the most grandiloquent stuff. Their relationship was balanced, affectionate, at times glowing. He called her Bricket, Hat, Hatrack, Hunky-Punky. She called him Sod, short for Sodder—baby talk for "Father." She tutored him in reading and writing, often correcting his pronunciations and the painful diction she heard. (It mirrored, she said, the "that-there" speech patterns of his family.) She handled the finances, keeping their surplus money, what there was of it, in a little cloth bag. She even began juggling to pass the time and mastered a few of her husband's tricks, though he was never fond of watching her do them. Fields, said Hattie, had a seemingly effortless command of the objects his delicate hands set into motion. "They were wonderful hands, so long, so slender, so quick, so graceful—I used to watch him by the hour when we were touring. The things he juggled seemed to go to his hands. His hands never went out to them." He juggled hats, cigar boxes, India rubber balls. He explained to an interviewer how "you don't hang on to what you catch. You just sort of brace it and start it up again. You keep the rhythm and timing in your hands."

W. C. Fields, *komischer jongleur,* opened at the Winter-Garten in Berlin on January 1, 1901. Days of confined practice on the ship combined with a bad case of nerves to sabotage the performance. "When you juggle, you judge the height of your throws by the ceiling," he explained. "But stages don't have orthodox ceilings. And the ceilings they do have are different heights in different theatres. Not only that, but you have spotlights in your eyes, blinding you. . . . I threw my hat up in the air. I was going to catch it on my head. And I lost sight of the hat after I tossed it. The lights blinded me." The act was a fiasco. "The opening night in Berlin in those days usually set your bookings for the rest of the Continent. All the agents were on hand to watch me, and did they have something to watch? Practically nothing went right." Still, his comic recoveries made a terrific hit with the audience, and, according to an account in the *Clipper,* "they would not let him off before he responded to several encores." He was astonished. "Practically nothing went right," Fields said, "but the net result was that the act was so much funnier that all of them offered me dates."

The Germans tried extending his stay, but British bookings prevented it. He topped the bill after the first night, moving from the No. 7 spot on the program to No. 12, and the European correspondent for the *Clipper* called it "the biggest hit ever made over here by a comic juggler." Hattie was enormously proud of the triumph and relished her role as wife and assistant to the new toast of Berlin. Celebrating after the show, someone induced Fields to try a glass of German beer, but he didn't much like it and, wary of his off-kilter performance, declined to finish it. "Sometimes he would drink a glass of beer at night after the performance," Hattie said, "and, as is often usual, when theatrical people get together after the performance for what they call a little supper, he would have a glass of beer, but he never drank anytime while he was juggling." Toward the end of their stay in Berlin, Hattie entered their hotel room one morning and looked behind the chairs, under the bed, in the closet. "What's the matter?" he asked. "S-s-h!" she hissed. "There's a man in this room!" Sure enough, it was January 29, 1901, and Claude Dukenfield had finally come of age.

He managed to postpone his London opening by two weeks, permitting him to play the Krystal Palast in Leipzig. Again, he topped the bill and was wildly successful. Moving on to the land of Dickens, he was one of the star attractions at the Palace Theatre of Varieties in Cambridge Circus. "The Palace Theatre in London was like the better American music halls," Fred Stone recalled, "but a little fancier in some respects. There were a barroom and a promenade on the balcony. The card boy—the one who removes the cards announcing the various acts—was a full-grown man in satin knee breeches and a court wig, and had a disturbing resemblance to my schoolbook pictures of George Washington."

British audiences were downcast over the death of Queen Victoria—Biograph pictures of her funeral cortege were used to close the show—and didn't feel much like laughing. Fields' four-week stand, with an additional four in the provincial music halls of Ireland, Scotland, and Wales, was successful enough, but never the triumph it might otherwise have been. Moreover, Harrigan, William Ritchie, and other tramp performers had preceded him, and the similarity of their characters was widely noted in the press. "It is always the same," one critic complained. "Hairy and florid face, seedy attire, grotesque movements. Sometimes it is a juggler, at others a cyclist, anon a musician. Take Ritchie, Harrigan, and Fields . . . place them in a row, and lo! 'Tom, Dick, and Harry!' As like as three peas."

Hattie's presence in the act helped distinguish it from the others. Fields' entrance, his costume, his mute demeanor, were all in direct and laughable contrast to her efficient, eager, immaculately attired helper. Wrote one observer, "Should he happen to drop anything, he promptly orders his charming lady assistant off the stage with such a comic absurdity that we want him to drop something else." He'd begin with three balls, casually running them as if they were not even there, occasionally dropping one and then waiting for the rebound, progressing to four, five, six, shifting positions, using both hands and feet in flawless manipulation. The balls would bounce into his back pocket and, in the words of H. L. Adams, "fly about all over his body, resting now and again in the most inconceivable places, with a maximum of movement to a minimum of effort."

Battered hats would come next, one black, one white. Throwing them both into the air, he'd catch one on his head, the other on the toe of his shoe. Then, in a single motion, he'd exchange them once, twice, three times. Taking the black hat in hand, a wooden cigar from his vest, and a whisk broom from his hip pocket, he'd juggle all three as if they were balls and, finishing up, land the hat on his head, the cigar in his mouth, and the broom back in his pocket.

Finally, he'd turn his attention to a small table onstage and the five cigar boxes resting atop it. Taking them in hand, he'd offer them forth to the crowd and make a great show of preparing them for an astounding feat. With a drum roll and a twist of the wrist, the boxes would suddenly shoot into the air and come to rest in a stack, end upon end, and the audience would go wild with applause. When the commotion had reached its peak, he'd allow the boxes to fall over toward the floor and reveal that they had been linked with an elastic cord. He'd walk offstage with a shrug—as if to say, "Suckers!"—but would return moments later with the dozen boxes he had filched from Harrigan's act, drop them to show they were definitely unconnected, and then, slapping the boxes together as if they were coated with glue, he proceeded to work the crowd into a frenzy all over again. For background music, the band would play "The Fatal Rose of Red," "The Man Who Broke the Bank at Monte Carlo," and, for the cigar box routine, "Coming Through the Rye."

Despite comparisons with other American acts, Fields' notices in England were fine and admiring. He gave his first interviews to British journalists, demonstrating a new trick he was perfecting for the act. "Every now and then I strike an entirely new idea," he told a writer for the *Blackpool Times and Fylde Observer,* "and if it can be carried out, I keep at it until I can rely on myself, and then I practice it all over again. You see, I have not only to practice the trick until I have got it perfect, but I have to practice it with the same nonchalant or contemptuous expression I intend doing it with in order to make it go with the audience."

The custom in London was to group the music halls into circuits, and Fields characterized the dizzying process of playing three houses a night as "no fun." The performer, he explained to an American journalist, "goes first to one, does his turn, takes a cab to the next, performs, and then goes on to the third, in order. His appearances are timed and he makes up once for all, every evening. But he generally only gets one salary for all three performances." Fields preferred playing the provinces, where two performances—one from seven to nine, the other from nine to eleven o'clock—were given nightly.*

He returned to Germany in April, where Martin Beck reached him with an offer of a thirty-six-week tour of the United States at $175 a week. He jumped

---

*There was a tax on matinees, so few were given.

to the *Folies-Bergère* in Paris and, as America's famed *jongleur comique,* topped
the bill for two full months. "Have been a tremendous success everywhere I
have played and have return engagements at each place," he boasted in a dispatch to the editors of the *Clipper.* "Had to postpone 20 months' engagements
to accept Mr. Beck's offer, and will return to Europe shortly after closing with
the Orpheum show. I will do a somewhat different act when I return." Few Continental houses remained open over the summer, requiring Fields and Hattie to
return to England to play out the balance of their time abroad. They finally
sailed from Liverpool aboard the RMS *Majestic* on the thirty-first of July.


The stars of Martin Beck's Orpheum Show were Jim McIntyre and Tom
Heath, two blackface comedians who had been working together since the
1870s. They were top-billed with a gambling hall routine called "The Man from
Montana." Joe Welsh, who did a Jewish hard-luck monologue ("Maybe you
tink I'm heppy?"), was featured second, and Fields and Hattie, billed for the
tour as "W. C. Fields and Wife," were third. Unlike some performers, Fields
liked Beck, a hard-nosed German who helped organize the theaters between
California and Chicago under the Orpheum banner and eventually built up a
circuit of seventeen houses. "He didn't like anything cheap," said Joe Laurie Jr.,
"and he liked class." And, like Fields, he believed in delivering the best-quality
product. The show traveled as a unit of ten acts, beginning in Cincinnati in
October 1901, and continuing into May 1902.

Conscious of keeping the act fresh, Fields was always devising new tricks
and figuring out ways to improve the ones he already had. The intended highlight of the Orpheum tour was a variation on the battered hat exchange, with
Fields balancing a cane sideways on the toe of his shoe, a hat resting on top of
it, and a wooden cigar on the brim of the hat. At the crack of a drum roll, he
would kick all three into the air. The hat would do a complete revolution, landing on his head, the cane would land horizontally on the bridge of his nose, and
the cigar would drop neatly into his mouth. It was the most difficult feat he had
ever devised—surely beyond the skills of any other comedic juggler—and it
took ten months to learn, practicing every day for a quarter hour. "It's no use
practicing any longer than 15 minutes at a single trick," he said, "or you get disgusted with yourself, and with it, too."

The trick required a special shoe with a toe broad enough to hold the cane,
and Fields paid $35 a pair. Occasionally, he felt confident enough to demon-
strate the new stunt in private, but he refused to do it onstage until he could
make it appear effortless. "I never go before the public until I am sure of it. I
don't care to see anyone merely trying to do a thing, and I know the public feels
the same." The trick finally made its debut at the Philadelphia Bijou on the

*Tramp juggler with hat, cane, and cigar*

night of August 17, 1901. Fields brought it off on the very first try, evidently making it look too effortless in the process. "I waited for the explosion of applause," he told J. P. McEvoy in 1932. "I might have been waiting yet." The effect drew polite, insignificant applause from a packed and otherwise enthusiastic house. Fields was mortified; the absence of an ovation that night threw him off. Even the critic for the *Inquirer*—who should have known better— failed to mention it in his notice. Adding insult to injury, he misidentified the author of the turn as one "W. S. Fields."

"That experience made me very bitter for a while," said Fields. "What's the use of burning out your soul for people who don't appreciate the better things of life? I could have juggled five rubber balls and got a bigger hand, but was it art?" Stubbornly, he dramatized the effect, taking as many as four tries to accomplish the feat and keeping up a running-fire commentary that could be heard in the orchestra pit.* But emphasizing the exertion of the trick ran counter to the casualness of the act. "Americans don't like to see a man working hard on the stage," he told a British journalist. "Physical exertion, such as is necessary in struggling with heavy weights, is not really appreciated. They like lightness, crispness, humor, and vivacity in their entertainment." Having created the trick on the assumption that its complexity was self-evident, Fields now decided it wasn't showy enough to captivate most crowds. "It is the same the world over. They simply want their fancies tickled, and won't exercise their minds to try and think which tricks are really difficult of execution."

His mood sank as the tour progressed, and he must have wondered if there was any future for him with American audiences. For Hattie, the sentiment he expressed in Pasadena—to quit touring and settle down—still resonated, and although she loved show business, she hated the travel, the insecurity, the unsettled nature of it all. They quarreled—violently at times—and she almost pushed her highly strung husband to the breaking point. Grant Felton sensed the danger, reacting to one soul-bearing letter from his nephew with justifiable alarm. "I see you are having a hell of a time with Hattie," he wrote, "but, as a brother, don't do any harm to her that you will get yourself in trouble way out there, but wait till you come east and settle things right up with her. Because, Claude, if anything happens to you out there, how would I get to your side? Now, for God's sake, hold your temper till you get home, and don't get into trouble for my sake."

Restless and unhappy, Fields left the Orpheum tour and made plans to return to Europe, where he considered the audiences friendlier and more appreciative of difficult tricks. If the Americans had failed to appreciate the improve-

---

*Given Fields' dogged devotion to this particular trick, it is interesting to speculate if this was one of the hat, cane, and cigar effects alluded to in the *Eight Bells* script.

ments he'd made in his act, at least some of the critics had taken notice. "Fields has individuality," wrote Epes Sargent, the pugnacious "Chicot" of the *New York Morning Telegraph,* "and if he keeps at work on this line he will have an act that stands alone." Sargent, like most writers of the day, mentioned Hattie's contribution, noting that while she looked rather uncomfortable in her tight-fitting knickers, "she got about the stage spryly and helped create an impression."

Fields' pursuit of technical excellence is no more evident than in an unlikely story he related to Jim Tully. He didn't date the incident, but if it did occur, it probably happened in July 1902, when Fields and Hattie had returned to Germany and toss juggling was still an important part of the act. "Being young and not widely traveled, and able to juggle six balls from any position, I considered myself among the masters of my craft.* I went into a small theatre in Hamburg and saw a midget, standing on a moving horse, juggle eight balls. Mortified, I hurried from the theatre and got eight balls. I spent all my waking hours in practice until I had mastered the midget's feat. I would return each day to watch him. Unknown to fame, he was a very great artist."

While comedy was always the primary focus of Fields' act, he was the most technically ambitious of all the comic jugglers. Doing tricks in a funny way made them, in the words of Paul Cinquevalli, "much more difficult to do." By mastering six balls in a comedic fashion, Fields had achieved a much greater feat than their mere manipulation. Cinquevalli, perhaps the greatest of all jugglers, considered the juggling of up to five balls a learner's progression. "When he can juggle with absolute certainty with five balls," he wrote, "he will have acquired a very fair facility with hand and eye, and he may proceed to learn more difficult feats."

Six balls were considerably more difficult than five, and Fields had developed a preference for odd numbers that made his mastery of eight even harder. "It's all rhythm," he explained of his preference. "And spacing. Or perhaps you'd call it timing." His genuine mastery of eight balls becomes suspect, however, when one considers another comment he once made about juggling: "You do your designs, and get up your speed, with uneven numbers of balls, or whatever you're juggling, but you do your faking with the evens." By "faking," Fields may well have been referring to a technique known to modern jugglers as "multiplexing," the act of catching and throwing the balls in pairs. To the

---

*Fields' comments suggest he was unaware of any jugglers who could handle more than six balls, but according to juggling historian Andrew Conway, the best ball jugglers of the day were "certainly performing seven or more."

casual observer, the performer appears to be catching and throwing each ball individually, an effect usually achieved with an even number of balls.

Seeing the midget was a harbinger of the ordeal to come. Fields arrived in Berlin with high expectations, but in comparison to his triumphant opening at the Winter-Garten in 1901, his reception on August 15, 1902, was exactly the opposite. He performed the act flawlessly, but couldn't seem to get the people excited. There were no laughs, and the applause was decidedly weak. "This time I didn't get a tumble. My act was as good or better. They just didn't like me." Fortunately, the second night went considerably better than the first, and by the third, Harry Houdini, writing from Dusseldorf, could truthfully report to the readers of the *New York Dramatic Mirror* that Fields had scored yet another hit. He was held a total of six weeks and, as the bill shifted, he decided his opening-night performance must have been impaired by the fact that he had followed a horse act. "Maybe they figured the horse could've done my tricks better," he said. The clatter of hooves rang in the ears of the audience, he theorized, distracting them from the relative quiet of his juggling. Later, he noticed this to be a problem whenever he followed a noisy act, and his reception usually varied according to the commotion that preceded him. Still, in spite of having determined that the problem was not his, the stigma of having flopped on opening night, when he was on display before all of western Europe, poisoned his ability to land subsequent dates on the Continent. When he tried to get a booking changed in Vienna to accept an extension on his Berlin engagement, Fields was told the manager had already caught his act at the Winter-Garten and decided he'd "rather have the horse." Then he was asked what Fields would take to break the contract entirely.

For once, Fields was thunderstruck. "Ever have an experience like that? It's an internal earthquake, it's the end of the world, it's hell. Here you think you're the king of the roost and babies cry for you, and all of a sudden you're a frost." It was his first inkling that a straight juggling act would not sustain him indefinitely, even if he were the best in the world. "I told him I'd take $500 for the contract, and for two weeks I suffered as I never suffered before."

*Four*

# An American Baby

Variety, as it made the gradual transition to "refined" vaudeville, gained in respectability. Audiences became more sophisticated and less accepting of grotesque character turns, and the so-called "rough" acts that had prospered in the beer halls of the 1880s and '90s slowly faded from the scene. New York's legendary Koster and Bial's closed for good in 1901, and the 1,200-seat Bijou in Philadelphia was replaced by B. F. Keith's lavish new Chestnut Street theater, French Renaissance in decor and a full city block in length. Show business was getting so dressy that Fields feared his tramp persona was all washed up. "Even acrobats were getting snooty and doing their stuff in evening clothes instead of pink tights," he said.

Fields brooded over the settling of his Vienna contract and decided that, despite his best efforts, his material had gone stale. "I was seeing the world and the world was seeing me, but was I getting anywhere? I went around the globe twice. But when I came back to the same old place, I was just the same old Bill Fields, doing the same sort of thing—a comedy juggling act, that was all."

He wrote letters, sent frantic cables, and finally lined up some work in Vienna with an itinerant company of *The Messenger Boy*. The idle time weighed heavily on him, and, eschewing elaborate new stunts after the failure of the cane, hat, and cigar effect, he decided instead to rely on his burgeoning skills as a pantomimist—"dress suit comedy," as he put it. Inspiration came in the form of a childhood memory: "While hanging around pool halls as a kid, I noticed that every player went through the same gyrations. He elaborately chalks his cue, he sights the ball, he wiggles around and sights it again, and he always preens and struts when he makes a shot." Stranded in Europe, Fields began working out the details of a completely new and unique character turn. "I just copied their mannerisms and people thought it was funny."

He went from Vienna to Prague, and from Prague to London, where he found a spot on the bill at the Hippodrome. At Christmas, he was one of the many performers to volunteer their services at Queen Alexandra's dinner for the families of soldiers killed in the Boer War. In England, he had time to over-see the design and construction of a collapsible pool table—shorter than the regulation length and with rounded cushions to facilitate some imaginative bounce tricks. Gone would be the shabby tramp with the cigar boxes, replaced by a somewhat more refined version in dress shirt, vest, and string tie. Fever-ishly, he worked away at the new act through January 1903, sailing for home with fresh time booked on the Keith and Orpheum circuits.

It was in New York that word reached him that his beloved grandmother had died, at the age of seventy-two. Annie Felton was buried in the family plot at Greenwood Cemetery alongside her bibulous husband, Tom. Fields sent flowers and regrets and regaled Hattie with admiring stories of her indomitable spirit. It is not known if Annie ever saw her grandson perform onstage, but she must surely have been pleased with the news of his success. Whatever her faults, she always gave him the hope of a better life through education and self-reliance, and her death closed a chapter in his life. Never again would anyone push him so forcefully in the right direction or so unquestionably have his own best interests at heart.

Before leaving for Rhode Island and the start of his new tour, Fields placed $5 ads in both the *Clipper* and the *Dramatic Mirror.* They read:

W. C. FIELDS

ECCENTRIC JUGGLER

NOW DOING THE NEW ACT

The pool table routine was first performed before a paying audience at Keith's Providence on February 9, 1903, and Fields couldn't have asked for bet-ter circumstances. Arthur and Jennie Dunn topped the bill but flopped miser-ably, and it was left to Fields to salvage the second half of the program. Manager Charles Lovenberg moved him to the No. 13 spot—prime position-ing—when he saw what he had, and the preceding act, James Richmond Glen-roy, proved a good lead-in by performing a familiar Irish monologue that droned on for eighteen interminable minutes. The new Fields act opened with a little ball juggling and the battered hat exchange, pretty much as before, then the pool table was brought forth, and, with a mirror suspended over the stage, he lighted a cigar and casually assumed the posture of a small-time hustler.

Starting off, Fields selected a cue from a grotesquely warped assortment, studying each successive one sagely before casting it aside. Settling at last on the least ridiculous, he chalked up, took aim, drew back for the break, and watched helplessly as the tip of the cue escaped his fingers and bobbed tauntingly out of reach.

Bearing down, he removed the cigar from his mouth, parking it on the rail of the table and fussily positioning and repositioning it between two well-worn pieces of chalk. Then he chased the cue with his hand as if pursuing an elusive thread with a needle, encircling the butt end with his fingers and running them along the shaft as if to sneak up on it. He seemed to have the cue under control when, ready to shoot, he took careful aim and watched again as the tip veered defiantly out of reach. Agitated, whacking the cue against the side of the table as if to knock some sense into it, he distractedly put the chalk in his mouth and ground the cigar into the tip of the cue. The audience roared as the stogie collapsed in his hand, and, after a moment, his face contorted hideously as he spat the chalk out onto the floor.

Capturing the tip of the cue at last, his first shot ricocheted off the opposing rail and hit him in the forehead with such force that it nearly knocked him senseless. On the rebound, his second shot landed the ball on his shoulder, where it hesitated, dropped to his inner knee, then fell to the back of his shoe, from where he was able to neatly kick it into the pocket of his coat. Retrieving the ball, he positioned the cue for a vertical massé shot, missed it entirely, and drove the stick clean through the table.

Working it from its hole, growling epithets under his breath, he mounted one final assault on the ball and, on the break, cleared the table in one spectacular shot. As the audience gasped at first and then erupted in applause, he threw the cue down on the table and sauntered triumphantly offstage. "People laugh at another's embarrassment, at frustrated plans, at timidity, at the underdog," he said. The percussion of the balls, the banging of the cue sticks, the broad facial expressions and muttered oaths ("Cu-urses!") were musical in their rhythms. The final clearing of the table, accomplished with a spring-loaded mechanism that yanked the racked balls, individually tethered to green strings, to their appointed pockets, was, in the showbiz parlance of the time, a "wow" finish.

"W. C. Fields, the eccentric juggler, deserves the title 'great' before his name," the reviewer for the *Evening Telegraph* announced. "His act was intricate, yet carried out with such ease, and his side play was so laughable that everyone gave him an ovation." Manager Lovenberg was equally impressed. "This act will probably be of most value to us of any on the bill," he wrote in his weekly report. "He has a lot of new tricks which he presents better than before and has improved in his comedy, as well as having added to his work some billiard double shots that are most surprising, among them that of shooting a ball on the table and having it bounce back and go over his head, falling into his hip pocket."

Fields took the new act from Providence to Boston, where he made a "big laughing hit," and then on to Philadelphia, where he and Hattie bunked with his parents. He spent the week of March 2 on the bill at B. F. Keith's with strongman Eugene Sandow, "the physically perfect man," whose act, consisting mainly of weightlifting and muscle flexing, was described by the *Inquirer* as "edifying and instructive." The management found Fields "absolutely without qualification" the best in the business. "In our estimation he is good enough for a headliner in any show." Flush with the success of his new routine and on the verge of a lengthy tour of Australia, Fields felt secure enough to make a $2,400 down payment on three adjacent lots on the west side of Warnock Street, just south of Venango, within easy walking distance of his uncle Will's house. Upon their return from Australia, he told his wife, they'd get busy and start a family.

When Fields and Hattie left Philadelphia on March 9 for Omaha, Walter was with them, lugging the crates, assembling the table, cutting the string that sprung the ball mechanism at the end of the act. "He asked me if I wanted to take a trip," Walter recalled, "and I said, 'Certainly.' He said, 'I have got this pool table. I will show you what to do, take it apart and put it together.' " There were fourteen pieces of luggage to carry. Congenial, unschooled, almost as lacking in ambition as Claude was driven, Walter idolized his older brother and began using the name Fields in place of Dukenfield. Hattie didn't travel well on the water and, despite her husband's entreaties, refused to accompany him on the trip down under. The tour had come about when impresario Harry Rickards was scouring the United States for rough acts to export to Melbourne and Sydney. He was urged to catch Fields' turn, which he eventually did at the Grand Opera House in Indianapolis. Rickards was a former star of the English music halls—he sang "Cerulea Was Beautiful" and "Captain Jinks of the Horse Marines"—who was dragged through the bankruptcy courts of Basing-hall Street before reinventing himself as an Australian manager. He loved the Fields act and promptly booked it for its first open dates—eighteen months hence.

Fields played Kansas City and New Orleans in March, jumped to San Francisco for two weeks in April, and finished up at the Orpheum in Los Angeles, where the billing read: "Last Week in America." Returning to San Francisco, he bought a copy of Stevenson's *Treasure Island* to augment the books Hattie had already gathered for him and, for one last time, implored his wife not to stay behind. "He begged me to come, to the last minute," she said. "He said it wouldn't take long for Walter to go back to the hotel and get your things and pack them, but I said no, I was afraid of a long trip."

Fields and Walter sailed first cabin for Honolulu, Pago Pago, Auckland, and Sydney aboard the SS *Sonoma* on the night of Friday, May 15, 1903. Hattie saw them off: "I stood on the dock and waved until the boat was way far out and I couldn't see him anymore." Four days later, on May 19, Kate and Jim Dukenfield celebrated their silver wedding anniversary at their home in Philadelphia.

Present were their two daughters, Adele and Elsie May, their son Roy, Will Felton and his wife Christianna, and a small gathering of friends and neighbors. Inconceivably, the two eldest Dukenfield boys were on their way to Hawaii.

Fields arrived in Auckland in time for the Grand National Steeplechase on June 3, and opened in Melbourne on the thirteenth as part of Rickards' New Tivoli Vaudeville Company, "absolutely the highest-salaried company of brilliant star comedians, pantomimists, and gymnastic eccentrics in the vaudeville world." He did a good deal of the old act—the one Rickards had seen in 1901—making his entrance in a sleighing costume with fur coat, cap, dark goggles, and carrying a driving whip. Separated from his wife for the first time in three years, he found himself dissatisfied with Walter's onstage work as a foil. He had been in Australia for only a few days when he sent a prepaid passage to Hattie in Los Angeles with strict instructions—for the sake of the act—to leave for Sydney at once. He played Rickards' Tivoli in Adelaide, and was in Sydney when Hattie finally arrived, in late July. So buoyantly happy was he to see her, he made a spectacle of himself at the pier. "Before the boat docked," she remembered, "he jumped up from the pier over the railing and everybody howled when he did." Fields embraced his wife extravagantly, toting flowers and presents and grandly arranging for her trunks.

Hattie came prepared to rejoin the act and once again filled a role the pool table had rendered obsolete. The critics in Sydney hailed Fields as an inspiration, a sensation, a miracle of originality. They swooned over Hattie as well. As one reviewer wrote: "His dainty little wife, clad in white satin breeches, coquets as much with him as with the audience, and helps materially in the decided success of the feature." Said another: "About the nearest thing to an artist's dream the critic has seen for some time is the natty little lady who acts as assistant to W. C. Fields at the Tivoli. She's as modest as she's handsome, too."

Inspired, perhaps, by the new roughhouse image of the American male as put forth in the ascendancy of Teddy Roosevelt, Fields spent five months learning to shoot and ride in the trackless prairies of Australia, acquiring a fiery mustang named Fluke in the process. He enjoyed such unprecedented acclaim for his work that, according to the Australian magazine *Theatre,* "Fields may safely be said to be about the biggest draw, both from a public and managerial point of view, that there is in the whole world of vaudeville and variety."

Fields approached the institution of marriage with the same youthful intensity he applied to his work. He was a passionate, excitable, temperamental man, and weeks of separation had sharpened his devotion to his wife. They conceived a child in Australia, and he became wildly jealous—often to the point of violence—over the slightest attention paid her, however innocently, by another man. Nearly a decade of juggling had strengthened him, and, like his father, he found himself repeatedly in trouble over hothead altercations. In

*The Dukenfield family, circa 1903.*
*From left to right: Elsie May, Adele, Kate, Leroy, and Jim*

Berlin, he slugged a Prussian officer after hearing an anti-American remark
and was thrown into jail for it. In London, a bobby shoved him into a muddy
gutter and got socked as well. In Paris, two gendarmes were blackjacking an
acrobat, Fields waded in, and was jailed for his trouble. Now, in Sydney, Hattie's mere presence occasioned two of the most serious eruptions.

"My husband," she said flatly, "was a coward. He liked to bully people—
waiters particularly—and it didn't matter whether they had been mean to him
or not. But he couldn't take a chance on his hands; they were as important to
him as the hands of a pianist. So he had this special cane, and it became a part
of him on stage and off." The cane had a gold head and was heavily weighted.
In Sydney, he used it at the racetrack to beat up the grandson of Lord Byron,
who had spoken to Hattie when she bet a pound on Lord Cardigan against the

favorite, Little Nell, and won. Overhearing an innocent remark, Fields came unhinged and had to be pulled off the man. An even worse event occurred on a city street, when Fields was in the midst of his shooting and riding phase and at the peak of his Australian popularity. Walter, Hattie, and he were out walking when three Cockneys, clustered on a street corner, made what Hattie later described as "rude remarks." Walter said, "Hey, Bill," and gave his brother the nod. Fields said, "Hattie, get back to the hotel," and, within moments, a brawl ensued. Two of the men escaped, but the third had a blackjack, and Fields and Walter worked him over to the point where he hung between life and death for nearly six weeks. Back at the hotel, Walter gave Hattie the blackjack. Using her husband's razor to cut it open, she disposed of the lead under the carpet in a neighboring room. (Afterward, Fields wondered why his razor was so dull.) They were detained—they couldn't leave the country—but the man eventually recovered and was quietly paid off.

By the time he left Sydney for Melbourne on October 2, Fields was being hailed as the greatest drawing card Rickards had ever brought to Australia. The sendoff that Friday evening was extraordinary by any standard. "The Redfern Railway Station was crowded with friends and well-wishers to see him away," reported the *Music Hall and Theatre Review,* "and when the time came for the train to start, the handshaking, hurrahs, and waving of hats and handkerchiefs, as the train sped away, must have been, to say the least, very gratifying to Mr. and Mrs. Fields."

Leaving Australia, they spent thirty-three grueling days crossing the Indian Ocean to South Africa and, according to Fields, "had the racks on the table nearly every day." Fields, Hattie, and Walter arrived off the province of Natal in early December and, appropriate to the small boat, were unloaded like cargo—they were herded into a gigantic wicker basket and lowered by cable to avoid £80 in port duties. Hitting the mainland at Durban, they thought it best to keep moving: "When we espied the giant Zulus in their weird makeup, legs and bodies covered in various designs in whitewash, horns adorning their heads and bone handkerchiefs or scrapers hung in their ears, we climbed into a rickshaw and let the luggage go to pot."

The siege of Mafeking was long over, the Boers had been routed, and the Treaty of Vereeniging had ended hostilities more than two years earlier. Still, Fields was advised by the American consular agent—who was an Englishman—that only thirty foreigners were allowed permits into the Transvaal at any one time. The man said he would write to Cape Town, but it would take five or six weeks to get an answer. Moreover, Fields was told that the Empire Theatre in Johannesburg, where he was scheduled to open, had burned to the ground. He smelled a rat: "I do not think the management welcomed my presence in the Rand, as I had a play-or-pay contract." He signaled Walter to lam, and they made their way to the railway station, where they learned a man needed a citizenship card to even purchase a ticket. "Here I was with a contract for Johannesburg and unable to reach the place." A train pulled in, and the first person off was a hunchback whom Fields instantly recognized as having sold candy and magazines on a train in California. The man was a repatriated Boer, and it was with his card of citizenship that Fields was finally able to buy the tickets. Arriving, miraculously, a few days ahead of schedule, he joined the bill at the Standard Theatre in Johannesburg on December 14, 1903. A full company, headed by comedienne Peggy Pryde, followed in three days.

After a lackluster week in Johannesburg under the Hyman banner, Fields and company made the eight-hundred-mile jump to Cape Town, where they played eight dismal weeks at the new Tivoli. He and Hattie took a suite at the International Hotel, where the mosquitoes were ferocious and the netting over the beds largely ineffectual. "They would rip the netting from its hangings and bite you to the bone," he said. It was a miserable stay, leavened only by a cheering letter from Jim McIntyre of McIntyre and Heath. Still with the Orpheum tour, the team was planning a new show for the 1905–06 season incorporating the minstrel company of George Primrose and wanted to know if Fields might be available as a specialty. By this point, Fields had had enough of foreign travel: "All you have to do is to say the word," he said in reply, "and I will be there with my new act, which is meeting with much success throughout the world."

Fields loathed South Africa, where prices were high, crime was rampant, and the food was terrible. "We are in the dead of summer down here now and it is hot if we are not getting south-eastern wind. And, if we get the south-easter, it blows us off our feet." Business for the new theater was lousy as well. "There is one theatre that furnishes the vaudeville and another that furnishes the dramatic and comedies, and the people have that old English way about them that they won't go to see anything else, as they have been going to these two houses and have been pleased and they won't change. They think everything else is inferior and they won't come in on a free pass." Yet, he had to admit the place had its charms. "This town, Cape Town, is situated at the foot of Table Mountain, and when the wind blows from the south-east, it blows the clouds over Table Mountain until it looks like Niagara Falls—the most beautiful sight I have ever seen."

Fields, Hattie, and Walter fled to England in March, where Fields shared the bill at the London Hippodrome with Eugene Sandow and Houdini, the Handcuff King. Hattie, now five months pregnant, was beginning to show, and her participation in the act was curtailed. The couple argued over where the baby should be born: Hattie was determined to return to the United States ("I wanted to have an American baby"), but Fields, with contracts extending into

# THE TIVOLI

Proprietors ... ... ... ... ... ... ... ... Tivoli Co., Ltd.
Manager ... ... ... ... ... ... ... ... EDWARD A. PICKERING.

## Wednesday, February 3rd, 1904.

## GRAND NEW COMPANY.

### UNPARALLELED ATTRACTIONS.

# W. C. FIELDS.

## HAYDAS TROUPE.

## The SISTERS FLEXMORE.

### Miss NINA CARLTON.

## BERT. BRANTFORD.

## THE SALVAGGIS.

**THE BIOSCOPE.** | **Miss Vivian Dell.**

### Miss

# PEGGY PRYDE.

## FAMILY MATINEE EVERY SATURDAY.

**NO SMOKING.**
**LIGHT REFRESHMENTS ONLY.**

BOX STALLS, 3s.     ORCHESTRA STALLS, 5s.     BOXES, £2 2s.
Children, Half-Price.

Doors open 7.30.     Commence 7.50 sharp.     Carriages at 10.45.     Telephone No. 992.

STABLEFORD, LTD., PRINTERS, CAPE TOWN.

the fall, urged her to remain with him in Europe. Said Hattie, "He made a suggestion to me, 'Why not stay in London and have the baby, or in Germany? There is only 12 hours' difference.' And I said, 'No, I would rather go home to my mother,' which I did." She stayed in London through the end of May, standing firm on her conviction that the child be born on American soil, and, grudgingly, her husband gave in. Walter left for home on the first of June, with Hattie following a week later. Fields went on to Birmingham alone, his first stop on a lengthy tour of the Empire circuit.

A dumb act went over well in the provinces, where, in some of the houses, brawls in the gallery drowned out what was being said on the stage. In the orchestras, men rarely removed their hats, and the auditoriums smelled of fried fish, which the spectators ate like popcorn. Fields wrote Hattie most every day, flooding Lizzie Hughes' New York apartment with concerned, solicitous, sometimes agonized correspondence. No detail of news was too small to report, no thoughts or feelings too trivial to express. The tour ground on: Edinburgh, Glasgow, and Bradford in June, Liverpool, Newcastle, Leeds, Hull in July. He was in Sheffield, appropriately enough, with the remnants of the Dukenfield family, when a telegram arrived from his sister-in-law, Kitty. Hattie had given birth to a son at her mother's home on West Twenty-seventh Street on July 28, 1904. At nine and three-quarter pounds, he was destined to be almost as big as his uncle Walter. His name was William C. Dukenfield, but he would be known for the rest of his life as Claude.

Fields was "struck speechless" by the news of his son's birth. In Sheffield, they all had a drink on the head of the kid—a boy too—and that night at the theater he was, by his own admission, "next to the worst thing that ever went on stage." His letter to Hattie, a breathless effusion of love and relief, was penned the next day: "It is impossible, Hat, to tell you how glad I am to know all the worry is over. You are well, and we have a little baby boy. Ain't it great, Hat? Bring him over until I kick the stuffing out of him. Have wired all my intimate friends, but have received no congratulations, not up to now anyway, but I suppose they will come to and send me some telegrams soon. You keep well and get over this O.K. I suppose all the worst is over, don't discharge the nurse or Dr. too soon. Keep them until everything is just right. Stay in bed and wrap your Zennie up well. Don't get up too soon. Soon as you are able, write me a long letter explaining all. Tell me how it all happened, how you feel, if you are thin or fatter. Tell me *all.*"

On payday, he dashed off a check for $50 "for some fine clothes for to bring him over with." Exhilarated, he moved on to Manchester, where he stayed with friends in Brooklins and made the twelve-mile commute by rail. He closed at the Palace Theatre on August 13, 1904, and was en route the next day, a Sunday, to Shepherds Bush when Hattie, in New York, had their son baptized at Guardian Angel Church. It was the baby's first outing, and the sponsors were Hattie's sister, Kitty, and her brother, James. Fields had always been tolerant of his wife's Catholicism, occasionally even accompanying her to mass, though he was usually content to let her go it alone, shooing her out the door at the last possible moment. According to Hattie, they had discussed the matter of the child's religious upbringing in Cape Town, and her husband had approved of the baby's baptism—knowing full well he could not reasonably expect a practicing Catholic to forgo the sacrament. "He said, 'You have him baptized in your church, because I have no religion,' and he knew I was strict."

The birth of Fields' son had the happy effect of bringing him closer to his family in Philadelphia, for Hattie and the baby spent a lot of time with the Dukenfields. The illiteracy of Jim Dukenfield and his children made it difficult for Fields to communicate by mail, and his letters—as if taking up the mantle of his late grandmother—gently urged them to better educate themselves. He expressed satisfaction when he received some "very creditable written letters from my sister May" and promised to help her and Adele form a singing act when he returned from Europe. "What's the use of their working in a mill for four dollars per week when they can get seventy dollars a week on the Buhne?"

Fields also felt that his brother Walter had a future in show business, due more to his good looks than any talent he possessed. Walter had a fine complexion and was as handsome as any matinee idol. Fields had seen a man named Tom Hearn, who billed himself as "the laziest juggler on earth" and whose act consisted of throwing household breakables into the air and allowing them to crash noisily to the floor. "There isn't any juggling in the act to be noticeable," he wrote Hattie, "and Walter could do the act great. He must be able to read and write though, and be able to do a bit of juggling if necessary."*

Fields approached the challenge of his own literacy with the same tenacity he applied to his juggling, spending hours scouring the dictionary for fresh words with which to build his letters. "I wrote a beautiful letter to Uncle Willie and Aunt Crissie," he boasted in a note to Hattie. "They won't understand it, for I didn't myself after I had written it. I used nine different dictionaries to write the letter, and when I finished I had to get them all out again to see what I had written, and what it meant."

Fields' reconciliation with his father may have been his proudest accom-

---

*Fields had been after Walter to learn to read for years. He had worked with him aboard the ship to Australia, and Hattie had purchased a book for him to read. "Walter must have been practicing his writing," Fields reported, "for he has that book down pretty fine. He read me one whole page in it this morning without one mistake. He surprised me to death."

plishment, for he achieved dominance over the old man by simply assuming his role as sole provider to the family. He made him retire and bought him a summer place across the river at Penns Grove, New Jersey. Jim Dukenfield learned to read and write in his late fifties, and his son always remembered the first letter he ever received from his dad. When he later assured him that he was able to decipher it, Jim expressed both amazement and delight and said, "That's the first letter I ever wrote, son."

After the birth of the baby, Fields found himself in an unusually relaxed and garrulous mood. "There's no place in the world where you can book so much time and have such small railway journeys," he said of England. In Nottingham, he took special care to praise the audience ("one of the brightest I have performed to"), telling a local journalist their smartness was evinced in their appreciation of difficult tricks. "That trick, for instance, of kicking the hat from the foot and catching it on the end of a 3½ foot cane balanced on the chin took me longer to learn than any," he said, describing his latest variation of the vexing hat, cane, and cigar effect. "You see, there's a double balance to maintain. I have to balance myself on one foot with the hat on the other while balancing the cane on the chin, and when I kick the hat up, I throw both balances out. Then I have to recover myself, get the two balances again, and try to push the cane, while balancing it on my chin, into the hat. It's a very complicated trick, and yet in some towns it wouldn't be applauded at all. . . . That's why you have had some of the better-class tricks."

Dreading another ocean voyage, Hattie was resisting the idea of bringing the baby to England when Fields hit upon the notion of having his parents accompany her on the journey. Jim Dukenfield hadn't seen his homeland in half a century, and Kate had never been there. But Hattie vetoed the scheme, saying it was in the boy's best interests to stay put, and then the sedentary Kate chimed in and said she wouldn't go either. Jim was less recalcitrant and took his son up on the offer, though being alone with his pugnacious father in Europe for two months wasn't exactly what Fields had in mind. Jim's arrival in London was set to coincide with the end of Fields' provincial tour on October 8, 1904. "Let me know all about Papa's departure," he wrote Hattie on September 14, "if you can keep track of the fights he has, etc., and see that he brings enough clothes with him. I think I'll take him with me for a week at Paris, and would you suggest taking him about the town one night or not? Paris will be upside down when Pa's there." Sourly accepting Hattie's decision not to participate in the trip, Fields urged her to at least send photos of the baby. "He must be a pippin. I am crazy to see him." It may have been his almost daily entreaties, or maybe it was just simply Hattie's perverse sense of humor—which sometimes revealed itself in the most awkward of moments—but when Jim Dukenfield stepped off the boat train in London, he did indeed have his daughter-in-law in tow, and Fields, after an excruciating wait of nearly three months, finally got a look at his son.

The party decamped almost immediately to Paris, where they put up at the Hotel Franklin and Claude, whom Fields insistently took to referring to as Billy, got his first pair of shoes. Fields had time booked at the *Folies-Bergère,* which kept them in Paris through most of November, then he left Hattie and the baby in their suite at the hotel while he took his father along for quick stands in Marseille and Milan. Returning to England in December, the family settled in Manchester, where Fields joined the *Cinderella* pantomime at the Prince's Theatre, incongruously performing his pool table routine. Jim quickly got his fill of the city, where the Sunday closing laws played hell with his good nature. Said Adele Dukenfield, "When our father saw there was no place he could get a drink on New Year's Eve, he had W.C. put him on the first boat home. He arrived at our house . . . and went to the kitchen. The first thing he said was, 'What's for dinner?' Our mother scolded him for not even asking how we were, but he remarked, 'I knew you would be okay.' " Never again would Jim complain about life in the United States.

In England, Hattie was taken ill with rheumatic fever, and the family found themselves stuck in Manchester until spring. "I couldn't walk," she said. "I was on the crutch and cane." Fields stayed with the *Cinderella* pantomime, but it wasn't his regular act, and by the time Hattie was able to get around, he was once again in a slump. At the Scala in Copenhagen, he went before a packed house and botched the troublesome hat-and-cane effect an unprecedented

*Fields with his father in Paris, November 1904*

seven times. "I always had a running comedy gag to use in such cases, trying to cajole the audience into believing these delays were intentional. But when I missed the trick the eighth time, I gave up and, tossing the hat into the air, I smacked it viciously with the cane. It soared high above the stage, twirled dozens of times, hit the back curtain, and bounced right onto a peg in the hat rack placed beside me. It was the most spectacular thing I ever saw. The audience went wild."

The hat-and-cane effect, in all of its variations, had never come close to sparking the kind of ovation that one impulsive whack engendered, and Fields instantly decided to add it to the act. The following night, he arranged to have a net strung high above the stage to catch the hat. Batting it with his cane at the appropriate moment, it turned the requisite number of somersaults and disappeared into the flies, where a stagehand was waiting to drop a well-timed replica onto the rack. After four years of trial and error, Fields had finally made a crowd pleaser of the most difficult trick of his career . . . by missing it.

On he moved to Berlin, where one of the cases holding the pool table was misdirected to the Russian border and impounded for duty. He couldn't do the pool act without rails, and used some ill-fitting substitutes until the originals could be ransomed and retrieved. Earlier, he had announced that he would spend the month of May in Moscow, but now the incident with the rails focused his attention on Russia's festering civil discontent—sparked by the infamous "bloody Sunday" shootings in St. Petersburg—and quickly he changed his mind. Speaking to the *New York Dramatic Mirror,* he said he would continue to amuse the people of "the more peaceful European countries" and hastily set time with a Madrid circus instead. The crowds weren't particularly friendly in Madrid, harboring a lingering resentment over the Spanish-American War. When he finally returned to New York aboard the German liner *Deutschland* in July 1905, W. C. Fields had been absent from the American stage for more than two years.

When "nigger singers" Jim McIntyre and Tom Heath first joined hands in 1874, they made a pact. For the sake of the act, they agreed that never, under any circumstances, would a woman be allowed to meddle or otherwise interfere in their business affairs. They also agreed, after studying the sorry fates of other partner acts, to settle all disputes with a coin toss, and to prudently set aside a portion of every week's earnings to invest in real estate. They broke into New York in 1879, playing the Bowery's London Theatre for $80 a week. Tony Pastor jumped them to $150, and by the mid-1880s they were touring the South with their own minstrel company. In vaudeville, where they were billed as the "world's greatest Ethiopian comedians," they performed a small library of routines, all featuring their familiar blackface characters, the blustery Henry (pronounced "Hennery") and the whiny, compliant Alexander. They married, bought lots of property on Long Island, and, although it was said they rarely spoke offstage, remained a team for half a century.

McIntyre and Heath had already been together nearly thirty years when Jim McIntyre wrote Fields in the fall of 1903, inviting him to do a specialty in their new show. Originally, it was to be called *Primrose, McIntyre and Heath,* but George Primrose, who was partnered with Lew Dockstader, dropped out of the project, and the show evolved into a long-form version of "The Georgia Minstrels," a popular sketch of theirs in which Henry recruits the wary Alexander as an end man. *The Ham Tree,* as the show came to be known, was described with considerable accuracy as a "musical vaudeville" crammed with ear-splitting songs, polite dances, boisterous specialties, and the barest hint of a plot. The title derived from an exchange between Alexander and Henry which centered, like most McIntyre and Heath routines, on the matter of hunger. Lost among the trees, Alex predictably turns to the subject of food and asks his partner, "How could a man find a ham sandwich in the woods?" to which Henry, the know-it-all, replies, "Drops off a ham tree!"

While still in England, Fields asked $275 a week to appear in the show, and McIntyre balked, telling him it was more than they could afford to pay.* A flurry of letters ensued, and eventually they agreed to Fields' terms, knowing their audiences, and what they liked, all too well. Rehearsals for the show, with a book by George V. Hobart and music and lyrics by William Jerome and Jean Schwartz, had already commenced when Fields arrived stateside on July 22, 1905.

*The Ham Tree* posed a major challenge for W. C. Fields. Cast as the kinetic detective Sherlock Baffles, he would be delivering lines onstage for the first time in his life. Previously, he had spoken only in ad-lib, and only for punctuation or emphasis. "He would reprimand a particular ball which had not come to his hand accurately, whip his battered silk hat for not staying on his head when it ought, mutter weird and unintelligible expletives to his cigar when it missed his mouth," recalled his friend and British agent, W. Buchanan-Taylor. Fields found the learning of lines a torture and had to work hard to avoid throwing them away—as he had always done with the audible comments he made in his act. He was the first character onstage and delivered the first lines of the show. His terror was evident during the first public performance in Rochester, on August 17, when he hurried onstage and just as quickly hurried off again. "I

---

*It is interesting to note that while they quibbled over Fields' rate, the partners themselves split a salary of $10,000 a week and collected an additional 25 percent royalty on their material.

came on, wearing a pedometer, and said, 'I've walked 968 miles.' It seemed an innocent piece of foolishness, but the audience roared. I thought I had done something wrong and had better make myself scarce, so I ran."

Baffles was always lingering at the periphery of a scene, hectoring the other characters and generally making a nuisance of himself. "I am John W. Gates—bet a million! I'm a mystery! I'm here, there, and everywhere—nobody knows who I am—and I know who everybody is. I'm covered with rubber shoes. I butt-in everywhere and nobody can put me out. I'm the best-natured man in the world, but whenever I get mad you can hear the ambulance bell. I'm six and carry two. I am—and I'm on the trail!"

Fields' specialty came at the top of the third act, in the handsome drawing room of Mrs. Nicklebacker's Fifth Avenue mansion. He worked in evening clothes and did a routine remarkably similar in setting and tone to the one performed by James A. Byrne a decade earlier. It was a high point of the show, went like wildfire, and prompted the critic for the *Rochester Evening Times* to suggest that Fields "be given more to do, more lines to speak and more 'business.'"

As *The Ham Tree* was readied for its New York opening, Hattie took the baby to Philadelphia and then, in the company of the Dukenfields, on to Atlantic City, where they stayed at the Biscayne. From the tone of their letters, there were problems between Hattie and Fields. She registered hurt at his leaving the salutation off one of his letters, and he brusquely scolded her for spending too much money. She sent him a peace offering, a book called *Sandy* by Alice Hegan Rice, and when her rheumatism flared, he gently urged her to "find some fine place where they have baths" and drive it out of her system while it was still young. "You know your Pop cashed in with it, and while I am in a position to pay for having you cured, you had better attend to it."

*The Ham Tree* opened at Klaw & Erlanger's massive New York Theatre at Broadway and Forty-fifth Street on August 28, 1905. With its eleven musical numbers and chorus of forty-eight, the show managed to fill the landmark house and its 124 boxes to capacity. Fields' part had been trimmed to keep the show to three hours, but his reviews were nonetheless outstanding. The *News,* reacting to the overall volume of the show, praised his "light and whimsical comedy method that had nothing of noise or bombast in it," while the *Globe and Commercial Advertiser* said his juggling "far surpassed in intellectuality anything in the way of lines uttered during the entire performance." Still, the show belonged to McIntyre and Heath, who had been doing this sort of thing since before he was born. Even in the most glowing of reviews, he couldn't touch them for popularity. The trade notice in the pragmatic *Clipper* put it bluntly: "Clever work was done by W. C. Fields in his bits of comedy and juggling, and there was a number of pretty stage pictures and pretty girls galore.

But McIntyre and Heath, with their old act, the old trunk, and bass drum, were what the people want to see, and they don't care a rap about anything else." Wrote Hartley Davis, "There isn't an act on the vaudeville stage so familiar as that of McIntyre and Heath, and none that is in greater demand."

Fields took a suite at the Markwell Hotel, four blocks up Broadway, and Hattie joined him there when she returned from Philadelphia with the baby in September. For the first time in their five years of marriage, they stayed comfortably put for nearly two months, Hattie regularly visiting her mother (who had turned her hand to playwriting) and Fields enjoying the relatively stress-free life of a Broadway performer. Matinees were Wednesdays and Saturdays at 2:15. There was time to sleep in, take breakfast as a family, and go on long walks in the park. Most important, there was time for a little white-haired boy who was doted upon and spoiled shamelessly. (An item in the *Clipper* identified Master W. C. Fields Jr. as the youngest possessor of a thirty-six-inch Taylor trunk "which alone carries his wardrobe and a collection of toys he got while abroad.") Fields declined an engagement at the London Hippodrome, ostensibly because he was having such a good time in New York, but also because it had been rumored that Klaw & Erlanger had a show for him—a starring show—after the first of the year.

*The Ham Tree* was set to go on tour in November, and Hattie, having sampled family life as non-theatricals lived it, adamantly refused to go back to living out of a trunk. Fields chided her at first, figuring she'd come around as she always had in the past, but as the date drew closer she grew more obstinate, and any pretense of marital harmony went quickly out the window. When *The Ham Tree* opened in Pittsburgh, on November 26, Hattie and the boy were still ensconced at the Markwell—and the tone of Fields' letters, always loving and solicitous, had suddenly turned ice cold.

*Five*

# *Watch Your Step*

Fields settled into a solitary winter touring *The Ham Tree,* playing weeks, split weeks, and one-night stands, riding the owl train again as if he had never left burlesque. The show was designed for travel, with four simple sets and a scaled-back chorus, but the task of moving it from town to town was still considerable. Most cities, excepting a few in the East, permitted Sunday performances, and it was only when the company hit places like Philadelphia, Baltimore, and Washington, D.C., that the cast enjoyed a day off. He dutifully sent money to Hattie, rebutting her "bombast" in his accompanying letters and complaining bitterly when she didn't answer him promptly. Where before he had always signed off "love to you both," he now pointedly ended his letters, "love to my boy," and wrote the words "your husband" in place of "Sod." Sometimes he addressed the boy directly, as if to alert the toddler to some possible chicanery. "Wired your ma twenty five for you," he advised in a Christmas telegram. "See that you get something nice or start a bank account."

Hattie knew the theatrical lifestyle when she married her husband, knew constant travel was part of the deal and that home would always be some dingy hotel room in an unfamiliar city. She was better off as part of the act, but now there was the boy to consider, and her intransigence was often couched in terms of his best interests. It was as if she really believed this ambitious and talented man, with at best a grade school education, would abruptly give up an income of $275 a week—at a time when whole families were comfortable on $30—and quit the performing life to settle down in one place and have more kids and a stable, respectable job. "I loved children and wanted more than Claude," she said sadly, "and he had other ideas and lived an entirely different life." By refusing to travel, she denied her husband the company of the wife he so adored and the child who was now the center of his life. Yet, being a Catholic, a divorce for her was out of the question. It was an untenable situation, a betrayal of the marriage vows, and Fields, at the age of twenty-five, reacted with an anger that was both righteous and unremitting. She stood firm, irrational in her uncertainty and terror, and egged on—as Fields' letters sometimes imply—by her own domineering mother, Lizzie Hughes, who, as long as they remained in New York, had unlimited access to the only grandchild she would ever know.

After the first of the year, Hattie abandoned the Markwell and went to live with the Dukenfields in Philadelphia. She made a disruptive presence of herself, taking every opportunity to carp about her husband's stubbornness and his miserly ways. By April, Jim Dukenfield had become concerned enough to write to his son, but Fields, as the recipient of weekly harangues from Hattie, had grown tired of her moans. "Regarding a certain person," he said in reply, "I don't care to know any more about her, and am positive Mother gave her all she gave Mother."

Walter was with him, and the two were in Hartford when *The Ham Tree* laid off for the summer. Fields dragged his pool table out of storage and hit the Keith circuit for a couple of months, stopping in Philadelphia in June and putting up at the same tiny house on Marshall Street where Hattie was staying. He snapped pictures of the family, his wife posed primly with the baby in the center of each shot, surrounded by Kate and Jim and Roy and the girls, and, in some shots, even their revered uncle Will. The tension between Hattie and Fields was palpable, and their being under the same roof for a week caused an uncomfortable strain for all. Fields returned to *The Ham Tree* in July, settling back into Klaw & Erlanger's New York Theatre through August, then making his way to Toronto, where the tour officially picked up again on the third of September.

It was during the second season of *The Ham Tree* that Fields began traveling with another woman. Maude Fendick was the same age as Fields, a hairdresser he brought over from England. Exactly when she entered the picture is uncertain, but it was an oft-repeated legend about Fields that when he discovered another music hall performer using his material, he retaliated by having an affair with the man's wife. Eddie Cantor directly quotes Fields on the subject in his 1957 autobiography, and George Burns told a similar tale, although he had the British comedian Harry Tate stealing Fields' wife away—an unlikely scenario—and Fields responding by lifting some of Tate's material. Those in the *Ham Tree* company who had come to know and like Hattie disapproved of the arrangement, and it wasn't long before word got back to her. Comedienne Belle Gold, who played the blackface maid Desdemona in the show, kept up a running correspondence with Hattie and was apparently the first to advise her that Fields was registering Maude at hotels along the route as Mrs. W. C. Fields. Hattie, at a loss over what to do, kept the knowledge to herself.

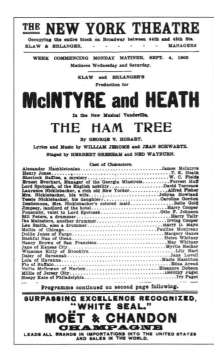

*The Ham Tree had a long life on the road under the management of Klaw & Erlanger, then John Cort bought the show and revived it in 1913.*

With Maude on the scene, Hattie softened the rhetoric between them, and by the end of the tour, she was coyly ghosting letters for her son, expressing the boy's love for his father (and, by insinuation, her own) and having Fields play along, compliantly responding in kind. "I am more than pleased to know you love Papa so and always want to see him. And I assure you Papa feels the same about his son. I am very proud of my little boy."

Fields stuck with *The Ham Tree* through the rest of the 1906–07 season, playing San Francisco and Los Angeles and the Deep South, and finally leaving the show for good when the season closed at Plainfield on May 11. Returning to Manhattan, he took a booking on the roof of the New York Theatre, where *The Ham Tree* had resided and where, five stories above Broadway, producer Florenz Ziegfeld was now inaugurating a policy of vaudeville. The New York, originally known as the Olympia, was part of a block-long entertainment complex built by Oscar Hammerstein in 1895. It contained two huge auditoriums, a concert hall, an oriental café, and, below street level, a bowling alley. Atop all this sat the glass-enclosed roof garden, spanning the entire length of the building and seating nearly a thousand. The flamboyant Ziegfeld, recently returned

*With son Claude, circa 1907*

from Paris and now, by his own admission, flat broke, renamed the place *Jardin de Paris* and imported a series of "living pictures" from London as its opening attraction.

The first night, May 27, 1907, was a rainy Monday, but the New York Roof was still packed with customers eager to examine the British cast, who, in various states of undress, posed in simulation of twelve works of art and statuary.

There were several nudes, but most of the applause was held for Gainsborough's "Duchess of Devonshire." The surrounding acts fared better than the pictures, even though Fields himself had an off night and, by the account of *Variety*'s Sime Silverman, "misses more than is bargained for, and persists in continuing the attempts after the house has lost interest." Fields remained with Ziegfeld, who didn't seem to find him particularly funny, through most of June. The next attraction on the New York Roof would be Ziegfeld's *Follies of 1907,* a new kind of revue that dressed burlesque up in jewels and evening wear and took New York by storm. It would be another eight years before the paths of the two men would cross again.

Hattie had hoped that when Fields returned to New York he would stay with them and that the love and affection they still harbored for one another would somehow be rekindled. But Fields remained aloof, living near the theater in an apartment with Maude and only occasionally coming to call. "I didn't know what he was going to do," said Hattie, "and I waited, and I didn't say very much about it either, but we never had any violent quarrels. . . . I just waited. I would ask him, 'When are you coming again?' and he would give me a definite date or say, 'I can't come tomorrow; I'm doing a new trick and I'm practicing,' or 'We have a rehearsal,' or something like that."

Fields played vaudeville in and around New York, boldly announcing plans at one point for an ambitious tour of the Orient. Bookings were set for Honolulu, Yokohama, Shanghai, Hong Kong, Manila, Singapore, Rangoon, Calcutta, and Bombay, and he had assembled a company that included British comedienne Renata Maud and dancer Carolyn Gordon, the female lead of *The Ham Tree.* Hattie was alarmed at the prospect of a lengthy tour, for Fields told Tom Heath he would be gone for three years. If he took Maude with him, as in all probability he would, Hattie feared it would mean the end of their marriage. "This woman has him completely under her control," Belle Gold warned, "and he will do anything she asks. . . . [I]f you permit him to leave this country, he will in all probability secure a divorce in England or the continent on the grounds of desertion."

The plan was evidently scuttled by logistical problems and Fields' own lingering distaste for touring a company on foreign soil. In August 1907, Fields spent some recreational time in Philadelphia and wrote to Hattie, asking that she bring the boy to him. She took special care in preparing herself for the occasion, with new clothes and a new hairstyle, and had the satisfaction, when he finally laid eyes on her, of seeing him stare, openmouthed. "Perhaps if you ask him to come back, now that he thinks you are looking so well, and is behaving more like a man, you might gain your paint and get him to leave her," Belle Gold advised after Hattie had related the incident in a letter. "I am afraid, if I had been in your place, I would have 'queered' myself by asking what Maud[e] would say if she knew how he was acting. You must have considerable willpower to be able to keep your tongue between your teeth."


By fall, Fields was touring for Klaw & Erlanger. The old act was comfortable and familiar to the critics, but the business of vaudeville was changing. The new vogue was for continuous performances and "Advanced Vaudeville" that put opera singers, sketch artists, celebrities, and imported companies of actors and singers—many of whom had never set foot on a vaudeville stage—ahead of traditional fare. He saw a lot of acts that were considered the mainstays of vaudeville just a few years earlier—the blackface, Irish, German, and Hebrew comics, the clog dancers and banjo players—relegated to the Columbia burlesque wheel or put out of work entirely. And he found himself billed under such nonvaudevillians as James J. Corbett, who spoke an awkward monologue about his exploits in the ring; the Romany Operatic Troupe, which sang "gems" from popular grand operas; and actor W. H. Thompson and Company. In fact, Fields realized he was now virtually unknown to a large segment of the audience that had fueled vaudeville's most recent growth. He also found himself under attack from competitors who were either lifting his material outright or accusing him of stealing theirs. Jim Harrigan, who saw no mystery in the origins of Fields' tramp juggling act, once waited for him in front of Miner's Bowery after a performance. According to O. K. Sato, another juggler, Fields made a hasty exit out the back door, armed to the teeth in the event he was caught. He managed to elude Harrigan during his various tours of England—where the "original" tramp juggler was already an established attraction—but then a feud erupted in the pages of the *Clipper* when an American juggling team, Lavine and Leonard, played the London Palace for the first time and performed a variation of Fields' own pool table routine. "Yes, Harrigan the Tramp Juggler presented to us the Pool Table Trick," they boasted in an ad. It was followed by another, signed by Harrigan himself, confirming the appropriation and asking, "How does it feel?"

Fields, to his credit, refused to get suckered in by the older man's taunts. He maintained that Harrigan and he were the best of friends and likened their brief altercation to a "lovers' quarrel." In another few years, Harrigan would retire from the stage altogether, becoming the president of the Empire Sand Company in Buffalo, New York. In 1912, while playing Mike Shea's theater there, Fields would be invited to dine at the Harrigan home and, still later, in 1943, twenty years after Harrigan's death, he would admit privately, in a letter to a friend, that Harrigan's act was indeed the basis of his own. "I think he accused me of filching some of his tricks, and now that I give the matter more consideration, I know he was right, but like the big man he was, he forgave me."

Of far greater concern to Fields than Harrigan's belated accusations of piracy was the theft of his own genuinely original bits, both at home and in Europe. Fields referred to the thieves as "nibblers," even though, in some cases, they stole the entire act. "There was a time when he was the most copied man in the whole world of variety," Buchanan-Taylor recalled. "Dozens battened on his style and inventiveness. One, a German, not only stole his makeup and his routine (avoiding the tricks that were uncopyable), but his lithographic poster as well. . . . When I saw it on the boardings in Germany, the name W. C. Fields had been excised and another name substituted." Fields took indignant ads out in the trade papers—as did dozens of other performers—declaring such bits to be his and warning of dire consequences should he learn of others doing them.* Such tactics had a limited effect, however, and it was pointless, due to the expense and time involved, to take the infringers to court.

The pressure to keep the act fresh was constant, but Fields always managed to deliver the goods. "It doesn't make any difference how many times you see W. C. Fields, the juggler," *Variety*'s Dash Freeman wrote, "he will always have a little something to show that was not there the last time." As a boy, J. B. Priestley saw him perform in Bradford, West Yorkshire, and a simple enhancement Fields had made to the cigar box routine stayed with him for decades. "He was very funny even then, and I seem to remember him balancing a number of cigar boxes and staring with horror at a peculiar box, in the middle of the pile, that wobbled strangely, as if some influence were at work. All his confidence, which you guessed from the first to be a desperate bluff, vanished at the sight of this one diabolical box, which began to threaten him with the nightmare of hostile and rebellious things."

Fields was settling into a comfortable pattern of summer trips to England, where the halls were open, the audiences good, and the jumps relatively brief. Moreover, the ocean voyages afforded him time to read and relax. Already he had learned the promotional value of self-portraiture, doodling stiff little cartoons of himself on the backs of envelopes and feeding them to the local papers. The British press seemed to find him good copy, and he obliged by giving interviews in which he emphasized his British heritage and exaggerated his childhood to Dickensian extremes. He found that giving a journalist a good story counted for more than simply telling the truth, and interviews and feature

---

*In one such ad, Fields claimed a piece of business in which he took curtains by walking offstage as the curtain rose, and walking on as it descended—apparently forgetting that he himself had stolen the bit. Sime Silverman diplomatically waited a year before identifying pantomimist Joe Jackson as the true originator.

profiles were cheaper than paid advertising. Many feature writers doubled as critics, and staying on good terms with them usually ensured a friendly notice.

Fields always traveled with a trunkful of books, an eclectic mix of popular and classical fare that belied his public image as an uneducated man. "In the three decades of our friendship, we have never stopped swapping books," "Bucky" Taylor wrote in 1942. "Before O. Henry had been published in England, I received the works of that supreme story-teller from Fields. He introduced me also to Rex Beach, George Ade, Irvin S. Cobb, Stewart Edward White, Eugene O'Neill, Theodore Dreiser, and many others." Fields' own traveling library, which he reconstructed from memory in 1934, included a Webster's dictionary, several books on grammatical construction, translations of Homer, Ovid, and Virgil, and copies of Dickens, Thackeray, Shakespeare, Ben Jonson, Milton, Thomas Paine, Washington Irving, and, of course, Mark Twain. He also carried his own hand-lettered dictionary, a loose-leaf notebook in which he recorded words he found particularly interesting, sounding them out in capital letters (PAN-E-GYRIZE, PA-NEG-Y-RIS, PER-TI-NA-CIOUS) and adding terse definitions to guide their usage.

Fields used books to assuage his loneliness on the road, retreating into one between shows and rarely acknowledging the surrounding commotion. "No one ever knew him," said Marty Lynch, another juggler of the period. "I was playing in London a long time, and so was Fields, at different theatres, and all the performers used to gather after their shows at the German Club on Lisle Street, in back of the Hippodrome. Fields would be there too, but all alone always, sitting at a table, reading and drinking, all alone. I would ask different actors if they knew him. Well, I met a few that played on bills with him, but hardly anyone knew him, to speak to."

Fields preferred the company of nonperformers, and in 1907 had become a Full Mason. "An actor has not the time in which to meet people and make close friends, as does the man in business life," he noted. "I used to fill in the lonely times with reading. One day I happened to pick up a book in which was the story of those workmen who built Solomon's Temple. . . . And how these masons kept in contact with one another, how they became organized, and when a brother mason was traveling from one locality to another, he was received, entertained, and taken care of by another brother mason. The significance and beauty of the whole thing dawned upon me. That was just the sort of thing I needed, so I joined a lodge as soon as I returned to my home town."

At the E. Coppee Mitchell Lodge in Philadelphia, one of Fields' recommenders was Will Felton, who had taken his own degrees in 1900. Fields could not have been prouder to join fraternal hands with his uncle Will, who had always set an impossibly high standard for integrity, and who had risen from

*William C. Felton, circa 1910. Kate Dukenfield can
be glimpsed through the doorway.*

street huckster to deputy sheriff to inspector for the Department of Public
Works, and, finally, to the office of chief of the infamously corrupt Bureau of
Street Cleaning under reform mayor John Weaver. Due to Fields' time on the
road—he was stopping in *The Ham Tree*—the mayor arranged for him to be
entered, crafted, and raised in one evening.* Weaver's flirtation with independence was brief, however, and Felton was returned to the inspector's position—
and the bureau to business as usual—when his term expired in 1908. It was the
buffeting his upright uncle took in the business of hardball politics that
prompted Fields to begin referring to Philadelphia as the "City of Brotherly
Graft." It sealed his fate as a political cynic: "I think Philadelphia was the first
town where the bosses all were contractors or in cahoots with contractors." For
the rest of his life, he was adamantly opposed to any and all political incum-
bencies. "I never vote *for* anybody," he once told his friend Gene Fowler. "I
always vote against."

---

*In due course, he also joined the Lambs Club, the New York Athletic Club, the Holly-
wood Athletic Club, the Masquers, and the Kiwanis.

Even as the affair with Maude Fendick continued, Hattie held out hope for a reconciliation. "I was rather naive in those days," she admitted. "I did my best—when Claude was very young and Mr. Fields wasn't too far away by train, we'd go and spend the weekend with him. I thought maybe this added up to something." She took an apartment at 706 Amsterdam and couldn't understand why he wouldn't give the marriage a second chance. "I questioned him and I said, 'Why haven't you come back? This is your home,' and we had in New York a little apartment, and most of the time he would cry. He just said, 'No,' and then he would cry and then he would play with the little fellow, and sometimes he would ask me, 'Let me take him out.' "

Fields and Maude Fendick were still together in 1910 when Halley's comet was spotted and the world mourned the death of Mark Twain. The relationship was on the wane, however, and he played England and France without her. Fields was in Chicago at the end of 1912 when Maude finally broke it off. "There are three women in your life," she wrote, referring to both Hattie and a new girl with whom he had taken up. "One, I'm afraid, is a barnacle that you'll never rid yourself of. The last, by all evidence, is the one you wish to cling to. And so I'm going to step out of it as quietly as possible."

Hattie had long since given up on the marriage, Claude being their only point of mutual interest, but when she announced in 1910 that she was taking him to California to ensure "every advantage for the welfare and education of our boy," her correspondence with her husband sank to an acrimonious new low. Fields, who was sending her $35 a week, refused to pay any relocation expenses. "Isn't there a school this side of the Sierras?" he demanded. "Don't quote that cheap literature. Tell the truth, once in a while anyway! You are going just to prove to May and your social circles that you can go. You are not thinking so much of Claude's education, or else you would take care of your pennies. Money is the only thing that will buy an education for him."

As hateful as Fields' relationship with Hattie could sometimes be, he was unfailingly gentle with their little boy. His treatment of his son came in marked contrast to the rough handling he gave his brother Leroy, who was only nine years older than Claude and never really qualified as a sibling in the way Walter did. Roy was more like an orphan left on the doorstep, a pet for Kate amid the attrition of her household. She babied him shamelessly, and there was a suspicion within the family that Roy wasn't all that bright. Fields' patience with him was decidedly limited, and he used to keep Roy tethered to a tree in Penns Grove so he wouldn't walk off the dock and fall into the lake behind the house.

Walter, the practical joker in the family, once asked Roy to check the coffee pot to see if it was hot, and he obligingly did so by grasping it firmly with both hands.

When he was older, Roy asked his eldest brother for a bicycle, and in the rough tradition of the Dukenfield clan, Fields took him to Wanamaker's to buy one. Out back of the store, in an alley known as Juniper Street, he steadied the boy on the new bike, gave him a shove, and told him if he could stay on he could keep it. Roy sustained his balance long enough to be granted full title, then crashed noisily to the ground. Emboldened, he petitioned his brother for a motorcycle, a request that was summarily denied. "If I want you killed," came the reply, "I'll do it myself!" Roy was seventeen, playing baseball at Philadelphia's Central High, when the family was hit with the death of Jim Dukenfield, on April 15, 1913.

Jim had settled into a comfortable retirement, enjoying his summers at Penns Grove, toasting his pension of $18 a month, and tending to a thoroughbred racing horse he kept in the stable out back of the house. "He never raced it, but he had it," Leroy said. "The first snow up at Valley Green Inn, the first sleigh that gets there gets a bottle of wine. He always tried to get that." In light of his father's illness, Fields curtailed his bookings, taking cut weeks to remain nearby, and held off the start of an overseas tour. The old man was now a frail shadow of his former self, placid and oddly compliant as the cancer ate away at him. He had grown to be enormously proud of his son's success, the comradery and honor that came from his Civil War service, the relative affluence he had achieved after a lifetime of struggle. Fields had him buried in the family plot at Greenwood Cemetery, a GAR insignia adorning his grave. He attended the funeral, according to a cousin, in the company of a beautiful French girl, and when he sailed for Europe the following month aboard the *Kaiser Wilhelm II,* it was presumably she who appeared on the passengers' manifest as "Mrs. W. C. Fields."

Fields remained a standard act in vaudeville, even as he sought to distance himself from the confining label of juggler. "I wanted to become a real comedian," he said, "and there I was, ticketed and pigeonholed as merely a comedy juggler." In 1910 he began billing himself as "the Silent Humorist," and by 1912 he was making some headway. "He is a juggler who is a real comedian," wrote Waldemar Young, "and a comedian who is a real juggler. His equal as the possessor of these two talents does not exist in the realm of the two-a-day. In his own line, to put it differently, Fields is the best in the world, bar none, and I want to drive that fact home and make it stick."

The real turn for Fields came in 1913, when he was invited to appear at the

*Self-portrait, 1913*

New York Palace on the same bill as Madame Sarah Bernhardt. The great actress was touring vaudeville for Martin Beck, who had made headlines the previous year by offering her a heart-stopping $7,000 a week.* At age sixty-eight, hobbled by a bad knee, Bernhardt was one of the most famous theatrical figures in the world. Her contract with Beck prohibited animals, jugglers, and

---

*This was at a time when salaries ranged from $2,500 to $4,000 a week for top draws like Elsie Janis, Eva Tanguay, and Nora Bayes.

acrobats on the bill, and she had final approval of all surrounding acts. At the Palace, she appeared before a largely Continental audience—the "Marseillaise" was played at the start, and half the crowd instantly rose to their feet—but if the bill was appropriately dignified, it was also quite lifeless.

At the start of Bernhardt's third week at the Palace, the Monday matinee began with Italian musical turns in both the first and second positions, and she refused to play the evening performance until the conflict was resolved. The Bernivici Brothers, who opened the show, were let out of their contract, and Fields, who had just finished a week at Hammerstein's, five blocks away, was engaged to replace them. Bernhardt was evidently familiar with his work, for when his name was broached, with the caveat that he was, unfortunately, a juggler, she replied that although her objection to jugglers held, she could not disapprove of Fields because "such an artiste could not fail to please the best class of audience." He stepped into the No. 3 spot on two hours' notice and delivered a performance that, in the words of Sime Silverman, "fitted the Palace as though built for it." Bernhardt herself struggled through twenty-three minutes of *Lucretia Borgia,* moving delicately between objects to either lean or sit upon, but was cheered nonetheless. Her third week at the Palace grossed an impressive $22,000, at a top ticket price of $2 a head.

Fields left for England within a week of the Palace engagement, and was touring the provinces when it was announced that Madame Bernhardt's sixty-ninth birthday would be celebrated at a performance before the king and queen. Britain's foremost musical comedy artists were expected to participate, and twelve of England's greatest composers were being asked to occupy the conductor's podium for fifteen minutes apiece. "It will probably be the greatest entertainment ever put together—greatest in point of importance through the list of artists that will appear," *Variety* enthused. That same issue reported that Fields had been approved by Bernhardt to appear on the bill when she played a month's stand at the Coliseum, bracketing the royal event on October 11. The performance began at 8:30, and it was nearly midnight before the spectacular parade of comics, actors, singers, and musicians ended with the playing of the French and British anthems. Presentations followed, and Fields, who had done his signature pool table routine, was honored—along with Bernhardt, Ellen Terry, Harry Tate, George Robey, Yvette Guilbert, Robert Hale, and a score of others—with a personal word of appreciation from George V. Fields would later describe the event, coming as it did only six months after the death of his English-born father, as the peak of his variety career.

In the afterglow of the royal performance, Fields accepted an offer to play Australia again, even though Harry Rickards was now dead and the time lost in transit deplorable—four weeks to South Africa, another three to Sydney, then seven home. He spent the month of December in Paris, playing the

Alhambra with his friend Harry Fragson, the influential Anglo-French come-dian who sang "All the Girls Are Lovely by the Seaside." A genuine Cockney, Fragson had a Belgian father in the early stages of senile dementia. By the man's later testimony, the father had grown jealous over a girl his son was see-ing and, on New Year's Eve, produced a gun and threatened to kill himself—a proposal that Fragson, weary of his father's increasingly irrational behavior, apparently greeted with a measure of enthusiasm. Enraged, the father abruptly turned the weapon on his son and fired a single shot into the back of his head. Fields was in the middle of his act on the stage of the Alhambra when a com-motion backstage brought the performance to a halt. The house manager emerged from the wings to announce that Harry Fragson had been killed by his father, and as Fields gazed out over the packed house in a state of shock, the audience, thinking it was a joke, burst into laughter.

Shaken by the Fragson murder, Fields left for Johannesburg in the foulest of moods. He dreaded the South African leg of the journey, even as it made the trip to Australia feasible. There was tension between him and his traveling com-panion, as evinced in his testy communiqués with Hattie. "Aren't you afraid people will point you out as the wife of a juggler if you continue to put 'From Mrs. W. C. Fields' at the back of your envelopes?" he asked in a letter from Paris. She ignored the comment, and he underscored his next reference to the matter with a threat: "Please drop that 'Mrs. W. C. Fields' on the back of the envelope. Just put Hattie Fields—I like it better. A little thing like that might make me forget to send you my route." Still later, in an Australian interview, the "Mrs. Fields" he was traveling with complained about his "wanderlust" and said she would prefer that he "stayed home and raised a family." Clearly, the relationship with this woman was not to survive the trip.

The pair arrived in Johannesburg in late January and found the city in the throes of a general strike and under martial law. The music halls were closed, and two companies were lying idle. "The place is full of grim-faced Boers with double-barreled guns and thickly-bearded faces," Fields reported in a letter to a friend. "They pass the lonely hours waiting for trouble by vying with each other to look the dirtiest. It is now eight o'clock and the quiet is absolutely appalling. Not a soul on the streets except soldiers and policemen with guns slung over their shoulders. They stand about in groups and remain perfectly silent. The railway is guarded by burghers all the way from Cape Town."

Work was irregular, and though Fields managed to get paid on the last day of January, he was in misery and plagued by the recurrent illness—"grippe"—that afflicted him through much of his adult life. To Hattie, he described eating food that "would not tempt the palate of a respectable canine" and moaned that his expenses alone "would eat up a year's savings." Earning a living at the age of thirty-four was getting progressively tougher for him, and he yearned for another shot at the legitimate stage. "My lot isn't a bed of hollyhocks and every year the task becomes more difficult, and I am not getting younger." He played his time in Durban, Germiston, and Pretoria, but was happy to be done with the place when he sailed for Australia in March 1914. From Sydney, Fields jumped to Melbourne and then Adelaide. He spent the month of July reading of the mounting tensions that stemmed from the assassination of Archduke Ferdinand at Sarajevo, on June 28, and then of the shelling, on July 29, of Belgrade and the eruption of war between Russia, France, Germany, and Great Britain. On August 10, as he was sailing the Great Australian Bight to Fremantle, Britain formally declared war on Austria-Hungary and all traffic emanating from Australian ports suddenly became subject to hostilities. "On account of the European war, I may have some difficulty getting money to you," Fields warned Hattie in a letter. "I hope you will be able to realize enough on your jewels to tide you over for a few weeks in case it is necessary. I tried to cable money from Adelaide, but the offices refused to take the money on account of the war."

He had planned to jump from Perth to Ceylon, and from there to India, where he had six weeks arranged in Bombay, Calcutta, and Madras, but on the first day out, his steamer was intercepted by the German cruiser *Emden*—which had been ravaging British shipping in the Indian Ocean—and chased back into port. His only hope for work would be to return to the United States as quickly as possible. "From the time I left England to go to Africa, I did not know what a contented mind used to be. They had me sweating blood." On August 29, Fields and his companion sailed for San Francisco aboard the TSS *Ventura,* an arduous journey that took forty-one days. He was alone by the time he reached Philadelphia, where he maintained his business address at the home of his mother. It was there that an extraordinary offer of work found him.

At that time, Charles B. Dillingham was America's leading producer of musical comedy. A respected drama critic before he made the transition to manager under the aegis of Charles Frohman, Dillingham had a particular passion for the people of vaudeville. By 1914 his shows had featured such variety favorites as Elsie Janis, Blanche Ring, Louise Dresser, Eva Tanguay, Nat Wills, Walter Kelly ("the Virginia Judge"), Nora Bayes, and the team of Dave Montgomery and Fred Stone, who had started with him in 1906 and continued until Montgomery's death in 1917. "He was what, in those days, we called a swell," Stone said of Dillingham. "Dapper, meticulously dressed, his hat always tilted a little over one eye, he was a unique figure in the theatre. He knew more of the important society people than any other producer, but he preferred the company of prize fighters."

Dillingham had opened *Chin-Chin,* the story of Aladdin, at the Globe Theatre in New York, and had another show in preparation for the New Amsterdam. Conceived as a showcase for the acclaimed ballroom dance team of Vernon and Irene Castle, *Watch Your Step* was destined to make theatrical history as the first show with music and lyrics throughout by Irving Berlin, the famed composer of "Alexander's Ragtime Band." The surrounding cast would include Frank Tinney, Harry Kelly, and Elizabeth Murray, all well known to vaudeville audiences. Ever conscious of bolstering the plots of his musicals with well-regarded specialties, Dillingham added Fields to the mix as well. The part wouldn't be as showy or as significant as the one he had played for Klaw & Erlanger in *The Ham Tree,* but the offer was a godsend nonetheless. After nearly fifty days of travel, Fields was tired, in need of money, and facing a domestic vaudeville market hit hard by an unseasonable spell of hot weather. Salary cuts had been initiated by a committee of managers, and the $400 a week Dillingham was offering was substantially better than the rate Fields was likely to command on the two-a-day. The deal was set by November 7, when Bruce Edwards, Dillingham's general manager, cabled Fields at his Marshall Street address requesting pictures.

*Watch Your Step* was set for its first public performance at the Empire Theatre in Syracuse on November 25, 1914, but the show refused to jell and the mood around the company was grim. "I went to church this morning and burned candles for the success of this piece," Elizabeth Murray told the librettist, Harry B. Smith, "but, personally, I think it will be a [goddamned] failure." Irene Castle blithely disparaged such prognostications of doom, even as she reportedly contributed to the atmosphere with her heavy-handed wielding of a star's prerogative. "From the very beginning, *Watch Your Step* was a sure thing," she insisted, "and everybody connected with the show knew it, even before it opened. . . . I couldn't imagine what everybody was so nervous about."

A private train carried the cast to Syracuse, where the curtain rose the first night on sixteen secretaries seated at sixteen identical typewriters, tapping out the first of twenty-five new Berlin tunes. This syncopated "law office de danse" set the stage for the reading of a will which bequeathed a $2 million inheritance to any relative who could avoid falling in love. Vernon Castle was Joseph Lilyburn, the principal claimant, and Renee Gratz, as Ernesta Hardacre, his rival for the estate. Mrs. Castle made her entrance halfway though the first act, bellowing out the refrain to the song "Show Us How to Do the Fox Trot" ("You'll have to watch your step . . .") in a voice that, she later admitted, had all the subtle qualities of "a foghorn at sea."

When the audience recovered from the shock of the willowy Irene Castle's low-throated phrasings, the scene reverted to an unusual automat where, instead of sandwiches and slices of pie, sections dispensed such unlikely items as escorts, umbrellas, affinities, ladies' hats, and cigars. Elizabeth Brice and

Charles King sang the pleasant "When I Discovered You" and then, at the conclusion of the number, poked a nickel into one of the slots, causing Fields and his pool table to be dispensed through a door in the wall. Nothing was particularly special about what he did that night, but the gloss that came from ten years' experience in performing the routine was enough for *Variety* to declare him "the individual hit of the evening."

Act 2 opened with the most popular song of the show, "Let's Settle Down in a One-Horse Town," and continued with Elizabeth Murray's Irish specialty. Frank Tinney, in blackface as a doorman at the Metropolitan Opera, didn't make his entrance until 10:30, but scored heavily with the first of two monologues. The second act ended with the clever "Old Operas in a New Way," in which Berlin ragged familiar themes from Verdi while the ghost of the great composer loudly protested, pleading with the chorus not to "hurdy-gurdy Mr. Verdi." It brought the house down, and Berlin was forced to take a curtain call so the performance could continue. The third act contained the one Berlin song of the show that has become a true standard, "Play a Simple Melody." Tinney made his second appearance at 11:20, and by the time the surprisingly simple finale had played itself out, it was well past midnight. Berlin came onstage for yet another ovation, and the notices the next day were uniformly fine.

Dillingham's gamble on a Tin Pan Alley composer had paid off handsomely; *Watch Your Step* would change the face of musical comedy for all time. Fields was jubilant. After the toughest year he had ever spent as a performer, he was the "undoubted hit" in the initial performance of a groundbreaking new musical. He had managed to jump from vaudeville to the legitimate stage at a time when salaries on the circuits were at an all-time low, and was now assured of a comfortable six-month run at one of the most prestigious of all Broadway venues. He treated himself to a quiet meal and slept better that night than he had slept in months. The next morning, Thanksgiving Day, 1914, he was fired.

# Six

# The Main Stem

While the war raged, the European market was effectively closed to American acts. The resulting glut of talent drove prices down and made work harder to come by. Competition was fierce, and moving pictures, which had been part of most every vaudeville bill for nearly a decade, were drawing crowds to fancy theaters that no longer featured live acts, just films. The days when picture companies roamed the country like nomadic tribes, rolling into towns with brass bands and lady orchestras and stretching sheets between trees on which to project their reels, were over. Movies were a very real threat to the survival of variety; New York's first prominent arcade, which opened on Fourteenth Street in 1904, was ominously called Automatic Vaudeville.

Fields had been traveling too long and too far afield to fully appreciate the impact movies were having on the domestic market for live entertainment, but when he saw how rates had plummeted and time had dried up, he considered the offer from Charles Dillingham—and the move to legitimate—a stroke of unbelievably good fortune. Getting fired after a single performance was a terrific blow, and Dillingham was maddeningly evasive as to why he had been dropped. "The pool table is too big," he said uncomfortably. "We have to cut down." It was only years later, at a party in Hollywood, that Fields learned what actually had happened: "Ran into Irving Berlin out here one evening and we got talking of old days, and he said, 'Bill, did you ever find out why you didn't stay with the Dillingham show? I'll tell you. Tinney and the Castles read the reviews the next day and got sore. They made up their minds they weren't going to play second fiddle to a juggler, and they told Dillingham it was either you or they'd quit. That's what happened.' "

The cut was generally assumed to have been made for pacing and length, and Sime Silverman said as much, noting that Fields' specialty, good as it was, slowed up the first act. From a comfortable distance, Fields himself had to admit that was true: "[Dillingham] had to do what he thought was right by the show. It wasn't his fault. But it wasn't mine either." Dillingham, who genuinely admired Fields, didn't try settling the contract, as most producers would have done. "Go back to New York, if you like, and draw your salary," he told Fields. "Or stay right with the show and we'll have a high time together." After having just steeled himself for a fight with one of the most powerful of all New York producers, Fields was taken aback by the offer. "I came as near blubbering then as I ever did," he said. "There never was a whiter guy than Charlie Dillingham."

Hattie, oblivious to the crisis, peppered her estranged husband with demands for more money, claiming she needed furniture for a new apartment in Brooklyn. Dillingham, fortunately, was true to his word and arranged to book Fields on the two-a-day, making up the difference between the fees he could get and the $400 a week he had guaranteed. He even spoke of mounting another show in which Fields would be the key attraction, keeping his itinerant juggler's spirits up even as he returned him to the grind of the small-time circuits. "Have a partial route from [Canadian] United [Theatres]," Fields reported in a hopeful letter to Hattie on December 12, "so may be able to help you with furniture suggestions in a few weeks." The Canadians paid the Dillingham office $350 a week and, after two weeks, came back with an offer to cover the full twenty-week commitment, but Fields resisted the idea. "I do not wish to establish my salary at $350 a week with the United Booking Office," he wrote Bruce Edwards from Ottawa. "After I finish these 20 weeks I wish to make a fresh contract with them. I couldn't afford to play the Orpheum circuit for the salary mentioned on the slip containing my route. I would be out-of-pocket after some of the railroad fares and excess baggage was paid."

Though Fields was never in the really big money in vaudeville, he worked almost constantly and, between the United States and Europe, could book more time than most American acts. Still, as a journeyman entertainer at $400 a week, he had considerable expenses to cover. Every theater was a separate corporation and required a separate contract. From his weekly check, the house deducted a 5 percent commission for the circuit and another 5 for the Buckner Agency in New York, which handled his affairs. The $320 that remained had to cover living expenses, tips for the stage crew, travel, and charges for excess baggage. In addition, he carried an assistant—either his brother Walter or a man named Ed Roach—whose travel and salary had to be paid as well. Then, of course, came Hattie's stipend, usually $35 a week, sometimes $25 when things weren't going so well. And a little something extra for his mother. With Scotch economy, he could save as much as $5,000 in a good year, but not every year was a good year.

The Dillingham contract was an Equity contract, and all travel expenses, baggage, and assistant's fees were covered under the agreement. The routes were hard—sometimes the only work available was in "cut" houses that paid as little as $150 for a split week—but Fields kept working, kept to the road, kept looking for another break. To Dillingham he wrote: "I am greatly pleased to know the *Watch Your Step* show has been such a colossal success. Hope you will continue to pack 'em in all winter." He went on to say how he had declined an offer to go into the Shubert Brothers' new show at the Winter Garden because the money wasn't particularly good. "Am doing nicely here this week," he continued, "but there is a vast difference between vaudeville and being with Mr. Charles B. Dillingham's company. However, as you say, 'Things are coming out all right sometime, somewhere, somehow.' " The Shuberts finally came to Fields' terms—$400 a week for fifteen weeks—but Fields wondered tactfully if Dillingham "felt safe" placing him with the Shuberts instead of back again in vaudeville. Disappointingly, Dillingham replied that he was pleased with the arrangement, and Bruce Edwards chimed in with some notable advantages: "It keeps you in New York without traveling and, as you are sure to make a hit, you will probably be there next year, or with the traveling company next year." Clearly, there would be no Dillingham show in Fields' immediate future, so he committed, without enthusiasm, to the Winter Garden Show, joining a vaude-villian cast that included Valeska Suratt, Gertie Vanderbilt, and Joe, Myra, and Buster Keaton. To Hattie, he wrote he had at last settled some consecutive time "and considering what a bad season it is, I feel very lucky."

What we know of Fields' appearance in *Watch Your Step* comes mainly from Sime Silverman, the unpredictable editor and founder of *Variety,* who reviewed both the Syracuse tryout and the subsequent New York premiere of the show. Silverman was reared in Syracuse and treated any excuse to revisit the place as a kind of homecoming, making the late-night rounds and hailing old friends, his trademark Perrier and scotch always at hand. For the *Watch Your Step* sojourn, Silverman was accompanied by Gene Buck, lyricist and right-hand man to Florenz Ziegfeld, producer of the annual *Follies* that bore his name. Buck had written, in collaboration with Dave Stamper and George V. Hobart, the last two editions of the *Follies,* and had just drawn an assignment to write the next. The two men, both of whom cut formidable figures, were enjoying a late supper when they saw Fields, sitting alone at another table, a book insis-tently propped in front of him. Buck correctly observed that if the show needed cutting, Fields' number—however well received—would be the easiest to drop. He sent over a card with the following note scribbled on the back: "SEE ME IN NEW YORK IF ANYTHING GOES WRONG."

    That next week, Fields presented himself at Buck's office at the New Am-sterdam, a brick and limestone monument to l'Art Nouveau on Forty-second Street, where the *Follies* had moved for the 1913 edition and where *Watch Your*

*In a New York photo studio, circa 1914*

*Step* would open in a matter of days. Still smarting at his dismissal from the Dillingham show, Fields came off to Buck as "tough, bitter, and cynical in an odd, humorous way." They had a pleasant, noncommittal sort of exchange, Buck speaking of the possibility of bringing Fields into the next edition of the *Follies,* and Fields just as casually suggesting his fee for such an engagement would be $400 a week. They parted company with an agreement to keep in touch.

Fields hit the road again, accepting the two weeks of Canadian time Dillingham had arranged, then joining the Keith circuit, starting back in Syracuse with a week's stand over Christmas. A local reviewer took the opportunity to write: "Mr. Dillingham's mistaken judgement as to the amount of specialties he could exhibit in *Watch Your Step,* now triumphantly successful in New York, resulted in the release of W. C. Fields after the premiere performance. . . . He is on this week's bill at the Grand, and for his kind of an act, which blends cigar boxes, tennis balls, old hats, lighted cigars, and billiard cues with silent comedy, there is nothing better on the stage."

Fields regarded the approach of his thirty-fifth birthday with an element of dread that bordered on morbidity. He was at an age when younger comedians, with fresh ideas and seemingly endless reserves of energy, were competing for laughs, and he'd had enough of sleeping on trains, curling himself into knots to save the price of a sleeper. He was tired of baggage delays, cold audiences, bad food, and slow laundries. Fed up to the gills with living in a trunk, he became desperate for something different to do. In Columbus, where he opened at Keith's on January 11, 1915, Fields suffered the humiliation of being slotted to close the show, something he hadn't done in years. It was bad time on any bill, as audiences invariably started to clear out after the headliner, and although it was often the curse of a dumb act, Fields had successfully avoided first and last positions since the time he worked the opening spot for Fred Irwin in burlesque. What made the situation worse in this particular case was that he would be following a team of raucous "nut" comics in their twenties who headed a noisy company of thirteen and were collectively known as the Marx Brothers.

The Marxes were touring in a musical comedy sketch called "Home Again," which audiences seemed to like but critics took as thin and undisciplined. "The comedy, in two scenes, has little in the way of plot, and the whole affair is rather nondescript," said the *Columbus Journal.* "A very clever pair of dancers appear, but their work is marred for the audience by the clowning of other performers, which is allowed to go on at the same time." The bill was "hardly up to Keith standards," according to the *Journal.* "One has to wait till the last act for a really finished and expert performance. Then W. C. Fields, the well-known juggler, pantomimist, and comedian, delights everyone with his clever and laughable manipulation of hat, stick, cigar, etc., concluding with his now famous exploits at the pool table. He is continually funny in a way that has been widely imitated."

Unhappily for Fields, the laudatory *Journal* review couldn't keep people in their seats after the assaultive Marx act had run its course. "Most of the time," said Groucho Marx, "Fields would find himself playing to only half a house because a lot of people would leave after our act. Especially if it was a matinee performance because most people would leave to go home to dinner. And very few people were interested in seeing some guy juggle after the stage had been full of our act." Fields played three performances in a progressively aggravated state, then threw in the towel—the only instance in his entire career when he actually walked out on a show. According to Groucho, he faked an injury called "noxis on the conoxsis" and told the skeptical house manager he just couldn't continue. The *Journal* reported it as a badly bruised hand, saying that Fields had left for New York to seek special treatment. "He injured his hand last week while playing his celebrated billiard game and has been suffering considerably with it ever since."

The following Monday, however, Fields opened at Keith's Louisville in the No. 6 spot and displayed no apparent signs of physical distress. Never again would he play the opening or closing position in vaudeville, and never again would he appear on the same bill with the Marx Brothers, the only act he could not follow. The episode was fortuitous, however, in that during his brief stopover in New York, he had another encouraging talk with Gene Buck. He elected, in fact, to withdraw from the Shubert show at the Winter Garden, hoping instead to land a featured spot in the *Follies.* Ziegfeld himself was noncommittal, but the soft-spoken Buck, Jesuit trained and an illustrator by trade, thought Fields just about the funniest man in the world. "His gifts and talents as an entertainer were born in him, I think. Some guys learn through experience and practice being comics. Not Bill. God made him funny."

The *Follies* always came together in an environment of barely controlled chaos, Ziegfeld starting with a core group of performers and ten thousand ideas, and Buck lending form and continuity to the various elements as they were thrown at him. Flo Ziegfeld was mostly interested in glorifying the American girl and had little time for the surrounding acts—particularly the comics. Buck wrote songs, oversaw rehearsals, and scouted new talent, which he spoonfed to "Ziggy" as the show took shape. He acted, said Eddie Cantor, "as a kind of check and stabilizer for Flo." Ziegfeld himself once said that *Hamlet* without Hamlet would be a perfect and complete thing compared to a *Follies* without Gene Buck.

By late February it was clear that Buck needed help, and on the night of March 5 he commenced work with critic and playwright Channing Pollock and his collaborator Rennold Wolf, a critic who had an ambition to write a revue. The three men got together in Pollock's study for a marathon conference and, incinerating enough tobacco to stock a small shop, threshed out a schedule of twenty scenes. Fifty pages in length, it contained far more material than could ever be crammed into one show, and yet not one scene was ever put into rehearsal. "Ziegfeld telephoned us nine times during the evening," Pollock recounted. "We got used to that. The furniture in the Ziegfeld apartment consists principally of telephones. . . . Every time Flo has an idea—which is three every five minutes—he telephones someone about it." The producer scheduled a general conference the next day, at which he had two composers, a scene builder, a property man, the inventor of a device that could float people above the stage on wires, and a scenic designer named Joseph Urban, who was just beginning a long and historic association with the *Follies.* "While we were asleep," said Pollock, "Urban and Ziegfeld had conferred, and Flo had accepted designs of a dozen scenes that were not in our schedule. They were inserted, and we were pledged to write a few pages of hilariously comic dialogue to fit them. . . . Conferring came to be the business of our lives."

According to Ed Wynn, who was touring with the 1914 *Follies* at the time, Ziegfeld didn't want Fields in the show because his act "was not tied into the rest of it." By April 9, the cast was practically complete: Bert Williams, Leon Errol, Louise Meyers, Anna (later Ann) Pennington, all from the 1914 edition, and a novelty dancer named Bernard Granville, who did a celebrated drunk routine. To the press, Ziegfeld indicated he was still looking for a "big" female name and mentioned Kitty (Lady) Gordon, who, in the words of music publisher Edward B. Marks, possessed "the most beautiful back in show business." Britain's Phyllis Dare, who, along with her sister Zena, had made a spectacular leap from the music halls to the world of musical comedy, was another possibility. A week later, Ziegfeld had forgotten about both ladies and settled instead on diver Annette Kellermann. He was also reported as dickering with monologist Sam Bernard.

Fields allowed Dillingham to finish his commitment by booking him through on the Orpheum time: Sioux City on March 14, Omaha on the twenty-first, Kansas City on the twenty-eighth, Des Moines on April 4, St. Paul on the eleventh. He was in Duluth, at the very end of his stretch, when the following item appeared in the *Herald:* "W. C. Fields 'The Silent Humorist' now playing at the Orpheum, will close his vaudeville work after next week and it will be the last vaudeville audiences will see of him for some time, as he will go immediately to New York for the new *Ziegfeld Follies,* which will open in New York June 1. This show will run through the summer in New York, and make the tour to the coast and back during the winter."

Ziegfeld was still in search of a star comedian, however, and Fields, by any reckoning, was not his man. There was Bert Williams, of course, as there had been most every year since 1910, but he was a special case—a light-skinned Negro who worked in blackface, singing, dancing, and performing exquisite feats of pantomime. He was, by 1915, a *Follies* regular, but his name alone would not carry the show. Ziegfeld made a desperate grab for Charles Chaplin, tramp comic and graduate of the British music halls, who had become a star attraction for Essanay. He offered the picture comedian $1,800 a week, and Chaplin, unhappy with Essanay, was reportedly willing, but the company, with expectations of two comedies a month, was not. Ziegfeld traveled to Chicago, where Essanay was based, to plead his case, pointing out that Chaplin could film in New York during the day and still play the *Follies* at night, but Essanay held options on Chaplin's services for the next two years and could not be persuaded to release him.

Ziegfeld continued to resist the notion of adding Fields to his cast. As J. P. McEvoy, who later wrote three shows for Ziegfeld, learned, Ziegfeld hated pantomime, and Fields was perhaps the greatest pantomimist in vaudeville. Ziegfeld liked color, music, laughter, but not silence. He was cold to it and convinced the public didn't like it either. Not that there wasn't pantomime in the *Follies*. Bert Williams, the previous year, had performed a poker routine, sans cards, partners, or dialogue, that was one of the undisputed hits of the show. But Williams was Williams, part of the Ziegfeld family, and Fields was not.

Rehearsals began with only random parts of the book settled, and Ziegfeld, foiled in his attempts to recruit Chaplin and Sam Bernard, finally contracted with Ed Wynn for another season. Fields was very much a last-minute addition. "We were told Mr. Fields couldn't speak a line," Pollock remembered, "but he had been promised a part, and we must provide one that would be silent but sidesplitting. On his account, all the dialogue was taken out of a bit satirizing the smoky atmosphere, the scant dancing space, the waiters and the coat-room boys of the cheap cabarets, and the pool table was put in its place." Fields reported to the New Amsterdam on May 19, 1915. By June 1, the show was in its seventh revision and Ziegfeld was still making additions to the cast. Rehearsals were spread over four theaters, with the first performances less than two weeks away. Julian Mitchell, who was deaf as a post, directed the musical numbers by pressing his head tightly against the back of the piano to catch the rhythm of the music.* Leon Errol, an impish Australian comedian Fields had first encountered on his tour for Rickards, was in charge of the comics: Fields, Bert Williams, Ed Wynn, Phil Dwyer, Will West, and himself.

---

*Mitchell, sixty-one at the time, had, in collaboration with Herbert Gresham, staged the first edition of the *Follies* in 1907.

Fields' participation in the show was almost punitive in that, having worked exclusively as a single since Hattie left the act in 1903, he was now, as a member of the cast of the *Follies,* never to be left alone onstage. His famous pool table routine would be performed in tandem with Ed Wynn, and he was to be part of a sketch with Bert Williams, Ann Pennington, and Leon Errol in which he would be required to speak lines. The *Follies* would mark his permanent exit from vaudeville and occasion one of the signal events of his life—his first appearance before a motion-picture camera.

Early one morning, thirty principals and chorus assembled outside the New Amsterdam for a momentous bus trip to Fort Lee, New Jersey. The call was for 7:30 a.m., but by the time everyone arrived it was after nine. Fort Lee, with its famously bad roads, was an easy ferryboat trip from Upper Manhattan, as rural as its neighbor across the Hudson was metropolitan. It was a favorite location for studio-bound film companies, and both Mary Pickford and D. W. Griffith had shot their first movies there. The business at hand was to create a quick parody of Griffith's twelve-reel epic *The Birth of a Nation,* which was playing to capacity houses at New York's Liberty Theatre. The girls donned ballet costumes as the bus crawled along, silk-clad legs flailing in all directions, until a suitable battlefield could be found. By all reports, Fields spent just a few fleeting moments in front of the camera, playing himself, a *Follies* cast member still slightly bewildered by it all. It was not clear to anyone, except maybe Gene Buck, how the stuff they were shooting was going to fit together, and when they lost their light, at about four o'clock in the afternoon, they all piled back into the bus and returned to town.

With just a week left before the first performance, Annette Kellermann backed out of the show and Ziegfeld frantically contracted with singer-dancer Ina Claire as her replacement. Claire, like Fields, had just returned to American vaudeville after an extended period abroad, and three days before the opening the authors were busy writing a song for her to sing. Ziegfeld said the new *Follies* would surpass anything he had done before and would, in fact, eclipse any musical show New York had ever seen. The company numbered 150—some reports said 175—with the payroll alone amounting to $8,500 a week. By the time it rolled into Atlantic City for its dress rehearsal, the show represented a $150,000 investment.

The ninth edition of the *Ziegfeld Follies* hit the stage of Nixon's Apollo Theatre on June 15, 1915. The script was in its sixteenth revision, and the show was more than four hours in length. The week in Atlantic City dragged on like one endless rehearsal, with Pollock and Wolf feverishly trying to eliminate two hours of material. Leon Errol dislocated a hip, the chorus girls functioned on three hours' sleep a night, and songs were written and discarded in a matter of hours. Every morning, they gave Ziegfeld a timetable of the preceding night's performance, setting forth at what instant every song was sung, how many encores it took, and how many minutes it consumed. Laughs were remembered and guarded like the Hope diamond.

Amazingly, Fields' specialty toward the end of the first act survived relatively unscathed. He had little interaction with Flo Ziegfeld, other than to field an objection to a new pool table he had commissioned in London. "The makers gave me the table on the condition that the firm name should be prominently displayed on the side and that the firm should get program credit. . . . When I showed up for rehearsals in my outfit, Ziegfeld said, 'Take that name off the table. No one's going to get any free advertising in a Ziegfeld show.' I mentioned the program agreement, but that was out too, so the firm sort of lost out." The company returned to New York on Sunday, June 20, and launched into an all-night dress rehearsal that ended just hours before the first spectators took their seats. The house was packed, tickets were being scalped at $20 to $25 apiece, and representatives of at least one agency were offering as much as $15 a seat with little success. The curtain rose sharply at 8:00 p.m., a promptness necessitated by the elaborate rigging needed to float the chorus—costumed as mermaids—through a submarine tableau. "The stage setting is the greatest Mr. Ziegfeld has ever presented," the program boasted, and the audience seemed inclined to agree. The first sight of it brought an audible gasp from the crowd, as did many of the subsequent settings, especially a Gates of Elysium number in which a pair of golden elephants flanked the entryway and spouted real water into a pool from which Aphrodite emerged.

The *Follies* consisted of twenty-one scenes, ranging from Ann Pennington and George White performing the Flirtation Melody Dance to Bernard Granville and Ina Claire commemorating the new transcontinental phone line with the singing of Gene Buck's "Hello Frisco!" The comedy was supplied by Leon Errol (as Rip Van Winkle), the droll and understated Bert Williams (whose rendering of "I'm Neutral" stopped the show), and Ed Wynn, whose direction of the "Commotion Picture" was praised in nearly every review. On the screen appeared Granville, Mae Murray, Fields, Errol, Bert Williams, Gene Buck, Ziegfeld, Julian Mitchell, the stagehands, and an electrician—all intent on making a movie about the Civil War. Wynn stood in the left-hand aisle, next to the orchestra rail, shouting instructions at the projected figures, some of whom would walk to the side of the screen and bend down to hear him more clearly. The stage was set and the brief plot worked out in a scene so perfectly timed and executed that *Variety* described it as "one long scream."

The 1915 edition of the *Ziegfeld Follies* became a classic of its kind—destined to go down in the history books as the first of the eight great *Follies* that burnished the legend of Florenz Ziegfeld Jr. and carried the series through its 1922–23 season. It would take in over $260,000 in its thirteen-week run at the New Amsterdam, a 12 percent increase over any previous year's receipts. "Everybody is going to see it," said Sime Silverman, "not because it is the *Follies,* but because it is the *Follies* outdone."

If Philadelphia gained a reputation as "the Cradle of Vaudeville," it might have laid similar claim to moving pictures as well. Never really a center for production, Philadelphia was nonetheless at the fore of exhibition, first when Keith's Bijou introduced the Edison Vitascope to local audiences, in May 1896, and later, in 1899, when Siegmund Lubin's Cineograph outgrew temporary quarters atop the Ninth and Arch Dime Museum and moved to a separate building on the midway at the National Export Exposition, thus establishing one of the first motion-picture theaters in the nation.

The movies had come of age while Fields was perfecting his own stage technique and were always looming as a principal attraction wherever he played—whether the Winter-Garten in Berlin, where the show concluded with thirteen Biograph subjects, or the Melbourne Opera House, where he shared the bill with Méliès' *A Trip to the Moon.* In 1901, while Fields was touring Europe for the first time, the White Rats of America, the principal vaudevillians' union, walked out on the eastern members of the Association of Vaudeville Managers and cleared the nation's stages of variety acts—most of which were hastily replaced with films supplied by the Biograph and American Vitagraph companies. Yet film work lacked the respectability of big-time vaudeville, and popular acts weren't commonly seen before the cameras until 1912, when Adolph Zukor founded Famous Players and imported *Les Amours de la Reine Elizabeth,* a four-reel subject starring Madame Sarah Bernhardt. It was a terrific success, and, coupled with Bernhardt's tour for Martin Beck the same year, it caused the floodgates to open, and major stage attractions began signing on for appearances. By 1915, several brands had been created around the "Broadway" name to showcase distinguished stage actors with appeal to urban audiences.* Universal offered "Broadway Features," Vitagraph had "Broadway Star Features," and Kalem sold three-reel subjects as "Broadway Favorites." The trend extended to shorts as well. In August 1915, Paramount, which released the Famous Players product, was reported as planning a series of one-reel comedies featuring "a big Broadway name star." That same month, Mutual announced "All-Star Comedies, featuring Broadway comedians in a new variety of comedy films."

The Mutual had been forced into a particularly aggressive posture by the

---

*Before the star system, movies were sold under brand names, like soap flakes and citrus fruit.

departure of president Harry E. Aitken, who left the company in May 1915. Within two months, Aitken had formed the Triangle Film Corporation to distribute the productions of Thomas Ince, D. W. Griffith, and Mack Sennett. Abruptly, Mutual was deprived of Sennett's Keystone comedies and had to scramble to replace them. The company's new management, headed by John R. Freuler, Aitken's former partner, contracted with the French Gaumont Company, which had been producing films in the United States since 1913, to provide three-reel features "with distinguished Broadway players," one-reel "All-Star Comedies," and a weekly split reel—half scenic ("Seeing America First") and half animated cartoon ("Keeping Up with the Joneses").

Gaumont had been making one-reel comedies under the Empress brand since the first of the year. Now, under the new commitment to Mutual, their output accelerated. To meet the initial mandate of delivering Broadway comedians for All-Star Comedies, general manager F. G. Bradford scoured the Main Stem for likely names. Ziegfeld, of course, was the gold standard, but the services of his biggest comedy star, Bert Williams, were reserved to Klaw & Erlanger, who would soon expand into film production as a partner of Biograph. Ed Wynn, who relied much on his voice and would become a major radio star, wasn't particularly suited to silent pictures, and Leon Errol was on the verge of a nervous collapse that would take him out of the *Follies* altogether. Fields, therefore, became the logical choice to kick off the series, playing off the fame of his now classic pool routine. A deal was announced through the Mutual press office: "As Mr. Fields' theatrical contract calls for his exclusive services, it is only through the courtesy of Florenz Ziegfeld that the Mutual Corporation is enabled to present this star feature on its regular program."

In later years, Fields would disparage *Pool Sharks,* his first film, claiming he spent "less than four hours" making it. "There was one camera and fifteen-hundred feet of film," he said. "If I missed my trick, I spoiled the picture." The film was shot at the Gaumont studio in Flushing, Queens, most likely in August 1915. Diminutive Bud Ross played Fields' rival for the hand of the girl, and Edwin Middleton, a Philadelphia stage actor used to making prestige features with the likes of Lillian Russell and Lionel Barrymore, directed. The impossible maneuvers of the balls were accomplished with stop-motion animation.

The first W. C. Fields movie ever made begins with a hauntingly autobiographical bit of action. An aggrieved boy (we never see why) is emptying a wooden water bucket when he spies Fields, smug and high-hatted, wooing a girl on a nearby patch of lawn. The boy rears back, heaves the bucket at Fields' head, watches it shatter, then runs like hell. It plays like a statement of principles, made as if to put all authority figures on notice and, at the same time, as a homage to the late Jim Dukenfield, a sort of symbolic evening of the score, his son on the receiving end, immortalized on film.

Ross appears, loud and dandified, and the battle is joined. There is considerable cane whacking and eye poking as they vie for the attention of the unidentified girl, who generally gets the worst of it. Doused with coffee and the water from a goldfish bowl, she is at once distinctive and funny. A child attacks Fields with a peashooter, and a theme that would carry through the rest of his career—the menace of the not-quite-so-innocent—is born. One of the men proposes "a friendly game of pool," and the action reverts to the hall, where Fields assiduously avoids any hint of his stage routine. There is a brief flash of ball juggling, but most of the scene is given over to the two men trading shots, sending the balls on intricate breaks, marching them around the table, and then reassembling them as if they had never been moved. The final scene has Fields making off with a bottle, an increasingly valuable commodity in a world of dry states and prohibitionist fervor. All in all, it was a remarkable bellwether of things to come.

"Admirers of Fields will find his screen work neither as subtle nor as laughable as his stage performances," the reviewer for *Motion Picture News* reported. "There is plenty of good fun in the picture, however, and much of the business is new." *The Moving Picture World,* with its usual restraint, described the film as "an eccentric comedy number with amusing spots in it" and said it contained some "good nonsense" but little else. As dissatisfied as Fields may have been with *Pool Sharks,* he was back making a second movie for Gaumont within days. *His Lordship's Dilemma* was more of a story film, directed this time by William F. Haddock, who was, even more than Middleton, a specialist in three-reel features. The film had Fields playing a remittance man down on his luck. He lets his valet, played by Bud Ross, go, then meets up with the man on the sidewalk—both of them straddled by sandwich signs. Fields invites Ross into a saloon for a drink, and in another deft autobiographical touch, engages the genial bartender, played by his brother Walter, in conversation while Ross stuffs his pockets with free lunch. In the course of the action, Fields manages three drinks for the price of one, and, on the way out, even recovers the dollar he used to pay for it all.

Sleepily, the men retire to the park to enjoy the spoils of their labors. Fields pinches a newspaper and reads of Lord Swan, who has captured the heart of a Fifth Avenue heiress with his mastery of golf. Pulling up a warm bench, he dozes off and imagines himself a titled nobleman, impressing his girl and her family not so much with his playing as with his bravery when he deflects a bomb thrown by a couple of blackhanders. As they embrace, he awakens to find himself in the arms of his valet, whom he throws into the lake. As the air bubbles rise to the surface, he strolls off, energized and renewed by his heroic dream.

Though more ambitious than *Pool Sharks, His Lordship's Dilemma* was

scarcely more pleasing to Fields, and he rarely, if ever, spoke of it. Following the release of *Pool Sharks,* on September 19, 1915, the name of the series, to complement the company's line of Rialto Star Features, was changed from All-Star to Casino Star Comedies. *His Lordship's Dilemma* became the first Casino release on October 3, but there were no further Fields pictures to follow.

His Lordship's Dilemma *had more of a storyline than Fields' previous film for Gaumont,* but the annual tour of the Ziegfeld Follies *prevented him from making more one-reelers.*

Unhappy with the dizzying rate at which the movies consumed new material, Fields went on tour with the *Ziegfeld Follies,* deferring any further talk of film production until his return in the spring. By then, Gaumont would have abandoned the American market. "[Paul] Gaumont quit this country because he refused to pay any more than ten dollars for a story," Bill Haddock said. "Bradford told me he had informed Gaumont that no one could get stories for that price. Gaumont's response was, 'In that case we will leave this country,' and they did."

John Freuler, left to fill the void, entered into a twelve-picture contract with Chaplin that paid the comedian a salary of $10,000 a week and a signing bonus of $150,000. It was the richest deal in the history of the movies, and it rendered moot the subject of further comedies from W. C. Fields. The whole experience was trying and unsatisfactory, and it would be another decade before Fields would return to the business of making pictures in earnest. For now, he would have to content himself as a star of the *Follies.*

# Seven

# Exclusive Services

Hattie, who had gone to California seeking a new life, was dragged back to New York in 1913 when her mother suffered a debilitating stroke. Forced to make do on $40 a week at a time when her husband was touring the British Isles and his letters sometimes went astray, she borrowed some furniture from her sister, Kitty, and set up housekeeping in an apartment on West 175th Street, in the Washington Heights area of Manhattan. In September, she went to Philadelphia looking for a place to live, and Fields, remembering the cramped quarters of his own childhood, chastised her for wanting a six- or seven-room house for herself and Claude. "There are lots of small, comfortable, up-to-date houses in sedate neighborhoods available for $18 to $20 per month. If you expect me to furnish a home for you, and a continuance of $40, you are mistaken."

Fields found himself continually frustrated by Hattie's seeming inability—or refusal—to get on with her life, get a job, find another man. He knew she would never consent to a divorce, and, according to her, the subject hardly ever came up. "He never wanted it," she said flatly, "and I never wanted it." When she saw him with another woman at Jim Dukenfield's funeral, her embarrassment and mortification were evident to all. He studied her quizzically. "Don't you ever get lonely?" he asked.

Hattie had long since become a martyr to her manipulative mother—first as a young girl and now as a caretaker—and was well suited to assuming the same role in the life of her son. The fissions that would fragment and eventually destroy the Hughes family would do the same to her own family as well. "Your mother's methods will not work with the present generation," Fields warned her, but instinctively she knew they would work just fine. And so they continued, week in and week out, their rancorous correspondence, Fields dependably sending his checks from whatever part of the world he was in, and Hattie always beseeching him for more money, more recognition, more love as she had once known it. Through it all, Claude was put in the position of choosing between warring parents for whom he was the sole point of rational contact, but there was never really any choice. Before he was two, the marriage of his parents was effectively over and his father had assumed the role of an infrequent visitor in his life. What he knew of Fields and his work was subjected to the filter of his mother's almost pathological hatred. His father wanted to steal him away, to take him to live with his concubine and never to let him see his mother again. Her screed was horrific, relentless, and, over time, fostered a dependence that was irrational in its intensity.

To her credit, Hattie did keep her son in close contact with his paternal grandparents—to the point, in fact, where Claude's childhood memories of Kate and Jim Dukenfield were more vivid than those of his own father. Hattie was friendly with Elsie May, who became a showgirl herself, and took up with the Underkoflers, close friends of the Dukenfields who became like a second family to Claude and herself. Every summer, they would meet Jim and Kate in Atlantic City, where Jim would take to the water, carrying his grandson into the waves on his broad shoulders, bobbing and splashing, a big, effusive smile on his face. Kate would remain on the shore, huddled toadlike in the sand, continuing, in her grandson's words, "her running commentary on persons, places, and things." She kept everyone laughing, even as she was, oddly, a more distant figure to the boy than the redoubtable Jim, who died when Claude was just eight. "Although she was a devoted mother," said Claude, "she had no capacity whatsoever for demonstrative love." Leroy, who was more like a brother to Claude than an uncle, once confided that he could not remember his mother ever kissing him.

Hattie knew that Claude was the one soft spot in her husband's hardened shell of indifference, and she cloaked whatever she wanted in terms of the boy's welfare rather than her own. Fields tolerated the tactic, biding his time until the boy was old enough to think on his own, and expressed unbridled delight when, in September 1913, he received his first-ever letter from his nine-year-old son. "I am pleased you are having such a fine vacation," he wrote jubilantly in reply. "Play lots of baseball and do a lot of swimming. It will make you strong. . . . Wish you would write me from time to time, letting me know what progress you are making at school and how healthy you are keeping." He signed the letter, "All love, Papa."

Claude's letters, though infrequent, were refreshingly free of Hattie's bombast. They continued through 1914, the first tentative exchanges between a father who was never prouder of anything than having a son, and a boy who knew his male parent only as a pinchpenny and a brute—the man who stood between his mother and the things she needed. In January 1915, Claude wrote a long, enthusiastic letter about the piano lessons he was taking in Brooklyn, and Fields was inspired to make him an offer: "If you get real good and would like to go, I will let your mother, or give her the money to take you to Europe—when the war is over and you can study under one of the big teachers in Paris, Berlin, or Brussels. The teachers there do not charge more than they do here, and the living is just as reasonable, if not a bit cheaper."

To his surprise, the boy's response to the idea was decidedly cool, and Fields detected the unwelcome incursion of Hattie into their dialogue. She told Claude she wanted him to have an American education, and rather than speaking for himself, the boy parroted her words. Wounded by the rejection, Fields wrote an intemperate rebuttal: "I agree with you, you will find teachers here that are just as good, but when your mother says: If you went abroad you would lose one of the greatest privileges this country gives, i.e. an American education, she failed to mention she has caused you to be denied THE GREATEST—that of becoming president of the U.S.A. when she made you a votary of the Catholic church."

The following month, during a lull in rehearsals for the *Ziegfeld Follies,* Fields called at the apartment, anxious to see his son and buy him "everything a boy of his age could desire." He was peeved when the boy told him that he preferred a home—which was, of course, what Hattie, off at a dental appointment, would have wanted him to say. She had left strict instructions for Claude to remain indoors, and his refusal to go out with his father on a crisp spring afternoon, even for a brief walk to the park, was wounding. When Hattie returned, an ugly scene ensued, precipitating a melodramatic fainting spell on the couch. Claude told his father that when he grew up he would not look at him, and the visit ended on the landing with Hattie heaping abuse on her husband, in Fields' words, "before a lot of stupid people with flapping ears." Retreating to the theater, he penned an angry note: "Your low cunning and scheming will some day cause you no end of grief. You will never be happy so long as you practice your perfidy upon your young son. You have taught him a hymn of hate, likewise tried to make him a Christian—the two do not blend."

Hattie made the mistake of apologizing for Claude's disrespectful behavior, as if she had no real part in the matter. Her letter just compounded the problem and brought a stinging rebuke:

> I do not feel offended with my son or his actions. . . . You have him so scared that he is afraid to even think without consulting you first. This state of frightened obedience is only accomplished by unkind treatment. . . . When son is older he will then think and see for himself. I will talk to him and he will understand, but it is useless for me to talk seriously to him now, for he has been punished until you have his very heart and soul in your hands through fear. If I ask him a question, he looks at you for his cue as to his answer. You have him fright-

ened of me by your imaginary tales, which haven't the slightest foundation, of me stealing him. Son has no desire to please me, and he only
thinks of me as the bad man that steals little boys. You manufacture a
lot of father and child stories which any fool can see through. I don't
blame son, and please get this through your brain—I love him irre-
spective of what you have taught him to believe I am.

Hattie's reaction to the second letter was to send Claude around to the
Bushwick Theatre, where Fields was rehearsing, to tell him that when he grew
up, he would pay back every cent his father had paid toward their support. This
was more than Fields could tolerate, and he curtailed further efforts to see the
boy. "Let him prospect by himself," he told Hattie, "and when he gets to be
about twenty he might look me up some day and want to know what it was all
about, or perhaps he will be satisfied with your version. You have put the jinx
on anything I wanted to do for him, and, incidentally, not improved your own
case. Now when he asks if I have anything to say about him in my weekly letter,
just say no! that I have left everything to you."

The *Follies* left the New Amsterdam on September 18, and the first stop, as
always, was the Colonial Theatre in Boston, where the show was scheduled for
four weeks and wound up staying for six. Receipts in Boston averaged $17,500
a week, and the show's popularity caused the entire tour to be telescoped and
considered anew. Ziegfeld dropped plans to play the West Coast—always a
dubious proposition for a lavish New York production—and chose instead to
concentrate on the major cities of the East, Baltimore, Detroit, Chicago, and
Philadelphia, where traveling expenses could be contained and anticipation
was strong. Fields became an audience favorite in the *Follies*, but consistently
found himself overshadowed in the press by the attention paid to Bert
Williams. Williams, of course, was one of the true stars of the *Follies*, and his
yearly appearances were eagerly awaited, but the praise lavished on him was
almost always at the expense of Wynn, Fields, and the other, lesser comedic
lights of the show. When attention did focus on Fields, it generally concerned
the novelty of hearing his voice in the Bunkem Court sketch. "Sure enough,"
said the *Detroit News,* "in his scene with Bert Williams in the Bunkem apart-
ments he says words right out loud. When you hear him, you hear a lovely voice
which reminds you of stripping gears on a flivver."

Despite Fields' success in the show, Flo Ziegfeld had little time for his new
comic, and Fields soon became convinced the boss didn't like him. "Ziegfeld,"
Fields said, "was a weird combination of the great showman and the little
child. He really did not like comedians and tolerated them only because of the

public. His forte was beautiful girls and costumes with elaborate settings." An impossibly elegant man in his late forties, Ziegfeld would lean against a post in the back of the theater, his eyes intently fixed on the performance, a cigar in his mouth pointing skyward and a smile never crossing his face. "Ziggy hired the best comics, disliked them all, and Fields more than any of them," J. P. McEvoy said. "His greatest pleasure was putting them all on the stage at once and watching them kill each other's laughs."

When Fields was engaged for the *Follies,* the pool table routine was added to a scene about life in a midnight cabaret. Ed Wynn claimed to have rewritten it: "Mr. Ziegfeld did not like straight vaudeville acts, which Bill Fields' act really was, so I rewrote his act—as a matter of fact, I wrote a complete new act and put his vaudeville act in it." Wynn had first encountered Fields at Kid McCoy's New York rathskeller in 1906, when Fields was appearing in *The Ham Tree* and Wynn was "just a punk kid" making out in vaudeville. "I had seen him a couple of times before that on the stage in our home town, Philadelphia." Integrating Fields into the cabaret sketch meant injecting Wynn's buffooneries into a turn that had always before been a solo. According to Gene Buck, Wynn had a history of stealing other people's laughs, and during the previous season, the ever patient and forbearing Bert Williams had actually led a delegation to Buck's office to complain of his habits. Buck had a word with the comic, and the situation calmed temporarily, but Wynn was back at it again by the end of the run.

In the midnight cabaret skit, Wynn played a sleepy pianist accompanying the Oakland Sisters as they rehearsed their farcical songs. Wynn's principal business came early on, and he was supposed to remain on the periphery, with a minimum of mugging, as Fields launched into his portion of the scene. Wynn, however, was an inveterate flycatcher, and it was not in his nature to remain in the background. Tensions flared between the two men during the first performances in Atlantic City. Fields knew where every laugh in the act was, and he was thrown by the laughs Wynn was eliciting from the sidelines. The men, who shared a dressing room, had an angry exchange, and Fields went to Buck, threatening to kill Wynn if he spoiled the act again.

Buck took Wynn aside, had yet another talk with him, and elicited a pledge of cooperation, even though the cabaret scene was designed for a certain amount of interference on Wynn's part. Fields did an admirable job of controlling his temper throughout the New York run, and Buck thought the problem had finally resolved itself when he was urgently summoned to Boston by wire. Wynn, he learned, had gotten particularly aggressive during the opening days of the tour, and Fields, discovering laughs once again where there shouldn't have been any, found him under the table making faces at the audience. Inverting his cue, Fields brought the butt end down on Wynn's skull with an ear-

*Fields was a pool player and Ed Wynn a waiter named Al A. Cart in the*
*"Midnight Cabaret" scene of the* Ziegfeld Follies *of 1915.*

splitting crack and continued the routine as his colleague lay out cold on the
floor. Back in their dressing room, Fields, who was too much of a professional
to hit Wynn in the face, seized him by the throat and beat his head against the
wall.

When Buck arrived, he found Wynn in "bad shape" from the encounter

("He killed me!" Wynn shouted. "He killed me!"), but Fields was in a genial, even conciliatory mood. "Let's keep it in," he urged. "It was the biggest laugh we got." Later, Wynn, with understandable embarrassment, denied the event had ever taken place—once even under oath. "It is true that I was under the table," he said in a 1956 radio interview,

> but I always was under the table. Now, a strange thing happened. We went to Boston to open our engagement there for four weeks, and on Tuesday morning, after our Monday night opening, one of the Boston newspaper critics, in writing about the show, said the Ed Wynn scene, "in which he was ably assisted by William C. Fields," was one of the hilarious scenes of the show. Well, this actually was William C. Fields' scene, it was not my scene, and Bill got very angry and wanted to smash me in the nose that night. I didn't know what it was about, because I never read criticisms in newspapers. Bill Fields was so angry at me because he thought I actually did something I had not been doing in the 16 prior weeks to our Boston engagement. . . . He never hit me with a pool cue; we allowed that to remain as a good story to be published once a year about both of us.

Amazingly, the hardheaded Wynn wasn't permanently dissuaded from poaching on Fields' act. In November, when the *Follies* opened in Detroit, the critic for the *News* wrote, "Mr. Fields is losing some laughs in the pool game because Ed Wynn, who is funny too, is cutting up at the same time. Fields is comical enough to hold any stage; has been, in fact, for many years with the same act. Wynn has plenty of opportunity to make 'em laugh during the entertainment and Fields would go better if Wynn left him alone. Trying to watch both is like trying to smoke two cigars at once—you don't enjoy either as much as if you could devote your time to them singly."

Fields' attack on Wynn became part of the lore of show business and was dutifully reported, with suitable embellishments, time and again—though never by Fields himself. "It was as if a common curtain of secrecy dropped," Joe Mankiewicz said. "It was never mentioned." In a private letter to the comedian, however, Fields reminded Wynn that physical violence was a common remedy for encroachments in vaudeville, and that Wynn himself had once discouraged Leon Errol from pinching his cheeks onstage with the aid of a baseball bat. "I sincerely hope you never suffer any more physical or mental pain than you did the night of the bloodthirsty encounter with a pool cue in 'fifteen,'" Fields concluded. "Did your head ever heal up?"

———

As successful as the *Follies of 1915* turned out to be, there was no guarantee that Fields would be retained for the next edition. Flo Ziegfeld was not one to be pinned down about content, and his top people scattered to other shows. Ina Claire entered into negotiations to star in a play for Archibald Selwyn, and Ed Wynn was picked up as the principal comedian for the Shuberts' *Passing Show of 1916.* Fields was anxious to remain with the *Follies,* but Ziegfeld complained about his performance and told him he was scarcely worth the money he was asking. On April 28, 1916, Ziegfeld wrote Fields at the Hotel Cumberland, formally engaging him for the new *Follies* "on the same terms, salary, and conditions as your contract of the past season." Pointedly, he added: "It is agreed and understood that during the term of this agreement, I am to have absolutely your exclusive services, and without written permission from me, you have no right to appear in moving pictures."

Ziegfeld had already committed to leading parts for Bert Williams, Carl Randall, and comedienne Fannie Brice. On May 20, it was announced that Ina Claire had re-upped for another season—the negotiations with Selwyn having fallen through—and the rest of the show took shape overnight. Bernard Granville, Ann Pennington, and actor Sam Hardy were added to the cast. Fields put the pool table in storage and retired the cigar boxes, concentrating instead on making himself an integral part of the annual revue. With his appearance in the previous *Follies,* he had exhausted a repertoire that had taken him fifteen years to build. Now he needed a showy new specialty.

The *Ziegfeld Follies of 1916* was written by Gene Buck and George V. Hobart, who, as the author of *The Ham Tree,* had written Fields' first speaking part in 1905. Hobart gave the show a classy Shakespearean theme, but, like Channing Pollock and Rennold Wolf the previous year, he found that holding Ziegfeld to a single theme was a challenge of almost insurmountable proportions. Much was made of the fact that this was the tenth anniversary of the *Follies,* and the prologue, titled "The Birth of Elation," became a pageant of girls representing previous editions of the show. Although Fields had been restricted to just three scenes in the 1915 *Follies,* he was on view throughout the 1916 edition. Among the various Shakespearean travesties, he appeared as Hamlet, played a recruiting station sketch opposite Sam Hardy and Bert Williams, and was part of the "Blushing Ballet," in which Williams danced outrageously while Fannie Brice, backed by an all-male chorus, put across a boisterous tune called "Nijinski." He also impersonated Teddy Roosevelt and ex–Secretary of the Navy Josephus Daniels in "Puck's Pictorial Palace" and sang a verse as each, getting away with it, as Sime Silverman observed, "but looking shocked himself after the final line and dazedly excited."

Learning to get laughs with words as well as actions took time for Fields, as he had to master an entirely different form of comic timing. In his years as a juggler, he never considered speaking onstage because so much of his work was in Europe, and pantomime, as he was quick to point out, was a universal language. "You're funny in English, but where does that get you in France or Germany?" he'd say. "Whereas, if you're a funny juggler, you're funny all over the world in every language." Moreover, pantomime had the advantage of never interrupting the audience. "You can't talk through a laugh," J. P. McEvoy explained. "If you do, you kill it. But a pantomime comedian can continue to build up one laugh on another until the audience is hysterical."

For his solo turn in the second act, Fields decided to revisit an aborted croquet effect he had first conceived for a tour of England in 1908. Working with a trick course, he had planned to make the ball shoot all the wickets in one shot—after the manner of his pool routine—but could never quite figure out how to bring the thing off. For the *Follies,* he abandoned the one-shot idea and developed instead a magnetized mallet that would attract the ball whenever he drew back to strike it. "Mr. Fields has given up his pool table for a croquet court," Alexander Woollcott reported in the *New York Times.* "He is funny, but not so funny as last year."

Fields formed abiding friendships with some of his fellow cast members, notably Sam Hardy, with whom he played the croquet bit, and monologist Will Rogers, who was added to the show after its New York opening. According to Fields, Rogers, who was appearing on the roof in the *Midnight Frolic,* wanted a spot on the main stage and had asked Fields to intercede on his behalf. "He offered to pay his own fare down to Atlantic City for the opening of the *Follies,*" Fields remembered, "and asked for no salary but only the opportunity to go on in case there was a stage wait. Ziegfeld couldn't see it. He told me he had $75,000 invested in the show and couldn't take the chance." Rogers was a straight roping act when he came to Ziegfeld in the fall of 1915, garnishing his tricks with the same jokes night after night. Ziggy wasn't impressed and, after a two-week trial, told Gene Buck to get rid of him. Fortunately, Rogers' wife Betty had already sensed the problem of playing to the same people—the Roof was a nightclub—time and again, and suggested he look to the newspapers for fresh material. "Why don't you talk about what you read?" she asked. "Goodness knows you're always reading the papers." Rogers went out onstage that night with a topical joke about Henry Ford's attempt to bring the war to an end and brought the house down. Ziegfeld, who still wasn't too keen on him, had to concede his popularity with the patrons and kept him on.

The *Frolic* was an intimate affair, and Ziegfeld was convinced that Rogers wouldn't go in the big room with its 1,675 seats filled to capacity. Betty Rogers remembered him halfheartedly offering her husband a late place in the show (at the urging, no doubt, of Gene Buck), but the money wasn't right, and touring would, after all, take him away from his family. She urged him to pass, and the couple attended the opening-night performance as civilians with $12 seats in the orchestra. Both were dismayed at what they saw. "Certain scenes were long and a little dull," said Betty. "Will grew nervous and irritable as one top-heavy number followed another, and he was cross with me because he was not in the show. . . . In the midst of all that glittering splendor, dull for want of contrast, Will's homey, down-to-earth act would have been a tremendous success."

A few nights later, Rogers went on unannounced, and the audience broke into spontaneous applause as he took the stage. Other parts of the show were trimmed, rewritten, dropped altogether. "Can't predict what will draw laughs or what song will be a hit," Ziegfeld said. "That's why the show is better after three weeks than it was at opening. We watch audience response and adapt [the] show accordingly." Fields, who was virtually ignored by the critics in the 1915 edition, came into his own as a returning favorite. ("To the show business, the wonder of this season's Ziegfeld show will be Bill Fields' singing and impersonating," Sime Silverman wrote.) Not only did he find his voice, but he settled on a look that made himself appropriate to most anything Ziegfeld could require of him. He wore a tuxedo in the 1915 *Follies* and, having abandoned the tramp's whiskers in 1912, experimented with a series of phony moustaches in various sizes, favoring, for most occasions, the "hook-and-eye" type that attached to the nose and wiggled as he spoke. It looked not so much like facial hair as a caterpillar that had suddenly been struck dead while traversing his upper lip. Though repulsive close up, it worked onstage, and he ignored repeated entreaties from friends to get rid of it.*

Fields had always avoided dissipation when juggling, but the *Ziegfeld Follies* marked a turning point in his life. He abandoned the juggler's mantle, working instead as a sketch comedian. He no longer had to worry about missing elaborate tricks, concentrating instead on actions and dialogue written largely by others. He became part of an ensemble, relieved of the considerable pressure of working alone and, in a sense, was liberated as a performer, able to relax and take a drink before the show—something he would never have contemplated doing before. In his twenties, Fields hadn't been much of a drinker, refusing to touch alcohol before a performance and only occasionally permitting himself a beer on the back end. "After a tough performance I'd have trouble settling down. I was on edge, overstimulated. Often, I'd be able to read, or walk it off, but sometimes it took a few beers to calm me down." He became less circumspect with the disintegration of his marriage, but into his thirties, he

---

*The bushy moustache—flared sideways—he wore in *Pool Sharks* and *His Lordship's Dilemma* was glued on with a glob of spirit gum. The appliance he wore in the *Follies* was briefer and of the clip-on variety.

could still truthfully describe himself as "a moderate teetotaler." Now that he was part of the *Follies,* liquor helped even him out and made him less subject to the violent fits of temper he had exhibited in his youth. It also loosened him up, making him less self-conscious about his voice and his singing and more likely to remember his lines. Life, he found, was more agreeable with a little buzz on. Unfortunately, with his natural tolerance for strong drink, it took a lot to make a difference. "Fields probably wasn't the biggest drinker in vaudeville," George Burns said. "He just had the biggest reputation." There were, of course, others: comedian Jim Thornton; Bert Fitzgibbons, who liked to drink his whiskey out of a water glass; Duffy and Sweeney; and, later, the columnist Mark Hellinger. Unlike these men, though, Fields was never visibly drunk, no matter how much he consumed, and since he slept very little, he rarely suffered the hammering effects of a hangover. There was also a social component to his drinking, for unwinding after a late performance was best done in the company of one's peers.

Touring, moreover, enhanced the camaraderie, for a traveling theatrical company was like an extended family and more time was spent at the theater—especially in the wintertime—than in any hotel room. Both Bert Williams and Fannie Brice were accomplished cooks, and Brice even made clothes for other women in the cast. Although the company had its own special train, Fields bought a huge 51 Series Cadillac to shuttle himself and his friends (Rogers, Hardy, occasionally Arthur Rosenbaum, the *Follies* stage manager) from city to city, and he began carrying a trunk stocked with liquor to pass the time between performances.* His dressing room became the social center of the *Follies,* where cast members knew they could always find a congenial gathering and a bracing libation. He was no snob, and members of the chorus were just as welcome as the principals. In time, he took up with one of the girls who had signed on for the tour, a leggy, long-faced brunette by the name of Bessie Poole.

Born on Cape Cod, Elizabeth Chatterton Poole first came to Broadway in 1911, when she was just sixteen years of age. She tried giving herself an exotic edge by spelling her name "Bessi," but supported herself dancing in nightclubs. "She was the best dancer, the most beautiful, with her long legs," said Faye O'Neill, who performed alongside her in the "Birth of Elation" number. "With Bill it was always 'Dear' this and 'Dear' that. You can tell when people are in love. Bessie's dressing room at the theatre was always covered with gifts from Bill—flowers, all kinds of perfume."

Fields was an excellent catch for a girl like Bessie. Not only was he a star

---

*In Europe, Fields had driven an American Underslung, but he got hung up in Antwerp when he couldn't get the forty-inch tires it took.

performer, but at the age of thirty-six he was still lean and muscular. "Bill was rather weight conscious," said his friend Billy Grady, "and I don't think Bill weighed over 160 pounds, 165 tops in New York. If he did, he went to the athletic club and worked it out." Fields was self-conscious about his looks, owing, in part, to the nose he inherited from the Felton side of the family and the bad complexion that came with the Dukenfields. Once he linked up with a woman, he tended to stay with her. "Bill was a one-gal guy," said Grady. "I never knew him to two-time."

After Hattie, he favored women who wouldn't compete with or correct him. Bessie was quiet and uncomplicated; anything he said or did was just fine with her. She asked nothing of him other than to just be with him, and as a member of the company, she was constantly around. When the show played Boston, Bessie, fairly obsessed with Fields, took him to meet her mother. They shared a rented house in Onset, near the home of actor Victor Moore, and Mrs. Witherell, Bessie's mother, served scallops for dinner. "He ate at least 15 scallop dinners that I cooked for them—how that man loved scallops!" He had a bad chest cold—a common occurrence—and Mrs. Witherell, who suspected he might be tubercular, warned her daughter not to kiss him. "My daughter answered, 'Mama, if I knew I would catch it and *die,* I wouldn't refuse to kiss him.' That is how much my daughter loved him—she was perfectly infatuated with him—crazy over him."

The *Follies of 1916* scored another record season, playing a total of forty-five weeks and grossing close to $1 million. Profits were thinner, as the costs were some $2,500 a week greater than for any of the previous editions of the show. Even as salaries and expenses soared, Ziegfeld was expected to continue to outdo himself with more beautiful girls, more lavish settings, better songs, funnier comedians. It was a cycle he couldn't sustain indefinitely, but Fields' participation in the 1917 edition of the *Follies* helped make it the greatest assemblage of comedic talent in the history of the New York stage. Bessie would play no part in it, though, for by the time the show opened at the New Amsterdam Theatre, on June 12, 1917, she was pregnant with Fields' second child.

# Eight

# A Game of Golf

In March 1917, Ziegfeld had cabled Fields in Indianapolis: "Have you anything to suggest for next season? Do you think you can do anything with golf?" But having mined comedy from the games of pool and croquet, Fields was already constructing an act around the game of tennis. It was a sport for which he had developed something of a passion; he used the courts at 119th Street and Riverside Park in New York and was, by all accounts, an expert and fiercely competitive player. His bit for the *Follies of 1917* was created in the same manner as his famous pool routine—through simple observance and exaggeration. Still, there was nothing easy about the process, and he spent nearly eight months perfecting "A Game of Tennis" before putting it in front of an audience at the Apollo Theatre in Atlantic City.

Fields' partner in the sketch was Walter Catlett, an actor and able comedian who was to enjoy a long and distinguished career in motion pictures. He was, in fact, so perfectly suited to Fields' particular brand of comedy that it is both surprising and unfortunate they never teamed again. From the moment he first sauntered onstage, littering a banana peel for Fields, who was burdened with an armful of tennis rackets, to slip on, Catlett helped make "A Game of Tennis" a deft ballet of petty annoyances, the pool act in white shorts with a pair of admiring girls thrown in for good measure. Using a racket strung with yarn, Fields palmed a white billiard ball for his opening volley and ran it clear through the mesh as he attempted the shot. A second ball made of dough fell to the stage with a leaden thud. "We minced around emphasizing the dainty aspects of the game as it was played at polite upper-class parties of that time," Catlett recalled. "Occasionally we'd have elegant little arguments but allow people to understand that we'd really like to break each other's necks." Fields would juggle when the notion struck him, and, as with the pool routine, no two performances were exactly alike. "Mr. Fields plays a comedy tennis match with himself—Walter Catlett assisting—in which he catches the returning balls in his hat, on his head, in the side pockets of his coat, and occasionally on his racket," Burns Mantle observed of the opening-night performance.

The 1917 edition of the *Follies* was historic in its concentration of great comedians. Every night at 8:10, with matinees on Wednesdays and Saturdays, the casual theatergoer could enjoy Fields and Catlett in their tennis sketch, comedy and songs from Bert Williams, the *Follies* debut of Eddie Cantor, Fannie Brice's turn as a Yiddisher dancer who was "all Egyptian but her nose," and the impromptu observations of Will Rogers—all for just $2. The *Follies* was a topical show, and Fields began seeing the value of developing and owning his own material. He saw how Bert Williams, despite his brilliance as both a physical and verbal comic, had left himself too dependent on Ziegfeld's harried writers, and so when Ziegfeld renewed Fields' contract for a third season, on May 2, 1917, his wire—at Fields' insistence—specifically affirmed that the "Tennis game that you are to introduce as specialty remains your property at the end of season." It was a practice that would continue throughout the rest of Fields' association with the Great Glorifier.

Required to perform in sketches and blackouts and even sing a little, Fields grew more comfortable with the spoken word and began embellishing the dialogue scripted for him.* In the "New York Streets and Subway" episode, Walter Catlett played a stranger bewildered by the high costs of the city. Enter Fields, trundling a small pushcart with a whistling peanut roaster. The line he was scripted to deliver was "Peanuts!" but in performance it became: "Seeking sustenance from peanuts, friend? Those small yet succulent morsels of tastiness?" This led to an elaborate exchange over the identity of a mutual acquaintance. "Ah yes, Charles G. Bates. A bell seems to tinkle. I concede the name might in truth be familiar. Perchance you too have a moniker?" Three lines and seven words grew to twenty-one lines and more than a hundred words as Fields put his own distinctive spin on the text.

With the *Follies of 1917,* Fields embraced writing with a zeal unmatched since his early days as a juggler. An unproduced sketch for the show, "One of the Six Best Cellars," survives, as does a movie scenario titled *The Man with a Grouch.* Fields apparently offered the latter to Gaumont (which had briefly reentered the American film market) in May 1917, sketching the first tentative characteristics of a man he would play for the rest of his days: "The birds are singing, the flowers are in full bloom—all is at peace with nature—but the grouch does not know it." Unproduced, *The Man with a Grouch* is a veritable

---

*Fields' changes may have been the result of a famously bad memory. He had a trick of writing out scripted dialog in order to memorize it, but when he got onstage, he would catch the meaning of the text while framing it in his own unique manner. His fascination with two-dollar words served him especially well.

catalogue of sight gags that were to become recurring staples of Fields' comedy routines: the hat that finds the tip of the walking stick instead of the head . . . the paper that sticks to the hand and everything else in sight . . . the dog that gets blamed for the innocent sprinkle of water . . . the limb that finds itself caught in the cuspidor . . . all make their first scripted appearances in this amazing document. As it ends, the grouch is on the sidewalk in front of his hotel, his precious grip is full of broken bottles, and a cop is pinching him for toting booze in a dry state.

At first, Bessie Poole denied that she was ever going to have a child. "Who's pregnant?" she erupted when Billy Grady dared to suggest the obvious. "I ain't pregnant, never was pregnant, and never will be pregnant—I hate kids!" When the *Follies of 1917* went into rehearsal, though, she was in no condition to participate. "Bessie and I lived together in the Bristol Hotel in New York during June and July," Faye O'Neill remembered, "and it was obvious she was expecting a baby." Through Lou Martel, another Follies girl, Bessie met Lou's sister-in-law, a quiet nonprofessional named Rose Holden. Rose and her husband were childless at the time, and when Bessie, upon meeting her, asked if she would take the baby, Rose thought about it, talked it over with her husband, and eventually said yes. Fields arrived to collect Bessie after the show, and upon hearing the news thanked Rose profusely. "That will take a lot off our minds," he said, "because Bessie wants to go with the show in the fall."

In August, Fields took an apartment for Bessie at the St. Nicholas in upper Manhattan under the arbitrary name of Morris, and on August 15, 1917, she gave birth to a baby boy at Stern's Sanitarium. The father on the birth certificate was given as one William R. Morris, an actor. Bessie had a brother named Rexford who lived in Boston, and so the baby's name became William Rexford Fields Morris. A month later, on September 12, just as the *Follies* was set to close in New York, Fields and Bessie brought the baby to Rose Holden's home on West 130th Street, near St. Nicholas Park. The child may well have been premature, for Rose remembered Fields commenting specifically on his size and color. "He was talking about the baby being so red, and I made some remark about mentioning his nose. I always called him a rummy nose, you know. He took it in a joke, but maybe I shouldn't have said that."

Fields asked Rose what she wanted, and she said, "Well, it isn't that . . ." She was in good circumstances at the time. "I will leave it to you. I don't know."

"Will twelve dollars be all right?"

"I suppose so."

The baby was never a replacement child, in the sense that Fields was seeking another chance at parenthood. He never expressed an interest in the boy as anything other than an obligation, and seemed merely to be indulging Bessie for the sake of the relationship. Still, he was in a naturally paternalistic mood when the *Follies* rolled into Boston for the start of its annual tour, and young Eddie Cantor became the beneficiary of his largess. "What he saw in me," said Cantor, "I don't know." Cantor, who had just turned twenty-five, had a wife and a new daughter, and was, by his own admission, "pretty cocky." He had been onstage since the age of sixteen, working his way (just as Fields had) through burlesque and vaudeville to a spot in the fourth edition of Ziegfeld's *Midnight Frolic.* For the *Follies of 1917* he did a blackface turn, putting his songs over by prancing about the stage, his banjo eyes rolling behind an outsized pair of white eyeglasses and his gloved hands clapping excitedly. "I'd been good enough on the Roof to make the big show," Cantor said, "and I reported for rehearsal in jig time. But when I was introduced to a sandy-haired fellow with a nasal drawl, I was so scared I shook."

Fields, whom Cantor had first seen in *The Ham Tree,* could be a forbidding figure under the most cordial of circumstances. He had a reputation as a quick temper, and the Ed Wynn incident was legend already. He watched as Cantor rehearsed a scene with Bert Williams, and saw how Williams tried unsuccessfully to tone him down. When the rehearsal ended, Fields motioned him over. "You don't have to bang that line over, boy. When you're on stage with Bert Williams, there's no other place for the audience to look except at you and Bert. You don't have to grab the audience by the collar." He showed the hyperkinetic kid how to get his points across through gesture rather than volume. Cantor was not a well-educated man, and when he made a grammatical error, Fields corrected him. "Each night he would get out the dictionary and pick out three words that he made me use in sentences." On the road, Fields permitted the young man to room with him—something of an honor—and started talking to him about literature. "He went over to one of his big trunks and flipped back the lid. Not a thing in it but books! What he was looking for wasn't in that trunk, so he flipped the lid of the next one, fished out a copy of *Oliver Twist* and gave it to me. The next night, when we got back after the show and had ordered up some food, he sat and questioned me about what I'd read. 'Just why did Nancy feel any loyalty to Bill Sykes?' " For the duration of the tour, Cantor became Fields' project. *Les Misérables* followed *Oliver Twist,* then Dumas, George Eliot, Mark Twain—the works. In the morning, they'd review the local papers. Fields was an astute, albeit cynical, analyst of the news. "It wasn't enough to read the story," said Cantor. "What was behind it?"

When the company arrived in Philadelphia for a two-week stand at the Forrest Theatre, Fields stayed, as he usually did, with his mother on Marshall Street. Virtually the only time Kate Dukenfield got dressed up was to see her son in the *Follies.* She lived alone, Leroy having married in 1915. Adele, also married, lived one door down, at 3921 Marshall. Kate rejoiced when her eldest son came to town; she kept the front bedroom reserved for him, and he always felt obliged to use it, even though she made it nearly impossible for him to sleep. In at one or two in the morning, Fields was invariably awakened at daybreak, his mother's voice cutting through the ambient sounds of the neighborhood like a foghorn, admonishing all who came within earshot—milkman, newsboy, neighbors, tradesmen—to keep their noise down, lest they wake her famous boy. "Yes, he's up there now," she'd say. "Got in late. Needs his sleep."

The *Follies* settled into its traditional holiday mooring in Chicago, where it remained until March 1918. Spring took the show to St. Louis, Cincinnati, Indianapolis, Columbus, Buffalo, Toronto, and, lastly, Montreal, Fields making the jumps at the wheel of his open car, bundled in an outsized raccoon coat and seemingly oblivious to the elements, Bessie at his side, their passengers protected by a tarpaulin stretched taut across the automobile, slits cut to permit their heads to peep through, and fortified against the cold with an inventory of premium stimulants. Their frequent stops to reconnoiter and indulge (or to "feed the rabbits," as Bessie so eloquently put it) could stretch a three-hour trip into six or eight hours and make commuting with Fields a trial for all but the heartiest of souls.

When the weather was fair, in September and October and sometimes in late spring, he would have the boot packed with groceries and keep an eye out for an open field. "He had all the equipment Lewis & Conger stocks, the baskets, the thermos jugs," said Cantor, who, along with Fannie Brice, was a frequent passenger during the 1917–18 tour. "He'd build a fire and fry potatoes and broil steaks. It was fine traveling in good weather, but he didn't care what the weather, rain or shine. You don't know what cold is until you've traveled across country at seventy miles an hour in zero weather in Fields' open car."

When it came time to design a specialty for the *Follies of 1918,* Fields recalled Ziegfeld's suggestion of a golf routine and created an act variously known as "A Game of Golf" and "An Episode on the Links." Briefly, he had flirted with golf as a source of comedy in *His Lordship's Dilemma,* but he hadn't yet become an ardent follower of the game. It wasn't until he assembled the eighteen-minute scene at Ziegfeld's behest that comparisons invariably turned to England's Harry Tate.

A renowned comedian, Tate's pattern of work in the music halls very closely presaged Fields' own trajectory. His early hits were all grandly verbal, but he eventually abandoned mimicry for a series of sporting sketches—the first known as "Motoring"—that established his character as a bumbling, bombastic autocrat who could reduce any situation to chaos. "Fishing" came after "Motoring," and, by 1906, Harry Tate's Company was playing New York, Africa, and Australia. His golfing sketch, introduced in 1907, was widely taken as the model for Fields' own "A Game of Golf," but their similarities were more coincidental than plagiaristic. Tate had a trademark moustache—as did many comedians of the period—that hung off the nose and rocked from side to side, but where Tate's moustache was long, bushy, and waxed at the ends, the one Fields wore, though of the same hook-and-eye variety, was briefer and less animated. There were also fundamental differences in the material each man could perform, for while Tate distinguished himself with memorable commentary in the face of calamity ("always in control of the situation"), he had no skills as a juggler and could never have worked anything as adroit as Fields' pool, croquet, and tennis acts. Conversely, Fields would have been profoundly uncomfortable with the large amounts of dialogue that routinely issued forth from Tate.

In "A Game of Golf," Fields' dialogue was brimming with braggadocio and clearly not in the Tate mold of comedy: "I haven't played since playing in the Canary Islands many years ago," he booms as Colonel Bogey, entering stage left with a partner, Miss Green, and his caddy, Willie Sniff. "In the early days we used to tee up on one island and drive to the other." Miss Green asks, "How far is it from one island to the next?" and Bogey replies, "Oh, about four or five miles." He works his way through a series of defective clubs in much the same way he worked through his pool cues. One bends. Another breaks. A third telescopes and collapses on cue. The caddy's shoes squeak. The greenkeeper's lunch includes a pie wrapped in crisp paper, and it sticks to everything in sight. At the end of the sketch, Fields has a hunter, Fred Shootem, walk into the scene and fire into the sky, bringing a stuffed turkey down on Fields' head. Amid the ensuing commotion, Miss Green's dress is torn off, and as she darts from the stage, Fields and his caddy take off in hot pursuit.

In "A Game of Golf," Fields used a character with a defiantly belligerent attitude toward life. Like Tate, he was beset by irritations firmly beyond his control, but where Tate was merely trying to cope, Fields was always fighting back. The caddy, who is the source of much of his irritation, bears the brunt of his abuse, and when the little man tries to pull the sticky paper from his shoe, Fields wrestles the shoe from his foot and then, distracted by a hole in his sock, brings the club down on his big toe. After months of work and rework, Fields showed the sketch to Ziegfeld, who regarded it glumly and made a suggestion for the part of the hunter: "Use a girl for the role."

"It's a man's role!" said Fields.

"I know, but who wants a man?"

Ziegfeld also decreed a Russian wolfhound appear in the scene. He had seen a picture of a society girl with one in a newspaper and, according to

*"A Game of Golf" was originally suggested by Flo Ziegfeld, who proceeded to cast a woman in the part of the hunter. From left to right: John Blue, William "Shorty" Blanche, Fields, Allyn King, and Martha Mansfield as Miss Hope I. Shootem*

Fields, "dropped the paper, ran out, bought a wolfhound, and told me he was going to have one of his glorified girls, Dolores,* walk across the stage, leading the hound, in the middle of my act!" Again, Fields squawked, but it did no good, and at the next performance, just as he was building up a laugh by stepping in the greenkeeper's pie, the regal Dolores emerged from the wings leading the Russian wolfhound and walking in the trademark Ziegfeld manner (back arched, chin held high). "I lost my audience instantly," said Fields.

> They didn't know what it was all about. I wasn't going to give up my scene without a fight, so I looked at Dolores in amazement, and then at the audience as if I, too, were shocked at this strange sight on the golf course. When she was halfway across the stage, I said, "That's a very beautiful horse."
>
> It got a big laugh. Dolores was so indignant, because I had spoiled her parade, that she grabbed the hound around the shoulders and ran off the stage with him in her arms—and that was another laugh.

---

*Dolores (1892–1975), like most showgirls, could neither sing nor dance. She distinguished herself in the *Follies* by moving across the stage in expensive costumes.

Ziegfeld and Dolores raised the very devil. I maintained I had improved the scene. They said I had ruined it, and finally we compromised. I was to let her have her moment, and was not to speak the line until she was one step from her exit. It turned out that the suspense made it all the better.

Fields had grown fascinated with the sounds of words and why audiences found some words funnier than others. "I experimented night after night to find out what animal was the funniest. I finally settled upon, 'That's a very beautiful camel.' " The line stayed in the act, but when Fields had the script copyrighted, in August 1918, he returned the hunter's role to that of a man's. "Ziegfeld spent fortunes on comedians but never liked them," he said reflectively upon the great showman's death, in 1932. "Why he tolerated me for so long, I do not know."

The 1918 season of the *Follies* was turbulent, and Fields finally tired of Ziegfeld's seeming indifference to his work. During one rehearsal, the boss called the assistant stage manager over and asked how long it took the girls to dress for the next number. "Five minutes," came the reply. "Cut Fields' number to five minutes," he said.

"Whenever Ziegfeld had a mood, which was often, he took it out on me," said Fields. The annual renewal of his contract was virtually the only inkling he ever had that Ziggy was pleased with his work. Even that was a grind: "When we play Columbus at the end of the run, Ziegfeld'll start sending you critical telegrams," he warned Eddie Cantor. "He'll criticize you to the point where you'll be glad to work next year for the same money you got this year. Don't be fooled like I was. You're working for four hundred dollars this year, hold out for six hundred."

The annual tour of the *Follies* opened in Boston on September 16, but the worldwide pandemic of influenza hit the United States so hard that theaters all along the Eastern Seaboard were closed to help stifle the spread of infection. The company was chased back to New York, where it spent most of October in residence at the Globe Theatre. Performers were expected to play Sunday afternoons for the troops shipping out overseas, and Fields found himself working seven days a week. On October 15, 1918, he accepted an offer from Hugh D. McIntosh, governing director of Rickards' Tivoli Theatres, Ltd., to make yet another tour of Australia over the summer of 1919. Fields informed Ziegfeld he would be unavailable for the thirteenth edition of the *Follies* and arranged international copyrights for his tennis and golf routines. He also began assembling a company that included Bessie Poole (under the name Elizabeth Chatterton) and William Blanche, a toothless dwarf known as "Shorty."

Blanche had been with Fields since 1915, when he was hired as a valet for the road tour of the *Follies*. "I was a stage clearer at the New Amsterdam," he told a reporter in 1924. "[Fields] was playing there then, and I used to stand in the wings every night . . . and laugh my head off. I guess he appreciated my appreciating him, because he took me with him after that, and I've been with him ever since." Blanche, then twenty-nine, was present one evening when Fields had a violent eruption with comic Harry Kelly over the latter's handling of the caddy's part in the golf scene. Kelly was arguably a bigger name than Fields, having been a star in the legitimate theater when Fields was still tramping it in vaudeville, but, like Ed Wynn, Kelly was incapable of playing in support of another comedian.* The two men came to blows in the wings, and Fields sprained a wrist in the melee. "Anybody will do!" he shouted as Kelly brusquely tendered his resignation. "Anybody will be better than Kelly!" The next time the curtain rose on "A Game of Golf," Shorty was playing the part instead.

Fields delighted in putting the little man onstage. Not only did he have absolute control over his performance, but the dwarf's grotesque appearance offended the superstitious Ziegfeld, who wanted him removed from the act. Shorty, according to Billy Grady, "looked as though someone had started pushing his head down and someone else his feet up, much like an accordion. They stopped when they got halfway." Ziegfeld prevailed for at least one performance and persuaded the elfin-faced comedienne Ray Dooley (who, at five feet, was not much taller than Shorty) to appear in Shorty's place. Unaware of the switch, Fields began his nightly ritual of abuse and had pretty well beaten her up when he realized that it was she, and not Shorty, in the costume. Visibly upset, he almost fumbled the act, and followed her around the theater the rest of the evening begging her forgiveness.

Shorty Blanche had lived the same kind of hardscrabble life as his employer and was indulged accordingly. He helped himself to loose change whenever the opportunity arose and got into Fields' liquor reserves on a regular basis, selling drinks to the chorus girls and refilling the empty bottles with water. Nevertheless, Fields entrusted him with every key he owned and treated him as he would an ill-trained pet, merely punishing him for the bad behavior into which he invariably fell. "Anytime you heard a lot of noise around the the-

*Especially irksome to Fields was Sime Silverman's comment in *Variety* that whatever "genuine humor" the scene contained had been the work of Kelly.

*"Any Old Time at All" had Fields, Will Rogers, Eddie Cantor, and Harry Kelly*
*in support of Lillian Lorraine, 1918.*

atre," said Ray Dooley, "you knew it was Fields and Shorty having an argument." Shorty's best attribute, apart from being an ideal stooge for Fields' relatively unique brand of rough humor, was his punctuality and absolute
dependability in matters of business. He loved being in the *Follies* and prided
himself on never missing a performance. Despite their almost constant bicker-
ing, he and Fields were devoted to one another.

In the year following the birth of their son, Bessie and Fields settled into a
comfortable pattern of absentee parenthood. When in town, they would visit
the boy at Rose Holden's place, where they came to be known as Aunt Bessie
and Uncle Bill. Fields made sure Rose got her $25 every two weeks, usually giv-
ing the money to Bessie to pass along in cash. He spoke hopefully of their son,
as if to somehow ameliorate the painful memory of Claude's rejection. Within
the *Follies* company, Bessie was known as Bill's girl, and there were rumors of
an illegitimate child, but no one openly broached the subject. "Bessie, in my

recollection, never put herself forward," said Doris Eaton, who, at the age of fourteen, was touring as Doris Le Vant. "She was sort of retiring. She had a good sense of humor and always made us laugh, but she never tried to be one of the important chorus girls." Bessie was an imp in a scene set in Hades in which Fields portrayed the renegade Republican senator Robert Marion La Follette, and Will Rogers was His Satanic Majesty. Fields and Rogers were further on display, in white ties, top hats, and tails, as members of a male chorus flanking longtime *Follies* beauty Lillian Lorraine as she sang "Any Old Time at All." Despite Lorraine's newsmaking return to the *Follies* after an absence of six years, the most comment in the press was generated by the balleretic Marilyn Miller, a veteran of the Shuberts' *Passing Show* who would go on to star in some of Ziegfeld's greatest successes of the 1920s.

In anticipation of his Australian tour, Fields spent much of his time on the road writing, and in the spring of 1919 was able to copyright three new works. The most important of these was "An Episode at the Dentist's," which was too gruesome for Ziegfeld but rough enough to appeal to the raucous audiences to which Rickards had introduced him in 1903. Fields passed the time sitting in hotel lobbies, watching the people and taking down notes. "I'd had wonderful opportunities to study people," he later said, "and every time I went out on the stage I tried to show the audience some bit of true human nature."

Worried that he was producing a generic brand of comedy that could be performed by just about anyone, Fields began work on a scene based on a definite character, a harried family man named Mr. Fliverton whose new car was his pride and joy. The scene was similar in tone and content to Harry Tate's 1903 classic "Motoring," which had fixed Tate's character in the public mind for all time. Now, upon leaving the *Ziegfeld Follies,* Fields would attempt to do the same thing for himself.

*Nine*

# *The Family Ford*

Fields applied for a new passport on April 29, 1919, and his impending tour of Australia was announced the following week in the pages of the *New York Dramatic News.* Ziegfeld went ahead without him, engaging composer and lyricist Blanche Merrill to write the entire first act of the new *Follies* and Irving Berlin to do likewise for the second half. The *Follies of 1918* gave its final performance in Boston on May 10, 1919, and the cast was hustled back to New York for the annual Follies–Frolic Ball atop the New Amsterdam. Rehearsals for the *Follies of 1919* were set to begin on June 2, with Ziegfeld, who had been the first to raise the price for seats on the lower floor to $3 the previous year, rumored to be considering a top of $3.50—a move that brought gasps from the ticket agencies and was front-page news in *Variety.*

Fields was set to sail on June 6 when news of a new tax imposed on foreign workers by the Australian government reached him. Hugh McIntosh showed how the commonwealth had allowed an exemption of £156—roughly $780—on earnings and that the tax payable on the balance would likely be less than $500 on a twenty-week tour. "This," McIntosh wrote, "is by no means an excessive charge and is considerably lower than the English Income Tax." Yet any foreign tax was too much for Fields, who had watched domestic tax rates rise to 77 percent during the war. Communication with the Rickards organization was cordially but summarily terminated, and Fields made plans to return to vaudeville over the summer with Bessie and Shorty Blanche.

The coincidence of the Australian tour and its subsequent cancellation saved Fields from getting caught in one of the bitterest labor struggles of the twentieth century—the great Actors' Equity strike of 1919. It drove a wedge between Flo Ziegfeld and Eddie Cantor that took years to repair, and brought the *Follies*—along with some forty other shows in New York, Chicago, and Boston—to a screeching halt. Fields had earlier been a member of the White Rats, an organization formed for the protection of vaudeville artists, but had gone with Ziegfeld, who was considered legit, and therefore Equity, by the time a prolonged strike irreparably weakened the Rats in 1917. Largely apolitical, Fields seemed to regard the unions he joined as fraternal, since he made his own contracts and drove his own bargains, but he was, given his sympathies for the underdog, naturally disposed to collective bargaining throughout his adult life. Because of his relationship with Bessie, he was particularly cognizant of the abuses traditionally heaped on chorus girls—weeks of uncompensated rehearsal time, arbitrary dismissal, pay cuts, and contracts broken at will. When the strike began, on August 7, 1919, he was not only foursquare behind Equity but an active supporter of the cause.

The strike broke on a Thursday night, and twelve theaters immediately went dark. Ten others, including the New Amsterdam, stayed open, the executive secretary of the Actors' Equity Association explaining, with some embarrassment, that it was "a rather big task" to close the whole street down in one blow. The *Follies* played according to program that night, a surprise to some because Eddie Cantor was a member of the Equity Council. The next afternoon, though, Cantor was announcing the show would not go on that night and intimating that other cast members would join him in a walkout. He did sit out the first half, playing the second half of the show only after Ziegfeld gave his assurances that he was not a member of the Producing Managers' Association and, therefore, exempt from a work stoppage. Over the weekend, the PMA claimed Ziegfeld as one of their own, a point Equity, on Cantor's assurances, was at pains to refute. The tug-of-war intensified, and it fell to Ziegfeld to declare himself publicly, which he finally did on Monday, first by obtaining a court injunction against the AEA and its specific members in the cast, and then by announcing to the press that he had indeed joined hands with the producers.

Cantor understandably felt double-crossed and played the Monday- and Tuesday-night performances under protest. When, on Wednesday, the order restraining the performers was modified, he walked out on Ziegfeld, pausing only to draw his salary at the box office, which he promptly turned over to the Equity strike fund. John Steele, Van and Schenck, Johnny and Ray Dooley, and Eddie Dowling followed suit, forcing the house manager to announce that the performance had been canceled "owing to several desertions," a declaration that was greeted with cheers, jeers, and laughter from the audience.

Happily, Fields could support the strike without putting himself in the uncomfortable position of actually having to walk out on Flo Ziegfeld. Six days after the *Follies* closed, he performed his golf act at a benefit for the AEA at the Lexington Opera House, sharing the bill with Marie Dressler, Charles Winninger, Eddie Foy, Pearl White, Frank Tinney, and Cantor, who, a couple of days earlier, had said he would "go back to the cloak and suit trade" if Equity lost its battle with the producers. Ed Wynn, who was appearing in the *Gaieties* at the time, was enjoined by the Shuberts from appearing onstage at the Lexington, so he took a seat in the orchestra and did his talking turn from there instead. After the performance, Fields took Wynn's head in his hands and kissed him on the forehead, ending nearly three years of silence between them.

With Cantor's withdrawal, Fields did not, as widely expected, step into the *Follies of 1919* when the strike had been settled, choosing instead to work the Roof, where a new edition of the *Midnight Frolic* was scheduled to open on October 2. The New Amsterdam had always had a rooftop performance space (as did most of the major New York theaters in the days before air conditioning), incorporating an open-air café and a charming jewel box of a theater that seated nearly seven hundred. The Aerial Gardens had been dark for several years when Ziegfeld moved into the building in 1913 and decided to turn the room into a nightclub, adding a dance floor, a stepped platform for a stage, and glass runways suspended out over the main floor so that the audience could look up the girls' dresses. He renamed it the *Danse de Follies* and staged his first midnight revue there in April 1915. Bucking the trend toward free entertainment where food was served, Ziegfeld charged $2 for the *Frolic*—the same price he got for the *Follies*—and gave good value in packing the rooftop show with many of the same performers he used in the big room. Within a month, he was boasting that the "free" shows on other roofs were driving patrons to his aerial resort in such numbers that he couldn't handle them all. Regulars at the time included William Randolph Hearst, tenor John McCormack, and Diamond Jim Brady.

Fields had remained aloof of the *Frolic* for four seasons while Will Rogers, Bert Williams, Eddie Cantor, and Fannie Brice played in various editions, sometimes doing so in addition to their regular duties in the *Follies* downstairs. In December 1918, while the main show was out on tour, Ziegfeld decided to add a dinner show he called the *Nine O'Clock Frolic,* a hedge against the looming ratification of the Eighteenth Amendment, which would likely kill any demand for a midnight revue. Fields contributed his golf act while dedicating his daylight hours to the refinement of his Fliverton sketch, which he registered with the U.S. Copyright Office on October 15, 1919.

"The Family Ford" was unlike anything Fields had ever attempted. Instead of being either a tramp or a dandy—someone to be laughed at but not identified with—the character of George Fliverton was a family man out to enjoy one of the great recreational privileges of the modern middle class—the country drive. The influence of Harry Tate is obvious, but so is the influence of Jim Dukenfield, after whom the short-fused character of Fliverton was patterned. When Tate's "Motoring" was first conceived, the motorcar was still something of a novelty in Britain, and not many people had actually had the experience of riding in one. By the time Fields tackled the subject, some fifteen years later,

Henry Ford had made popular ownership a reality through mass production of the Model T, and the frustrations of owning one were familiar to all. Tate's sketch grew over time as characters were added—the twit of a son, the know-nothing chauffeur, the abusive schoolmaster—and as the car was finally made to move, a policeman appeared to issue a citation. But where Tate was a master of the slow burn, Fields came out swinging with his very first line, shouting down his wife and telling his little daughter to shut up. "Someday you'll learn it's very bad policy to monkey with the machinery of a high-powered motor-car!" he yells as the car comes to a halt. "When I sold our small car and bought this Ford . . ."

"When you sold your *small* car?" says Mrs. Fliverton incredulously. "They don't build anything smaller than a Ford, do they?" As the couple argues, a blind man enters the scene and pokes one of the headlights out with his cane. Fliverton's bratty daughter taunts him with a tin horn, his father-in-law tosses food on the ground, and his wife bursts into tears when Fliverton blames her for the breakdown. "Never mind what I told you to do!" he bellows. "You do what *I* tell you!" A woman pushes a baby carriage into the scene and knocks a fender off the car. Fliverton jacks the car up to replace a tire, and his little girl drops ice cream down the back of his neck. When the Ford suddenly rattles to life, everybody jumps in, Fliverton yanks the jack out from under it, and the whole thing collapses in a heap.

With "The Family Ford," Fields did violence to the twin illusions of prosperity and marital harmony, serving them up on a platter for the common man. No one had ever experienced a day quite like this one, but everyone had fought with their spouse, whacked their kid, had a Sunday picnic ruined by a breakdown. Fliverton's irrationality and irritability brought howls of recognition from the women in the audience, and more men knew about the failures of Fords than any other make of automobile. Fields had finally stepped away from the pool table, the tennis court, the golf course, and taken a place at the kitchen table of everyday life. It was nothing short of revolutionary for a scene in the *Follies,* and Ziegfeld hated every minute of it.

Flo Ziegfeld wasn't interested in the common man; he was interested in the uncommon woman. Besides thinking it was as unfunny as anything Fields had ever attempted, Ziegfeld found the constant nattering in "The Family Ford" grating and unpleasant. He told Fields he wouldn't allow it in the *Follies of 1920* and urged him to come up with something else instead. Fields, who at the time was performing his croquet act in the *Nine O'Clock Revue* (which actually started at 8:30) and doing a juggling turn for the *Midnight Frolic,* was disinclined to go along with the boss and, convinced "The Family Ford" was surefire, dug into his own pocket to finance the construction of a trick car. In May, he hired a hall away from the New Amsterdam—and Ziegfeld's baleful gaze—to privately rehearse the company, which consisted of Fannie Brice, Ray Dooley, Shorty Blanche, and Jessie Reed. He eventually got Ziegfeld to permit it for the first Atlantic City performance, which traditionally ran long and was pared for New York. The audience, Ziggy grudgingly allowed, would decide for itself.

Fortunately, "The Family Ford" was a sensation. The advance word from New Jersey, where the show opened at the Apollo Theatre on June 15, 1920, was that the fourteenth edition of the *Ziegfeld Follies* was the most lavish and tuneful in history, and that Fields' new act was downright riotous. "Not even the famous golf scene . . . was as funny as Fields' adventures with this Ford," Philip Scheuer of *Variety* reported. "It will be safe to call it the funniest stage sketch in five years." Ziegfeld's response to its tumultuous reception was hardly encouraging: "It slows up the show," he complained. Rolling into New York, the *Follies* caught the attention of Sime Silverman, who cut nobody any slack and delighted in news of backstage chaos: "Stories wafted back from the seashore that Ziegfeld has sent for Ren Wolf to doctor up the comedy end and finally got George V. Hobart, that $75,000 worth of scenery and costumes had been stored away after the Atlantic City opening, and that the show was in bad shape. The show was in bad shape in comedy when starting off at the Amsterdam. It was badly off in all other departments as well, other than production." One report had Ziegfeld dropping a $25,000 Gilbert and Sullivan scene after one performance and likened Atlantic City to a political convention as far as the flock of authors was concerned.

To everyone's surprise, Eddie Cantor stepped into the second act of the *Follies* to fill a bad wait and justify a $4 admission price—the steepest on Broadway. "Cantor would have stopped the show if it could have been stopped," said Silverman, "for the applause was deafening." Like Ziegfeld, *Variety*'s editor disapproved of "The Family Ford," describing it as "closely resembling Tate's 'Motoring' in idea and execution." Moreover, the collapsible car failed to work on opening night, resulting in weak applause for what should have been a socko finish. Ziegfeld again made noises about cutting the scene, but Cantor only worked out the week, and the Fields scene stayed through necessity. Ziegfeld's distaste for the piece only strengthened Fields' resolve to create more scenes for Mr. Fliverton and his dysfunctional family. "There are many little incidents in a street car or elsewhere that are full of natural humor," he told a reporter, "and I want to crochet them together into acts."

Fields' taste for alcohol was no doubt sharpened by the fact that it was becoming an increasingly notorious commodity. Some states had never permitted the stuff, while others had gone dry before the Civil War. The Woman's Christian

Temperance Union and the Anti-Saloon League of America became political forces in the late 1800s by electing dry legislatures in the key states that remained wet. Twenty-one had banned saloons by 1916, and the elections that year returned a Congress in which the prohibitionists outnumbered wets two to one. Soon they were fashioning the Eighteenth Amendment—commonly known as the Volstead Act—to insert into the Constitution a nationwide ban on the manufacture, sale, and transportation of intoxicating liquors. Nebraska became the thirty-sixth state to ratify the measure, causing America to officially go dry on January 17, 1920.

Fields began traveling with liquor in 1916, fortifying himself against the arid counties in which he was compelled to play as a star of the *Follies*. His earliest writings for Ziegfeld displayed an abiding faith in the comedic properties of alcohol and its consumption. In 1917, he wrote a sketch for Walter Catlett as a dipsomaniacal businessman called "One of the Six Best Cellars," and the creeping criminalization of booze contributed a sock payoff to the scene in which he played the circumspect peanut vendor ("Seeking sustenance from peanuts, friend?"), and in which the cart, with the simple pull of a lever, was transformed into a fully stocked bar. "Name it, brother," was the curtain line.

Prohibition, for a time, made liquor less funny, and audiences—at least on the Roof—less responsive to good material. There was serious talk of eliminating the intermissions at burlesque and vaudeville houses, because the purpose of having them—so a man could run next door and down a highball between acts—had evaporated. "Since the installation of the torrid legislation a noticeable change has come over the complexion of the properties adjoining theatres," *Variety* reported. "Ice cream parlors and orange juice booths have supplanted the saloons." Sunday performances also enjoyed a brief vogue—the prohibitions on baseball and vaudeville having been lifted—and Fields appeared in a Sunday concert series at the New Amsterdam called *Tonight at 8:10*.

Ziegfeld was never much of a drinker himself and grew increasingly skittish about booze as the decade drew to a close. Bert Williams sang "You Cannot Make Your Shimmie Shake with Tea" in the *Follies of 1919*, but the 1920 edition was scrubbed free of Prohibition references. However comical the country's accommodations of the Volstead Act were, with hotels suddenly charging twenty-five cents a bottle for ginger ale and most dealers going underground with virtually the same clientele as before, none of it found its way into Ziegfeld's topical revue. Fields blithely maintained his backstage routine, keeping his door open to visitors and his trunk, which he called his "dispensary," close at hand, eschewing bathtub gin and bootleg beers for only the finest of imported labels (ofttimes supplied by stewards from ocean liners). "Newspapermen and others were welcome at all times," Marc Connelly remembered. "It was a great haven when Prohibition came along." Fields remained steadfast in his hospitality, even as he endured price hikes of 500 percent and more. "I'll say this about Fields' money," said Eddie Cantor. "He lived well."

Fields and Ziegfeld arrived at an accommodation for the *Follies of 1921,* Ziegfeld permitting another Fliverton sketch and Fields participating more fully in the show than he had the previous year, when "The Family Ford" was such a point of contention. His deal called for a salary of $800 a week, $25 extra for Shorty, and an additional hundred should he furnish a second scene of acceptable quality. Thus motivated, Fields stepped up his writing output, churning out at least five sketches (including two or three Flivertons) for Ziggy's consideration. One, called "Spring," was set in the yard of a Philadelphia row house, and the set he sketched bore a striking resemblance to the scene on Goodman Street the day his father stepped on a garden spade and then hurled it at his son. Fields loaded the scene with familiar business, puns, and at least one Prohibition joke:

WOMAN

Do you know where Dr. Shugg lives?

FLIVERTON

No, but you can buy some hundred-proof stuff at that grocery store without a prescription.*

Ziegfeld preferred "Off to the Country," in which the Flivertons repeatedly attempt to board a subway train while laden with fishing rods, worms, tennis rackets, birdcages, hatboxes, "impediments of every sort." It was the same comedy of frustration that had distinguished "The Family Ford," and Fields' character was just as irascible as before. The abrasiveness that so offended Ziegfeld was somewhat mitigated by Fields' other appearances in the show, the most prominent of which was an impersonation of John Barrymore in a burlesque of *Camille* that also featured Fannie Brice and Raymond Hitchcock as the actor's siblings, Ethel and Lionel. Singer-comedian Hitchcock, who was a particular influence on Ed Wynn, had joined the *Follies* after several seasons of his own revue, *Hitchy-Koo.* Like Fields, he was a student of the language, and the two men appeared in a total of five scenes together. "Mr. Fields juggles nary a jug on this occasion," Alexander Woollcott wrote with his customary disappointment. "Mr. Ziegfeld's rounding off process, continued through the years, has finally brought him forth merely as an actor."

---

*Under the new law, doctors were allowed to prescribe up to one pint of alcohol, for medicinal purposes, every ten days.

*Fields' handwritten notes for a Fliverton sketch entitled "Spring"*
*included this drawing of the proposed set.*

The first-act finale, a sendup of the Dempsey-Carpentier fight by Gene
Buck and Victor Herbert, cast Fields as the referee, with Brice, as Georges Car-
pentier, duking it out with Ray Dooley in what Woollcott regarded as "a
remarkably lifelike impersonation of Jack Dempsey." Fields worked hard
throughout, always helping the book laughs and always feeding as well as par-
taking, but it was Brice who was far and away the star of the show. She

appeared a dozen times and, in the words of Jack Lait, "guzzled the gravy and gobbled the apple sauce." For all its distinguished content, the *Ziegfeld Follies of 1921* has always been remembered as the show in which Fannie Brice first sang her two signature tunes: "My Man," adapted by Channing Pollock from "Mon Homme" and performed, at Ziegfeld's insistence, in tatters; and the Hanley and Clarke standard, "Second Hand Rose."

The *Follies* left for Boston on October 2, Fields piloting a new high-powered Lincoln for the occasion. His driving was never noticeably affected by the alcohol in his system, a fact evinced by the willingness of stars such as Fannie Brice and Eddie Cantor to ride with him. He was, in fact, a bold and assured driver who always acted decisively in times of peril. Leaving Cleveland one time, he noticed another car passing frequently, slowing down, accelerating, and figured it was a stickup. On the outskirts of Detroit, he rounded a bend and saw the car parked lengthwise across the road, two of the bandits standing next to it and a third at the wheel. He called to his passengers, "Want to take a chance with these thugs?" Not waiting for an answer, he floored the pedal. "I headed for the two feet of road that was behind the car and give my buggy all the gas it would take. Those two holdup men scattered as fast as they could—they didn't even stop to fire—and the driver shot his car in low and pulled out. We whistled by them at least 60 miles an hour, and I never took my foot off the throttle for miles."

The only time he left so much as a scratch on one of his cars, his drinking wasn't a factor at all. A blowout sent him careening into a ditch on a *Follies* jump between Washington and Pittsburgh, distributing his passengers about the landscape. Nobody appeared to be hurt except Will Rogers, who had a broken leg, and it was Fields who took command, hailing a passing car and getting his friend to a nearby hospital as quickly as possible. "As soon as he was taken care of, I heaved a sigh of relief. I started to take off my hat, but the thing wouldn't budge. I suddenly discovered that my head ached painfully. I finally got the hat off and discovered I had a bump on my head about twice the size my head normally was. And I didn't even think I had been hurt!"

Fields' mood during the 1921–22 tour of the *Follies* was not helped by his worsening relationship with Ziegfeld, who hated his material and threatened a salary cut. In Boston, Fields received a stern warning: "From your attitude and unwillingness to play the scenes fast that you are in, I came to the conclusion it was your desire to get out of the show. I admit you furnished some very good scenes for the show from time to time; some of them were great, some fair, and some not so good, and I want to remind you that I paid you—and paid you well—for every one. . . . I realize the contract you have with me and that you are loathe to give it up, but if you could arrange to release me immediately after the opening in Chicago, I would appreciate it, for I think you are doing yourself harm every time you go on in a performance, because the material you have for yourself this year is very punk, and my expenses being out of all proportion—hence this letter."

The *Follies* played an extra matinee in Pittsburgh on Thanksgiving Day, and Fields, as the Equity deputy on the show, demanded an extra one-eighth salary for the eleven chorus girls, including Bessie, who were Equity members.* Ziegfeld, who paid well above the Equity minimum of $35 a week, submitted the matter to arbitration and lost. Relenting, he ordered an extra dividend paid the entire company—not just Equity members—then required them all to sign new contracts agreeing to a 10 percent reduction in salary in any city where the *Follies* played more than eight performances a week. Bessie, in Cleveland, was one of only two girls in the chorus who refused to sign, and when Ziegfeld caught up with the company in Detroit, he directed that she be given her two-week notice.

Bad weather and heightened competition contributed to a rough season on the road, and as a hedge against dismissal, Fields arranged to sell his properties in Philadelphia, pressing Hattie to sign the papers by telling her he had an eager buyer in a difficult market. "And, as you probably know, I have been a flop in this season's *Follies* and will not be with the show after the opening in Chicago unless I take a cut in salary. Maybe they won't have me for the cut, so this money will come in handy." Fields prepared to declare war on Ziegfeld, using Ziegfeld's assault on the Eight Performance Clause to enlist Equity's help in the battle for Bessie's job. Investigations by three Equity representatives sustained Fields' contention that Bessie had been let out solely because she insisted on Equity conditions, and Executive Secretary Frank Gilmore approved secret plans for a job action to take place in Chicago on December 25, 1921. The AEA's Chicago representative mustered the support of the musicians' and stagehands' locals, and just moments before the curtain was set to rise on Christmas evening, he walked backstage at the Colonial Theatre and notified the company that unless the extra eighths awarded the chorus were paid and Bessie restored to her rightful place in the show, the *Follies* would not be permitted to open. With a $4,500 house already in the theater and $60,000 in advance sales, Ed Rosenbaum, the burly company manager, had no choice but to sign under duress, and the show went on as planned.

Fannie Brice, who had held out for an increase of her own before taking

---

*Equity's basic agreement with the producers defined a full workweek as eight performances, and the so-called "Eight Performance Clause" required members to be paid pro rata for any extra performances.

*Elizabeth Chatterton "Bessie" Poole*

the show out on tour, disowned the move, phoning Ziegfeld to emphasize she wasn't even in the theater at the time. Boiling mad over the controversy, Ziegfeld told *Variety* he had been unjustly treated, that conditions in the modern theater were deplorable, and that no self-respecting manager could tolerate them any longer. "So when the Equity Shop goes through in 1924," he said, "I am through with the show business in America."

Fields expected to pay a price for his defense of Bessie Poole, and he did so when Ziegfeld closed the show a month early and announced that no one concerned with the Chicago action would be retained for the *Follies of 1922*. Fields dusted off "The Family Ford" and, through Billy Grady, assembled a company to tour the sketch with comedian Jim Harkins in the role of Mr. Fliverton. Fields himself played the Keith circuit in "An Episode on the Links," and set about preparing his subway, tennis, and croquet acts for similar treatment. He told Hattie, in fact, to send their seventeen-year-old son to him and that he would put Claude to work in one of his touring companies. After seven years with Flo Ziegfeld, Fields' love for Bessie had landed him back in vaudeville, where, at the age of forty-two, he would attempt to make a new beginning for himself as a writer and producer.

*Ten*

# The Beloved Mountebank

Alexander Woollcott blamed Ziegfeld's "rounding off" process for turning one of the world's greatest jugglers into a mere actor, but Fields himself was only too happy to take credit for the metamorphosis. "I realized that if I was ever to get the chance I wanted, I would have to work it out for myself," he told an interviewer. "So I began to change my methods. . . . Little by little, I built up various acts. . . . I still did the juggling tricks which were expected of me, but more and more I subordinated these to real human comedy in gesture, expression, and action. . . . I tried to deal in ideas, not in mere mechanical stunts."

By the time Fields parted company with Ziegfeld, he had an inventory of some fifteen sketches in various stages of completion, including nine registered with the Copyright Office. Most were scenes he had written for himself, but he was trying his hand at other material as well and producing sharp satires of stage and screen conventions. The most bizarre of these experiments was an absurdist masterpiece called "What A Night!," in which lamps light from across the room, overcoats come off in halves, and sunfish are placed in the sun parlor, fed sunflowers, given their sunbaths, and taught to do the sun stroke. Police pound on the door of Lord Biggleswade's mansion: "We came here to smell your cellar." He calls back, "I haven't a drop in the house!" and the sergeant responds, "Do you want to buy some?"

Fields was still in the process of setting up his touring companies when hoofer George White offered to return him to the legitimate stage as a star of the *Scandals.* Of all the Ziegfeld imitators, White was probably the most highly regarded. He knew music like Ziegfeld knew girls, and where Victor Herbert's melodies and Joseph Urban's designs had come to define a sort of neoclassicist style for the *Follies,* White embraced the jazz age, hiring George Gershwin to write all of his music and importing Erté, the Russian-born designer of the *Folies-Bergère,* to invest his annual revue with an art deco sleekness. White had never had a formal dance lesson. Like Fields, he was completely self-trained, coming up through burlesque and vaudeville and landing in the *Follies of 1915,* where he was paired with luscious little Ann Pennington and quickly became the love of her life. White was in another Ziegfeld show, *Miss 1917,* before striking out on his own, taking Pennington with him and opening the *Scandals of 1919* at the Apollo Theatre—almost directly across the street from the New Amsterdam—a full two weeks ahead of the *Follies.* Apoplectic, Ziegfeld wired that he would pay White and Pennington $2,000 a week to close their show and return to the *Follies.* White responded by offering Ziegfeld and his wife Billie Burke $3,000 a week to join *his* show instead.

Still smarting from his tussle with Ziegfeld over Bessie Poole and the Eight Performance Clause, Fields considered his joining the *Scandals* to be an excellent way of rubbing Ziggy's upturned nose in it. And since White had kept the *Scandals of 1921* on tour well into July, the 1922 edition would get a convenient late-summer start at the Globe Theatre just as the *Follies* was clearing out of town. Plagued by the mounting cost of trying to match Ziegfeld for opulence— Paul Whiteman's orchestra alone cost $2,000 a week—White sought the financial help of his friend Al Jolson, who put a reported $25,000 into the show. The new *Scandals* would set a record for Broadway by charging $5.50 for *standing room* on opening night.* White upped the price of seats for subsequent performances to $4 and tax.

To write the show, White hired monologist Andy Rice, who, in his years as a performer, had revolutionized the traditional "Hebe" act by toning down the broad accent and harsh makeup of earlier times and delivering wickedly subtle accounts of family weddings and funerals. Initially, Rice was given Ann Pennington as the star of the new *Scandals,* but after quarreling with White, she returned to Ziegfeld, and Irene Castle was briefly attached to the show as her replacement. The cast wasn't complete until late July, when Winnie Lightner was announced in lieu of Mrs. Castle. Then Rice saw some of his prime material eliminated to make room for Fields and his scenes.

Rehearsals for *George White's Scandals* were as chaotic as any of Ziegfeld's, and Fields went about the staging of his own material as he had in previous years, hiring out a separate hall and remaining as aloof as possible from the musical elements of the show. Since White himself was also a performer, there was little time for him to lord over Fields or make the arbitrary cuts for which Ziggy was famous. As a star of the *Scandals,* Fields enjoyed a level of independence he hadn't known since his days in vaudeville, but a lack of supervision resulted in some decidedly uneven material. Fields wrote and

---

*Top for standing room had previously been $1.50 for important openings.

copyrighted several sketches for the *Scandals,* but they were thrown together quickly and were mostly derivative of earlier works. "The Sport Model" was an amalgam of "The Family Ford" and "Off to the Country," with the Bimbos overloading the old family heap on their way to Absess on the Hudson. A baseball sketch, apparently inspired by a similar scene in the *Follies,* was little more than the old tennis routine with a Louisville Slugger in place of the racket. Fields was much better served by a topical idea he called "Ten Thousand People Killed" (retitled "The Radio Bug"), in which he lampooned the national obsession for picking up broadcasts by turning the Shuggs' tiny one-room apartment into a spider's nest of wires. "I don't know why they call it wireless," moans Mrs. Shugg. "They ought to call it 'nothing but wires.' " Mr. Shugg strings still more cables, hoping to get a recital by a Mrs. Whiffin from Upper Sandusky. Of course, the radio continuously cuts out, so all the Shuggs hear are commercials, interspersed with tantalizing fragments of actual programming. It is the panic-inducing announcement "Ten thousand people killed . . ." that sends Mr. Shugg flying out the door for a paper, convinced another earthquake has hit San Francisco, only to miss ". . . ten million flies with the Cadula fly swatter last year."

On opening night, the radio bit was one of the few genuine hits in a decidedly ragged show that ran for almost four hours. White had traded a week of tryouts in Atlantic City for three inadequate days in New Haven, and what he delivered was a revue painfully in need of trims. Gershwin's "I'll Build a Stairway to Paradise," which closed the first act, was a genuine sensation, but, ironically, the most important piece of music in the show was eliminated entirely. "Blue Monday" was a gloomy concert piece for the Whiteman orchestra, an "Opera à la Afro-American" that presaged the composer's triumphant *Porgy and Bess.* It was an obvious cut at the time, overlong and out of step with the rest of the revue, and it wasn't until much later, when it was reorchestrated and retitled "135th Street," that it found its way to a more appropriate venue at Carnegie Hall. Whiteman's numbers dominated the program as well as the notices, and Fields was regarded as something of an afterthought. Woollcott happily noted that at least Fields provided a juggling specialty—the cigar box routine—but suggested that he should have stopped short of the unfortunate baseball sketch, which he tersely labeled as "stupid."

After the first night, White flew into action, reordering the progression of the show's twenty-three scenes and cutting, among other things, the dismal baseball routine, which he replaced with one of Andy Rice's deleted segments. Despite its problems, the *Scandals of 1922* carved its own niche in the marketplace, never attempting to compete with Ziegfeld in terms of pulchritude, but turning in a performance that was nonetheless livelier and, in some respects,

*Fields' work in* George White's Scandals
*was somewhat overshadowed by Paul Whiteman's band
and the music of George Gershwin.*

more entertaining than the tradition-bound *Follies.* It ran eleven weeks at the Globe, then was away on tour for the balance of the year.

Today, Philip Goodman is better known as one of H. L. Mencken's closest friends than for anything he ever did on his own, but in 1923 Goodman was one of Broadway's hottest new producers. His history is vague. He claimed to be descended from Portuguese Jews and one Isaac Abarbanal, a noble and a savant. He spent his childhood in Philadelphia, where his father, according to one report, was a prosperous banker. Goodman went to New York as a young man, where he worked for Theodore Dreiser and eventually opened a small advertising agency on Thirty-third Street in the garment district. Through Dreiser he met Mencken and printed two books authored by the Sage of Baltimore during a brief flirtation with publishing. He was nearly forty when he suggested to Don Marquis, a columnist for the *Tribune,* that the character of Clem Hawley, a comical drunk Marquis called "The Old Soak," would make a good basis for a play. "I didn't know anything about the show game," he admitted, "but I slipped Marquis $1200 advance royalty to write the piece. When it was finished it sounded good, and I wanted to see it presented on the stage, never figuring it would land the way it did."

Goodman took the play to Arthur Hopkins and worked out a fifty-fifty split of the ownership. *The Old Soak* opened in August 1922 with actor Harry Beresford in the title role and became an immediate hit. Two road companies were spawned and a third was in the works when Goodman procured a second play to produce entirely on his own. *Poppy Comes to Town* was the work of an actress named Dorothy Donnelly, who was famous for her harrowing performance in the original New York production of *Madame X.* Ill health forced Donnelly into retirement at the age of thirty-six, and she turned to playwriting, collaborating on prim melodramas like *Flora Belle* and *The Riddle Woman.* Her new play was a Cinderella story, but what attracted Phil Goodman's attention was not so much the plight of the heroine, born to a circus worker and the unwitting heir to a fortune, but rather the character of her disreputable father, Professor Eustace McGargle. In McGargle, Goodman saw another indelible character along the lines of the Old Soak and, best of all, he knew exactly who could play him.

Assembling a road company of *The Old Soak,* Goodman had hit upon the idea of putting Raymond Hitchcock—who had done some credible drunk scenes in the *Follies of 1921*—in the part of Clem Hawley. "Hitchy" had become so strongly identified with musical comedy that his casting in a straight play was considered something of a stunt, but his work was phenomenal and Goodman was widely praised for his trouble. Encouraged to further flights of nontraditional casting, Goodman next thought of Fields, Hitchcock's comedic colleague in the *Follies,* when the part of McGargle presented itself. Goodman may have been inspired by Fields' work opposite Hitchcock as the blustery Elderberry in the Willard Mack scene "The Professor," but he also claimed to have been a Fields fan of long standing. "For twenty years," he told *Variety,* "I have thought him to be the funniest man in the civilized world."

There was a bit of the Old Soak and McGargle in Goodman himself. He was a man of enormous charm, impeccably tailored and conversant on most any subject. He was also a liar, a con, a raconteur of the worldliest sort. He weighed close to three hundred pounds, drank extravagantly, and liked to say that he didn't believe in working too hard. "You can make money not by working, but by getting others to work for you," he once told an associate. He got Fields to work for him because he offered him a chance that no other producer had dared to offer—a plum part in a Broadway play. "The gods certainly were good to me," Fields said, "for my part was one that had splendid possibilities."

The two men bonded instantly, Goodman being as nocturnal as Fields and rarely rising before noon. He appreciated good liquor and had a capacity that met Fields' own considerable facility. They dined regularly at the Colony, discussing the play (which was badly in need of some doctoring) and trading fanciful anecdotes about their vastly different childhoods in Philadelphia. "[Fields] was marvelously funny," said Goodman's daughter Ruth, who was fifteen at the time, "but there was never a dirty story—no smut. The humor was tender and humane." Afterward, they would often repair to the Goodman apartment for some low-stakes poker, Fields grandly shuffling the cards, sending them cascading into the air and catching them in his opposite hand. He was enchanted by Goodman's beautiful wife, Lilly, who had spent much of her youth in Berlin, and he found he could even trade a few words in German with her. He was particularly pleased to meet the revered Mencken, with whom he could discuss the brutal realism of Ibsen at length.* "He *knew* his Ibsen," Ruth Goodman said of Fields. One night, as he sat playing cards with her father, Ruth innocently made the comment that she didn't quite understand Ibsen, and Fields was caused to pause and lay his cards on the table. "You must never say a thing like that about Ibsen," he said to her solemnly.

*Poppy Comes to Town* was a challenge for Goodman because Dorothy Donnelly would brook no interference in her first solo effort as a playwright. Donnelly had set her play in the present day, but Goodman sensed its characters would play better in a period piece. Howard Dietz, who had earlier worked

---

*Mencken had edited translations of *A Doll's House, Little Eyolf,* and *Hedda Gabler* and was considered an authority on Henrik Ibsen and his plays.

*Fields and Philip Goodman, the producer of* Poppy, *became fast friends.*

for Goodman as a copywriter, was given the task of backing off the action fifty years, substituting horses for automobiles and revising the dialogue where necessary. In exchange, he was allowed to contribute the lyrics to a song called "Alibi Baby," one of six in the show. "Miss Donnelly said she would use the dialogue and the lyric," he recalled, "but would not give any credit in the program." In the end, she took credit for the book as well as the lyrics, leaving Stephen Jones and Arthur Samuels to share credit for the music. It would not be until Goodman's next show, *Dear Sir,* that the future lyricist of "Dancing in the Dark" and "That's Entertainment" would see his own name in print.

As pleased as Fields was with the part in *Poppy,* he was also terrified at the prospect of having to remember his lines. In the past, he had only had to learn enough to get himself through an eighteen-minute sketch, and in most of his own scripts he emphasized physical business over the spoken word. *Poppy* would run two and a half hours, and Fields would be onstage for a considerable part of that time. His only defense would be to influence the character, allowing himself a certain latitude to vamp as the need presented itself.

In bringing McGargle to life, Fields added elements of people he had known—Bill Dailey, Jim Fulton, even the rotund and autocratic Phil Goodman, whose habit of spinning elaborate stories of questionable veracity was rolled into the character. The play began with McGargle's arrival in the village of Green Meadow in 1874. He sells patent medicines at the county fair, works the shell game, and juggles to attract the crowds. Poppy, his adopted daughter, assists in the juggling act but disapproves of his swindles. Even so, she loves McGargle, and he obviously adores her. Opportunity knocks for them both when McGargle learns that a wealthy old man has died, leaving his fortune to a distant relative because the whereabouts of his own daughter, who ran off years before with a circus man, are unknown. The constable, one Amos Sniffen, suggests to McGargle that he forge a marriage certificate asserting that he had been married to the old man's daughter so that Poppy can claim the money. McGargle knows he must do so quietly, because Poppy would never go along with such a scheme were she to know about it. The upshot, of course, is that Poppy McGargle is indeed the genuine heir to the man's estate, her mother having been the man's daughter—a wardrobe mistress who died, leaving her friend McGargle, an old circus hand, to care for the child.

Rehearsals for *Poppy* were tense and unpleasant, and Fields quit several times over his inability to remember lines. This would have been just fine as far as Dorothy Donnelly was concerned, for she had come to loathe him and the violence he did to her text. Goodman, however, knew he was onto something and permitted Fields free rein over the script. From the evidence of his "sides" (half sheets, in booklet form, containing only his own lines and cues), Fields removed, rewrote, or amended entire sections of the part. When, for example, in describing his late wife, he was given the line, "Why—why—her teeth were perfect—except—except for a gold plug in her upper left molar," he added the words, "both of them." He eliminated a two-page pitch for Purple Bark Sarsaparilla with the notation, "Just use lines absolutely necessary." And he employed the use of sight gags to take the curse off Donnelly's most purple passages. "Go—Have your will!" he was required to say to Poppy at one point. "I shall not blame you! Go on to a brighter, happier life without me! But some day when you stumble upon my emaciated, deserted frame lying in the gutter, say to yourself, 'This is my work,' and then step over me." In pencil, Fields added: "Have button burst on suspenders. Pants drop. Catch them in time."

The show was set to open in Atlantic City for a week of tryouts on August 13, 1923, but Fields still didn't have his part down. Goodman had prompters stationed in the wings to feed him his lines, yet Fields, in a bustle of avoidance, continued to busy himself with sight gags. Shorty Blanche was added to the cast, playing a peanut vendor, and Fields told him on the night before the dress rehearsal that he wanted to shoot off a shotgun at a specific point in the story and have a swan drop from the flies—a gag lifted from "An Episode on the Links." Comedian Robert Woolsey, who was playing the part of Mortimer Pottle, the estate lawyer, witnessed the argument that ensued between Fields and Dorothy Donnelly, and Bert Wheeler, Woolsey's partner, remembered hearing about it. "This woman who wrote this beautiful play says, 'What do you mean, swan?' He says, 'Well, I shoot a gun, it goes through the roof, and a swan comes through.' This woman walked out, saying, 'You can't do this to my beautiful play!' Bobby Woolsey told me, 'This'll ruin the thing.' You know, it would be all right in a sketch, but not in a real dramatic play. Woolsey told me, 'That swan came through the roof and the audience laughed for five minutes. It never hurt the play.' "

Another argument erupted over Fields' embellishment of a particular line at the climax. "I had stolen a horse," he said, "and was trying to get it over the border into Canada. I said an affectionate farewell to my daughter, and disappeared into the wings, but came back in a few seconds, handcuffed and in the custody of a policeman. My daughter uttered the single word, 'Pop!' She spoke this with heartfelt dismay, and there was not a sound or motion in the audience. They were liking us and caring what happened to us. I said, 'Fortunes of war, my dear! I never did think much of that horse, and he dropped dead right in front of the police station!' That was one of the big laughs of the piece, but there was warm feeling in it."

Donnelly hated the line, insisting the audience wouldn't laugh if the words "dropped dead" were used: "It will make them think of their mother's ailing kidneys, the little daughter that got run over, Uncle John's heart trouble—no, you can't say things like that in comedy." Fields put up a spirited fight, and they finally agreed to a compromise: "The mare succumbed in front of the police station." Fields uttered the line with perfect fidelity in rehearsals, then conveniently forgot the pledge on his first night in front of an audience. The words "dropped dead" brought a roar from the audience. Later, when he saw Donnelly in the wings, he threw up his hands. "I *am* so sorry," he said with as much feeling as he could muster. "I got excited and forgot about our little agreement." The performance had gone so well that all the hostility had drained from her. "It's all right," she said graciously. "I'll forgive you."

The notices in Atlantic City focused their praise on thirty-one-year-old Madge Kennedy, a popular movie star who took top billing as Poppy McGargle. Kennedy, a winsome brunette, had plenty of stage experience and was known to a broader audience through the films she made for Samuel Goldwyn. She had drawing power—more so than Fields—but Goodman had been warned that she belonged in straight drama or comedy, for she had never sung or danced onstage. "But I saw her do both (and cleverly too) one night in her home," Goodman said, "and that settled it for me. Then to convince Miss Kennedy, we came down to the Apollo the next afternoon, and I sat in the farthest balcony seat, hearing every line of a song she tried out."

Fields and Kennedy formed an instant rapport that told Goodman that, whatever else happened with the play, the father-daughter relationship, the core of the story and its audience appeal, was solid. Fields took to calling Kennedy "Daughter," and she soothed him during the arduous rehearsal process when his self-confidence was at such a low ebb. "When he did *Poppy,* it was something very new to him. And frightening," she said. "You see, he had always just done his own thing; it was very, very different to learn lines and have to speak them. Bill kept saying, 'Take the lines away from me. I can't say all those things.' And I said, 'Bill, wait until opening night and you'll see how good you are.' "

Opening night was August 27, 1923, and Fields was as scared as he had ever been in his life. Goodman kept a watch on him to make sure he didn't drink himself into a state of total dysfunction—an apparent impossibility—and Bessie Poole was on hand in the dressing room, running lines with him. Curtain time came and went, and it wasn't until nine o'clock that the show finally got underway. Fields made his entrance some eighteen minutes into the performance, clad in the checkered pants, spats, and stovepipe hat of McGargle, a cane at his side and all the wounded dignity of the world on his shoulders. "This is evidently the scene of our future labors," he says to Poppy, surveying the fairgrounds and immediately taking command of the audience. He tells Sniffin, the constable, that he dispenses "healing roots and herbs" in the company of his daughter, "the well known cantatrice and songbird, professionally known as the girl with the double larynx."

His pitch for Purple Bark Sarsaparilla (colored water, wintergreen, and a few drops of ginger "to make it taste important") is a masterpiece of con-nivance. "Are you ill? Are you lonely? Ladies and gentlemen, has your daily dozen of buckwheats lost its zest and that pillar of our ancestors, the boiled dinner, relinquished its punch? Can you no longer saw off your morning cord of wood or join the gay revelers in the light fantastic toddle to the stirring strains of the parlor organ? Be of good cheer, ladies and gentlemen! Again you can crochet lamp doilies, make and eat beaten biscuit, cut the ice and kill hogs like a boy of 18. And what is this great discovery, you ask? Why, ladies and gen-tlemen, it is Purple Bark Sarsparilla, the greatest discovery in the scientific world of medicine since Hippocrates discovered the onion!"

The words that had so thoroughly defied Fields in rehearsal came flooding back to him in perfect sequence. And when occasionally they left him for a moment, he was so completely at one with the character that his ad-libs were invariably better than the lines he had forgotten. Madge Kennedy was charm-ing, delightful, a wonderful counterpoint to his dandified rogue, but through nearly three hours of performance, top-heavy with numbers and a chorus of sixteen, it was Fields who literally stole the show. "He has never been quite so amusing as he is in *Poppy,* nor so versatile," Woollcott announced in the *Times.* "His comicalities range from his accustomed juggling to untold difficulties with some bits of tissue paper. But added to all of these not unfamiliar maneuvers is a hitherto unrevealed facility with the spoken word. Mr. Fields creates comedy where certainly none existed in the libretto, for it can never be claimed that Dorothy Donnelly's book is funny per se."

The entire critical community rose up as one to praise his work. "Miss Kennedy was the star of the evening, a beautiful star," wrote Alan Dale in the *New York American,* "but the better-than-star of the evening was W. C. Fields. Mr. Fields was so tremendously funny, and so outrageously clever, that he car-ried everything away from everybody. It was a W. C. Fields evening with a vengeance." Charles Darnton, in the *Evening World,* agreed: "W. C. Fields makes *Poppy* gorgeously funny. He turned the trick of his life at the Apollo Theatre last night by scoring a hit bigger than his hat as a genuine comedian. He is a whole side show in himself." George Jean Nathan, Mencken's partner on *The Smart Set,* polished off his laudatory notice by calling Fields "the most gorgeous scaramouch of the season, a creature of infinite drollery, a fellow out of the pages of Mark Twain, and, what is more—he nonchalantly throws it into the bargain—an actor of genuine parts."

That morning, with the line at the box office stretching around the block and eight weeks of capacity business ahead, Madge Kennedy got Phil Good-man on the phone and said, "Put his name up with mine." The billing had been "Madge Kennedy in Poppy with W. C. Fields," but now she did the unheard-of thing of asking that the name of W. C. Fields be moved from under the title to over it. "I was starred in it and he was featured. I said, 'Put it right up there, please. He is magnificent!' "

The rousing success of *Poppy* gave Fields the confidence he needed to take full ownership of the role. Long after the cheers of opening night had faded, he was still regarding the show as a work in progress, adding bits of business to what had already been hailed as a perfect performance. To Madge Kennedy, Fields' tinkering was exasperating. "He would do the most incredible things. He would come on in that funny coat and they arrested him—we were what they call 'grifters'—and I would say to the constable, 'Look at him. He's a child. You can't take him away.' And I would look at him—it was a very touching moment, really. So one night, I said, 'Look at him. He's a child . . .' I turn to him and from out of this great overcoat that would stand alone, he took out a lollipop that big. Well, of course, the audience and the cast just burst into laughter and the play went out the window. I said, 'Bill, if you'll play that one scene and mean it, it won't matter what you do.' He said, 'Daughter, you're right.' And we'd be all right for another month or so, then he'd come out with a trumpet or something."

Fields also became more comfortable with his ad-libs, sometimes covering the most unpredictable of accidents. "In one scene I was alone in a dark library," he remembered, "hunting on tiptoe for cards I intended to mark so that later I could cheat in a poker game. One night, as I was stealing around the stage, being careful not to wake up anybody in the house, somebody offstage accidentally knocked over a pile of boxes with a crash that shook the theatre. My scene was ruined for the moment. I had an inspiration. I stole down to the footlights and whispered across to the audience, 'Mice!' "

For many, the most memorable moments in *Poppy* were Fields' wordless interludes of pantomime. Actress Jane Wyatt saw the show as a kid: "He had a scene where he was trying to play an instrument while fighting off a roll of fly-paper. Just as he'd get it unstuck in one place, it'd attach itself somewhere else. It was one of the funniest things I've ever seen in my life." James M. Cain, the future author of *The Postman Always Rings Twice,* was writing for Mencken's *American Mercury* and could remember Fields' handling of the kadoola kadoola, a rickety sort of box instrument he played with a bow. "Halfway through *Poppy,* he would come out with [this] skeleton cello, sit down with it after putting his silk hat on the floor, and start 'Pop Goes the Weasel.' But he would barely play three notes before the silk hat would start to roll, and continue around the back of his chair, to stop on the other side. He would put it in place again, again, again, and have to stop again. That was the whole sketch, but it was sheer delight, and I don't know anyone who ever figured out how he did it—how he made the hat roll, I mean, on cue, in exactly the right way."

The show gave birth to certain catchphrases that have clung to Fields ever

*Madge Kennedy was the official star of* Poppy,
*but the "better-than-star" was W. C. Fields.*

since, the most famous being his parting advice to Poppy on the day of her
wedding: "Never give a sucker an even break." Wilson Mizner is usually credited with originating the line, although there are sources that contend that
Fields actually got it from Nick Arnstein, Fannie Brice's larcenous husband.
Others, like "You can't cheat an honest man" and "It's the old army game," had
entered the vernacular long before *Poppy* hit the boards, but all were of a type,
all in step with Fields' character, and all immediately and for all time associated

with him.* Even Phil Goodman contributed one when, while watching a performance, a Donnelly line given the rich boy suddenly struck him as silly. Entering the scene, the boy asks, "May I come in?" though he already is. Goodman went to Fields and said, "Next time he asks that, tell him, 'You *are* in.' It could get a laugh—who knows?" Fields used the line, dripping with annoyance, and brought the show to a standstill. "Paul Palmer, Sunday editor of the *New York World,* told me about it first," said Cain, "before I ever knew Fields, and with tears streaming down his face at the mere recollection of it. He said, 'Jim, what it was about it I don't know, but that was the funniest thing I ever heard in the theatre.' " Other comics picked up on the line, and for years it was heard in every variety sketch that could possibly accommodate it.

Most important, *Poppy* helped fix an image of Fields in the public mind as the high-hatted con man with a marked deck in his pocket. At the age of forty-three, Fields had grown portly from too many lavish meals with Goodman, too many beers with Mencken, too many nights when the most exercise he got was playing the kadoola kadoola. The family nose asserted itself, round and red from the winter winds and exaggerated, according to his brother Walter, by his habit of sitting before the dressing-room mirror, where he would "squeeze his nose, squeeze the blackheads out." Caricatures Fields drew of himself show that he was fully aware of its prominence, and his continued use of a moustache (he couldn't grow one of his own) may have been an attempt to diminish the attention naturally drawn to it. "The moustache I wear . . . isn't ever supposed to look as though it belonged to me," he told Sally Benson of the *Sunday Telegraph.* "It is a black one and it falls off. It seems careless and therefore funny. It is not subtle, yet it makes people laugh."

Business for *Poppy* was strong through the rest of the year, with the weekly take hovering around $20,000 at a top price of $3 ($3.50 on Saturday nights). It might have run longer, but Goodman milked the holidays, running ticket prices up to $4.40 on Thanksgiving and $5.50 thereafter, hurting the word of mouth and eventually short-circuiting the show's popularity. Sales began to sag after the first of the year, and by March the cast had been asked to take a cut. When that didn't help matters and a second cut was ordered, Madge Kennedy gave notice, saying she'd rather go back to making pictures. Fields elected to stay, as Kennedy's resignation meant that he would be starred for the first time in his life. He took sole possession of *Poppy* on June 2, 1924—the same night, ironically, that the Marx Brothers attained similar stature in *I'll Say She Is.* Will

---

*Vaudeville historian and comic Joe Laurie Jr. once credited the "army game" line and the admonition "Go away, boy, you're bothering me" to Charles Kenna, who did a "low pitch" right off the streets of New York and was a standard act for decades.

Rogers, who was appearing across the street in the *Follies,* came onstage at the conclusion of the performance to read congratulatory wires from Fred Stone, Eddie Cantor, Leon Errol, Harold Lloyd, Mack Sennett, Al Jolson, Walter Catlett, Oscar Shaw, Raymond Hitchcock, Jerome Kern, Buster Keaton, Lee Shubert, and E. F. Albee, among others. Rogers christened Fields a star by breaking a trick bottle of ginger ale over his head, and then explaining to the audience that it hadn't hurt "because it was a soft drink."

Fields' newfound celebrity wasn't good for his relationship with Bessie Poole. He was, for a brief time, the toast of Broadway, and his world now included the expansive Goodman and his literary circle of friends—Dreiser, Sinclair Lewis, Nathan, and Mencken when he was in town.* Fields remained on the periphery, reluctant to speak in such august company, and he felt his lack of a formal education more acutely than ever. Bessie wasn't a part of *Poppy,* and therefore became less and less a part of his daily life. Ruth Goodman could remember the suite they shared "high up" in the Astor Hotel, where one day Bessie tried to teach her how to high-kick. Ruth liked her, but Bessie still was an ignorant chorus girl, as lacking in education as Fields but without the native intelligence that made him conversant on so many subjects. She was still attractive in her own way, and her quiet nature tended to keep her agreeably in the background.

Bessie's devotion was intense and unwavering, but she knew that he could never marry her, and the hopelessness of the situation began to consume her. In the aftermath of their battle with Ziegfeld over the Eight Performance Clause, when he knew their days with the *Follies* were numbered, Fields had put "The Family Ford" in her name, giving her an income of $75 a week whenever Jim Harkins and the company were playing it on the two-a-day. He made her a part of the *Scandals* as well, but her drinking had worsened and her inability to hold her liquor had become an embarrassment to him. The end was already in sight when Fields took up with a broad-beamed chorus girl named Linelle Blackburn. Billy Grady got a look at her for the first time when Fields asked him, after a performance of *Poppy,* to go sit with her at Billy Haas' restaurant while he took Bessie home. "I was warned to watch my language in the lady's company," Grady remembered. "I was told she was a Southern first-family belle, a college graduate who dripped with degrees." Grady took an instant dislike to the woman.

---

*"Will you please give Bill Fields my kindest personal regards?" Mencken once asked Goodman in a letter. "Tell him he is one of the few artists I really admire, and I am delighted to hear that he still maintains his old interest in malt liquor."

"Putsie," as Fields called her, was substantial where Bessie was petite and, according to Grady, had a fondness for premium cigars. Actress Louise Brooks, who later met her on a shoot, described her as a "large, plump blonde who wore ruffled pink organdy dresses with matching hat, gloves, shoes, and parasol." She had an accent as thick as her beefy arm, but Fields was smitten and in a quandary over what to do with poor Bessie. The breakup was not easy, and when "The Family Ford" wore out, he established a $50,000 trust fund in order to furnish her with an income. In June 1926, he sent her to Europe, hoping she would get a grip on herself and meet somebody new, but Bessie carried a torch, and when she underwent a serious operation and feared she might die, she wrote to Fields, telling him where he could find the letters he had written her and leaving her diamond ring to him as something to remember her by. "And darling," she concluded, "I love you, and have never loved anyone else and never will. And all the luck and love in the world to you dear, is my last wish."

As business for *Poppy* was weakening, J. P. McEvoy was putting the finishing touches on the script for a new show. McEvoy, at thirty, was a graduate of Notre Dame and the first writer of greeting-card sentiments to be admitted to the Authors League. His gift for pithy get-well rhymes enabled him to buy a typewriter and pursue more serious verse. His 1919 collection *Slams of Life* ("with malice for all and charity toward none") was culled from a syndicated feature of the same name and offered cynical takes on the mundane matters of everyday existence—cops, movies, brothers-in-law, wives who must always be right. In McEvoy's world, nothing ever worked the way it was supposed to and the poor working schlepp always took it in the shorts.

By 1923, McEvoy's attitudes and theories had given birth to *The Potters,* an American working-class family with a drone of a husband, a frumpy wife, two snotty kids, and an ugly apartment. It began as a Sunday feature in a Chicago newspaper, then blossomed into a hit play in which Donald Meek and Mary Carroll played the leads. McEvoy didn't write real people by looking for their finer attributes. In dialogue, he used the stock phrases "that constitute 90 percent of daily speech" and adhered to a limited vocabulary "because average speech and thought are limited." He developed *The Potters* logically, with episodes in place of scenes and acts. "When people come away from *The Potters* saying, 'Why, they might be three-fourths of the families I know,' that is literally what they mean," wrote Heywood Broun.

Joe McEvoy always derided the conventions of the Broadway revue, and with *The Potters* playing to standing room only, he set to work on a new kind of show—topical in terms of what it had to say about contemporary life, but limited to the things that mattered to the Ma and Pa Potters of the world. For his framework, he chose the bright colors and petty frustrations of the Sunday funnies, where any man could feel superior to the characters on the page. "I am not making any efforts to adopt comic supplement technique to the stage or materialize comic supplement characters," he stressed. "Rather, I am going back to the original idea of caricaturing life, which all the cartoonists started out with, but from which many, too many, have allowed themselves to be beguiled for artificial reasons." He called his show *The Comic Supplement* and gave it to the New York producer least likely to stage such a thing—Florenz Ziegfeld Jr.

There are differing stories of how Ziegfeld and McEvoy got together. McEvoy remembered Ziegfeld coming to see him at the Plymouth Theatre, where he was rehearsing a new actor for *The Potters,* and asking him to write some sketches "like the Potter scenes" for the new *Follies.* McEvoy said that he would, but, to his everlasting regret, he wasn't satisfied with just writing a few simple sketches. "Listen," he said to Ziegfeld, "how would you like me to write a whole new show for you? Something entirely different." Gene Buck recounted it differently. According to Buck, a meeting had been arranged after Buck had seen a performance of *The Potters.* McEvoy turned out to be a rumpled little man with wild hair and a bushy moustache. He and Ziegfeld talked at cross-purposes, and when he finally left, Ziegfeld turned to Buck and said, "You should know that a fellow that looks like that couldn't possibly write anything I would like."

That Ziegfeld ever seriously entertained the idea of producing a show like *The Comic Supplement* is less a tribute to consummate salesmanship than a sign of his own extreme desperation. Ziegfeld was, by 1924, a man on the ropes, his *Follies* having diminished in both artistry and popularity, and his all-star casts having deserted him for book shows like his own *Kid Boots.* The *Follies* was no longer touring, and Will Rogers was the sole star of the new edition. Nothing about *The Comic Supplement,* which, in McEvoy's draft, was a series of sketches with just the barest intimations of songs and dances, would have appealed to Ziegfeld just a couple of seasons earlier, but with the *Follies* past its prime as a franchise and costs ever mounting, he needed to confront the changing tastes of his audience or risk going out of business.

The two men worked a deal, McEvoy requiring a $3,000 advance for his material, and Ziegfeld, putting a brave face on the project, issuing a statement: "Here is a theme untouched by the revue or musical comedy stage. I mean realism. An entertainment built around the eccentricities of everyday life, deriving its humor from the familiar incidents of the city's day, would be a vital contribution to the stage." Said McEvoy: "Mr. Ziegfeld's beautiful and exotic interpretation of the American scene, his utilization of the sybaritic note which sounds above the industrialism of our age, is one reaction to the modernism of our day. *The Comic Supplement* is another. That these opposing versions of life both appeal to Mr. Ziegfeld is in itself the most interesting critical commentary yet made upon his creative mind."

There was no opening number to *The Comic Supplement,* and where the family in *The Potters* was merely common and unrefined, the Jones family was downright crass and unpleasant. McEvoy makes reference to the "father and his terrible little male offspring" as well as the "mother and her equally terrible little female offspring." Customers are unfailingly rude and demanding to the put-upon druggist, and in the end he erupts in rage, leaping on one offender and attempting to beat him to death with a handful of hot water bottles. *The Comic Supplement* was clever in an obnoxious sort of way, but the simmering anger of its characters threatened to poach the show in its own considerable bile. Ziegfeld must have recognized this, for the first casting suggestion he made was to put the wonderfully benign Bert Wheeler and his wife Betty into the show as the mother and father.* This held until the start of the new season, when *Poppy* folded while on tour and Fields suddenly became available.

If Fields hadn't been in mind when McEvoy wrote *The Comic Supplement,* it isn't apparent from the evidence of the first script. The show seems tailor-made for the Flivertons, if not actually inspired by them, and Ziegfeld, despite their past differences, had a grudging respect for Fields' abilities as both a writer and performer. For his part, McEvoy wanted someone to play the man in the street, good-humored, frustrated, slightly bewildered by it all, and Fields struck him as ideal. "He is the average American upon whose simple features life has placed a vaguely comic mask. He is the surprised and blinking troll entangled in the details of his day, who fights to get into crowded elevators, who sometimes falls down a flight of steps, who, in short, is forever raising his head out of what the alarmists call the debacle of modern civilization to crack a joke."

Fields set to work on a revision of the *Supplement,* replacing McEvoy's generic Jones family with the Flivertons in his handwritten drafts. He extended the drugstore scene with bits of physical business and embellished a picnic routine in which the family crashes through a fence and onto a private estate. ("Now why do you suppose people are always putting up fences around their place?" Pa wonders. "I'll bet I've busted more fenders on fences!") To these he added his old pool table routine (having come to believe that audiences expected it of him) and a Sunday-drive event called "The Joyride" that owed much to "The Sport Model." The physical design of the show was based on the "flat brutal colors" found in actual comic strips, and throughout the tone was

---

*The Wheelers had performed a popular ten-minute number in the *Follies of 1923* in which Bert sang an emotional "Mammy" song while eating a ham sandwich.

quietly malicious, without any of the grating qualities that distinguished McEvoy's initial draft or, for that matter, the earlier Fliverton exchanges that had so offended the sensibilities of Flo Ziegfeld.

In Fields' version, Gertie, the little daughter, is a disruptive brat, and her brother George can't stand her:

GEORGE

Why don't you put a little poison in her milk?

MA (to PA gaily)

Isn't he the joker?

PA (seriously)

On the contrary, I think he's got hold of a darned good idea.

McEvoy, for his part, concentrated on the connecting numbers, giving the show more of a musical framework than he originally intended and turning *The Comic Supplement* into a savage satire of all New York revues. Where Ziegfeld glorified the American girl, McEvoy sent her slumming. There was a ballet number for scrubwomen, and a cafeteria march of counter girls. (They danced with trays.) He began with a brassy opening number in which the chorus comes rushing onto the stage in bright costumes that, when reversed, reveal effigies of popular characters of the period—Mutt and Jeff, Barney Google, Jiggs and Maggie. As they part, a double quartet comes down the aisle singing: "Oh, this is the thing we always do / In a musical show or new revue / They rush out here with a hullabaloo / and kick their girlish legs at you." The chorus dances madly, works itself into a frenzy, and then drops from exhaustion. Ziegfeld was destined to hate *The Comic Supplement* under the best of circumstances. Even the beach scene, which McEvoy conceded to him and which had a tableau of genuine beauties, was balanced by a song that lamented the "hoi polloiters" that "show their rickets, glanders, adenoids, and goiters."

Fields' most original contribution to the show was a brief bit toward the beginning in which, tormented by a toothache, Pa takes to the porch in his pajamas and bedding to try and get some sleep while, below, his son and a girl-friend play out a noisy love scene. If Fields felt at all burdened by McEvoy's material, he never let on, as both men had such convergent views of the world they formed an almost perfect collaboration. If anything, Fields had a leavening effect on McEvoy's material, bringing to the proceedings a more rounded sense of character, as Fields, in the final analysis, lacked the utter contempt for his fellow man that McEvoy so obviously felt.

Ziegfeld, to his credit, backed the production to the hilt, committing $120,000 to *The Comic Supplement,* hiring Norman Bel Geddes to design it, Julian Mitchell to stage the production numbers, and cartoonist John Held Jr. to draw the costumes. He never read the script, relying instead on what McEvoy and Gene Buck were able to tell him and on his own observations whenever he happened in on a rehearsal. One day, he saw Fields developing some wordless business to go with the "Back Porch" routine and came storming down the aisle. "Off the stage, everybody! Stop it! I won't have it!" What he wouldn't have, McEvoy learned, was a moment of silence. "I've lost a hundred and seventy-five thousand dollars on pantomime," he informed the playwright. "Pantomime comedy won't go. The public won't stand for it."

McEvoy stood his ground, sarcastically suggesting they warn Charlie Chaplin before it was too late. "And anyway, this is a pantomime comedy part, it was written that way, it was read to you that way, and that's why we decided to get Fields for the role, and whether you think it's funny or not, Fields thinks it's funny and I think it's funny, and suppose we let the audience decide whether or not they think it's funny." Ziegfeld could not be persuaded. "It's terrible," he said flatly. "Nobody will laugh." He fought constantly with McEvoy and made little show of liking Fields, either. "It was almost impossible for Ziegfeld to carry on a conversation with Bill," Norman Bel Geddes observed. "He acted as though Fields had done something terrible to him." By the end of the third day of rehearsals, Ziegfeld had dispensed with four comedy sketches and ordered Bel Geddes to design the sets for four new "girl numbers" to replace them. He developed the show the way he would build a new edition of the *Follies,* but he seemed detached from it all in a way he never would have been with a revue of his own making.

*The Comic Supplement* had its first public performance on the night of January 20, 1925, before a packed house at the National Theatre in Washington, D.C. With all the additions Ziegfeld forced on McEvoy and Fields, there was enough material and scenery to keep the show running for nearly four hours. Programs contained the following statement:

PUBLIC DRESS REHEARSAL

Mr. Ziegfeld offers his new entertainment tonight in its entirety and will abide by the verdict of the Washington public as to its eliminations.

Blackouts, played in slapstick pantomime, were used to separate the various sketches, actors clad in the bright greens, yellows, and reds of the funny pages and holding up word balloons to indicate dialogue and sound effects. Instead of the customary half-dozen times a star might appear in a conventional revue,

Fields found himself onstage for ten of the show's twenty-five scenes. The much disputed "Back Porch" bit was first up, lengthened by a parade of disturbances from the ice man, an organ-grinder, and an array of other early-morning pests. Ziegfeld was standing with McEvoy in the back of the house as a milkman in wooden shoes clomped up three flights of stairs, delivered a minuscule bottle of cream, and clomped back down again. "See?" he said to the author as the theater literally rocked with laughter. "I told you!"

"But the people are laughing their heads off," McEvoy protested.

"They don't mean it," he said sadly.

According to Bel Geddes, *The Comic Supplement* was greeted as one of the true wonders of the new year. "The audience was howling to the bitter end and beyond. Ziegfeld was horrified. He had spent most of the performance in the lobby, wincing, and had come in at one point to find the audience laughing at one of his chorus numbers. This was the height of disrespect and proved that the whole show was a monstrous joke." *The Comic Supplement* wasn't done until the stroke of midnight, and reactions the next morning were vividly mixed. The *Washington Post* printed a rave, John C. Daily calling it "the greatest extravaganza ever assembled on the stage." The notice in the *Star* was in a similar vein, saying it "sparkled with newness" but portraying—despite Bel Geddes' rosy memory of the evening—an audience that was "far from satisfied." Then there was the man from *Variety,* who clearly hated the show and everything about it: "This one comes closer to being a complete flop than anything Ziegfeld has ever sponsored. . . . If ever a man labored loyally and faithfully, it was Fields. But Fields for a solid three and one-half hours is too much Fields. That goes for Ray Dooley too, who trailed along with the star throughout the show."

Ziegfeld's relationship with McEvoy disintegrated into an exchange of vituperative telegrams. He was threatening to close the show out of town when Bel Geddes offered to buy it for $100,000.

"You got the money?" Fields asked him.

"Yes."

"Then go to it. You're my man. I'll back you to the limit, and if you need a little more money, let me know."

At first, Ziegfeld agreed to the sale, perhaps thinking Bel Geddes wasn't good for the money, then backed off when actually proffered a check. "The sight of the check restored some of his confidence in the show," Bel Geddes said. *The Comic Supplement* did a $26,000 week in Washington, a record for a tryout in that city. The first night played to capacity, but the numbers dwindled as word spread that for $4.40 it wasn't much fun to sit through a dress rehearsal. Ziegfeld decided to prune the script himself, trimming it to just twenty scenes by the time it rolled into Newark on the twenty-sixth. It played

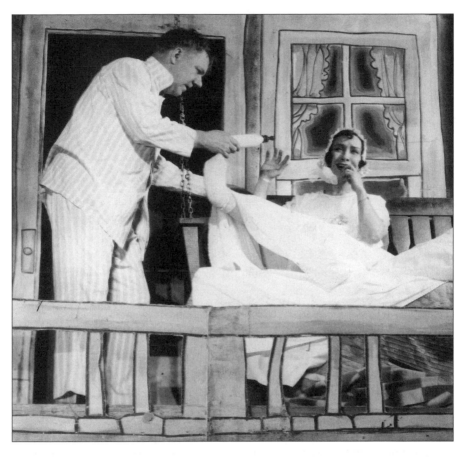

*Fields performs the "Back Porch" scene with Ray Dooley*
*in Ziegfeld's* Comic Supplement, *January 1925.*

out the week at the Shubert Theatre while publicist Bernard Sobel did advance work in Philadelphia, the final stop before its scheduled opening on February 16 at the Cosmopolitan Theatre on Columbus Circle.

The company never made it to Philadelphia. Ziegfeld pulled the plug on January 31, 1925. The closing announcement was issued from his offices atop the New Amsterdam: "*The Comic Supplement* closes at Newark tonight. Mr. Ziegfeld has decided, however, not to bring the production to New York in its present condition. The notices in Newark and Washington were remarkably fine . . . but Mr. Ziegfeld did not deem the entertainment typically enough Ziegfeld to open at the theatre which he has just acquired." The *Times* column "Gossip of the Rialto" reported the next day that "reliable information" held that the closing had less to do with the shaky structure of the show than the "unending conflict" that existed between the producer and author McEvoy.

The cast and chorus, which included Betty Compton, the milky-white girl-friend of Mayor James J. Walker, were all wonderfully supportive of the show and shocked by the news of its closure. "I think the problem was that it was way ahead of its time," said Nona Otero, a dancer in the show. "We thought the show was good and, in fact, it was good. We were sorry to see it close." Norman Bel Geddes, however, wasn't all that surprised: "All Flo Ziegfeld could understand was his *Follies* formula. A show like *The Comic Supplement* was beyond him." Fields was, perhaps, the most shaken of them all, for he knew the stuff in the *Supplement* was fine and important and, most of all, new. Ziegfeld's abrupt move brought memories flooding back to him of *Watch Your Step* and his firing at the hands of Dillingham. "There wasn't a damn thing I could do about it," he later told an interviewer. "There never is. So now you know why I'm nervous—or crazy and nuts, as some of my good friends call it—why I never feel safe in this blankety-blank business I juggled myself into."

The postmortem in *Variety* took all of two sentences: "*The Comic Supplement* was rated as having great possibilities, the show being regarded as top heavy in comedy, but shy of production numbers and sight diversion. The principal trouble with the revue appears to be that it afforded no change of pace." Ziegfeld may well have taken this item to heart, for within days of its appearance, he reverted back to his original intent, which was to have McEvoy write some scenes for the *Follies*. He sent much of *The Comic Supplement* to the storehouse, retaining four key scenes he inserted into the new "Spring Edition" of the show pairing Fields once again with his old friend Will Rogers. But Fields' tenure as a star of the New York stage was quickly drawing to a close. The day after the opening of the new *Follies,* on March 10, 1925, he began work on a feature film under the direction of the great D. W. Griffith. It would be the first of thirty-two starring features he would make over the next twenty years.

*Eleven*

# Common Picture Making

One of the fringe benefits of being a Ziegfeld girl was being put on display before some of the wealthiest and most influential men in New York. Ziegfeld's glorified golddiggers were squired around town by lawyers, bankers, playboys, and picture makers. Many of them married well, and sometimes—as in the case of Peggy Hopkins Joyce—often. "We have a hard time keeping our girls together," Will Rogers once remarked on tour. "Every time we get to a new town some of them marry millionaires, but in a few weeks they catch up with the show again." Jessica Brown became Lady Northesk, Justine Johnston wed film executive Walter Wanger, and the stately Dolores retired to Paris, where she married one Tudor Wilkinson and held fashionable salons in the Rue St. Honoré. Peggy Fears' marriage to real estate magnate A. C. Blumenthal made her a successful stage producer. Mary Lewis became a star of the Metropolitan Opera, and Dorothy Mackaill, Lilyan Tashman, Mae Murray, and Billie Dove all went to Hollywood.

But it was Marion Davies—nee Douras—who caught the eye of newspaper and magazine publisher William Randolph Hearst and made the most of it. In the *Follies of 1916,* she was just another teenage member of the chorus, with long curls trailing down her back, until Ziegfeld picked her out of the line and decided to feature her in the "Birth of Elation" number. "I was supposed to walk down a staircase in a gorgeous costume of blue tulle with sparkles on it and a marabou hat and say, 'I am the Spirit of Spring.' " She made it as far as the first performance in Atlantic City, when it became apparent that she had a bad stammer. "When I got down the stairs—this was the curtain, the finale—I looked around and I started, 'I-I-I-I-I-I-I . . .' So they pulled the curtain."

Unable to speak onstage, she went back to being a pony, but that was enough to appeal to Hearst, fifty-three at the time, who haunted the front rows of the New Amsterdam. "The girls in the show told me who he was. They said, 'Look out for him—he's looking at you.' " She made the transition to films the following year in an independent feature called *Runaway Romany,* financed by an old boyfriend. "I couldn't act," she said, "but the idea of silent pictures appealed to me because I couldn't talk either." The Marion Davies Film Company was established in 1918, and Cosmopolitan Productions followed the next year. The new company was ostensibly formed to make movies from stories published in the Hearst magazines, but Davies, by virtue of her relationship with the old man, was by far its most important asset. Nobody accused her of being a great actress, but she had an undeniable flair for comedy that was rarely exploited in the costume dramas for which she became best known. After starring in twelve movies, she made a genuine hit in *When Knighthood Was in Flower,* and at the time Fields was making news in *Poppy,* she was preparing to shoot the most ambitious picture of her career, an adaptation of Paul Leicester Ford's Revolutionary War romance, *Janice Meredith.*

Filming precipitated a clash with D. W. Griffith, who was shooting *America* on some of the same locations and staging some of the same events—Paul Revere's ride, Washington's crossing of the Delaware, Cornwallis' surrender. Griffith met with Hearst's people to dissuade them from making the film, but nothing came of the appeal, and as the year ended, U.S. infantrymen were working as extras in both productions. Davies began work on her own scenes in January, filming at Hearst's International Studio on the Harlem River. In March, the company adjourned to Plattsburgh, where the village of Trenton had been reconstructed from antique maps and prints. Washington's spectacular crossing of the Delaware required the cutting of a channel four hundred feet wide in the ice of the Saranac River, where exact reproductions of the original flatboats were used. No expense was spared, and the cost of *Janice Meredith* was approaching $1.5 million when Fields joined the cast, on April 1, 1924.

He had given little thought to movies in the years since his Gaumont subjects had been so quickly filmed and forgotten. For the time and trouble pictures represented to him, it was far more lucrative to write for the stage, where a good piece of material could generate income for months, if not years. "The Family Ford" was worth $800 a week in the *Follies* and another $75 a week in vaudeville—a grand total in excess of $40,000. The same material, written and performed as a one-reeler, would bring one tenth the amount. *Poppy,* however, had established Fields as a legitimate stage actor, and since most features shot in New York were populated with theatrical personalities, it was only natural for offers of character work to come his way.

There were no fewer than thirty-three featured players in the cast of *Janice Meredith,* including Harrison Ford, George Nash, Tyrone Power, and Douglas Stevenson. Filming was spread over five studios in the New York area, and Fields' showy cameo as a bungling tosspot of a British sergeant was shot in three succinct days at the Tilford Studio on Forty-fourth Street, across the Queensboro Bridge on Long Island, where he guzzled whiskey, puffed away at a big cigar, and flirted with the title character as she struggled to free the young soldier she loved. The sequence gave the 153-minute film its only genuine burst of comedy and ended with Davies desperately clinging to Fields' leg as he tried to give chase to his fleeing prisoner. The film opened at Hearst's Cosmopolitan Theatre on August 5, 1924, and *Variety*'s Robert Sisk, who waited a couple of days before taking it in, described an audience "unaffected by first night enthusiasm" responding to Fields' appearance to such a degree that he was "the momentary hit of the film." By virtue of the Hearst publicity machine, *Janice Meredith* promptly supplanted *Pool Sharks* as the official screen debut of W. C. Fields.

By the time of his break with Ziegfeld, Fields had worked himself up to a salary of $800 a week. He took less to land the part of McGargle, and although the show failed on tour, the concession paid off handsomely in other respects. Phil Goodman, more convinced than ever of Fields' gold-plated potential as a legitimate draw, declared his intent to star him in a new musical called *The Showman* during the 1925–26 season. Fields signed a three-year contract with Goodman on June 3, 1924, calling for a guarantee of $2,500 a week, plus a 1 percent royalty for "comic scenes and sketches," commencing September 1, 1925.

A week after Fields signed with Goodman, D. W. Griffith entered into a contract of his own to direct three pictures for Famous Players–Lasky. Griffith was one of the founding partners of United Artists, but his five-year contract with UA was at an end, and the twin failures of *The White Rose* and *America* had left him in desperate need of cash to sustain both his company and a picturesque studio he had established near Mamaroneck. Adolph Zukor stepped forward with the offer of a $250,000 loan, guaranteed by Famous Players, that would enable Griffith to make the ninth and final film of his UA commitment. Zukor's deal with Griffith called for a substantial salary—up to $200,000 on "big" pictures—and a 20 percent share of the net profits. But *Isn't Life Wonderful* wasn't the hit it needed to be, and UA came after Griffith on the basis of an informal commitment he had made to remain with the company. He lost his cherished studio on the Long Island Sound, and it wasn't until April 11, 1924, that he publicly announced, after rejecting several properties, that his first film under the new pact would be a project entirely of his own choosing—*Poppy*.

Griffith was already familiar with Fields' work when he saw him in the role of Eustace McGargle at the Apollo Theatre. In 1920, actress Mary Hay was playing a small part in *Way Down East* and singing nightly on the Ziegfeld Roof. When Hay asked Griffith what she could do to improve her screen technique, he told her to look no farther than the star of her own show. "Watch W. C. Fields," he said. "His timing is perfect." In fact, Griffith said he'd like to have tea with Fields sometime and discuss the possibility of a role in one of his films, but nothing ever came of it.

Later, when *Poppy* fell apart on tour, Fields was called on by a man named Charles Walton. "He introduced himself saying he was a booking agent and thought he could put me in a picture which Mr. Griffith was planning to make. He wanted me to come over and meet Mr. Griffith. He stated to me that he would accept a ten percent agent's commission if he secured my employment in that picture, to which I agreed." Walton arranged an appointment, and Griffith told Fields he'd like him to make a test. "We talked over salary, and I suggested $1,200 per week. Mr. Griffith thought that amount too high." The test was made late one afternoon on Long Island, but it apparently didn't go very well. Fields rode back to town with Griffith and actress Carol Dempster, who was to play the part of Poppy in the film. "Mr. Griffith said that after two or three years in pictures I would probably be all right. A few days after the test, Walton came to my room at the Hotel Astor and said that it was doubtful whether Mr. Griffith would do [the picture] at all and that the whole proposition might be off." Subsequently, Griffith was able to see *Janice Meredith,* and his interest in Fields was rekindled. "He did not have much to do," Griffith recalled, "but I thought he was good in what he had. . . . I thought he got over in the picture."

Fields was in rehearsals for *The Comic Supplement* when Walton took him to meet Edwin C. King, general manager of the Famous-Lasky Eastern Studio. King told him that $250 a day was all he could afford, but Fields held out for $300 a day on a four-day guarantee.* Filming got underway on March 9, 1925, at the cavernous Astoria studio where the company produced features under the Artcraft and Paramount brands. Fields ended up cutting his stage price "almost in half" for the opportunity to work with Griffith, whom he would later remember as "one of the finest men I ever knew." Griffith, a fan of low comedy, returned the compliment, saying, "W. C. Fields was always my idea of an artist, even in the days when he never spoke a word."

Unfortunately, the twenty-three-year-old Dempster was also Griffith's idea of an artist. A dancer by training, she had first come to Griffith's attention on the set of *Intolerance* in 1916. He was fascinated by her odd, angular features and, beginning with *The Girl Who Stayed at Home* in 1919, she played increasingly prominent roles in his films. Blessed with a modicum of talent, she had the misfortune, as Kevin Brownlow has pointed out, of being associated almost exclusively with Griffith's flops. Her one standout performance in a string of eleven features was as Inga, the Polish refugee, in *Isn't Life Wonderful.* Staff

---

*He also brokered the sale of the silent-picture rights for $15,000, splitting the commission on the deal with Walton.

and technicians at the Famous Players studio were shocked by Dempster's hold on the fifty-year-old director, whose earlier films had soared with the likes of Lillian Gish, Mae Marsh, and Mary Pickford. "She ruined him," said Rudy Koubek, a projectionist at the studio. "Christ, when she came in, he had to drop everything." Ed Flaherty, chief electrician on the film, was equally unimpressed. "She had nothing," he said.

Predictably, Griffith chose to showcase Dempster's gamine over the rascal McGargle, who was relegated to a secondary role in the film. Fields fought back by injecting as much stage business as possible, taking full advantage of the fact that even while Griffith's approach to film comedy was leaden, he was, in Fields' words, "the most wonderful audience in the world." According to Frank Nelson, a carpenter on the picture, Griffith did not use a script, but came to the set with everything planned in his head and expected his assistant to know what he wanted. Under such informal conditions, it was easy for Fields to insert his old cigar box routine or plant the peanut cart gag from the 1917 *Follies.* He could persuade Griffith to shoot practically anything, but the material ofttimes ended up on the cutting-room floor. "Much of my work was eliminated because it diverted attention from the star," he said tartly. Only glimpses of Fields' juggling specialty remained in the finished film, while a tedious dance number by Dempster was covered in full.

Griffith bleached any element of suspense from the plot, setting it forth from the very beginning that McGargle knew of the girl's origins. In fact, the first scene Fields played under Griffith's direction was the death of Poppy's mother—an event merely alluded to in the play. McGargle enters the tent, adorned with top hat, cigar, stick pin, and cane. Stepping clear of a passing dog, he twits the little girl, blows smoke rings to her delight, then seats himself at the bedside of the dying woman. "Since my husband was taken, you have been my only friend, McGargle." She hands him the girl's birth record, the document that will prove her true identity. "Perhaps my people in Green Meadow might help." Tenderly, he calls the little girl to her bedside. The scene fades.

The company had to cleave to Fields' stage schedule, which meant he could work only mornings on Wednesdays and Saturdays, and no evenings past six. His first shot was on a matinee day, and Griffith pretty much left him to his own devices. Fields played the scene as he would onstage, working to an audience of some thirty crew members and timing himself to the sound of their laughter. Griffith sat under the camera, rapt, delighted, egging him on: "That's fine . . . great . . . couldn't be better." When the company broke for lunch, Fields left for the New Amsterdam, where he and Ray Dooley were breathing new life into the moribund *Follies.*

Ziegfeld's plan to make the show a year-round attraction required seasonal changes, but the version playing New York in early 1925 contained nearly two

hours of material left over from the wildly unexceptional *Follies of 1924.*
Critics found the policy intolerable, the numbers having fallen to a kind of glit-
terless precision and the comedy having dwindled to practically nothing.
Ziegfeld's flagship revue was getting by on reputation alone. "It is this charming trait in the American people, this shut-eye acceptance of anything so long
as it has the right name, that makes it so easy to sell them bad liquor, bad styles,
and bad presidents," said Robert Benchley. The addition of scenes from *The
Comic Supplement* had the immediate effect of raising the show from the dead,
and Benchley, for one, said that if McEvoy's experiment had been as good as its
individual bits "it would have been better to close the old *Follies* and bring *The
Comic Supplement* in." Indeed, the *Supplement* had developed such a potent
word of mouth that Ziegfeld took out full-page ads assuring the public they

could see "all the comedy features" of *The Comic Supplement* in the new edition of the *Ziegfeld Follies.* Said *Variety,* "Here, at last, is a laughing *Follies.*"

The critical hit of the show was the "Back Porch" scene, which owed little to McEvoy and which Fields revised and copyrighted himself prior to the opening. All the careful additions over weeks of rehearsal time—the milkman, the newspaper boy, the ice man, the squawking baby—amounted to a brilliant burst of comic invention. "The physical accuracy and rhythm of [Fields'] past make his pantomime now absorbing and unerring," Stark Young said in his *New York Times* review. "He holds your eyes by his timing of his expressive movements, the timing of the change and flow in them. And meanwhile he juggles our philosophy and his humor seems to show us our absurd human life somersaulting and turning back and making flat falls in a droll, expert brain."

Business shot to capacity the night Fields rejoined the show, and standees were two deep the following day. Yet he was never relaxed, chain-smoking on the set of *Poppy* and pacing in short, jerky steps with an unused cane in his hand. Alfred Lunt joined the company on March 26, playing Carol Dempster's rich admirer by day and, like Fields, working on the Broadway stage at night.* Lunt's part was not very strenuous, and his first day's work amounted to little more than establishing shots for a society ball. Eighteen days into production, Lunt observed a Griffith who was ill with a cold, tense and distracted. He was given no script, and when he asked what to say when delivering his dialogue, he was told to simply speak gibberish. "It was quite paralyzing, to tell the truth." Yet Fields, said Lunt, was an absolute riot. "His ad libbing, which he was doing constantly, was just about the funniest stuff I ever heard in my life."

Barnet Bravermann, Griffith's putative biographer, was keeping a diary on the making of the film and observed Fields performing for the camera various bits from the stage version of *Poppy*—the "newspaper gag" and his "flirtation and fly paper gags"—and noted how he "made them all laugh" as he rehearsed. Griffith contributed nothing to Fields' scenes and had very little to say to the others. "He'd set up the scene," said Lunt, "and that was it." He never acted out a scene himself, as some directors were inclined to do. "He explained the situation," wrote Bravermann, "and relied on their feelings" to put the thing across. Fields added his gags to the film in such a casual manner that they all seemed spontaneous. The bit where the trickle of water is blamed on the dog was finally put before the cameras on May 15—eight years after Fields had first conceived of it. "Scenario?" Bravermann wrote in his diary that day. "Doubt it. If so, it read 'Fields ad lib.' " Griffith shot the gag with the dog and the garden hose even

---

*Lunt was appearing at the Garrick in *The Guardsman* with his wife, actress Lynn Fontanne, and took on the thankless role of Peyton Lennox for some extra cash.

*Fields is flanked by D. W. Griffith and actress Carol Dempster on the set of*
Sally of the Sawdust, *1925.*

though he disapproved of it. "Now you'll be ashamed of that mean act some day," he warned Fields. "That's not nice. Don't do anything that you'll be ashamed of." Yet it remained in the film because it played well in early screenings.

Fields proved incapable of playing a scene without flair or invention. Griffith had yanked *Poppy* back into the present day—apparently on the conviction that Dempster, after the failure of *America,* would play better in a modern setting—and Fields availed himself of paraphernalia that would have been absent from the original show. He'd scour the set for inspirational props; even his ever-present cigar became an appendage with a life all its own. As Alfred Lunt said, "If it wasn't his hat, or a towel, or a shoe, or a boot, or a billiard cue, or a table cloth, he would use anything, and he was always funny." Toward the end of production, the Sparks Circus came to Jackson Heights, and Griffith seized the opportunity to shoot the raising of the tent, the parade, the acts—nearly four thousand feet in all. With such an abundance of legitimate color, the decision was made to retitle the film *Sally of the Sawdust,* and it was under that name that Griffith first showed it to an audience on June 3, 1925.

Fields was pleased to be finished with the tandem grind of both filming and playing the *Follies* at night. He seemed to relax, and Bernard Sobel wrote fondly of the final days he spent under Ziegfeld's employ: "Every memory I have of Bill Fields is filled with kindness, an earthy wisdom, and his willingness to comply with any request that I made concerning publicity." The door to Fields' dressing room, just off the first landing of the staircase, was always open, and the chorus girls would call out to him as they rushed past. Fields, who conducted interviews while flicking ashes on Ziegfeld's No Smoking sign, would crook his head to ask, "What's on now?," and every once in a while, he would get up ponderously, shed his terrycloth robe and put on a coat, casually slap on a moustache, and head toward the stage as if he were a shopkeeper about to wait on a customer. Occasionally, when he had a particular glow on, he would sing a bawdy song about a French soubrette who fended off admirers on the beach with a strategically placed handful of sand. One night, Sobel spotted Charlie Chaplin in the audience and asked Fields if he would sing the song for Chaplin if he brought him backstage. "Certainly," said Fields, and at intermission Sobel fished Chaplin out of the audience and took him to the dressing room, where Fields gave a spirited performance for just the two of them.

Ziegfeld churned the *Follies* again that summer, leaving the comedy scenes from the *Supplement* intact but adding a half-dozen numbers to replace the holdovers from the previous season. He also declared the year-round policy at an end, announcing the show would again tour in the fall. Fields was in a quandary over what to do about Goodman, who had taken no substantive steps to make *The Showman* a reality and who, with the impending release of *Sally of the Sawdust,* wanted to put him back on the road again in *Poppy.* Fields balked at the notion, pointing out that he was still owed $750 for his last week in Newark, but Goodman held firm, threatening to hold Fields to the fanciful contract he had signed more than a year earlier.

Fields was looking forward to the Chicago premiere of *Sally of the Sawdust* when news reached him on July 11 that his mother had died. Kate Dukenfield was just days shy of her seventy-first birthday and had been under a doctor's care for nearly a month. Her death at Penns Grove still came as a jolt to her eldest son, who played both Saturday performances of the *Follies* in something of a daze and then left for home to take charge of the arrangements. Just weeks earlier, he had covered for his friend Will Rogers when Rogers' sister died after a long illness at her home in Oklahoma. Now Rogers did the same for Fields, taking on his roles in the back porch, the drugstore, and the picnic scenes, and dancing with Ray Dooley in the ridiculous "Waltz of Love" number. Kate's funeral took place in Philadelphia on July 13, 1925. She was laid to rest at the same Knights of Pythias cemetery near Feltonville that held her parents, her brother Grant, her stillborn son, and her husband, Jim. Fields had matching stones cut, honoring his mother's agreeable nature and his father's service in the Civil War:

| DUKENFIELD | DUKENFIELD |
|:---:|:---:|
| JAMES L. | KATE S. |
| FATHER | MOTHER |
| 1841–1913 | 1856–1925 |
| A GREAT SCOUT | A SWEET OLD SOUL |

Side by side, the markers remained in place for more than half a century, and Jim's GAR insignia was still on display in the overgrown plot at the turn of the millennium.

Fields arranged to close the house at 3923 Marshall, where he had kept his trunks and received his mail for nearly twenty years. He asked if he could move his things to his brother Walter's house in Waterford Works, New Jersey. "I said yes, I was tickled to death," Walter remembered. "He brought his clothes and trunks and books and kept different things he had in his room." In the attic were trunks packed with shoes, clothes, hats, and, of course, books—five big boxes of them. Walter worked for fight promoter Tex Rickard and was gone much of the week. His wife, Lily, an ex–chorus girl, was delighted when Adele, who was living with Kate at the time of her death, moved into a two-room cottage on the property.

Fields was back in the *Follies* by Wednesday, relieving Rogers after just two performances and working his way through a pile of sympathy telegrams that had accumulated in his absence. He wired D. W. Griffith on July 19: "I hope the picture proves to be even greater than the critics predict if that is possible I would give Shorty's right arm to be in Chicago with you tonight." At 113 minutes, *Sally of the Sawdust* was extraordinarily long for a comedy and pricey at a cost of $336,000—twice its original estimate. Adolph Zukor viewed the film on June 30 and wrote Griffith a laudatory note, suggesting trims that would make it "perfection itself" and calling Fields' scene in a balking Ford, which he helps along with a walking stick, "one of the funniest parts I have seen on the screen in a long time." As part of the effort to land Griffith's services, Zukor permitted the release of *Sally of the Sawdust* through United Artists, arranging a split of the rentals and placing it on display at New York's Mark Strand Theatre just prior to Chaplin's *The Gold Rush*. Perceived as a program picture, despite the Griffith name attached, the film did extraordinarily well, returning its cost by the end of the year and ultimately posting a profit of around $200,000.

"D. W. Griffith is down to common picture making in this one," Sime Silverman wrote. "While it is strange to witness a Griffith film directed by him in a straightaway manner, so foreign to his far-advanced ideas and ideals for the average picture fan, still Griffith with all of this and all of what he must have suppressed or suffered in the making of this picture, has sent many a wallop across for first aid at the box office. As W. C. Fields made his legit stage hit in the musical *Poppy* as the carnival showman, so does he here scream his screen debut as a film funnyman in *Sally*. Mr. Fields has put in bits of business and gags that will make the Chaplins and the Lloyds bawl out their gag writers. And Fields plays them as well as though on the stage. He gives a smoothness to his comedy stuff and his playing that cannot be missed."

The critics were unanimous in lauding Fields' performance. Even negative reviews, such as Robert Emmet Sherwood's dirge in *Life* ("Among the major tragedies of movie history has been the decay of David Wark Griffith"), praised the warmth and inventiveness Fields brought to an otherwise bloodless story. Carol Dempster fared well also, her ragged exuberance tapping into the authority Fields so naturally exuded in the role of McGargle. Like Madge Kennedy before her, Dempster had taken to addressing Fields as "Pop" on the set, and a genuine affection came through in the scenes they shared. "Famous Players–Lasky wanted to sign her as a featured player with an eye to stardom after that picture," Griffith revealed with pardonable pride. "I signed her again instead."

In fact, Griffith had Dempster back before the cameras on July 6—barely a month after the final shots had been made for *Sally of the Sawdust*—shooting a potboiler called *That Royle Girl*. She was cast in the unlikely role of a Chicago jazz baby who sets out to clear her lover when his estranged wife is murdered. Griffith knew the story was a stiff and had rejected it on several occasions, but Famous Players thought enough of the novel, serialized in Hearst's *International Cosmopolitan* magazine, to pay a whopping $35,000 for the rights to it. The part of Dempster's no-account father was perfect for Fields, but reports were that he was asking too much money, and actor Erville Alderson, who had played the pivotal role of Judge Foster, the unwitting grandfather, in *Sally of the Sawdust,* was handed the job instead.

Alderson worked on the film until it was clear from the Chicago reception of *Sally* that Fields was going to be a major hit. Earlier, Fields had declined Griffith's invitation to visit the set, saying he would have felt "foolish" in light of his inability to come to terms with Edwin King, but now, with renewed interest on the part of the company, he met with King, Walter Wanger (who was in charge of East Coast production), and Jesse Lasky in the latter's Fifth Avenue office. As they needed him to start work the next day, they agreed to a five-week guarantee at $2,500 a week, and Fields began filming the father's part on Saturday, August 1, 1925. The next day, Fields' friends from the Lamb's Club banded together to parade him down Broadway to Forty-seventh Street, where he joined Dempster and Griffith on the stage of the Strand, and a capacity audience, having just witnessed the New York premiere of *Sally of the Sawdust,* cheered the arrival of an important new screen comedian.

*That Royle Girl* was a more arduous shoot for Fields than *Sally of the Sawdust,* but the results weren't nearly as satisfactory. Unlike *Sally, That Royle Girl* was a melodrama, and Fields' addition to the cast was gratuitous in that, however perfect he was for the character of the father, the part was too small to merit his participation. He stepped into the role when filming was almost a month along, and his work, without the anchor of a previous stage characterization, was perfunctory at best. "In a vain effort to make a comedy," Robert Sisk wrote in *Variety,* "Griffith has dragged in W. C. Fields as the girl's father, but he doesn't belong in the picture, no matter how you look at it. He has nothing to do, and does it just like a man with nothing to do would do it." Mordaunt Hall said, "Fields frequently gives one a little too much of his comical conduct for a melodrama of this type. One is prepared to laugh and enjoy a scene in which he is punched and laid low, but when the same thing occurs seven or eight times it loses its humor."

Fields readily admitted to being off his game, blaming his distraction on an extraordinary late-summer burst of activity at the studio. "The racket made by carpenters, the yelling for lights to be switched on and off, the blowing of the director's whistle . . . those were some handicaps to doing my stuff right." An organ was routinely played setside to battle the noise, but there were simply too many companies working on the same stage to make the careful improvisation of comedy possible. "The studio is like a madhouse," Bravermann noted in his diary on September 2, "with seven pictures being made at the same time: D. W. Griffith, Gloria Swanson, Adolphe Menjou, Thomas Meighan, Richard Dix, Monta Bell, and Herbert Brenon.* Jazz bands, brass bands, symphony orchestras all trying to outdo each other, and the carpenters and props drowning out the lot with hammers, tearing down sets, dragging in properties and furniture."

The most strenuous part of the film was a climactic cyclone inserted by Griffith and supervisor William Le Baron to give the picture some size. It had the effect of nearly doubling the budget and making *That Royle Girl,* with rentals comparable to *Sally of the Sawdust,* a commercial loser at the box office. Fields spent five days working under storm conditions, braving sand and debris blown by a bank of Curtis airplane propellers and allowing, in one shot,

---

*There were several basement stages at Astoria, and it was once generously estimated that twenty production companies could share the building simultaneously. There were, however, rarely more than two or three pictures working at a time.

a breakaway wall to be blown down around him, an open doorway just saving him from being flattened.* Another scene had him blown into a lake, where he was supposed to bob comically amid a gaggle of geese. Conditions were brutal, and the shots took an eternity to make. "To my mind they were not very satisfactory," Bravermann observed. "Mr. Fields, not doing his stuff in the water, looked as though he was scared. We had four airplanes to create the wind but these did not seem to be enough." Griffith wasn't happy either and had Fields immersed in a tank on three subsequent occasions to get the scene more to his liking.

If Fields' comedy wasn't up to par, at least his spirits were bolstered by the release of *Sally of the Sawdust.* Sara Redway, in a September profile for *Motion Picture Classic,* praised his work: "Both Mr. Griffith and Mr. Fields should be crowned with laurel wreaths . . . for Mr. Fields has dared to be vulgar and Mr. Griffith has dared to let him." When Redway told Fields she liked him in the picture because he was "such an old bum" from start to finish, he was pleased. "That's the way I should be, but I don't think audiences like it. Just the way a girl will marry a bad egg because he is a bad egg, and then want to reform him, the audience will like some no-account character, but they want him to turn out all right in the end. . . . I don't like to have to be too nice. I'm not. No one is, or if they are, no one likes them. Things should be a little rough on stage or in pictures just to be consistent."

Demand for Fields' services suddenly intensified. With the completion of *That Royle Girl* he became embroiled in negotiations with Famous Players–Lasky over a three-picture agreement. He went to Boston with the *Ziegfeld Follies,* but left the show when a $4,000-a-week film deal was set, choosing to interpret his February 17 contract with Ziegfeld as having run its course. Desperate to keep him through the lucrative Chicago run—Rogers had declined to tour—Ziegfeld cried foul and accused Fields of "contract breaking." The settlement they agreed to paid Ziegfeld $500 a week out of Fields' share of the picture money, while Ziegfeld committed to the same rate Phil Goodman would have paid under the ill-fated *Showman* contract: $2,500 a week. Lasky agreed to back off until January 6, 1926, and Fields rejoined the *Follies* in Philadelphia on October 26, 1925.

Goodman, watching from the sidelines and incensed at Fields' refusal to tour in *Poppy,* filed suit in superior court eleven days later, alleging breach of contract. By the time Ring Lardner had stirred up a deal to write a revue for producer Harry Frazee—who was making millions off *No, No, Nanette*—if Lardner and composer Jerome Kern "could land Bill Fields," it was too late.

---

*This was two years before Buster Keaton inserted a similar stunt into *Steamboat Bill Jr.* As the Griffith film no longer exists, it is impossible to make a comparison.

"Bill said it was all right with him and I started to work," Lardner recounted in a letter to Scott Fitzgerald, "only to discover that Bill had already signed contracts (synchronous contracts) with Goodman, with Ziegfeld, and with the Famous Players. He's going to spend the winter in court. Goodman is suing him for $100,000, Ziegfeld has him, and he is supposed to be working for Famous Players and getting $6,000 [sic] a week."

Fields seemed genuinely surprised at Goodman's action but refused to back down. *Poppy,* after all, had closed in the red, and he was still owed for that last week he had spent on the road. He tried cajoling Goodman into dropping the suit and, after some hesitation, sent a Christmas greeting in the form of a telegram:

DEAR PHIL

THE SPIRIT OF CHRISTMAS IS PROFOUND. THE PRESENCE OF OUR OMNIPOTENT BLESSED SAVIOR JESUS CHRIST IS FELT BY ALL. WANTED TO WIRE YOU AND LILLY AND RUTH LAST NIGHT AND ALL DAY TODAY BUT WAS TIMID. IF YOU WIRE I'LL LAUGH AND HAVE THE GREAT FRIENDSHIP I HAVE ALWAYS HAD FOR YOU ALL. IF I WIN I HOPE YOU WILL FEEL THE SAME. BETTER LUCK NEXT TIME SHOULD BE SPOKEN CHEERILY BY THE WINNER AND THE VANQUISHED SHOULD SAY SOMETHING EQUALLY AS CLEVER IF HE CAN THINK OF IT. MY SINCERE LOVE TO LILLY RUTH AND YOURSELF. BACK IN THE TRENCHES TOMORROW.

BILL

Despite the bravado, Fields was genuinely shaken by Goodman's lawsuit. The Eddie Cantor musical *Kid Boots* was in Chicago when the *Follies* hit town, and Billee Blanchard, a member of the chorus, found herself seated next to Fields at a holiday dinner. "I was surprised by how quiet he was. He was very well liked, but he seemed reticent and withdrawn. I remember they asked him to say something—make a little speech—and he declined. He seemed like such a sad man."

Hattie had never been happy with the amount of the check her husband faithfully sent each week. In bad times, it was as low as $25, but mostly it rose—$35, $40, $50, and finally to $60 a week. She pelted him with news of dire poverty, of ragged clothes and jobs cleaning houses. "I have not worked in two weeks because I have not been able to," she wrote to him in 1917. "I am nearly blind as a result of illness, and I could hardly read the menu prices when I worked as a waitress. I am mad, almost, trying to know how to meet expenses. . . . We don't even have curtains in our bedroom. Please send me some old clothes you no longer need, so Claude can wear them. His suit now is so patched."

Fields had long since inured himself to such pleadings. "Your monologue containing 'shoes and the dollar per week you have been paying off on a piano for thirteen years' gets awfully monotonous," he said. "Especially when you have the boy tell me the price of food going up and the dollar per week on the piano, etc. The prices have gone up on me, too. My salary has come down. Still I advance you the same each week and never let a peep out of me." He was especially intolerant when Hattie invoked the power of prayer in her letters. "Know positively if you would do a little work you would not have to take the shot in the arm so often. That would help you a great deal more than all the prayers offered to some imaginary power residing somewhere in the upper ether."

Fields was driven by the example of his own father, who, as intemperate as he was, worked hard into his sixties to keep his family together and achieve some measure of security. He ridiculed the old man onstage but shared his impatience with inaction, laziness, stupidity. He belittled Hattie for her sure sense of entitlement, and could not help but compare her to the two most influential women in his life—his mother, Kate, who never had a job but amassed a small fortune through low cunning and frugality, and his grandmother Annie, who never let anything stand in her way and who made things happen by the sheer force of her personality. Hattie was neither frugal, nor industrious, nor making a thing happen for either herself or her son. Worse, through the smothering intimacy of her relationship with Claude, she was molding him as her own mother had molded her.

When Hattie started pestering Kate Dukenfield for money, Fields did his best to shut down the relationship. "You have been a lazy, ignorant, bad-tempered, arguing, trouble-making female all your life," he seethed. "You [will] find yourself friendless in your old age. . . . I haven't one good thought or memory of you, and the very thought of an interview with you fills me with rage." For a while, their correspondence dwindled to terse one- and two-line notes ("Enclosed please find check . . .") and little more. Claude Fields grew into manhood without much contact with his father. Hattie would send him to the theater, but the dialogue invariably came around to money, illness, Hattie's struggle to survive on such a meager stipend. Fields got so he couldn't stand listening to such a relentless diatribe and told Hattie to keep their son at home.

"Just about the time I get ready to do something nice for him, he spills the beans." The two had only sporadic contact in the late teens and early twenties, yet Fields always took care to send Claude a check at Christmas.


Fields was weary of the *Follies* grind and looking forward to making pictures at least part of the year. "I've been on the stage a long time and I'd like to try something else," he said. "Besides, I'm tired of doing a set act." When Dave Stamper asked if he'd miss the audience, Fields hooted. "Miss the audience? With all the people that stand around and watch you on a movie set? Sometimes 30 people!" *Sally of the Sawdust* had the effect of focusing more press attention than ever before on Fields and his work. He spent much of his last tour holding forth in his dressing room on the subject of comedy in the movies. He declared his allegiance to slapstick because life, he said, was slapstick. "It's the best sort of humor because it gets down to real things. Anybody can understand its broader lines. Yet it gives a chance for social satire, like the drawings of Hogarth. Look below the surface, if you care to, and you will discover the satire." On a more practical level, Fields knew that slapstick was surefire with most audiences. "I don't care how nice anyone is trying to be, a funny fall can always get a laugh."

Niceness, in light of the Griffith rebuke, became a pet peeve of his, and he went on about it at length. "I have talked to several successful moving picture comedians about this same niceness that is in such great demand. I have suggested things to them that they might use, and they have told me that their audiences would not stand for anything vulgar. Yet Chaplin, the greatest of all comedians, is vulgar. I think the funniest scene I almost ever saw was in one of Chaplin's old pictures. He is eating some ice cream and it falls down his trousers." When Fields signed with Famous Players, Adolph Zukor gave him a piece of advice: "You hear a lot about people being helped to high places in pictures, but the only person who can really help you is yourself." Fields took it to mean that only he could be responsible for the quality of his work, because the average filmgoer would see it that way. "People who come to see me don't come to learn a lesson. They don't come to be uplifted. They come to laugh at me. So I do the things that make them laugh the hardest and enjoy the most." He told one interviewer that he had a lot of gags and "several scenarios" tucked away—an unlikely boast—and an "idea for subtitles that I don't believe has been used."

The movies, he opined, weren't so different from stage work, and the lessons he had learned before live audiences would serve him well in the studio. "What is there of art, or of acting either, in simply responding to the director's orders like an automaton operated by a push button? Like Merton—'Walk on—go over to table left—pick up picture—look at it—lay it down—three steps to the left—walk off through this door.' That's why directors are so important in the film industry. If more picture actors had stage training, they would not have to be told how to do every least little thing. Pictures would not be so artificial and stilted. The best actors on the screen do not need directors. Ernest Torrence and Adolphe Menjou direct themselves. That is the only way to real success—success that you yourself know is success, artistically if no other way."

Mindful of Zukor's admonition, Fields would set his own course in pictures and dare to be different. He finally left Flo Ziegfeld's employ in Chicago on January 16, 1926. Within a month, he would be back before the cameras at Famous Players making the first of his starring vehicles.

# Twelve

# Apothecary and Humanitarian

William Le Baron was the managing editor of *Collier's Weekly* when he got sucked into the movie business. The year was 1919 and his boss, William Randolph Hearst, had him look at a Cosmopolitan picture titled *Dark Star.* "What do you think of it?" Hearst inquired. Le Baron, who was a playwright by trade, said, "Terrible!" And Hearst said, "You fix it up."

Le Baron became director general of Cosmopolitan in July of that year and proceeded to build Marion Davies into a star of some rank. *When Knighthood Was in Flower* became their breakout hit in 1922. Cosmopolitan was distributing through Paramount at the time, and when Hearst brought a new studio manager in during the filming of *Janice Meredith,* Le Baron left to join Famous Players–Lasky as head of their scenario department. Within weeks, he was producing, along with Hector Turnbull, the entire output of the eastern studio at Astoria, Long Island. Le Baron was a plain-spoken man, but his literary background gave him a certain cachet with creative people that most picture executives lacked. A graduate of New York University, he was one of them, an elegant guy with an earthy sense of humor, someone who had actually had a hit of his own on Broadway. Le Baron was gone from Cosmopolitan by the time Fields shot his cameo for *Janice Meredith,* but his appreciation of Fields' talent stemmed from years of watching him in the *Follies* and, before that, in vaudeville. Le Baron was a prime mover in bringing Fields to Famous Players, correctly reasoning that Fields did not need D. W. Griffith nor a $400,000 budget to build a sizable audience.

Famous Players–Lasky was in its tenth year as a producing entity, having incorporated the combined assets of Adolph Zukor's Famous Players Film Company and the Jesse L. Lasky Feature Play Company in 1916. Previously, both Zukor and Lasky had distributed their films through Paramount, and they acquired that company and its memorable brand as well. In the next seven years, Zukor and Lasky spent an estimated $6 million building recognition for the Paramount name, a tactic that backfired when the company went public in

1919 and investors looking for Paramount stock couldn't find it. In 1924, the relationship between producer and distributor was more carefully delineated, with all advertising carrying the slogan "A production of Famous Players–Lasky, a Paramount Picture." It was too late to make much of a difference, though, and where Famous Players–Lasky was indeed the parent company, anyone lacking a legal reason to know better always referred to it as Paramount.

Fields came to the company at a time when management was scrambling for new talent and a boost in prestige. Paramount was known for Gloria Swanson and Rudolph Valentino and the biblical epics of Cecil B. DeMille, but the vast majority of Paramount releases were programmers starring the likes of Richard Dix, Pola Negri, and Thomas Meighan. Valentino and DeMille both left the company in 1925, and the drive to replace the latter was evident in the zeal with which Zukor courted D. W. Griffith. Harold Lloyd, America's favorite comedian, began distributing through Paramount in 1926, and Eddie Cantor made his feature film debut that same year in Paramount's *Kid Boots*.

*It's the Old Army Game* was settled upon as the title of the new Fields picture, and the announcement was made from Los Angeles on December 1, 1925. It would be based on the core elements of *The Comic Supplement*—as transplanted to the *Ziegfeld Follies*—but the public would be led to expect another round of sucker-fleecing at the hands of a McGargle-like character. Fields was plainly uncomfortable with the bait and switch, not wanting to play variations on *Poppy* for the rest of his days, but film marketing was still a mysterious form of commerce to him, and Le Baron assured him the public would forgive a misleading title if the picture itself were up to snuff. Clarence Badger, who directed most of Will Rogers' early films, was assigned to direct, and a starting date was set for February 8, 1926.

The supervisor on *It's the Old Army Game* was an ex–newspaper reporter named Tom Geraghty. It was Geraghty's job to concoct a story for Fields, and he put the task off for as long as possible. According to his daughter Sheila, Geraghty was the first writer to stress the use of doors in motion pictures. "He said all he needed really to make a picture was a set of a door. . . . there is always an air of excitement in a house when the door bell rings." Geraghty's scenario for the Fields picture would begin with the frantic ringing of a doorbell in the middle of the night. Eventually he'd have a plot to go with it.

Clarence Badger was trained as an engineer and preferred his scripts finished. Geraghty sensed Fields was best suited to a looser structure and decided he needed a director with more of an improvisational bent. Badger went off to direct a remake of *Brewster's Millions* with Bebe Daniels, and Geraghty went with one of Daniels' previous directors, a young hotshot by the name of Eddie Sutherland. The nephew of Thomas Meighan, Sutherland had been an actor, gag man, and stunt double prior to scoring a hit on the coast with a modest service comedy called *Behind the Front.* Previously, he had worked as an assistant to Charlie Chaplin on *A Woman of Paris* and, more significantly, *The Gold Rush.* Sutherland stopped in Chicago, where Fields was appearing in the *Follies,* and the two men sized each other up over lunch at the Drake Hotel. Sutherland was an intense, compact young man with hazel eyes and wavy brown hair. He had seen how Fields worked Griffith on the set of *Sally of the Sawdust*—he was directing *Wild Wild Susan* on an adjacent set—and wanted no part of it. "He was an ugly man," Sutherland said of Fields, "and he was telling me what he was going to do and I was telling him what I was going to do, so we didn't like each other at all."

*It's the Old Army Game* would be an epic of the American druggist, with Fields playing Elmer Prettywillie, "apothecary and humanitarian." Famous Players had a habit of rewarding its producers when they brought their pictures in under budget. Tom Geraghty got the bright idea of setting the film in Florida, where the land boom was in full swing, and shooting on location to save money. Le Baron approved the scheme, and plans were made to leave for Ocala in late February. The film was cast inexpensively enough, with Josephine Dunn and Jack Luden each getting $75 a week. Sutherland hired his aunt, Blanche Ring, to play the role of the ditzy Tessie Gilch, and her niece Marilyn was played by Louise Brooks, a promising young contract player who had worked as a dancer in the summer *Follies.* Fields liked Brooks, who roomed with Peggy Fears, because she was literate and had a reputation for being a troublemaker. The same qualities appealed to Eddie Sutherland, who, within a few months of having wrapped production, would ask Brooks to be his wife.

The challenge of the film was in adapting the McEvoy scenes—especially the "Back Porch" sequence—to the silent screen. Fields knew where the laughs should be, but knew nothing about the camera or how to communicate sound through image. Any change the director made in timing or staging was rigorously challenged. "Management," said Sutherland, "meant anybody who said 'no.' " A drugstore set was built on the main stage at Astoria, and much of the film was completed before the company adjourned to Florida. Sutherland freely admitted to not liking Fields ("I hated his insides"), but the set was untroubled by open hostilities. He sat seething as Helen Hanemann, a writer for *Motion Picture* magazine, visited the set and observed that Fields was "practically" undirected. "There was an occasional suggestion of 'Bill . . .' from Klieg-bronzed young Edward Sutherland, who spoke from the eminence of a stool beside the soda counter and from the deep absorption of folded arms and bent brow." Louise Brooks, who had watched Fields play the same scene from the wings of the New Amsterdam, knew Fields' frustration at trying to put the same gags across for the camera. "He never really left the theatre," she observed. "As he ignored camera setups, he ignored the cutting room, and he could only curse the finished film, seeing his timing ruined by haphazard cuts."

The second assistant on *It's the Old Army Game* was Joseph Pasternak, a busboy in the studio restaurant who kept pestering the directors on the lot for a job. Sutherland gave him one, and it was Pasternak who went to Florida with the company and tried so earnestly to make things happen on schedule. They spent a month in Ocala, an inland farming town near Gainesville, where, between bouts of hospitality on the part of the natives, love scenes between Brooks and William Gaxton were shot. "Nobody in Ocala seemed to have heard of Prohibition," Brooks observed. Tom Geraghty and Fields amused themselves by pacing off large parcels of swampland, tantalizing local realtors with talk of hotels and housing projects. The only substantive portion of the film actually made in Florida was the picnic scene, which was set at the Palm Beach estate of Edward T. Stotesbury, a Philadelphia banker who loved hobnobbing with the stars. By all accounts, the filmmakers behaved irresponsibly, trashing the immaculate front lawn that faced the ocean as the servants looked on in absolute horror.

"Of course, Bill Fields was a great enough comedian to realize that precisely because it *was* the Stotesbury estate, it would be funny if he made a hash of their lawns," Joe Pasternak said. Fields did three takes of the introductory shot in which he drove his old Ford through the gates of the magnificent estate, plowing clean through a hedge and digging deep into the lawn as he bounced toward the house. "During the five days of shooting the litter converted it to a garbage dump," said Brooks, "and when the trucks and forty pairs of feet finished their work it looked like the abandoned site of an old soldiers' reunion. But Mr. and Mrs. Stotesbury were thrilled. 'Everybody,' said Mrs. Stotesbury, 'everybody in Palm Beach is driving by to see what is going on here!' "

Fields tried springing the same impromptu ideas on Sutherland that Griffith had so agreeably shot, and Sutherland decided the old master's way of handling him was probably the best. "There was a scene in Florida where a kid was flying a kite," Sutherland remembered, "and Fields was going to take a cap pistol and shoot it down, and I knew this gag was too broad to be put into a story that you had to believe. This was a cartoon thing. I didn't want to take the time, and I said, 'Bill, I don't think I can get a cap pistol down here.' Sure enough, five minutes later, Mr. Pasternak, the eager beaver, says, 'Here it is! I got your cap pistol!' I could have killed him. So I shot it and cut it out, which was the easiest way to do it."

As was his habit, Fields made the trip to Palm Beach at the wheel of his Lincoln, Linelle Blackburn at his side and Billy Grady in the backseat. When he wasn't needed on the set, he busied himself sightseeing. One night, he and

*While filming* It's the Old Army Game *(1926) in Palm Beach,*
*Fields took particular delight in trashing the Stotesbury estate.*

Grady drove all the way to Miami to buy six cases of Gilbey's Gin—the real
thing—from a young hoodlum Grady had known in New York. Fields packed
a .38 for the occasion, and rode with the cases flanking him in the backseat.
"He looked like Queen Victoria," Grady remembered, "seated with the ends of
his coat hiding the gin and he, erect and regal, staring straight ahead." According to Louise Brooks, Le Baron pulled the plug on the Florida location shoot
when the effects of hard drinking began to show on film. "He said, 'What are
you doing in Florida? Your rushes look so peculiar. They're all tilted.' And
Sutherland, of course, said, 'Oh, gee, that was the day the cameraman had a
slight hangover.' So finally Le Baron said, 'I don't give a damn. What you're
shooting down there doesn't make any sense. Come back.' "

Fields wasn't happy with *It's the Old Army Game,* telling at least one writer
that not enough time was spent on story development. Geraghty never did
work out the entire story—a Florida land swindle turned on its ear—and
Sutherland wasn't up to faking it on the set. "Those young comedy directors—
Eddie Sutherland, Mal St. Clair—they thought they were geniuses, like Chaplin and Sennett," said Brooks. "What they didn't know was that when they were

out drinking and playing around and dancing all night, Chaplin and Sennett were thinking about tomorrow." The result was as disjointed as *The Comic Supplement*—individual scenes of great invention framed by the feeblest of plots. The film had a patched-together quality, and there was virtually nothing effective that hadn't previously been done onstage. Rushed into the action was an incongruous glimpse of the shell game, barely justifying the title, and the concluding moral, as Fields jauntily walks out of frame, is once again his curtain line from *Poppy:* "Never give a sucker an even break."

*It's the Old Army Game* was a blatant attempt to establish Fields in pictures on the strength of *Sally of the Sawdust,* and from a commercial standpoint it worked. Sold to exhibitors as a "long-run Paramount special," it was considerably less expensive to make than either *Sally* or *Royle Girl,* yet business was largely consistent with those two previous films. In Chicago, it bested comparable films starring Lon Chaney and Colleen Moore. In Los Angeles, where it played Grauman's Metropolitan, it performed respectably against competition from Richard Barthelmess and Norma Talmadge. The film's performance in New York City, however, was an entirely different story. Notices were mixed, as all the critics had seen Fields perform the same business onstage in the *Ziegfeld Follies. Variety* dismissed the film as a "gag picture pure," and Mordaunt Hall of the *New York Times* wasn't quite sure what to make of it. "The trouble here is the lack of anything substantial in the shape of a plot," said Laurence Reid in *Motion Picture News,* "which placed quite a burden upon the scenario writer and director to dress it up for laughs."

*It's the Old Army Game* played the week of July 10 at the Mark Strand and registered just about the lowest gross of the year—$23,300 for a 2,900-seat house.* Fields found himself compared to the established comedians of the screen—Harry Langdon, Harold Lloyd, Buster Keaton—but knew their films were better jobs of story and construction. Langdon's *Tramp, Tramp, Tramp* had preceded *Army Game* at the Strand and done well; *The Strong Man,* which followed in September, did better still. Lloyd's first Paramount release, *For Heaven's Sake,* played six strong weeks at the Rialto and smashed all opening-day records. Keaton was in Oregon shooting his masterpiece, *The General,* and the trades were carrying news of the Marx Brothers' impending debut for First National.

Competition, in other words, was fierce, and Fields knew he would need better material to last long in the picture business. "I don't want to go back to the stage—not for a long time, anyway. There're so many things I'd like to try out in pictures first. I want to do some slapstick comedies, but also some work

---

*By comparison, *That Royle Girl* drew $38,300 and *The Black Pirate,* with Douglas Fairbanks in Technicolor, did $50,600.

of a more subtle character." Tom Geraghty, with his wild Irish imagination, couldn't invent a viable plotline for *Army Game,* so Fields insisted on a ready-made story for his second movie, something airtight and solid. "A comedian should be given a well worked-out skeleton framework," he said in an interview with *Motion Picture Classic,* "and then told to add the bricks and ornaments as he goes along." The framework for his next film would be supplied by an award-winning short story, and his character would work in service of the material, not the other way around. "I intend to make the development of the character I'm playing more important than the registering of my own personality," he said.


*It's the Old Army Game* paid Tom Geraghty a $5,000 bonus, and he used the money to send his wife and daughter to London. By the middle of May, he was at work on another Fields vehicle. Geraghty thought his first Fields script a "knockout," but his star wanted something with a bit more shading to it. "I might make an instant success," Fields said, "if I were to continue making pictures in the makeup of Eustace McGargle, for instance, yet I might be just a fad and die quickly as they always do. But the basic human types never become old and stale—no more than landscapes do."

The "basic human type" Fields would play in his new picture was as far removed from McGargle as possible—the small-town Babbitt of Julian Street's "Mr. Bisbee's Princess." The story, published by Doubleday, had won the O. Henry Memorial Prize as best short story of 1925. The character of Bisbee was tailor-made for Fields, timid and self-important and yet achingly vulnerable. He meets a beautiful woman on a train, builds a longing acquaintance with her, then learns as she disembarks that she is Princess Lescaboura, returning to Europe and her playboy husband after a very public separation. At home, Bisbee faces rumors of a romantic liaison, and a scandal sheet's allusions to her "taste for bizarre associations" holds him up to ridicule. The gossip boosts his silverware and jewelry business—the largest in the southeastern part of the state—but threatens his marriage. In the end, an innocent note from the princess herself clears the matter up, and, once again, in his imagination at least, Bisbee is her loyal and devoted servant.

This was sterling material for Fields, admirable and meaty. Where as Prettywillie he largely reflected the sensibilities of Joe McEvoy—threatening babies, kicking dogs, aiming to blast noisy interlopers with a shotgun—as Bisbee he would be more nuanced and believable, less reactive and belligerent. Geraghty's adaptation was gagged up by Howard Emmett Rogers, a specialist in vaudeville acts, and laid down in shootable form by J. Clarkson Miller. As with the previous film, Fields was saddled from the beginning with a popular but contextually inappropriate expression for a title: *So's Your Old Man.*

Following his marriage to Louise Brooks, Eddie Sutherland returned to Los Angeles to make a sequel to *Behind the Front.* Direction of the new Fields picture fell to Gregory La Cava, a cartoonist and gag man who had distinguished himself at Astoria with the popular Richard Dix comedies. La Cava was given a new two-year contract on the basis of his success with the square-jawed Dix, and he set about to make an honest film of "Mr. Bisbee's Princess." In Fields, La Cava knew he had an actor who was high-strung and difficult to please, yet one who could also live in the skin of a character like Bisbee and make him breathe. At first, Le Baron feared La Cava might have met his match. The director found Fields intractable and downright mean at times, but it wasn't long before the defensive gruffness Fields displayed to most authority figures gave way to a grudging respect and, finally, when he began referring to his director as a "dago bastard," outright affection. "The peculiar thing," said La Cava, "is that although he thought he was being pretty mean there wasn't any real sting in it. It was only funny. Bill never really wanted to hurt anybody. He just felt an obligation." They would make only two films together, yet Fields would come to regard La Cava as his favorite director. "Not only is he brilliant," he said approvingly, "but he is the most thorough workman in anything he attempts of anyone I know."

*So's Your Old Man* went before the cameras in August 1926, with La Cava determined to tell a story true to its origins. Fields came armed with thirteen pages of notes—bricks and ornaments—most of which never got used. Geraghty went to work on other stories for Fields, most notably *Sweethearts in Every Port* and *Are You a Mason?,* and supervision of the new picture fell to Ralph Block, the story editor who had worked so effectively with La Cava on the Dix comedies. Le Baron had the good sense to leave them alone. "What was wonderful about Bill Le Baron," said Louise Brooks, "was he never left his office, he never came down onto the set, he never policed anyone."

The entire film was made on Long Island, in close proximity to the Famous Players lot at Pierce and Sixth. The first sequence to be shot was Fields' famous golf act, which was filmed on the first tee at the Deepdale Country Club in Great Neck. The film had not yet been completely cast, and La Cava realized only at the last possible moment that he needed a juvenile for the day. Twenty-two-year-old Charles "Buddy" Rogers was a student at Paramount's short-lived School for Screen Acting. "They were testing us a little bit," he said, "not using too expensive a film. . . . [T]hey called one day and said, 'Buddy, you have a pair of knickers?' Well, of course. That was what I was wearing at university at that time. They said, 'Wear 'em tomorrow because we're going to use you.' "

Early the next morning, Rogers was driven out to the course and introduced to La Cava. "He put me in front of the camera right then, without knowing anything, because it was silent, and Fields mumbled, 'You're going to marry my daughter in the film.' "

Fields went through the routine as it had been performed onstage, with Shorty at his side and actress Alice Joyce, playing Princess Lescaboura, looking on. The pie pan clung to him as usual, the tissue blew in his face, the ball got stuck to the head of the club. Five straw hats were crushed by Shorty, and an old whiskey bottle decorated the set. A writer for the *New York Times* was among the spectators: "Behind the camera, players and extras were convulsed with laughter each time Mr. Fields, with a very serious face, went through his harrowing experiences of a golfer about to make a drive." Rogers, in a crowd of onlookers, was talked through a series of reaction shots by La Cava. Fields, he observed, "had the most amazing set of clubs, some of 'em made out of rubber, some of 'em made out of tires. They would jump, they would fly, they would wrap themselves around trees." Just before the first shot of the afternoon, Fields discovered that his clip-on moustache was missing, and production was halted until Shorty could locate it.

In his journey to the screen, William P. Bisbee, successful jeweler, became Samuel Bisbee, an out-of-work inventor. Fields, having largely abandoned the adversarial stance he had assumed with Sutherland, was a "funny, sweet guy," as Rogers remembered him, who actually seemed "timid" under La Cava's gifted direction. The town of Huntington was dressed as Waukeagus, New Jersey, and Bisbee's invention of an unbreakable windshield for cars was played out in its neighborhood streets. Bisbee demonstrates his miraculous discovery by repeatedly ramming his Model A Ford into a tree. He is congratulated by his colleagues as the rest of the car falls apart. Kittens Reichert, a former child star, made her return to the screen as Bisbee's dreamy daughter, Catherine. Marcia Harris played Bisbee's downtrodden wife, and Julia Ralph was the snobbish Mrs. Murchison, society matron and Buddy Rogers' disapproving mother. Bisbee's demonstration to a group of auto executives fails when the car with the correct windshield is towed and another takes its place. On his way home, Bisbee contemplates suicide, meets the princess, and mistakenly thinks that she, too, is about to off herself. Earnestly, he talks her out of it, then tells her of his own troubles. She's taken aback by Bisbee, a good man who's hit a patch of bad luck, and determines to use her celebrity to give him another chance.

*So's Your Old Man* was released in October 1926, and *Variety* hailed it as Fields' funniest picture. It did an excellent week at the Rivoli on Broadway, where it pulled nearly $30,000, then spread to other cities and, finally, the neighborhood houses, where reports to the editors of *Moving Picture World* were ecstatic. "A comedy that will stand all the praise you can give it, and if you give it enough you are bound for a large crowd," came a manager from Rensselaer, New York. "Fields shows a big improvement over his last picture," said another from Texas. "This is a delightful comedy. Lots of laughs and amusing situations. Two or three more pictures as good as this and Fields will be a box office star."

Fields was starting to get noticed and remembered beyond the insular world of the New York stage, though the character of McGargle still colored the public's perception of him. Iris Barry, in her 1926 book *Let's Go to the Movies,* wrote of a class of comedian quite different from the Chaplin-Lloyd-Keaton variety. "The fathers of this school were [John] Bunny and Sidney Drew, character comedians of a Falstaffian or Quixotic build. Of these, W. C. Fields is, though a newcomer, the greatest. He has Pickwicks, Micawbers, and Marie Lloyds up his sleeve; he is supremely the charlatan who deceives only himself and appeals to everyone by a genial, if not exactly impeccable behavior."

Now completely divorced from stage work, Fields took a split-level frame house in northeastern Queens, next to Ray Dooley and Eddie Dowling on Little Neck Bay. The rural community of Bayside was full of summer homes for the theatrical elite and surrounded by a plethora of golf courses. In the winter months the place was practically deserted, affording good access to Astoria, ten miles to the west. When filming, Fields observed a rigorous schedule, rising at 7:00, breakfasting on orange juice and Postum, leaving for the studio at 8:30, and arriving on the set at a little after 9:00. Lunch consisted of orange juice and ice cream, followed by more work, then a four-course meal at home. He rarely went to bed before midnight, and then it took him a couple of hours to read himself to sleep. "For one who has played on the stage some thirty years, never getting to bed before two or three in the morning, it's hard as the dickens to turn up for work each day at nine," he said.

Le Baron took good care of his new comic, flattering him with solid material and supporting him with reliable directors. In October, he paid $25,000 for the rights to *The Potters,* the hugely successful play that begat *The Comic Supplement,* and assigned Fred Newmeyer, Harold Lloyd's frequent collaborator, as director. Fields was ideal casting as Pa Potter, and Ray Harris' respectful adaptation made the character less a drudge, more a dreamer than in J. P. McEvoy's original.

*The Potters* was made at the Astoria studio and the Long Island City Railroad yards during the month of December 1926. The modest cast was comprised of Mary Alden, Ivy Harris, Jack Egan, and Richard "Skeets" Gallagher, another graduate of the Paramount school. Newmeyer handled Fields well and brought the film in at a cost of $227,000. It had its first showings in January 1927. Fields, said the *Film Daily,* was "better than ever" as the henpecked Pa

*Shooting* The Potters *at Famous Players' Astoria studio, December 1926*

Potter, and Laurence Reid, in the *Motion Picture News,* agreed: "For one thing, he is not so dependent upon his stage gags." Sid Silverman of *Variety* saw *The Potters* at the new Paramount Theatre on Times Square and said they "ate it up" at a Sunday matinee. "There may not be enough slapstick in it to thoroughly amuse the shooting galleries, but it's human and everyone can understand it. Which may explain Fields' brilliant performance. He's human here, and funny. So much so it may prove a lesson in pantomiming to many of his contemporary screen comics." Mordaunt Hall, who witnessed the same showing for the *New York Times,* decided that Fields had "struck his stride" as the whimsical, daydreaming stenographer who invests the family savings in a pair of worthless oil leases. "His performance is a real achievement, for he has resisted the temptation to be extravagant. The moods of Pa Potter are reflected admirably by Mr. Fields, and whether it is the lowering of an eyelid, a gesture of his right hand, a frown or look of exuberance, one feels delighted with this Mr. Potter."

Fields, clearly on the ascendancy after a decidedly rough start, settled into an easy lifestyle at Bayside, making two pictures a year for Paramount and golfing whenever weather permitted. Compared with his time on the stage, he found filmmaking a far less taxing assault on the nerves. "On the stage it is such a strain to be on time for every rehearsal and performance. You have to be right on the dot. They won't wait for you a fraction of a second. But now here—at the studio—I can arrive at ten o'clock when I'm supposed to arrive at nine and it doesn't make much difference. There's no hurry, no worrying about being on time. It gives you a nice comfortable feeling."

But there was trouble brewing. B. P. Schulberg had rejoined Famous Players–Lasky after a six-year stretch as an independent producer and was in charge of the company's new West Coast studio. Larger and better equipped than the old ramshackle lot on Vine Street, the new twenty-six-acre facility was big enough to meet all the company's needs. Schulberg, who, in the words of Ivor Montagu, "resembled an amiable efficient crocodile smoking a large cigar," started angling to consolidate all production under himself in California. About a quarter of the company's feature output came from New York—a disproportionate share of which were moneymakers—but in light of expanded capacity in Los Angeles, the bicoastal arrangement came to be seen as more of an accommodation to overpriced stage talent than a matter of practical necessity. Le Baron, who was a Lasky man, successfully fought off a move in December 1926 to close the Long Island studio by pointing out that stars like Thomas Meighan and Richard Dix actually had New York production written into their contracts. Schulberg, however, having been with Zukor from the outset, had greater credibility and political clout, and Le Baron knew it would only be a matter of time before he would prevail.

With *The Potters* a hit, Fields returned to La Cava for a second picture. In February 1927, Le Baron approved the $5,000 purchase of "Fearless Finch," a modest original by a man named Roy Briant, who wrote vaudeville acts. La Cava massaged Briant's material into a script he called *The Timid Soul.* But before the film could get underway, the boom got lowered on the Long Island operation, and one by one the various stars were ordered to California to finish their contracts. Not a word of the decision leaked out until the general manager made the stunning announcement on a cold Wednesday afternoon in March, effectively ending feature production on the East Coast. Contract players were called into Le Baron's third-floor office the following morning. Thomas Meighan agreed to make his last two pictures in Hollywood, but the upcoming Richard Dix film, *The Roughneck Gentleman,* was called off entirely. Director Frank Tuttle was dispatched to Los Angeles to start work on a new Raymond Griffith comedy; Griffith himself was caught in his compartment on a train headed east when word reached him. By Saturday, several hundred workers had been idled, their closest job prospects suddenly three thousand miles away.

At first, Fields and La Cava were told they could finish *The Timid Soul* on Long Island, but later that same week, the announcement came that it would be filmed instead in Los Angeles. Le Baron, for his part, would stay behind in New York, squandering his talents on "research work and [the] preparation of stories that will be made on the Coast." According to press agent Irwin Zeltner, Fields was "stunned" by the decision and only "somewhat" calmed by Le Baron. He objected to the heavy-handed way in which the closure had been accomplished, and lamented the fact that Le Baron's careful nurturing of his career would now be denied him. Sets for the new film were already under construction, and there were several months left on Fields' lease of the house at Bayside. Jesse Lasky, to whom both Le Baron and Schulberg reported, personally approved the making of the film in New York, an act which always endeared him to Fields. When shooting commenced in early April, La Cava had the deserted lot practically to himself. Actress Mary Brian, who had been brought east to appear in a Dix comedy, was permitted to remain in New York in order to play Elmer Finch's devoted daughter.

Fields described the project to a visiting journalist: "I play the part of a man who is afraid to walk across a lawn that says KEEP OFF, afraid to ask his wife for another piece of pie at the dinner table. Then I get mixed up with a hypnotist and things happen. It's more of a character study than any part I've ever had." Mary Brian perceived an uncertainty in the way Fields and La Cava approached the material. "I knew Fields was a great stage comic," she said, "and because this was a new medium to him, he was listening—sort of—to La Cava. I don't think he had really developed the character that he perfected later on. He was more intense about it at that time because this was a whole new thing that he had started."

Under the influence of Arvo the hypnotist, Finch rips and roars his way through a demanding day at work, braying all the while, "I'm a lion!" Then he heads home to straighten out the loveless family that has made a fine art of browbeating its sole provider. Finch has married a widow with a grown son, a pantywaist and a slacker who hollers "Ma!" at the slightest provocation.* "I've always thought," Brian said, "that if it was just the awful stepmother and the dreadful stepson, and if he was not close to the daughter, then it made him a monster." The father-daughter relationship was the key to the humanity of Elmer Finch. "We had sort of a thing going that you could tell even when the lines weren't there."

Fields tore into the character with a ferocity that was sometimes surprising to the cast and crew. As one observer noted, "There he was, tearing around a three-walled living room, up on the sofa, down on the floor, all the while roaring, 'I'm a lion! I'm a lion!' letting himself go so completely, so thoroughly, that even a director, who is never supposed to be satisfied, and a company of picture-wise prop boys and gag experts burst out in the same kind of applause that you would expect to hear from a ten-cent Saturday afternoon audience of grade school children."

La Cava's tentative approach to the material actually seemed to energize Fields. "I think comedy—out and out comedy—was not [La Cava's] strong suit," Brian suggested. "And I think he was trying to learn from Fields, and Fields was trying to learn from him." Filming was brought to a satisfactory conclusion on April 28, 1927, at a final cost of $179,000. The handful of remaining employees on the lot were let go with two weeks' severance, and by June the five major New York studios—including the Jackson, the Pathé, and the Biograph in the Bronx—were idle.

*Running Wild,* as the film came to be known, was the most successful of all of Fields' silent pictures. Its opening in New York, on June 11, 1927, coincided with a ticker-tape parade honoring Colonel Charles A. Lindbergh, and the throng, after several hours of waiting in the hot sun, filled the Paramount on Times Square to overflowing. Sime Silverman said the film would send Fields "quite some forward in starring picture circles, besides giving him most likely a wider circulation than any or all of his previous picture productions have done." It returned a tidy profit, with domestic rentals amounting to $328,000 and another $92,000 coming from foreign territories.

---

*There are echos of Hattie in Mrs. Finch's plaint, "My boy and I wear rags—you and Mary dress like millionaires!"

*"I'm a lion!" Fields, Mary Brian, and Marie Shotwell in* Running Wild

As Finch said at the fadeout, "From now on, I'm the big noise in this house!" But the release of *Running Wild* was soured when Fields was hit with a $7,500 judgment in the breach-of-contract suit that had been brought by Philip Goodman. The award stunned him, partly because he was genuinely fond of Goodman and his family, and partly because Goodman still owed him $750 back salary on *Poppy* (a matter that went unaddressed by the court). Fields asked Goodman to take $6,750 to make it square, and was fried when the perennially hard-up producer refused. The judgment was considerably less than the $100,000 Goodman had sought, but any sum—to Fields' mind—was gallingly unreasonable. Fuming, Fields abandoned all pretense of friendship and fired off a cable:

DEAR PHIL:

DON'T YOU THINK IT A BIT PIGGY ON YOUR PART TO WANT ALL THE MONEY? I DO, SO I'VE DECIDED IF I DO NOT HAVE

YOUR LITTLE CHECKIE IN MY LITTLE HANDIE FOR UNPAID
SALARY YOU STILL OWE ME BY WEDNESDAY AT THE LATEST,
I SHALL BEGIN HOSTILITIES BY FIRST GOING TO EQUITY. I
HAVE DEFERRED DOING THIS SO LONG ON ACCOUNT OF
THE UNPLEASANT PUBLICITY ATTACHED TO THESE THINGS,
BUT NOW THAT YOU HAVE RECEIVED YOUR BALM I MUST
INSIST THAT I GET MINE. LOVE AND SWEET FORGET-ME-NOTS,
AS ALWAYS,

W. C. FIELDS
WORLD'S GREATEST COMEDIAN

# Thirteen

# *Vanities*

There was little about Ben Schulberg that suggested a robust sense of humor. He was a man of pretensions, literate and well read, a college graduate who got his first break as a publicist. He was also an ambitious man who took no prisoners in the internecine warfare that passed for office politics in Hollywood. He knew good material when he saw it, but didn't always think the moviegoing public was interested. His output at Paramount was an odd brew of hokum and prestige. He backed Ernst Lubitsch and Josef von Sternberg and brought Emil Jannings to America, but he also made Clara Bow one of the biggest stars in pictures.

Schulberg had a tin ear for comedy. For all his elegance, William Le Baron had the sense of fun that Schulberg intrinsically lacked. The modest films Le Baron made at Astoria were consistently funnier and more profitable than anything that issued forth from Hollywood. Schulberg hated Le Baron, not only for the success of his pictures, but also for the easygoing management style that made working in New York such a pleasure. He encouraged the suspicion that Le Baron didn't run a tight enough ship, and with the acquisition of a roomy new lot in California, there was no longer any need for a studio in the East. With Adolph Zukor's blessing, Schulberg moved Richard Dix and Thomas Meighan to the West Coast and set about, either by design or incompetence, to destroy them.* His greatest bonehead move, however, was reserved for W. C. Fields.

*Behind the Front* had been the surprise comedy hit of 1926—a surprise in no small part due to the fact that it was made in Hollywood. Eddie Sutherland quickly ground out a sequel that proved nearly as popular, and Schulberg put him in charge of a newly created "comedy unit," asking him to come up with

---

*Meighan announced his retirement, but Dix followed Le Baron to RKO, where he made a new career for himself in talkies.

another team that had the box office punch of Wallace Beery and Raymond Hatton. Nothing came of the scheme, at least at first, but then Schulberg looked at *Running Wild* and came up with the bright idea of pairing Fields with Chester Conklin, an old Sennett comic who had been effectively teamed with George Bancroft in La Cava's *Tell It to Sweeney.* The hulking Bancroft had been such a hit in Sternberg's *Underworld* that Schulberg decided he was more valuable to the company as a dramatic lead than as a comedian. The announcement of Fields' pairing with Conklin came in June 1927, but Fields was told not to worry himself with matters of story or content. "All I had to do, I was told, was to go out and play golf. When they were ready for me, they would let me know, I would come to the studio, make a few faces and a few previously written remarks, and I would be paid regularly. I tried it, and in six months I was out of a job."

Schulberg turned over responsibility for the Fields-Conklin pictures to Louis D. "Bud" Lighton, a tall, well-liked man whose every decision had to be blessed by his fast-talking wife. Fields didn't like the woman, a scenarist named Hope Loring, and her antipathy toward him may have hastened his downfall. Lighton did well with Westerns and social dramas, where a studious respect for source material gave his films a veneer of quality that others lacked. But, like Schulberg, Lighton had no experience in comedy, and his ignorance was exacerbated by a rigid hierarchy that was supposed to take the guesswork out of pictures. As Fields observed, "Hollywood, it seemed, was a community of specialists. There were specialists who did nothing but sit down and think up plots for stories, others who embellished these into screenplays, still others to write dialogue, and more to think up funny situations."

Fields arrived in Los Angeles on June 9, 1927. He installed himself in a suite at the Ambassador Hotel and reported for work at the new Paramount lot on Marathon Street, where the property, appropriately enough, abutted the Hollywood Cemetery. Where before he had been used to the cramped, communal feel of Astoria, Fields now beheld a virtual city for the making of movies. Four steel stages had been moved from the old Famous Players lot to augment the seven already standing, and the property surrounding them was crammed with exteriors. On September 6, he went before the cameras with his first West Coast film, an ill-conceived affair entitled *The Side Show.*

Mindful of Fields' impact in *Sally of the Sawdust,* Bud Lighton had commissioned a circus story from Percy Heath, the man who had written *Tell It to Sweeney* and who had, therefore, made a team of Conklin and Bancroft. Over the summer, the producer ran the material through no fewer than eight writers, Grover Jones, Norman McLeod, and Julian Josephson among them. What he got for his trouble was a hodgepodge of dusty business. Fields was, once again, called upon to clip someone at the shell game, and a poverty of inspiration

*Fields invested* The Side Show *with ball juggling and the most complete version of his cigar box routine ever captured on film.*

resulted in the most extensive demonstration of his juggling skills ever captured on film.* He played Gabby Gilfoil, the owner of an impoverished circus which has been dispossessed of all its animals, leaving only its sideshow freaks. Stranded in Arkosa, Gilfoil matches wits with Ben Holden, the local sheriff, for the hand of the town widow, a giggling antique played by Cissy Fitzgerald.

All the tried-and-true elements were there, excepting, of course, Le Baron's keen understanding of what made Fields and his characters tick. Mary Brian was his daughter once more, but this time there was no discernable affection between them. (The script, in fact, had her so ashamed of the old man that she elopes with the sheriff's son.) Much was made of Fields' pairing with the

---

*For this reason alone, it is a tragedy the picture no longer exists.

walrus-faced Conklin, but at no time were they permitted to actually function as a team. "I think Conklin was rather in awe of Fields," Brian said, "but their relationship was very congenial. They didn't compete." Indeed, Conklin proposed Fields for membership in the Masquers Club.

The director was a man named John Waters, whose few films were action pictures and whose true calling was as a second-unit man. Waters had been an assistant to men like Sam Wood and Raoul Walsh and had an assistant's way of inhabiting the background. "I hardly remember him on the set," Brian said, "so he wasn't very visible." Waters, by most accounts, had little talent for the staging of comedy and displayed more interest in the half-dozen freaks that populated the film. "We went far from the beaten path in order to line up a menagerie of unusual human oddities for the side show scenes," he said to one of the publicity men with obvious relish.

The system of production at Astoria was vastly different from the way it was handled in California. "In New York," said Mary Brian, "everyone had theatre tickets, so we rarely worked past six." Hours in Hollywood were completely unregulated and could stretch far into the night. Louise Brooks was shocked at the contrast: "We had complete freedom [in New York]. Of course, I didn't know [that] until I got to that police state in California, the California studio, which was really just a factory."* Ironically, the regimentation seemed to instill a false sense of security in Fields. The temperate climate agreed with him, and friends like Will Rogers were close at hand. "He was a very funny man," said Jim Rogers, the comedian's youngest son, who remembered Fields as a guest in their Beverly Hills home. "We were sitting there having dinner. Dad had given Mother some plates from Europe, and Fields picks up these brand-new glass plates with lace in them and starts juggling them. She just about had a fit." Fields impressed the boy by taking the time to talk to him, something few of their notable guests did. "He was like most all the comedians I have ever known—men with very deep feelings and tremendous compassion. I never got the impression he had an axe in his pocket to chop off every kid's head."

Relaxed after the tension-filled days in New York with Sutherland and La Cava, Fields suddenly became a press agent's dream. Publicist Cecil "Teet" Carle, new to Paramount and the movie business in general, was assigned the task of compiling an official biography. He was driven out to Lasky Mesa near Calabasas (officially known as the Paramount Ranch), where the company was filming on a midwestern street. He found Fields, hot and bored, sitting off to

---

*Schulberg was, in the words of David O. Selznick, "a great mill foreman."

one side on a make-believe porch. He was, said Carle, "kind, considerate, and talkative" over a two-hour interview and gave more than an inkling of his fascination with the sounds of words.

"That day he remarked how amusing it was to be working in Calabasas, with the closest town being Agoura and Malibu just over the ridge of low mountains, and Point Hueneme just up the coast. He said he had been musing about Cucamonga kumquats and rutabagas grown in Azusa." Fields told Carle he ran away from home at the age of eleven—conveniently forgetting to mention that he also returned—and talked of sleeping in cellars and sheds. "He told me to touch the wood railing of the porch. I noticed its warmth. He said he had learned early that wood quickly absorbs, then holds, warmth from the sun. 'Some mornings after I came awake I used to sit for hours with my back against a board fence,' he said softly." Carle came away with a score of human-interest items and enough material to produce a 2,500-word biography that would form the basis of Fields' personal history for the decade to come. "Fields was very easy to work with in terms of publicity," he said, "because you could write anything you wanted and he never complained. In other words, we could sit in an office and we could publicize a Fields picture and never go on the set, never have to talk to him, because we knew his type of humor and could make things up."

To Schulberg's credit, *The Side Show* had every apparent advantage. The $235,000 budget was comparable to Fields' priciest Astoria subjects, and the comfortable schedule permitted a generous twenty-four days of filming. Waters was nearly $13,000 under budget when the last bits of a climactic chase scene were shot at the ranch on October 3, 1927. Fields and Conklin were racing back to Arkosa and the widow, Conklin on horseback and Fields at the wheel of a truck loaded with angry, unpaid freaks. When the truck broke down, Conklin passed and hooted; Fields stole a bicycle and took off in hot pursuit. When Conklin fell into a stream and clung to the bank, Fields paused long enough to step on his fingers. Conklin proceeded to float downstream, where he was able to get the truck started again. Moments later, he passed Fields, still feverishly pedaling the bicycle, and this was where the script called for Fields, unaware that Conklin was now in front of him, to ride up into the bed of the truck as Conklin threw it into reverse and attempted to back over him.

The studio driver passed out of camera range, but as Fields looked back he misjudged the distance between himself and the ramp. He struck his head against the undercarriage of the truck, and the bicycle flew out from under him. "I should have been able to roll between the back wheels without trouble," he said, "but I couldn't move. Everybody yelled at the truck driver, but he couldn't hear." Johnny Sinclair, a stunt double, pulled Fields clear of the wheels and, in effect, saved his life. It would take a set of radiographs to confirm what Fields already knew—that he had broken his neck. "I heard it snap, and many things went through my head. I suddenly recalled what my friend, Dr. Harry Martin, had said, that he had held his head perfectly straight with both hands when the same accident had happened to him. So I cautioned everyone to keep away from me and immediately held my head with both hands until I reached the hospital, fifteen miles away."

A man sat on each side of him, and he was still bracing his head in his hands when he arrived at Hollywood Hospital. Dr. H. J. Strathearn conducted a lengthy examination and determined he had indeed fractured his third cervical vertebra. The injury was thought to be life threatening and initial reports were dire. Two days later, the *Los Angeles Times* carried an item under the headline: "Film Actor Will Survive Injuries." Strathearn told the press that Fields would be confined to his bed for at least five weeks.

Bessie Poole read of Fields' injuries in one of the New York dailies and wired her concern. He had kept her afloat over the years with a series of $500 checks, but had ignored her pleas since her return from Europe. Then their ten-year-old son was hospitalized in November 1927 and, after covering $100 of Mrs. Holden's expenses out of her own pocket, Bessie traveled to California for a "showdown" with the father. Armed with a sheaf of letters he had written over the years, she got a lawyer and threatened to sue him in open court if he didn't make good on his responsibilities. Fields retained an attorney of his own and dictated an affidavit which included, in part, the words: "W. C. Fields is NOT the father of my child." Upon a negotiated payment of $20,000 ($13,000 in cash and a note for the balance), Bessie relinquished all claims and walked out of Fields' life forever.

Fields enjoyed a steady stream of visitors during his recovery, and left the hospital, over his doctor's objections, after only three weeks, with a stiff rod strapped to his spine. "I had to carry my head braced in an upward position," he recalled, "as if I were counting the stars." He and Linelle Blackburn took a Mediterranean-style house on Wedgewood Place in the Whitley Heights section of the Hollywood Hills, where the location afforded them a spectacular view of the Cahuenga Pass. Fields had a barber's chair installed in the living room, for he could get no sleep in a conventional bed. He also ignored his doctor's orders to avoid strong drink, and one of his first acts upon settling into his new home was to fix himself a highball. He was, in fact, descending the staircase with one, eyes firmly fixed on the ceiling, when he slipped on an unfamiliar step and bounced all the way to the bottom, breaking his coccyx in the process and knocking his sacroiliac out of alignment. The neck, thanks to the brace, was still mercifully intact, and he endured the ordeal, he later claimed, without spilling a drop.*

After some troubling previews, *The Side Show* was trimmed to fifty-five minutes and renamed *Two Flaming Youths.* (The title itself was a nudge in the ribs, *Flaming Youth* having been a harbinger of the flapper age and a hit for Colleen Moore a few seasons back.) Paramount did its best to promote the new Fields-Conklin combination, having obviously written Fields off as a single, but the new team was a low-wattage attraction alongside the likes of Harold Lloyd, Clara Bow, Emil Jannings, and the aforementioned Beery and Hatton. In a full page ad in January's *Photoplay,* they shared the bottom row of the company's roster with cowboy star Fred Thomson, Florence Vidor, and Esther Ralston. "You've no idea what a great comedy team they make together!" the copy enthused.

And they didn't. Having grown used to Fields in films like *So's Your Old Man* and *The Potters,* there was virtually no appeal in watching him compete for screen time with Chester Conklin. The reviews were better than the film deserved; Abel Green gave what amounted to a rave in *Variety* because Jack Conway, a fellow staffer, had contributed the titles (". . . the gags and all the laughs are in the *Con.* style," Green wrote). Partly on the strength of the New York reviews, *Two Flaming Youths* played the week of December 31 at the Paramount Theatre and did extraordinarily well. The take amounted to some $83,000, with only *The Docks of New York* besting it for the year. A week's stand at the Oriental in Chicago proved almost as lucrative, but in most other markets—Los Angeles, Boston, Atlanta—the results were dismal. *Variety's* man in San Francisco described the film's performance at the 2,700-seat Granada as "pitiful" and tagged it a flop. "The public just didn't want W. C. Fields and Chester Conklin in *Two Flaming Youths.* [The] picture didn't mean anything to [the] sophisticated mob who play this big house." It took in $19,000 for the week and was "lucky to get that." Clara Bow, at the slightly smaller Warfield, grossed $31,000 for the same seven-day period.

If *Two Flaming Youths* was not quite the comedy sensation Schulberg had envisioned, it was a laugh riot compared to the next Fields-Conklin offering. Al Christie, who made his name in two-reel comedies, occasionally turned out a feature as well. He held the rights to such staples as *Charley's Aunt* and *Up in Mabel's Room* and made creditable screen versions of both. He also owned the rights to *Tillie's Punctured Romance,* the landmark slapstick feature directed by Mack Sennett. Christie proposed a remake for Paramount release, and Schul-

---

*Liquor was expensive in Los Angeles, but the supply of genuine or slightly cut goods was steady. It seemed that fully half the mechanics, doormen, chauffeurs, and office boys at the studio were dealers.

berg agreed to fund the project, contributing Fields, Conklin, and director Eddie Sutherland to the package. There was, however, no story to the first film, which had starred Marie Dressler, Mabel Normand, and Charlie Chaplin, and so all Christie really had was a title. He sent for Sutherland and said, "What do you know?" Sutherland, seemingly fed up with Schulberg, said, "I know I'd like to go to Europe."* Christie arranged for a long weekend in Paris with Harry Edwards and Sutherland's writing partner, Monte Brice. On the second day out, Sutherland said to Brice, "Gee, I think Al is kind of worried because we haven't come up with anything." Brice agreed. "I sense that," he said. Christie was hoping the trip would produce a storyline. "So," said Sutherland, "we got up promptly at five in the afternoon, as we'd stayed up till eight or nine in the morning, but between five in the afternoon and seven, when we met Christie, we dreamed up a story. We came down and Al said, 'How've you boys been all day?' We said, 'We've been working.' You could see his eyes light up at that."

The story they told Christie reflected the time they put into it. It was, once again, a circus story, with the second half a retooled bit of *Behind the Front* with Fields and Conklin in place of the Beery and Hatton characters. It was a dreadful piece of tripe, but Christie embraced it like a drowning man. "Boys," he said, "I owe you an apology. I thought you were loafing and I was getting worried to death. I didn't want to say anything, but now I'm just in Heaven. This is a great, wonderful story. Let's relax. Let's have some wine." Christie never drank, but he saw to it that they always did. "So then work ceased," said Sutherland. "Nothing happened until we got back to New York. We were supposed to go out on the train with Christie, and I stalled and wiggled out of that, so Mr. Brice and I could do some work on the train for four days. So now this story, that Brice and I knew wasn't very good, became, in our minds, really good. We got to Hollywood and went to two or three of our pals and they didn't like it much, but we were sold—convinced that it was good." Fields came to the house Sutherland shared with Louise Brooks in Laurel Canyon one afternoon to hear the same pitch that had sent Al Christie to heaven. Said Brooks, "I remember Bill sitting quietly, listening and drinking martinis from Eddie's two-quart cocktail shaker; I remember him teasing me by dropping my fragile Venetian wineglasses and catching them just before they hit the floor; but I can't remember one word he said about the idiotic plot contrived for the remake of the film."

Production got underway in December at the Christie lot on Sunset, where, in 1911, a remodeled roadhouse had become the first permanent studio in Hol-

*Sutherland had volunteered to deliver his young sister-in-law, June Brooks, to a finishing school outside Paris while his wife, Louise, was shooting a film in Hollywood. Christie's interest in developing a story provided a convenient way of financing the trip.

lywood. Fields, shielding his eyes with a derby and gnawing on the butt end of a toothpick, spent his time between shots balanced up against a palm tree in an undertaker's chair, bathing his tender neck in the weak afternoon sun. Conklin was more gregarious, reminiscing about the original film (in which he also had appeared) and talking over old times with plain-faced Louise Fazenda— "Tillie" in the new film—and Bob Kerr, a Sennett gag man who was now directing for Christie. Sutherland, who considered Al Christie a "dear pal," did his best to make something out of it all, but his inspiration deserted him, and Brooks would remember the experience as "the worst mess of filmmaking that I have ever observed." Fields played his early scenes with Babe London, a 250-pound comedienne who, at one point, roughly gave him a chiropractic adjustment. The pair, according to the plot, were trying to destroy Conklin's circus by feeding the lions cream puffs to make them sleepy and inert. When war is declared, Conklin takes the circus to Europe, where he, Fazenda, and Fields end up masquerading as German soldiers. For the climax, the lions are sent over the top to scatter enemy troops.

After nearly losing his life on the previous film, Fields seemed to take this benighted remake in stride. He showed none of the trademark intensity for which he was known in New York, and his relationship with Sutherland could almost be described as congenial. Anything the director suggested appeared to be okay with him. Standing in the middle of a faux battlefield at Studio City, he agreeably juggled hand grenades while awaiting his cue. He even appeared in shots with the lions and, in at least one instance, narrowly escaped a mauling. "He was fun off screen," Sutherland admitted, "but he wasn't funny. He was a great drinking companion, an earthy man. We used to go to the fights together and have all kinds of parties together, play good pool, good ping-pong, good golf—a very fine athlete, you know."

*Tillie's Punctured Romance* wasn't a cheap film to make—the mob scenes and war effects were genuinely impressive—but it previewed so badly that no amount of cutting could help. It premiered in Los Angeles and did withering business, prompting the distributor to offer it almost immediately on split weeks. It flopped in New Orleans and Boston in March, and didn't find its way to New York until June. The Paramount wouldn't touch it—preferring Clara Bow instead—and *Tillie* landed in a second-run house on Lincoln Square. It sank quickly and didn't resurface again until 1932, when producer Charles R. Rogers paid $30,000 for all rights to the original Sennett production and got the camera negative of the remake as well. That was the last anyone ever saw of *Tillie's Punctured Romance,* and today it is thought to be lost.

Lighton, meanwhile, had a second story for Fields and his partner, a moldy original about a land swindle that was patterned after the "Get-Rich-Quick Wallingford" stories. He tinkered with the thing while Fields convalesced, put-

*Eddie Sutherland did his best to make something of*
Tillie's Punctured Romance, *but the "idiotic" plot defeated him.*

ting Sam Mintz on the script just as *Tillie* entered production. As with *Two Flaming Youths,* Lighton had a multitude of indifferent writers on the scenario: Harry Fried, J. Walter Ruben, Hank Mann, Grover Jones. Then, suddenly, there was a perplexing urgency to the project, and Fields began to smell a rat. *Two Flaming Youths* had flopped, *Tillie's Punctured Romance* was awful, and there was no reason to believe *Quick Lunch* would be any better. Fields figured he was getting the bum's rush and told the people at Paramount he would only work for cash on the barrelhead. When *Quick Lunch* entered production barely two weeks after *Tillie* had finished at Christie, it became the job of Paul Jones, the assistant director on the film, to draw $1,000 from the bursar's office at Paramount each morning and drive it over to the house Fields shared with Linelle in Whitley Heights.

The director of *Quick Lunch,* Chuck Riesner, had been a prizefighter, vaudevillian, songwriter, and actor. He was eight years with Chaplin and had just come off the spectacular *Steamboat Bill Jr.,* which he directed in collaboration with Buster Keaton. His talkies were undistinguished, but as a director of silent comedy Riesner was straightforward and accomplished. Under different circumstances he might well have done something memorable with Fields, but *Quick Lunch* was situational and bereft of gags, and the best he could do was simply to get it done. He opened the film with a pool hustle, but it was basically all story, no character, the product of a producer who knew nothing of comedy. In later years, Fields would express such contempt for Lighton that he could not even bring himself to utter the man's name. "All I've got to say is God help anybody who trusts his career to somebody else—particularly when the person in charge knows no more about pictures than my supervisor, or whatever he was."

*Quick Lunch* was completed on March 14, 1928, and Fields was promptly let out of his contract. "They were plenty fed up with me," he said. "Not only was my option not renewed, but nobody else would hire me." In three years, he had worked himself up to $45,000 a picture. Yet it had taken only six months for Schulberg and Lighton to utterly destroy him in pictures. It would be another seven years before he would see that kind of money again.

Fields did not remain long in Hollywood. While *Tillie's Punctured Romance* was crawling its way through the second-run houses, the big news on Times Square was talking pictures. *The Jazz Singer* was charging through the relatively few houses wired for sound and shattering records everywhere. Paramount, Metro-Goldwyn-Mayer, and United Artists signed contracts with Western Electric, joining Warner Bros., Fox, and First National in the race to be all talking, all singing. When the 1928–29 season was announced for Paramount in April, Fields' name was nowhere to be found on the schedule.* He fished for other offers, but the industry was in turmoil, and his currency as a solo attraction was greatly diminished. He was playing golf at Lakeside, opposite the First National studio in Burbank, when a message came through. Earl Carroll was calling from New York with an offer to star in the *Vanities.* "Tell him to go to Hell!" said Fields, returning to his game.

---

*Chester Conklin, who, at $2,000 a week, was a much cheaper commodity, was demoted to featured player.

Fields didn't like Earl Carroll, didn't like the way he did business or the type of show he staged. Delicate and balding, Carroll was a predatory businessman with a distant manner and a clammy handshake. His *Vanities* was a leering knockoff of the *Follies,* built around showgirls he managed to lure away from Ziegfeld. He worked in a tam and a pale blue artist's smock and required his girls to audition in the nude. Fields once dismissed him as "a preacher with an erection." In Atlanta, Carroll had done time on a perjury rap, and the stretch had almost killed him.* It was six months before he could even think about staging another edition of the *Vanities,* and then he maintained that it would be his last. Wanting to make it the greatest production of his career, Carroll at first tried negotiating with the Shuberts for the services of Al Jolson. Rebuffed, he then conceived of a historic pairing between Fields and Beatrice Lillie. Lady Peel was mildly interested, but Fields had no intention of working for Carroll and refused under any circumstances to even take his calls. The producer, who had a well-known disdain for agents, finally turned in desperation to Billy Grady for help.

"I went to see Carroll," recalled Grady, "and I had to level with him. Bill Fields had always expressed his violent dislike not only for the man but for any Carroll operation. I felt it hopeless for Carroll to seek Bill Fields' talents and told him so. I also said that Fields' demands would be such that he could not afford him. But Carroll would not take 'no' for an answer." At Carroll's insistence, Grady met with Fields, who had returned to New York and taken a suite at the Hotel Astor. The third picture with Conklin, retitled *Fools for Luck,* had just opened in Boston and taken a well-deserved nosedive. ("The comedy team pictures are fast losing their sting," said the *Motion Picture Herald.*) Fields also was in the process of being sued for back commissions by Charles Walton, who claimed, on the dubious merit of his association with D. W. Griffith's brother, Grey, to have been Fields' agent on all three of his Paramount contracts. (In May, Fields settled for just the $1,950 he owed on *That Royle Girl* after Walton took the stand in a jury trial and, in Fields' words, "topped the truth into the rough every time he swung at it.") Despite all this, Fields was adamant: "I wouldn't work for the son of a bitch if he gave me his theatre."

Grady persisted. The most Fields had ever made on a stage contract was the $2,500 a week he extorted from Ziegfeld in his final days with the *Follies.* Now Grady suggested that he could get even more. When pressed, Fields outlined a deal certain to repel Carroll—$4,500 a week and a royalty of $150 for every new sketch he provided. "I never did like that guy's setup," Fields said of

---

*Carroll had served champagne at a private party and then denied it under oath. The champagne was in a bathtub, as was a nude showgirl named Joyce Hawley.

*Earl Carroll reminded Fields of "a preacher with an erection."*

Carroll. "He's a sensation and publicity seeker. All he knows is to put a lot of bare-assed dames on the stage and call them Carroll Beauties."

Grady thought the demand excessive but dutifully presented it anyway. When Carroll, who had the seemingly unlimited backing of a Texas oil million-aire, agreed to Fields' terms, Grady nearly fainted. "Believe it or not," he reported back to his client, "Carroll said he'd do it." Astonished, Fields upped his demand to $5,000 a week and asked for a thirty-week guarantee. Moreover, he wanted his name above Carroll's in any and all publicity. "I took the offer to Carroll," said Grady, "but I knew it was complete nonsense, so I didn't make any effort—in fact, I told Bill I was resigning."

Talks continued through May 1928, with Fields dickering directly with the producer and hoping nothing would come of it. "God! How I miss California and am going to miss it until I get out there again," he said. Casting agents were puzzled by Carroll's gargantuan plans, which called for salaries of up to $200 a week for the right showgirls. When Fields learned that Bea Lillie had been offered $5,000 a week, too—she was seeking a percentage from the Shuberts— he demanded still more. Grady was certain that Carroll's ardor had cooled when he saw an item in the May 30 issue of *Variety:* "$5,200 FOR W. C. FIELDS." "I told you how I nicked Earl Carroll for fifty-two hundred per week," Fields gloated in a letter to Tom Geraghty. "I think it is next to the record—Jolson out-salaries me." He got a lawyer who was friendly with Linelle's family to do the contract, and Grady, with his Irish temper, had screwed himself out of nearly $20,000 in commissions.

Fields had returned east for the Walton trial, but also in the sincere belief that talkies would revitalize New York as a center of production. In fact, he made permission to do "movies and talkies" part of his *Vanities* contract. From Elmer Pearson, Moran and Mack's manager, he heard that Harold Lloyd was willing to back a talking picture starring the Two Black Crows and himself. He also knew he had backing for his own vaudeville company should he choose to tour again. "This is the Sabbath," he wrote solemnly to Geraghty, "and it is raining. What a great country for the farming—but you can't raise a thing in my room at the Astor Hotel. Consequently, I am very low and ugly about weather conditions. We have had one nice day since we left Los Angeles. They can have New York and 'stickit.' "

In anticipation of doing a film with the Crows, Fields reluctantly agreed to a series of one-nighters for a promoter named Francis Coppicus. The tour would hit nineteen cities in three weeks, beginning in Roanoke in early June and finishing up in Dayton, Ohio. "I hope to the redeemer we will get some sun there," he said. Charlie Mack, who owned all rights to the characters, had quar- reled with partner George Moran and set out to find a replacement. Protective of his newfound prestige as Broadway's top-salaried performer—Jolson was on the road—Fields refused to share billing with a fill-in and was therefore accorded the top spot on the program. He and Mack split $7,000 a week between them, but there was trouble from the very beginning. Fields performed his pool and golfing routines with Linelle in the girl parts but hated the grind, and after a couple of days it was obvious that he was looking for a way out. In Wichita, an ad mistakenly billed him second to the Crows, and he immediately took the opportunity to allege breach of contract. The road manager offered an additional $1,000 a week as "heart balm," but it wasn't enough. At the age of forty-eight, Fields was off touring for good and had no stomach for it. The company played Saturday shows in Des Moines as scheduled and then hope- lessly fell to pieces. Coppicus was forced to sue.

Back in New York, Fields settled down to the business of crafting new scenes for the *Vanities,* the first he had written in four years. The Moran and

Mack debacle only served to sharpen his appetite for talking-picture work, and he proposed to open the *Vanities* with a Movietone clip of himself in which he would argue with the director, the higher-ups, even himself, and eventually step off the screen in a Keatonesque manner. "Possibly Carroll is standing on side lines near [the] camera, and during argument with director and heads of film company, Carroll suggests that I go into *Vanities* until argument is settled."

Carroll's show was a crass affair, and it brought forth a certain crassness in Fields as an artist. Among the results of an intensive month of writing were "My School Days Are Over," a snickering blackout, and "Fido the Beautiful Dog," a fifteen-page manuscript in which the owners of a "big and frightfully dopey-looking" dog try desperately to rid themselves of the animal. The most substantive of the new sketches were "The Stolen Bonds," a straight-faced burlesque of old-time melodrama, and "The Caledonian Express," for which Fields created four separate roles for himself. The rambunctious "Episode at the Dentist's," which closed the show and garnered the most attention, was a trunk item he had originally written for the aborted Australian tour of 1919. As a group, the *Vanities* sketches were a departure for Fields in that they depended more on dialogue than action for their impact. In the past, lines had been mostly functional and perfunctory for him, merely working in service of the physical business. Now, with talkies in the offing, he turned away from the pantomime that had always been his stock in trade and built characters defined as much by what they said as what they did. Rehearsals got underway in July, with the New York opening set for August 6 at Carroll's self-named theater on Seventh Avenue.

Conscious of giving good value for what amounted to a record salary, Fields spent more than an hour onstage, bolstering a lavish revue in which the material was thin, the songs unmemorable, and the length interminable. Fifty scenes comprised the two acts that unfolded before a packed house in Atlantic City on July 30, 1928, and, as one critic put it, "life and verve" substituted for genuine content in carrying the day. Fields' scenes were the best received, supported as he was by Ray Dooley and Joe Frisco, but he was also saddled with Dorothy Knapp, a spectacularly untalented woman whom Carroll billed, with some justification, as the most beautiful girl in the world. Unburdened by clothes she posed well, but movement and speech were more of a challenge for her. She bounced from the wings in a negligee to serve up occasional straight lines, and was in a wedding-night blackout entitled "All Aboard." Fields' gift for ad-libs served him best when Knapp was onstage, and he cloaked her awkwardness with a genial, almost fatherly indulgence. She played a patient in the dental scene and practically pulled down the set one night as she made her entrance. Fields caught the flat as it began to fall and held it until the stage crew could pull it back into position. Dusting his hands, he turned to the audience, which was momentarily unsure of how to respond, and said, "They're not building them like they used to." The laugh that followed was so long and sure-fire that Carroll wanted the bit retained.

Trimmed to forty-seven scenes, the so-called Seventh Edition of *Earl Carroll's Vanities* (it was actually the fifth) was still in rocky shape when it rolled into Manhattan on a fleet of flatbed trucks. One onlooker, observing the procession and noting the absence of Fields' name on an adjoining billboard, stopped a stagehand to ask, "Isn't W. C. Fields in the show?" The man at first regarded him as if he were nuts, then thought better of it and just gave him a tremendous, "An' how!" It was perhaps the most appropriate summary comment ever made about the show. "The *Vanities* has a cast size of 7⅝," Jay Kaufman wrote in the *Telegraph,* "but Fields is the 7."

The curtain rose at 8:49 the following evening. Anticipation ran high, and the audience was fairly oozing goodwill. They applauded the first notes from the Vincent Lopez Orchestra and kept on applauding for the next three hours. "Say It with Girls" opened the show, and seventy-five of them populated the stage. Carroll's strong suit was never the elegance or taste that distinguished the Ziegfeld productions, but he had money to burn and wasn't shy about using it. His "living curtains," scattered throughout the show, were a *Vanities* tradition, nude girls dangling from the flies, serving as tassels or decorated in jewels and shimmering blades of silver and gold. By the time Fields made his first appearance, at approximately 9:30, the crowd was primed and ready to laugh.

In "The Stolen Bonds," he faced the audience in the tippet and mackinaw of a gold prospector, uttered the immortal line, "It ain't a fit night out for man or beast and it's been astormin' for a fortnit!," and took a handful of snow in the face.* In "The Caledonian Express," Breeze (Joe Frisco) occupied the reserved compartment of Lord Derby and refused to vacate. Fields based the piece on an actual event that occurred aboard a crowded train between Glasgow and London when he appropriated a compartment reserved for actor Seymour Hicks and refused to budge. There was no payoff to the scene, but he managed to put it over by appearing in four different guises—guard, conductor, stationmaster, policeman—and using actors in masks to sustain the illusion.

The familiar "School Days" came near the top of the second half. Another scene, "The Mormon's Prayer," set Fields as a herculean Brigham Young amid a roomful of wives. ("Brigham Young and tell 'em nothing.") The critics on tight deadlines had mostly fled the theater by the time Dr. Pain, the incompe-

---

*The snow was made of diced paper. A ten-pound bag cost $14 because it had to be fire-proofed.

tent dentist, took the stage at approximately 11:30. Unhindered by Ziegfeld's relentless meddling and empowered by a sense of desperation on the part of Earl Carroll, Fields put across one of the rawest exhibitions of slapstick butchery ever seen on a New York stage. ("Have you ever had this tooth pulled before?" he inquired pleasantly.) Women screamed, drills whirred menacingly, bits of teeth flew in all directions. The revue came to a clamorous end about midnight, when Carroll himself was pulled through a trap door on the stage and, blinking into the spotlight, told the cheering crowd that he was "terribly glad" his comeback production had been so well received. He kissed Ray Dooley and triumphantly rang down the curtain on the most troubled period of his professional life. Reviewers the next morning weren't quite as laudatory as the audience had been. Most all were of a mind, however, that the new edition of the *Vanities* was the best ever. Wrote Heywood Broun, "There is no song in all the *Vanities* to haunt your nights of dancing. The singers fail to set each idle foot to tapping. I even think there may have been girls more glorified and charming. But this is a funny show and so it seems to me a triumph."


Much as Fields disliked the weather in New York, he enjoyed the nightlife. He frequented old haunts—Dinty Moore's, where he often ate in the kitchen, Leone's, on Forty-eighth Street, Henri's on Long Island—and renewed his wounded friendship with Philip Goodman. Fields expected relief from the high prices of California liquor, but found supplies of scotch and rye at historic lows in the East and still paid upward of $90 a case. Champagne, which he kept for guests and rarely drank himself, cost even more—$120 a case, regardless of quality. In the daytime, he indulged his passion for golf on Long Island, playing shirtless to soak up the sun. "You know, when I first took up the game, I went around in little more than a pair of trousers," he told Fred Crosman, Carroll's press agent. "Now I have cut that down to knickers. I can go around any old course in knickers almost any time."

Fields was jubilant as the *Vanities* played to capacity business, and he reveled in newspaper accounts of his fabulous salary. But as the new theatrical season took flight, he suddenly experienced a spate of bad publicity. The first event was absurd. In the dentist sketch, Gordon Dooley, Ray's brother, was a patient with a thick set of long, bushy whiskers. Fields had a gag in which he palmed a canary and made it look as if the bird flew out of the beard as he probed for a mouth. The canary—there were five kept in a communal cage backstage—would typically fly out over the audience and then disappear into the wings. On the night of September 13, two publicity-hungry officers from the Humane Society witnessed the show and decided Fields was mistreating the bird. After the performance, they appeared at the stage door and demanded his arrest. The scene, similar to one in *My Little Chickadee* a dozen years later, had Fields being marched to the Forty-seventh Street station as an angry mob of friends gathered and cameras flashed furiously. The next day, Fields was arraigned before a magistrate in the West Side court, where it came out that, far from mistreating the birds, he had a specially prepared salad brought over for them each day from the restaurant next door. "They get the proper apples," he told the court, "and they do not eat pears. They do not like them. They get all the seed and some delicacies that canary birds eat." He was acquitted of the charge, and an item in the *New York Times* the next day carried the headline "W. C. Fields Not Cruel."

The second event was not so easily laughed off. Having severed all contact with Fields in the aftermath of their Los Angeles showdown, Bessie Poole returned to New York and descended into an alcoholic haze from which she rarely emerged. Late on the night of Saturday, October 6, 1928, she was in the company of Joseph Whitehead, philanthropist and heir to the Coca-Cola fortune, and his brother-in-law, a shipping executive by the name of Eddie McCarthy, at a West Forty-eighth Street nightspot called the Chez Florence. Robert Neilly, a retailer known around town as "the Orangeade magnate," was at an adjacent table in a state of semiconsciousness. Someone poured spirits of ammonia into a glass and was holding it under his nose when Bessie yelled, "You're burning him!" and tried to yank the glass away. In the process, she tipped over the table and a fracas ensued. Bessie was punched in the face, and her escorts were beaten as they rushed to her aid. Bleeding profusely, she was bundled into a cab and returned to the Hotel Dorset, where she was staying in the suite of former *Follies* star Lillian Lorraine. A doctor who examined her there said her nose had been fractured. "I guess I forgot to duck," she said.

Bessie's condition worsened, and she complained of abdominal cramps, as if somehow she had been poisoned. On Monday, she was removed to Park East Hospital, where she lapsed into a coma and died. The word on the street was that she had succumbed to bad booze, but the attending physician gave the cause of death as myocarditis, an inflammation of the heart muscle, aggravated, he told the press, by acute alcoholism. She was thirty-three years old. The tabloid press, particularly the *Daily News* and the *Graphic,* had a field day with the story, implicating Tommy Guinan—brother of Texas Guinan and the reputed owner of the club—as the man who pasted her. The district attorney weighed into the fray, declaring such clubs to be the natural byproduct of Prohibition. "Persons who patronize night clubs associate with criminals of the worst type. The night clubs are hangouts of criminals who watch for women with jewelry and men with money, follow them when they leave, and rob them or else blackmail them." He stopped short of calling for their closure, but said personally he wouldn't mind seeing them all put out of business.*

Fields managed to keep his name out of the papers until Bessie's will was filed for probate in November of that year. Of the $20,000 payoff he had made the previous year, only $7,000 remained. The papers picked up on the fact that she bequeathed him a ring "with a diamond in the center and small stones set around it." No provision, the *Times* reported, had been made for William Rexford Fields, the decedent's eleven-year-old son. In Philadelphia, the *Evening Bulletin* was less circumspect: "A romance that flourished when Bessie Chatterton Poole was 16 [sic] and Broadway was a glitter of promise may have languished in later years, but that it never died completely was revealed in pitiable fashion in the short, simple will of the showgirl just filed."

Friends told the paper that Fields and Bessie had once been married, but Fields himself ducked the reporters and refused to comment. When finally cornered, he said only that she had been a friend whom he had tried to help when she was broke. "Some years after I first helped her, she began demanding money. I got threatening letters from her and a lawyer. I concluded she was being made the tool of blackmailers. Her son is now ten years old, but I never met her until six or seven years ago." In desperation, Bessie had signed away her son's birthright, and in death Fields held her to the bargain.

He sank into a deep funk over the Bessie Poole affair, and business at the *Vanities* began to falter. He talked of leaving the show and going to Florida to sit out the winter. Ray Dooley left in December, and the *Vanities* went dark the week before Christmas. Competition was stiff: Will Rogers was starring in *Three Cheers* at the Globe, Eddie Cantor was around the corner in *Whoopie,* and uptown at Fifty-fourth Street, *Show Boat* had been standing them in the aisles for more than a year. Carroll arranged for Frank Fay to take over the show, but amid wholesale changes in the cast, Fields eventually decided to stick it out. His traditional ad in the holiday issue of *Variety* was succinct. "Happy new year," it read, "to almost everybody."

---

*Guinan closed the Chez Florence within days of the incident and, blaming the *Graphic* for his troubles, fled to Cuba. He was never charged in the death of Bessie Poole.

# Fourteen

# *Ballyhoo*

Fields stayed with the *Vanities* through January 1929, but business never improved. Carroll closed the show after a run of twenty-five weeks and, with receipts off by as much as 30 percent, declined to send it out on the road without a sharp concession in salary from its star. Fields, however, was in no mood to tour and removed himself to Palm Beach to play a benefit instead. "I am constantly ill with grippe," he complained in a letter to Hattie, "which becomes worse each year—four attacks last year. If it recurs as many times this year, I am going to live in Phoenix, Arizona, open some small business, or manage a theatre. The lungs can't stand the strain."

In 1901, Fields had been diagnosed as consumptive by a doctor in Berlin. "I had . . . one lung completely out of commission," he remembered, "and the other doing half duty. . . . He said I must stop smoking, refrain from drinking all cold beverages, and must retire before sundown and take plenty of rest." The doctor, a Professor Fischer, also advised him to go to Milan and "eat" raw wine. "Raw wine. Ever hear that one? He meant grapes. 'Eat raw wine,' he says, 'or you'll die.' Well, I couldn't afford to go to Milan and eat raw wine—or cooked either—so I stayed where I was." He suffered from congestion almost continually for twenty years, but never had a thorough physical examination until he had settled in New York with the *Follies*. Dr. Jerome Wagner put him on a fluoroscope. "Hey, Bill," said the physician. "About twenty years ago, you had consumption." His lungs were full of scars, the doctor said, but Fields wasn't surprised. "Am I okay now?" he asked.

"Sure. The scars are all dry."

"That's fine. That's what I get for eating raw wine in Milan." He told Wagner what he had done—continue to work and smoke cigars and refuse to believe he was sick—and remained convinced to the end of his life that his devotion to cold air (he slept with the windows open and always rode in an open car) is ultimately what cured him.

Fields' relationship with Hattie stabilized in 1927 when he established a drawing account to manage her payouts. He had her sign a signature card and told her that she could thereafter stop by the Harriman Bank every Monday and collect her money. "Do not tell them the history of your life," he instructed. "Just say what I have told you. When you have signed the card return it to me. I will O.K. your signature and return it to the bank." News of the *Vanities* deal caused Hattie to lobby for an increase in her "salary." Her demands grew more vociferous when the New York dailies printed their thinly veiled reports of a son by Bessie Poole. "I have worked exactly 17 weeks this year," he responded, deftly dodging the specific issue of income. "I have worked my brain and worried the whole year, but received 17 weeks salary. Do not be so gullible when reading about the press agents' extravagant statements regarding salaries."

Hattie held dreams of showbiz glory for her son, Claude, and drilled him in much the same way that she and her sister Kitty had been drilled by their late mother. Claude was trained on several instruments, and, as early as 1923, Hattie had tried to lure Jim McIntyre and his wife to her Bronx apartment for a recital. Mrs. McIntyre, who had stayed in touch with Hattie over the years, had given her some glasses and a blue cape, and now Hattie tried to reciprocate with "one of those famous house-made dinners" and the opportunity for them to hear "the loveliest boy in the whole world" play the piano.

Fortunately, Claude was good enough to earn his way through school, because his father steadfastly refused to help. Fields was genuinely proud of being a self-made man (he sometimes referred to himself as "the Kensington Paradox") and doubtless thought that Claude, who had grown into a terrible mama's boy, could only benefit from the struggle of having to pay his own way. "My old man never helped me," he told his son gruffly, but when advised by wire of Claude's graduation from Columbia University in 1928, he nonetheless responded with a check for $200. Claude fronted a little jazz band and played dates at the local hotels. His father came to hear him one night. "The boy has talent," he conceded, "but I think he should find a more stable profession." When Claude declared his intention to study law at Yale, Fields was pleased but refused to contribute a dime. For a while, Claude lived in New Haven and commuted to weekend jobs in Manhattan, but eventually switched to NYU to devote more time to his studies . . . and to be closer to his mother.

Fields said he would go to New Mexico to "try to have my tubes and chest dried up" but spent two months in Florida instead. When he and Linelle returned to New York, it was to a house in the Russell Gardens section of Great Neck, Long Island, where he would spend the summer golfing and working up ideas for films. "I have several offers to do talkies," he advised Tom Geraghty, "including one from Famous [Players] to do some shorts and two longies

'IN N.Y.' but I want to get to California." The Astoria studio had become home to feature-length talkers with prominent stage stars like Jeanne Eagels, Walter Huston, and the Four Marx Brothers. Moreover, MGM and Vitaphone were making New York a center of production for noisy short subjects. The flurry of production was merely a stopgap, however, with new construction centered in Los Angeles. Paramount alone was building four new stages specifically designed for the recording of sound. Nearly half the 1928–29 season's output would be all-talking—as opposed to containing just music and sound effects—and the trend was toward more talking pictures.

Geraghty collaborated with Fields on the screen treatment for a talkie about a traveling company of actors at the turn of the century. They called it *The Great McGillicuddy* and based it, in part, on Fields' own experiences as a young juggler in burlesque. The title character owed much to the tradition of McGargle and *Poppy,* a point the authors made abundantly clear in a foreword: "He is at once self-confident, pompous, and dignified, whether he is reveling in success or sinking to the depths of despair. We love him for his faults and blunders as well as for the tenderness he shows when his big heart is so easily touched." The two men hoped to get D. W. Griffith interested in directing *The Great McGillicuddy* and made its melodramatic finale reminiscent of Griffith's own *Way Down East.* McGillicuddy's troupe is playing *Uncle Tom's Cabin,* but the line between fact and fiction blurs as bloodhounds are put on the track of a man lost in the snow. McGillicuddy leads his people across a river of ice, just as he has so often done onstage. "Aside from real thrills, there is a comedy element in back of it all as the Great McGillicuddy and his troupe are in very bad repute when he volunteers for this heroic action." Fields wrote Geraghty: "I have a former manager named Goodman who has a company formed to make pictures. He wants to start immediately but his stories are no good. Will you please send me on a copy of *The Great McGillicuddy* at your earliest convenience? I am sure I can get him interested in it."

Goodman was indeed interested and commissioned James M. Cain to work with Fields over the summer of 1929. They wrote nights, sequestering themselves in Cain's tiny apartment on East Nineteenth Street. "I quickly found out," said Cain, "that on story, on plot, on structure, Fields drew a complete blank—and in fact could hardly make himself get his mind on it. He thought in terms of gags, which followed a set pattern: annoyances of one kind or another." Fields spent his mornings golfing, cheerfully hustling his pal Charley Mack. When once he shot a 79 at Deepdale, he was careful to keep the news to himself. Mack, he said, was worth too much to him. "I wouldn't sell him for $250 per week, cash paid in advance."

Goodman, Fields soon learned, had taken a financial drubbing on a show called *Rainbow* and was in no condition to back his own films. Nothing further came of *The Great McGillicuddy,* and, toward fall, without anything else in play, Fields agreed to tour for Earl Carroll at a discount. The money wasn't as good as before—Carroll pared him back to $3,500 a week—but the tour was scheduled to go all the way to Los Angeles, and Fields saw it as an opportunity to display himself to an industry that had all but forgotten about him. Without Ray Dooley or Joe Frisco to help shoulder the burden, he made the *Vanities* a personal showcase and was on and off the stage a dozen times. In addition to "The Stolen Bonds," the "Episode at the Dentist's," and "The Caledonian Express," he did his golf act and the bit as the peanut vendor whose roaster doubled as a full-service bar. In the cast were Ben Blue, Dorothy Britton (Miss Universe), Al Trahan, acrobatic dancer Dorothy Lull, Joey Ray, and the Vercell Sisters. To play the caddy's part, Fields recruited Allan Wood, who was part of an eccentric dance act known as the Bennett Boys. As Wood's principal qualification for the job was being short, it took time to whip him into shape. "I was so bad in the first rehearsal of the sketch," said Wood, "that Bill didn't think I could handle it and told me so. I begged him to give me another chance, and he did."

When it came time to leave for New Haven and the start of the *Vanities* tour, Fields took Cain and the Goodmans to dinner at a little Italian joint to show there were no hard feelings over the demise of *The Great McGillicuddy.* Cain had spent hundreds of hours with Fields and had marveled at impromptu performances of such variety and richness that he had come to regard him as a great actor as well as a great comedian. "Once he was struck by the harangue of a rubber he had had at the Turkish bath he patronized, and sat there reciting it, working on himself, kneading his leg, as he did, and becoming so wrapped up in his tale as to be transformed. Actually, I sat there staring at him, asking myself, 'Is that *Fields?*' He didn't look like himself at all, but exactly like the rubber."

Nothing Cain had yet seen, however, prepared him for the performance Fields gave that particular evening at the restaurant. It started when the proprietor's ten-year-old son walked up to Fields and said, "Hi, Big Nose." Fields returned the greeting, and that would have been the end of it had the waiter not ratted the boy out to his father. Suddenly, the man appeared in a fit of rage and whisked the boy off for a noisy thrashing. Memories of the countless beatings Fields suffered at the hands of his own father must have flooded back, for he listened uncomfortably to the performance. "Jim," he said quietly, "that's all for my benefit. What kind of imagination is it that thinks I will get pleasure, or satisfaction, or whatever I'm supposed to get, at hearing a boy punished? I have a big nose, and I suppose to him it's a fact of life like the Grand Canyon or Niagara Falls, or some other natural wonder, and so . . ." Presently, the boy was hustled back into Fields' presence to tearfully whimper an apology. "I'm sorry,

Mr. Fields. I didn't mean it, honest I didn't." Fields ignored the boy's father and said, "Come here, son." He then proceeded to give a performance unlike any he had ever given in his life. "In addition to being a juggler," Cain recalled, "he was also a master magician, and he made half dollars come out of the boy's nose, letting him keep the half dollars. He stuck toothpicks into the dinner rolls and made them dance on the table. He came up with a yapping dog between the boy's feet then, and went tearing into the boy's pocket when the dog took refuge there, finally fishing him out, a two-inch thing of red flannel, and letting the boy keep him, too. It went on and on, with the boy utterly entranced."

Fields' work in the *Vanities* wasn't quite so inspired, but he dutifully played weeks and split weeks for Carroll for the rest of the year. The show finally came to rest in Chicago in January 1930, just as the ramifications of the great stock market crash were beginning to be felt. Fields had never had much luck with the market and was relatively unhurt by the October slide that wiped out a good number of his friends. Eddie Cantor, who barely survived the crash, was always proffering tips. "Eddie," Fields would respond, "if these stocks are so good, why do the presidents of these companies want me in on it? They don't know me, don't give a damn about me. Why the hell do they want me as a part-ner?" Eventually, Fields did buy shares in a few companies, halfheartedly, and found their volatility unnerving. "They were terrible," he later said of his stocks, wincing at the memory of a modest portfolio. "They went from $100, some of them, down to $6. They didn't pay any dividends at all." He was much happier with the interest he was earning at the Harriman Bank, where the vast majority of his fortune was tied up in cash.* He had a laugh on everyone when the bottom fell out of the market. "He was hysterical!" Cantor said. "After he finished laughing he offered me any amount of money I wanted, but I was enough in debt without incurring more."

Fields was comfortable, but he wasn't getting where he wanted to go. The *Vanities* never did make it to Los Angeles, and the tour came to an abrupt end in February 1930. Nothing he could do seemed to move him closer to another contract in Hollywood. He even found, much to his frustration, that his own material was being filmed without him. News of the indignity had reached him in August 1929, when a lawyer trying to close the Bessie Poole estate made an inquiry through Lou Frohlich, Fields' New York attorney, asking if Fields had

---

*It was known that Fields had accounts in a number of banks, some of which undoubt-edly failed. When the crash hit, he called his sister Adele in Philadelphia, where she was a telephone operator for the Land Title and Trust Co., and asked about the banks. Specifi-cally, he wanted to know about the Philadelphia Savings Fund Society and the Corn Exchange Bank. When told they were still up, he said, "That's fine. Those are the only two I'm interested in."

any interest in buying back the rights to "The Family Ford." Bessie had owned the prop car, the scenery, and the costumes, as well as the material, and Fields saw a chance to turn a venerable sketch into a talking two-reeler. He sent word back through Frohlich that the stage rights were practically worthless—Jim Harkins' years of touring had seen to that—but that he would be interested in the motion-picture rights. On October 25, Harkins signed a release, authorizing the estate to receive the "physical parts" of the act, which were in storage at a theatrical warehouse on Forty-seventh Street. Then he dropped a bombshell—"The Family Ford" had already been filmed as a Vitaphone subject and was awaiting release.

Fields hit the roof. The lawyer for the Poole estate immediately wrote to advise Warner Bros. that Harkins, who thought he controlled the act, had never had the authority to dicker away the movie rights. A hold was placed on the film's release, and it wasn't until July 1930—fourteen months after it had been shot at the Vitaphone studio in Brooklyn—that Warners finally purchased the rights to "The Family Ford." The film got shown, but Fields received no credit on it, and one of his most enduring sketches was lost to him forever.

Returning briefly to the two-a-day, Fields booked himself into the RKO Palace for a week at $5,500, playing "The Stolen Bonds" and the golf act and, in essence, bidding farewell to vaudeville. Within a month, the Palace would be wired for sound, signaling the end of live performances. With Fields in the golf act were Linelle ("a looker," according to *Variety*) and Al Wood, who, despite the rigorous training to which he was subjected, never quite filled the squeaky shoes as well as the deadpan Shorty had. Fields liked a tight act and hewed to the script, Wood observed, and was a soft touch at the stage door, where performers put out of work by closures and talkies tended to congregate. "After every show he would send Asa, his chauffeur, to the box office with a $100 bill, and Asa would bring back tens. Bill would crumple them up and put them in his pockets. He knew all the old timers from vaudeville and the stage, and when he met them on the street or at the stage door after the show, he'd pass one of those crumpled bills when they shook hands."

Fields' sense of charity never extended to the unauthorized use of his material, and, within days of his Palace bow, he was back raging against nibblers and defending his turf. The artist in question was Ben Blue, a lanky dancer and sketch comedian who was notorious for appropriating other people's gags. Having toured with Fields in the *Vanities,* Blue followed him into the Palace and did a comedy bit that borrowed elements from the "Waltz of Love" that Fields and Ray Dooley had performed in the spring and summer editions of the 1925 *Follies.* A pal at the Lamb's Club tipped Fields off to the pilferage, and he went the next night to have a look for himself. Blue lifted his partner, a comely tap dancer named Floria Vestoff, to his shoulder and waltzed her around the stage. Back to the center, he brought her down, only to have her foot become caught in his trousers. Trying to extricate her, he carried her around again and again. Finally, her foot dislodged but her slipper got lost, sending Blue on a frantic search of his lower regions. Fields, who never had much liked Blue, was livid and eager to avenge himself. Hattie, who heard all this second-hand, later claimed he went around to confront Blue in person and knocked a front tooth out with the same gold-handled cane he had used to beat Lord Byron's grandson to a bloody pulp. But Fields was now fifty, less impulsive than he was at twenty-three and able to hire his dirty work done. Billy Grady was present when Fields, bundled in his raccoon coat, drove up within whistling distance of the stage door of the Palace in his open Lincoln and waited for Blue to emerge. "There's the son of a bitch!" he shouted. "Get him!" Two hoodlums emerged from the shadows and gave Blue a good working-over. "They belted him to the sidewalk," Grady recounted, "and were about to give the foot-stomping routine when Fields yelled, 'Hold it—that's enough.' The roughnecks ceased their belaboring of Blue and disappeared as quickly as they came."

With the loss of "The Family Ford" still fresh in his mind, Fields arranged to commit the golf act to film before that too became valueless. Louis Brock, an independent producer of short comedies, was based at the Ideal Studio in Hudson Heights, New Jersey, where sets for his two-reelers were sometimes recycled from the old Herbert Brenon features shot there back in the teens. Brock owed six "Broadway Headliners" to Radio Pictures for the 1929–30 season, and he was anxious to add Fields to a roster of talent that included the comedy team of Clark and McCullough. The picture that resulted, *The Golf Specialist,* was a static rendering of "An Episode on the Links," stretched to twenty-one minutes with the addition of a lengthy prologue. Ironically, it was this new material, set in the lobby of a swank Palm Beach resort, that worked best onscreen. Fields' jaunty entrance, singing to himself, and his first words to the desk clerk ("Hello, Walter. . . . Any telegrams? Cablegrams? Radios? Televisions?") recorded beautifully on the famously temperamental Photophone equipment. Whatever else the film proved, it showed that Fields was a natural for the talking screen.

*The Golf Specialist* gave the old routine a backstory, thinly concealing the fact that it was essentially a filmed vaudeville act. (There had been a backlash against these after the novelty of talking shorts wore off.) Fields played J. Eppington Bellweather, a con man and gigolo whose laundry list of petty crimes included bigamy, passing as the Prince of Wales, eating spaghetti in public, using hard words in a speakeasy, trumping a partner's ace, spitting in the Gulf Stream, jumping board bill in seventeen lunatic asylums, failing to pay installments on a straitjacket, possessing a skunk, and revealing the facts of life

*Fields made his talking-picture debut in* The Golf Specialist. *Left to right: John Dunsmuir, Naomi Casey, Shirley Grey, Johnnie Kane, Fields, and Bill Black*

to an Indian. The film reportedly drew laughs in its initial showings—it played the Globe Theatre in New York—but its value today rests almost entirely in its record of one of Fields' best-known specialties.

The stretch with the *Vanities* had been marred by the absence of Shorty Blanche, who appeared in several of Fields' Astoria features but never made the trip to California. Shorty spent time with Harkins in "The Family Ford" and then went back to being a stagehand when times got tough. He wasn't in *The Golf Specialist*—that was Al Wood again—but his absence did not go unnoticed by critics in New York who knew the original turn by heart. In the summer of 1930, with audiences thinning and theaters going dark in record numbers, Fields and Shorty reconnected, and when Fields left for St. Louis in July to appear for the Shubert office in the Municipal Opera production of *Show Boat,* Shorty was once again at his side.

The Muni in St. Louis occupied a ten-thousand-seat amphitheater in Forest Park. Tickets were sold in conjunction with low-priced railroad fares, drawing visitors from as far away as Kansas, Arkansas, Louisiana, and Texas. Fields had Shorty cast as Rubberface and played opposite Sammy White and Eva

Puck, the Frank and Ellie of the original New York production; Charlotte Lansing, who went on to a brief career on the New York stage, was Magnolia. *Show Boat* was always a sore subject with Fields, for in 1927 he had been Flo Ziegfeld's original choice for the part of Cap'n Andy. He passed on the role because he was weary of stage work and, at the time, was making $45,000 a picture at Paramount. "I regret it now," he told a St. Louis publicist. "The pictures weren't so hot, as they say. And Cap'n Andy is a great character. Great." He accepted a fee of $4,000 for the two-week engagement and claimed that he learned the part in five days when, in reality, he never learned the part at all. Shorty's job was to stand offstage and feed his lines to him, a ruse that did not endear him to the cast and crew. One night toward the end of the run, stagehands locked Shorty in a trunk, and Fields, onstage, made an elaborate show of looking for him in the orchestra pit, behind the scenery, under a hoop skirt. "Someone's absconded with my dwarf!" he exclaimed.

With his juggling and his imperfect command of the part, Fields' interpretation of Cap'n Andy was, according to one account, "more grotesque" than that of Charles Winninger, the actor who ended up playing the role in New York. Fields might well have continued on to California from St. Louis, but there were still no nibbles from Hollywood. Instead, there was a new show in the offing, and it seemed certain that Fields would be spending yet another dreary winter in the East.


*Ballyhoo* was Fields' last Broadway show, his only flop in fifteen years of playing the Great White Way, and its failure was so personal, so inconceivable that he refused to abandon it until long after its original producer had given it up. His determination came partly from desperation—he had no other place to go—but also from the firmly held conviction that *Ballyhoo* was a good show that merely needed time to find its audience in a market that had always embraced him in the past.

The producer was Arthur Hammerstein, brother to the late Willie Hammerstein and heir, therefore, to his throne as king of Broadway showmen. A specialist in operettas, Hammerstein had made $2.5 million on *Rose Marie* and sunk most all of it into a new theater at Fifty-third and Broadway. The intent was to perpetuate the name of the father, the great theater impresario Oscar Hammerstein, and for a while, the cathedral-like Hammerstein's housed a steady stream of hits. But *Ballyhoo* came along at the wrong time, as 1931 turned out to be the most dismal year for the legitimate theater in nearly two decades. Half the theaters on Broadway were dark, and there was a surfeit of excellent shows—*Smiles, Tonight or Never, The Green Pastures, Five Star Final*—to attract what customers remained. Hammerstein formally engaged Fields to star in the show on October 21, 1930, agreeing to pay him 10 percent of the gross receipts against a guarantee of $4,000 a week.

The closing days of the Roaring Twenties had given rise to spectacles like dance marathons and flagpole sitting. The specific inspiration for *Ballyhoo* was one C. C. Pyle, the big-wind promoter of a cross-country foot race derisively known as a "bunion derby." Fields would play Q. Q. Quale—promoter, financier, gyp artist, handyman—as a droll parody of the flamboyant Pyle, following the race, hitting one hick town after another, giving impromptu performances and fleecing the natives. There'd be specialties at every stop: acrobats and tumblers, elastic-limbed tap dancers, a fire eater in an Arizona opera house.

The book was by Oscar Hammerstein II, the producer's nephew and the celebrated author of both *Rose Marie* and *Show Boat*. Harry Ruskin, who wrote premium revue sketches for people like Ziegfeld and John Murray Anderson, was Hammerstein's collaborator. Together they crafted lines that were, in Fields' estimation, "banal, verbose, and prolix," and he rewrote them to such an extent that Oscar Hammerstein took his name off the show (substituting that of his longtime assistant and gofer, Leighton K. Brill). Fields embroidered the show with his juggling act, his pool routine, his druggist scene from *The Comic Supplement*. "What a hell of a thing it will be," said Arthur Hammerstein, "to pay these guys as authors and they can't write a goddamn thing."

When Tom Geraghty sent over a child-sized Austin for Christmas, Fields was inspired to compose his only original scene for the show, a memorable gloss on "The Family Ford" he called "The Midget Car." He tuned, babied, stuffed himself into the thing. It was sublime bit of comedy, his hat poking through the canvas top of the tiny roadster, his knees up about his ears, the girl at his side adding her cat, a birdcage, and luggage to an already impossible load.

The additions crowded a book that was already overlong. There were two postponements before *Ballyhoo* finally barged into Philadelphia on December 1, 1930. Fields staged his entrance atop a calliope, all stops out, preceded by a band, a drum major, and the moustache that always dangled so tentatively from his nose. Twenty-four dancing girls, young and eager, surrounded him as he tried to speak, insistent blasts of the calliope always drowning him out. The supporting cast included singers Janet Reade (from Ziegfeld's *Whoopee*), Jeanie Lang, and Grace Hayes, whose show-stopping "Blow Hot, Blow Cold" came toward the end of the first act. Fields' fingerprints were everywhere: a star football player patterned after Red Grange bore the name "Whitey Duke," and the part of "Shorty" was created for the ubiquitous William Blanche. Fields sang a number titled "Go!," the starting gun fired, and the race was on.

Musically, the show limped. The dance was mostly a spirited tap, but the

HAMMERSTEIN'S

GRACE HAYES, W. C. FIELDS AND JANET READE

BALLYHOO

*Fields' last appearance on Broadway was as the star
of Arthur Hammerstein's* Ballyhoo, *1930.*

songs, with a couple of exceptions, were slow and forgettable. Hammerstein signed just some of them, letting the credit for the others go to Brill. The composer, Louis Alter, was a twenty-eight-year-old songwriter and pianist, Nora Bayes' accompanist during the final years of her life. By the time of the incongruous finale, a spectacular ballet on a Hollywood soundstage, the audience was fidgety and restless. "It isn't altogether fair to blacklist a musical comedy premiere," said the *Philadelphia Record,* "for even the worst of them have been known to achieve success after revisions and recastings. But a tremendous amount of polishing, dressing up, and speeding will be necessary to make *Ballyhoo,* which opened at the Erlinger Theatre last night, into an attractive musical show." The *Inquirer* called it "huge and haphazard" and said that while last-minute changes put it at variance with the program, it still "lacked some vital spark of spontaneity to make it go." All concurred that Fields had done a herculean job of anchoring the thing. "Mr. Fields," said the *Bulletin,* "is riotous, mostly so when he steps out of the role of Quale and becomes W. C. Fields. His juggling, his subbing for the football star, his miniature auto stunt, his uproarious poker game with the cowboys (all revue stuff, you note) are the kind of things that make audiences get a stitch in the side."

*Ballyhoo* spent a week in Philadelphia, another in Baltimore, and was headed for Syracuse when it was decided to ditch the rest of the shakedown tour in favor of more straight rehearsal time. The show brought a top of $6.60 when it opened in New York on December 22, but it was still in shaky condition, and the New York notices mirrored the Philadelphia reviews. *Ballyhoo* wasn't a hit, but Fields, chomping an unlighted cigar and gamely carrying the weight of the entire enterprise on his considerable shoulders, was. "A masterly dignity surrounds his skittish gray derby," observed Brooks Atkinson. "The eyes burn with the fierceness of the practical philosopher. Although his financial affairs are in a desperate state, he is a man of principle. He will not rob a sleeping cowboy who carries a loaded pistol. 'A thing like that would be dishonest,' he says in a scornful tone as he scrambles clumsily through the furniture to get out of the way." Shorty's presence was hailed, just as some of the absences were mourned. "Miss Ray Dooley sat in the row with me," said Alexander Woollcott, now writing for the *New Yorker,* "and, I thought, looked a little longingly at that extra seat in the Austin beside Mr. Fields. Or maybe my wish was father to the thought. Don't you suppose Miss Brice, Miss Dooley, and Mr. Fields are *ever* going to get into the same automobile again?"

Heywood Broun was moved to write a thoughtful and laudatory piece for the *Nation:*

Fields is, as far as I know, the only one who is able to introduce a tragic note in the handling of a dozen cigar boxes. When they are pyramided, only to crash because of a sudden off-stage noise, my heart goes out to the protagonist as it seldom does to Lear or Macbeth. If one thinks of art in terms of line and movement, then I suggest that there is present in this juggling act as much to please the eye as when Pavlova dances. Like the best of modern painters, Fields can afford to depart from the orthodox, because he is heretical from choice and not through incapacity. It is amusing when he muffs a trick because you know he could easily complete it if he cared to. Certainly, there is something admirable in the ability to emotionalize the task of tossing spheres into the air and catching them in rhythm. Possibly there is even profundity in such a pastime.

Such magazine appreciations came too late to help. Business went slack almost immediately, dropping from $20,000 in the first week to just $15,000 in the second. (By comparison, *Girl Crazy,* a solid hit, did $37,000 for the same one-week period.) Fields pressed for changes, but Hammerstein was distracted and on the verge of financial ruin. "No one in authority paid the slightest attention to the show," Fields lamented. Hammerstein went off to the races and took his nephew Reginald, who was in charge of the book, with him. "Consequently, we all sat around inert and didn't even rehearse," said Fields. On New Year's Day, 1931, he wrote to the producer, offering to work at half salary and urging immediate, wholesale cuts in the book. "I still think that by the process of elimination the show would have had a great chance. There are many fine things in the show, but they need to be brought closer together, bunched as it were." Under Equity's agreement with the Managers' Protective Association, Fields was compelled to report that he had not been paid for the previous week. "This is a hell of a letter to be writing on New Year's Day," he said.

Hammerstein made his reply the next day. The show had lost $33,000, he reported, as of the previous Saturday, and the current week, "which should be the biggest in the year," would lose another $10,000. Salaries for the musicians and stagehands amounted to $5,000 a week, and he didn't know where he was going to get the money. "I have sold everything in my possession and the only thing I have left is this theatre, on which I owe back interest and taxes. . . . I have one satisfaction, and that is that I am now in the class with the big financiers—busted." With receipts not much over $13,000, the closing notices were up before Broun's paean in the *Nation* ever made it to the stands. *Ballyhoo* gave its last performances under Arthur Hammerstein's management on Saturday, January 3, 1931. Having already endured the twin failures of *The Lottery Bride,* his first film venture, and *Luana,* his previous show, Hammerstein publicly declared his disgust with Equity minimums, union scales, high-priced musicians, and feather-bedding electricians. He averred he had been able to run *Rose Marie* on what the labor outlay alone was for *Ballyhoo* and bitterly announced his retirement. Over eight productions, Hammerstein had sustained losses of $1,350,000.

Agent Walter Batchelor, who was married to Janet Reade and had a number of clients in the show, was the first to broach the idea of reviving it on the commonwealth plan. Manufacturers Trust, which held the mortgage on the building, was willing to go along if the show paid for the heat and the lights, approximately $750 a week, and Hammerstein agreed not to take a share of the profits until the show had put itself on a paying basis. A meeting was held on Sunday, January 4, at which nineteen of the principals took control of the show and elected Fields as their business manager. Batchelor brokered a deal with Equity and the unions, arranging for the first $8,000 to go to the stagehands, musicians, wardrobe women, and chorus girls. After that, the principals would evenly split whatever was left. "If we go broke," said Fields, "we won't have to walk home. We *are* home!" Eight men were dropped from the crew, and the orchestra was similarly pared. With Hammerstein's name off the playbill, *Ballyhoo* reopened on Thursday, January 8, with a leaner, tighter book and a new top of $4.40. After the performance, Fields counted the till in full view of everyone. The arrangement, virtually unique in the annals of Broadway, drew some badly needed publicity. In the half week following the takeover, *Ballyhoo* split $2,000 after expenses, paying the principals, other than Fields, 84.2 percent of their regular salaries. Encouraged, Fields persuaded baritone Gus Van, an old *Follies* colleague, to come into the show as a guest star. Eddie Cantor went on for the Saturday matinee, and Moran and Mack played the following week. Will Rogers wired to say he would throw in as well.

*Ballyhoo* finished its first full week under the new arrangement with a respectable $13,900 in receipts. Fields, who was due 10 percent if the take exceeded $13,000, took just $700 and gave the rest back to the chorus.* By mid-February, the show was averaging $13,500 a week and paying the cast 50 to 75 percent of their contracted rates. But the gate never went any higher, and Fields took little or nothing most weeks. "I remember one matinee," he said, "when the house was so small that the performance was costing each one of us a lot of money because we had to pay the electrician, stagehands, musicians, and chorus girls and men no matter what happened. Not only were we getting nothing for our work, but we were digging into the sock to get cash to pay our bills. Do you think the crowd crabbed about it? Not a bit. They gave all they had, and the few people that watched us had a swell time. They saw as good a show as though the house had been jammed."

*Ballyhoo* played a total of six and a half weeks as a co-op and might well have lasted longer had it not been for Lent and a traditional dip in business. The electricians also rankled because the Theatrical Protective Union had refused to make any concessions to help keep the doors open. "I'm for the unions," Fields declared. "Why, in the old days when a stagehand got about four bits a night, we'd get into our costumes and go on the stage, and while we

---

*There was grumbling when some of the principals figured they were getting less than the ponies, who, at $45 a week, were making $10 over the Equity minimum.

were there somebody would steal everything in our dressing rooms. After the men got a union, this never happened. Oh, I'm for the unions, all right. But listen to this: When we were fighting along to hold on with *Ballyhoo,* using waterfront language to express our thoughts about the electricians, they stuck a poster up on the bulletin board by the stage door. It told us there was going to be a benefit for the unemployed stage electricians and asked us would we contribute our services to make the entertainment a success. Funny?"

The quixotic run of *Ballyhoo* ended on February 21, 1931. The following Monday, the dressing rooms were padlocked over a $21,000 claim on the costumes, and the Manufacturers Trust began foreclosure proceedings. Through Equity, Fields initiated a claim against Hammerstein for $8,000 in back salary, an obligation assumed, under the circumstances, by the Managers' Protective Association. Frank Gilmore, Equity's president, warned Fields that "drastic action" would probably be necessary before he saw any money, but Fields said he had "every confidence" in Gilmore's judgment and felt comfortable in leaving town. Ill with grippe, he was back in Miami Beach by March 5, en route to Cuba to ponder his next move. A few days later, Arthur Hammerstein formally declared bankruptcy.

Fields' theatrical career ended with *Ballyhoo,* and there were no prospects for work on the West Coast. Like a number of high-priced acts, Fields did business almost exclusively through lawyers like Robert Burkhalter and didn't need an agent in New York. But Hollywood was different. *The Golf Specialist* hadn't brought him much attention—despite a full-page ad in *Variety*—and as a calling card it was both stilted and stagebound. Fields decided his only hope of breaking back into the movies was to return to Los Angeles and make the rounds on his own. He put the pool table, the midget Austin, everything he owned, in storage, and packed up the Lincoln for one more drive to California. He talked of sending for Shorty when the money got steady, but talk was unfortunately all it was. Shorty would go back to working as a stagehand, and within six months he would be dead of tubular meningitis. Two-a-day vaudeville was all but gone, and there was a steady migration west, where performers could find work as extras, makeup artists, dance coaches, musicians. The Broadway Fields had known was quickly vanishing from the scene, and he felt oddly estranged from it. He left $50,000 with the Harriman Bank and consolidated the rest of his savings in $1,000 bills. By Eddie Dowling's reckoning, Fields tooled out of Manhattan with some $350,000 on his person.* "What'll

---

*Doubtless this was an exaggeration, for Dowling had no way of knowing Fields' true worth at the time. After his death, the total of nine savings accounts held by Fields prior to June 9, 1927, was established at $115,505, but this, of course, was before his record deal with Earl Carroll.

you do if you get robbed?" Dowling asked. "What do the banks do?" Fields returned. Linelle Blackburn was with him as he crossed into New Jersey on a sunny spring morning. "When I got over the river," he said, "I twisted around for a last look at the skyline. I had an idea somehow that I wouldn't see it again."

In Los Angeles, Fields installed himself in a suite at the Hollywood Plaza Hotel and began setting appointments. "I did everything but hawk my wares door-to-door," he said. One of his stops was the compact RKO lot on Gower Street, the home of Radio Pictures. Dapper Lou Brock, the former exhibitor who, as an independent producer, had made *The Golf Specialist* for RKO release, was now on the West Coast and in charge of all shorts for the company. The meeting was cordial but strained, and it was clear to Fields that Brock was uninterested in using him again. Money may have been the sticking point, for Fields was asking $5,000 a week—pricey for a star of two-reelers. Fields did, however, come as a package. He brought his own material, copyrighted scenes from the *Follies, Scandals,* and the *Vanities,* and he could write finished scripts. He was also capable of directing his own stuff.

The meeting ended on a sour note. "In desperation," as Fields remembered it, "I . . . offered to write, direct, and act in a film for nothing." He would not ask a nickel. "All they had to do was put up the money, and a cheap two-reeler it would have been. I was confident it would be successful, and that they would hire me for more two-reelers." He thought it a swell proposition, but Brock wouldn't budge. "Being one of those men who knew exactly what the public wanted, he refused my offer." At the age of fifty-one, W. C. Fields had reached the point where he couldn't even give himself away. "They wouldn't take me as a gift," he said.

*Part Two*

# THE GREAT MAN

# Fifteen

# Rollo and the Road Hogs

"If the west didn't want me," said Fields, "I wanted *it*. I wanted sunshine and warm weather. I wanted a house and a bed to sleep in and a closet to hang my clothes in and a washing machine I could swear at if it didn't get my laundry back in time. I wanted to be out in the open and play golf and tennis and handball and squash. But for all that I had to have work. I couldn't get it."

Hollywood had yet to feel the full brunt of the Depression, and Fields, with no work on the horizon, cut back sufficiently by the simple expedient of getting rid of Linelle Blackburn. "Bill changed women every seven years," said Billy Grady, "as some people get rid of the itch." The relationship with Linelle had been on the wane for more than a year, yet she had insistently made the trip to California, neatly scotching his plans to stay rent-free at the home of his pal Charley Mack. Yet, eager though he was to make the break, Fields could never quite find the words that would humanely send her on her way. "Her composure was indestructible," Louise Brooks remembered. "All Bill's suggestions that she should leave him for her own good were deflected with smiling contentment."

In the end, Fields concocted an elaborate scheme to get himself out of town. He prevailed upon his friend Paul Jones to accompany him to San Francisco, giving an alleged business trip an air of legitimacy. Linelle saw them off at the platform, waving a fluttery good-bye with a pink lace handkerchief. Twelve hours later, safely ensconced at the St. Francis on Union Square, Fields placed a call to his Los Angeles attorney, Milton Cohen, who presented Linelle with a generous check and bundled her onto a train bound for Texas. Within weeks, she had married a man in San Antonio.

With Linelle now gone, Fields moved himself into a guest room on the Mack estate in Newhall, some thirty-two miles north of Los Angeles in the Santa Susana Mountains. Mack owned twenty-two acres across a small canyon from the white castellated mansion of William S. Hart. The comfortable house, built in the French Normandy style, boasted one of the area's few swimming pools, and Fields, who loved the dry heat and the cool evening breezes, spent considerable time in Mack's triangular pond.* He played golf and tennis as well, and occasionally drove up the coast to break the monotony. He drew national attention when he pressed his claim against Hammerstein and the Managers' Protective Association, and when the claim went to arbitration, in June 1931, it nearly resulted in the termination of Equity's landmark agreement with the MPA.

Fields' money from the *Ballyhoo* arbitration came through in July, and he took a few days in Santa Barbara to celebrate the win. The resort town, some ninety miles north of Los Angeles, was a favorite venue for picture folks and previews. The oceanfront Biltmore was usually crawling with movie stars, and it was on a Sunday night in the Biltmore lobby that Fields was spotted by Marilyn Miller and a clutch of film executives. Miller, of course, knew Fields from the 1918 *Follies,* where she created a sensation posing as Billie Burke and singing "Mine Was a Marriage of Convenience." She had scaled the heights of Broadway stardom in the intervening years, and was working off a three-picture contract with Warner Bros. "Bill!" she squealed. "You're just the man I've been looking for!"

He was indeed. Miller had committed to a picture called *Her Majesty, Love* and was in search of the proper actor to play the role of her father. It was a remake of the German musical *Ihre Majestät die Liebe,* an early talkie, and while there were plenty of character people to essay the part, few, if any, could play Dad Torreck as he was in the original film—an old showman who had been a juggler. Nobody had thought of Fields—Miller didn't even know he was in Los Angeles—but he was perfect for the role in every respect. The contract agreed upon called for star billing and a four-week guarantee at $5,000 a week. Fields was jubilant. The part wasn't big, but it was feature work at a respectable price, and he knew there'd be more. A French version of the story, *Son altesse l'amour,* had already been made, so the new picture would only be seen in the English-speaking territories. The rights were acquired for a paltry $5,000 with the proviso that the original director, Joe May, be brought to Hollywood to assist in the filming. Agreeably, May shipped the original negative on ahead so dupes could be made of the stock shots. An assignment from the composer, Walter Jarrmann, was obtained in August. The director would be yet another German émigré, the distinguished Wilhelm—later William—Dieterle.

Filming began on September 8, 1931, at the First National Studios in Burbank, where Stage 6 was crowded with interiors of the Roxy, the cabaret where Lia Torreck tends bar. Miller's well-known drinking habit—spurred, it was said, by the tragic death of her husband, vocalist Frank Carter, in a 1920 auto-

---

*Mack named the compound, which eventually grew to contain six houses, Tierra de Cuervo, which was as close as he could come in Spanish to "Crowland."

mobile crash—had, by the age of thirty-three, taken a terrible toll on her looks. She photographed older and stockier than in her previous films, and, struggling to flatter his fading star and still keep the film moving, Dieterle indulged in enough traveling camera work to put the company immediately behind. Consequently, Fields didn't start work until the seventeenth, when they moved to the modest Berlin apartment where Dad Torreck lives with his daughter. He was on his best behavior throughout the shoot, carefully memorizing his dialogue and obediently running lines with a coach. (Even the moustache he wore was realistic.) Dieterle, he observed, wore perishable eggshell-tinted suede gloves and was so tall ("at least six-foot-three") he tended to kneel when addressing the actors. He seldom spoke to Fields, but effectively encouraged him to underplay his part.

Fields' big scene in the film comes at a fancy buffet where he must prove himself to the snooty family of his daughter's fiancée. They own the Von Wellingen Ball Bearing Foundry and don't want their boy to marry Lia; Dad Torreck, on the other hand, runs a barber shop and likes the idea better than anything. ("After you're married and I come to visit you," he says dreamily, "I can just hear you say, 'Dad, how much do you need?' ") Thinking he must serve himself, Fields builds three plates in succession, only to have each carried away by a waiter. He flicks chocolate eclairs across the table at Chester Conklin. He does a bit of a drunk act, having downed "four or five cognacs" for the occasion. And, as he did at Will Rogers' home, he juggles the plates.

Most important, *Her Majesty, Love* restored the loving father-daughter relationship that had been so utterly lacking in the pictures Fields made under Schulberg. Surrounded with a wealth of comedic talent—Conklin, Ford Sterling, Leon Errol—he was a standout in what was otherwise a routine story. His work on the film was over by October 2, and, still lacking an agent, he sat back to wait for the film's release and the inevitable flood of offers to follow. To be closer to the studio—the drive in from Newhall took almost two hours—he signed a year's lease on a four-bedroom house on Toluca Lake, where a flagstone patio and adjacent garden shared the protection of a giant oak tree and the vast lawn sloped gently toward the water. Before long, he had imported a girl from New York, a pretty blond stenographer by the name of Grace George. Bob Burkhalter had first met her during the two-week run of *Show Boat* in St. Louis and took to calling her "Little Bright Eyes." (Fields' own nickname for her was "Wiggle.") She was lovely and quick-witted, a young woman of Italian descent who very openly wanted marriage and children. Burkhalter warned his client, who was twice her age, that she would be "very difficult" should they ever come to a parting of the ways.

Fields deflected an offer to do another vaudeville turn in New York, this time with Ray Dooley performing the back porch and picnic scenes on sets bor-

*With Marilyn Miller in* Her Majesty, Love, *1931*

rowed from Ziegfeld. Instead, he tried lining up a deal for a series of shorts at Warners, but found them curiously uninterested in the idea. Miller, he came to realize, was at the end of her contract and would never make another picture. He was simply part of an obligation for which there would be no commercial payoff. When the first previews came and *Her Majesty, Love* was still overlong, the *Hollywood Reporter* called it "good light entertainment" and nothing else. "The comedy is shared and shared alike by Leon Errol, Ford Sterling, Chester Conklin, and W. C. Fields—but, on second thought, it is Fields who has the lion's share and he is a scream." If there was any buzz from the *Reporter* review, it dissipated with the film's New York opening at the Winter Garden on November 26. The *Herald-Tribune* thought it "clumsy," the *Sun* "skimpy and commonplace." The *Times* threw its praise to Dieterle and hoped that he would one day be rewarded with a narrative "more worthy of his artistry and fertile brain." All lamented Marilyn Miller's profound lack of screen presence.

Worse, Fields found himself buried in the incidentals, his billing super-seded by the studio's abiding interest in actor Ben Lyon, who had just signed a term contract. In the ads, he was clustered with Errol, Sterling, and Conklin, all freelancers, as one of the "four kings of comedy," an obvious attempt to liken them to the phenomenally popular Marx Brothers. He rightly saw this as a breach of the billing clause in his contract, which required that he receive the first featured position, and he had Loyd Wright, a prominent Los Angeles attorney, draw up a sharply worded letter of protest. Nothing came of it, as the film was already a flop, posting a $135,000 loss. Consequently, the exposure Fields got from it was practically nil. "I hadn't a hell of a lot to do," he admitted in a letter to a friend, "but in these depressing times a fellow is glad to get anything. I hadn't done anything since *Ballyhoo* laid an egg last February. I was about to apply for a position as chauffeur or dresser when this thing came up."

Pushed to the wall by industry indifference, he mitigated his longstanding distaste for agents by signing with a former actor named Charles Beyer. In 1929, Beyer had established an agency with producer Arthur MacArthur and taken offices in the new Taft Building at Hollywood and Vine. Fields, who knew Beyer from New York (he played a small part in *So's Your Old Man*), asked if he could get an old juggler some picture work. The client list at Beyer-MacArthur included May Robson, Lowell Sherman, Richard Dix, and Victor McLaglen. "He said if I couldn't get him picture work, could I get him some stage work in New York," Beyer remembered. Fields had a healthy distrust of the film industry in all its various aspects and thought he would always be more marketable on the stage than on the screen. "At all times up until almost the time of his death, I would say within a year or two of when he died, he asked me if I could get him a good New York show he could go into, but it would have to be something within his liking."

Fields, Beyer discovered, was adamant about keeping his price up, and this turned out to be a problem. Beyer told Fields he could probably get character work for him at $2,500 or $3,000 a week, but not at the $5,000 that Fields seemed to regard as a floor. With business getting worse, not better, it was easy to plead poor-mouth to Hattie. "Health not so 'Be Jesus,' " he wrote her in February 1932, "what with recurring grippe attack and now an infection of the index digit of my left hand which may necessitate amputation of my left mitt. . . . Last year I worked nine days in a picture called *Her Majesty, Love,* and a few weeks in a flop called *Ballyhoo.* . . . The little nest egg I had cached for inclement weather almost entirely disappeared with the bond crash." He shamelessly asked if she could manage with $50 a week until things looked up. "And this seems very remote and indefinite at this time."

In New York, Billy Grady pressed Fields to accept an engagement at Lou Holtz' Hollywood Theatre (where he currently had Clark and McCullough on a four-week stretch), and Fields, weighing continued unemployment against the dead of the New York winter, was almost desperate enough to take it. He asked $3,500 a week on a six-week guarantee, but Holtz was only willing to go to $3,000 and four weeks on the deal. "With salaries as they are," Grady advised Fields, "this is a very fair offer. Come on back to the street." Fields dawdled, waiting for something to come up in California, and, when it did, he settled for the same money Holtz had offered. Grady again tried in April, this time dangling the prospect of a revue with material written by S. J. Perelman. "New York craves the beetle puss for the winter season," he declared. But as long as he was getting work in Los Angeles, Fields was evasive and uninterested.* He wired back:

DEAR CATHOLIC

WIGGLE AND I HAVE JUST COME OUT OF THE DESERT. MUST DO PICTURE FOR PARAMOUNT SOMETIME NEXT MONTH. I AM SORRY BUT THE PROTESTANTS ARE THE BEST PEOPLE. A GOOD OLD FASHIONED HUG.

BILL FIELDS

The picture at Paramount was an absurdist comedy that carried the working title *On Your Mark.* The producer was Herman J. Mankiewicz, a journalist who had known Fields in New York and had, in fact, once written a profile of him for *Vanity Fair.* The story was by Herman's brother Joe, who at age twenty-three was the youngest staff writer on the studio payroll. "One day," Joe Mankiewicz remembered, "Ben Schulberg, who ran production, sent a note around saying that the 1932 Olympic Games were to be held in Los Angeles and how could we get a story out of that? Well, I went up and talked with him about it, and I said there were only certain set plots for athletic pictures— would Jack Oakie carry the ball over the goal line for a touchdown and win Mary Brian, and that sort of thing—and I suggested to Schulberg that he let me do a comedy about the Olympic Games, poke fun at the whole thing, and B. P. went along with it."

Mankiewicz recalled the shambles of the 1928 Amsterdam games—in which the Americans won exactly one race—and envisioned a delicious satire. *Million Dollar Legs,* as it came to be known, took eight months to evolve, even though it was ultimately robbed of much of its subtlety by the casting of Jack Oakie.

The politically unstable Klopstockia, a mythical country of goats and nuts,

---

*The show was *Walk a Little Faster,* into which Grady inserted Clark and McCullough in lieu of Fields. A modest hit, it starred Beatrice Lillie and introduced Vernon Duke's "April in Paris" to the world.

enters the games at the behest of an American brush salesman named Tweeny. Mankiewicz, by his own admission, set out to write a "nut" picture for Schulberg and, working with playwright Henry Myers, achieved the effect largely through dialogue. All the men in Klopstockia are named George, and all the girls are called Angela. ("Why?" asks Tweeny. "Why not?" comes the response.) Myers, who had also written for the Marx Brothers, invested the script with an anarchical mixture of non sequiturs and puns that were not merely reserved for the comics but evenly distributed among all the cast members.

"If you laid all the athletes in this country end to end," says Susan Fleming, the president's daughter, "they'd stretch 480 miles."

"How do you know?" asks Oakie.

"We did it once."

The role of the dimwitted president, described in the first draft of the script as "a comedy heavy," was not an obvious fit for Fields, but Herman Mankiewicz was somehow seized with the notion that he should play the part. "Bill loved it," said Joe. "He even read the dialogue the way it was written." There was considerable revision, mostly by a genial gag man named Nick Barrows, and in the end the film's comedy came as much from broad sight gags as from the farcical lines. The ensemble cast was loaded with comics of the Mack Sennett school—Andy Clyde, Hank Mann, the perennially cross-eyed Ben Turpin. The director, Eddie Cline, was a Keystone alumnus as well. "He was very much of the old, old comedy school," Mankiewicz said. "He didn't know what was happening in *Million Dollar Legs*. At all. But he enjoyed doing it, because he had Andy Clyde. And Ben Turpin. And Bill Fields."

The long gestation of the script paid off in an unusually quick, efficient shoot for a comedy of this sort. Cline shot the film pretty much as written but was unable to sustain the madcap tone of its opening minutes. On June 23, *Million Dollar Legs* was shown to representatives of the Motion Picture Producers and Distributors of America, commonly known as the Hays Office because it was headed by former U.S. postmaster general Will Hays. James B. M. Fisher and Lamar Trotti, two administrators of the MPPDA's largely toothless Production Code, found it silly and unfunny. "I think children will like it very much," Trotti allowed, "but I have a fear that adults would be bored with it." The trade papers and preview audiences seemed to enjoy it, but the film clearly wasn't to everyone's taste. Reviewers, who generally regarded it as an admirable experiment, cut *Million Dollar Legs* a lot of slack. "Mankiewicz . . . and his adapters have clearly fallen short of producing a masterpiece," Alexander Bakshy said in the *Nation*. "But they did let their fancy run as far as it would carry them, and the result is a film that at times has a quality of freshness and genuine imagination much too rare in Hollywood products."

Fields got little play in the notices. The bombastic president was a broadly

*The surreal aspects of* Million Dollar Legs *(1932) came primarily from
a screenplay credited to Joseph L. Mankiewicz and Henry Myers.*

comic character with none of the human traits that made Elmer Finch and
McGargle so appealing. And with little to do after the first twenty minutes of
the picture, he wasn't around to relieve the tedium of the boobish Oakie. He
took second billing in the film, a considerable feat under the circumstances, and
apocryphal stories of his Philadelphia youth filled the pressbook. *Million Dollar Legs* did adequate business in the big eastern cities, where it was seen as a
sophisticated swipe at the overhyped Olympic Games, but it died like a dog in
the sticks. Its reputation as a lasting work of art stems primarily from its having
been embraced as a surrealist masterpiece by Man Ray when the film hit Paris
in 1933. It played more than a year at a Left Bank theater and later became a
favorite of Pauline Kael, who called it "one of the silliest and funniest pictures
ever made."

While *Million Dollar Legs* was being shot, Fields learned of a deal Mack
Sennett had made with Paramount to produce thirty two-reel comedies for the
1932–33 season. Having learned from the failure of *Her Majesty, Love* to strike
while the iron was hot, Fields lost no time in throwing his own battered hat in
the ring. On June 9, 1932, while the new picture was still in the cutting room, he
wrote to Al Kaufman, Schulberg's executive assistant and the son-in-law of
Adolph Zukor, fishing for a deal for his own series of shorts. "I was thinking

that if you contemplate doing any more two-reelers than you have contracted for with Mack Sennett, you might be interested in my doing a half dozen for you. I have in mind incorporating into two reelers some of the scenes I did in the *Vanities, Ziegfeld Follies,* and *George White's Scandals.* And some of the scenes I did in *Ballyhoo* and *Poppy.*"

Fields' peremptory strike was ineffectual in that Kaufman waited a full month—until *Million Dollar Legs* had previewed solidly and was almost in release—before making his reply. In the interim, both Schulberg and Jesse Lasky had been deposed in a palace coup engineered by Chicago theater mogul Sam Katz, and Kaufman was now effectively running the studio under Schulberg's replacement, Emanuel L. "Manny" Cohen. "Regarding your letter of June 9," Kaufman wrote, "our contract with Mack Sennett provides that he will make two-reel comedies exclusively for us for the coming year, and I suggest that you take up with him (at an early date) the matter you wish to discuss with me." He added: "In view of the enthusiastic manner in which the audience received you in *Million Dollar Legs,* I feel certain that Sennett will be interested."

The timing of Fields' note to Kaufman was fortuitous in another sense as well, for it got the deputy production chief thinking about him at a time when the studio he ran was the world's leading purveyor of laughter. "The entire atmosphere at Paramount in the early thirties was right for comedy," Joe Mankiewicz said. "We had expert prop men, technicians, and directors who really knew their craft, and a whole group of comedians—Hank Mann, Andy Clyde, Edgar Kennedy, Hugh Herbert—all of whom had their characteristic bits and gave us guaranteed laughs. There were writers, like Grover Jones and William McNutt, who really knew their business. I was lucky to break into picture writing around all those people."

Kaufman was preparing a remarkable film based on an obscure book called *Windfall.* The idea was that a dying millionaire, surrounded by his grasping heirs, gives his fortune to complete strangers in $1 million increments. Ten individual episodes of eight to twelve minutes each would highlight the studio's sizable stable of contract players. A different director would be in charge of each segment, and the authors would include Harvey Thew, Nina Wilcox Putnam, and Oliver H. P. Garrett. One of the episodes, an original by Putnam that carried the title "Good Company," was written for Alison Skipworth and Roland Young. At an early point in its development, however, it became a feature all its own, and Skipworth (Young was a freelancer) was left with nothing to do. Kaufman caught a glimpse of Fields eating dinner at the Brown Derby one night and stopped by his table. "Bill," he said, "I think I've got an idea for you. I'm going to double you up with Alison Skipworth."

The idea, at first, brought Fields up short. He knew Skipworth as a grande dame of the American theater, a regal beauty at the time of her London debut who graduated to formidable character roles as age and weight caught up with her. Nearing seventy, she was hired by Paramount to play the same kinds of lofty matrons and seriocomic hags that Marie Dressler had popularized at MGM. Dressler had reached her greatest heights as a foil for Wallace Beery (first in *Min and Bill,* later in *Tugboat Annie*), and it was only natural that Kaufman think in the same terms for Skipworth when considering potential costars. In *Madame Racketeer* she was paired with Richard Bennett, and for *Sinners in the Sun* she was the wife of Reginald Barlow. Fields had a different sort of potential, though. Like Beery, he was a name and a presence to be reckoned with, and although Skipworth was old enough to be his mother, they seemed a good match.

Joe Mankiewicz was given the job of coming up with a suitable script for them. "I adored Bill Fields as a performer, because vaudeville for me was something almost mystic in its appeal." In 1923, as a fourteen-year-old student at New York's Stuyvesant High School, Mankiewicz had been granted a backstage audience with Fields at the Apollo, but had managed to blurt out only a couple of questions. "Other members of the cast came in, in search of liquid refreshments of one kind or another, because it was in between the matinee and evening performance, so a lot of activity was going on in his dressing room. I'd never been in a dressing room before or back stage, excepting for student productions, in my life." The resulting article, "An Interview with Comedian W. C. Fields," appeared in a fall number of the *Caliper,* the school's student monthly. "It was a very nice interview, I thought, and I wrote it up and sent him a copy and, lo and behold, I received what most people deny could exist—a handwritten letter from W. C. Fields, thanking me for the interview, complimenting me on my style (at the age of 14, style is the last thing you're after). That was it. I did not know that eight years later, I would be writing for W. C. Fields at Paramount Studios in Hollywood."

Mankiewicz built the episode around Fields rather than Skipworth, writing him as the old juggler he was and turning his costar into a retired vaudevillian who had worked herself a bird act. Like so many old troopers who watched the circuits go talkie, Emily and Rollo have moved to California, where she runs a tea room and he handles the kitchen. She's got everything she's ever dreamed of—except one. With the delivery of a shiny new Ford sedan, she glows with joy. Rollo bustles out from the back, lovingly settles her into the passenger seat, and takes the wheel for their first-ever drive together. Cautiously, he inches out onto the street, and he carefully looks both ways when pulling away from an intersection. Despite his best efforts, the car is broadsided within blocks of the house. Emily is devastated—until the visit of Glidden the industrialist and his check for $1 million. "You must use this money, my sweet, to satisfy your every whim," Rollo tells her. "You have earned it."

"But Rollo, it's your money, too. What do you want?"

"Nothing my pet," he says. "I—" Then he looks darkly out the window at the wrecked car and his eyes suddenly light with a malevolent glee. "I have some idea of what I would like to do—something I would like above everything else in the world right now."

The deal for *If I Had a Million* went together quickly, with Charlie Beyer settling a contract that called for a fee of $5,000 for up to a week's work, and $833.33 for each additional day.* Mankiewicz did a polish on his nineteen-page script, and it was sent to the MPPDA for review. Filming began on the morning of Friday, September 9, on the Paramount lot in Hollywood, where the interior of Emily's tea shop had been constructed on Stage 7. Mankiewicz drew the Fields character as an affectionate nod to the entertainers of his youth; Rollo is an exuberant old goose, still brimming with love and consideration for his darling Emily after twenty-five years together. "There is a courtliness and a grace of speech and gesture about him that belong to another day," Mankiewicz noted in his screenplay. The part gave Fields a lot to work with, and one line in particular caught his eye. When Emily calls to him to come see the new car, he erupts with, "Coming, my little bird!" Rollo's dialogue was sprinkled with endearments of the commonest kind, but "my little bird" had color and character, and Fields, as he often did, tinkered with it. He had, observed Mankiewicz, "this incredible punctiliousness about material that is one of the great attributes of the old-time vaudevillian. . . . Material to the vaudevillian was his bread and butter."

When Fields appeared at the writer's office, he had a set of Audubon's *Birds of America* slung under one arm.

I was glad to see him—always glad to see him—and he says, "Kid, I want to buy that material." I said, "What material, Bill?" And he said, "The stuff you wrote for me for Rollo and the Road Hogs. I want to buy that routine." I said, "Well, it's not a routine. Besides which, it doesn't belong to me. It belongs to Paramount." He said, "I don't want to have anything to do with their lawyers. No, no, no. *You* wrote it. I want to buy it from *you,* and that's all the proof I'll need. I want to own it." And, to my amazement, he pulled out a fifty dollar bill and, as they say in Victorian novels, he pressed it upon me. He insisted that I take that fifty dollar bill. Well, since I could put up only so much resis-

---

*Since Fields wasn't under contract to Paramount, he became the most expensive member of the cast. Everyone else in the film got the weekly rate stipulated by contract. Charles Laughton, for example, was paid $1,875 for his sequence, which was directed by Ernst Lubitsch.

tance at that age—it was almost my full week's salary at Paramount—
I took it. I said, "Now Bill, really, there's no legal reason for me to have
this." He said, "I want to know I paid you for this routine."

Having satisfied himself that the material was now his, Fields went about
revising lines. He added, "Did you chirp for me, my little wren?" to his clamorous
entrance, and where Mankiewicz had written "my little bird" he changed it to
read "my little chickadee." Emily became his little fledgling, his little penguin,
his little turtle dove.* The episode of "Emily, Rollo and the Road Hogs" was
made under the direction of Norman Z. McLeod, the man who had helmed the
two previous Marx Brothers pictures and would go on to make some of the best
comedies of the 1930s and '40s. McLeod was a laconic, ruddy-faced man who
sketched his setups in the form of cartoons. His reticence hid a brilliant mind; he
was a Rhodes scholar, trained as a scientist, and was a combat pilot during the
war. He had the good sense to let Fields have his head, thereby making the first
episode shot for the film the most memorable. "[Fields] expected people to take
him the way he was," said publicist Teet Carle. "I think the great directors were
the directors who understood Fields and didn't try to change him."

Fields found an instant rapport with Alison Skipworth, who was well read
and extremely funny in her own right. ("I'll bet she drank drink for drink with
him," remarked Constance Binney, who played opposite the actress in a play
called *39 East*.) Their scenes in the tea room went quickly enough, but the
stunt-driving effects, staged on the surrounding streets of Los Angeles, took
considerably more time to film. Rollo and Emily use their money to buy a fleet
of used cars, and they prowl the streets looking for road hogs. "Beaver!" cries
Emily, pointing excitedly, and Rollo responds by running the offending driver
spectacularly off the road. "Take that, you great snorting road hog!" he calls
out as they drive off.

The "Road Hog" sequence took ten long days to shoot and brought the
money Fields received for the film to an even $10,000. While it was still in pro-
duction, the *Hollywood Reporter* caught wind of Paramount's "odd experiment" with its fourteen writers, seven directors, and twenty "names" and
marveled at the audacity of it all. With the Fields sequence now almost in the

---

*Mankiewicz always remembered the bird endearments as his own invention, and he did
indeed give Emily a bird act ("Emily's Educated Birds"). He never, however, carried the
idea through to the famous bird lines, and none appears in the final script, dated September 8, 1932. Yet Fields spoke the line, "Coming, my little chickadee!" on the set the very
next day. The inescapable conclusion is that it was Fields, and not Mankiewicz, who substituted the word "chickadee" for "bird" and thus created a catch line that would follow
him through the rest of his life.

can, the paper revealed other prospective names in the cast: Miriam Hopkins, Gary Cooper, Fredric March, Sylvia Sidney, Clive Brook, Wynne Gibson, Charlie Ruggles, Richard Bennett, Richard Arlen, Mary Boland, Cary Grant, Jack Oakie, Gene Raymond. It wasn't the first omnibus film in memory but it was the first talkie to attempt the stunt on such a stellar level, and, in that sense alone, it was news.

Fields was finishing his work just as other performers and directors were commencing theirs: James Cruze with Gene Raymond in a death row story; Stephen Roberts with Wynne Gibson as a streetwalker who longs to spend the night in a bed by herself; George Raft as a bank forger who is unable to cash the millionaire's check. Some episodes were discarded, others recast, but remarkably, *If I Had a Million* finished on October 25 at a negative cost of just $300,000. It was shown to representatives of the Hays Office on November 2, and they predictably urged the elimination of the Gibson sequence. The *Hollywood Reporter,* in a wildly enthusiastic notice the next day, called it "one of the best pictures of this or any year."

*If I Had a Million* was officially released on November 16, 1932, when it opened a nine-day run at the Paramount Theatre in Los Angeles. The notices

*Pairing Fields with Alison Skipworth in* If I Had a Million *was a stroke of genius on the part of Paramount executive Albert A. Kaufman.*

were good—LA was never known for its penetrating criticism of the local out-put—but business was flat from the start and both a flu epidemic and the USC–Notre Dame game got blamed for the dip. It moved to New York's Rivoli Theatre, where great things were expected from the cast, the concept, the undeniable power of the sum of its parts. The "Road Hog" sequence was cheered by an opening-day audience whose members, in Abel Green's words, "seemingly nurtured the same inhibitions," and Fields was a standout in most every review. Then, after a relatively strong initial weekend, *If I Had a Million* did a brodie in New York as it had done in LA. Again there were credible reasons: the usual pre-Christmas slump and a devastating snowstorm that all but eliminated the automobile trade. Receipts for its second week at the Rivoli fell to just half the first week's tally and continued to fall as the weather refused to break. The film did no better in other cities, and what had once seemed a surefire box office hit became the season's most puzzling flop. For its minimal cost, *If I Had a Million* could hardly have posted a loss, but the meager $65,000 profit it eventually earned was substantially less than anyone had anticipated. In places like New Haven, Buffalo, Denver, and Cincinnati, both audiences and exhibitors found the film curiously uninvolving. Paramount's great all-star experiment—and Fields' best appearance yet on the talking screen—was greeted by the filmgoing public with profound indifference.

Yet, the Fields of *If I Had a Million* is, in many respects, the prototypical Fields of the sound era. Battered but unbowed, he strikes back at a world that has dealt him an injustice. He is expansive, solicitous, the old vaudevillian eager to please, but with a survivor's instinct and a sort of half-assed dignity that keeps him from sliding into pathos when things go bad. The florid language, almost completely absent from his previous talkies, begins asserting itself, and Fields, despite his theatricality, is a more fully rounded character than ever before. With *If I Had a Million,* Fields abandoned the trick moustache for good, a signal he was growing comfortable in his new screen persona, his voice lending a presence and individuality he somehow lacked in silent pictures. He seemed to understand that the job of making himself memorable to notoriously fickle movie audiences required the same degree of consistency he applied to his stage career. He would mine the depths of his trunk for material to put before the cameras, but never again would he deviate from a character that seemed so beautifully suited to both himself and the times.

# Sixteen

# *New Deal*

Mack Sennett first met W. C. Fields in New York when Fields was appearing in the *Ziegfeld Follies.* Sennett was rich, powerful, a legend in the picture business. "Like everyone else," he said of Fields, "I thought his routines were uproariously funny." The two men talked casually of making a film together, but nothing came of the idea.

They reconnected in California nearly a decade later. Sennett was no longer rich and powerful and Fields was no longer thought to be uproariously funny, so they played a lot of golf. "During our games [Fields] used to say, 'Mack, I'm having difficulty out here trying to get into the movies and I'd like to get in your studio. Now I don't care what you pay me or what you give me, I'd just like to be busy.' " Sennett was having trouble delivering his films to Paramount because his financing hadn't come through. "Since money was no object," he reasoned, "I arranged an appointment for the following morning."

What Fields proposed was essentially the same deal that had put Lou Brock on the defensive, offering to write and direct two-reel comedies for whatever his quarry was willing to pay. But Sennett already had good men on the payroll—Arthur Ripley, Del Lord, Leslie Pearce, Clyde Bruckman. "I said, 'There's only one thing, naturally, that I want you to do and that is get on the screen. You're a great artist. Perform.' So he said, 'Now wait a minute—' His whole personality changed. I could feel the adding machine go click-click in his mind. He said, 'You know, I get $5,000, of course, when I perform.' I said, 'What do you mean? Five-thousand dollars a week?'

" 'A week—$2,500 when I start, and $2,500 in the middle of the week.' I said, 'What's the matter? Are you afraid of fire or something?' "

The deal for *If I Had a Million* had driven Fields' price back up to $5,000 a week, and he was loath to accept any less. Sennett, on the other hand, populated his two-reelers with low-priced veterans from the silent days and up-and-comers like singers Bing Crosby (whom he paid a less debilitating $500 a week) and Donald Novis. "Bill went to work on me while I was still anesthetized by his salary demand," he said. "He bullied me, cajoled me, and charmed me." Both parties wanted desperately to do business, so an accommodation was reached: Fields would accept $2,500 for turning one of his copyrighted stage routines into a screenplay, and another $2,500 for performing it on film. This was still a hard pill for Sennett to swallow, but Al Kaufman was bullish on Fields, and Sennett, on the verge of defaulting on the lucrative Paramount order, needed all the goodwill he could muster. The contract with Fields called for a single picture, with options for up to five more at $5,000 apiece, then another six at $7,500. On September 15, with just five films delivered, it was announced that Paramount would step in and fund the next two shorts on the Sennett production schedule.

The best screen material Fields owned at the time were the noisy sketches he did for Earl Carroll in 1928, and the one that seemed closest to Sennett's tradition of broad physical comedy was "An Episode at the Dentist's." Fields went to work on an adaptation, expanding the material to include a golf scene at the beginning. (In the *Vanities,* the sketch opened and closed with Dr. Pain practicing his swing.) The thirty-one-page script was ready for production by the end of October, and Fields' agreement with Sennett was formally announced to the trade on November 3, the same day the *Reporter* ran its glowing opinion of *If I Had a Million.*

Everything went smoothly at first. *The Dentist* proved a nearly perfect rendering of the riotous and ribald stage success, and Fields managed to complete it in the space of six days. The director, Leslie Pearce, contented himself to sit quietly under the camera and advise the star if he happened to step out of frame. He seldom spoke to the rest of the actors, leaving Fields to block the action and coach delivery himself. The largely female cast was headed by Babe Kane as his willful daughter, Zedna Farley, Dorothy Granger, and a long-faced beauty named Elise Cavanna, a Philadelphia native who went back to the days of *The Comic Supplement* and was known more as a painter with a bent for the erotic than an actress in short comedies. Fields knew the family (her mother was Mrs. Flora Seed) and her husband, author-designer Merle Armitage, and gave her work whenever he could. It was she who was cast as the dour woman with the stubborn molar whom he dragged around the floor, her long legs wrapped around him as in a fit of passion, a scene that nearly sent the staid representatives of the MPPDA into cardiac arrest.*

Sennett was pleased with *The Dentist,* its violence and misanthropy harkening back to the days when it was conceived as a rough act for the rowdy Australians and the producer himself was in full flower as the knockabout King of Comedy. It previewed well—Al Kaufman laughed his head off—and

---

*Most localities cut this scene, and it was subsequently snipped from the negative for a reissue.

*This scene with Elise Cavanna in* The Dentist *was so raw it was cut in many locales.*

earned rave reviews in the local papers. "First picture with Sennett, *The Dentist,* has been acclaimed as revolutionary by the *Hollywood Reporter, Times,* and *Examiner,*" Fields reported in a self-congratulatory wire to Bob Burkhalter. "Sennett immediately took up [my] option." The film, he added, "paid for itself three days after its release." With Sennett momentarily convinced of the infallibility of his new comic star, Fields went back to the well and came up with the vastly different "Stolen Bonds" as his second effort. Sennett was dubious about material so clearly lacking in the qualities that had made *The Dentist* such a crowd pleaser, but believed in Fields' conviction that the sketch itself was an absolute riot. "Sennett," said Fields, "shared my belief that a comedian should do what he thinks is funny and not worry about the reaction of the audience."

Denied the laughter with which he timed himself in silents, Fields was forced to rely in talkies on his sense of where the laughs should be and his memories of how the stuff had played onstage. He lengthened "The Stolen Bonds" with a sober rendering of monologist Charley Case's old temperance put-on, "The Fatal Glass of Beer," singing of a callow young man of sturdy upbringing who goes to the big city and is set upon the road to ruin when induced to take a drink. Fields sings gravely:

*Once upon the sidewalk,*
*He met a Salvation Army girl,*
*And, wickedly, he broke her tambourine.*
*All she said was "Heaven bless you"*
*And placed a mark upon his brow,*
*With a kick she learned*
*Before she had been saved . . .*

Accompanying himself for the scene on a dulcimer, he discordantly plucks away at the wires while a Canadian Mountie, overcome by the tale, sits beside him and weeps uncontrollably.

Where the roughneck *Dentist* was smart and fast and loaded with innuendo, tapping as it did into a commonly held loathing, "The Stolen Bonds" was a deadpan parody of antique stagecraft and had none of the cinematic zip of its predecessor. It went over in the *Vanities* with an audience primed to laugh at anything out of date, but it fell flat on the screen, where the proscenium vanished and visual effects of the stingiest sort were still more convincing than a handful of phony snow in the face. Fields exacerbated the calculated stupidity of the piece by making some genuinely awful process shots and working the line "It ain't a fit night out for man nor beast" to the point of tedium.

He completed the film, retitled *The Fatal Glass of Beer*, on November 28, 1932. Sennett got a look at it a few days later and hated every frame of it. No amount of cajoling on Fields' part could dissuade him from "fixing" it. He wanted to jazz it up, make it move, get it off its ass and make it go someplace. Fields, on the other hand, just wanted the audience to buy into the joke and let the film sweep over them like a bad dream. His straight-faced rendering of the title song was the key to letting them know how to take it, but Sennett wanted cutaways to break the monotony and give it some badly needed movement. On December 7, Fields warned in a letter to Sennett that cutting away from him during the song would "definitely kill the picture." But the producer was adamant and had the prescribed shots made by director Clyde Bruckman.

The film was released in March 1933 to glowering reviews from just about everyone. Theater owners loathed it ("This is the worst comedy we have played from any company this season," said one. "No story, no acting, and as a whole has nothing.") It received scant bookings and didn't play New York until June, when it showed up on a bill at the Rialto. Abel Green reported "no real laffs and hardly a snicker" in *Variety.* "In old-style manner of exaggerated dramatics it becomes a boresome, repetitious build-up until the obvious finale when both kick the prodigal youth out when learning he had none of the booty cached." Fields was past caring about the film at that point, and seventy years later it remains an acquired taste. "You are probably 100 percent right," he told

Sennett in a communiqué. "*The Fatal Glass of Beer* stinks. It's lousy. But I still think it's good."

When the two men first got together, Sennett assured Fields that he would get screen credit for stories and could do as he wished until he went wrong, but after one successful film, *The Fatal Glass of Beer* destroyed the bond of trust between them. With both *The Dentist* and *If I Had a Million* in general release, and an offer in hand from E. W. Hammons, Sennett's erstwhile partner, to make shorts for Educational, Fields asked to be released from his contract. "I am too good a friend of yours to make what you consider bad pictures," he told Sennett. The request was denied, and not wanting another disaster on his hands, Sennett inserted himself into the creative process, becoming a meddlesome terror. Bruckman had worked out a new story called *His Perfect Day,* but after ten days' work on Fields' part to adapt it to his character, Sennett made wholesale changes to the script without consulting him. He added, in Fields' words, "an indelicate Castor Oil sequence" and calmly advised his star that if he did not like the script in its revised state he would give it to Lloyd Hamilton.*

Fuming, Fields fired off another letter, this time saying that he was reluctant to resume writing until he had some assurances his work would not be molested. "You have been a tremendous success with your formula," he wrote, "but it is new to me and I can't change my way of working at this late stage of the game. When I have the stage all set for a Fields picture and you come in and have everything changed to a Sennett picture, you can see how you have rendered me helpless." To Bob Burkhalter he wired: "Might consider Hammons proposition five grand net, add your commission. I will write story for one thousand extra, or Hammons can furnish the story and I will work on it. I will direct the picture gratis if I write it. Have Hammons see *Dentist,* which I wrote, directed, and also picked the locations. Would also like to have him see *The Fatal Glass of Beer,* which I gave the same treatment to. Would only care to sign for one picture. He may not like me and terra firma. In these times of depression one bad or even just fair picture is too many."

Relations with Sennett remained frigid into the new year. There was talk of another feature at Paramount, but the company was in tough financial shape and nothing appeared to be certain. Rumored to be on the verge of bankruptcy, Paramount had lost nearly $12 million on its Publix theater operation and another $6 million on the movies it produced. Faced with the extraordinary popularity of *The Dentist,* Sennett softened his stance toward Fields and the creative freedom he sought and agreed to a new deal that gave him full con-

---

*He did indeed give it to Hamilton, who made the film as *Too Many Highballs* (1933). Though Fields always credited Clyde Bruckman with the story, many of his own contributions survived as well.

trol over the content of his films. Fields set to work on a third picture for Sennett, an adaptation of his drugstore scene from *The Comic Supplement.* "Finished two scenes for Mack Sennett," he jotted in a note to Phil Goodman. "Was to do 12 but called ten of them off when he wanted to rewrite everything. I'm back now again on a new understanding: One picture at a time and I have sole right of ruining them. Walk in when so disposed, kick out a short in four days, pick up six or seven grand, and then back to pick up my studies of the New Testament."

The feature Fields was booked into at Paramount was a wild exercise in modern burlesque called *International House.* The impetus came from the amazing impact of Mae West's debut in a film called *Night After Night.* Randy and wisecracking, the thirty-nine-year-old West wrote her own lines and easily stole the show from George Raft, Constance Cummings, Wynne Gibson, and Alison Skipworth. She dominated the film's reviews and made it one of the surprise hits of an otherwise dismal season. Manny Cohen bet the farm on West's lowdown appeal to audiences buffeted by unemployment and bank failures and approved a high-gloss version of her 1928 stage hit, *Diamond Lil,* as a followon. In true Hollywood fashion, Cohen then looked around for another scarlet woman to tap into the same market.

The woman he picked for the job had the same thick wad of tabloid press clippings that fattened Mae West's resume, but none of the talent or personality that made West so magnetic onscreen. Peggy Hopkins Joyce wasn't famous for what she did, but rather for whom she wed. Her first marriage, to Everett Archer, the American Borax scion, was annulled when she was found to be underage. Her family packed her off to school in Washington, where she met Sherbourne Hopkins and married again. Hopkins, the son of a wealthy society matron, kept her in jewels and furs but couldn't contain her wandering spirit. On a visit to New York—she knew Fannie Brice a bit—she was offered a job by Flo Ziegfeld, who apparently was titillated by her status as a Washington socialite. She went into the *Follies of 1917,* representing England in "The March of the Continentals" and decorating a couple of scenes with Fields, most notably as an onlooker in the tennis act he played with Walter Catlett.

Not wanting to tour, Hopkins stayed in Manhattan when the *Follies* left town and did a show for the Shuberts called *A Sleepless Night.* Then she made her way to Chicago, where she met Stanley Joyce, a rich lumberman of limited sophistication. Joyce showered her with gifts, wooed her from Hopkins, and got nothing but grief in return. She fled him for the Parisian playboy Henri Letellier, but, miraculously, didn't marry him. ("Frenchmen understand women too well," she explained. "A girl should never marry a man who understands women.") Count Gosta Morner of Sweden became her fourth husband, but only for a few months, and she was back in the headlines when a Paris blood thoughtlessly shot himself while registered in the same hotel. By 1922 she was probably the best-known woman in the country—if fame can be measured in column inches—but was being kept out of pictures by an industry weary of scandal and faced with calls for tighter controls at every level.

She responded with a plan, à la Marion Davies, to set up her own productions and buy the theaters in which to show them. In 1924, when P. A. "Pat" Powers went so far as to have a script written for her, the Wisconsin state legislature flew into action and introduced a bill advocating the censorship of all films brought into the state. "It was discovered," said *Variety,* "the drawing of the measure was brought about through the announcement that Peggy Hopkins Joyce would appear on the screen in a series of picture productions." Powers put her before the cameras under Marshall Neilan's direction in a predictable Hollywood tale called *The Skyrocket,* but little of her much-vaunted sex appeal came through on the screen. "From one end of this country to the other," a prominent press agent said at the time, "when you say Peggy Hopkins Joyce it means all that was ever written about charmers of men. Yet she's a darn long way from beautiful. How does she do it?"

How indeed. *The Skyrocket* was a flop. Her sizzling diaries, published in Paris and syndicated internationally, enhanced her notoriety, and she collected them into a book. When Paramount came calling, in November 1932, she was the same age as Mae West. She didn't need the money, but she did want to be a movie star (however unqualified she was for the job), and she jumped at a $1,250-a-week offer on a four-week guarantee. The template, patterned after *The Big Broadcast,* would surround her with various contract players and a selection of radio stars. The story, set in China, would cover one of the hottest and most controversial topics in the motion-picture industry—the invention of television.

With the start of *International House* looming, Fields dispensed with his third picture for Sennett in record time. His draft script, titled *The Drug Store,* was ready for notes on February 3, and the twenty-four-page shooting final was completed three days later. Filming commenced on the ninth of February, and the entire picture was in the can on the eleventh. Fields' character, Dilweg, seems to reflect the pressure he was under. He is short with his wife, irritable and combative with his two daughters, yet grossly forbearing when confronted with boorish customers. He doesn't go berserk in the end as McEvoy would have him do, but the store is virtually demolished in a violent gun battle. Babe Kane assumes the Ray Dooley part of the younger daughter, buoyantly spitting gum in her father's martini and eating the canary bird when her dinner isn't quite to her liking. Elise Cavanna stepped into the role of the put-upon wife, the part played originally on the stage by Alice Hegeman and, later, by Bertha Belmore.

As with the previous Sennett shorts, *The Pharmacist* (as it came to be known) was true to its origins. Fields never attempted to update the material, simply content in giving it one final airing before abandoning it for good. The familiarity of the Sennett releases instilled a certain monotony in the interested parties who had followed Fields' stage career and saw him as merely repeating himself. Eddie Sutherland, who had filmed a lot of the same business with him in 1926, made a generalization that came to be widely held: "Fields only had one story—an ugly old man, an ugly old woman, and a brat of a child."

Having rushed through the making of *The Pharmacist,* Fields found production on *International House* delayed due to script problems and the logistics attendant to using radio stars based in New York. Early announcements had Bing Crosby, Rudy Vallée, and the comedy team of George Burns and Gracie Allen in the cast. Then Crosby was dropped in favor of Stu Erwin, who, like Burns and Allen, had been part of the model *Big Broadcast.* But where the earlier film had some semblance of a plot (it was actually based on a play), *International House* would go it one better in having no discernable plot whatsoever.

*Fields' third short for Mack Sennett,* The Pharmacist, *was derived from the drugstore scene in* The Comic Supplement.

The film would sustain itself on a diet of specialties—which would conveniently appear on the television screen as programming—and a certain leering reverence for Peggy Hopkins Joyce.

Fields spent time with the writing team of Francis Martin and Walter DeLeon, ex-vaudevillians who spoke his language, and the result was a script so tailored to him that it could only be described as a stacked deck. He knew a term contract with Paramount hung in the balance, as Kaufman was expecting him to carry the picture. Joyce might bring people into the theater, Kaufman reasoned, but it would be largely up to Fields to keep them in their seats. Filming began on February 20, 1933, with Fields filling the role of Professor Quail and performing bits of business from *Ballyhoo*. His greatest single reprise was the return of the midget Austin, shipped out from New York, into which he stuffed the film's leading lady and antagonized the Hays Office by having her wonder what she was sitting on. "It's a pussy!" he proclaimed, hoisting a cat into camera range.

Given the studio's goal of creating another Mae West, Peggy Hopkins Joyce was a nonstarter. She could barely say her name for the camera, much less purr double entendres, and she didn't photograph particularly well. Like West, she was blond and blue-eyed, but she had a round face and didn't smile much. (She was insistently slugged in press releases as "internationally famous beauty.") The plan was to make her the brunt of all the jokes, surround her with people like Fields and Erwin, and hope she wouldn't get in the way. The cast was indeed eclectic: Joyce, Fields, Erwin, Burns and Allen, Sari Maritza, Bela Lugosi, Edmund Breese, Baby Rose Marie, Colonel Stoopnagle and Bud, Franklin Pangborn, and Sterling Holloway. Cab Calloway fronted his thirteen-piece band and sang "Reefer Man." It fell to Eddie Sutherland to orchestrate all these disparate elements into something cohesive, and he knew Fields was essential to pulling it off. That didn't make their relationship any less contentious. "Gradually we got to an armed neutrality which finally developed into a very interesting situation," he said. "In all the pictures I made with Fields, from nine in the morning till six at night we were bitter enemies—very polite to each other, but bitter enemies. . . . But eventually we became, though still enemies in the daytime, pals and drinking companions from six at night till the following morning. So it worked out pretty well."

Since Fields had taken the time to consult on the script, he rarely strayed from it once filming began. His arguments with Sutherland were over his infrequent ad-libs and some last-minute inspirations. Fields, the director found, had no problem going over his head when a solid laugh was at stake. Their fiercest battle was over a scripted line attached to the Rudy Vallée number. Vallée, who was a big star on radio but not much of a draw in pictures, wasn't keen on doing the scene—it kidded his trademark megaphone—but went ahead on

*With Edmund Breese and Peggy Hopkins Joyce in* International House

Sutherland's assurances it would be handled tastefully. Fields loathed Vallée's singing—as he was convinced most men did—and thought there was a big laugh in his coming on after the song, bellowing, "How long has this dogfight been going on?" and sticking his cane through the video screen. He prevailed with producer Al Lewis on the matter, and Vallée discovered the enhancement only after the film had been completed. "So," Sutherland remembered, "Mr. Vallée sent me a wire saying, 'Thanks for the usual Hollywood double-cross.' I couldn't blame him a bit."

*International House* was made at a time of terrific turmoil for Fields, for Paramount, and for Hollywood in general. Franklin Delano Roosevelt entered the White House on March 4, and bank holidays were declared around the nation. Fields, who kept vast amounts of cash in the house, was less worried than most about the outcome, but he nevertheless cast a suspicious eye on the New Dealers in Washington. Production ground on until the evening of March 10, 1933, when a 6.3-magnitude earthquake hit the city of Long Beach and killed fifty-two people. "It was the last shot of the day," Teet Carle recalled, "and it *was*. The shake scared hell out of everybody." The only visible sign of damage on the Paramount lot was the loss of two votive urns and a bell tower atop the main gate, but nobody would have known it from the reaction. "That quake was a dilly," said Eddie Sutherland. "The big lamps on the top of the set were just remaining in their standards by about a half inch, and Fearless Fosdick Sutherland was the scaredest man in Southern California, but we got through it."

Workers flooded the studio streets, waiting for the tremors to pass, but Fields wasn't among them. Al Lewis sent an assistant to look for him, and he was discovered napping in his dressing room, having slept through the entire thing. A quick check of the camera crews—*The Eagle and the Hawk* was filming on an adjacent stage—revealed that no one had actually captured the quake on film. Sutherland huddled with Ralph Huston, the unit publicist, and got an idea: "As you all know, we have a little larceny in our souls, so I got the prop man to rig up some threads on the lamps, etc., and we all pulled on the strings gleefully and shook the camera. Next, I had the scene sent to Paramount News and, to my great surprise, it played in all the theatres in the country."

Three days after the quake, Fields got another, even more significant jolt when word came from New York that the Harriman National Bank had been placed under conservatorship and J. W. Harriman himself had been arrested, charged with the misuse of depositor funds in a scheme to bolster the stock price and repurchase large blocks of it for himself. Fields, who began buying Harriman shares in 1928, reportedly had $50,000 in cash deposits and another $25,000 in preferred stock that carried a double-jeopardy clause. Normally, he avoided securities as he did most all speculative investments, but he admittedly was taken in by the charismatic Harriman, who entertained lavishly and held directorships with a variety of intriguingly named companies, including Consolidated Cigar and the Philippine Desiccated Coconut Corporation. "The bank president was my pal," Fields told Jim Tully without a trace of rancor. "He gave me a lot of inside tips; everything was jake. I was sorry that I hadn't met him sooner."*

The day after the bank failed, the beleaguered Paramount-Publix Corporation filed a voluntary petition for bankruptcy as a protective move against a spate of shareholder suits. No paychecks were issued that week, and all the assets were placed under the administration of the court. Contracts became subject to cancellation, and Manny Cohen used the opportunity to, as *Variety* put it, "clean out the deadwood." Litigants who had actions pending against the company, such as Jesse Lasky and Walter Wanger, became creditors. Al Kaufman urged calm amid the chaos, assuring everyone that the company was still solvent and that production would continue as usual, but with mortgages, debentures, bank debts, and royalties amounting to some $113 million in obli-

---

*Harriman was convicted on all counts and sentenced to four and a half years in prison. Fields later claimed he lost $250,000 in the failure, but the figure was evidently closer to $100,000.

gations, only the book value of the company's real estate holdings—an estimated $150 million—justified claims of solvency.

The mood around the studio was gloomy. Audiences had dropped 40 percent, and pictures were taking a terrific beating at the box office. Admission prices were down, with theaters closing their doors in record numbers. Warner Bros. had carved itself a Depression-era niche with stories drawn from the headlines and scripted by journalists who knew the mean streets of Chicago and New York. Paramount, with *International House,* made a similar claim for topical comedy, pushing the limits of the Production Code and fishing for a younger, more urban audience. Fields' character was a gruffer, less theatrical version of the role he played in *If I Had a Million,* still spouting endearments ("my little begonia") but more a sophisticate, less a rube. The top hat wasn't battered this time, and he made his entrance at the controls of his own gyrocopter, landing on the roof garden of the gigantic hotel in the middle of a performance. "Hey, where am I?" he shouts from the cockpit. "Wu-Hu!" returns Joyce, meaning Wu-Hu, China. "Wu-Hu to you, sweetheart." He looks over at Franklin Pangborn, the prissy hotel manager. "Hey Charley, where am I?" Pangborn says, "Wu-Hu!" Fields glares at him and plucks the carnation from his lapel. "Don't let the posy fool you."

The first glimpse audiences got of Fields showed him downing the last of innumerable beers. It was the first time he worked booze into the act in a big way, and he stayed pleasantly snockered throughout the film. Quail wasn't a drunk by any means, but he kept a glow on, cheerfully celebrating the agreeable effects alcohol had on a man of capacity. En route from Juárez to Kansas City, his progress is traced by the empty beer bottles tossed from his copter. Taken for the rep of the North American Electric Company, he is allowed to wreak havoc on the hotel and its occupants as sealed bids are collected for Dr. Yu Too Wong's amazing radioscope.

Happily, *International House* was the beneficiary of fortuitous timing. While the film was still in production, Roosevelt sent a request to Congress calling for a modification of the Volstead Act to permit the manufacture and sale of 3.2 beer as a source of "much needed revenue." The legislature, over the shrill protests of Billy Sunday and the WCTU, swiftly complied. On May 15, 1933, Fields happily reported the return of real beer to Los Angeles. "Prohibition ends today," he said in a celebratory letter to Phil Goodman. "We will be permitted to buy any quantity of real stuff from drug stores. You can buy 100 cases on one prescription. The beer here is really grand already. Porter, the mayor, has turned wet and given the town over to the yeggs. Everything wide open; you wouldn't know the place."

A week earlier, *International House* had been seen by Dr. James Wingate and representatives of the MPPDA and subjected to a hefty list of proposed cuts. The Hays Office was merely advisory, and the studio, fighting for its very existence, was shocked at the suggestion of vulgarity in the picture. "We are very much perturbed by the suggested deletions," A. M. Botsford responded, "which we feel eliminate considerable comedy, and comedy which is, we believe, entirely innocuous." The notice in the *Hollywood Reporter* the same day suggested their man had seen an entirely different film: "The gags are very funny and there are millions of 'em, and the lines are funny, too—and plenty blue."

All this advance word had the effect of making the picture a hot ticket on the preview circuit. Within days, Fields had two offers in hand: "J. D. Williams [of First Choice Pictures] wants to tie me to a five-year contract. Paramount wants a three-picture contract. Twenty-five Gs per picture. Have just finished *International House* for Paramount and stole the show, so the papers say." The papers, in fact, did say. *International House* was promoted as an all-star picture ("The *Grand Hotel* of comedy"), but Fields clearly dominated. "With his regal and somewhat beery manner, his precious silk hat, his frozen face, and his unlit cigar, he keeps his audience in perpetual roars," Andre Sennwald said in his review for the *New York Times*. "His athletic argument with the hotel clerk,

*Commemorating the end of Prohibition in this publicity shot outside Hollywood's Brown Derby*

which brings most of the International House thundering about his ears, is the funniest thing in the picture, unless it be his clandestine rendevous with Miss Joyce in her boudoir."

A week's run at the Times Square Paramount turned into a rare holdover for the 3,600-seat showplace. *International House* did solid business in Chicago, San Francisco, and Boston, but less well in the heartland, where risqué humor was usually met with cuts and objections. Ed Kuykendall, president of the Motion Picture Theatre Owners of America, told Carl Milliken of the MPPDA that executives responsible for the production of films like *International House* ought to hear "what the average decent-minded exhibitor thinks of their product and why." The MPPDA's James B. M. Fisher was similarly moved to object to the word "pussy" when it became apparent that the studio had "pulled a fast one" and used an alternate take in the review print in which Fields had used the word "cat" instead. "From various comments, it appears we are taking a terrific beating in allowing something to pass which is unmistakably vulgar."*

Fields reveled in the attention. His attorney, Loyd Wright, advised him to pass on Williams' tempting offer of $45,000 a picture. ("He is primarily and fundamentally a promoter," Wright warned.) So on May 25, 1933, playing it safe, Fields signed a contract with Paramount to appear in four pictures over a ten-month period, with an option for a fifth at the discretion of the corporation. At a rate of $4,375 a week, he would make slightly more on his next picture for the studio than the $15,000 he was paid for *International House.* Five long years after he was let out of his first contract, Fields was back at Paramount, albeit at less than half the money he was getting before. That day, he took a half-page ad in the *Hollywood Reporter:*

W. C. FIELDS

THE NEW DEAL

Giving the Suckers a Break

---

*They had their revenge in October 1935 when Paramount applied to the newly established Production Code Administration for a reissue certificate. Joseph I. Breen, director of the PCA, responded with a suggestion that the application be withdrawn. "*International House* is filled with gross vulgarities in both action and dialogue," he noted.

# Seventeen

# *Grubbing*

*International House* quickly became the most widely seen of all of Fields' pictures, and the image of him as an irreverent, beer-guzzling eccentric was suddenly fixed in the public mind. It wasn't exactly how he cared to be thought of—he preferred the earnest family man beset by life's frustrations—but it was what people seemed to respond to, and he took the Paramount contract as a way of building his stock with an audience that didn't know him. Fields hadn't been onscreen in a big way since 1927, and hadn't toured in a show in three years. His vaudeville days were a dim memory to people his own age, and to most everyone outside of New York he was an entirely new commodity.

In some ways, it was good that Fields left silent films when he did. Many of the most popular stars of 1928 had since faded from the scene, victims of changing tastes and the new enthusiasm for dialogue. Clara Bow, Milton Sills, Pola Negri, Colleen Moore, Ramon Novarro, Gloria Swanson, Douglas Fairbanks, Mary Pickford, and Rod La Rocque were all on their way out. Raymond Griffith, Paramount's urbane comedy star, couldn't talk above a hoarse whisper and ended his career playing a corpse. Even John Gilbert, the most popular of all male leads, was doing a fast fade. Sound did less damage to the ranks of the great comedians, in part because there were fewer of them. Chaplin refused to talk, Buster Keaton talked too much, and only Harold Lloyd seemed to embrace it completely. Comedies with sound took more time to produce and cost more than their silent counterparts. Laurel and Hardy were advanced to features in 1931, their voices perfectly suited to their familiar characters, but kept cranking out shorts at the rate of six per year. Bert Wheeler and Robert Woolsey were a hit in Ziegfeld's *Rio Rita* and stayed on at RKO. Slim Summerville and ZaSu Pitts were popular with rural audiences at Universal. Fox had El Brendel, Warners had Joe E. Brown. By far, the biggest draws came from the Broadway stage: Eddie Cantor, Will Rogers, the Four Marx Brothers.

Fields had proven himself, but would still have to rebuild his worth with the picture-going public. He sculpted vagabond stories of his Philadelphia youth for Paramount publicists at a time when tramping was a national obsession and school closures were putting hundreds of thousands of kids on the road. His age at leaving home dropped to eleven, and he said he got his first booking as a juggler at the tender age of fifteen. "Without money to buy tights, I had to do a tramp act in my old tattered clothes," he said pitifully. He claimed to have lost money in the stock market and that the Harriman Bank scandal had cleaned out the rest. Where, in the late 1920s, whole press releases were constructed around his fabulous salary for the *Vanities,* he now discouraged such talk on the grounds that no one could have spontaneous sympathy for a man who had lots of money. "There was nothing funny about Midas, you know. He was tragic. And if a comedian doesn't excite your sympathy, you don't laugh at him." It became one of his dictums: "A comedian is best when he's hungry."

Fields cooperated fully with men like Ralph Huston and Teet Carle, urging them to talk him up at the studio as well as in the press. Some people were leery of him because he made a show of his drinking, but his working habits hadn't changed since the *Follies,* when he kept a fully stocked bar in his dressing room. "He *was* a heavy drinker," said Teet Carle, "but so were a lot of people in motion pictures in those days." Word of Fields' behavior reached New York, and a concerned letter arrived from Hattie and Claude. It brought a typically sanguine response: "I note the derogatory rumors concerning my use of alcoholic stimulant and lavish living. It is the penalty of greatness. [Raymond] Hitchcock was accused of being a drunkard and the very odor of liquor nauseated him. I would have sworn, when these rumors reached you, that you would have retaliated as did Lincoln, when informed by some nosy parker that Grant was continually in his cups, 'Find out the brand of whisky he drinks and send a barrel to each of my generals.' For Grant was making good, and I have made good as far as you are concerned ever since I have known you." He concluded the letter by cutting Hattie's stipend to $50 a week.

The rambling wood-frame house on Toluca Lake became a lively center of operations. Fields kept an office on the lower level, just off the main room, where he held court from a huge swivel chair, the bar positioned directly opposite his desk so that he could reach it by simply rotating. Bing Crosby was a neighbor, as were Joe Mankiewicz, Norman McLeod, and Jim Tully. Mary Brian lived directly across the lake on Navajo and could observe him in his pajamas and robe, chipping golf balls into the water: "Once in a while he'd hit one of the swans and they would come up to him, furious." At first, Fields liked the birds on the lake, found them pastoral and soothing. He fed the ducks every day. "Fields would come out with a pan and the ducks, all together, would roll up the banks and right up to his door. I once said to Norman McLeod, who lived just a couple of doors down, 'My feelings are hurt. The ducks love Fields and they won't have anything to do with the food I put out for them.' He said, 'You should put rye in the pan like he does.' "

When it came time to make another short for Mack Sennett, Fields conducted auditions in his enormous living room for the role of his son. "There were about ten of us kids, who had all been in motion pictures, and we walked in the door and lined up," said Harry Watson, who was twelve at the time. "Fields was sitting there with the director, Arthur Ripley, and he pointed to me and said, 'Come here, my boy.' I looked around. 'Yes, you,' he said. I walked over to him and he handed me a martini glass—I didn't know what it was then—and said, 'Walk over there and come back.' So I walked across the room and came back, and he filled it up. 'Now repeat the process.' So I did it again. He turned to Ripley and said, 'What a talent. We could have searched years for a boy like this.' Then he looked back at me and said, 'You've got the part.' "

Having exhausted his backlog of suitable stage routines, Fields dug into his trunk for one of the many scenes he had sketched but never developed beyond a promising idea. The original version of *The Barber Shop* was penciled on the back of a 1917 letter from F. G. Bradford of the Gaumont Company, suggesting that Fields had envisioned it as a film from the very beginning. The complete text of his note went as follows:

Sits in chair. Rips collar off. Puts necktie on back of chair. Uses it for razor strap. Gets brush full of soap. Slaps soap in face. Puts towel over legs. Tries to get brush in mouth. Shaves him with razor. Hooks razor under nose and pulls. While he is strapping razor on tie, [the customer] looks up. He throws tie around his neck and pulls him back. As he shaves him, [the customer], in pain, raises his stomach. Fields pushes it down with his fist. Finally sits on him. Business with hot towels. Gets them out of heater with tongs. . . . Finish: Throws powder in face.

As initially conceived, *The Barber Shop* was as rough as *The Dentist,* and Bradford may have been put off by its cheerful sadism. Certainly Ziegfeld wouldn't have gone for it, and by the time of the *Vanities,* Fields had the copyrighted script of the dentist scene already at hand. But the idea stayed with him, for the twenty-five-page screenplay (his only original for the Sennett studio) was completed within a week of his finishing *International House.* It was a sterling piece of work, cohesive and assured in a way the others were not, and he obviously benefited from the counsel of director Ripley, a former cutter and screenwriter who later progressed to moody dramas like *I Met My Love Again* and the richly textured *Voice in the Wind.* Ripley had been responsible, in col-

*Owing little to his past stage routines,* The Barber Shop *was the most original of Fields' four short subjects for Mack Sennett.*

laboration with Frank Capra, for some of Harry Langdon's best work, and the tone he established for Fields was gentler, less aggressive than before.

With *The Barber Shop,* Fields erased any doubt about Kate Dukenfield's lasting influence on his style of delivery. Waxing nostalgic, he opens with an exterior shot of a banner being hoisted across a dirt road: "YOU ARE NOW ENTERING FELTON CITY." "Pretty good town you've got here," a voice says offscreen. "You bet," returns one of the workmen. "A public library and the largest insane asylum in the state."* Cut to Cornelius O'Hare sitting out front of his barber shop, sharpening his razor and greeting passersby in the best manner of his late mother. "Good morning, Mr. O'Hare," says a well-dressed woman.

"Good morning, Mrs. Goggin. How's Mr. Goggin?"

"He's not so well this morning."

"Oh, that's unfortunate," he says without a trace of concern. "I'm sorry to hear that."

"I'm worried about him."

---

*Norristown, where Fields made his professional debut in 1898, had the largest insane asylum in the state.

"Yeah, I am too."

As she disappears up the street, he turns to a frozen figure reading a paper off to one side. "He was out on one of his benders last night again. How he can drink that raw alcohol and live I don't know. Fine mayor he is." Kate's influence doesn't stop with the opening. O'Hare is a genuinely sweet-natured man, a good father and an agreeable husband to the domineering Elise Cavanna. The affection he displays for his riddle-happy son is genuine and heartfelt, and he at last emerges on the talking screen as a true family man.

"I never knew he had been a juggler," said Harry Watson.

In fact, I didn't know anything about him. My dad, who was always on the set with us, said, "Mr. Fields used to be a juggler. He's the only man who could juggle nine balls at the same time. Why don't you go over and ask him to juggle something?" I went over, and he acted surprised when he looked up at me. I said, "My dad says you're a good juggler." He had a pack of cigarettes in his hand—he had just emptied one—and he crumpled it up. He picked up a piece of carbon trim from the floor, about two inches long, and a pencil, and he started juggling. I said, "That was great. Thank you." The stories about him not being nice to kids, I never found that to be true.

As for working with him, he was kind of hard. "Don't jump on a line," he'd tell me. "Wait until the line drops. Wait for your cue." We were rehearsing a scene at the dinner table, and my line was, "What looks most like a cat looking out of a window?" My answer was, "Another cat looking in!" When we got to that point and I asked my riddle, he changed it around. He said, "I don't know. What looks most like a domestic feline contentedly gazing from the window?" And I'm waiting for my cue. He said, "Don't you know your line, my boy?" I said, "I'm waiting for the cue." He thought a moment and said, "Tell you what we'll do. From now on, when I start talking, don't do anything until I kick you under the table. Then you come back with your line." So that's how I got my cues.

Fields cheerfully sliced away at his customers, sandpaper effects accompanying every swipe of his razor, and occasionally he would burst into the "Grubbing" song (a one-word lyric with no discernable melody). The film wrapped on May 4, 1933. When Harry Watson asked Fields to sign his autograph book, he got a warm and generous inscription: "To my side-splitting son Ronald with appreciation for your fine talent." (At his father's urging, Watson asked him to sign it "W. C. Fields" instead of his customary "Bill.") "Funny thing," said

Watson, "when I went back to school after the picture, they had to have a slip saying you were working as an excuse. (Of course, you went to school on the set.) When I showed it to the teacher, she was livid. She said, 'Your father let you work for a man like *that?*' "

*The Barber Shop* was well received, with *Variety* going so far as to declare the shorts Fields made for Sennett "the most consistently entertaining line of two-reelers currently coming to the trade." Sennett, of course, wanted more, but Fields, by then, had been signed by Paramount and had his hands full with a demanding slate of features. *The Barber Shop* became the last and, in many ways, the best of his short films.

While awaiting the start of the first picture under his new contract, Fields devoted his time to the golf course. He lived within walking distance of Lakeside, and could be found most mornings playing alongside Greg La Cava, Charley Mack, Eddie Sutherland, and sometimes Sennett or Harold Lloyd. "When he finished the ninth hole," said Lloyd, "he had to have his snort. And he wasn't happy to have his snort alone. I drink very little, but he would go into the locker room and say, 'Come on, Harold, take one.' Well, I'd take a couple of swigs. And by the time I got out there on the course again, everything was uphill. But it didn't seem to bother Bill."

Having come to the game relatively late in life, Fields refused to take it very seriously, enraging some of the more intense players in his circle and giving rise to occasional accusations of cheating. Traipsing the course in silk shirts and floral ties—he was not allowed to play shirtless as he had on Long Island—Fields cut a colorful figure. He played in the high 70s and was good enough to appear with Bobby Jones in one of the famous instructional shorts Jones made for Warner Bros.*

"He couldn't hit a long ball," said Bing Crosby, "but he was marvelously clever with his hands. And he was a terrific putter." According to golf pro Leo Diegel, Fields didn't get the full power of his swing because he couldn't pivot properly off his left foot. "It's a left-footed game," Fields insisted with a trace of resignation, but Diegel said it was possible to play a good game on the right foot, too. To prove his point, Diegel suggested they play for $2 a hole, the pro standing only on his right foot when swinging. Fields, who was used to playing for as much as $100 a hole, called a halt to the game after just two holes. Diegel had scored a birdie on the first, and hit the green on the second with a forty-

---

*Hip Action* was third in a six-part series for Warners called *How to Break 90.* "All the stars were eager to take part," the director, George Marshall, said. "They donated their time in order to have the chance of Bobby Jones working on their game."

*As a golfer, Fields made up in accuracy what he lacked in range.*

nine-yard drive. "I'll play you some more," Fields told him, "but you've got to play on both feet."

Fields' conviviality knew no bounds that summer. The door to the house on Toluca was always open, and he kept a personal trainer on duty for whoever wanted to stop in for a drink and a massage. "I try to keep as fit as possible," he told Elsie Janis. "I don't stay up late anymore. Play a bit of golf. I like to putter around the place, eat a bit, drink a bit. It's a great life!" The seventeenth annual convention of Kiwanis International came to Los Angeles in June 1933, and Fields, who had come to the service organization through Will Rogers, took advantage of his brief respite from filming to become a delegate-at-large. Dutifully, he attended business meetings at the Biltmore Hotel and participated in nightly programs at the Greek Theatre and the Hollywood Bowl. "We're expecting three-thousand-five-hundred Kiwanians and their families in town by Sunday for a big outdoor meeting and barbecue," he told Phil Goodman excitedly, "and we're going to have a swell time. Singing and speeches and dancing by the children. Grace is getting up a little thing, a recitation which I have written called 'Why I am a Kiwanian.' If Ruth was here I know I could get her a fine spot on the program doing most anything she wanted. Even if she just showed up they would be tickled to death."

Amid the confusion that followed the Paramount bankruptcy—lawyers were swarming—it took nearly a month for Al Kaufman and his staff to find something suitable for Fields to do. At first, it was an all-star musical called *The Funny Page.* A deal was struck with the King Features Syndicate to acquire the screen rights to Popeye, Blondie, Boob McNutt, and other characters made famous in the Hearst papers. Then there was *Every Man for Himself,* with Eddie Sutherland directing Fields, Jack Oakie, and Sari Maritza in an original by Joe Mankiewicz. For a few days, Fields was even part of an ad hoc trio of comedians set to take over *Grasshoppers* when the Marx Brothers quarreled with management.* Finally, it was announced that Norman McLeod would direct Fields and Alison Skipworth in *Tillie and Gus.* Along with *Death Takes a Holiday, Design for Living,* De Mille's *Four Frightened People,* and *I'm No Angel,* it was one of sixty-five features set for Paramount's 1933–34 season.

*Tillie and Gus* was based on a story by Rupert Hughes, but little remained after Fields got involved. It was originally conceived as a comedy for Skipworth and Mary Boland, two old ladies who return to a small town to claim an inheritance and find it consists solely of an orphanage. The Hays Office was queasy over a plot point that had the ladies mistaken for missionaries. They also didn't like the title: *Don't Call Me Madame.* When the MPPDA declined to register it, the film got shelved and the producer, Bayard Veiller, went on to other projects. Yet Fields had been an undeniable hit with Skipworth in *If I Had a Million,* so in July he was persuaded to work with Walter DeLeon and Francis Martin, the authors of *International House,* on an entirely new version of the story. It barely resembled the original in any significant respect, other than the authors took care to preserve the "dangerous element" that had so distressed the administrators of the Code—both Fields and Skipworth were to appear as bogus missionaries.

---

*The walkout was over the percentages owed them on their previous pictures. The crisis passed when the Marxes agreed to accept a flat fee of $300,000 to make the film, which was released as *Duck Soup* (1933).

Fields liked working at home, where the bar was close at hand and the serenity of the lake was conducive to creative thought. He sometimes held story conferences on the water. "I used to see him out there in the middle of the lake with the writers clutching the sides of the canoe," said Mary Brian. "The swans would swim over and he would stand up and mock them. The writers were sure they were going to get dunked in the lake, because the swans had necks so strong they could have tipped the canoe over." The script that emerged from these sessions on the lake, *Odds Are Even,* began and ended, appropriately enough, with a duck. Fields was Augustus Q. Winterbottom, a frock-coated cardsharp on trial for the attempted murder of one High-Card Harrington. Skipworth was Mathilda Winterbottom, proprietress of the Soo Chow Club and ex-wife of Augustus. From different corners of the globe they are summoned to the small town of Danville to share in the estate of Tillie's late brother. But all that remains, they discover, is a rundown ferryboat, a legacy they must share with their young niece, her husband, and their infant son. The Winterbottoms deduce that the money has been appropriated by a crooked executor and they set about to fix the boat up and retrieve it.

Fields didn't get on well with the new producer, whose sense of comedy was gentler than his own. Douglas MacLean had been a star comedian in silent pictures, but he seemed more interested in telling a story than making it funny. Fields tried softening him up by sending him a copy of the gambling scene from *Ballyhoo:* "I have many little bits of this sort and many scenes and sketches I have written which you may have for *Tillie and Gus.* If you will let me see the story I may be able to make some suggestions with regard to my part, if you would welcome them." MacLean objected to a six-page scene in which Fields mixed paint to the instructions of a radio announcer ("Pour in the linseed oil . . . two cups of benzine . . . three scoops of white lead . . . the small can of turpentine . . ."). As the pace quickens, Gus throws in everything he can lay his hands on—including the pet duck. MacLean thought the scene wasted too much screen time without advancing the story. But Fields didn't care about story. The bit was a fresh and funny sendup of "Handy Andy" shows, and he wanted it in.

The first script, dated August 7, 1933, was virtually shot verbatim, though MacLean put them through two additional drafts that were subsequently discarded. Fields sensed disaster at hand; Norman McLeod, who was preparing an ambitious live-action picturization of *Alice in Wonderland,* begged off as director, and Francis Martin, who had directed short comedies for Educational but never a feature, stepped in as his replacement. Filming was set to begin on Monday, August 14, and the cast was hurriedly completed with Jacqueline Wells and Clifford Jones as the young parents, and a toddler named Baby LeRoy.

LeRoy Weinbrenner was a phenomenon, a photogenic blue-eyed boy with a winning smile and a seemingly inexhaustible library of expressions. He debuted with Maurice Chevalier in *Bedtime Story* and, at sixteen months, became the youngest person ever put under term contract by a major studio. Chevalier was so taken with the baby—officially the result of a doomed marriage but actually the product of a rape—he reportedly tried to adopt him. The part of "The King" in *Tillie and Gus* was specifically written for Baby LeRoy, and Fields was required to play a couple of brief scenes with the child nestled restlessly in his arms—an unattractive prospect to any actor who knows how an infant can draw an audience's attention and leach the energy from a scene. "In the beginning, I did have the feeling that he did not like working with Baby LeRoy," said Jacqueline Wells. "I thought he might be afraid the child would steal some of their scenes together. He was adorable. But all at once, everything changed. He was actually playing with Mr. Fields, who seemed to really love the little boy. And there was harmony all around."

Harmony, that is, until the two were finally put before a camera together. At close range, Fields' face seemed to terrify Baby LeRoy, and he would break into a protracted crying fit whenever Fields drew near. "He couldn't stand the kid," said Clifford Jones. "I was the only one who could do anything with him. I was a new father at the time. I'd get him calmed down and shove him into the scene before he could get a look at that bulbous beak and let out a yell. The baby didn't seem to like him too much, either."

Most of *Tillie and Gus* was shot at Malibu Lake, thirty miles west of the studio, where the *Fairy Queen,* a rattletrap steamer, had been fabricated on a set of pontoons. The schedule was a brisk three weeks, so the delays caused by Baby LeRoy's tantrums resulted in longer hours for the adults. One scene that ran far into the night called for Fields to be submerged in a diver's suit, sabotaging the rival boat for a big race. Having had pipe smoke introduced into his air supply, Fields rises to the surface, pops the helmet open, and, as the smoke streams out, gasps the line, "Is there a doctor in the house?"

With the clock approaching midnight, Fields inexplicably began to ad-lib. Pointing to his weighted boots, he said, "Primo Carnera's carpet slippers!" Martin yelled cut. "Why, that's funny," Fields protested. "Everybody knows about Carnera's big feet."* Again. "Charlie Probischer's bedroom slippers!" he exclaimed on the second take. Martin again cut the shot and wanted to know what the hell was wrong with him. "Don't you know," said Fields, "that the name 'Charlie Probischer' always gets a laugh? People will howl at it." Unconvinced, the director called for yet a third take, and Fields uttered the line exactly as it appeared in the script. Nobody seemed to notice that it was now

---

*Carnera, an enormous Italian, was the world heavyweight boxing champion.

past midnight . . . and the studio was contractually obligated to pay Fields an $800 penalty for working him into the next day.

Taking monetary revenge on Paramount couldn't lessen the toll Baby LeRoy took on the schedule, and Fields was, at times, forced to resort to extreme measures to keep things moving. "I was naturally the cause of all his grief," he said, "and each time he saw me he bellowed loud and long." The principal shot in which Fields held the child lasted just forty seconds, but it began to look as if it would take an entire day to make. "We took the scene over and over again for hours on end. They gave the child a drink of water. . . . They gave him his milk bottle. . . . I told his nurse to get me a racing form and I would play nurse until she returned. I quietly removed the nipple from Baby LeRoy's bottle, dropped in a couple of noggins of gin, and returned it to Baby LeRoy. After sucking on the pacifier for a few minutes, he staggered through the scene like a Barrymore."

By all accounts, Fields had much to do with the direction of *Tillie and Gus,* and Francis Martin rarely opposed him on matters of staging or dialogue. Indeed, much of the camera work had already been built into the script, leaving the men free to fight with MacLean and the front office over the footage they delivered. Fields got his back up over any suggestion that the rushes weren't funny. The constant nattering ate away at his confidence, and by the end of production he was sure they had a dud on their hands. The Hays Office passed the film on September 28, and it was put before a paying audience the same day. Fields had a lot riding on this screening, for he would finally demonstrate his viability as a topliner in feature comedies. More important, he would accomplish the feat with none of the recycled material he had so heavily relied upon in the past. Other than a stray endearment for Alison Skipworth ("my little water lily"), the lines and situations in *Tillie and Gus* were entirely new and original. Fortunately, the picture scored big. Fields admitted to Bob Burkhalter that, going into the screening, he considered *Tillie and Gus* "very bad" and that he had endured "many arguments" over the direction, supervision, and writing. "The picture had a preview at the Criterion Theatre in Santa Monica and the audience screamed all through the picture, much to my surprise and amazement. *The Hollywood Reporter* raved about it, as did Will Rogers, who attended the preview with us. Bill told me that he had just done a picture called *Dr. Bull* and told me that his was stinko, but the critics claimed his was good. I hope we are both wrong."

The notice in *Daily Variety* was lukewarm, asserting the film rarely got above the "titter and chuckle" level, but the review in the *Reporter* fully corroborated Fields' account. "All the laughs that can be safely crowded into one picture and still leave the audience able to stagger home are packed into *Tillie and*

*Fields' first starring picture of the sound era was* Tillie and Gus (*1933*).
*From left to right: Baby LeRoy, Fields, Clifford Jones, Alison Skipworth, and Jacqueline Wells*

*Gus.*" The paint-mixing routine was "a riot," and Fields, the film's star, never gave the audience a dull moment. "*Tillie and Gus* is as sure a winner for the showman as one of W. C. Fields' four-ace pat hands." Better still, the top brass from Paramount were all present to witness it for themselves. "I went to the studio the day after the preview," said Fields, "and was told by the head of the studio, Albert Kaufman, that from now on all directors and writers having anything to do with pictures that I play in would be given instructions to lay off and let me do exactly as I please."

*Tillie and Gus* was released on October 13, 1933, just after Mae West's hotly anticipated *I'm No Angel* and shortly before the Marx Brothers' *Duck Soup.* Though infinitely more modest in terms of size and budget, it held its own in a difficult market where hit pictures were doing better than ever, but for every hit picture there were twenty flops. Restless exhibitors—especially outside the big cities—were demanding films with fewer pretensions and greater entertainment value. *Tillie and Gus* seemed to fill the bill.

Fields' relationship with Grace George was an on-again, off-again sort of thing. "Gracie is back again," he informed Goodman in one letter, "because she thinks I have changed . . . or did she say change?" She willingly took dictation and signed some of his letters "Secretary to Mr. Fields," but by September 1933 he was ready to throw her out. Gracie wanted $5,000 and some clothes to leave the house, but Fields thought $300 sufficient. A ninety-minute conference ensued at Loyd Wright's office, and Fields ended up giving her the $5,000 she wanted, plus $500 for clothes and the price of a new Buick (which was $1,379). Linelle was in the background as well, having gotten a quickie divorce in Texas. "Unhappy Linelle!" said Bob Burkhalter. "She is, no doubt, making a brave effort to forget, but with unavailing success. Such is life."

Fields' relationship with his family was similarly unsettled. He kept in regular touch with Walter and Adele and occasionally sent them checks, but rarely communicated with either Leroy or Elsie May. Roy actively resented the brusque treatment he had received as a child and was sure he had lost out on a career in baseball by staying at home with their mother. May, on the other hand, simply married well and didn't need her brother's money. Usually, he received news of them through Mabel Roach, a cousin who kept in touch with everyone. Fields maintained an impressive correspondence with his friends, however, exchanging books and lengthy letters with Phil Goodman in New York, Burkhalter in Chicago, W. Buchanan-Taylor in London. He sent funny notes to his cronies in Hollywood, using insults as salutations and always signing off with an old-fashioned hug. Billy Grady was the Catholic; Eddie Cantor, the Christ-killer; La Cava, a wop. When Wiggle was in one of her snits, he wrote letters in longhand and didn't bother to make copies. When it was something more formal, he found himself a typist and had a carbon made.

He flexed his newfound muscles by getting out of *Funny Page*—in which he was supposed to play Wimpy—and attempting to remove himself from *Alice in Wonderland* as well. He had been tapped to replace Charles Laughton in a cameo as Humpty-Dumpty, but regarded the prospect of being glued into a rubber mask with horror. He rarely wore makeup of any kind, and after years of avoiding elevators and constricting booths in restaurants, he had come to the realization that he was claustrophobic. He was, however, prevailed upon to do the film for the exposure—Gary Cooper and Cary Grant would be in it as well—and so, two days after the triumphant *Tillie and Gus* preview, he dutifully reported to Wally Westmore's studio above the dressing rooms on the Paramount lot to have a plaster cast made of his face.

The procedure of smearing the face with wet plaster went surprisingly well until the very last portion of the Fields countenance—the great nose—was covered. Soda straws had been poked up his nostrils to facilitate breathing, but that couldn't forestall a raging panic attack. "Fields went berserk," said Frank

Westmore, who, as a ten-year-old child, witnessed the event. "He began clawing at the still-damp plaster on the rest of his face, pulling it away from his mouth and emitting unearthly howls. The hardening plaster began to adhere to Fields' hands, and he jumped from Wally's chair and struck them against the walls, trying to get the plaster off his fingers."

He was subdued with an injection, and Westmore eventually got the mold he needed by making the cast in two vertical sections, leaving the face at least partially uncovered at all times.* A worse ordeal was yet to come when the filming of the *Alice* sequence came in October. The young daughters of William Cameron Menzies (who was codirecting the film with Norman McLeod) were on the lot that day, and their host, a studio functionary, asked if they'd care to meet Humpty-Dumpty. Having answered in the affirmative, they were led onto a darkened soundstage where they observed a grotesque figure in a canvas chair, an egg-shaped prosthesis glued to his head and a set of spindly legs dangling lifelessly from his chin. "I guess it was W. C. Fields," said Suzanne Menzies, who was eight at the time. "He was evidently drunk, sitting there and bellowing something. We were ushered out quickly."

Fields had faced the day with a fortification of strong drink, but it barely calmed him for the brief scene he played with Charlotte Henry, the twenty-year-old actress cast as Alice. He spoke his lines with absolute fidelity to the script and was finished in a few hours, but the trauma of the job stuck with him for years. When, in 1939, he was asked to name his least favorite role, he replied without a moment's hesitation: Humpty-Dumpty in *Alice in Wonderland.*

Fields' pal La Cava was under contract to RKO, where he worked under William Le Baron and, later, David O. Selznick. RKO was next door to the Paramount lot, and Fields spent much of his time drinking and talking story with the director in the latter's disheveled office. It was there that Fields met Gene Fowler, a tall and articulate Irishman hired by Selznick to turn his best-selling book *The Great Mouthpiece* into a script for John Barrymore. Fowler had a rich contempt for Hollywood that appealed to Fields, and was a literary man of the first rank. The two hit it off right away, and when Fowler sent Fields a copy of his autobiographical pamphlet, *A Solo in Tom-Toms,* Fields responded with a laudatory wire. Fowler was the kind of writer Fields yearned to work with, and when he followed Selznick to MGM, in 1933, he promoted the idea of pairing Fields with Marie Dressler in a picture called *Fericke, the Guest Artist.* The source material was a German play, and the project was seri-

---

*Fields later told him, somewhat apologetically, that his fear of confinement was so great that he couldn't even stand to wear a ring on his finger.

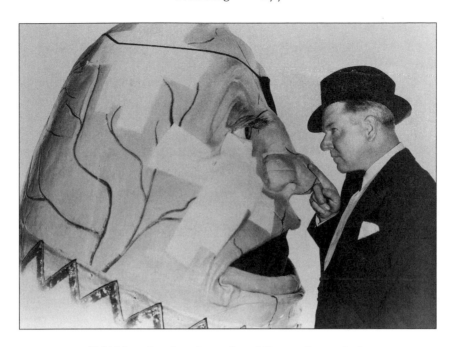

*Fields' least favorite role was that of Humpty-Dumpty in the*
*William Cameron Menzies version of* Alice in Wonderland.

ous enough for Metro to enter into negotiations with Paramount, proposing the loan of Jimmy Durante in exchange for Fields. Fowler and Ben Hecht began work on a screenplay, and George Cukor was pulled off another picture in order to direct it.

Fields, in the meantime, was set for a third film at Paramount with Alison Skipworth. *Six of a Kind* was designed to showcase three sets of couples who had already established themselves in Paramount comedies; Charlie Ruggles and Mary Boland and George Burns and Gracie Allen were to be in it as well. The script, by Walter DeLeon and Harry Ruskin, began under Douglas McLean's supervision while Fields was on location with *Tillie and Gus.* It was sent to the Hays Office for review on November 9, just as talk of the MGM deal was intensifying. Production was set to begin the following Monday, but Fields expressed no interest in the film, provided minimal input to the writers, and, according to director Leo McCarey, didn't even bother to read the script until Sunday night. The next morning, there was hell to pay.

"He didn't show up at all," said McCarey, who knew Fields socially but had never worked with him.

I was told he was in the front office complaining about his part. I found him in the boss' office with his feet on the desk and a quart—or rather a half a quart, to be exact—beside him. "Come right in," said Willie. "I was talking about you. I was telling the boss here that I'm twice as old as you and I ought to know twice as much. I just got around to reading your story last night, and I came to the conclusion you were trying to kill me in pictures. I thought you and I were good friends, but Caesar thought Brutus was too." I asked him what he didn't like about the story. He said, "I'm coming to that. Last night, I started reading your story in bed, just me and a quart of whiskey. I want you to know I finished three-fourths of the story and all of the whiskey before I got to my part."

Indeed, Fields did not make his first appearance until Sequence D, forty pages into the script. Worse, the film clearly had been thrown to Burns and Allen, who had just been awarded a three-year contract with the studio. The part of Sheriff "Honest John" Hoxley was devoid of color or, for that matter, the distinctive patterns of speech that only Fields could bring to the material. Working in a vacuum, the writers had sketched in a perfunctory version of the famous pool specialty, providing the germ of a monologue but little else, and a scene at a roulette wheel that gave all the laugh lines to Gracie Allen. It was a punk job, careless and unfunny, and Fields steadfastly refused to play it. The film was postponed, and, as blue pages flew, Fields girded himself for making the Dressler picture instead. However, Manny Cohen wasn't keen on a loan, apparently worried that Fields would be a hit at Metro, and he put the kibosh on the deal. Incensed, Fields retaliated by refusing to appear in *Six of a Kind* under any circumstances and was threatened with suspension. Cohen tried getting Fields on the telephone to iron things out, and his star comedian refused to take the call. "Give him an evasive answer," Fields instructed his cook. "Tell him to go to Hell!"

Without Fields, Fowler and Hecht were dispersed to other films, and *Fericke, the Guest Artist* was history by the end of November. The episode damaged Fields' relationship with Cohen, whom he considered a pain in the ass, but the issue of a loanout was, in the end, moot; Marie Dressler was ill with cancer and would never make another movie. There was little Fields could do but honor his contract and make *Six of a Kind*. For the first time on a talking picture, he prepared to ad-lib extravagantly. The roulette scene was junked, and when filming finally got underway on December 4, 1933, a new ending was still in the works. Angry with Fields over the delay, McCarey went toe-to-toe with him on nearly all his ideas. Reacting to one scene Fields had written, McCarey told him flatly it was no good. Fields responded by telling the director he wouldn't continue on the picture unless the scene stood as written. "What have you got to say to that?" he demanded. "Lunch!" shouted McCarey, and within moments the stage was cleared of personnel and bathed in darkness. Fields stewed for the better part of a day before admitting that it was a good retort. "The hell of it," said McCarey, "was that he was basically so funny that I'd start to wail to the Front Office about how difficult he was, and I got no sympathy."

The centerpiece of the film became the pool act, which was originally written as a dialogue between Fields and Alison Skipworth. She was to ask how he came to be known as Honest John, and he was to tell her how he had once declined to steal a red-hot stove. Fields took this one line and spun it into a five-minute scene in which the element of the stove was replaced with something equally unstealable but more palpably repulsive—a glass eye. He then removed Skipworth from the scene entirely and replaced her with Tammany Young.

Stooging for Fields was a job the Runyonesque Young had coveted for nearly a decade. Short and round with a pug face and vacant eyes, he had appeared in the New York productions of David Belasco, George M. Cohan, Jed Harris, and Gilbert Miller, usually as a racetrack tout, a tramp, a mug, a face in the crowd. He had a showy bit in *The Front Page* and can be glimpsed in Chaplin's *Making a Living,* but his true fame lay in his ability to crash any gate. He was a favorite of sportswriters, who turned out reams of copy on the twenty-five years he spent cuffing his way into major sporting events. He was a hanger-on, always at the periphery of things, and he first put in for Shorty's job around the time of *Poppy.* Fields, out of loyalty to Shorty, rebuffed him, but he was still at it when he showed up in Los Angeles to crash the Olympic Games. Al Jolson spotted him at the Brown Derby ("I have about three bucks in the kick") and gave him nine weeks of steady work on *Hallelujah, I'm a Bum.* Subsequently, Young got jobs at Warners, Goldwyn, and Paramount, where he played a minor role in *She Done Him Wrong.* "I meet Fields every once in a while and I always brace him for the stooge job, but he says he's not using any stooge. One day I meet him and I brace him again and he says to me: 'If you work with me, you gotta keep your mouth shut because you do not have a word to say. Can you do that?' I say I can, so he says come over to Paramount where he's working in *Six of a Kind* and doing the old pool table act."

Left entirely to his own devices, Fields begins the scene complaining of a hangover ("I feel as though the Russian Army has been walking over my tongue in their stocking feet") and then remedies the spell with a pint of rye. Tam says, "Tell me, Sheriff, how did you ever get the name of Honest John?" and Fields is off and running. "At the time of which I speak," he begins, "I'm tendin' bar up at Medicine Hat. Well, a guy used to come in there with a glass eye. I used to wait on him. Wasn't a bad guy . . ." He lines up his shot fastidiously. "He used to take this glass eye out and put it in a tumbler of water. Wait until I break these balls . . ." He draws back his cue, and it, of course, escapes him. He chases it, doffing his hat and coat in the process. "He comes in one

*Fields performed his classic pool routine with Tammany Young in* Six of a Kind *(1934).*

d—" He puts the chalk in his mouth, spits it out, replaces it with his cigar. "He comes in one day and he forgets the glass eye." He finally makes the shot, the ball rebounding and knocking him squarely in the forehead.

"But tell me," presses Tam, "how did they come to call you Honest John?"

"As I was saying, one day he forgets his glass eye. I found it. Next morning when he comes in, I said, 'Young man, here's your glass eye,' and I gave it back to him. Ever since that time—" He sets up the massé shot and runs his cue clean through the table. "Ever since that day, I've been known as Honest John."

McCarey wasn't particularly keen on the pool routine, but he was fond of a line Fields delivered to Alison Skipworth just prior to it: "According to you, everything I like to do is either illegal, immoral, or fattening." The director reasonably took the line as an ad-lib, and his admiration for Fields' improvisational skills grew accordingly. McCarey said,

> Sometime later, I was making a picture with Irene Dunne and Charles Boyer* and I thought it would be very effective if Irene were to tell the joke to Boyer. We all knew that Willie was full of larceny and couldn't be trusted, so I got him to sign an agreement that he would convey to

---

*Love Affair* (1939).

me all of his right, title, and interest to the joke. The price he asked was quite reasonable—a case of branded whiskey.

Then, feeling perfectly safe, I had Miss Dunne speak the line. When the picture came out it was quite successful, but the critics panned the life out of me for one thing: Why did I steal Alexander Woollcott's line, "Everything I like in life is either illegal, immoral, or fattening"? I got very angry and I called Willie on the phone. "I thought you told me that joke was yours!" I shouted at him. He said, "All I assigned to you was any right, title, and interest I had in the joke. As it turned out, my rights were nil. So you bought nothing!"

*Six of a Kind* finished just short of the new year and, despite McCarey's misgivings, performed wonderfully at a January preview. "Rarely has this reporter seen a crowd so enthusiastic in the appreciation of screen amusement as was the preview audience," said the ensuing notice in the *Motion Picture Herald*. "Clocking the laughs was impossible; they came so fast and furiously." The film was released in Los Angeles on February 9, 1934, rocking the opening-day crowd with the kind of belly laughs of which most producers can only dream. "One particular scene, when W. C. Fields is trying to hit a billiard ball, that and nothing more, really has the audience in hysterics," Sidney Burke reported in the *Post-Record.* "People gasp for breath, double up into weird shapes, cry. The rest of the film is funny and well worth seeing, but that scene is a classic."

The New York notices and grosses were equally favorable, and the studio quickly announced plans for a followup, *Three Pair,* with the same sextet and MacLean again functioning as producer. But Fields had other plans, for he had re-teamed with William Le Baron to remake the best of their Astoria productions. Over the course of three pictures, Le Baron had built Mae West into a commercial powerhouse, setting records across the nation, and now he was poised to do the same for W. C. Fields. The audience for Fields' fresh, irreverent brand of comedy was obviously there, and it was time once again for him to go solo.

# Eighteen

# The Old Fashioned Way

When William Le Baron returned to Paramount in May 1932, he was on the rebound from RKO and glad to get the job. Twelve months hence, having produced *Night After Night, She Done Him Wrong,* and *College Humor,* he found himself deluged with offers. Le Baron chose to remain at the studio for another year, agreeing to a slate of six films with the right to make an additional two if he so wished. On his schedule were two Mae West pictures, an all-star musical, and a pair of comedies starring W. C. Fields. Once again, Le Baron was a man with clout, and Fields took the liberty of "bawling on his shoulder" and telling him what he thought was wrong with his movie career. "After all, I was no tenderfoot. I'd been entertaining people for 30 years. I knew what I could and couldn't do. I begged him to let me have my head. Lord bless him, he did."

The key to putting Fields across as a solo attraction was in delivering his pictures for a price. Fields had a modest following—nowhere near as large as West's—and his comedies had to be budgeted in the $125,000 to $150,000 range. (West's pictures, by comparison, were $300,000 affairs that grossed in the millions.) Mining the Astoria legacy made good economic—as well as artistic—sense. It offered proven story material from properties already owned by the studio, and at $22,500 a picture, Fields' salary would constitute the largest single line item on the budget.

In December, as Fields was filming *Six of a Kind,* Le Baron put Walter DeLeon and Paul Jones on a talking-picture adaptation of *So's Your Old Man.* In January, he brought J. P. McEvoy in to tinker with the dialogue. Production was ready to begin on January 24, and Fields was on his best behavior, anxious to bring the film, titled *You're Telling Me!,* in on schedule and budget.* Erle C.

---

*The title reflected Le Baron's habit of hanging popular catchphrases on Fields' pictures on the theory that they connected with the public more than did a merely descriptive title. There was hardly a film in release over the 1933–34 season in which someone didn't say, "You're telling me!"

Kenton, a Sennett alumnus, was assigned to direct. Having both acted in and directed slapstick comedies, Kenton experienced none of the haggling that had worn down some of Fields' previous directors. "Bill was a great guy in my book," he said.

Fields softened the character of Samuel Bisbee for the remake, pulling him still farther away from the protagonist of the original story. "It is a queer experience to see a story one has written produced on the screen with Fields as star," Julian Street observed. "The story becomes unrecognizable, but it is always funny. One feels at once indignant and amused." For *You're Telling Me!* Bisbee was inexplicably made an optometrist, though no refractions got performed onscreen and there was no connection between the profession and his resume of eccentric gadgets. The shatterproof windshield of the original film became a puncture-proof tire in the talking version, and Fields used an absurd contraption called a "murder chair" (designed to subdue unsuspecting burglars) to experiment with the technique of telegraphing a laugh.

"It seems in general as though people laugh only at the unexpected," he said, "and yet sometimes they laugh still harder exactly because they expect something. . . . [In that scene] I explain to the audience how I shall make friends with the burglar, and invite him to sit down and talk things over, and I show how the instant his rear touches the chair bottom, a lever will release a huge iron ball which will hit him on the head and kill him instantly. From then on the audience knows what's coming. They know that I am going to forget about my invention and sit down in the chair myself. They begin laughing as I start toward the chair, and their laugh is at its peak *before* the ball hits me." The seeming perverseness of a laugh based on anticipation rather than surprise fascinated him. "If I sat in a chair and the ball fell on my head, and *then* it was explained that it was a burglar alarm, the scene would fall flat. The success of the scene depends upon the absence of surprise."

Exteriors for the film were shot in Sierra Madre, a little bedroom community at the upper end of the San Gabriel valley. After the ordeal of shooting *Tillie and Gus* on location, Fields had a trailer outfitted that permitted him to exit the house in his pajamas and robe and sleep en route to the set. It contained an electric stove, a refrigerator, a buffet, and a fully stocked bar. The studio rented a frame cottage on a tree-lined street, but the first day of shooting was like a scene out of one of his own movies. The woman in the house next to the cottage turned her radio up when filming began and refused to douse it until paid a $10 bribe by the assistant director. The following day, it blared again, and her children played hockey in the front yard with broomsticks and tin cans. The demand this time was for $100, and a studio emissary was dispatched to the Chamber of Commerce for help. An appeal to civic pride brought her price down to $15, but Paramount nevertheless put an embargo on further uses of the neighborhood.

It was in front of the Sierra Madre cottage that Fields played one of his infrequent drunk scenes, a nighttime ballet of unsteady footwork performed coat in hand, a cigar determinedly sticking out of his mouth and a straw boater on his head with a life all its own. Carefully seating himself on the front steps, Bisbee noiselessly removes his shoes and makes a wobbly approach on the front door, using a funnel-like device of his own invention to navigate the keyhole.* Inside, Mrs. Bisbee (Louise Carter) is awaiting him, considerably more shrewish—thanks to Joe McEvoy's retooling of the dialogue—than Marcia Harris had been in the original. She complains of the late hour and her husband's habit of spending time at the shop while working on his inventions.

"If you were married to Thomas Edison—" he begins.

"You're no Edison, Sam Bisbee."

"No, and you're no prophet, Mrs. Bisbee."

She frets over the whereabouts of their daughter, Pauline, and scolds him for the shame his slovenly behavior has brought to her. "Look at you. Suppose she were entertaining a nice young man in her home and you came in looking like that, with your shoes off, your suspenders down, and your breath smelling of cheap liquor?"

"Cheap?" he erupts. "Four dollars a gallon!"

The early minutes of *You're Telling Me!* were used to establish Bisbee's character, his loving relationship with his teenage daughter, and his dream of selling his miraculous tire and the wealth it will bring. After the all-important demonstration goes awry, he tries poisoning himself aboard the train home and botches the job with equal measures of cold feet and incompetence. When subsequently he meets Princess Lescaboura and talks her out of taking her own life, he achieves a sublime pathos rare in the annals of screen comedy, at once both ridiculous and wise. If ever Fields came close to showing his true potential as a dramatic actor, it was in this brief but affecting exchange between European royalty and a failed small-town inventor who has suddenly realized the true value of things. As with *So's Your Old Man,* Fields ended *You're Telling Me!* with his celebrated golf routine, shot at the Lakeside course with Tammany Young stooging in the best tradition of Shorty Blanche. The pie tin still sticks to his hat, the tissues still blow in the breeze, and the ball still resists every conceivable effort to drive it off the tee. Like Shorty before him, Tam became inseparable from Fields and could usually be found at the house on Toluca Lake when filming wasn't in progress.

---

*This wordless three-minute sequence is underscored with Gounod's "Funeral March of a Marionette," later the television theme music of Alfred Hitchcock.

*Dispensing autographs while on location in Sierra Madre for*
You're Telling Me!, *1934*

*You're Telling Me!* closed on February 20 after twenty-four days before the cameras, and was previewed to a chilly audience on March 19 at the Ritz Theatre in downtown Los Angeles. The opening scene played sluggishly, and at seventy-one minutes the film was simply too long. Back in the cutting room, editor Otho Lovering worked with both Kenton and Fields to sweat five precious minutes from the picture. Lovering was not well versed in comedy and had a tendency to stifle the laughs with cuts that were too quick for the audience. Fields came armed with notes from the preview, and by the time the negative was ready to ship, it was in solid shape.

The first talking film to bill W. C. Fields over the title was released on April 6, 1934, when it opened jointly in both Los Angeles and New York City. Cued by the billing and the film's undeniable quality, the critics on both coasts greeted *You're Telling Me!* with unbridled enthusiasm and a sense of Fields' growing importance to the moviegoing public. John Scott in Los Angeles said it had been "many months" since he had heard such laughter in a theater.

"W. C. Fields, who achieved considerable fame for his pantomimic talents on the stage, emerges after considerable grooming as a ranking screen comedian." In New York, Eileen Creelman of the *Sun* neatly distilled Fields' evolving screen persona when she described Bisbee as "one of those quietly harassed men whose greatest efforts are met with futility and laughter. It is essentially a character quite as tragic as Chaplin's little tramp, much more credible, and, thus far anyway, much less self-conscious."

To fully comply with the terms of his Paramount contract, Fields needed to complete yet another picture by May 27. By Le Baron's reckoning, this should have been a remake of *It's the Old Army Game,* but Fields insisted on "The Great McGillicuddy" instead. This was an ambitious undertaking, for there was no basis for success in this untried story and only three months in which to have it written and shot. Moreover, Le Baron had his hands full with the new Mae West picture, *It Ain't No Sin* (released as *Belle of the Nineties*). Largely on his own, Fields went through a dozen writers in as many weeks.

Revising "McGillicuddy," Fields removed the tragic ending and overt action of the second half that would entitle Tom Geraghty to a writing credit. He added the kadoola kadoola routine from *Poppy* and a double wedding at the fade-out. Significantly, he injected the kind of texture that could only come from someone who had lived the nomadic life of a traveling player. Owing to its nostalgic roots, he retitled the story "Playing the Sticks" and firmly set it in the year 1898, when, as an eighteen-year-old boy, he first hit the road with Fulton and his Monte Carlo Girls. Going over the typescript, he made still further emendations in ink, adding bits of dialogue ("On our last appearance here, the house was so crowded they couldn't applaud horizontally, they had to applaud vertically . . .") and shortening the name of the character from McGillicuddy to McGonigle.

The film would cover a one-night stand in the life of the Great McGonigle's traveling repertory company, rolling into town one step ahead of the law, wooing the local widow ("leg-pulling") for the money to move on, drumming up the bluster and ballyhoo that feed the performance, and hastily withdrawing upon its conclusion. The screenplay went through three successive drafts, each somehow weaker than the last. Writers on the project included Joe McEvoy, Lex Neal, Garnett Weston, Walter DeLeon, Paul Jones, Jack Cunningham, and Ralph Ceder. Each contributed bits and pieces, but when the time came to assign final credit, only Weston and Cunningham were named onscreen. (Fields himself took a story credit under the pseudonym of Charles Bogle.) Weston wrote murder mysteries and horror films and was brought in to lend story and structure to the script. Cunningham was more of a comedy hand, having worked with Harold Lloyd and Douglas Fairbanks, and he concentrated on dialogue and bits of physical business.

When shooting began on April 18, the script (retitled *The Old Fashioned Way*) was talky and action-starved, an idea in search of a plot. Fields began improvising and rewriting on the set, something he had done in New York but never before in Hollywood. The subject matter was rich with possibilities, but a strong central character was needed to lend focus. Fields instinctively knew McGonigle—more than any screenwriter could—and understood the story would grow naturally from his efforts to keep his extended family together. McGonigle was no crook (as Jim Fulton had obviously been) but a man bent on survival in a hostile and unwelcoming world. Working out the particulars was a nightmare. Long stretches of dialogue between the various members of the company were shot and discarded. Fields made his own scenes unsure of where they would go in the film. "I am in a louse now," he reported to Phil Goodman on the tenth day of production. "We have the 17th author on it and just concluded our second week and no story has been written. I write my disconnected scenes in the morning and shoot them in the afternoon. It's Hell."

Directing *The Old Fashioned Way* was William Beaudine, a man not particularly known for his handling of comedy but something of a specialist at working with children. Included in the cast was Baby LeRoy—now two years of age—whose scripted activities were limited to a running gag in which he mistook the Great McGonigle for "Dada." Fields thought there was something more to be done with the child, and worked up a dinner scene in which the two were seated side by side. But playing such a scene would require more than the simple reaction shots the tiny thespian was used to contributing, and nobody was sure he was up to it. In order to put the baby under contract, Paramount had been required to get approval from a Los Angeles court. Then the agreement was submitted to the Board of Education for stipulations regarding his education, feeding, sleeping hours, and time before the camera. A teacher, Rachel Smith, was on the set at all times, and it was up to her to teach him his "piece" through play. However well or poorly he did, she enforced a strict limit of five consecutive minutes under the lights, making any scene of extended length a tedious job of work.

In the dinner scene, LeRoy was called upon to splash soup on the star, dip his pocket watch in molasses, and yank coarsely on his nose. Each of these actions was carefully rehearsed with Fields' stand-in, Murray Keever, taking the abuse. Then Fields would step in for the actual shot. Keever wasn't Fields, however, and Fields ofttimes engendered a different kind of reaction in the child. Taught to smear Keever's coat with pie, LeRoy repeated the action perfectly until Fields took the stand-in's place. Then, with film rolling, LeRoy grabbed a handful of custard and threw it in Fields' face. The finale of the scene, in Fields' conception, had McGonigle giving the kid a swift kick in the rear.

He was told not to do it, that it wouldn't be funny. Fields had contended with belligerent children before—most notably in *It's the Old Army Game*—but never had he retaliated in kind.* "The studio was in an uproar about that scene," said William Beaudine, who took a neutral position in the matter. "They said, 'You can't do that. People won't stand for it. You can't kick a kid.' Bill said, 'What the hell? It's what any ordinary human being would do. Look at what he's done to me.' " Harold Lloyd thought Fields' reasoning sound: "A lot of people would like to give troublesome children a swift kick. But none of us dares. When a child gets into mischief, who among us wouldn't want to do what Bill Fields did?" According to Fields, the shot had to be made twice because he kicked Baby LeRoy too far on the first attempt. As it appears in the film, the kick does send the child to the floor and the soundtrack is blooped to erase any sound of his landing. Tacked on is a reaction shot of the boy looking around with a big smile on his face, assuring the audience he had sustained no injury or discomfort. Fields objected to these last few frames, concerned they might kill the laugh, but a preview audience in Glendale erased any fears. "It gets," said Beaudine, "the biggest laugh in the picture."

With content in such short supply, *The Old Fashioned Way* required a certain amount of padding. Joe Morrison, a soloist with the George Olsen band, was permitted two songs, and the film laboriously encapsulated an entire performance of *The Drunkard,* an ancient melodrama that had become a hit with smart audiences at the Los Angeles Theatre Mart. Fields picked up several cast members from the Galt Bell production (which was performed in a music hall atmosphere with full olio) including Samuel Ethridge, Ruth Marion, and Jan Duggan, "The Bowery Nightingale," who played the pivotal role of Cleopatra Pepperday in the film. It was Duggan's nightly rendering of "Gathering Up the Sea Shells" that inspired a scene in the movie in which she sings for McGonigle and seems to go on forever. "Wonderful, wonderful," he says, finally cutting her off. "You make Jenny Lind sound like a mangy alley cat with asthma."

Fields, by necessity, improvised much of the dialogue and business surrounding *The Drunkard,* a feat that impressed scenarist Jack Cunningham no end. "He's got more natural feel for pungent line and spontaneous talk than anyone I've ever struck," Cunningham said admiringly. In his desperation, Fields looked anywhere for help, and at one point turned to John Coogan, an ex-vaudevillian who had gained national prominence as the father of actor

---

*Chaplin had played a similar scene in *The Pilgrim* (1922), but the willingness to boot a child was never an essential part of his character.

*The dinner scene in* The Old Fashioned Way *set the tone for all future encounters between Fields and LeRoy Weinbrenner, known professionally as Baby LeRoy.*

Jackie Coogan. "Dad went over," said Jackie, "and Bill said, 'I don't care what kind of deal you make with them, but I want you to direct this movie. These [guys] don't know what I'm trying to do.' Dad said, 'Bill, I want you to juggle. Just for 40 feet of film. I want people to see you actually doing it.' So Bill did four or five of his old tricks, stuff that other jugglers hadn't done before." And so the troubled making of *The Old Fashioned Way* resulted in Fields doing his original juggling act for one final performance, cigar boxes and all. He worked in some hat business, some ball juggling, some byplay with Tammany Young. At the age of fifty-four he still had his chops, and it was a glorious moment.

The ending, pieced together with string and sealing wax, showed the Great McGonigle learning that the rest of his tour has been canceled. With his beloved daughter about to be married to the socially prominent Morrison, he makes a hasty exit to save face, claiming a prestigious engagement in New York City to ensure her happiness. "Fields had played the buffoon all through the picture," Beaudine said. "The audience was expecting a funny twist to this scene too. And if Fields had made the slightest false step, the whole tragedy of his parting would have gone to pieces in a burst of laughter. But he didn't make that false step. He acted with the pathos of the true clown. He held his audience and conveyed to them the sadness of the old man's parting from the only person who meant anything in his life. That was a great bit of acting."

*The Old Fashioned Way* was completed on May 24, 1934, after thirty-two grueling days in production. Fields left immediately for the desert to recuperate, convinced beyond any doubt they had a dreadful picture on their hands. His contract with Paramount expired three days later.

The desert, to Fields, was a stretch of resort property along the base of the San Jacinto Mountains. Soboba Hot Springs was owned by John Althouse, a Los Angeles hotelier and candy merchant, and his formidable wife, Tillie. They leased the property in 1919 and developed it as a destination for Angelenos seeking the healing ministrations of the mineral springs. The water, according to an early brochure, had "a marked effect on the stomach and digestive organs, increasing the flow of saliva and gastric juices, and benefitting the appetite and general health."

During the 1920s, Soboba became a retreat for Hollywood stars, who would rent the rustic two-room cottages built of hollow tile and dip their pampered physiques in the sunken tubs of the famous bathhouse. At night, the kitchen rustled up food in the European tradition (John and Tillie both being German) and bootleg liquor imported from Kentucky. After exercising an option to buy the 320-acre ranch in 1929, the Althouses built a cluster of fourteen premium units on a rise overlooking the San Jacinto valley. They called it the Indian Village, and the new cottages were designed after the native architecture of Mexico and the Southwest. Each had a different design and was named for a particular Indian tribe—Siwash, Paiute, Maricopa, Hopi.

When Fields discovered the place in 1931, he wasn't so much interested in the waters as the wild grapevines that garnished the trails, the subtle music of the tumbling streams, the arid climate and year-round sun that baked the congestion from his lungs. Soboba had a nine-hole golf course, presided over by a stocky Indian pro known as Lubo. The springs were adjacent to the Soboba Indian Reservation, and the resort was staffed with a combination of Filipino and Indian workers. The reservation was anything but prosperous, yet Fields learned early on that liquor was more highly prized among the natives than money. The Indians were supposed to run dry, so Fields took to tipping them with the little single-serving bottles of scotch that were made to be sold on trains. He would arrive at the springs with flats of them. "Fields was always very kind to Lubo," said Steve Fairfield, who, as a kid, hung around the pro shack and occasionally caddied for Fields. "I remember one day when Fields came in. He said, 'Good morning, Lubo.' Then he tipped his ever-present straw hat. Lubo reached up and, from the top of Fields' head, removed a railroad-size bottle of scotch. He said, 'Thank you, Mr. Fields, for saving my life this morning.'"

The drive out to Soboba was a rigorous four-hour trek over a two-lane highway, out California Route 60 past Riverside and then south at Beaumont on Route 79, past Gilman Hot Springs—the Jewish resort*—and up the circular driveway that led to the main building. A dining room on the second level afforded a spectacular view of the valley, and, across the road, a landing strip awaited private planes. Fields loved Soboba because the Indians weren't celebrity-struck and the townspeople in nearby San Jacinto were mostly farmers and ranchers. His routine every morning was to rise early and make the two-mile walk into town, where he'd buy the *Riverside Enterprise,* sit on the curb, and wait for the barber shop to open. He'd get a shave, have breakfast, and be back on the grounds by ten.

The golf course was rarely crowded, and he always got preferential treatment. "Between my friend Albert Collins and myself, Fields would pay us one dollar for shagging a five-gallon pail full of balls," Fairfield remembered. "He stood up on number one green and teed off across Soboba Road onto the airstrip. He would spend an hour or two driving the balls and he was really— I'm sure—aiming at us. Fields, to my mind, was a wonderful golfer. He could put that ball just about any place that he wanted. We had to keep on the move so as not to become a good target for him."

It was in 1934 that Fields arrived at Soboba with a new girl in tow. Carlotta Monti was a raven-haired beauty in her late twenties, a sometime actress and model who played ethnic bits in films like *Deadwood Pass* and *King Kong.* She was discovered by Fred Niblo, a film director who had formerly done a patter act in vaudeville. (When Fields played Koster and Bial's in the summer of 1900, Niblo was on the bill.) Carlotta had a part in Niblo's production of *Ben-Hur,* and by 1931 was registered with Central Casting. "She loved attention," said actress Rosita Del Mar, who met her on a set at MGM that year, "and she loved to shock people with her audacity. She told everyone she planned to marry a 'rich old man' because he would die and she would be rich while she was still young. She was very proud of that plan."

In 1931, of course, Fields was just fifty-one and struggling to find work. Being neither old nor particularly rich, he was not on Carlotta's radar. How he came to her attention three years later is a matter of conjecture, for she told conflicting stories in interviews and in a memoir she wrote. Supposedly, she posed in a set of stills with him around the time of *Million Dollar Legs,* but none of the photos has ever turned up. She also credited the writer Gene Towne

---

*Althouse had a discreet way of observing the registration of a new guest, and if the name Liebermann, for instance, ended in one "n" instead of two, he would helpfully mention that good kosher food was served down the road.

with delivering her to Fields' doorstep, but Towne was never particularly close to Fields, so it is unlikely he would have been used to make such a procurement. It is far more probable that she met him through his friend Niblo, though she was also supposedly involved with William Le Baron for a time. In her sworn testimony before the Los Angeles Superior Court in 1949, she said she began "working" for Fields in 1934—two years later than her book would have it— and that date appears to be accurate.

Fields' love life was in a state of flux that spring, with Gracie still around— alternately threatening to leave town and stopping by at all hours demanding to see him—and Linelle Blackburn writing from Texas to say that she might marry an army officer and abandon the country for good. Gracie did leave, returning to New York and Long Island City, though keeping in touch for a considerable time. Fields squired around starlets like Judith Allen (who, by her

*Carlotta Monti*

own admission, dated many of the men with whom she worked) and Marion Ladd, who, for a brief time, was under contract to Fox. Carlotta fell into this group, but she had tenacity and wit and apparently decided that Fields, by 1934, was indeed the rich old man for whom she had been looking.

It wasn't long, however, before Carlotta learned that Fields could be tight with a buck. It wasn't so much that he was cheap, but Fields was always on the lookout for the scam, the con, the flimflam. Hollywood was full of predatory types, and he wasn't about to be played for a sucker. Keeping a tight grip on his poke always kept him in control. "Bill," said Joe Mankiewicz, "was almost psychotic about money." The same was true of most comedians, Eddie Sutherland observed, and he once worked up the nerve to ask Fields exactly why. "Well," Fields told him, "most of us are not very good looking, and we like girls like everybody else, and we need a little money to be able to buy the necessities for the ladies and ourselves. Also, we guys who are funny men, comedians, think we give enough of ourselves by just being funny."

Yet, protestations to the contrary, Fields could be a soft touch when he reckoned that somebody was truly in need. "All you had to do was go to him," said Harry Caplan, a prop man at Paramount, "and say so-and-so is in the hospital, or his wife has had a baby, or something in which money was involved, and Bill would say, 'Don't tell 'em who did it—find out the doctor and I'll take care of the bill.' He was generous to a fault there." Out at Soboba, Steve Fairfield was at the caddy bench one morning when Fields ambled into the pro shack to give Lubo his tip. "He was a little more serious and dignified than usual," said Fairfield. "He said, 'Lubo, I went out to the reservation yesterday to watch the kids play ball. They had a two-by-four whittled down for a bat, and the ball was a roll of tape wrapped around a ball of twine. No one had a glove of any kind.' Then he said, 'Lubo, here's some money. I want you to go over to town, buy balls, bats, a catcher's mitt, a pitcher's glove, and take them out to the reservation and give them to the kids. And Lubo, if you ever tell a soul I did this, first I'll never supply you with any more booze. And you never know. Sometimes I'm a dangerous man. I might even kill you.' " Said Magda Michael, the woman who would shortly become his devoted secretary, "If you met him halfway and gave no evidence of trying to put something over on him, he was really a prince of a man."

Despite the chaos under which it was made, *The Old Fashioned Way* turned out better than anyone expected. It previewed to screams from an overflow crowd at the Alexander Theatre in Glendale, and the inclusion of the juggling act sparked a flurry of letters from boys who were enchanted by the ancient art and inspired to become jugglers themselves. Fields answered them all, telling them he was glad for their interest. "It's a bunch of fun," he advised one boy, going on to tell him how he could buy a book on the subject at a local bookstore.

*The Old Fashioned Way* had a sock opening in Los Angeles, bettering the theater's previous attraction by a considerable bit. It had a tougher time in New York, where the papers were nonetheless beginning to recognize a following. "The great man, the omnipotent oom of one of the screen's most devoted cults, brings with him some new treasures," Andre Sennwald averred, "as well as a somewhat alarming collection of wheezes which, ten years ago in the vaudeville tank towns, must have seemed not long for this world. But somehow when Mr. Fields, in his necessary search for comic business, is forced to strike up a nodding acquaintance with vintage gags, they seem to become almost young again. There have been funnier Fields pictures, but the master himself, with his borrowed cigar, patrician cane, and medicine show clothes, is so much greater than his material that scarcely anything in which he appears can afford to be ignored by students of humor."

The picture finished the job *You're Telling Me!* began by proving that Fields could sustain a line of films in which he was top-billed and present in most every scene. Will Rogers, in his weekly newspaper column, hailed the fact that Fields had at last come into his own as one of the great comedians of the time. "He is going like a house afire, and how he deserves it, for he has had the training." Paramount picked up the option on Fields' contract, setting him to appear in a remake of *Mrs. Wiggs of the Cabbage Patch.* Fields wasn't happy with the assignment, knowing he would be billed second in the cast and confined to the last third of the story, and he signaled his dissatisfaction by joining hands with Bing Crosby, Gene Fowler, Jim Tully, and Mack Sennett in a scheme to make feature pictures on an independent basis. Nothing came of the plan, but it did set Charlie Beyer to work on extorting a new contract from Paramount, something Fields had been angling for since the completion of *Six of a Kind.* ("I haven't made a new deal with Paramount yet," he had advised Loyd Wright in a January letter, "but I know everything is going to be O.K. as there are several companies bidding for me here and one or two in Europe, and as soon as I knuckle down to one of them, I'll need you and need you badly.") The deal memo drafted by Beyer endorsed a drop in Fields' weekly rate in exchange for guaranteeing a straight fifty-two weeks of employment instead of the usual forty. Manny Cohen rejected the proposal, insisting that Fields work out the option period as contracted, and Fields punished Beyer by trimming his commission. "Almost everyone I know in the motion picture business in the important money pay no more than five per cent commission," he said in a terse note. "I am going into the extra heavy elusive from now on. So what?"

Paramount was on a new course, returning to profitability under Cohen's determined leadership. He was able to cut production costs by $5 million during his first year at the helm, and managed to produce a full slate of pictures without a dime of outside capital. He rid the company of George Bancroft, Nancy Carroll, Clive Brook, and Tallulah Bankhead—high-priced stars who were no longer pulling their weight at the box office—and took care of proven attractions like Marlene Dietrich, Gary Cooper, Claudette Colbert, and Sylvia Sydney. He also brought along such up-and-comers as Mae West, Bing Crosby, and Cary Grant. Even so, he was an object of fun, a production executive with virtually no experience in production whatsoever. "He was strictly a newsreel editor, great with a pair of scissors," said Eugene Zukor. "He could deliver you a story out of a batch of film that would be very striking and important." He was also, like Al Kaufman, quite short in stature. "He was about four feet tall," said Sidney Salkow, who worked as an assistant to producer Barney Glazer. "When he sat at his desk, he disappeared behind it." Fields enjoyed tweaking Cohen's various pretensions, not the least of which was his fondness for big cigars. At a party thrown at Cohen's home for Gary Cooper, Fields was prevailed upon to perform, something he hated doing at social gatherings. Cohen had a table stacked with a dozen boxes of imported cigars, and Fields scooped them up as if he were back onstage at the Orpheum. "I'll only use the sealed boxes," he assured his host, deftly removing the pins in the process. He then reprised his cigar box specialty, with Cohen watching in horror as the boxes flipped open and his precious Havanas were flung about the room.

It was Cohen who wanted Fields to do *Mrs. Wiggs* as box office insurance, for its star, Pauline Lord, had never before appeared in a picture. She was revered on the New York stage, where she had starred in O'Neill's *Anna Christie* and *Strange Interlude,* but she was completely unknown to movie audiences, despite the fact that it was considered something of a coup to have landed her for the part. The story, derived from Alice Hegan Rice's 1901 novel and a subsequent play of the same title, had already been filmed twice. Paramount made the 1919 version with actress Mary Carr (who had created the role onstage), and, with the rights already in hand, a talking version had first been contemplated under the Schulberg regime. Filming got underway on July 9, 1934, with Fields playing Mr. Stubbins, the homely old tramp who comes to the Cabbage Patch with designs on Miss Hazy. Doing the film was a painful trade-off for Fields, for he loathed the material and considered the entire enterprise detrimental to his career. On location at Lasky Mesa, where a small grouping of shacks had been built, the accommodations were unpleasant and downright rustic. "There were no honey wagons in those days," said Ed Montagne, an assistant director on the film. "They'd go out and dig one hole for the cast and two holes for the rest of the crew. Consequently, when people had to relieve themselves, they weren't too particular about where."

Fields stayed mostly in his tent, a canvas dressing room with a cot and an end table, drinking and stewing. The children in the cast were warned about rattlesnakes and ordered not to wander far from the set. An open tent served as a schoolroom for the five young actors, their stand-ins, ten mothers, and a couple of teachers. "I was on my way to the school tent," remembered Edith Fellows. "I was passing a dressing room when I heard a voice call, 'Little girl, come here.' It was W.C. He told me about danger and possible death if a rattlesnake bit me. He said he wanted to give me some medicine that would protect me. He poured something into a small Dixie cup. It looked like water. I took a drink and I screamed. It burned my mouth. I ran out of the tent to my school teacher and told her what happened. She went to W.C.'s tent and let him have it. She asked what he had given me. He said, 'Gin! The snakes couldn't hurt the child!' The teacher didn't buy, and warned him to stay away from the children except when in a scene."

Fields knew he was behaving badly on *Mrs. Wiggs* and didn't care. He made a great show of his drinking, something he always did when he wished to express his utter contempt for something. "[He] was always fried before noon," said Evelyn Venable, who played Lucy Olcott in the film. "When we started shooting at 8:00 a.m., he had his drink already half-gone." Filming ceased momentarily to service the equipment, and when the soundman hollered, "Sound reloading!" Fields, off to one side with Tammany Young, took an exaggerated sip from a tall glass and called out, "Fields reloading!"

"He was a very strange man," said Fellows. "The kids on the film were a little afraid of him. His *nose* alone was frightening." Fields had endured surgery on his nose to relieve a sinus condition, requiring much of the cartilage to be removed in the process. The procedure caused it to lose definition and appear far rounder than it had before. Coupled with the roasting it took at Soboba (despite a generous dusting of foot powder) it came to resemble, in the words of Kenneth Tynan, "a doughnut pickled in vinegar." According to Carmencita Johnson, who at the age of eleven was playing Asia, the eldest of the Wiggs girls, Fields was much nicer after the scolding he caught from the teacher.

We had box lunches, which we loved and the parents hated, and one day I got a slice of cantaloupe, which was a great treat then. I can remember saying to my mother, "When I'm grown up and rich, I'm going to buy you all the cantaloupe you want." It was hot as heck that summer, and [Tammany Young] said, "Who's the little girl that likes cantaloupe?" I said "Me" and he said, "Come with me, please, Mr. Fields wants to see you." So I walked out obediently. I had no idea what was going to happen; he never talked to us on the set. I followed him into this trailer, and Fields had his back turned to me. He was sitting in front of the dressing table. He said, "Take as many as you somewhat amused by the unexpected eruption. "I have a feeling I could have blackmailed Bill Fields merely by knowing he had a son named after him."

Not only did audiences know W. C. Fields by the latter days of 1934, they had a strong perception of his character as well. He was expected to be brow-beaten and gruff in his modern persona, effusive and crooked in period garb. His voice had the range and distinction of an antique pipe organ, and he used it to best advantage when wrapping it around a ten-dollar word or a surname he recalled from his Philadelphia childhood. Linguistically, he showed the patterns of the Philadelphia dialect, though his private speech was devoid of the volume and flourishes that made him one of the most imitated of personalities.* The way he spoke on camera was Victorian and mannered, and he seemed to have an infallible sense of what sounded funny. " 'Charley Bogle,' spoken slowly and solemnly with a very long 'o,' is a laugh. 'George Beebe' is not funny, but 'Doctor Beebe' is. The expression 'You big Swede' is not good for a laugh, but 'You big Polack' goes big. . . . Usually towns that have a 'ville' on the end of the name—like Jonesville—are not to be taken seriously, while those that begin with 'Saint' cannot be joked about. But will you tell me why St. Louis goes well in a gag and Louisville does not?"

He was proud of the fact that the preposterous names he employed in his work—a habit he cheerfully appropriated from Dickens—were nearly always real. "Every one of them is an actual name that I have seen somewhere. I think they're funny and remember them." The name "Prettiwillie," for example, was on a lumber yard outside of Detroit. "Peppitone" was a dentist in Washington, D.C. Charley Bogle and Dr. Beebe were bootleggers in upstate New York. "Posthlewhistle" (as in Messrs. Posthlewhistle and Smunn) was discovered in England. "Almost the entire population of the village of Barrow-in-Furness is named Posthlewhistle." Chester Snavely was an undertaker in a small Pennsylvania town. Junk and Limberger were lawyers he used in Germany. "Fuchswanz" and "Muckle" were neighbors of the Dukenfield family and can be found in U.S. Census records.

Booze had not yet become an integral part of the act, but Fields made such bald-faced exaggerations in print that he was widely thought to have an unlimited capacity. "I'm an advocate of moderation," he told Jack Grant in *Movie Classic* magazine. "For example, I never drink before breakfast. During the

---

*"Fields is a Philadelphian in his dialect pattern," according to Dr. William Labov, a linguist at the University of Pennsylvania. "This shows up clearly in two crucial features: The vowel of *caught, hawk, off, lost,* etc., is an 'upper mid ingliding' vowel in Philadelphia, as in New York. Fields does not have the New York City r-lessness or short -a pattern. Also, the post-vocalic /r/ is consistently pronounced. There is almost no trace of the British vocalization of /r/ in stressed vowels. Fields' use of /r/ is characteristic of Philadelphia."

*Fields improvised his introduction in* Mrs. Wiggs of the Cabbage Patch *by getting himself tangled in a wire fence.*

want," and he pointed to this big washtub, filled with ice and piled high with cantaloupes. I took just one, because I was very well behaved, said, "Thank you," and went out. That was a really sweet thing for him to do.

Director Norman Taurog, a recent recipient of an Academy Award, found Fields cooperative but distant and allowed him to do largely as he pleased. Ed Montagne witnessed the shooting of Stubbins' introduction:

[Fields] went to the prop man and said, "Build me a three-strand wire fence here," pointing it out. "And make me a kite out of newspaper." My memory is that he wanted a dead horse blocking his path, but the prop man wouldn't have had that. (Normally prop boxes had everything in those days.) Norman just started the camera on his feet as he walked, tilted up, and here comes this figure, who sees this unpleasant whatever it is, sniffs, walks around it, and starts to climb through this fence. And, of course, that was five minutes between the cane getting caught in the fence, the hat coming off and his picking up the hat, and his finally getting through the fence only to have the kid run through with the kite and get him tangled up in the kite. This was all improvised on the spot.

Making her film debut at the age of forty-four, Pauline Lord was overwhelmed by the mechanics of moviemaking. She was nervous and fidgety and needed idiot boards to remember her lines. "Norman," Montagne said, "had to nurse her along." Fields was required to play just one exchange with her, confining the bulk of his participation to an extended kitchen scene with actress ZaSu Pitts. Lord's understated work as Mrs. Wiggs helped take the curse off the antique sentiment of the play, with its squalid poverty and consumptive children, but she made just one more film before returning to the relative comfort and security of the stage. *Mrs. Wiggs of the Cabbage Patch* played badly in a preview at Westwood Village and was sent back to the studio for trims and additions. It was released in October 1934 to surprisingly good notices, but when Jim Tully wrote the following month to tell Fields that he and his wife had seen the film, Fields was anything but happy about it. "I feel very ashamed that you and Myrtle saw me in *Mrs. Wiggs,*" he replied. "I saw it for the first time a few nights ago in North Hollywood, but when I came on the screen I stunk so badly the police came in with the impression that someone had been throwing stink bombs around. Fortunately, I had my false moustache with me. I turned up the collar of my greatcoat and did a 'vanishing lady' before I was discovered."

*Nineteen*

# It's a Gift

Of all the movies Fields made for Paramount, he was the most proprietary about *It's a Gift.* It was a remake of *It's the Old Army Game* and, as such, contained more personally authored material than any of his previous features. At its core, of course, were the *Comic Supplement* scenes he had crafted and honed and performed in the *Follies,* but where some—such as "The Sleeping Porch"— had worked beautifully on the New York stage, they fell flat when translated to film. The missing element was synchronous sound, and Fields was finally in a position to do them correctly. "If I flop now," he said, "it'll be my own fault, and I'll have no kick coming."

He also had the advantage of being better known to moviegoers. *Photoplay* ran a profile in January 1934—his first appearance in a fan magazine since 1927—and multipart biographies were in the works for both *Screenland* and the *New Yorker.* He took some of these interviews quite seriously (he spent a good deal of time with Alva Johnston on the *New Yorker* series), but most were done solely for their entertainment value, and, under such circumstances, Fields never let the truth stand in the way of a good story. He gave streamlined accounts of his running away from home, keeping the action broad and comic and making an ogre of his late father. Yet he rarely mentioned his mother, for whom he had only the tenderest of memories, and never spoke at all of his uncle or grandmother, two of the most influential people in his life.

There was a suspicion among journalists that Fields had been married at some point, but he steadfastly refused all comment on the subject. He told Max Eastman he would never try to make love funny. "I was in love once myself and that's too painful—that's too painful!" Joe Mankiewicz once said to him, "You know, Bill, there was a fellow in my English class at college who sat two rows in front of me. His name was W. C. Fields, Jr. Now, that's quite a coincidence. That must be a relative." Fields said, "Relative???" His face went bright red and he let loose with a stinging volley of obscenities, capping the tirade with the words, "That was my son!" Mankiewicz was taken aback, both shocked and

morning, I have 15 or 20 highballs. Then comes lunch. But I don't eat lunch. Bad for the waistline. I drink it instead—oh say, a gallon of cocktails. In the afternoon, which is longer than the morning, I have possibly 30 or 40 highballs. With dinner, I have ten or twelve bottles of wine or something to drink. In the evening, I like a case of sherry or maybe 50 to 60 highballs." A more reliable account of Fields' drinking came in 1951 from Norman McLeod. "After breakfast he downed a solid glass of bourbon with one-half inch of water in it," he told columnist Ezra Goodman. "He said he didn't want to discolor the bourbon. He had four or five of these until noon. He drank on the set. He was one of the few actors I knew of who was allowed to drink on the set. Then he had lunch. After lunch—he always ate big meals—he began imbibing again at 2:30. He would have four or five more bourbons until 5 p.m. At 5 p.m. he started on martinis. He'd have five or six martinis—he made a very good martini—before dinner. He was never drunk unless he consumed liquor after dinner. If he did, he went back to bourbon."

*It's a Gift* started out as a costlier proposition than any of the previous Fields vehicles. To begin with, Paramount only held silent-picture rights to *The Comic Supplement,* and a new deal had to be struck with Joe McEvoy. The $15,000 purchase of the talking-picture rights was finalized on June 25, 1934, and Fields went to work massaging the *Supplement* into a new eleven-page story outline to which he affixed the title *Back Porch.* "The opening scene is in a grocery store," he began, laying the groundwork. "I own the store. I have a wife and a young daughter, about 17 years of age (Joan Marsh type) and a younger daughter (about the age of Shirley Temple). A little boy is never so funny with me as a little girl. I can't explain very well why. The little girl is annoying the father all the way through, and the wife is the type that is bullying me all the time." He went on to detail an elaborate gag in which a blind man, Mr. Muckle, lays waste to the store while his character, Mr. Fliverton, attempts to wait on a customer. Muckle enters, poking his cane through the glass window. As Fliverton tries to seat him, Muckle steps in a basket of eggs. "Now this guy is a son of a bitch. He'll ruin something else. I'm trying to be kind to him." The blind man ambles out of the store after ruining $100 worth of stock, disgruntled that Fliverton can't split a box of cough drops. And Fliverton loses a $78 sale from the frustrated man at the counter. "I think this should be funny," Fields concluded. "Should give me some sympathy. Anything else we get in it is gravy. I have many more gags that will fit."

Next came the "Back Porch" scene, which he thought "really was awful" in the first film. "This is where a baby works. I feel Shirley Temple wouldn't hit me over the head. She's a little too old, but a baby would. So have Baby LeRoy in

*Director Norman McLeod sketched Fields
and Baby LeRoy in his trademark
stick-figure style.*

this sequence." At the end of the porch business, Fliverton gets a letter telling
him an uncle has died in California. The estate is valued at $6,482.10 and it's all
been left to him. "My wife comes out and gets the good news, and, as in everything else, *she* decides what we will do." They load up the car—incorporating
gags from both "The Family Ford" and "The Sport Model"—and the rest of
the film is a road picture. At nightfall, they pass a campground, and Fliverton
attempts a U-turn. "Cars are blowing their horns and I am ultimately caught in
a whole pack of cars, and the wife and I are very embarrassed. The only natural thing to do is fight with each other. It's unfortunate and you feel sorry for
the poor sons of bitches and their wives who get caught that way."

They pass through Philadelphia (in slow motion), Pittsburgh (it's black
outside), and Chicago, where the wife wants to stop and buy herself a spool of
cotton. At an Indian village, they get caught up in a marathon. Fliverton thinks
it's an Indian attack and pulls out his gun, opening fire. "My family is rather
proud of me as a warrior, and my daughter says, 'Remember how we laughed at
Pop and thought he was lying when he told us that he was in the Army and the
Captain once came to him and gave him a week's holiday, saying, 'You killed
enough men last week. You don't have to fight next week!' I make some remark
to the effect of, 'Some day you folks are going to appreciate me!' " Finally

reaching California, the Flivertons play out the picnic scene on the lawn of a Pasadena estate as debutantes and liveried servants look on. When Fliverton gets his inheritance money, he buys a new Ford just as the old one collapses. Fields concludes the outline with a disclaimer: "Of course, you'll see that there are no details or attempt made to build up the boy and girl or any of the scenes. It is merely to give you a very vague idea of what it's all about."

The outline was turned over to a set of writers and gag men, the order of which has been lost over time. The screenplay is credited to Jack Cunningham, but, according to studio records, contributors included Garnett Weston, Claude Binyon, *Follies* veteran Paul Gerard Smith, and the amazingly prolific Howard J. Green, who authored comedies, plays, vaudeville acts, and grim social dramas like *I Am a Fugitive from a Chain Gang.* Conferences ensued with both Fields and Le Baron, and the result was a thirty-nine-page treatment that expertly fleshed out the scenes Fields had proposed, attaching dialogue that, to a considerable extent, is heard in the finished film. The structure of the family unit remained as Fields dictated, but his character evolved somewhat from the passive-aggressive Fliverton to the more benign Harold Bissonette.* A shaving scene, first performed in *The Potters,* was added. The grocery scene with the blind man was embellished with both dialogue and business. (The impatient customer is trying to buy ten pounds of granulated sugar and an order of kumquats, and Harold can never seem to get to him.) A wild car chase came next, Harold rushing a woman to the maternity hospital in the mistaken belief she is about to have a baby. The noisy porch scene followed, with every interruption meticulously detailed. Added was a man searching for a Carl LaFong—capital "L" small "A" capital "F" small "O" small "N" small "G"— and then trying to sell Harold an annuity. In classic McEvoy fashion, Bissonette explodes and repels him with a meat cleaver. The baby is brought in—he bonks Harold over the head with the cleaver—and then the parade of tradesmen begins—the vegetable man, the ice man, the scissor grinder. Harold disappears into the house and returns with his gun. It goes off, blowing a large hole in the ash can. He picks up a fly swatter, kills a fly, dozes off.

With the treatment having established (and filled in) the major comedy sequences, the buff script was completed in a matter of days. Jack Cunningham jettisoned the car chase, wrote parts for the girl and the boy, and authored the few connective scenes in which Fields did not appear. The eighty-six-page screenplay was ready for submission to the Breen Office on August 22. Fields seemed to be testing the new guardian of the Production Code when he

---

*Fields lifted the name from a man who golfed at Lakeside. The real Harold Bissonette pronounced it "Bisson-ette," which gave Fields the notion of having the snooty wife in the film pronounce it "Bisson-ay." It became a running gag.

inserted the old spray-and-dog gag into the script. A revision was submitted and passed on August 30. Five days later, on September 4, 1934, the cast and crew assembled on the interior set of the Bissonette store and rehearsals began.

Although the store sequence had been written out in considerable detail, Fields wanted to see how it would actually play on the set. With him were Tammany Young, actors Charles Sellon and Morgan Wallace, Jack Cunningham (who would be present throughout the shoot), and director Norman McLeod. Over the course of the morning they tightened the scene while adding bits of physical business. Then they adjourned to the exterior of the Bissonette store on the studio's New York street and repeated the process. No film got exposed until 2:00 p.m. A gag man was added the next day to make further suggestions. It was common at Paramount for the director of a major comedy or musical to have a gag man at his side. Le Baron usually budgeted for three on a Fields picture: one to work with the writers, and two to be present during shooting. For the store sequence in *Back Porch,* Fields retained Johnny Sinclair, the stunt double who had, back in 1927, saved his life. Sinclair still earned his living doing stunts, but also had work as a gag writer as a result of Fields' patronage. Good ideas were always valued, no matter where they came from. "He always tried to improve any gag he did," said Harry Caplan, who was one of the two prop men on the picture, "and he was very open to suggestions. In fact, any time I came up with an idea, I was rewarded with a hundred-dollar bill."

Fields worked his way through the next day of filming with Young and Morgan Wallace, the demanding customer with a taste for kumquats. They eliminated the order for granulated sugar, leaving Wallace to repeat the word "kumquats" with an ever-escalating tone of exasperation. Bissonette changes into his workday smock with Tam's dimwitted assistance, pausing to gaze longingly at an idyllic magazine picture of the "typical California orange grove." He turns his attention to Wallace, unwilling to admit that he has no kumquats. On the third day of production, Sellon, as Mr. Muckle, made his entrance, and progress slowed to a crawl. The entire morning was lost perfecting the shot in which Fields dashes toward the door as the blind man's cane comes poking through the glass. More time was lost as they refined the business of Muckle's stepping in the basket of eggs—a shot ultimately cut from the picture. The following day, still more time was lost replacing breakables and working out Fields' wrapping of the gum. Most of this action was not in the script.

The company was already behind on the fifth day of shooting. It took two hours to rehearse Muckle's exit from the store, in which a frantic knot of traffic threatens to flatten the old man. Still more time was lost as exteriors were shot with the Bissonette family—Kathleen Howard, Jean Rouverol, Shirley McClellan—and both Fields and McLeod came to the conclusion that they needed a boy instead of a girl for the role of the youngest Bissonette child. Nearly eight

*The Mr. Muckle scene in* It's a Gift *was dangerous in that it made a blind man the butt of the jokes. Fields got around the problem by writing the character as "a son of a bitch."*

hours of camera time would be lost discussing and interviewing children before settling on the precocious Tommy Bupp as McClellan's replacement. Actress Jane Withers responded to a cattle call on the Paramount lot and was rewarded with a small part in the film. "There were over one hundred children there," she remembered, "and I was one of the ones selected. Just really for extra work and atmosphere. When Mr. Fields first came on the set, he said, 'Oh, it's one of those days with children again.' That was the first thing I heard." As Bissonette approaches the store, he avoids the cracks in the sidewalk. The script called for a little girl to follow alongside him, and Fields was trying to make something more of the shot. Selecting Withers from a group of kids, he said, "Do you play hopscotch?"

> I said, "Well, I know how, but I don't play that often. But I can learn. What do you want me to do?" He said, "I want you to jump in front of me as I start to move. You're playing hopscotch, but I want you to jump right in front of me so I can't get past you." I said, "That's a cinch." He said, "Oh, you think so?" I said, "Yes, sir. It is. Would you like to try it?" So we did it. I kept jumping in front of him. He said, "Oh, that was fine, little girl, just fine. Do you think you could do it

again?" I said, "As many times as you like, sir." So we did it again, and then something happened—there was noise or something—and he went, "Oh—!" and said something appropriate. "I really liked that last take." I said, "Don't you worry about it. I can do it again. Honest I can." So we did it again and he said, "You know, little girl, that was even better than the first time." I said, "Well, we've had a little rehearsal." He said, "How old are you?" I said, "Seven and a half, sir. How old are you?"*

Baby LeRoy joined the company on the sixth day of filming, continuing the attack on Fields that had commenced five months earlier with *The Old Fashioned Way.* The image of Fields kicking the child was still fresh in the public mind, and their cinematic rematch was a hotly anticipated event. Although LeRoy would work only half a week on the picture (and collect just $30 for his efforts), he would receive second billing on the film, a circumstance that riled his costar. Fields regarded the infant as a useful prop, but Baby LeRoy cried a lot and Fields hated the tedium involved in the filming of his scenes. "I don't dare talk about the language he used off stage about the child," said Harry Caplan. "And the kid wasn't that bad. He was a little baby." Said Norman McLeod, "Fields had a phobia about the baby. He not only hated infants in general, but he believed that Baby LeRoy was stealing scenes from him. He hated that little [bastard]. He used to swear at the baby so much in front of the camera that I sometimes had to cut off the ends of the scenes in which they both appeared."

The shots with Baby LeRoy involved a certain amount of violence, but all the scripted action was tentative and dependent on what they could persuade him to do. The screenplay had him opening the spigot on a barrel of molasses, holding Fields off with a knife, pulling a crockery shelf down on his head. The company lost six hours shooting the equivalent of two and a half pages of unscripted dialogue, and when the slapstick worked out to no one's satisfaction, it ended on a quiet note with Bissonette exiting the store and posting a hastily lettered sign: Closed on Account of Molasses.

On the twelfth day of filming, the company rehearsed and lined up a new set. While Harold is shaving with a straight razor, the bathroom is invaded by his daughter Mildred. She brushes her teeth, combs her hair, and applies her makeup, completely oblivious to the fact that she's blocking the mirror. Harold

---

*The bit was cut from the film, but Fields remembered the little girl. When Jane Withers got her first starring picture the following year, he had a beautiful bouquet of roses delivered to the set.

tries to see around her, nearly cutting his throat in the process, and when she opens the medicine cabinet, he follows his image to one side, only to have it snatched away from him when she closes the door. Seventeen-year-old Jean Rouverol was making her first movie and was not very happy about it. Having been cast as Hermia in Max Reinhardt's production of *A Midsummer Night's Dream* at the Hollywood Bowl, she was plucked out of rehearsals to satisfy an obligation to Paramount Pictures.* "Here I am going from Shakespeare to this drunken vaudevillian," she said. "I wasn't sophisticated enough, or knowledgeable enough, or even smart enough to know that I was working with one of the great comic geniuses of the twentieth century."

Ironically, it was Rouverol's greenhorn status that helped put the scene across. Fields told her to simply do what she'd do normally and he'd be where he needed to be. "I did everything right because I was literally deadpan. I didn't know that I was playing comedy, and that what I was doing was laughable." The only direction she got was from Fields himself. "I think everybody maintained the fiction that Norman McLeod was the director. I think that Fields maintained the same fiction. But it was Fields who knew what he wanted and what was necessary to get it. I remember witnessing some of the shooting of that great scene in the grocery store with Mr. Muckle. He choreographed that."

The stress of shooting visibly affected Fields, who would sometimes break out in a rash during the course of production. Faced with the start of another workday, he would shamelessly procrastinate. "Fields would have his call at nine o'clock in the morning," said Ed Montagne. "Tammany Young would drive him. We'd be on the stage at nine, and about nine-thirty or quarter of ten, Fields would come on the lot in the car, Tammany driving him, and go to his dressing room. We'd sit for fifteen minutes, then Norman would say, 'You'd better see what's happening down there.' I'd call and Tammany would say, 'Well, we'll be there in a few minutes.' To make a long story short, they'd show up about eleven. Norman and Fields would have a few drinks. (He used to call it 'Pine Tar.') We'd get ready to shoot and it'd be lunchtime. We wouldn't get a shot until three."

*Back Porch* was scheduled for a total of twenty-seven camera days— fourteen in the studio and thirteen on location. The company shot in Glendora, Calabasas, and at Seventeenth and Oak Streets in Los Angeles, where the exterior of the Bissonette home stood. The scene in which the family trashes the lawn of a private estate was shot at Busch Gardens in Pasadena, where the former mansion of St. Louis brewer Adolphus Busch was frequently used for filming. The Busch location was plagued by clouds and bad weather, and with the

---

*She was replaced by the understudy, Olivia de Havilland.

*The shaving scene in* It's a Gift *was inspired by a similar bit in* The Potters.
*Fields improvised while actress Jean Rouverol played it straight.*

working out of new gags, the sequence took four long days to complete. Nearly three pages of dialogue were written on the set. "The thing that astonished me," said Jean Rouverol, "was the way Fields used to work. He always kept a thesaurus with him. He would sit in his chair, the script open in front of him, and thumb through the thesaurus looking for words. Those ad-libs of his— sometimes they were spontaneous, and sometimes they were as carefully crafted as a fine jewel."

Jean observed Fields at his most spontaneous when making the shot in which he drove the family car onto the lawn and into a replica of the Venus de Milo. Kathleen Howard's scripted line, "Goodness! You've broken that beauti- ful piece of statuary!" was to have been followed by Fields' response: "It's bro- ken already. Someone hit it before. Look at the arms." Said Rouverol, "He had a perfectly legitimate written line, and that's what we heard in rehearsal. But when we were actually rolling and she delivered her line, he said, 'She ran right in front of the car!' A wonderful line, and I swear we never heard it until that moment." Fields was at the peak of his improvisational powers, and many of his best lines came to him when the cameras were grinding. For the largely unscripted sequence in the store, they had Tommy Bupp run in to tell his pop the orange ranch he wanted to buy was no good. "We needed a line to put over just what the grocer felt about the orange grove," Jack Cunningham remembered. "We'd racked our brains for days, and couldn't get the right line. So they decided to shoot without it. Well, just as the director was about to yell 'Cut,' Bill the grocer says, as quietly and naturally as though he'd been that grocer all his life, 'I've got my heart set on it. I'm going through with it.' Sounds simple, doesn't it? Just what that grocer would have said. But the rest of us who were smart enough to learn our lessons at school were too dumb to figure it out."

When the time came to shoot the "Back Porch" sequence itself, the company was six days behind schedule and under pressure to pick up speed. "It was on that picture that they decided to use three cameras on intimate shots," Ed Montagne said. "Three cameras were not unusual on long shots—chases and that sort of thing—but for intimate shots we'd use three cameras like they did in television later. So we'd get the coverage on the scene and we wouldn't have to break it up." Originally, the plan was to build the back porch set—a three-story affair—on the Paramount lot in Hollywood, but Fields wanted to shoot the scene out at Lasky Mesa, where he could take his time developing the bit and not have the front office breathing down his neck. The ranch was quieter, too, and he wouldn't face the distractions he'd have at the studio. To offset the additional cost, McLeod cut a scene set at a gas station in Albuquerque in which the car gets put on a hoist and abandoned, leaving the Bissonette family stranded ten feet in the air.

On the twenty-fifth day of shooting, the title was officially changed to *It's a Gift.* Fields didn't particularly care for the title, a line spoken by Mae West in *She Done Him Wrong,* but had grown pragmatic about picking his battles. Twenty-eight days into production, the company lost yet another half day rigging the back porch set for gags. The script called for a coconut to roll down the stairs, one step at a time, "the effect of an amateur picking out a tune on a dull xylophone," and it was up to Harry Caplan to make it work. "I had the art director and the construction man groove the center of the stairs. And then I had to work out, when it made it to the second landing, how to make the turn. So I went to the cameraman and I said, 'Is it possible for you to set an angle so that I can get behind a post (and we'll make the post thicker than it is) and get a cue stick and, at a given point, hit the coconut and start it down to the next landing?' I drilled out all the meat and we put a certain amount of mercury in it. We practiced it, because we didn't want it to flop. We wanted it to roll nice and easy and even to hesitate. So we balanced the mercury and kept working on it until it was the way we wanted it, and then we plugged it up." After two successful takes, Fields got the idea to make the coconut teeter, and Caplan tied a thread around it in order to make it rock. The result, when assembled, was everything Fields felt it should be, and he pronounced it "a very fine scene."

*It's a Gift* closed on Thursday, October 11, seven days behind schedule and some $17,000 over budget. The next day, October 12, 1934, a minor item appeared on page seven of the *Hollywood Reporter:*

> "MICAWBER" GETS TO WORK
>
> Charles Laughton reports to M-G-M Monday to start work in the episodes of *David Copperfield* in which Mr. Micawber appears. On his clearance from the Selznick picture, he returns to Para[mount] for *Ruggles of Red Gap.*

The film version of *David Copperfield* had been in the works for nearly a year. Producer David O. Selznick had cherished the book as a child: "When most people were reading Frank Merriwell—which, believe it or not, I never read—I was reading *David Copperfield* and *Anna Karenina.*" Selznick abandoned the job of executive producer at RKO—a post he inherited from his predecessor William Le Baron—in early 1933 and joined Metro-Goldwyn-Mayer, where his father-in-law, Louis B. Mayer, was in charge of the studio. Even so, his dream of adapting the Dickens classic to the talking screen met with resistance. "I am sure that the opposition to filming *David Copperfield* was based largely upon the fact that both classics and costume pictures had been taboo in the industry for a long time."

To write the script, Selznick engaged Howard Estabrook (who had authored the screenplays for *The Virginian, Cimarron,* and *A Bill of Divorcement*) and put him to work on a complete structural digest of the book. In May, Selznick, claiming that he could not find a Betsey Trotwood, Uriah Heep, or Daniel Peggotty in Hollywood, traveled to England with Estabrook and director George Cukor to scout locations and consult with Dickens scholars. The trip resulted in the discovery of Freddie Bartholomew, who would play the part of the young David, as well as the engagement of novelist Hugh Walpole, vice president of the Dickens Society, to "edit" the dialogue and vaccinate the production against inevitable charges of Americanizing the text. In June, Estabrook compiled a summary of the principal characters, drawing descriptive lines from the book and making suggestions as to the casting of each, the plan being to populate the entire film with MGM contract players or free-lancers who could be placed under contract. The first choice for Wilkins Micawber, the man with "a certain condescending roll to his voice" who welcomes the young Copperfield into his home and his heart, was Charles

Laughton. One of the top British stars of the time, Laughton had recently finished *The Barretts of Wimpole Street* on the MGM lot. Others on Estabrook's shortlist (in order of preference) were George Robey, Lennox Pawle, Burton Churchill, Lynn Harding, Nigel Playfair, Nigel Bruce, and Cedric Hardwicke. Occupying the second position on Estabrook's list was the only American— W. C. Fields.

Fields had been considered for the role, but fell far outside the studio's casting parameters. Not only was he under contract to another studio, but he wasn't British either. Selznick had wired Mayer from London, anxious to confirm Laughton for the part of Micawber: "If Laughton unavailable for Micawber, might like W. C. Fields. Can we get him? To avoid necessity of trying Paramount, think we should get word to Fields direct, who would probably give eye tooth to play Micawber." Mayer wasn't enthusiastic about the idea, but the choice of Laughton never sat particularly well with Selznick and his advisors. "Charles Laughton as Micawber is a dangerous proposition," G. S. Marlowe wrote after reviewing a set of tests. "At his best, it would be Henry VIII all over again, besides he could never look the part. W. C. Fields—infinitely better." Laughton himself wasn't enthused with the assignment, either. "I didn't like the idea because I had vivid memories of my last attempt at a Dickens character, when I played Pickwick at the Haymarket Theatre, and literally cringed at the remembrance. Mr. Walpole himself said at first he didn't think I could do it, but he later changed his mind, and finally I weakly agreed to have a shot at it."

Laughton was announced as Micawber, but the subject of Fields, who was deep in the shooting of *It's a Gift,* was still in the air. By the time filming of *David Copperfield* began on September 17, 1934, Laughton was ill and reportedly confined to a hospital bed. Ten days into production, Selznick cabled New York, warning that he might not be able to deliver Laughton at all. "What I would like to know immediately is whether if it comes to issue, how much difference commercially would there be having W. C. Fields instead of Laughton? Of course, not certain we can obtain Fields, but am raising question in hope we could. Fields would probably make better Micawber, but we've always felt we required the one important name in cast in Laughton."

The consensus in New York was that Fields, on the strength of *You're Telling Me!* and *The Old Fashioned Way,* was more valuable in the domestic market, while Laughton was probably a bigger attraction in the United Kingdom. There was little star power in the remaining cast, with Lionel Barrymore, Edna May Oliver, Maureen O'Sullivan, and Roland Young (as Uriah Heep) being the most prominent.* "Charles Laughton looked wonderful," said

---

*The embargo on contract players from other studios was broken when Frank Lawton was borrowed from Universal to play the part of the elder David.

George Cukor. "He really didn't want to do it. He said, 'I'm not genial enough, I'm not right for it . . .' And they persuaded him to do it, David Selznick. And he really wasn't right for it." The actor finally went before the cameras on October 15, 1934. "We started the picture," he said, "but after the first day that Haymarket feeling came over me again, and I felt sure my Micawber would be worse than my Pickwick. Cukor agreed with me. So, hand in hand, Walpole, Cukor, and I approached Selznick, and told him our troubles. He insisted we should try another day, and after that it was worse, and I finally insisted that I be allowed to drop out." Everyone on the set could plainly see that Laughton wasn't fit for the role. "He was good at what he did," said Joseph Newman, the assistant director, "but he would have to go off behind the set and almost crack his head against the wall before he could do a scene." Selznick persuaded Laughton to work another day with Hugh Walpole, trying to get into the spirit of the thing, but the writing was very clearly on the wall. "Charles lost his confidence completely," said Elsa Lanchester, who was married to the actor and had a small part in the film. "The more he tried, the worse he felt he was."

Talks were quietly opened with Paramount, where Fields was scheduled to take part in *Mississippi* with Bing Crosby and Joan Bennett. At first, Selznick wanted Fields so badly that he was willing to close down production on *David Copperfield* and wait until February when Fields would be free to do it. The front office at Metro nixed that plan, however, and two alternates came briefly into the running: Walter Connolly, who was in the process of filming *Father Brown, Detective,* and Guy Kibbee, who was out of town on a promotional tour for Warner Bros. Then, at Fields' urging, Manny Cohen agreed to hold the start of *Mississippi* on the condition that MGM pick up Joan Bennett's salary for the seven days she would be left inactive, and that Fields be back on the Paramount lot no later than November 12 for the start of the new picture. The charge for two weeks' work would be $50,000.*

Fields had little time to contemplate the job; he had to report for fittings immediately and was told his head would have to be shaved (as Laughton's had been) to match the image of Micawber as laid forth in the book. He was horrified. Dickens himself had described the character as having "no more hair upon his head . . . than there is upon an egg," yet Fields told Selznick that Micawber had often been portrayed with hair and offered to produce such an illustration as proof. This was easier said than done, but Fields pored over numerous editions of Dickens until he finally found a picture of Micawber with a full head of hair. Faced with such stirring evidence, Selznick relented, and

---

*The terms of Fields' contract with Paramount called for an even split of any monies received by the studio for his services, above and beyond his weekly salary of $6,875. On *Copperfield,* his share of the excess amounted to some $18,000.

*Charles Laughton was MGM's first choice for Wilkins Micawber in* David Copperfield; *Laughton worked three days before relinquishing the role.*

*Fields was horrified at the prospect of having to shave his head for the part and played it with hair intact.*

Fields triumphantly pasted the picture in his scrapbook. There was also the issue of an accent. "He never attempted one," said Cukor. "He always spoke with a slightly bogus accent . . . so you would think that that was an English accent. . . . It wasn't American, it wasn't anything." Selznick, on his English journey, had dismissed the notion out of hand of using an American in the part. "We shouldn't dare," he said. "But, anyway, we don't want to." Fields wasn't English, but he was undeniably Dickensian. *David Copperfield* was a favorite book, and enough of Micawber had invaded him over time so that it became a perfect marriage of actor and role. "I've been playing Micawber all my life, under a lot of different names, and never knew it," he said. "He's the kind of guy who is always expecting something to turn up to help him out of his present difficulties, and is always having difficulties waiting for something to turn up. You know the type. Of course, this is the first time in my life I ever played a character part. . . . At first, I was a little wary about playing Micawber, but as soon as I got into the part, I knew it was made to order."

People who had heard stories of Fields' drinking and his irascible nature were surprised at the conscientious way he approached the role. "I have always admired the works of Dickens," he explained, "and decided not to take any liberties with his character. I studiously learned the dialogue and rehearsed it diligently."* Cukor found him amiable, modest, and hardworking, and Freddie Bartholomew, who was, at first, admittedly terrified of him, decided he wasn't so bad after all. "He would say something snide like, 'Tell me, son, are you a midget or am I overgrown?' Then he would smile and pat me on the head." One day during the shooting of the film, Fields lunched at the MGM commissary with Chico Marx and his daughter, Maxine. "To play Micawber has been my lifelong dream," he told the girl. "I can't believe my good luck. MGM trusts me with this part."

Apart from the traits they both obviously shared, Fields and Micawber were naturally funny characters, and Fields was able to embellish the role with the same bits of business he might have thrown into any of his other pictures. A shaving scene came to near-suicide as he took repeated, misdirected passes at his own throat, and a rooftop scene in which Micawber eludes his creditors gives him the opportunity to lose his hat on the tip of his cane. "He was charming to work with," said Cukor. "His suggestions and ad libs were always in character. There was a scene in which he had to sit at a desk writing, and he asked me if he could have a cup of tea on the desk. When he got agitated, he dipped his pen into the teacup instead of the inkwell. Another time, he was sitting on a high stool and asked for a wastepaper basket so he could get his feet stuck in it. Physically he wasn't quite right, wasn't bald as Dickens describes Micawber—but his spirit was perfect."

Just as Fields was winding up his work on *David Copperfield, It's a Gift* was previewed before a paying audience in Glendale. More than 133,000 feet of exposed film had been whittled down to 6,030 feet of surefire comedy. It was a cold Wednesday night, and the crowd was in a mood to laugh. "Fields runs riot in the grocery, manages with the aid of a blind man to wreck the place," the man from *Daily Variety* reported the next morning. "It has been a rule in pictures never to try for comedy through an infirmity or a physical defect. In this case, there's nothing about the man's blindness that will make the audience stop laughing. Norman McLeod has handled the situation so well that Charles Sellon, the sightless one, poking his cane through Fields' plate glass windows, is one of the picture's howls." The *Reporter,* which also had a reviewer present,

---

*He also relied on the use of cue cards, employing a man to walk ahead of him in traveling shots, just out of camera range, wearing a sandwich sign on which Micawber's lines had been printed.

called it "a gorgeous piece of nonsense" that would stand by itself in every class house. "Some of the material is superannuated, but Fields, adroitly as usual, wrings every last laugh out of it, stuff you haven't laughed at in years."

Though buoyed by the response, Fields was dog-tired from two months of constant filming. Producer Arthur Hornblow Jr. promised him a week off before the start of *Mississippi,* and Fields used the time to contract a bad cold. The start date had to be pushed back a second time, and Fields didn't actually begin work on the film until November 27, 1934. *Mississippi* was a period musical based on a twice-filmed play by Booth Tarkington. Fields was to be top-billed, but the story actually revolved around the exploits of a young easterner in the antebellum South. The role of Tom Grayson had been written for Lanny Ross, a radio tenor who had come to national prominence as the featured singing star of the Maxwell House *Show Boat.* Ross had a five-year deal with Paramount, but he didn't have the presence onscreen that he had on radio, and after two pictures he bolted. Bing Crosby was substituted, dropping Fields back to second position in billing but bolstering the film's overall appeal at the box office.

Fields didn't like *Mississippi,* even though the part of Commodore Orlando Jackson was the closest he'd ever come to playing Cap'n Andy on screen. After commissioning treatments from both Dore Schary and librettist Herbert Fields, Hornblow had a screenplay drafted by Francis Martin that was subsequently revised by five additional writers in a futile attempt to make Fields happy. Crosby's addition to the cast complicated the job, and shooting began with absolutely no concurrence from anyone as to content or balance. Fields took his anger out on the producer. "He was a mean man," Hornblow later said of him. "He was difficult to work with. There was nothing funny about him as a human being. He was ill-tempered [and] drank much too much. But one's respect for his talent was so enormous that it all didn't seem to matter very much."

As Fields struggled with *Mississippi,* his confidence in his work on *David Copperfield* seemed to ebb. The film was being readied for previews, yet there was no word from Selznick or the brass at Metro, and rumors were that the picture was much too long for general release. Selznick floated the idea of distributing it in two parts, but there wasn't much enthusiasm for the idea. "I hope I have done a good job as Micawber," Fields said in a note to Elise Cavanna, "but I doubt it very much. Trying to memorize early pedantic English, got that stuff in the neck, which I hope will not show in the picture." As 1934 drew to a close, Paramount was estimating profits of $5 million on the strength of better pictures and lower production costs. Mae West was still their top draw, but Crosby was gaining on her, as were Gary Cooper, Claudette Colbert, and now

Fields as well. Will Rogers and Eddie Cantor were still the biggest of all comedy stars, but neither was doing the sheer volume of movie work that Fields was taking on. Since January, he had filmed *You're Telling Me!*, *The Old Fashioned Way*, *Mrs. Wiggs of the Cabbage Patch*, *It's a Gift*, and *David Copperfield*, and was in the process of making—and largely ad-libbing—*Mississippi*. The cumulative effect of all this exposure would be to drive him to the top ranks of screen comedians in 1935, but it would come at a terrible price.

*Twenty*

# Swan Song

Fields might have lived on Toluca Lake indefinitely had it not been for the swans. He liked the tranquility and the sense of community, but by golfing into the water as he did, he led the mute swans to believe they were under attack. Territorial and ill-tempered, they retaliated by waddling up on shore and driving him back into his house. Fields tried feeding the birds, as he did the ducks, but that didn't work, and it got so he could go into his backyard only at his own peril. One great bird, who seemed to be the ringleader, had a wingspan seven feet across and quills as thick as pencils.* "The swan was a killer," said Bert Wheeler, who lived around the corner. "We all knew about it. Fields had been out shooting mud hens out there one day, and he was trying to collect them, and this swan came at him in the canoe, and Fields took a swipe at the swan with his paddle and fell over. Boy, this swan nearly killed him."

Joe Mankiewicz didn't know of Fields' history with the swans when he rented Charles Farrell's house on the lake.

> I was awakened one morning about 2:30 by the damnedest noise I had ever heard in my life. It sounded like the bombardment of Rotterdam. All this beating and screaming and language and thrashing around wasn't far from me, so I looked out the window and all I could make out was a kind of feathered riot—these enormous swan wings beating on somebody and somebody beating back with a golf club—and I could see vaguely that Bill had taken on these two swans. He had drank himself a good dinner someplace, and he was out there with a golf club. Then the phone rang, and it was Bing Crosby, who lived down at the end of Toluca Lake Avenue. I said, "Well Bing, Fields is out there beating the hell out of these swans with a golf club, and I

---

*Boris Karloff, who also lived on the lake, named the swan "Edgar" after the famous London store, Swan and Edgar.

can't tell who's winning." Bing said, "What kind of club is it? Can you see?" I said, "I don't know. It's an iron—maybe a four iron or a five iron." And Bing said, "Tell him he's over-clubbed!" and hung up. I grabbed a tennis racket and went down there, but by the time I got there, the swans had retreated and Fields was a mess.

It wasn't long afterward that Bert Wheeler met producer Milton Bren for breakfast at the Hollywood Brown Derby: "He was white, he was so mad. I

*The swans on Toluca Lake ultimately drove Fields from his home.*

said, 'What's the matter?' He said, 'A terrible thing happened this morning. I went out to see W. C. Fields today. Got there about nine o'clock in the morning. He had a big bottle of whiskey out in the back yard, and we're drinking out there—he is—and all of a sudden a swan came up out of the lake. And Fields got a baseball bat and hit the swan over the head!' I started to laugh right away, but Bren says, 'I told him, Mr. Fields, that's the worst thing I've ever seen in my life. So Fields says, 'Well, I told that so-and-so to keep off my property!' "

When the lease was up, in the spring of 1934, Fields was ready to move. He put the house on a month-to-month and began looking for a place to build. "I want to put on my rompers and play," he said. He liked the San Fernando valley, where it was warmer, quieter, and farther from the studio. He asked Loyd Wright to find a parcel of land in the Van Nuys area, but work interfered and nothing ever looked quite right. Just before production on *It's a Gift* began, Fields took a year's lease on a hilltop citrus ranch in Encino. On its seven and a half acres grew oranges, lemons, Mexican limes, apples, pears, peaches, avocados, grapefruit, mangos, guavas, walnuts—and, yes, kumquats. The last scene of the picture, in fact, was shot on the Encino property.

Long after he had decamped from Toluca Lake, the legend of Fields and the swans remained. "Spec" McClure, a legman for Hedda Hopper, spent time at Jim Tully's house in the 1940s. "Late one afternoon, Jim and I were quaffing some scotch on the terrace overlooking the lake. A flock of swans cautiously waddled into Fields' yard with their long necks stuck forward suspiciously. Jim studied the fearful antics of the swans for a while and then said to me, 'For Christ's sake, they must be looking for old Bill Fields!' "

*It's a Gift* arrived in New York on January 4, 1935, and advance word—the picture had been in release since November 30—made it the hottest movie ticket on Broadway. It opened at the 6,200-seat Roxy Theatre to rave reviews and ran a solid $30,000 on the week. The following morning, a full-page ad depicting a bottle of patent medicine graced the *Hollywood Reporter.* On its label was a drawing of the man Douglas Churchill declared "the second most important male star" on the Paramount lot. It said:

W. C. FIELDS

ELIXIR OF

LAUGHTER


PRESCRIBED BY

BEYER & MacARTHUR

That night, Fields witnessed a showing of *David Copperfield* at Grauman's Chinese Theatre. The place was crawling with press, and the 133-minute cut was the result of five previews that had been held over the previous month. He had not seen the picture in any coherent form, and was shocked to find that his performance had been cut to the bone. Out were the early scenes in the Micawber home, the debtors' prison, the shots at the writing desk that Cukor had so praised. Worse, the scenes that remained left the spectators curiously restless and unsatisfied. After the screening, the audience split into two distinct factions, one favoring Selznick's idea of lengthening the film and releasing it in two parts, the other believing it was already too long and in serious need of trimming.

All agreed that the first half of the picture, with Freddie Bartholomew as David, the boy, was stronger than the second half, and those who favored cutting the film wanted Frank Lawton's scenes removed in their entirety. Fields thought the emotional core of the story was the relationship between little David and Micawber (a character Dickens had clearly patterned after his own gregarious father), and he fired off an impassioned wire to Selznick urging the reinstatement of all the scenes he had shot. Selznick replied at length a few days later, sadly informing Fields that the Chinese showing was the official press screening, not an editorial preview, and that the film would open in New York as shown. "If I may say so," he added, "I think you come out extremely well in the picture, and I am most grateful to you for your performance. I can say in all sincerity that I know of no other actor in the world who would have been even comparable as Micawber."

Fields was unswayed. He wrote Roland Young saying he thought Young's performance as Uriah Heep marvelous and that he liked Edna May Oliver and little Freddie as well, but that the rest of the characters had been so badly cut they couldn't register. "There is a shipwreck scene with combers a mile high, and some melodrama about the city slicker who steals the girl from the honest seafaring man. He takes her to France, tires of her when her apron strings don't meet, and gives her the boot, gate, air, or you name it. The old uncle who has been her guardian displays a determined jaw through a wealth of meticulously glued crape hair. He grinds his hands and stares into nowhere. The big lunk who was to marry the girl sobs and cries as only big strong honest men can. It takes about six reels to tell this and, as my old Sunday school teacher used to say, it's bloody monotonous."

Young responded by saying that he thought the film held up amazingly well for its extreme length and that Fields had, in spite of vigorous cutting, "walked away with the picture." Micawber's scenes were few but memorable, and his climactic confrontation with his villainous employer ("If there is a scoundrel in all this world with whom I have talked too much, that scoundrel's name is . . . Heep!") was electrifying. Fields was singled out for praise by every reviewer, and there was talk of an Academy Award nomination. "I don't believe," said Will Rogers, "there has been a picture made where one character-ization stood out like Micawber's. That's to say nothing of the fine comedy of it, I mean the real clear-cut character. It was great."

*David Copperfield* went on to earn nearly $3 million in foreign and domes-tic rentals, returning a respectable profit on a $1 million investment. Fields cooled off enough to appear at the Los Angeles opening of the film, and was pleased to learn that Loyd Wright liked it. "I had some wonderful scenes in the picture which were cut out," he responded, "and whilst I left the audience the first night in high dudgeon, I have since calmed down and feel very proud and happy that I'm in the picture at all."

With the New York releases of *It's a Gift* and *David Copperfield* coming within two weeks of one another, assessments of Fields and his work were suddenly everywhere. Andre Sennwald, in the *New York Times,* who had just days before delivered a somewhat measured response to *It's a Gift,* emerged from the closet as an idolater himself, suggesting that an affection for Fields was a "form of confessional." He devoted a full Sunday column to the great comedian who "traffics in high and cosmic matters relating to man's eternal helplessness" and who "presents for our amusement that part of the human composition which is plagued by persistent frustrations, bullied by an inescapable sense of inade-quacy, and tormented by the problems involved in complex associations with other human beings." To Sennwald, Fields' character was present in every man and dominant in many. "When Mr. Fields cringes before the rage of a bullying wife, scrapes the floor in his hasty salaams to someone who is his superior only in lung power, or asserts his stunted ego in cautious admonitions to unarmed babies, he is distorting a universal characteristic so meagerly that only the fool in his audience is deceived. In short, this sublimated Caspar Milquetoast is holding the mirror up to nature."

Sennwald's column, however well intentioned, was so far over the top that J. C. Furnas, in the *Herald-Tribune,* offered a counterpoint the following week in which he said that it was precisely the tragedy of the Little Man, as put forth by the critical establishment, that had ruined Chaplin (who, after taking their serious commentary so very seriously, had become "a tear-jerker first and a comic second").* To this veteran Fields admirer, who could remember waiting

---

*"It has been Fields' great and individual improvement on the Chaplin pathetic ne'er-do-well," wrote Alistair Cooke, "that instead of fading away up a lonely road poor but blithe, he ends by winning decisively for the first time in his life."

for his New York stage appearances "the way a pup waits for supper," Fields had more in common with Sancho Panza than Don Quixote. "For . . . it seems that the essence of his comedy lies in his bewildered and outrageous kickings against the pricks. He is not the timid soul—he is the worm who can be pushed just so far and no farther, and then turns on his persecutors in a muddled but definitely berserk rage. Thick-headed, even vague, if you like, but always tenaciously set on some personal satisfaction, always bluffing, always the underdog, but always biding his time and then squaring his reckoning with the world. If the world bars him from the cookstove, he will ruthlessly burn down the house to roast his pig, and even take particular satisfaction in the damage wrought."

It is uncertain whether Fields ever saw the Furnas piece, but Elise Cavanna sent him a clipping of the *Times* column, and he regarded it with satisfaction. "This Andre Sennwald certainly knows his business," he said. "I wish all critics were just like him. I have just sent him a letter telling him I hope he is right for both our sakes."

Production on *Mississippi* was impeded by an extraordinary run of trouble. Two days were lost because of cast and director illnesses, and Wesley Ruggles briefly replaced director Eddie Sutherland in order to keep things moving. Bing Crosby, difficult under the best of circumstances, refused to work for parts of five days. Script changes and rewrites cost eight days, and Fields himself delayed two critical scenes due to his own dissatisfaction with the dialogue accorded him. (Jack Cunningham, who was remarkably adept at writing in the Fields vernacular, was on the set constantly.) There were a number of retakes. Bad weather hampered exterior scenes, and the company had to work around Crosby's NBC radio schedule.

The team of Richard Rodgers and Lorenz Hart had written a total of eight songs for the film, including a spirited number for Fields entitled "The Steely Glint in My Eye." (Rodgers actually recorded a demo of the song in August; Fields said he was "highly pleased," thinking he could do a lot with it.) A good deal of material was filmed and discarded, and *Mississippi* became not so much a musical as a melodrama with songs. Fields worked a total of thirty-two days on the picture—more than Crosby—but was beginning to show the strain of the previous year. "Fields was all right from about nine in the morning till two," Eddie Sutherland recalled. "He'd just go out, and I'd stall around and shoot other stuff, or not shoot anything, because if he wasn't any good I'd have to shoot it over."

Crosby would go to the racetrack and leave the company in a lurch, but if Fields caused a delay, it was nearly always over the quality of his material. "There were a lot of other stars who were very famous for causing a lot of lost time, which is probably the greatest sin that can be committed by an actor," Teet Carle said, "but I don't remember any stories coming out about Fields costing the studio a lot of time." Generally, Fields could ad-lib his way out of a bad scene, but he was never happy about it. "He'd very rarely know the lines of the script," said Arthur Hornblow. "But whereas I have very little respect, as a rule, for changing lines on the set, and have had very little respect generally for actors attempting to improvise lines, Fields is the one exception. Fields really could improvise lines and make them much better than anything anyone ever wrote for him." Sutherland agreed: "I remember Bill Fields ad libbing a line: 'I'd no more think of [harming a hair on a red man's head] than I'd think of sticking a fork in my mother's back.' That's thinking funny."

There was, however, at least one scene in *Mississippi* that Fields couldn't salvage with improvised dialogue. Someone had come up with the idea for him to play a calliope, and he just couldn't see it. "If I have any kind of fame," he explained to Sutherland, "I'm dexterous. I'm a juggler. I can do the kadoola, play the pool room act, do golf, anything I can do with my hands. But when I have to sit down at the piano and play it and steam comes out the whistle, that won't go over. That's for Ed Wynn, that isn't for me." Sutherland was willing to drop the seven-page scene, but Hornblow, the producer, was not. He embraced the idea and went to work on Fields, telling him how wonderful it would be, but Fields, who had a genuine disdain for the producer, wasn't listening. "I knew Mr. Fields like a book," Sutherland said. "I could see those snake eyes watching the man. He's nodding, but that doesn't mean anything. So finally [Hornblow] said, 'Will you do it?' Fields said, 'Oh sure.' We walked out of the dressing room and I said, 'He's not going to do that, you know.'

" 'Oh,' he said, 'that's utterly ridiculous. He said—'

"I said, 'I don't care what he said, he's not going to do it.'

"He said, 'Well, we'll see about that.' "

They built the calliope at a cost of $15,000, but when it came time to shoot the scene, the normally inventive Fields became a blank slate. The script suggested that he play "with sweeping gestures of his hands, crossing them and spearing at the notes with one finger and his thumb cocked as though he is shooting them," but it was devoid of actual business. "Tell me what to do," Fields said.

"Well, like playing the piano," Sutherland said.

"I don't know how to play the piano."

"Take one finger and play."

"No, I don't think that's very funny."

"Well, what do you want to do?"

"I don't understand this routine at all. Can you explain it to me?"

Sutherland eventually gave up and got Hornblow on the phone. "Maybe it's because I'm inarticulate, or maybe it's because you have a great fondness for this thing—at any rate, I can't convey to Bill what's on my mind about this.

*Fields worked more days on* Mississippi *than Bing Crosby,
but wasn't happy with the result.*

Maybe you'd like to take this over?" And Hornblow said, "I'd be very happy
to." The attempt to shoot the scene stretched over three days. "The calliope was
hooked to a boiler powerful enough to drive the Leviathan," Idwal Jones
observed while visiting the set. "Steam hissed out from the stops, ruining Fields'
cigar, but he jabbed manfully at them and evoked fortissimo the river bravura,
'Farewell, brothers, if you's gwine fo' to go, We'll weep fo' to see you' face once
mo'.' The effect on all eardrums within a radius of a mile was direful in the
extreme." The entire calliope scene had to be junked. "Fields had no intention
of doing it," said Sutherland. "He didn't want to and he wasn't going to."

With suitable content at a premium, Fields made drinking and braggadocio the key elements of his character. A running gag had him telling a somewhat less than enraptured audience of his days as an Indian fighter and how he
had once confronted the entire Shugg Indian tribe with a canoe under one arm
and a Rocky Mountain goat under the other. "Unsheathing my Bowie knife,"
he growls, "I carved a path through this wall of human flesh . . . dragging my
canoe behind me!" When Bobby Vernon came onto the film as a gag man, he

got the idea for an introductory shot of the commodore piloting his boat, the cigar in his mouth carefully dodging the spokes in the rotating wheel. Fields was so pleased, he leapt at Vernon and kissed him on the cheek.

Inspiration aside, *Mississippi* played itself out like a jinx, and it was reasonable to expect the film to be a complete flop. It came in fourteen days behind schedule and, at a finished cost of $694,000, more than $100,000 over budget. Fields thought it would get by on the strength of Bing Crosby's burgeoning popularity and, indeed, saw it as a chance to ingratiate himself with a largely female audience. Consequently, he became alarmed when Arthur Hornblow decided to eliminate the one serious scene he played in the picture.* After viewing a rough cut at the studio, Fields clipped an item from the *Los Angeles Examiner:* "*One Night of Love* was considered by Columbia (before its trade showing) to be a complete white elephant in every key. Since the trade showing, the rest is history."

He sent the clipping to Hornblow and begged that the scene—an impromptu speech in which he tells Crosby what the boat means to him—be reinstated: "Please, please, Arthur, don't cut out the scene where I sit on the steps and tell Bing to continue on in case I should not continue with the boat. It is your wish, also Al Kaufman's, Eddie Sutherland's, and mine that the comic should get a bit of sympathy. You were all delighted with the rushes, and I can't understand why you soured on the scene when the film was assembled. Please give it a chance in the first preview." He then sent a copy of the letter to Eddie Sutherland. "I was hippodromed into playing this part," he said in an accompanying note, "and, as you know, it was nothing to write home about when they put it on paper. I can't afford, at this critical moment, when things are going right for me, to show up at a disadvantage in any film. I need every little bit of comedy or pathos I did in this film. . . . Please, for Christ's sake, protect me in this one."

Fields' timing could not have been worse. The studio was in turmoil that very day over the ouster of Manny Cohen, who was abruptly dismissed after it became known that he had signed some of Paramount's biggest stars, including Crosby and Mae West, to personal contracts. Cohen was replaced by Ernst Lubitsch, who didn't care much for *Mississippi* and wasn't inclined to arbitrate disputes over content. When the picture was previewed at the Wilshire Theatre

---

*Fields' own audience skewed heavily to males, who seemed to respond to an element of cruelty in his work. "I like, in an audience, the fellow who roars continuously at the troubles of the character I am portraying on the stage," he once said, "but he probably has a mean streak in him, and if I needed ten dollars, he'd be the last person I'd call upon. I'd go first to the old lady and old gentleman back in Row S who keep wondering what there is to laugh at."

on February 20, 1935, it was eighty-five minutes long and contained the scene for which Fields had so strenuously lobbied. But the balance between him and Crosby had been so carefully managed that the audience seemed confused over how to regard the film. "Before releasing," said *Daily Variety,* "Paramount should decide if it wants a romantic feature starring Bing Crosby or a hokey comedy starring W. C. Fields. Picture as it stands is neither, [and] has little hope of getting but average grosses." A full ten minutes of footage were removed from *Mississippi,* and Fields' part was cut strictly for laughs. Hornblow thought it was Lubitsch's antipathy that kept the film from getting the kind of handling by the New York office that it clearly deserved, but the reviews were universally favorable, if not ecstatic, and with the double attraction of Crosby's singing and Fields' comedy, it became a considerable hit. It pulled more than $30,000 in its first week at the New York Paramount, where seats ranged from thirty-five to eighty-five cents each and the four days of Lent cut heavily into attendance. It was held over in Los Angeles, Denver, Kansas City, and New Haven, and Fields, who was preparing to negotiate a new contract with the studio, had high hopes it would boost his next starring picture, which carried the prophetic title *Everything Happens at Once.*

Fields dubbed his Encino ranch "The Crossroads" and took up the pose of a gentleman farmer. Every morning when he wasn't filming, he could be found ambling about the premises, a golf club in one hand and pruning shears in the other. The vast living room, with its arched doorways and hand-carved beams, was fitted for an office—desk, files, a typewriter. The rest of the house came impeccably furnished in the heavy woods and wrought-iron accents of early California. There was a tennis court and a swimming pool framed with lattice-work and a litter of kittens that had the run of the property. The clocks ran slow, and, when it rained, the dirt road leading up to the house sometimes became impassable, but on a clear day Fields could see the sun set over the ocean, and the only noises in the air were the sounds of cattle and poultry on the adjoining estates. At the completion of *Mississippi,* Fields retreated to his hilltop hacienda to begin work on his next script, the long-delayed remake of *Running Wild.* "I have never had so much work in all my life," he wrote Maude Fendick. "I like to work, but you can really get too much of it." His original intention was to make the film after *The Old Fashioned Way,* but the story, with the added dimension of sound, presented an almost insurmountable series of problems. Neither Fields nor Le Baron was comfortable with Finch's incessant brayings—limited to title cards on the silent screen but shrill and irritating when amplified on a soundtrack—and the delicate whimsy of the worm having turned was almost impossible to sustain in a feature-length talker.

The solution was to take the characters from *Running Wild* and drop them into a story he and Clyde Bruckman had fashioned for Mack Sennett, *His Perfect Day.* Sennett hadn't much liked the story, in which the Fields character used his mother-in-law's supposed death as a cover for a day at the fights, but it was perfectly suited to the plight of Elmer Finch and his devoted daughter. In working it out, Fields used his pal Sam Hardy as a sounding board; the two men had shared the stage in the *Follies of 1916,* and Hardy was, like Tammany Young, a perennial in Fields' relatively small circle of friends. In Hollywood, Hardy sustained himself with character work, but Fields found his years on the legitimate stage, first as a Belasco player, later as Lenore Ulric's leading man, valuable on points of three-act structure. They played tennis every day, and when the time came to make the film, Fields got Le Baron to put "Sambo" on the payroll. "Sam Hardy looked and dressed like the city slicker who was always going to con you out of something," said Mary Brian, "but he was a good writer and gag man."

Fields had long been accustomed to using his girlfriends as secretaries, but the latest, Carlotta Monti, was an actress, not a stenographer, and refused to take dictation. He ordered a Dictaphone, thinking he could sit out by the pool and work, but there was no electrical outlet, and the machine, he decided, would just make him nervous. So he hired the Dictaphone rep instead, a thirty-five-year-old divorced mother working for $5 a day. He doubled her rate to $10 a day and, because she was so quiet, took to calling her Mickey Mouse. Over time, Magda Michael would become the most trusted person in his life.

"On my arrival in the morning when I first came to Encino," she remembered,

> the matter that always took priority was a discussion of the dinner menu for that evening. The selection of the evening's fare took considerable time as W.C. would mull over each course and decide exactly which food would complement the others. "Let's make it prime rib of roast beef tonight with Yorkshire pudding, string beans with tiny mushrooms, Waldorf salad, and trifle for desert . . . yes, that will about do it." I would relay the gastronomic selections to the cook in a rather unfeeling way since, at that early hour, my taste buds were not yet awakened. Of course, I deduced from the minute attention he gave the matter that he was a real gourmet and epicure, and that food was very important to him, but as time went on, I discovered this conclusion was wrong. He derived pleasure from the contemplation of food, rather than in participation in it, for about 4:30 each afternoon, he would announce that he was "beautifully tired" and wanted to go to bed without his supper, and he would ask me to see that the meal was

served on time and that his guests were properly treated. During this period, I never remember him sitting down to eat one of those elaborately planned meals.

Fields was, by the time of his fifty-fifth birthday, a desperately ill man, but he ignored the symptoms of exhaustion that troubled his sleep and ravaged his appetite. He kept at it, eager to complete his Paramount contract and then stick it to them when a new deal got made. "It seems my pictures are going equally as

*At the Encino ranch he called The Crossroads with secretary Magda Michael*

well in Europe as they are in this country," he confided in a note to Philip Goodman. "I had Tammany Young steal the books of the Paramount Company, and we looked them over and found that I am making a lot of money for them. So much that I am compelled to charge them 100 Gs a picture on my new contract."

Fields dubbed his new story *The Flying Trapeze*. "That title was the working title on another picture," Mary Brian recalled. "He used it on three or four pictures, and then he put it on this picture, which had nothing to do with the circus. He loved that title, and I don't know why." Perhaps his affection for it came from happy memories of the song, "The Daring Young Man on the Flying Trapeze," which was based on the exploits of the great acrobat Jules Léotard and could be heard throughout Europe when he first arrived there in 1901. He objected when the title of the film was changed to *Everything Happens at Once,* and was successful in getting it changed back only after the picture had been completed. "Fields also persuaded the studio to credit Sam Hardy as co-author of the story with Charles Bogle (i.e. W. C. Fields)," an item in the *Reporter* noted.

The cast of *Flying Trapeze* was largely made up of players from Fields' previous pictures. Mary Brian reprised her role as the daughter, Grady Sutton was the shiftless stepson, Tammany Young played an applejack-guzzling burglar, and Kathleen Howard was once again the nagging wife. As a private joke, Fields wrote the part of Wolfinger's loyal secretary for Carlotta Monti, and various bits were contributed by Billy Bletcher, Rosemary Theby, and Mickey Bennett. The screenplay, with a generous assist from Jack Cunningham, was subtler and more richly textured than any of his earlier features. There were no blind men, no dogs or combative children, no crooked poker games or bally-hoos. "I never go out for a gag," Fields told a magazine writer as he was preparing the script. "I base my comedy on humanness, so I just watch people. We're all very funny, only we don't know it. No one is original, and we all do about the same things, so I take the simplest everyday incidents, exaggerate them and turn them into an act, and people, seeing themselves, laugh."

Significantly, the people he was watching for *Flying Trapeze* were the members of his own family. The prune-faced, disapproving mother-in-law, Mrs. Neselrode, was clearly patterned after his wife, Hattie, and the unemployable mama's boy played by Sutton was deliberately named Claude. Fields hadn't laid eyes on his family in nearly twenty years, and yet the painful memories lingered. The loving daughter Hope was named after Maude Fendick's niece (with whom he exchanged a series of affectionate letters). In the film, Hope is always on his side, understanding and levelheaded, grateful to have such a dedicated provider. The parallels to his own life could not have been more obvious.

Filming began on April 27, 1935, with Clyde Bruckman directing a story

*Dictating script revisions to production secretary Dorothy White during the making of* Man on the Flying Trapeze. *Collaborator Sam Hardy (with cigar) can be seen in the foreground.*

that he had originally conceived as a two-reeler. Scheduled for twenty-four studio days and three location days, most of the film would be shot on Paramount's Stage 11, where the interiors of Ambrose Wolfinger's home had been erected. Ten days were spent on the leisurely setup, in which Leona Wolfinger hears a pair of burglars in the cellar and demands that Ambrose go down to investigate. One burglar appears, then another, and when they discover a keg of applejack, they begin to sing "On the Banks of the Wabash Far Away." Amid Leona's moans of dire peril, Ambrose blows his socks out, dons his old robe, swats a fly. Opening the drawer of the nightstand, he retrieves his pistol from a tangle of suspenders. "It's unloaded," he assures his wife. "There's nothing in it." The gun goes off, of course, firing off into the wall, and Leona faints dead away. "Did I kill you? Good, good, good, I didn't kill you. That's fine." The family hears the gunshot and rushes into the room one by one. Claude won't go down into the cellar with Ambrose. ("I know you have the heart of a lion," Mrs. Neselrode tells him sternly, "but if you want to see your poor old mother die of heart failure, you go down into that cellar!") So Ambrose phones the neighborhood patrol. The officer sent to arrest the burglars samples the apple-jack and joins in the singing. And, when Ambrose himself finally descends into the cellar—head first, after catching his foot on the staircase—so does he.

Most mornings on the set began with a story conference. Fields and his associates viewed the rushes after lunch. More often than not, the rushes inspired a second conference, and new dialogue and retakes generally resulted. Fields wrote on the fly, consulting with Bruckman, Hardy, and Johnny Sinclair. After two pictures with Fields, Kathleen Howard was used to the drill: "Bill likes to play with me because I don't get upset. And I don't get upset because I was an opera contralto used to prima donna sopranos.* One must never hamper comedians or sopranos. Bill's stuff is spontaneous; he ad libs as he goes, and if he changes the lines in every take, it is up to a good little contralto to think quickly and make a suitable response." Fields found himself writing just ahead of the action, and on the twelfth day of production, a Friday, the company caught up with him. There was nothing more to shoot until he arrived on Saturday morning, and he did not get to the set until 10:30. He brought seven and three-quarters pages with him, but they too were gone by the end of the day. The next two days were dedicated to writing, with the lower floor of the Wolfinger house cordoned off as a "hot" set. Production reports for the rest of the shoot noted lost time virtually every day, and the words "waiting for script" were ubiquitous throughout.

Despite the considerable demands imposed on Fields by going into production with an unfinished script, he remained fully involved in the staging of his scenes. Mary Brian said,

> He had directors who had done comedy, not making things for him to do, but seeing if the whole ensemble worked and if the scene was funny. You could see his serious face when he wasn't actually working. He was looking far ahead. Was this coming off? Was this funny? He was much more serious about his work than people would expect him to be. Lots of times he had a drink in his hand, and occasionally he started directing with a drink in his hand. But I never saw him drunk,

---

*Kathleen Howard (1884–1956) began her opera career in Berlin in 1906 and joined the Met ten years later. She became fashion editor for *Harper's Bazaar* in 1928, a position she held until 1933, when she resigned to take a role in *Death Takes a Holiday.* She was president of the Fashion Group, an association of 450 of the most important women in fashion, and a frequent lecturer on the subject of historic costumes.

and I never worked with him when he was tipsy. He would sip casually someplace along the line, but not continually, just to keep a little glow on. We worked a long day's work, and if he were to drink continuously, he couldn't ever have made it past lunch. This was a long tall glass, and it lasted him for quite a while.*

Kathleen Howard adored Fields and told the *Los Angeles Times* her greatest challenge in working with him was in not laughing during a take. "When we ask him how he wants us to play a scene, he will usually say, 'Oh, do it your own way.' He won't call us down, but tells us to do something as well as we did some other scene—which, of course, is subtly flattering. Once I asked him, 'Bill, do you want me to cut in when you say that line?' He just put his hand on my shoulder and said, 'You know very well how we work.' "

Grady Sutton believed it was necessary for Fields to take an active hand in the direction of his pictures because no director could fully anticipate what he was going to do. "We had a scene [at the breakfast table] where I played a glutton. I ate all my food and part of his, and we had some dialogue. Fields never said a speech the way he rehearsed it, and I got so fascinated listening to him I forgot my line. The director yelled 'Cut!' and started giving me what-for. Fields cut in, 'Leave the boy alone—I didn't give him the cue.' Then, in an aside to me, he said, 'Son, when you think I've said enough, just break in.' " Said Mary Brian, "They lit every corner of the set because sometimes he would think, 'If I did this . . .' And if I'm in the scene, I'm just going to stand there looking dumbstruck. So I'd find little things to do that are not distracting and let him embroider until he gives me that little key word or key phrase, and then I'd come up with what I was supposed to do. That was one of the reasons he always wanted me in his films."

On the twentieth day of shooting, the company went on location while an office set was being readied on Stage 4. Fields was planning to make Carlotta's first scenes that evening and was already in a high state of agitation. As Brian remembered it, "The same automobile would pick the two of us up and we'd talk along the way. It was so funny. He would say to me, 'Mary, if you ever do'—it was something I never had any intention of doing—'I will give you a spanking myself!' This was something Carlotta had done. I'd say, 'Mr. Fields, I'm not going to do that!' I would hear what had happened the night before, and it was always rather rocky. Every once in a while, I got lectures of what not to do." Fields fretted all day over Carlotta's dialogue, and at 5:00 p.m. the company was dismissed for lack of script.

---

*"His timing was better when he was drinking," Mack Sennett said. "Often when he hadn't had a drink he seemed indecisive, other times he was sharp, sure, positive."

Three days later, he fell ill with grippe and was plagued by back trouble for the duration of the shoot. The remaining exteriors were hampered by bad weather. The production went five days over schedule, though it was, miraculously, within $2,500 of its $268,000 estimate. *Man on the Flying Trapeze* was sneaked in mid-June, and a few retakes were ordered to punch up the dialogue. Another preview took place in Glendale on June 26, but the results were still pretty mixed. *Daily Variety* thought it "a very bad, if not hopeless, comedy concoction," while the *Reporter* took only partial exception: "When Bill Fields is on the screen, the howls are frequent. When he is absent, there are long, dull periods that fall flatter than yesterday's pancakes." There would be no further refinements, however. The constant, unrelenting pressure of having to be funny in every frame of film he was in, combined with sleeplessness, malnutrition, and an unprecedented volume of work, had finally taken their toll. Shortly after finishing the picture, Fields injured his back while playing a strenuous game of tennis with Sam Hardy and was laid up when the flu struck again. His heart and mind racing, he could not get to sleep, and the sleep he did get was so shallow and sporadic that it barely qualified as rest. By the time of the first preview of *Man on the Flying Trapeze,* he was laid up at home with around-the-clock nursing. "I have a bad case of nerves," he confessed in a note to Elise Cavanna, "just one jump ahead of a nervous breakdown, and have thrown my sacroiliac out, which is the most painful thing I have ever known in my life." Paramount held an option on a fifth picture, but plans for the film were quietly dropped. In July, the studio promised exhibitors three W. C. Fields pictures for the 1935–36 season, but a new pact was still months away. Around Hollywood, the scuttlebutt was that *Flying Trapeze* would likely be the last film of his career.

# Twenty-one

# The Need of Change

The rest of 1935 was hell. In late June, the Associated Press reported that Fields' doctors had advised him to take an entire year off and rest. *Man on the Flying Trapeze* was released the following month to indifferent notices. Then Al Kaufman, the man responsible for Fields' return to Paramount—and his most indefatigable champion within the studio hierarchy—resigned to take a job with Myron Selznick. On August 15, Will Rogers was killed in a plane crash near Barrow, Alaska. Two months after that, Sam Hardy was stricken on the set of an Eddie Cantor picture and died after surgery to remove an abdominal obstruction. Fields rallied on October 4 to sign a new contract with Paramount that would pay him $100,000 a picture and a percentage of the gate, but he was still out of commission at the end of the year. "Just when I think I can sit down and do a little work . . . Grandpa Sacroiliac begins sticking pins in my back," he said.

Nothing hit him quite so hard as Rogers' death, at the age of fifty-six. Among the newspaper columns Rogers had filed during the trip—he worked several weeks in advance of publication—was one in which he made reference to "dear old" Bill Fields "who has been sick and I hope he is well—he is, next to Chaplin, the screen's greatest comedian." The column ran ten days after Rogers' death, and it led Fields to believe that, although he had not seen Rogers since the January opening of *David Copperfield,* his old friend had died thinking of him. "I was with him for years in the *Follies* and he did an entirely different monologue every night, a thing I have never known in my 37 years of trouping," Fields wrote in a remembrance. "Rogers was the nearest thing to Lincoln that I have ever known. His death was a terrible blow to me."

After Rogers was killed, Fields made the grueling trip by car to Soboba Hot Springs, where he lay in the late summer sun trying to bake the pain out of his back. Sam Hardy was with him until the end of September, when the Cantor picture started at Goldwyn. "He'd drive into town to see his wife once or twice a week," said Fields, "but he'd always be back by nightfall. He was my

friend, Sam was." Too ill to attend Sam's funeral at Forest Lawn, Fields sent
Magda Michael in his stead. When she returned to Soboba, he peppered her
with questions: "Did Sam have on his blue suit? He looked all right, did he?"
Fields was anxious to "steam the poison out" and get back to work not only
because he deplored inactivity, but also because he suffered an immediate and
precipitous dip in income whenever he was idle. His tax return for the year 1934
declared earnings of $162,811, but for 1935 he reported just $76,875 for a comparable period. Moreover, a year-end summary in *Variety* concluded that
Fields' popularity had suffered due to poor films—meaning *Mississippi* and
*Man on the Flying Trapeze*—and that he needed better handling from a studio
that kept putting him in cheap programmers. The anxiety over lost time and
money caused him to relapse. "I couldn't walk, I couldn't sleep, I couldn't do
anything," he said. One by one, the projects announced for him were canceled.

Ernst Lubitsch, the new production head, favored putting him in bigger,
more prestigious pictures. *Rip Van Winkle* and *Don Quixote* were both mentioned, and *The Count of Luxembourg* was proposed for Fields and Irene
Dunne. There were also plans to re-team him with Bing Crosby in *Anything
Goes* (playing the Victor Moore part). William Le Baron, meanwhile, stuck to
his strategy of putting Fields in remakes and forged ahead with plans to redo

*With Wiley Post and Will Rogers at the Los Angeles opening
of* David Copperfield, *January 17, 1935*

the most important of all the Fields properties—*Poppy.* Sound would enable Fields to recreate his legendary Broadway performance in full, and he was bucked up considerably at the prospect. "When you've got nothing to do but just lie down or sit for hours on end, you start thinking. I thought about my present and my future, and the whole thing looked pretty dismal, let me tell you. But the thing that bothered me more than anything else was the inactivity. I've been pretty busy all my life minding my business, or somebody else's, and I got pretty tired of just doing nothing."

In January 1936, William Anthony McGuire, who was writing *The Great Ziegfeld* at MGM, wired Fields at Soboba Hot Springs for permission to use his name and likeness in the film. (Producer Hunt Stromberg had previously vetoed the idea of using the genuine article because of the enormous cost involved.) "I would consider it an honor to be part of the picture you are doing," Fields replied. "Of course, I would like to see the material, not that I do not admire your material immensely, and I would like to see the double, [as] they usually get a double for me looking as old as Aga Khan."* Fields went on to report on his own well-being: "I have been out of commission, so to speak, for nine months, and my sacroiliac is still doing high and lofty tumblings and give[s] me pain no end. I even have to sneak whiskey against doctor's orders."

It was at Soboba that Le Baron and Eddie Sutherland found him, sent by Lubitsch to see if he was up to making *Poppy.* "So we get there," said Sutherland, "and Mr. Fields looks awful. He puts on an act for us, but he certainly doesn't look very well. So Fields goes to bed fairly early. Le Baron and I sit up and decide what we're going to say the next day. We decided we were not physicians, it wasn't our province to judge whether the fellow was too sick to do a picture, we thought it was a good story, *Poppy,* and we liked it. We went back and that's the way we played it; they sent a doctor up there. Fields conned the doctor, did a dance for him, and the doc said, 'He's great.' "

A treatment by David Boehm, which sensibly returned the story to 1883, was supplanted by a more cinematic version from Waldemar Young and Frederick Hazlitt Brennan. The full script was a collaboration between Virginia Van Upp, a specialist in romantic comedy, and Young, whose admiration for Fields extended back to his days on the *San Francisco Chronicle.* Filming was set to begin on February 19, then was pushed back a week when Le Baron was suddenly tapped to replace Lubitsch as interim production chief. The picture finally got underway on February 24, with Paul Jones, Le Baron's unit manager,

---

*Fields was referring to actor James May (1857–1941), who was, during his lifetime, the preeminent Fields impersonator. Scenes of May were reportedly shot for *The Great Ziegfeld,* but he does not appear in the final version of the film.

filling in as associate producer, and both Bobby Vernon and Jack Cunningham on the set to contribute gags and help polish the script.

The first days were the worst. Fields had been ill for nine months and was still a very sick man. Tottery on his feet, quiet and morose when on the sidelines, he was purposely surrounded by the people he trusted most—Cunningham, Sutherland, Jones (whom he loved), Tammany Young (who had a small part in the picture), and, of course, Johnny Sinclair. In full costume and a rubber mask, it was Sinclair who doubled him in most of the long shots. "Among other things," said Sutherland, "Mr. Fields had something wrong with his inner ear, so he'd walk along and just fall right on his face, sideways. I shot scene after scene with men lying along the sidelines of the picture to catch him when he fell." With Sutherland constantly cutting back and forth between Fields and Sinclair, getting a scene in the can was a slow, arduous process, and pacing, which was usually set by Fields and the tempo of his own performance, suffered accordingly. "I don't think Willie was in 25 per cent of this picture," the director later said. "For example, there was a scene where Willie was supposed to climb through a window, go under a sink because he heard somebody, come out, have a scene with his daughter, and go back out the window. It was a long shot. Johnny Sinclair with the mask came in. Close-up of Willie hearing the noise (sitting on a stool, which we couldn't see, out of camera line). Johnny ducks under the sink. He starts to come out—double—gets up and walks. Two shots, Willie sitting down, in this scene. Cut. He starts out toward the window. The double goes to the window. This was the way the whole picture was made. Fields could barely get around."

Fields' sale of a talking dog to a gullible bartender and his early pitch for Purple Bark Sarsaparilla ("good for man or beast, will grow hair and also remove warts") were by-the-numbers renderings of trademark routines, and his immobility gave the rushes a static quality that shot his comic timing all to hell. Rather than fold, he summoned the strength to sustain himself in extended takes and endured the sharp pain that came with most every movement. The carnival set filled a stage the size of an airline hangar and was populated with the kind of color usually found on a George Bellows canvas. Fortune tellers, wrestlers, snake charmers, and glass blowers practiced their bits, a brass band blew insistently, and the handsome calliope built for *Mississippi* finally came to some use. Extras bustled about in period garb, actors rehearsed their lines, and the din of it all was deafening until an assistant director hollered for quiet and all eyes went to the thick padded door at the far end of the stage.

"In the last two years," said Idwal Jones, observing on the set for the *New York Times,* "Fields has become a sort of myth or legendary character, entitled, therefore, to make his entry in a hush." He was outside basking in the midday

*Many of the long shots in* Poppy *were actually made
with Johnny Sinclair doubling for Fields. The studio
embargoed photographs of Sinclair in costume, but he can be
seen here with his back to the camera.*

sun, his reading spectacles perched lightly on his nose and a floppy cap pulled
down over his ears.

He rose with great weariness, flanked by two bodyguards and a valet
carrying a bottle of restorative and two canes. He had, it must be said,
the aspect of a convalescent, until the director, Eddie Sutherland,
shouted: "Grind!" Then the cameras turned in a burst of light and
Fields was himself again. You saw the pea trickle under the walnut
shell, but you did not see it shoot back into his palm. "Noble demonstration of physics, gents," goes his husky patter in accents that compel
full trust. "The eye can't be fooled—not mine. If you win, you're in
luck. If you lose, that's sportsmanship." The portentous nose twitched,

the smile, with the slit eyes, had the bland innocence of a man picking up the wrong change at the bank. The patter was artless, and the walnut shells were lifted and dropped with gaucherie as the sporting populace, in $11.75 mail order suits, hastened forward to be rooked.

McGargle is tipped off as the mayor approaches and shifts gears without so much as a pause. "Gambling, my dear friends, is the root of all evil," he intones, quivering with righteousness. "For years I was a victim of this heartless scourge—gambling—a helpless pawn in the toils of Beelzebub." The mayor comes forth to offer his hand, and McGargle asks if he has read his book on the evils of wagering. "No . . . ," says the mayor, to which McGargle registers mock surprise. "You haven't? It has a blue cover. Maybe that will recall it to your mind." A running gag has a yokel purchasing a bottle of patent medicine and tendering a $5 bill. McGargle quickly pockets the money and goes on with his spiel, seemingly oblivious to the fact that the man expects some change.

"But I gave you a $5 bill," he interrupts.

"You're quite right," McGargle replies, smiling tightly. "I catch on." He looks out over his audience. "The gentleman wishes five bottles," he announces grandly.

"But I don't want five bottles!" the man protests as McGargle gathers them up and loads them into his arms.

"No more!" McGargle says sternly. "Ladies and gentlemen, only five bottles to each person!"

Since the character of the yokel appears throughout the film—always wanting his money back—Sutherland arranged a small lineup of bit players he thought appropriate to the part. Fields looked them over like a despot reviewing his troops and selected Bill Wolfe, a cadaverous forty-one-year-old burlesque comic and sometime actor who could scarcely get his lines out. Sutherland wasn't happy with the choice, having had his own candidate in the group, but Wolfe appealed to Fields' sense of the grotesque in a way that no actor had since the days of the dime museum. He looked like a medical specimen, and injecting this walking sight gag into the film was one of the few genuine pleasures Fields seemed to derive from the making of *Poppy*. Wolfe, in fact, would appear in nearly all his subsequent films and become something of a Fieldsian trademark.

Because Fields' return to Paramount was an event, a number of celebrities were ushered onto the set to wish him well. He was photographed between takes with Adolphe Menjou, Mrs. Vincent Astor, Gloria Swanson, Herbert Marshall, and President-elect Gomez of Cuba, among others, and shots of him relaxing or clowning for the camera were widely circulated in the press. One day, photographer Jack Shallit persuaded him to crawl onto a flame-red horse

on the wobbly carousel and, after pausing to stick an unlighted cigar in the
horse's mouth, snapped a color photo of the imperious McGargle in high
beaver hat, checked trousers, and brown fur-trimmed coat that appeared in all
its glory on the cover of *Stage* magazine.

Toward the end of the story, McGargle makes his escape from the mayor's
house by stealing an antique bicycle. Feeling his oats, Fields insisted on performing the stunt himself, even though Eddie Sutherland was against it. "He
got on this high front-wheel bicycle, sweat pouring down his face, and I said,
'That's about enough.' He said, 'No, it's not. Let me do it again. I haven't got it
right.' Nothing would stop him." On the second take, the director's worst fears
were realized as Fields rolled out of camera range, lost his balance, and went
crashing to the floor. The stagehands detailed to protect him rushed to his side.
"Thanks, boys," he said as they gathered him up. "You caught me all right—on
the first bounce!" He was returned to Soboba on a stretcher, and the film was

*Fields' support team on* Poppy *included Jack Cunningham,*
*who cowrote five of his pictures.*

closed down. "Frankly," said Sutherland, "there were many friends who doubted if we could ever complete the picture." After ten days of "petrified jitters," Fields returned to the studio in the company of Carlotta Monti and his devoted brother Walter, who drew a monthly salary and had traveled all the way from Florida to get him through the ordeal.* From then on out, he had more good days than bad, but his strength always seemed to ebb after the shooting of an important scene. He managed an extended croquet routine in which the head kept falling off his mallet, but had to remain seated in an exchange with attorney Whiffen and the mayor. For a shot in which he struggled with a curled dickey, he was strapped into a harness to keep him from falling. Yet when the time came to recreate his famous routine with the rolling hat and the kadoola kadoola, he did so magnificently and entirely without the aid of a double.

Under the circumstances, Sutherland thought they had done pretty well. "We completed *Poppy* three weeks behind schedule," he said, "but I shudder to think of how many weeks behind we might have been if Bill Fields had not insisted upon working day after day when he should have been home in bed." The picture wrapped on April 22, 1936. Fields went back to Soboba in relatively high spirits, but he only had five days to recover before getting the terrible news that Tammany Young, the quaint little Irishman who had been at his side throughout the filming of *Poppy,* had died in his sleep at the age of forty-nine. Coming hard on the heels of the Rogers tragedy and the death of Sam Hardy, it was too much for Fields to bear. He sank into a deep depression, stopped eating and sleeping, and whatever progress he had made up to that point seemed to evaporate overnight.

Fields' back trouble flared, and the congestion in his lungs returned. Hypersensitive to any touch, he could barely stand the weight of the sheets on his bed. He stepped up his liquor consumption to help deaden the pain, and in the week following Tam's death, he was running a fever while killing two quarts of bourbon a day. Alarmed, Magda sent for Dr. Jesse Citron, an owlish man with a great pudding face who practiced out of a house on Florida Avenue in San Jacinto and had once tried, without success, to wean Fields off booze. Citron diagnosed his condition as polyneuritis, a painful inflamation of the nerves (not unlike a bad sunburn), coupled with a softening of the bones and joints, a condition known popularly as Paget's disease. The patient was weak from malnourishment and fatigue, and the doctor began a regimen of twice-daily injections of Pernoston, a barbiturate, to enable him to sleep. Magda stayed in the bungalow next door, Walter hovered constantly, and a nurse sat up with him at

---

*Fields had been sending Walter $60 on the first of each month, and his sister Adele was getting $50.

night. Carlotta, who was an excellent cook, oversaw the details of a vegetable-rich diet, and the doctor augmented her meals with iron and vitamin B supplements. But Fields was too stiff to walk or feed himself adequately, and he couldn't concentrate on anything related to work. The studio sent an insurance doctor out to look him over, and on June 1 suspended his contract for a period of three months. Abruptly, Fields' $6,000-a-week salary came to a halt.

In a letter to Bucky Taylor he wrote, "The various doctors have informed me that I have the following ailments: Paget's disease (which is said to make one's bones as pliable as an old rubber boot), must have all my teeth out (which I haven't), lacking in calcium (which would necessitate having a gland removed from my neck), sinus affection, a misplaced sacroiliac, catarrh of the stomach, arthritis, nervous breakdown, toxemia, and dehydration. I don't believe any of them—not even the one who came to see me at Christmas disguised as Santa Claus."

In the hope it would brighten his spirits, Le Baron scheduled a preview of *Poppy* at the Fox Theatre in Riverside, but Fields was bedridden on the night of the event and couldn't be there. The picture went well, considering the general sluggishness of the thing, and his winning exit, with his classic bit of fatherly advice—"Never give a sucker an even break"—had the audience cheering. McGargle steals Whiffen's top hat and cane, then helps himself to a fistful of the mayor's premium cigars. "Naturally, it would be ruinous for any other comedian to end a picture on such a note," Le Baron said, "but with Fields it was just the sort of thing that worked best, and the audience loved him for it."

Flat on his back, Fields deteriorated rapidly. On the morning of June 12 he was coughing up blood, and his breathing had become so labored that his lips and fingertips were blue. By noon he was delirious from the lack of oxygen and running a temperature of 104 degrees. Carlotta summoned Dr. Citron, and Magda told him she thought Fields should go to the hospital—an idea Fields had always rejected in the past, convinced as he was that his number was up and he would never come out of the place alive. The doctor called Walter into the room and, as they all gathered around the bed, said, "Bill, I think you are very ill, and we all think you should go to the hospital. Will you go?" Fields was listless, unresponsive at first. Then, after a moment, he said, "Well, all right." An ambulance was summoned, and Fields was taken to Riverside Community Hospital, where he was immediately placed in an oxygen tent. Citron brought in a local specialist, Dr. Philip Corr, and together they reached a diagnosis of bronchopneumonia in the right base. Because of the Paget's disease, a full set of radiographs was ordered—chest, dorsal spine, lumbar spine, pelvis, the right shoulder, left shoulder, legs, forearms, cervical spine, and the skull, right and lateral. At first, Citron downplayed the seriousness of Fields' condition, and the patient was left in the unheated X-ray room for nearly two hours. Consequently, the fever returned with a vengeance, and by June 15 Fields' condition was grave.

At Corr's urging, Citron phoned Dr. Roy Thomas, who was in charge of the pneumonia ward at Los Angeles General Hospital, and Dr. Thomas drove out to Riverside to consult on the case. "I don't think your patient is going to pull through," he said after a thorough examination. "We've had lots of men over 45 who have drunk two quarts in 24 hours, as you say your patient has been doing, and, especially [with] having polyneuritis and Paget's disease, I don't think there's any chance for him at all. His age is 56. They don't pull through after 45, even without his underlying conditions." The two men went into the adjoining room and told the others there was no hope for recovery. As he was leaving, Dr. Thomas paused long enough to give Citron his number. "You can send some sputum down to the hospital tomorrow, and we'll type it to see what group his pneumonia is, how it falls in the types of pneumonia that we have serum for, and we might give it to him. . . . I have nothing more to offer, but if he is still living tomorrow at four o'clock, call me up."

On June 14, 1936, the *New York Times* carried the following item:

> ### W. C. FIELDS HAS PNEUMONIA
> RIVERSIDE, Calif., June 13 (AP)—W. C. Fields, film comedian, was in the Riverside Community Hospital today suffering from pneumonia. His physician said he was not in critical condition. The veteran actor has been ill for about a year and had spent the last seven weeks at a hot springs resort near San Jacinto, Calif.

When a telegram arrived at the hospital from Claude Fields, Citron, who didn't know his patient was married, wasn't sure what to make of it. He showed the wire to Magda, who told him she would answer it herself. Knowing how Fields felt about his wife and son, she didn't think it would be helpful for them to come—especially if Claude, who had just earned his JSD at New York University, were to seek a conservatorship or involve himself in his father's business affairs. As a precaution, Loyd Wright set up a temporary account to keep the bills paid. Fields was too weak to write his own name, and the "X" he made on the bank's authorization form had to be witnessed.

*Poppy* opened in New York on June 17, and the crowds that queued up along Broadway were seemingly unfazed by the news of Fields' illness. Ozzie Nelson and His Orchestra were onstage, but it was clearly the man in the checkered pants that everyone wanted to see. "It's Fields day at the Paramount!" the ads proclaimed, and the elegant flagship of the Publix chain, with its marble statuary and l'Opera-styled lobby, did its best business of the year—"rather astonishing," *Variety* noted, for the first few days of summer.* Fields' condition added a certain poignancy to the notices, and the reviews were, at times, couched in the terms of a memorial tribute. "W. C. Fields nearly died before making *Poppy,*" James Agate wrote. "He has nearly died since, and I doubt if he will ever be well enough to make another picture. That alone gives *Poppy* special claims on our interest and sympathy. This may be your last chance to study one of the great comedians of all time—a figure comparable with Chaplin, in some respects even Chaplin's master. Chaplin, for reasons that seem to him adequate, shirks speech. Apart altogether from the excessive sentimentality of his outlook, this alone is enough to date him. Fields is essentially a modern, a realist who takes life as it is."

Citron issued nightly bulletins on Fields' condition, and a private phone line had to be installed at the hospital to handle calls from as far away as London. At first he reported "some improvement" in his patient, but there was no serum for Fields' type of pneumonia, and his temperature kept jumping back and forth. "The crisis in broncho-pneumonia does not completely drop as it does with lobar pneumonia," Citron later explained. "It comes down by lysis." Fields' treatment was largely confined to Pernoston injections, although both Seconal and Nembutal were tried because "it was so hard to find a vein in him." Fields slept fitfully. He wouldn't eat. He took small doses of bourbon to avoid the ravages of detoxification.

Carlotta, who had taken a room at the hospital and was never far away, weighed in on the treatment plan and asked the doctor, at one point, to consult with a spiritualist. "I was continually persisted in and bothered by Miss Monti," he complained, "who was always trying to tell me what to give him and what not to give him—making herself generally a pest. I could not keep her out of the room, yet Mr. Fields did not know anything about that." Finally, on June 23, Fields was well enough to take a regular meal, and Citron's update to the press that day said that he was "greatly improved." Carlotta objected to the sedatives that kept him listless and dull-witted, and Citron began referring to her, Ouija board in hand, as a "side-line consultant." Magda and Walter remained in the background, seemingly willing to let Citron direct the case as he saw fit, but even they joined with Fields when, on the night of July 2, he refused all medication. "Says he will have no sleeping tablet tonight," the chart read, "and no hypo unless he gets so bad he nearly goes crazy." The next day, July 3, was the first in which he maintained a normal temperature throughout.

---

*\**Poppy* was held four weeks on Times Square and took in nearly $150,000.

With the lessening of medication, Fields' mind cleared, and he no longer needed the oxygen tent. He was able to spend brief periods sitting up in a chair. Citron, anxious to retain control of the case, suggested he convalesce at Lake Arrowhead, in the San Bernardino Mountains, but Dr. Corr, sensing a growing dissatisfaction with Citron's handling of the case, recommended a private sanitarium in Pasadena instead. As the transfer was arranged, Citron had one final talk with his illustrious patient: "I told him he would have to eat more food, take more liver, capsules of liver after the injections of liver were given up, and I said, 'You will have to stop your continual drinking and, if you do that, you will continually improve, and you will be able to make a picture again.' "

Early on the morning of July 5, 1936, Fields was wheeled to a waiting ambulance and driven seventy miles to the Las Encinas Sanitarium in Pasadena, where he would spend the next nine months of his life. He was frail, almost ghostlike in appearance, substantially shrunken from the 190 pounds he weighed when he first entered the hospital. The Associated Press quoted his new doctor, Charles W. Thompson, as saying that he was "well on the road to recovery," but privately the doctor was alarmed at his patient's condition. Fields was barely recognizable as the robust man Dr. Thompson had seen in the movies. His color was bad, and his skin hung from him like an old suit of clothes. "When I first saw him, he was very feeble, confined to his bed," Thompson said. "His blood pressure was 124 over 64. Pulse 84. He was alternately clear and confused and cloudy, very greatly reduced physically." Dr. Steven Smith, the medical director at Las Encinas, said, "There were still areas of dullness and crepitation in his lungs. He still ran a temperature, so he was not cured of his pneumonia when he arrived with us."

Fields and his party were installed in a secluded bungalow, shingled in the rustic Arroyo style and graced with a commodious sitting porch that favored the morning sun. The daily press bulletins ceased, and Dr. Thompson set about ridding Fields' system of the drugs that had been pumped into him. "He looked dreadful," said actress Doris Nolan, who was with Gregory La Cava for a visit shortly after Fields' arrival in Pasadena. "They thought he was going to die. He'd lost a lot of weight. His neck was like a turkey's neck and his head— he had a big head—was bobbling all over the place. And he hadn't been drinking—they'd taken him off the booze. Greg and I thought this was going to be the end."

Citron was a one-trick pony, and his only avenue of treatment once Fields contracted pneumonia was to continue to do what he had done from the outset—administer Pernoston as a sleeping agent. And while Fields was able to sleep, at least initially, the extended use of the drug also lowered his blood pressure, weakened his respiratory system, and generally impeded his recovery.* As a final grace note to his apparent ineptitude, Citron nearly induced a relapse by submitting a $12,000 bill for his services. At first, Loyd Wright withheld news of the bill, concerned over the effect it might have on his client, and Fields did indeed suffer a slight chest inflamation and some temperature when the charge was at last revealed to him. Then, as if the Citron bill wasn't enough to rile him, Hattie and Claude appeared at his door, unmindful of Magda's advice to stay put and intent upon taking up permanent residence in Los Angeles. Fields did a slow burn, convinced they were circling like vultures, and Walter, who couldn't abide Hattie, beat a hasty retreat to New Jersey.

Fields had faithfully sent weekly checks to Hattie up until the time of his illness, but there had been virtually no contact between him and Claude since his move to California. Fields was clearly disgusted with his adult son, who was still so firmly under his mother's thumb that he allowed himself to be dependent upon her for money. As Fields once wrote in a letter to Hattie, "You claim you, with the money I earned and sent you, paid his way through college, [while Claude] claims he did it himself. Supposing he did or did not, why should a man 28 years old, with the advantage of a college and a musical education, not contribute to the upkeep of his home?" His objections did nothing to stop her pleas, and, as often as not, he responded with a check. "When he was just killing time with the cast [of *It's a Gift*], there were a lot of funny, bitter comments about his son," Jean Rouverol recalled. "My sense was he was having to support him unwillingly."

Fields' antipathy toward Claude had made for some tense moments in Encino one day when he was advised that his son was at the gate. Upon investigation, it was determined that the unexpected caller was not Claude at all, but rather Claude's seventeen-year-old half brother, William Rexford Fields Morris. Fields had contributed to Morris' support, and Mrs. Holden had kept the secret of the boy's parentage until he was a junior in high school. "It was kind of a shock to me," Morris said. "It was hard to fit it all together." In the spring of 1935, he drove to California to see the man he now knew to be his father, and their initial encounter gave rise to an oft-repeated story that generally is told on Claude. As Eddie Sutherland related it,

> [Fields] had a very formal Norwegian butler, and he used to play tennis with his pal, Sam Hardy. They'd summon the butler for a drink by tooting on a Halloween horn. It was that kind of establishment. This particular day, the bell rang at the gate, and this was quite a trek down

---

*Though not a narcotic, Pernoston was powerful enough to be used as an anaesthetic for minor surgery and as an induction hypnotic in major surgery. It was even known to cause death.

to the gate, and down went the butler and he came back and said, "Your son is here to see you."

"Tell him to go away!" said Fields.

He went down again, came back, said, "Mr. Fields, he came all the way from the east to see you," and he prevailed on Fields to see him. Now, Fields had no feeling about this boy at all. He was a stranger. How could he have much feeling about him? So they brought up the son. Fields got to questioning him. . . . Finally, he said to the son, "Will you have a drink?" The kid said, "Yes, thanks." So Fields' ears pricked up a little bit. He thought, "At least he's human." He said, "What'll you have?" The son said, "A Coca-Cola." That set Mr. Fields on a flat spin. Finally he said, "You say you're my son. Where are your credentials? Show me something." So the kid pulled out his driver's license. Fields said, "Get out of here!" and threw him right off the place and never saw him again.

Carlotta told her version of the story, in which Fields never saw the boy at all, but Morris' own account is the most credible, in that Fields received him but they were never able to speak to each other as father and son. "When I was there," he said, "there were always too many people around." The boy, feeling alienated from the woman he had always thought to be his mother, wanted to remain with his father in California. "After much discussion, W. C. told me the best thing for me was to go back east. He gave me $100 and I went." Fields occasionally gave him money "not over $250" and a pair of snowshoes, but they never again saw each other. In November 1936, when Morris was nineteen, Fields had him removed from his will.

Claude was an altogether different matter. He bore his father's name and came tethered to the dreaded Hattie. He was prepared to take the California bar exam and be of service to his father in his time of need, but Fields wasn't having any of it. Concerned that his legacy might be in danger, Fields had the will redrawn, reducing Hattie's bequest to $10,000 and leaving twice that amount—plus an income—to Carlotta. To Claude he left a single dollar with the following notation: "I have limited this bequest herein in this, my last will and testament, for my said son for the reason that I did not see him for a period of approximately twenty (20) years until a few months ago."

Plans were proceeding for another picture at Paramount, with Julian Street adapting his famed novella *The Need of Change* to Fields' style of comedy. The adventures of an American tourist in England, *Need of Change* had long held a special appeal for Fields, who, as a young American entertainer, had taken both England and Australia by storm. But his recovery was agonizingly slow, and he was too painfully thin to photograph. On September 1, the studio suspended his contract for another two-month period. "Bill Fields is a very sick man," Street wrote privately to Waldemar Young,

and it is still uncertain, when last I heard, whether he would ever make another picture. They barely got him through *Poppy,* and at that it makes a very thin picture. It will probably be as well for *The Need of Change* if he does not make it, though the version I made for them is carefully tailored to his measure. All it contains of *The Need of Change* is the valet sequence, and that, as done by Fields, would hardly be recognizable. . . . There's no English clergyman in Fields' version— instead a character known in England as The Juggling Earl. Fields, an American manufacturer of pinchbeck Midway products and juggling material and tricks, goes abroad with wife and daughter. They want social life out, but can't get it. They are down on Fields' juggling co[mpany]. But he meets the Earl and they become buddies; hence the visit to the castle and various happenings. Well, Paramount now owns all screen and talking rights, so that's that.

Fields wasn't happy with Street's treatment and signed an agreement with Paramount to write his own version of the story. He was not particularly eager to work, however, and applied himself to the job the way a fussy eater would pick at his food.* His regimen at Las Encinas took him completely off liquor and drugs, and he found himself, amid the gardens and towering oaks, able to sleep again for the first time in a year. His health gradually returned, and he abandoned, as much as he was able, the worry over money that had plagued him for so long. "It was really the first holiday I have ever taken in this young sweet life of mine," he said. "It would have been better, of course, to have kept fit and in perfect condition, but there has always been too much work to do."

Citron, in the meantime, wanted to know, like Bill Wolfe in *Poppy,* where his money was, and Fields, who thought the bill outrageous from a doctor who normally charged $4 for a house call, refused to pay. He countered with an offer of $1,000, convinced beyond a shadow of a doubt that Citron's care not only had retarded his health but actually had precipitated the pneumonia which he was now claiming to have cured. In November, Fields advised Loyd Wright that "our old nemesis, Dr. Citron, has been to my agent, Charlie Beyer, asking for some help, and he warned Beyer that he did not wish to be nasty, but he felt he would be compelled to take it to court if I did not pay him the four-hundred and some odd dollars a day, amounting to $12,000, that he demands for his services during my last days of illness in Riverside."

---

*The Need of Change* was eventually filmed as *I'm from Missouri* (1939).

In December, Citron followed through on his threat to sue, claiming he had treated the defendant for a period of twenty-five days "continuously and without interruption" and that the "reasonable value" of the services rendered was indeed the sum of $12,000. By taking such an action, Citron may have hoped to inspire a settlement, but Fields steadfastly refused to dicker, and on April 6, 1937, the case was set for trial in Department 2 of the Superior Court of the State of California, in and for the County of Riverside.

During his first four decades as a professional entertainer, Fields studiously avoided the medium of radio and made only sporadic appearances. In 1931, he was talked into doing his first broadcast as a promotional stunt for *Ballyhoo*. "Though he was evidently fearful of appearing on early radio, he did so because I requested him to do so," said Bernard Sobel. "And when he faced the microphone and balked at the encounter, he permitted me to lead him back, whisper an encouraging word, and start him on his routine."

Network radio in the early 1930s emanated almost entirely from the East—New York and Chicago—and it wasn't until Louella Parsons' *Hollywood Hotel* in 1934 that a major network show originated in Los Angeles. Parsons, however, didn't pay her big-name guests—they went home with a case of Campbell's soup—and radio was merely a promotional tool to most Hollywood stars. So Fields, who was nearing the end of his Paramount contract, was understandably surprised when, in March 1935, he was offered thirteen weeks on NBC at $8,000 a week. "I can't accept radio at this time," he responded. "It would interfere and break my price in moving pictures, and television is too close at hand."

He didn't have to rebuff many offers, though. Generally, Fields was thought to be too slow for radio, and he wasn't particularly interested in adapting. "I didn't think radio was a regular business—not for show folks," he said. He didn't even listen very much, though he generally made a point of catching friends like Eddie Cantor and Fannie Brice. It wasn't until he was sick, staring straight up at the ceiling for hours on end, that the radio turned out to be a valuable friend. At Las Encinas, Carlotta bought him a combination radio and phonograph for Christmas and a whole new world opened up to him. "That saved my life," he said. When the hospital's diathermy machine threw static into the signal as he was listening to Jack Benny, Fields threw such a fit that he had to be carried to a car elsewhere on the property in order to finish the show.

When asked to appear on a broadcast honoring Adolph Zukor's twenty-five years in motion pictures, Fields said he would be "tickled pink" to do so. The occasion was an elaborate banquet at the studio commissary, followed by an all-star performance before 1,400 invited guests. Though he was well enough, Fields was acutely sensitive to his emaciated appearance and didn't want to go before a live audience. "I told them I couldn't get out of the bed, so they brought a little black gadget called a microphone to me and everyone said I was good." The *Silver Jubilee* broadcast on January 7 marked Fields' first public appearance in more than a year. His brief comedy bit with a telephone operator was piped onto the Paramount stage from his room at Las Encinas at approximately 9:20 p.m.—well after midnight in New York—but the surprise of hearing his voice again delighted an industry audience that had long since bought into the notion that he had made his last movie. He still didn't take the medium very seriously, and went back to work on a story with Jack Cunningham after the broadcast.

"We were out, a couple of us, to see him at the sanitarium in Pasadena, a quiet place with lots of flowers and sun," Philip K. Scheuer, the film columnist for the *Los Angeles Times,* reported. "He was showing a fellow patient how to swing a golf club as we walked across the lawn. 'Well, for goodness sake,' said Bill, glancing up. He led us to the porch of his cottage without leaning on the cane he carried. He was dressed for summer: white trousers, white shoes, soft shirt. . . . [He] talked about everything, from Max Eastman's *Enjoyment of Laughter* to Jack Benny's latest broadcast. About laughter, he said he didn't think you could make rules; you did something because it struck you as funny, and if people laughed, that was it. As to Bill and the radio, which he listens to a great deal, I wish some of his contemporaries, the lesser comics, could have heard what he thinks of them."

Keen on radio and now eager to work again, Fields was surprisingly receptive to an offer from John Reber and Danny Danker of J. Walter Thompson to appear on the agency's new *Chase & Sanborn Hour.* Standard Brands, makers of Fleischmann's Yeast, Tender Leaf Tea, and Royal Baking Powder, had controlled a prime Sunday-night slot on NBC's Red Network* since 1929, but the glory days of Eddie Cantor and Major Bowes had given way to such specialized fare as *Good Will Court* and *Do You Want to Be an Actor?* Usually the market leader, Chase & Sanborn "Dated" Coffee had fallen to second place behind vacuum-packed Maxwell House. Reber, who headed Thompson's radio division out of New York, and Danker, the hard-drinking Irishman who ran the Hollywood office, aimed to put their client back on top with an all-star revue that, in the classic JWT tradition, would have something for everyone. Appearing on the program with Fields would be Don Ameche, radio's Mr. First

---

*NBC had two parallel networks—the larger, more prestigious "red" network, and the smaller "blue" network. The Blue Network, separated from NBC by order of the Justice Department, eventually became ABC.

Nighter and a popular leading man for Twentieth Century–Fox; Dorothy Lamour, "Dreamer of Songs" and the beautiful star of *The Jungle Princess;* ventriloquist Edgar Bergen, an overnight sensation on the Rudy Vallée show; and conductor Werner Janssen, who had a following among classical-music enthusiasts and was regarded as one of the world's preeminent interpreters of the works of Sibelius.

As the biggest name on the program, Fields commanded the highest price: $5,000 a week with a sixteen-week guarantee at a time of year when listenership was usually at its lowest ebb. He also built in several escape clauses, including one that allowed him to leave the show on ninety days' notice if he ever decided to star in his own series. Danker rolled the dice, committing his client to a $75,000 payday for a fifty-seven-year-old comedian who hadn't worked in a year and was virtually untried in radio. Paramount granted him another six-month suspension, and Fields applied for membership in the American Federation of Radio Artists (AFRA) on March 21, 1937. The contract, with options extending into 1942, wasn't signed until May 7, just two days prior to the initial broadcast.

Rehearsals for *The Chase & Sanborn Hour* took place at the NBC studios on Melrose, where Janssen's thirty-six-piece orchestra was crammed into the same room as the performers and a minuscule studio audience. Fields, who hadn't had a drink in months, tried calming himself by chewing on toothpicks and puffing on cigarettes poked into a filtered holder. Carlotta pulled one of her scarves around his neck to cover the loose skin, and he kept his hat on in the studio to help guard against the cold. At four o'clock on Sunday afternoon, May 9, 1937, a line was opened to sixty-two stations across four time zones and announcer Don Briggs stepped up to the microphone: "Ann Harding! Dorothy Lamour! W. C. Fields! Edgar Bergen and Charlie McCarthy! Richard Rodgers and Lorenz Hart! Ray Middleton! Werner Janssen! Don Ameche! This is *The Chase & Sanborn Hour!*" The orchestra launched into Jerome Kern's "The Big Show," and Fields was back before the public again in an entirely new role . . . as himself.

*Twenty-two*

# This Radio Business

Deprived of pantomime, Fields was a vivid presence in voice alone. However, a radio character had to be created to fit that voice. He was no longer the drinker he was once reputed to be, and there was only so much to be made of his recent illness. Dick Mack, imported from New York to devise routines for Edgar Bergen's impudent dummy, Charlie McCarthy, was assigned to work with him, and Mack discovered that Fields came off best in a reactive posture. He couldn't grapple with inanimate objects as he did in the movies, so the result was simpler—a bleary-eyed version of Fields' modern screen persona, reduced to its most basic elements.

AMECHE

I have the great pleasure now of welcoming back to good health and into laugh circulation our friend W. C. Fields, who makes his first appearance since a serious illness which kept him off stage and out of pictures for over a year. And now he returns fully recovered to say hello—W. C. Fields! (APPLAUSE) Mr. Fields, I'm sure you'll feel at home because here's your old Follies piano player, Werner Janssen.

FIELDS

Oh yes. Howare you, Jackson? I've known Werner Jackson for quite a spell.

AMECHE

Mr. Fields—the name is Janssen—Werner Janssen.

FIELDS

That's right, Janssen. How are you, Werner? Cute little fellow, isn't he? How is everything?

AMECHE

Mr. Fields, that's Charlie McCarthy.


FIELDS

Oh yes, so it is. So it is. How are you, Charlie?


CHARLIE

How do you do, Mr. Fields?


FIELDS

He's put on quite a little weight since I saw him last, hasn't he, Mr. Bergen?


AMECHE

Now, Mr. Fields, will you tell us about the accident that started your illness?


FIELDS

Yes, yes. Half a tick. You are Mr. Bergen, aren't you?


AMECHE

No, no, Mr. Fields. That's Miss Harding.


Charlie hadn't yet gone on the attack, so it was left to Fields to fire the first shot.


BERGEN

He's really older than he looks. He was hewn out of an old oak tree.


FIELDS

His face looks as if it were hewn out of a piece of sassafras root.


CHARLIE

Oh, is that so? If they had to cut your face out of a piece of wood, they would have to use redwood for a nose—and an ample bit of it too, I'd say.


FIELDS

You do, eh?

BERGEN

Charlie, Charlie.


AMECHE

All right, Mr. Fields, now about that serious illness of yours.


FIELDS

Yes—oh yeah—of course. Redwood for a nose! He's a fresh little punk, isn't he? Redwood for a nose! Take him away from me! He draws flies!


CHARLIE

He's drunk!


FIELDS

Yes, and I'll be sober tomorrow and you'll still be full of termites.


Fields went on to tell Ameche that he had "a very stubborn case of pernicious dandruff" and that while he was riding a bicycle, a Paramount truck loaded with props had backed over him and broken his neck. "I was ingurgitating an invigorating stimulant that I call Red Milk and I slipped down a flight of stairs. . . . I fractured the southern-most portion of my spinal column. And to my great dismay, I discovered I'd spilled half of the tasty nectar." To the hospital he went: "Clang! Clang! Clang!" And then: "Whilst cavorting in *Poppy*, I was again compelled to venture onto a high bicycle. I instructed the boys to catch me in case I fall off." Did they catch you? "Yes, on the first bounce. And this time, when I got out, I enjoyed my convalescence having a nervous breakdown. The run was curtailed on account of my developing lobar pneumonia. They put me in an oxygen tent. I thought I was camping—" Then: "After I played three weeks of Fields the Campfire Girl, I returned to play out my two open weeks of nervous breakdown." What next? "A pulled tendon—broken left foot—Paget's disease—double vision—infected toe—more nervous breakdown. They came so fast and furious it was difficult to distinguish them from perfect health. I had miff-and-tiff and Boffandill—" A . . . what? "Oh, don't ask me what they are—and a slipped sacroiliac." He concluded by noting that his ten-week stay in the hospital was complicated by "mogo on the gogogo and Ralphadaldo."

It was a surreal resume of ills trailing back over the last decade, delivered with more volume and bombast than Fields had ever needed onstage. The routine went over big, and he was the undisputed hit of the show. "No new show since broadcasting began has caused more favorable comment after its first broadcast than this fine new program," said the news columnist for *Radio Guide.* "Wherever one went, the talk was of radio's newest feud—that of the reconstructed Fields versus a ventriloquist's dummy. . . . Hollywood's latest super production is a smash hit." In New York, where *The Chase & Sanborn Hour* aired at 8:00 p.m., Maude Fendick heard the broadcast and sent an encouraging wire. "This radio business is a great racket," Fields responded. "Sometimes I'm not sure whether everything is a dream. I was a bit nervous last night, not having faced an audience in nigh onto ten years. How time flies. But soon as I hit them and got their reaction I calmed down. . . . I have only to crack the gate of television now and I will have run the whole gamut starting in pavilions, halls, circuses, concert tours, honky tonks, museums, variety, musical comedy, moving pictures, and radio."

Word of mouth bolstered listenership (which was estimated at eight million) for the second broadcast. Fields had no lines opposite McCarthy, whose spot was played with Carole Lombard, but instead delivered an old vaudeville wheeze about a pet snake that attacks an intruder, then sticks its tail out the window and "rattles for a constable." The material was considerably weaker than for the opening week, but *Variety* still predicted a big jump in the biweekly Crossley ratings. "Those who heard Fields for the first time on his second broadcast were promptly pooh-poohed. 'You should have heard him the first week,' said the good-old-days contingent. Those who heard him on the second broadcast, however, still seemed to feel that radio had brought in another entertainment dreadnaught."

Bergen's dummy made an excellent foil for Fields, and McCarthy's exchanges with him helped renew the public's perception of Fields as a hater of children. Coming from supper clubs and a string of Vitaphone comedies, Edgar Bergen had been a success on the Royal Gelatine show despite the widely held belief that a man who threw his voice for a living had no business on radio. It wasn't Bergen's virtuosity as a ventriloquist that put him over, but rather the vivid contrast between the soft-spoken Swede and a mouthy twelve-year-old carved of wood. In person McCarthy was an unlikely sight, dressed in tailcoat and top hat with a monocle glued to one eye, but on radio his appearance gave way to his character, which was so different from that of Bergen's that most people refused to believe they were one and the same man. "I don't know whether I ever had the feeling I was talking to a real person," said Don Ameche, "but I know I always talked to the dummy, never to Ed."


The Crossleys were inching upward as the Citron trial got underway in Riverside on June 15, 1937. Fields countersued for $25,000, claiming Dr. Citron's treatment had actually retarded his recovery, and he used his newfound promi-

*With Edgar Bergen, Charlie McCarthy, and guest Carole Lombard during a rehearsal for*
The Chase & Sanborn Hour, *1937*

nence on radio to fry his opponent. Just prior to going to court, Fields told
Ameche on the air that he was writing a new picture called *The High Cost of
Dying.* He refrained from mentioning Citron by name, but took enough pokes
at the medical profession to be asked by the sponsor not to dwell on the subject.
The trial itself made all the wire services, alongside news of Amelia Earhart's
last flight and the death of Jean Harlow.

Citron told the court that he had based his fee on a percentage of Fields'
annual earnings, knowing that Paramount paid his star patient $6,000 a week.
Seated at the defense table with Charles E. Milliken of the Loyd Wright office,
Fields chewed on a toothpick and watched the proceedings intently. Under
cross-examination, Milliken established that Citron had been trained as an
obstetrician and had practiced twelve years as one in Beverly Hills. In 1930, Citron was suspended from the staff of a Santa Monica hospital after a federal
grand jury indicted him on charges of having furnished drugs to actress Alma
Rubens.* "Citron ended up in Hemet because he had his license suspended,"

*Rubens, thirty-three, died of pneumonia the following year.

Steve Fairfield recalled. "There was a doctor by the name of Clark in Hemet who chose to bring him out here, and he was practicing under Dr. Clark's watchful eye. Most of the people in Hemet would have rather gone to the veterinarian than have gone to Dr. Citron." The revocation of Citron's license was vacated in 1934, and he was placed on probation for a period of five years. As a term of his probation, Citron could not apply for a federal narcotic permit nor work with narcotics in any way. As Citron lacked admitting privileges at Riverside Community Hospital, Fields, it turned out, was admitted as Dr. Corr's patient.

Citron's lawyers raised the specter of Carlotta and her Ouija board, and there was fear that she might be called upon to testify. Overly impressed with her own cleverness, Carlotta practiced her big scene for Dick Mack: "When they ask me, I am just going to say, 'What has THAT got to do with the price of eggs?' " Mack took Fields aside. "Bill, you had better do something about her." Fields was also warned about displaying his toothpick habit in court. "If a judge thinks a man is showing him disrespect," Milliken lectured, "he'll decide for the other side." Fields, the great cynic, had a childlike faith in the law and couldn't fathom such a thing: "The issue here is whether I robbed that man or he is trying to rob me. The issue is not whether I chew a toothpick or not."

Milliken had the goods on Citron all right, and he produced expert testimony to establish that not all doctors based their charges on the incomes of their patients. But Judge O. K. Morton resented a big Hollywood star and his high-priced lawyer coming to town to stiff a local physician, and, as Milliken had feared, the toothpick protruding from Fields' mouth may well have been the straw that broke the camel's back. Fields thought they had the case wrapped up when he took the stand at the end of the second day to deny under oath that he ever drank two quarts of whiskey a day. "It's a lie!" he shouted. "Why, I never drank two quarts a day, not even in the good old days. Right now, I'm a teetotaler." The judge found in Citron's favor, throwing out the countersuit in its entirety. "After all," said the judge, "when Mr. Fields entered the hospital, the testimony shows he had bronchial pneumonia and other ailments. He was 56 years of age. Physicians say he is lucky to be alive, but here he is. Dr. Citron must have done a good job. Nor am I one of those who think a small town doctor or lawyer should be paid less because he is such. I am more impressed by results than theories."

Fields was outraged by the verdict and said he would appeal through "the last court in the land." On Sunday's program—the Father's Day show—he slipped a line in about feeling "greatly relieved."

AMECHE

Relieved of what, Bill?

FIELDS

Relieved of twelve grand!


The demands of the Chase & Sanborn program forced Fields to seek larger quarters. "When things got too cozy for me over there in the hospital, I knew the time had come to get out—and I got." Just before he made his first broadcast for Standard Brands, he rented a house on Funchal Road in Bel Air. It was completely furnished in white under a pattern of red roses, and the floors were covered in a soothing layer of green carpet. He moved in a few personal things, a desk out of storage, some pictures, and his clothes, and had all his other stuff—his books, his trunks—shipped out from New Jersey. On a clear day, he could see the ocean beyond his own vast expanse of lawn, and he was within walking distance of the Bel Air Country Club. To Walter, he wrote that California was "the nearest place to Heaven I have ever seen." Magda Michael had gone off salary—there being little for her to do at Pasadena—and she had taken a job with John Monk Saunders, the author of *Wings*. But radio, the Citron trial, and an imminent return to pictures made her presence in the new household a virtual necessity. "I have never felt better in my life," he told Dr. Smith. "I even feel as though I had good sense. I am writing a book dealing with the Fields vs. Citron joust, and with your kind permission will dedicate the thing to yourself, Dr. Thompson, little Dodgie, etc., telling of your great kindness, even tenderness, and care." The book never got very far, but there were plenty of other projects to keep Magda busy.

When Mickey Mouse first came to work for Fields in 1934, his financial affairs were in chaos. "I tried to straighten them out and find out when his coupons were due, and things like that," she said. "I had worked in a bank and I tried to get him to put everything down in concrete form for income tax time. Mr. Fields didn't like people prying into his financial affairs. He once said it was unlucky to count his money. When he declined to discuss it, I stopped talking about it." Once she had established herself as honest and reliable, he entrusted her with the combination to his safe, the only contents of which were his assorted bank books—about thirty-five in all.

> When I observed that in most cases only one deposit was indicated and many of them reflected no action for over ten years, I told him it was essential that the books should be activated and by sending them to the various banks for at least entries of the interest which had accrued. Rather reluctantly, he consented to let me take care of this matter, but cautioned "only one or two at a time, registered mail, and wait for them to come back before we send out the next two." I proceeded to do

this, and as they came back, I would ask him, "How much money do you think you have in the Girard National Bank in Philadelphia or in the First National Bank of Memphis?" That would set him to reminiscing as to when he appeared in certain cities and, in each and every instance, he knew the exact amount he had deposited and what the interest accruals should have brought the amount up to. His memory when it came to money matters was unbelievable.

Eventually, Magda was able to collect all the information in a small black notebook. "That was the best I could do. After I made up the book in 1935, he seemed to think it was a good idea and kept it up." Fields, she said, often paid his bills in cash, cashing checks for $2,000 or $3,000 at a time. He was also in the habit, for all of his fabled stinginess, of paying double the quoted rate to any tradesmen who came to his house to perform a service.

"Every week," said Don Ameche, "Bill would reject the first script as terrible." Dick Mack, who drafted the routines Fields performed on the air, approached every Friday, when he offered the new script up for approval, with a growing sense of dread. Fields would read the pages in stony silence, convinced no writer could understand the character he played as well as he did himself. When he saw something he liked, he'd say, "Blowing hot, Dickie! Blowing hot!" but more often he'd say, "Blowing cold!" and Mack knew he was in for a weekend of frantic rewrites. So much did Mack come to loathe these weekly sessions with Fields that the feeling stayed with him to the end of his life. "He used to get the shivers just passing the Bel Air gate," said his widow, Naomi Lewis. Rehearsals took place on Saturday afternoons, and all the pauses and interjections were carefully written into the script. NBC's Program Acceptance Department had to pass on the lines before they were read on the air, and ad-libbing was strongly discouraged. "They would get a little nervous," said Edgar Bergen. "We would ad lib and have fun, and they would come in and raise two fingers, one finger—one minute to go, get back to the script and wrap it up! You didn't always have to come up with great jokes, you know. It was the maneuvering and the inflection and playing around that worked so well." Fields, as a point of pride, always maintained that he did more ad-libbing than he really did on the air. "I can't work without ad libbing," he said. "A lot of that stuff between Bergen and me was on the spur of the moment, and in pictures it has got so that they don't even write out my scenes. They just indicate them and I go on—sometimes forever, it must seem."

*The Chase & Sanborn Hour* became the most popular sixty minutes on radio, but the pressure on Fields to deliver eight funny minutes a week nearly sent him back to Pasadena. He coped with incipient mike fright by sipping on sherry, which, as a wine derivative, didn't qualify as hard liquor—a technicality he invoked when he claimed to be a teetotaler. "Haven't [had a drink] for nine months," he told Sara Hamilton of *Photoplay,* "and never will again. But, you see, if they knew that out there, they might think I'd reformed or something. They wouldn't like that. Best they think of Bill with his bottle." A typical *Chase & Sanborn* broadcast began with a tune from the orchestra, a routine from Bergen, and a song from Dorothy Lamour. After the first commercial break, Ameche would perform a twelve-minute playlet with the week's guest star, usually a leading actress like Ann Sothern or Constance Bennett. After the station break, Bergen would conduct an exchange between Charlie and the guest, followed by another tune from the orchestra. At 8:40 p.m. EST, Ameche would introduce Fields, who was spotted as the highlight of the program. Usually, but not always, he would spar with McCarthy, after which he would be played off to "He's a Jolly Good Fellow." Songs from Lamour and baritone Ray Middleton would follow, and, of course, the final commercial.

The show generated a lot of publicity for Fields, much of it tied to Bergen and McCarthy. A photographer for *Life* magazine came to an early rehearsal and made a series of shots in which Charlie was posed sneering at Fields, insulting him, and blowing his nose on his necktie. "No matter what crushing epithets Fields may hurl at him, Charlie is ever imperturbable and ready with a comeback. Fields' favorite insults concern the fact that Charlie is made of wood. ('Stop scratching, you're getting sawdust all over the floor.') Charlie picks on Fields' propensity for liquor and mocks his tall stories." Articles appeared in *Radio Guide, Screenbook,* and *Liberty,* and Fields made the covers of both *Radio Stars* and *Radio Mirror* magazines. By September, he and McCarthy could be seen endorsing RCA Victor electric-tuning radios in a nationwide print campaign, and there was talk of them doing a picture together. All this drove listeners to the radio on Sunday nights, where they were constantly reminded by Bergen and his alter ego that Fields was a heavy drinker and had a big red nose to prove it. The image stuck, much to Fields' chagrin. "I've been accused of being drunk all my life," he grumbled. "And I've never been drunk in my life. Once, in the early stages of my career, before I'd even so much as tasted a sip of apple cider, a fellow I was working with in a theatre went around saying, 'Bill Fields was drunk tonight!' Now, I'm a juggler. I do comic routines that demand every bit of concentration I have. How on earth could I do them if I had been drinking? I've never tried it, but I've got enough sense to know that it can't be done successfully. I've had enough trouble while stone sober with some of the goofy routines I've done without trying them while drinking. And, in all my years of trouping, I've never missed a performance and never let the public down while on the stage. You can't be a drunkard and have that record."

The matter of the Felton nose was no less vexing to him. "People are always referring to my nose. What's the matter with my nose? It's in proportion to my face, isn't it?" It was indeed in proportion to his face, but its shape and color somehow made it look bigger. "One time," said Magda, "several guests were present [at the house] and one of them made some crack about his nose and its pinkish color. He said, 'Yes, I don't use any makeup for it except nine bourbons a day, and I'll bet it isn't any longer than most anyone's here.' And out came the tape measure and we all measured noses and he was right—two of the guests' noses were considerably longer."

Paramount, eager to take advantage of all the free ink, wanted him back before the cameras by the end of summer. The latest of the contract suspensions ended on August 8, 1937, and Fields' final broadcast under the terms of his agreement with JWT took place a week later. The agency exercised the first of its option periods, but a new entry in Paramount's *Big Broadcast* franchise was also in the works, and William Le Baron had Fields hastily inserted into a story originally announced for Jack Benny. The *Big Broadcast* pictures were largely plotless affairs, with radio stars, musical numbers, and specialty acts all in a jumble. To cover himself, Danker added Nelson Eddy to the cast of *The Chase & Sanborn Hour,* causing immediate friction over billing and money. Eddy's singing genuinely irritated Fields, and the star of *Maytime* was reportedly getting $10,000 a week. "He was very jealous of Eddy," said Carlotta Monti. "He said he sang through one nostril. When Eddy's mother, who didn't know how he felt, asked Fields whether there was anything Nelson could do for him, Fields said, 'Yes, he can slit his vocal cords with a stiletto.' His mother said, 'What did you say?' "

With his weight back to a presentable 160 pounds, Fields began filming *The Big Broadcast of 1938* on September 11, 1937. His spot for Chase & Sanborn the next day was devoted to the spectacle of making a new movie, but he was tired and ill-prepared for the broadcast and saddled with weak material.

AMECHE

Well, Bill, now that your picture's started, how do you feel?

FIELDS

I feel all shot to pieces, Don. Close shot, long shot . . .

Unhappy with his performance, Fields left the studio that night and never returned. The people at JWT tried covering for him, and he was said to be "on location" in the ensuing weeks. Finally, on September 30, *Radio Daily* reported that he was off the show permanently "because it takes too much time and energy while currently engaged on his Paramount picture." Privately, Fields also complained that he was "unable to get good script material," but there was never much doubt that his principal concern was for his health. "I'd been ill for months," he said. "As soon as I was able, I started another picture, working on the script for weeks before the picture went into production. On top of all that, I took on the radio work. Doing double duty, I began to feel a collapse coming on as the weeks went by. It was either give up radio or pictures. The right choice was an obvious one for me. Doctors told me that if I didn't give up radio I was likely to injure my health permanently."

Fields walked away from the largest audience of his career, only to appear in one of the worst pictures he ever made. As the owner of a gleaming new luxury liner out to set a transcontinental speed record, Fields made *The Big Broadcast of 1938,* an appreciably better film with his participation, but it was a picture he had no business making. It represented a severe lapse in creative judgment on the part of William Le Baron, who, by forcing Fields to do the film for purely commercial reasons, distracted him from worthier projects. In the end it was a sorry mess, a commercial flop and a credit to no one. Jack Benny had starred in *The Big Broadcast of 1937,* and Frederick Hazlitt Brennan's original story for the 1938 edition was written with Benny, Martha Raye, and Burns and Allen in mind. In March, playwrights Howard Lindsay and Russell Crouse were put to work on a screenplay, and their draft stood until June, when it was determined that, on the strength of Fields' first few weeks with *The Chase & Sanborn Hour,* a picture featuring both him and Edgar Bergen would likely clean up. Le Baron's attempts to land Bergen didn't jell, however, and Fields was left to fend for himself amid an eclectic group of performers that extended from hillbilly comic Bob Burns to Madame Kirsten Flagstad singing Brünnhilde's battle cry from *Die Walküre.*

Once again, Walter De Leon and Francis Martin were charged with shaping a picture for Fields, but with so many conflicting interests—Burns and Allen, Raye, Dorothy Lamour, newcomer Bob Hope—there wasn't much left for him to do. Moreover, their material was unduly influenced by his radio work, and Joseph I. Breen, upon seeing the August 6 draft of the script, cautioned against the "excessive display and drinking of liquor." Fields responded by churning out his own set of specialties, none of which depended on booze or the shape of his nose for laughs. There were variations on his golf and pool room acts, a calamitous routine involving the ship's orchestra, and an elaborate scene staged at an overstaffed service station. "The Fields character," he wrote, "is sort of a composite character study, as might be reproduced in magazines like *Life* and *Look,* done rather with pictures and pantomime than with dialogue. The dialogue should be more in the nature of captions than actual conversation." He worked out the lines in considerable detail, while simply sketching in the physical business. "These scenes will be developed, as usual, on the set." For authoring a total of five sequences, Fields charged the studio $25,000, with the understanding that the leftovers could be used in other pictures.

As Fields tinkered with his scenes, the development of the rest of the script continued in bits and pieces. Burns and Allen dropped out, and numbers were added for Shep Fields, Tito Guizar, and Bob Hope, who was given the song "Thanks for the Memory" to sing with Shirley Ross. "After they had been shooting for a week or ten days," recalled Howard Lindsay, "Mr. Fields went on strike. His reason seems perfectly valid, although he arrived at it somewhat late. He went to the heads of Paramount and said, 'See here, I have always played a poor man. In this picture I am playing a rich man and I am not comfortable. Goodbye for now.' And he went home." Fields, who never made any secret of his conviction that rich men weren't funny, thought the conceit of his playing a shipping tycoon unworkable. "It doesn't make sense," he argued. "A guy wouldn't wreck his own $10 million boat to win a $10,000 bet." When he clashed with director Mitchell Leisen—who did not think him funny and described his golfing scene as "interminable"—Fields was assigned his own unit under the direction of J. Theodore Reed. "Ted" Reed had been everything in pictures from a scenario editor to president of the Motion Picture Academy. Working with Reed, Fields was able to solve the problem of playing a rich man in a diabolically simple way: he would play twin brothers, one rich, the other poor. The rich one would have the poor one dropped on the competing ship in a two-ship race with the expectation of his lousing things up. Landed on his own brother's ship by mistake, he assumes the authority of the owner, is treated as such, and unwittingly proceeds to sabotage the wrong vessel.

While tangling with Leisen and holding JWT's Danker at bay, Fields sought nothing more than rest and solitude at home, but his nerves got the better of him. "I never slept one whole night in the same bed with him," said Carlotta, who shared the house on Funchal. "Not that we didn't have an affair, but he couldn't sleep more than two or two and a half hours at a time. So he was up and down, and I was up and down. I had another bed set up alongside of his, in addition to having my own separate bedroom. When he got up at night, I'd make him a snack, and we'd stay up and talk." Carlotta, who could sing passably and hankered for a career as an opera star, was Jenny Lind, the Mexican, Diva, the Thrush. In turn, she called him Woody, drawing the "o"s out lengthwise as if pronouncing the word "moody." Volatile and disruptive, Carlotta's ministrations were always tempered with drama. "She was very beautiful and extremely vivacious and a true exhibitionist," said Magda Michael. "I think Carlotta's absolute refusal to be cowed or dictated to was one of her strong points with him."

Two weeks into production on *Big Broadcast,* Fields had a noisy row with Carlotta. The details were never entirely clear, other than that she claimed he hit her with a gavel and a cane and kicked her as well. Carlotta responded by summoning two radio crews and the police homicide squad to the house at 3:30 in the morning. She told the officers she had been hit when she came home late from a party. "She exhibited a black-and-blue bruise on a shapely leg in support of the kicking account," the *Citizen News* reported. Fields himself deferred any comment to the Paramount publicity people, who denied that he ever hit anyone. "It's all right to argue in the daytime," Fields was quoted as saying, "but at night I want to sleep." The dust-up made all the papers (as well as *Time* magazine), and Fields, mortified at having his private life displayed for a leering public, dismissed Carlotta from her $50-a-week position as a "writer." Incensed, she threatened to get a lawyer and sue him for $200,000. "Poo," said Fields. "I've been sued before—and by experts!" Boiling mad, she cleared out and followed through on her threat. She found herself a lawyer who, according to Fields, had been up for disbarment four or five times. "Nobody else would take the suit," he said. The attorney, one Clifford A. Rohe, entered into negotiations with Loyd Wright, who advised his client to settle. "Fields said he would pay $5,000 and not a cent more," Rohe's own attorney, Isaac Pacht, said at a subsequent disbarment hearing before the California Supreme Court. "Miss Monti declared that she had taken his dictation on what clothes to wear and what food to eat and this time he was going to dance to her music. She said that she didn't care how much it was, but that Fields was going to pay more than $5,000 just because he said $5,000 was all that he would give."

When Rohe heard this, he saw a chance to discharge some debts he owed attorney Wright by forcing Fields to pay those off in addition to any settlement. Fields called it "a blackmail arrangement" and, when the deal was finally struck, paid a total of $6,300 to send Carlotta away—$1,300 of which was retained by his own attorney. For his part, Fields wrote the entire amount off on his taxes, a maneuver that eventually came up in federal tax court. "I dispensed with her services," he testified. "And I gave her some advance salary on account of the fine treatment and meticulous work she did in the hospital. So I gave it to her with that understanding."

Production on *The Big Broadcast* continued, with Fields filming chiefly with Reed but still accountable to Leisen when appearing with the other principals. Philip K. Scheuer of the *Los Angeles Times* watched Reed shoot a pool sequence in relative calm, Fields trimming actor Lionel Pape by allowing the rolling motions of the ship to pocket the balls. "Bill came over when the scene was done and said that he's still off the hard stuff; hasn't had a drink in nearly two years, and wouldn't dare anyway for reasons of health and business." For Leisen, Fields played a wild scene with actress Grace Bradley in which he dodged icebergs at the helm of the ship, and he fought with the director constantly. "He was the most obstinate, ornery son of a bitch I ever tried to work with," Leisen said. Bradley, for her part, loved working with Fields, having first caught his attention while dancing in the chorus of *Ballyhoo*. "I used to stand in the wings and watch him," she remembered. "I just thought he was the funniest man who ever lived. When he finished, he would come off and walk right by me. Absolutely no attention. But then finally he began to recognize me, and as he came by he would pat me on the top of the head."

Fields had particular respect for anyone who had come up as he had—onstage before a live audience. "He wasn't an easy guy to get along with," Bob Hope said, "but he liked me because I was from vaudeville." Never hesitant to take on Leisen or Harlan Thompson, the producer, Fields was always friendly with cast members and crew. Producer A. C. Lyles, who was an office boy for Adolph Zukor at the time, recalled a typical act of kindness: "One of the crew—I think he was a grip—went over to him one day and said that it was his mother's birthday and that she liked him very much, and he wanted to know if he would sign a picture to her. He signed it, and then he said, 'Wait a minute.' He went over to the phone and said 'What's her number?' He called her and said, 'I'm here on the set with your son, and I just wanted to wish you a happy birthday.' He said nice things about her son, and then he said, 'Why don't you have your son bring you over to the lot so I can meet you?' He did that in a very sincere fashion, and I think he really meant it. And she did come over, and he posed for pictures with her. It was a very nice gesture."

Fields tried capping Kirsten Flagstad's performance (which had been filmed in New York) with a line about a parrot being on board, and Leisen opposed him bitterly. "I wouldn't direct it," he said, "so they must have gotten Ted to do it." Le Baron told Leisen it was just for the preview, but the director wasn't mollified. He went to the legal department and got the gag pulled. Fields was incensed: "It is entirely in character and should be tried in front of a regular audience. I have absolute confidence in it, and further confidence that it is not overstepping any bounds of propriety or good taste." Le Baron, said Leisen tartly, thought Fields "the most fascinating person in the world." A. C. Lyles observed the two men in rapt conversation one day, and the image stuck with him. "Fields was telling Le Baron a story," he said, "and Le Baron was just fractured by it. Now Bill Le Baron was a very dignified-looking man, and to see him doubled over in laughter was an unusual sight, yet it just underscored the admiration he obviously had for Fields, and vice versa."

*Fields loathed Mitchell Leisen, who directed*
The Big Broadcast of 1938, *and thought him unfunny.*

*The Big Broadcast of 1938* took a heavy toll on both director and star. When production concluded, on November 15, 1937, nearly five months after the first specialty had been committed to film, Leisen went home and suffered a heart attack. (His secretary, Eleanor Broder, blamed Fields for making the picture "an absolute nightmare.") Assembled in Leisen's absence, the picture ran an interminable 130 minutes. It was previewed in San Francisco, then trimmed considerably before Fields was able to see it on January 18, 1938. As was his custom, he sent notes to Le Baron, pleading the case for scenes that had been eliminated while suggesting judicious cuts in others. Harlan Thompson thought parts of the pool routine too drawn out, but Fields disagreed. "After thinking it over," he wrote, "I believe these bits of business should have another chance when previewed by the Los Angeles audience." Bad editing had ruined the service station sequence. The place was supposed to burst into flames as Fields drove away, a shot missing from the preview print. "You'll lose my trade!" he bellows.

Cut to ninety-seven minutes, *Big Broadcast* was next shown to an audience at LA's Paramount Theatre, a cast concrete barn of a structure where a comedy needed all the help it could get. Fields escorted Magda Michael and her daughter Ginger to the preview, taking them to the Trocadero for dinner beforehand. "He was very considerate of me," said Ginger. "I was 13 years old, with pimples and all, but he was still very solicitous. 'What would you like my dear?' For my sake, he even ordered cherries jubilee at the end. They came to the table, pouring in all this stuff and setting it afire. He never touched it himself, but afterwards I was *loaded.*" The reaction to the film that night was much improved, and it was finally deemed ready for release. All the trade papers welcomed it, though *Daily Variety* lamented the "new element of phantasy [that] runs through all the business." Heralding Fields' return to the screen, the picture and its all-star crush of performers couldn't satisfy a crowd that wanted Fields and only Fields. "It is a pity," said Howard Barnes, "that the entertainment was not built more surely around its star. It is forever going off at random and tiresome tangents."

Frank Nugent was perhaps the unhappiest of the New York critics, roundly panning the film itself and sensing at the same time a dangerous trend in the studio's handling of Fields. "Mr. Fields is not himself," he wrote. "The rasping voice has lost its fine nasal resonance, as though someone had scraped the rust from the old trombone. His golf and billiard routines—not the Honest John number this time—and his adventures at the super-service gas station, whither he had repaired to have his cigar lighter refilled, are almost up to par, but the rest is sub-strata Fields. The shadow of his radio debacle with Charlie McCarthy has fallen upon the script, and W. C., who never had to stoop so low before, makes a Durante-like play upon his nose and jokes morosely about strong drink and the DTs. We prefer to forget it."

The radio exposure that had caused Fields' stock to rise so precipitously now confined and dictated what he was expected to do in pictures. He was back to performing revue turns, displaying a character onscreen that had few of the mitigating qualities that had made Wolfinger and Bisbee and McGargle so real. It was a dangerous precedent, excusable in an expensive vaudeville like *The Big Broadcast of 1938* but unsustainable in the smaller pictures to which he would inevitably return. The time had passed for pool tables and golf burlesques, and bombast alone wouldn't carry the day. As Fields approached the age of sixty, he knew he would have to keep searching for those little bits of truth that made his characters resonate and his movies viable.

Fields had expected to start another picture upon the completion of *The Big Broadcast of 1938,* but grippe caught up with him again, and the story, which he had worked out in collaboration with Jack Cunningham, never resulted in an acceptable script. *Things Began to Happen* was a noble project, putting Fields in England as *The Need of Change* had proposed to do. It was set to costar the estimable John Barrymore, under contract to Paramount but principally on display in the studio's Bulldog Drummond mysteries. The Great Profile hadn't seen star billing in a picture since 1934's *Twentieth Century,* and now Fields offered him first position over the title, a selfless and heartfelt gesture from an unabashed admirer. Fields' payments of $6,000 a week shrank to $2,500 as he worked with the writers, but there was no inspiration in their pages and a tendency to inject an unwelcome element of fantasy into the sight gags. Fields complained of "unplayable, trite dialogue" and "impossible jokes" bodily lifted from other pictures. Ted Reed, set to direct, enthused over a scene in which the Fields character belched up explosives and demolished the English Channel, a gag not only completely out of step with the storyline but lifted almost in its entirety from Ed Wynn's network radio show.

After eight weeks of work, the script still wasn't in satisfactory condition and the studio agreed to an additional two weeks of writing that stretched into four and then six. By then, *The Big Broadcast of 1938* had established itself as a bona fide disaster, its reviews mixed and its box office tepid. On April 21, with only ten pages of dialogue in hand to show for his efforts, Fields was advised by Paul Jones, the producer, that Adolph Zukor "seemed disappointed" in his progress. Fields responded by writing to Zukor directly, detailing his frustrations with the writers and urging patience with the process. "I assure you those pages are really ten playable pages," he said, "and with the scenes I have already written, if I could keep up this good work, I could finish the whole job in less than ten days." In another five days, however, Fields had just thirty-five pages to show—approximately one quarter of a filmable script—and the studio was out over $50,000. With the failure of *The Big Broadcast* laid entirely at his feet ("W. C. Fields' long absence from the screen apparently has caused him to lose ground," said *Variety*), Fields had become an untenable liability to Le Baron, who was deep in discussions with Barney Balaban and Stanton Griffis over a new three-year contract. On April 28, he was given an ultimatum to shoot the script as it stood. He refused, causing his agreement with Paramount Pictures to be terminated.

*Fields planned to make* Things Began to Happen *with his friend
John Barrymore, but all that came of the project was a series of stills.*

Fields was paid in full, Le Baron using his clout to see that it was done, but the sting of having been fired by his old friend and mentor was something money couldn't salve. "What would *The Big Broadcast* have been," he asked, "had I not fought like a fiend with the supervisor, Thompson, and the director, Leisen? Yet when the picture is finished and my stuff proves to be the outstanding feature of the picture, what happens? I am given my congé and the director and the supervisor and the producer who are responsible for this $1,300,000 flop go calmly on their way, working for the studio making another picture. The star has flopped." The trades picked up almost immediately on the event, noting that Fields and Paramount had come to a mutual parting of the ways and that he would likely freelance. "I do believe that the motion picture business is on the downbeat," Fields wrote privately to Jack Norworth, "however, it may be that I have outlived my usefulness. Either way, it's O.K. with me. However, when they told me to screw, I had the presence of mind to grab the salary check for the whole picture and quite a goodly sum for some writing I did for them. And if that be larceny, let them make the most of it."

Not wishing to antagonize the studio, Fields had scrupulously avoided radio over the fall and winter of 1937, despite Danny Danker's constant entreaties to return to the Chase & Sanborn broadcast. As a gesture of goodwill, Fields did agree, in the spring of 1938, to do a tab version of *Poppy* on JWT's other big Hollywood show, *The Lux Radio Theatre,* but it was a commitment that required no writing to speak of, only a couple of rehearsals, and a single Monday-night performance. "I enjoyed doing the broadcast," said Fields, "and have abundant respect and appreciation of C. B. DeMille's ability and kindly, patient counsel. Everyone was so goddamned nice to me, I was afraid they wanted to borrow money." Reading lines on the Lux program was considerably easier than coming up with eight minutes of fresh comedy every week. Fields liked radio, but described it as "the toughest work I've ever had." Not only was the writing difficult, but the actual performance was deceptively stressful—more so than for either stage or screen. "The shorter the time you have to get laughs, the more difficult it is to get them," he said. "On the stage, if you flop in the first part of the show, you may make it up in the last part. But on radio, when you have just ten minutes, you have to make every minute count, squeeze down every gag to its minimum wordage, and, on top of that, be nonchalant. As if you're ad libbing."

In spite of the constant pressure, Fields had already agreed to go back on the air for Chase & Sanborn when the cancellation of *Things Began to Happen* left him free to do so on a full-time basis. No amount of time could compensate for the drudgery of having to write his own material—Dick Mack was essentially Bergen's writer—and so Fields offered a 25 percent split of his fee to Gene Fowler and Arthur "Bugs" Baer (author of the "Rough Town" series and the syndicated "Sunday Biographies") if they would write his weekly spots for him. It was a proposal both men regarded with horror. Fowler, for his part, urged Fields to pursue a film version of his novel, *Salute to Yesterday,* instead. A principal character in the book was the Fieldsian Captain Trolley, and critics wondered if there was a connection between Trolley and Fields. "Trolley *is* Bill Fields," Fowler confirmed. "So put on your asbestos jock strap and go into action. Yammer for the part like the foul monster you always have been."

Lacking the support of a dedicated writer, Fields pared his radio commitment to one appearance a month. The premise for his June 5 return to the show would be Charlie's birthday party, but Mack wanted to work his rupture with

Paramount into the exchange as well. Fields balked at the idea, and, as a result, the script became a hodgepodge of individual lines and retorts with no discernable cohesion. "On Sunday afternoon," said Don Ameche, "Danny Danker would come up to me and say, 'It's time to go up and tell the man that this script is okay.' So I'd go up to Bill, and Bill would listen to me, and then we'd get on the air, and I used to have to sit alongside of Bill, and Bergen and McCarthy sat on the opposite side of a very thin table, and the reason that I had to sit with Bill is that he would get so mad at Charlie McCarthy—and I mean actually mad—that he would look up from his script and lose his place all the time, so I'd always have to have my finger on the script and take Bill and put his eyes back to the script. Oh, he would get livid."

The show began well enough, with Fields delivering a genuinely affecting performance as the gentle grafter of O. Henry's "Exact Science of Matrimony." The much anticipated exchange with McCarthy did not come until the second half, but the results were predictably disastrous. In attempting to punch it up a bit, Fields made an unscripted reference to Bergen's toupee, and Bergen—America's most unlikely insult comic—immediately went on the attack.


CHARLIE

Say, why aren't you over at Paramount anymore?


BERGEN

Charlie, please—


CHARLIE

Well, why isn't he at Paramount anymore? Is he afraid to tell?


FIELDS

That Mexican situation is quite perplexing. Don't you think so, Charlie?


CHARLIE

Why did Paramount fire you?


FIELDS

Skip it, will ya? Everything you tell that kid goes in one knot hole and out the other.


CHARLIE

Well, why did they fire you? You must have done something.

FIELDS

I didn't do a thing. Now shut up. I asked them. I said, "Why did you fire me? I've done nothing." They said, "That's why you're fired. You do nothing."

CHARLIE

That's funny.

FIELDS

Not so funny. Shut up, will you? Edgar, keep him quiet.

But Bergen refused to let up. Charlie asked, "Do you think you'll ever get back to Paramount, Mr. Fields?" and, boiling mad, Fields threatened to saw off Charlie's leg "and use it to beat the sawdust out of his head." Then he abruptly terminated the spot—four and a half minutes into an eight-minute routine—by telling McCarthy he was going back to the Happy Hour Hotel. "Until we meet again, this is W. C. Fields saying good night. And I do mean *night!*"

It was a brutal session. After the broadcast, the hot-headed Danker went looking for Fields, but he had already left the building. In the years to follow, Danker let it be known around town that Fields had been sacked by JWT as well as by Paramount. And Fields, when he finally got wind of it, fired off an angry blast in return. "I was not let out of the Chase & Sanborn program," he corrected. "I resigned from a very fine program because of inferior material, not up to Chase & Sanborn standard. I practically wrote all my own material and couldn't stand the grind alone. . . . I have been in the top brackets in the amusement world since 1897, in every part of the world and every branch, and, if rumor be true, I am singled out and condemned to oblivion because I do not agree with the so-called writers, mostly males who sit down to pee. . . . I never desire to do any high and lofty tumbling for Chase & Sanborn again. I have plenty of moola—meaning spondulix—as we college boys say, and am not begging for a job."

# Twenty-three

# You Can't Cheat an Honest Man

Across town, just two days prior to Fields' calamitous Chase & Sanborn broadcast, the purchase of *The Wizard of Oz* was finalized by Metro-Goldwyn-Mayer. A script had been in development for several months, and plans were to shoot the film with Judy Garland as Dorothy and Ed Wynn in the title role. Wynn was the choice of producer Mervyn LeRoy, who was making his first picture for MGM, but Arthur Freed, LeRoy's assistant, and E. Y. "Yip" Harburg, the lyricist, both wanted Fields for the part. As early as 1933, Samuel Goldwyn, having acquired the rights to the book for Eddie Cantor, had similar designs on Fields, but Cantor was cool to the material and the film never got made. Now, six years later, W. C. Fields once again was being paged to play the Wizard of Oz.

With the abrogation of his Paramount contract, it was a job Fields was perfectly amenable to doing. The rate quoted by Beyer-MacArthur was the same as for *David Copperfield*—$5,000 a day for an estimated ten days' work. The screenwriting team of Florence Ryerson and Edgar Allan Woolf had already expanded the role for a player of Fields' stature, creating a real-world counterpart for the Wizard in the person of Professor Marvel. Actor Frank Morgan was on their minds when they first broached the idea of adding the Professor, an old medicine man, to the film, but by the time their first revision of the script was delivered, on June 13, 1938, Marvel had taken on a dwarf assistant and the Professor spoke with a distinctly Fieldsian bravado.

Fields began making notes on how he would play the character—brief scribbles on random bits of paper, carefully gathered together and typed by Magda Michael. He envisioned Marvel as an old con man working "the fortune telling racket like they do in Chicago" and sleeping on park benches. Among the ideas:

Oiling the Tin Man's joints.
When F. sees the lion—"My gosh, that's wonderful, he even smells like
  a lion."

Someone says, "I want to light a cigarette—put the cyclone machine in
reverse."

Re cyclone: Tell about the big wind in Ireland. It blew a cow up against
the side of a barn and he stuck there and starved to death.

Dorothy asks about Fields' dwarfed helper: "Is he a dwarf?" Fields:
"No, he's the smallest giant in the world."

When Prof. Marvel is telling Dorothy's fortune (aside): "Yes, your aunt
wants you back. She wants to put you in moving pictures like
Shirley Temple."

But Fields didn't expect *The Wizard of Oz* to lead to more work at MGM,
and he considered, for a brief while, making films in partnership with Harold
Lloyd. "I'll never go back on the stage," he declared. "I don't want to go back-
ward, but forward. Television—that'll be interesting."

As the role of the Wizard was being tailored to fit him, Fields was approached
by another producer, an independent named Lester Cowan. No Thalberg,
Cowan, at the age of thirty, had just one picture to his credit, a John Ford comedy called *The Whole Town's Talking.* Married to songwriter Ann Ronell,
Cowan had worked as an executive assistant to Columbia's Harry Cohn, trying
to set up a picture for himself and his wife. A joint project, *Champagne Waltz,*
ended up at Paramount, but without Cowan's participation or credit. Briefly,
with Ford, Dudley Nichols, and others, he was a principal in a production company called Renowned Artists. In May 1938, two events occurred that gave
Cowan an unexpected opening at Universal. One was Fields' very public rupture with the brass at Paramount. The other was the dismissal of Charles R.
Rogers as Universal's chief of production after two dismal years in charge.
Rogers left a legacy of anemic musicals, one of which, *Top of the Town,*
depleted his production capital for most of an entire season. He filled out the
schedule with programmers starring the likes of Nan Gray and Kent Taylor, his
only salvation being the surprise hit of *One Hundred Men and a Girl* and the
popularity of its cherubic fifteen-year-old, Deanna Durbin. During the lean
days of 1937–38, Durbin's contract was one of the few corporate assets against
which money could be borrowed.

Rogers was replaced almost immediately by Cliff Work, a big, ruddy-faced
Cincinnati theater man who had been western division chief for RKO and
manager of San Francisco's Golden Gate Theatre. Work was tapped for the
production spot by Nate J. Blumberg, the new president of Universal and
Work's boss from the old Orpheum circuit. Work, like Blumberg, brought an
exhibitor's perspective to the business of making pictures, and, to both of

them, the problem with Universal was painfully obvious—no stars. Reinforced with an additional $1 million in production capital (on top of $2.5 million already raised from British banking interests), Work set about lining up stars for the studio's 1938–39 season. Jackie Cooper was the first to be signed to a three-picture contract, the intent being to pair him with Deanna Durbin. Joel McCrea, Douglas Fairbanks Jr., and Basil Rathbone were retained under multiple-picture deals as well. The studio's new policy was still in its formative stages when Cowan proposed a novel arrangement designed to give Universal a W. C. Fields picture at a bargain outlay. "The front office had quite a lot of people who had been in the vaudeville business," said Edward Muhl, head of the contract department. "What the hell? His pictures had done well for Paramount."

Fields had been hankering to play the benevolent Samuel Pickwick—Dickens' first really great character—since emerging with plaudits from his work as Micawber. (In August 1935, in fact, Louella Parsons' column reported that he would play the part for Paramount as soon as his health improved.) Fields knew the part was rightfully his if a proper script could be written, and Cowan sensed this in dangling the Universal carrot before him. Cowan's plan, in a nutshell, was to have the major elements—namely Fields, himself, possibly the director—working solely for a percentage of the gross revenues. The studio would make a cash outlay of approximately $250,000, and Fields, with Cowan as his producer, would retain full creative control. Were the picture a hit, Fields stood to make considerably more than the flat $100,000 fee he had been receiving from Paramount. And, as a further incentive, the second picture of the two-picture deal could be the aforementioned *Pickwick Papers*.

Fields signed on in principle and began work on an original story, which he tentatively titled *You Can't Cheat an Honest Man*. It was a circus picture, with elements borrowed from the 1927 misfire *Two Flaming Youths*. Again, he would have a daughter in the Mary Brian tradition, and, again, he would be just one step ahead of the law. But where the earlier picture was a full-on farce, *Honest Man* would have interludes of genuine pathos. Its opening, with the accidental death of his wife, a beautiful aerialist, would recall Fields' affecting scene with the girl's dying mother in *Sally of the Sawdust*. And driving him to hold the circus together, by whatever means necessary, would be his love for his two kids, both of whom he must keep in college.

"Since your mother's passed on I get more of a yen to see you kids every day," he writes. "I guess it's either old age or something else sneaking up on me; at any rate, I get mighty lonesome for you both." The daughter is fiercely devoted to her father, but the son is in love with a snobbish society girl, the daughter of a wealthy banker, and worried about his father's "slangy" behavior. Fields had genuine contempt for the winsome tearjerking in which Chaplin so often indulged, but he also knew the value of staying in the audience's good graces while hoodwinking the populace. "We couldn't like the fellow that was all rogue," he once said, "but we'll forgive him almost anything if there's a warmth of human sympathy underneath his rogueries."

The arrangement with Universal didn't work out quite the way Cowan envisioned. Even at this early date, Cowan had acquired a reputation as a slippery character, and Work's deal kept him at arm's distance. Cowan would start work only upon the studio's acceptance of Fields' original story, and only then would he get the $5,000 advance he was due under the terms of the contract. Fields, on the other hand, would receive cash payments all along the way: $5,000 for his original story outline, $10,000 for a treatment derived from said outline, $15,000 for the completed script. He committed to engaging "competent and experienced writers" at his own expense, and agreed to pay for the director of his choice. As an actor, he would receive cash payments of $15,000 a week and a final payment of $50,000 upon completion of photography. He would then collect 20 percent of the film's gross revenues in excess of $600,000. This was, in itself, a historic arrangement.

Fields objected to provisions in the contract designed to protect the studio from what they perceived as a difficult and headstrong performer. He wrote Cowan, "After reading the contract, I already feel I have been up for larceny, petty and grand theft, assault with a deadly weapon, mayhem, etc., ad libitum. You make this contract so iron clad, and there are so many silly clauses in which you could claim damages, that I would feel so nervous, it would be impossible for me to go ahead and make a picture." He went on to iterate his own understanding of the agreement, which included the option of pulling the story and returning Universal's money if they couldn't agree on changes. He concluded by submitting a list of directors who would be acceptable to him: Eddie Cline, Malcolm St. Clair, Clyde Bruckman, and Edward Sedgwick.*

The contract was signed on August 4, 1938. At first, Fields thought he could work *The Wizard of Oz* into his schedule—Yip Harburg had written the Wizard's climactic speech with him in mind—but now he was, apart from Deanna Durbin, the biggest star on the Universal lot, and no time would be lost in announcing his engagement. After pained exchanges over conflicting dates—both pictures were set to start in October—Fields reluctantly withdrew from the *Wizard of Oz,* relinquishing the part to Frank Morgan. What followed was a gingerly give-and-take between Fields, representing the artistic integrity

---

*Fields, of course, had previously worked with both Cline and Bruckman and trusted their instincts. Bruckman had been Harold Lloyd's director at Paramount, while Sedgwick had been Buster Keaton's at MGM. And Mal St. Clair regularly accompanied him to the Friday-night prizefights at the Hollywood Legion Stadium.

of *Honest Man,* and Cowan, playing the difficult role of protector of both Fields' and Universal's interests in the matter.

On the studio's side, Cliff Work and Matthew "Matty" Fox, late of the Skouras circuit and Nate Blumberg's twenty-seven-year-old brother-in-law, were uncomfortable with the dramatic portions of the story—particularly the death of Mademoiselle Gorgeous—and wanted a straight comedy. Cowan, for his part, assured them that Fields could be maneuvered into delivering a more commercial picture and urged patience while the screenplay was being written. Fields selected George Marion Jr., who wrote a lot of Paramount's musicals, "to help improve, re-write, and adapt the story." Marion knew how to get the most out of episodic material and prepared a first draft of the screenplay that was delivered—in lieu of a treatment—on September 19. A bill for $10,000 accompanied it.

Having passed on *The Wizard of Oz,* Fields was surprisingly receptive to an offer from Lord & Thomas to go on the air for Lucky Strike. Perhaps it was his anger at Danker and the people at J. Walter Thompson that fueled his resolve, but another demanding picture would soon be starting and he had already found it impossible to prepare a weekly radio appearance while shooting a film. It is unclear whose idea it originally was to combine Fields' comedy with the popular song rankings of *Your Hit Parade,* but it may well have been the legendary George Washington Hill of the American Tobacco Company, who dictated every detail of the show down to the volume at which the music was played. ("I want it loud!" he declared.) Hill must have been a fan, for he met Fields' fee of $5,000 a show and also bore the substantial cost of shifting the New York–based program to Los Angeles for fifteen minutes a week. The contracts were signed on September 9, 1938, just as George Marion was immersed in the writing of *You Can't Cheat an Honest Man.*

Taking his cue from the Universal deal, Fields reserved the right to pick his own writers. A parade of agency-supplied talent marched through his Bel Air home in the weeks leading up to the first broadcast, but his reactions to the material they brought ranged from indifference to outright disgust. A man named Eddie Davis got the nod at one point, having written for Eddie Cantor, and Davis brought his young protégé, Hal Kanter, along to witness the meeting. "I remember Fields listened to us," said Kanter, "and nodded now and then to acknowledge the fact that he understood what Eddie was reading to him. We were taken to Fields' house by one of the agency men—they were like glorified pimps—and when we finished, he said, 'Well, Bill, how was that?' And Fields said, 'I heard a story the other day . . .' And he told a joke that had absolutely nothing to do with what we were discussing. The agency man said,

'Well, that's very amusing, Bill, but what about the script?' He said, 'The script will be fine. Thank you, gentlemen, and good day.' We started to leave, and as we got to the door, he said, 'But don't be surprised if I can't use any of this.' ' "

Unhappy with everyone the agency proposed, Fields finally pressed George Marion into service. Without a Charlie McCarthy to banter with, Fields decided he would play a continuing role on the series and awarded his character the unlikely name of Larson E. Whipsnade. (He had, coincidentally, given his character in the *Honest Man* script the same name. Whipsnade, Fields told his collaborator, was the name of a dog track near London.) "Larson," said Marion, "is an engaging rascal who owns a failing department store he knows nothing about running." The first script, concerning Whipsnade's efforts to find a job at the store for his nephew Chester, was rejected after someone at the agency put the names "Chester" and "Fields" together.* Another script, with Fields repeatedly phoning a man whose house is afire, was hastily substituted.

On October 15, 1938, *Your Hit Parade* officially became *Your Hit Parade starring W. C. Fields,* and its new attraction introduced himself by talking over the first number. The forty-five-minute show originated in New York, requiring a line be opened to the Vine Street Playhouse in Hollywood, where Fields appeared before a live audience. With him were announcer Harlow Wilcox and a cast of seasoned radio actors that included Hanley Stafford, Elvia Allman, and Walter Tetley. Though *Variety* thought the opener a "wham," the nation-wide audience for popular songs of the day was not necessarily Fields' audience, and when, halfway through the broadcast, they heard "We now switch to Hollywood and W. C. Fields," they tuned out in droves. "I am getting fairly tired," Fields confided to Ed Wynn, "and the kindest thing that could happen to me would be to have the great army of entrepreneurs play me for a chill and give me a rest. I have been top-flighting now for 41 years and I think it's time to move over. As our Sunday school teacher used to say: Pluckhit. If you do not hear me on the air on the 22nd, you will know I'm fired."

He did, in fact, appear on the twenty-second, then asked to be let out of his contract, citing the conflict with Universal and *You Can't Cheat an Honest Man.* The agency, however, would grant only an extension, not a release, and compelled him to do another two weeks at the mike. By the time of the November 5 broadcast Fields had given up on new material, playing instead a radio version of his old Sennett short *The Pharmacist.* The following week, *Your Hit Parade* unceremoniously reverted to its old format, and Fields' contract with Lord & Thomas was canceled. "In time," said Alton Cook, "Fields doubtless would have found the proper writing staff, a matter of long experiment with a

---

*Chesterfields were a competing product of Liggett & Myers.

*Fields moved to CBS as the unlikely star of* Your Hit Parade *in 1938.*

new radio program. In his month on *Hit Parade,* Fields was making no progress. Then came the decision to give up the whole thing."

Even before the failure of the Lucky Strike engagement, Fields was convinced of the need for a hit picture at Universal. The *Big Broadcast* debacle had seriously harmed his standing with exhibitors (who had not seen him draw customers since *Poppy* in 1936), and he wanted to win them back. At one point, Le Baron had conceived of pairing him with Edgar Bergen for a picture, and now Fields, anxious to show his stock with the public wasn't entirely in freefall, proposed adding Bergen and his dummy to the comedic stew he called *You Can't Cheat an Honest Man.* It wasn't an easy decision to make. There were still hard feelings from the last Chase & Sanborn encounter, when Bergen effectively ran Fields off the air, and Bergen's agent, Jules Stein of MCA, insisted on a star deal for his client that necessitated the amending of Fields' contract with the studio. When Universal agreed to foot the bill for the necessary rewrites, Fields permitted the threshold at which his percentage kicked in to be raised from $600,000 to 1.7 times the negative cost or $1 million, whichever was lower. In the end, inviting Bergen onto his picture cost him $25,000.

To further entice the ventriloquist, Fields, through Cowan, offered Bergen co-approval of the director. "Whatever rights Mr. Fields has in connection with the selection he wishes to share with you," Cowan advised him. Bergen, a relative novice at such things, permitted Dr. Stein to reject Fields' first choice for the job, choosing instead the highly inappropriate John M. Stahl, who had guided Bergen's feature-film debut in Universal's *Letter of Introduction.* Stahl's romantic dramas, including *Imitation of Life* and *Magnificent Obsession,* were big moneymakers for the Laemmle regime at Universal, but he was hardly a gifted director of comedies and made only a few. Eventually, the parties compromised on George Marshall, who had directed Will Rogers and Laurel and Hardy and seemed an ideal choice at the time. Bergen's scenes would be created by a writer or writers working directly under his supervision, while the scenes in which he appeared with Fields would be "created and written jointly." Naturally, Bergen selected the principal author of his radio scripts, Dick Mack, to compose his scenes for the film, while Cowan engaged scenarist Manuel Seff to work Bergen and his dummies into George Marion's screenplay. Fields himself thought in terms of character and gags rather than continuity and story, and whatever plot points he contributed to the script grew out of his need to put Whipsnade across. "Bill's best comedy is gritty, grim, basically anti-social," said Joe McEvoy, who might well have made the same statement about his own work. "The character he plays is an old rogue and a rascal; always drinking, never drunk; always sinning, never saved." Under Fields' direction, Seff made Bergen an itinerant performer who comes upon the circus caravan just as the bearded lady is giving birth to a baby. Whipsnade rushes in and, mistaking Bergen for the doctor, takes Charlie for the infant. "Born dead!" he exclaims. "And with clothes on!" An exchange with Charlie ensues as Bergen tries to explain that they are in need of a job. Suddenly, Whipsnade is called back to his own wagon, where his wife lies mortally ill. He hurries, mumbling her name over and over, as the others follow. Dissolve to the Mlle. Gorgeous poster coming down, replaced by one that pictures "THE GREAT EDGAR— ASSISTED BY CHARLIE McCARTHY." "In this way," Seff wrote, "we get over birth and death in our opening, the introduction of Bergen and McCarthy, and a prologue effect of the circus being chased across a state line. (This can be accomplished in about 700 ft. of film.)"

The first pages of the script, from Whipsnade's ballyhoo at the ticket window through the death of Gorgeous, went to the Breen office for review on November 18 with the expectation that production would commence on the twenty-first. Setting up Bergen as an equal partner in the creation of the film guaranteed a contentious shoot. The only copy of the script that can be described as anywhere near complete is Fields' own unfinished and heavily annotated draft, dated November 1, 1938. Officially, *You Can't Cheat an Honest Man* began without a script, and progress was, in the words of Martin Murphy, the studio's production manager, "exceptionally slow." Fields fought with Bergen, with Marshall, and with a studio hierarchy that seemed convinced that he was crazy.

Actress Constance Moore was, in her own words, "a fast seventeen" when she was signed—sans screen test—to a Universal contract in the waning days of the Rogers regime. A Dallas radio singer, Moore appeared in twelve movies over fourteen months, playing ingenues in the "B" programmers that passed for product at the time. In the one "A" assignment she got—Stahl's *Letter of Introduction*—she did an unbilled bit as an autograph seeker. "I was the leading lady in more tests," she said. "Before they would actually call Irene Dunne in, when they were looking for a new leading man, I was Irene Dunne, I was Deanna Durbin, I was—you name it. They were the best scripts, the best directors, the best cinematographers, and they were seen by everybody on the lot." Moore's tests caught the attention of Lester Cowan, who was casting the daughter's part in *Honest Man*. "I was between pictures, and I wanted so to do this 'A' lead. Oh, god, I wanted to play Victoria Whipsnade so badly. I could taste it. And that's when I first met Fields, for he had to say yea or nay." Their brief meeting took place in Cowan's cramped office on the Universal lot. Fields was quiet, cordial, not at all the man she expected, and by the time she left the room, she had the part. "I was so excited. It took me a year and a half to get it."

Moore, used to minuscule budgets and twelve-day schedules, was shocked at what she observed of the "A" filmmaking process. The writing of the script was a tense negotiation between Fields and Bergen, each with conflicting ideas of what the story was about. "Every morning, Mr. Fields had us all form a circle, with our little canvas-backed chairs, in full makeup and full costume, tissues around the collars, and he would hand in to the director the scenes that he had rewritten overnight. And then Bergen would hand in the scenes that he and his writers had written overnight." The group gathered every morning at nine, but rarely was a shot made before noon. "Edgar Bergen would read Mr. Fields' script and he'd say, through the dummy, 'I never call you Bergen, do I? It's either Mr. Bergen or Edgar, but I've never called you Bergen, have I?' Fields would say, 'I don't care what the hell you call him, okay? It's just a matter of reference. You're talking to Mr. Bergen.' Well, it got so terrible, they were really at sword's points. So much so that one day, Mr. Fields exploded and banished Charlie McCarthy from the set. That *piece of wood* was banished from the set. And his chair, too! That little canvas-backed chair that said 'Charlie McCarthy' on it was quickly picked up by one of the gofers and it was taken from the set. And, of course, Mr. Bergen had nothing else to say from then on."

Bergen, on his own, was a shy and reticent man, not given to confrontation, so it fell to Charlie, his alter ego, to fight the battles. A mild complaint from Charlie might be, "How long does this lard head expect us to keep working? It's time to go home, and by God I'm a-goin'!" Bergen always made a game effort to quell Charlie's temper, and those on the receiving end of Charlie's tart wooden tongue rarely blamed the man with his hand up the dummy's back. "It was just so horrible, these mixed emotions," Moore said, "because Charlie was a living creature." Indeed, Fields' annoyance with Bergen gave birth to one of the most memorable scenes in the movie, in which he performed a cruel parody of the ventriloquist's act using a dummy with a face like a melted candle. It rattles off a stale joke and sings while the Great Whipsnade hides his incompetence behind an outlandish moustache and a hideous set of buckteeth. The onlookers register their appreciation with stony silence.

George Marshall, who had directed some thirty features by this point, was driven to distraction by the "writing" process and dismayed at what radio had done to Fields. "After all the years he had taken to create a great and unusual talent," Marshall said, "overnight he decided to be someone else. Bill was the master of a frustrated attitude and, when he was cornered, no one could be funnier or better. Now, out of a clear sky, he didn't want to do these things anymore. He wanted to be a talking comedian. He started sitting up half the night listening to comics like Fred Allen, then sit down and write a couple of pages of his own jokes, bring them down to the studio in the morning, and insist on using them in the picture whether they would fit or not."

The early days of production were given over to the business of Whipsnade working the ticket window. "Count your change before leaving the window!" he booms. "No mistake rectified after once leaving the window!" Seeking to illustrate the meaning of the title, Fields carefully built this scene into his original story: "In bilking the gilpins, [Whipsnade] is constantly carrying on a conversation with either his assistant treasurer or some imaginary person, which leads them to believe that he is confused thereby, and by deftly manipulating the paper money, the customers are led to believe that they are getting the best of it. They do not count the money, but go off chuckling inwardly, thinking they have rooked the smart circus aleck. Were they honest about the whole procedure, they could not be taken. Hence, one of the diverse reasons why 'you can't cheat an honest man.' "

In the scene, Bill Wolfe is taken in much the same way he was in *Poppy,* and he spends the rest of the film, as one of the Pronkwonk twins, wanting his money.

DAVE

That guy talks too much. He counted three, four, five three times. Did you hear him?

BILL

Ain't it dishonest to keep it?

DAVE

He'd do the same to us, wouldn't he, if he had the chance? I'll split it with you. Two—why there's only five dollars here! He's doubled the bills! Look!

BILL

You mean he crooked us?

*On the set of* You Can't Cheat an Honest Man *(1939)*
*with writer Dick Mack and producer Lester Cowan*

Through December, the Fields unit averaged just one page of script a day, a dismal progression by any standard. After a lengthy session with Marshall and Lester Cowan on December 16, the production department reported "a form of script which both these gentlemen agreed would be adhered to after a fashion," but progress the following week showed only a slight improvement. "The constant change of routines and lack of a real, definite continuity makes it impossible for us to intelligently lay out any schedule or figure what the probable final cost might be." The company had been filming for six weeks when the end of the year came, and, frustrated with the sluggish progress and faced with mounting cost overruns, Cliff Work decided to shut the picture down. Having conferred with both Fields and Edgar Bergen, Cowan, on January 4, 1939, registered his emphatic disapproval. "Mr. Bergen is willing to give his time, gratis, to shoot a proper opening and finish the picture," he memoed, "and the services of Mr. Fields and myself are already available to you without additional cost."

Constance Moore recalled a palpable anxiety that pervaded the set: "Remember the fellow, Bill Wolfe, who kept saying, 'I want my money'? It became a running gag on the set. Someone would say, 'Got your money?' And you'd say, 'No, but I want my money.' Of course, it was divine for me, but the members of the company and the crew members really weren't kidding, because they expected it to go down the drain any second." A scene to which George Marshall was inexplicably opposed was the party sequence at the Bel-Goodie mansion where Vicky's engagement to Roger Bel-Goodie is announced. Recalling the luncheon scene in *Her Majesty, Love,* Fields arrives on the premises in his ringmaster's soup-and-fish, engages in a noisy round of Ping-Pong, loudly regales the crowd with his old snake yarn, and repeatedly sends the squeamish hostess into a screaming faint. The scene formed the crux of the third act, leading up to Vicky's renouncement of the stuffy Bel-Goodies and their money, but Marshall was loath to shoot it at all. "Mr. Marshall thought me most unfunny," Fields remembered, "and expressed himself quite audibly on the set, and, one day, at the top of his voice, called me an egotistical bastard."

Something obviously had to give. "I wasn't aware of [the trouble between them] at first," said Moore, "and then I became *very* aware of it. Marshall went into his little office on the set a couple of times. I thought that he was just angry with Fields, but maybe he didn't think it was funny." Fields began making a show of his drinking. David Butler, who was directing a Bing Crosby picture on the lot, got used to seeing him outside his bungalow at eight-fifteen in the morning. "He had one of those Spanish things you lift over your head and drank wine from," said Butler. "Every time he'd see me coming along, he'd say, 'Come on, Dave. Have a sip.' For breakfast! When I'd go home at night, as I'd pass the door going from the stage, I'd hear him arguing with Cliff Work, the studio manager."

In desperation, the studio retained Eddie Sedgwick as codirector of the film—giving Fields one of his original choices for the job—and the company was officially split into two units, Marshall directing Bergen and Sedgwick directing Fields. But Sedgwick, an ex-vaudevillian with a song-and-dance man's sense of comedy, had no better luck with Fields than Marshall, and his tenure on the film barely lasted two days. "Before Mr. Fields did the famous Ping-Pong scene," said Constance Moore, "he wanted Mr. Cline. He said, 'I've worked with Cline. He knows my work.' He first put out his feelers. Then he started asking for Cline. Then he demanded him, and, of course, each time Lester Cowan was brought down to the set. This went on for days and weeks. It was really an "A" picture in every respect. I was just bug-eyed, watching it all happen."

Eddie Cline joined the company on Tuesday, January 10, and immediately the production office noted "a very definite improvement on both quantity and quality of work." Congenial, distracted, the ashes from an ever-present cigarette trailing down his vest, Cline had the rock-solid instincts of an old Sennett gag man. Fields relaxed before such an appreciative audience, and when the *New York Times'* Douglas Churchill visited the set, he noted that Fields was allowing himself only the briefest nip of sherry before a shot. "The day we dropped in, he was doubling for Buffalo Bella, the bearded lady and trick-shot expert of the circus. There were five perfect takes of one gag sequence, but the first four of them were spoiled by offstage laughter. The grips, juicers, and director simply couldn't help themselves."

Concurrent with the hiring of a second director, Everett Freeman was brought over from MGM to help finish the script. Known principally for his short stories, Freeman was to "hold the story together" while Dick Mack churned out dialogue for Bergen and Fields crafted his own bombastic lines. Not exactly a fan, Freeman nonetheless claimed vivid memories of having ditched high school in order to see *It's a Gift* at Loew's Metropolitan in Brooklyn.* "I sat through two shows," he said. "My sides ached with laughter." At twenty-seven, he looked much too young to write the seriocomic opening of the film. Fields, who figured he was getting the bum's rush from both Cowan and Marshall, looked him over and said, "Where's your father?"

Working one day ahead of camera, Freeman was plainly terrified of Fields. "I would write dialogue furiously the night before each scene, then come in trembling and show it to him. Invariably, he would crumple it, throw it back at me, and growl, 'When do I play the death scene with my wife?' " The death of Mlle. Gorgeous had become the principal sticking point in the completion of

---

*Freeman, born in 1911, would have seen *It's the Old Army Game* during his high school days, not the remake.

the picture, and Marshall ignored Fields' entreaties to get on with it. "He told me he either played a death scene with his wife or he quit the picture," said Marshall. "What could I do? He had no wife in the movie, so I shut down production for the day before making my next move."

As Marshall was contemplating his next move, Fields was busy making his. David Lipton, West Coast publicity chief, witnessed the gesture:

> The studio sent him a telegram, or a registered letter, or whatever was required, and served notice that if he did not appear the following day, he would be in breach of contract, and so forth and so on. Now, Fields had his own way of dealing with it. It wasn't a case where he sent us any answer. But the studio heads and all the people involved waited at the door of the stage the next day to see if he would arrive or not. It was a showdown. The word came from the gate that Mr. Fields' car had just driven into the studio. Pretty soon, the car emerged down the street and pulled up right in front of the stage where the rest of us were all standing. The driver got out—in the old limousines you couldn't see into the back seat—and he walked around, opened the door, and stood there for a moment. Of course, no one emerged; no one was in the car. He shut the door, got back in the car, and drove away.

After ten days of filming, the Cline unit was summarily disbanded. Marshall presented the front office with a plan to finish the picture with a double to represent Fields. Martin Murphy reported: "After meeting with Marshall, who will handle the show from now until the finish, we mapped out a tentative schedule whereby it looks possible to wind up all remaining scenes with Bergen by Saturday, January 28th. On this basis, we feel the final cost will run in the neighborhood of $700,000, providing it is not found necessary to go into any extensive shooting beyond January 28th."

Lester Cowan registered a spirited protest in a letter to Cliff Work, fighting an uphill battle for the proper completion of the film.

> As the picture now stands, Fields is not the buffoon with the great and kindly heart which the public loves. Instead he is a buffoon who does shady tricks, and there is no explanation of the fact that he is doing these things so that his children may have a better chance in the world. The scenes which were written for the definite purpose of creating sympathy for Fields, our principal character, have not been shot. . . . Everyone who has had anything to do with this picture has been enthusiastic about the opening contained in our script and which has not yet been photographed. From the story standpoint, it represents a

*Fields' deal with Universal made him part of an eclectic star roster that included*
*Basil Rathbone, Bela Lugosi, Boris Karloff, Deanna Durbin, Jackie Cooper, and Bing Crosby.*

brilliant piece of construction. In a few hundred feet (not more than 600) it introduces Fields sympathetically, establishes his character and purpose in life, the condition surrounding his little circus, introduces Bergen and McCarthy in the right way and launches the feud. . . . I am convinced that if the picture is completed without these scenes, or their equivalent, we will have—no matter what devices may be used or what tricks employed with Bergen—no more than an enlarged two-reeler, without clear foundation in story or character.

Marshall worked all week to finish the film, ending it with Mortimer Snerd describing the final moments of action from aloft in a circus balloon. There was enough Fields footage to comprise the two main segments of the movie— the circus material Marshall had shot and the party sequence directed by Cline—but the rest of the picture had to be built around an unlikely love story between Bergen and Constance Moore. Fields' gambit to save the opening by withholding his services proved ineffectual, and when he got wind that Marshall was making new shots with a double, he erupted angrily. Firing off a letter to Cliff Work, he asserted that he had been available for work all along and threatened to "take such steps as may be necessary to protect my rights" if the shots were used.

> I suggest again that you shoot the opening scene in the wagon and the proper introduction for Bergen—the scene of Gorgeous' death. This is a transition from low comedy to pathos, which has been employed by the finest writers since the days of Indian and Chinese drama and has not been altered. The scene outside the Bel-Goodie home, with me apologizing to the children, baring my heart to them, and the children deciding in my favor and giving the reason for their coming back to the circus is most important. Then, in the midst of this scene showing the children's love for the father and the father showing his real love for the children, again we change from pathos to comedy when Whipsnade immediately switches to get money from Aunt Sludge to continue the circus. His children, with forbearance, try mildly to dissuade him.

There was no reply. Within days of Fields' letter, two previews were held under Marshall's supervision. Fields had no inkling of the first, and only found out about the second at the very last moment. Making one final attempt to salvage the film, Cowan asked Matty Fox to intervene with Cliff Work in permitting a meeting between Fields, Marshall, Bergen, and himself "at which everyone can lay his cards on the table so that we will know where we stand." All he got for his trouble was a sharp rebuke from Work for going "beyond the limits of the authority customarily vested in producers." Not only was the picture finished, Work advised him, but the New York opening was less than two weeks away. The negative, in fact, was shipped on February 10, 1939. *You Can't Cheat an Honest Man* opened at the Rivoli Theatre on Broadway nine days later.

# Twenty-four

# December and Mae

Fay Adler first came into Fields' life as part of the Earl Carroll *Vanities* of 1928. With partner Ted Bradford, she performed a spirited specialty number called "The Butterfly and the Spider." She had a talent for raucous comedy as well, and when Ray Dooley left the show, it was Fay Adler who took her place as the boisterous Baby Hubbard. A petite blonde, all of five feet, Fay had doll-like features and the tight, athletic body of a professional dancer. "She was very tiny," said Doris Nolan. "Somebody told me she had been a trapeze artist." In the early 1930s, as jobs dried up in New York, she came west and found work in Hollywood as a stunt woman. Light and dexterous, she worked steadily, and when Carlotta Monti was thrown out of Fields' house in 1937, she was there to fill the void.

To Fields, the pleasing difference between Fay and Carlotta was that Fay never seemed to want anything. Tough and independent, she had an earthy sense of humor. Of the two women in Fields' life, however, it was Carlotta who needed him the most and did her best to be helpful. "There was a big romance for maybe a year," she once said of the relationship, "but I was mostly a nurse-maid." When money from the settlement ran low, she returned to the house in Bel Air and was welcomed back as if nothing had ever happened. But the man she found inside was distracted, under siege at Universal and unhappy with the new picture. Unable to get his attention or work the old magic, she busied her-self in ways certain to cause a row. "I used to help people out with his money," she said proudly. "Once I ordered 20 turkeys for people who didn't have any for Thanksgiving. By mistake, they came to his mansion. Fields said, 'Carlotta, who the hell did you buy all these turkeys for?' I told him and he said, 'You're a philanthropist with my dough. Next time I'll throw you out!' "

As her thirty-second birthday approached, Carlotta lamented having wasted her life in a futile quest for a rich old husband. She wished instead that she had the dedication and commitment of her role model, Jeanette MacDon-ald, a chorus girl who had come to international fame at the age of twenty-eight. When Fields canceled a $25,000 life insurance policy in her name because she had worked the chorus of *La Bohème* for a paltry $2 a performance, Carlotta told him she would go to New York to study voice and turn professional, an idea in which Fields saw some genuine merit. "You say your voice has improved," he said. "But if you cannot commercialize on it, it will do you very little good and cause others who have to listen to it quite a bit of nervousness. Thank Christ you never took up the cornet." Seemingly glad for the opportunity to again be rid of her, Fields gave her $1,000 and sent her on her way.

Carlotta boarded the eastbound *Chief* on January 6, 1939. Fields wired ahead to the station at Raton: "Enjoy your trip and concentrate on your future. We are all pulling for you and send our love." Circumspect, he addressed the wire to Carlotta Douglas (her name from an early marriage) and signed it, "Mr. and Mrs. Carlotta Carlote." Another wire, also wishing her luck, found her aboard the *Twentieth Century Limited* in Pennsylvania. His ensuing letters offered money, help, and fatherly advice she was loath to take. He sent books on etiquette, fashion, and style, and small volumes of poetry. When he fled to Soboba after the showdown with Universal, he kept her apprised of the situation: "Had quite a fight on [the] picture and felt so tired I came here. Passed your hideout near the pool twice and thought of you. It is raining and I am enjoying it. . . . The picture is not finished and they are trying to give me the works. But I have every confidence of winning as usual. Even if I lose I always feel there will be a rematch. I will win that fight."

Ironically, Fields was at the very pinnacle of his fame. Radio shows clamored for his services, animated cartoons caricatured him grandly, and RKO wooed him with promises of generous budgets and creative autonomy. A popular comic strip, *Big Chief Wahoo,* featured a red-nosed grifter known as the Great Gusto, and a line of pop-up greeting cards displayed his likeness alongside lines like "GREETINGS MY LITTLE CHICKADEE." He appeared on magazine covers and sheet music, and in ads for radios and cigarettes. It was fame, however, born primarily of radio, and the image of the drunken miscreant was now impossible to shake. Interviewed frequently, he played fast and loose with the details of his life, going so far in one New York daily as to deny that he had ever been married. This brought a howl of indignation from Hattie, who was living at the edge of Beverly Hills as Mrs. W. C. Fields, and the demand of a retraction from his son Claude. In New Rochelle, Maude Fendick saw Claude's letter in print and fretted her family would find out that she had been involved in an adulterous affair. Fields waved her concerns aside. "It would be hell if I ever told the truth to the papers," he said. "No one has a worse reputation and has received worse publicity than myself. Some of the yarns are true, others are grossly exaggerated, as were the many rumors of my death, quoting Mark Twain."

When *You Can't Cheat an Honest Man* got underway at Universal, a studio publicist named Dan Thomas pitched dozens of ideas. One, a trumped-up search for an actress to play Whipsnade's daughter, got scuttled when Fields blithely approved Constance Moore for the part. Others met with greater success, and Fields was willing to proceed full bore until the picture was released in what he considered to be an incomplete form. Suddenly, all plans to promote the movie ground to a halt, and Fields even rejected a request from Lester Cowan to attend the San Francisco premiere. All such efforts to endorse the film, said Fields, would only add to their embarrassment and humiliation. "We certainly don't want to go on the air to advertise that we are releasing an obviously unfinished picture, or that Universal is heedless to the entreaties of the artists, producer, and staff who are offering their services without additional cost, so enthusiastic are they about the improvements that can be made with very little additional effort and expense."

The one exception Fields made to this policy of giving Universal "absent treatment" was for a testimonial dinner in his honor—largely because it was too late to call the thing off. Cowan had conceived of the idea of commemorating Fields' fortieth year in show business and prevailed upon the Masquers Club to host the celebration. A sponsoring committee, composed of Harold Lloyd, Charlie Chaplin, Jack Benny, Groucho Marx, Eddie Cantor, and Edgar Bergen, was assembled (although Chaplin, sensing a frost in Fields' attitude toward him, declined to attend the event). Fields himself agreed to show only if the dinner took place on a Thursday ("cook's night out"), and the customary testimonials were dispensed with. "I was just thinking that if anyone calls me 'great' or even 'good' I'll walk out and leave 'em without a guest of honor. I told 'em I didn't want to hear any of those fancy speeches, full of lies, like they make up when a man dies."

The stag tribute took place at the Masquers' Sycamore Street clubhouse, an English Tudor affair just north of Hollywood Boulevard, on the night of February 16, 1939. Tables were set for four hundred, but more than five hundred turned out, braving fierce Santa Ana winds that blew out windows and uprooted nearby trees. The room was aswarm with three generations of theatrical royalty, ranging from Weber and Fields and the seventy-three-year-old monologist Willie Collier, the club's Harlequin, to Fred MacMurray and Robert Taylor. Fields, sporting a pink carnation in his lapel and an ever-present glass of sherry in his right hand, was toasted by the likes of George Arliss,

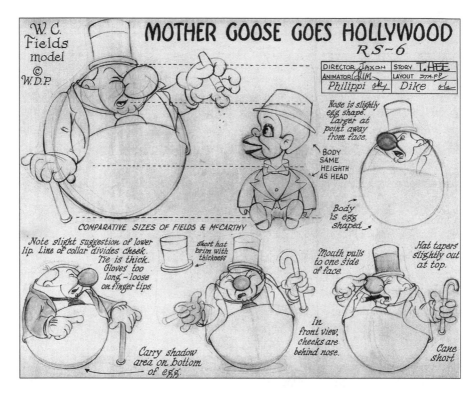

*By the late 1930s, Fields could be seen on his own line of greeting cards, in comic strips like* Big Chief Wahoo, *and in animated cartoons such as Walt Disney's* Mother Goose Goes Hollywood *(1938), for which this model sheet was prepared.* © *Disney Enterprises, Inc.*

Atwater Kent, Chico Marx, Joe E. Brown, Jesse Lasky, Gene Fowler, Herbert Marshall, Leslie Howard, and "Bringing Up Father" cartoonist George McManus.

After dinner, Collier stepped to the podium to characterize Fields as a man with "a jugular vein of humor" who owned "the world's finest traveling barroom." The first speakers of the evening were Groucho Marx (who said, "I feel like Chamberlain in Munich") and Dr. Leo C. Rosten, a Carnegie Foundation anthropologist preparing a book-length study of the motion-picture industry. Faced, in the words of *Daily Variety,* by "the hardest-boiled bunch of troupers ever gathered under one roof," Rosten chose to keep his remarks brief: "The only thing I can say about Mr. W. C. Fields, whom I have admired since the day he advanced upon Baby LeRoy with an icepick, is this: Any man who hates dogs and babies can't be all bad."

Rosten's line, though not particularly memorable at the time, has followed

Fields and his shade ever since. H. Allen Smith recalled it admiringly in his 1944 book *Lost in the Horse Latitudes,* and it eventually found its way into *Bartlett's Quotations,* where it was erroneously attributed to Fields himself. This caused Rosten, in the 1960s and '70s, to loudly proclaim his authorship of the line, first in the pages of *Look* magazine, later in his book *The Power of Positive Nonsense.* The saying took on a life all its own, cementing Fields' posthumous reputation as a hater of both children and dogs, a bum rap in the former sense, though reasonably accurate in the latter. (Fields did, in fact, own dogs from time to time, but he was not especially fond of them and liked quoting his mother's line: "I've got so much love for human beings that I haven't any left for dogs.")

The speeches that followed were anticlimactic in terms of posterity, though famed divorce attorney Dudley Field Malone, dispensing equal parts of wit, tearjerking, and flag-waving, brought the crowd to its feet. Malone felt sure he was the only one present who actually saw Fields make his debut. "The last time I saw Bill," he said, "he would not remember." By most accounts, however, the high point of the evening came when Collier called upon Bergen to produce Charlie McCarthy. "I hope you can't get him out of the box," Fields mumbled.

"I'm surprised you're here," Bergen commented to his wooden partner, hoisting him into view.

"I came just for the food," Charlie replied.

"But I've come to pay my respects to this actor, this friend, this philosopher—"

Charlie interrupted him with a well-timed belch.

"—I shall spend two or three minutes extolling Mr. Fields' merits."

"Then I've got time to go down to the bar!"

The men exchanged several minutes of endearments "too sweet to be sent through the U.S. mails," but at the end of it all, Charlie twisted himself around and spoke directly to the guest of honor. "Seriously, though, Mr. Fields, I'm only kidding. But I do have a lot of fun hating you."

When the time came to introduce Fields to the gathering, Collier again took the floor. "Before I offer our guest of honor and help him to his feet," he said, "may I offer a short biographical sketch? He was foaled in Philadelphia in 1879, which date can be changed later. When he was 11, his parents took one more look at him and ran away. . . . Now, Mr. Fields, if I've said anything that pleased you, anything at all, I'm sorry." Dabbing his eyes with a handkerchief, Fields rose to a thunderous ovation. He told the crowd he remembered seeing Collier onstage when he was a little boy, then warmly thanked the men on the dais for all their kind words. He even expressed his gratitude to Charlie McCarthy. "I hope Charlie and I are in another picture together, if either of us get in another picture after that last one." He removed some papers from his

*At the Masquers tribute in his honor with Leslie Howard, Fred MacMurray,*
*and George Arliss, February 16, 1939*

coat pocket and slowly unfolded them as he donned his glasses. "And now," he announced, "I'll read the telegrams of congratulations. Here's one that starts, 'You dirty, drunken—' I'll try another. It's signed **THE BOYS FROM UNI-VERSAL STUDIOS** and it says, 'So you've been in the show business 40 years; the two months you've been over here seem like 60.' "

Fields read more wires, then turned the room over to Eddie Cantor, who told how he had come to know Fields in the *Follies* by using his soap and towels. Bringing the evening to a conclusion, Collier adjourned the group to the cellar, where the bar, a Colonial tavern, was situated. Fields continued to fuss with his spectacles, which kept getting misty. "Sentiment," he growled. "I hate it."

The next day was spent dictating letters of thanks. "I never enjoyed myself quite as much, or your friendship any more, than I did last night," he wrote Collier. Similar letters went to Cantor, Marx, Bergen, and Arliss. "I felt very silly," he said in a note to Maude Fendick, "but managed not to get nervous. I, at least, was natural. Whether it went over or not, I do not know, but my friends all thought it did. While I was sitting at the speakers' table, one of California's junior lawyers, age about 35, came to the table and greeted me with, 'Hello, Father.' I returned the salutation and the matter was at an end."

———

The release of *You Can't Cheat an Honest Man* came two days after the Masquers event, following a studio press preview at which, according to the *Motion Picture Herald,* the attendees "laughed themselves into tears." However much Fields loathed the film, its comedy was potent even where the story was not. Predictably, notices were mixed. The *Reporter* thought it "hilarious" while *Variety* found it labored and disappointing. The principal difference, as seen by all, was in the broadening of Fields' character into something of a burlesque turn. This pleased some reviewers ("The W. C. Fields of this roaring comedy is the Fields of the unforgettable *Follies,* rakish, rowdy, and unpredictably funny"), but others were profoundly upset by an almost complete lack of humanity. Frank Nugent, usually an unabashed partisan, unwittingly validated Fields' vigorous battle over the original opening in accusing him, as author of the story, of being "singularly ignorant" of the qualities that had so endeared him to millions.

> His Larson E. Whipsnade, circus proprietor, is completely unsympathetic. He is a scamp, but not a lovable scamp; a blusterer who bullies for the sake of bullying and not to conceal a tender heart. In this strange guise, he canes his troupers when they ask to be paid; he flies into prodigious rages on no provocation at all; he tosses poor Charlie McCarthy to the crocodiles; and he sends Mr. Bergen, Charlie, and buck-toothed Mortimer Snerd aloft in a no-longer captive balloon while they are generously pledging their friendship. Whipsnade is not the Fields we have known. We want no part of him. He is something created by the radio, the result of nagging and being nagged by a pert ventriloquist's dummy.

Despite its obvious—and widely acknowledged—deficiencies, *You Can't Cheat an Honest Man* was a hit from the outset, drawing strong business in its first six openings and setting a house record at the Rivoli in New York. It did big weeks in Los Angeles and Chicago, and in Portland, where business was better than for any of the Deanna Durbin pictures, the house manager estimated that 30 percent of the Fields or Bergen gags were lost by "continuous laughter." The film doubled the average week's gross in Washington, D.C., and a theater in Massachusetts reported audiences so tickled they were actually rolling in the aisles. Pained by the patchwork condition of the film, Fields fled to Mexico with Charley Beyer and spent time aboard Eddie Sutherland's yacht in the Gulf of California. Feeling rotten, he slept twelve to fourteen hours a day, and was "much improved" by the time of his return. "Am all rested up and healed up and ready for a new jousting contest," he advised Cowan by wire.

On March 21, he made a last-minute guest appearance on the new Lifebuoy program, singing "The Fatal Glass of Beer" for host Dick Powell and drawing an offer to continue. "They want me on every week, but it's too tough. I'll take it once per month, but not oftener." After the Lucky Strike fiasco, he found himself no longer enthusiastic about radio. The writing had become more difficult than for pictures, and the precision of speech too dispensable to abide. "When I object to changing my gags around, the radio censors always try to come back with, 'But it won't make any difference, anything you say will be funny.' That's a lie. A man's only as good as his material. What we need in the business, both on the air and the screen, is somebody with guts. They're going to ruin every good show if it keeps up." He did Jesse Lasky's *Gateway to Hollywood* as a gesture of friendship to both Lasky and Al Kaufman and then declined all subsequent offers. In January 1940, he withdrew from AFRA with no intention of ever broadcasting again.

Rentals on the new picture were approaching $500,000 when Universal unexpectedly expressed interest in doing another. Fields wrote Carlotta, "That abortion, *You Can't Cheat an Honest Man,* is doing the second-best business of the year. Can you beat it?" Presciently, he added, "I will probably do a good picture some day and it will be the second lowest gross of the year." On April 17, 1939, the studio extended Fields' contractual deadline for proposing a new film, and he prepared to submit, through Cowan, a treatment screenwriter James Seymour had developed for *Mr. Pickwick.* There were alternate stories as well (including a South American tale and one about a theatrical mother and an infant prodigy with an "inebriate father who is aced out of the family"), but with such startling commercial results from *Honest Man,* the chance to make his dream of *Pickwick* a reality was finally at hand. "I recall your having mentioned Pickwick to me during the filming of *Poppy,*" he wrote D. W. Griffith in La Grange, Kentucky. "If I could interest some of these Eskimo people out here in the idea, do you still feel you would like to go through with it?"

But then something intruded, a purely commercial inspiration too potent to ignore. "Am busily engaged in lining up a picture for Mae West and myself," he told Carlotta in a letter on May 12. "The idea is hotter than a firecracker, but so many gilpins and muzzlers are trying to declare themselves in, the deal will most likely end up in the latrine." For the moment at least, *Pickwick* would have to wait.


Back in 1934, Fields had the dressing room next door to Mae West on the Paramount lot. She was the studio's biggest attraction at the time, earning $300,000 a picture. He, by contrast, was the star of modest comedies like *You're Telling Me!* When Manny Cohen was feted with a banquet at the Ambassador Hotel just days before his dismissal, both attended and posed for pictures. Otherwise, they rarely spoke. Fields once described West as "a plumber's idea of Cleopatra." Yet clearly she fascinated him. He wrote a poem about her, "Little Censor Annie," for the short-lived humor magazine *Ballyhoo,* and when he later answered a questionnaire submitted to him by the *New York Sun,* he listed his

*Fields and Mae West were first photographed together at a 1935 banquet honoring Emmanuel L. Cohen. From left to right: Cohen, Al Kaufman, actor William Warren, Fields, and Gary Cooper*

favorite movie as *It's a Gift*, his favorite actor as Roland Young, and his favorite actress as Mae West.

West didn't return the compliment. She seldom carried a high opinion of other performers and never gave Fields so much as a second thought. When she lost favor with a mercurial public that had tired of her act, Paramount unceremoniously dumped her after a string of eight features. There was talk of producing her films independently, but the funding dried up and she was left with no place to go.* West did personal appearances and tended her real estate investments, and it wasn't until eighteen months after she was cut loose that she accepted Universal's offer of $50,000 to costar in a picture with Fields. "I sorta stepped off my pedestal when I made that movie," she later remarked.

The idea for the teaming was apparently conceived while Fields was at Soboba Hot Springs, for he returned to Los Angeles with a story in hand. "December and Mae" concerned the laying of the first rails between Denver and Pueblo. "My suggestion for a writer is Gene Fowler, who was born and raised in Denver, worked on the local newspaper, and is familiar with the history of the building of these three roads," he wrote. In the story, Fields' relationship with West is similar to the one between Rollo and Emily in *If I Had a Million*—responsive, solicitous, chaste. At the end, West trundles off in a horseless carriage with her new husband, a handsome young rail engineer, and Fields is left alone with his dog.

"December and Mae" was not a particularly compelling story, but the idea of pairing the bombastic Whipsnade with the wisecracking Diamond Lil was the highest of high concepts, a surefire hit if ever there was one, and the management at Universal embraced it eagerly. Fields worked himself into such a frenzy putting the package together that by the middle of May he was back at Las Encinas fighting off "a parcel of bronchial pneumonia germs." Of necessity, he kicked the sherry habit he had maintained for two years, leading to the apocryphal but oft-repeated legend that he always checked himself into the hospital before the start of a picture in order to dry himself out. Indeed, once he was discharged, he went back to drinking I. W. Harper, sometimes spiking it with milk to ward off the effects of a hangover.

After some testy negotiations with Murray Feil, West's agent at the William Morris office, the project was announced to the press on June 30, 1939. Stolid Nate Blumberg posed for pictures with his two stars, and West told Hearst columnist Louella Parsons she thought Fields' screen character would

---

*This was after Harry Brandt's infamous ad in the *Hollywood Reporter*, in which he labeled West, along with Katharine Hepburn, Joan Crawford, and Marlene Dietrich, "box office poison." Hepburn eventually recovered (with the success of *The Philadelphia Story*), but West never did.

mesh just fine with that of her own. "There is only one Fields and why should I or anybody else try to change his style?" While both participants were described as "painfully gracious," there were observers who doubted that Fields could sustain the harmony of the occasion for very long. "I couldn't imagine him getting along with Mae West," said Joe Mankiewicz. "She was a pain in the ass." West, a lifelong teetotaler, had a well-known revulsion toward alcohol. (Her sister Beverly was an alcoholic.) She may have been pleasantly surprised, therefore, to find that Fields was not as physically repugnant as he seemed onscreen, nor did he fairly reek of liquor. "He was very meticulous about himself and his appearance," said Ginger Michael. "He was always clean and he smelled nice. And he dressed beautifully." The two old troupers hit it off, if only out of respect for one seasoned vaudevillian by another.

Fields' contract with Universal was held in abeyance for this "intervening photoplay," but he still retained the responsibility for hiring and paying the director. In exchange, he received 20 percent of the gross rentals (after 1.7 times the negative cost was recouped by the studio) and drew a salary of $150,000. The writing of the script did not, as feared, turn into a repeat of the Bergen-McCarthy negotiations. In a shrewd dicker with West, Fields had swapped first-position billing in exchange for story approval, though he was, by far, the bigger star of the two. Lester Cowan, impressed with Fields' willingness to give the story a historic context, chose Grover Jones to craft the screenplay. Jones, late of Paramount, was—by his own admission—virtually illiterate, but he was a great storyteller who specialized in period epics like *The Plainsman* and *The Buccaneer.* Mindful that both Fields and West would likely write their own dialogue, Jones pledged to give each a solid structure upon which to build.

Jones' original story, purchased by Universal on July 6, 1939, contained elements of "December and Mae" but added rousing action and the three-act structure Fields' stories typically lacked. In Cowan's words, the formula was "similar in many respects to that employed by DeMille in *The Plainsman, The Buccaneer,* and *Union Pacific*—namely to first give the story significance to national importance by opening in Washington, where national leaders are in debate and where the foundation of the conflict is explained, [then winding up with] our hero being sent to establish law and order and see the project through." To this, Cowan added a *Guardsman*-like twist of his own "wherein [West] is in love with two men, one of whom she sees and another whom she meets only as the Red Shadow. The audience knows that both are identical, and she claims in the end 'that she knew it all the time.' " This, he said, gave Fields the opportunity to disguise himself as the masked rider.

Suggestions came at Jones from all sides, and the scripting process quickly bogged down. At a conference on July 17, Cowan gently suggested that Jones "take the Fields character in detail, then discuss the West character in detail, then the relationship between the two, then tie this together in a plot." Jones did so, the result being an entirely new story set in the pro-slave town of Atchison on the Missouri River in the territory of Kansas. Tweedy the Crumb, "a card-sharper and carnival man, flowery of dress, speech, and manners," thinks Kansas Kate ("beautiful, but of unsavory reputation") is his former wife. Fighting alongside Abolitionist missionaries, Tweedy is killed in a battle with counterfeiters, and Kate goes off with a handsome young soldier of fortune. Jones, who had a reputation for talking his stories, read "The Jayhawkers" to Fields and director Eddie Cline on the morning of July 26. As one of his 1940 obituaries took care to note, "Mr. Jones had the reputation of being able to sell any star, no matter how temperamental, on doing one of his stories." Cline reacted favorably, but Fields disliked being read to, and no amount of selling would get him to like Jones' story.

"Where are the places to drop in Miss West's or my routines in this picture?" he demanded. "And I don't want 'Anyplace you want to put them in' for an answer. The story is so constructed that it's impossible to disentangle it, and it is only a rubber stamp of the Western moving pictures that have gone on before with Missouri and Kansas as the background rather than the Iron Horse. . . . Had I known Jones was going to read the story to me rather than tell it to me, I would never have gone over this morning." He then sent off a wire to Mae West: "I want you to know I had nothing to do with this script and you will note that it does not follow the outline of the epitome of the story that I suggested we do. . . . We will probably have to get together in the end and write the tome ourselves."

Cowan, having guided Jones down this particular path, took another look at "The Jayhawkers." Its theme, he allowed, was "a little too big and pretentious for our principal characters and tends to dwarf them." He thought the murder of a slave woman needed clarifying "so that she becomes the symbol of the slavery issue." And care had to be taken so that the low-comedy elements of the script were not "too out of tone for the rest of the picture." In short, he found he had straitjacketed the comedy of Fields and West with a story completely at odds with the intent of the picture. West, having read Jones' treatment for herself, had a phone conversation with Cowan in which she essentially seconded Fields' reaction. Cowan assured her the story was definitely out. "I told Jones to forget about history and write for the personalities," he said. "Jones is going to write a new outline." He also mentioned that Fields had written a story of his own. "Why don't you encourage him?" West suggested. "Let him write it and get it out of his system. Let him do it." Cowan, however, was committed to Jones and resisted the idea. "Bill is probably capable of writing," she continued, warming to the notion. "He knows what he wants. Personally, I don't like to write. I'm not happy when I write. Otherwise, I'd do it for a living."

Jones tried moving the story back to 1860, opening with Fields running his own medicine show and attempting to attract Indians, trappers, and bull-whackers to his tent while, inside, West prepares for her performance. On August 19, through Charlie Beyer, Fields submitted his own revised story, a circus tale—also in period—recycling many of the discards and trims from *You Can't Cheat an Honest Man.* "I did not attempt to write any dialogue for Miss West," he noted, "as that would be presumptuous on my part. She is too capable and she knows her character so much better than I do."

Cowan, however, was unwilling to consider an alternate story until Jones was finished working on his. Angrily, Fields went to Nate Blumberg: "This method is absurd and impracticable and a waste of time and money. Mr. Jones cannot write one story in [Pacific Palisades] and I another one in Bel Air and both of us expect to come out in the end with a finished story that will jell. . . . I conceived the idea of Miss West and myself making a picture and have devoted five months to thinking and writing on it, and am no nearer the starting point now than I was then." Blumberg's reply was noncommittal (". . . I want to give your thoughts the most serious consideration"), and Cowan was fried by Fields' attempt to go over his head. He informed his star, through Beyer, that he was contractually obligated to appear in the film no matter what and that he could be sued for refusing to do so. Predictably, Fields found the next version of the Jones script even more objectionable than the last, and underscored his disgust in an elaborately sarcastic critique he addressed to Cliff Work. "Even if Mr. Ripley himself were to read this new Mae West–W. C. Fields script, he would blink his eyes in sheer amazement and say, 'I DON'T BELIEVE IT.' Here is a motion picture story that will prove to the world that movies are still in their infancy." To Cowan, Fields was simply dismissive: "Come up and sue me sometime."

By this point, Mae West, embracing the masked bandit idea, had written a script of her own. Having taken story or screenplay credit on seven of her eight films, she wrote better dialogue than Jones and understood Fields' character as well as she did her own. Cowan, under siege, placed himself firmly in the studio's camp and dug in his heels: "[Jones'] script can be developed into [a] fine picture; [the] present plan is to consider no other script. If what Miss West has written can be successfully combined with this script, I will be glad to consider and recommend purchase of the material by the studio, but not for replacement of this script. The problem of selling Miss West's script to Universal depends first on her selling it to Fields, and Fields joining with her in requesting it. Secondly, the studio's willingness to purchase it in view of the investment made in the Jones script."*

---

*Jones was drawing $2,500 a week.

On August 30, Fields again wrote to Cliff Work and asked for control of the project. "The work I'm doing on the screen differs from that of anyone else," he said. "My comedy is of a peculiar nature. Naturally, no writers have been developed along the lines of my type of comedy, and that is why I sometimes have differences with writers, supervisors, and directors alike. . . . I know how to make a Fields picture. I know how to make a West-Fields picture. I know how it can be done with expediency and economy. . . . Give me the final say on the cutting, the supervising, and directing, and I will write the story gratis—free. Eliminate factional disturbances such as making it a director's picture or a supervisor's picture or a writer's picture. Make it a Mae West–W. C. Fields picture, and if *we* are outstanding in the picture, it will sell plenty."

In response, Work told Charlie Beyer to get Fields together with Cowan and Eddie Cline, but Fields refused to do so without the authority he sought. Cline, in trying to please all the warring factions, also incurred Fields' wrath: "I picked Mr. Cline as a director because I thought him efficient, inexpensive, and someone I could talk to and get a direct reply from, but recently, when he laughed so heartily at nothing when Mr. Jones read his first script to us and, in the presence of Mr. Jones, thought it a great story and later agreed that the story was impossible, and when I found he was making visits to Mr. Jones, who was not supposed to be writing a new script, and [he] did not acquaint me with Mr. Jones' activity, and let me go ahead writing my script in the dark, I felt he was not sincere."

Estranged now from Cline as well as from Cowan and Grover Jones, Fields felt he couldn't talk to West either, for she had never responded to his wire of July 26. "I feel so God-damned out of things and so alone and working so much in the dark that it's got me nuts," he told Work in a lengthy letter. Cowan, meanwhile, was trying to "close the door" on the West script by making it clear that no money would be paid her for writing it. He kept it from Fields by maintaining his allegiance to Jones, and Work supported him in the apparent hope that the problem would eventually solve itself. A few days later, Fields did indeed concede an impasse and vowed to live up to "every letter of the contract." At the same time, he made another attempt to connect with West, offering his own story up for review and suggesting a meeting. "I feel we understand each other thoroughly and that we must get together for a chat if we are to make this opus. I am so thoroughly disgusted I have asked them several times to let me out of my contract. When I am to be placed in the tender mercies and to be guided by the trio of Jones, Cowan, and Cline, it's time to take a laminster."

Lester Cowan made a game attempt to repair his relationship with Fields, first by inviting him to dinner (Fields declined) and then by urging Gene Fowler to take on the project as screenwriter. Fields, who correctly viewed this as a wan act of appeasement and not a genuine attempt to fix the script, instructed Fowler to do nothing. "He wishes to have a friend of mine—a most able scrivener—tell him the script is a good one. This he will use as part of his evidence when Universal sues me." Cowan tried to convince Fields that Fowler had seen merit in the new script, but Fowler, in reality, thought it "gorgonzola" and refused to fall into the producer's trap. "I withdrew rather than misguide my old elk-milking friend, Water Closet Fields," he said.

Fields then escalated the battle by forbidding the use of his copyrighted material, and Cowan, sensing erosion in his position with Work and Blumberg, finally asked that Fields get together with Mae West and read her script for himself. "We have been in the middle of a situation," he said, "where you offered to write the entire story and script as your suggested solution, while she, on the other hand, had already gone ahead and prepared a complete shooting script." Fields was plainly astonished at what he saw; not only had West constructed a story line that would accommodate the both of them, but she had also created a character that Fields could play almost verbatim. Her dialogue, typically spare and epigrammatic, was, for Fields, as rococo as anything he had ever devised for himself. "During my entire experience in the entertainment world," he said in all candor, "I have never had anyone catch my character as Miss West has. In fact, she is the only author that has ever known what I was trying to do."

On September 29, Fields dictated a searing indictment of Cowan's duplicity: "I felt I had in you a young friend, and to think you should align yourself with the director and writer and make false or evasive statements to me is inconceivable. . . . I will live up to my contract and it will undoubtedly be my swan song. Universal will dive at least part of the way with me, and you, Lester, will probably be able to explain your way out of it. . . . It could have been a great picture had you not been so ambitious and avaricious for power. . . . I have come to realize what you did to me in the last picture. It is very easy to deceive a friend. Friends are on their guard only whilst in the camps of the enemy."

Two weeks later, Fields asked Matty Fox to arrange for Cowan's dismissal. "It is my best judgment that for the benefit of the picture, Lester should be given another assignment. Or put me on another picture, but I insist on Miss West going along with me. I feel if Lester continues, the picture can only wind up in a farrago. I have no wish to disparage Lester's talents, but some of them are not for tranquility and coalescence." By the time filming began on October 30, 1939, Cowan was gone. "In order to make the picture," said David Lipton, "Mr. Cowan was asked to leave the studio, and he did." The publicity people let it be known that he had returned to New York to have his wisdom teeth removed, and Fields stuck to that story when queried by the editor of the *Reporter* one night while having dinner at Chasen's. Eventually, Cowan returned to Columbia, where he produced *Ladies in Retirement* and a lamentable Paul Muni vehicle titled *Commandos Strike at Dawn.* Contractually, he retained credit as the producer of *My Little Chickadee,* along with a 2.5 percent share of the gross receipts, but as far as anyone knows, he and Fields never spoke again.

## Twenty-five

# Snorts and Grimaces

Eddie Cline narrowly survived a move by Fields—with Mae West's approval—to replace him as director with Eddie Sutherland. "[Fields] loved Eddie Sutherland," said Harry Caplan, "because Eddie Sutherland was a playboy, and he loved hearing all the stories about Eddie Sutherland going out with the broads. He was one of those boys who could leave the set at ten o'clock at night, go out all night, come in at seven o'clock in the morning, take a quick shower, and be back on the set." Fields pressed Matty Fox for Sutherland's engagement: "I think he would do a hell of a job and, as Mae said, he's got plenty of class, and that's what we need in this picture." But Sutherland, who had been responsible for the direction of West's previous film, *Every Day's a Holiday,* had committed to making a picture for Lee Garmes' Academy Productions and was unavailable.

Fields accepted the news with equanimity. He had no illusions about Cline as either a story man or picture maker; he merely thought him friendly, resourceful, incapable of getting in the way. "Eddie Cline was unique," said A. C. Lyles. "He had a tic. He was always batting his eyes and scrunching them up." Director Jules White could remember Cline from the days when Cline's father owned the Edendale Meat Market. "He'd blink like an owl," he said. Cline joined the Sennett studio in 1914, later taking credit for the invention of the Sennett Bathing Beauties. In 1920, he began working with Buster Keaton, codirecting his early shorts and his first feature, *The Three Ages.* Eventually he freelanced, driving his price to $1,500 a week. He directed Irene Dunne's screen debut in *Leathernecking* (1930) and did the occasional melodrama, but mostly he stuck with comedy. Prior to coming to Universal to direct portions of *You Can't Cheat an Honest Man,* Cline had been filming the Bobby Breen features for Sol Lesser. In terms of both budget and stature, the West-Fields picture—still untitled—represented the absolute peak of his career.

"Do not waste time in a panegyric on Eddie," said Fields. "He has devoted many years to making pictures. Just ask yourself what salary does he receive and compare it with the honorarium of Messrs. La Cava, Leo McCarey, Frank Capra, George Cukor, and dozens of others who are virtually neophytes compared to Eddie." But Fields' anger with Cline subsided once Lester Cowan was gone and he realized the big Irishman was just trying to hang on to a job he desperately wanted. West, for her part, didn't much care who directed the film. "A director can't really tell me what to do," she said. "I look a certain way, and move a certain way, and talk a certain way . . . other actors have to move around me." Fields seemed content to move around her in their early scenes together, saving his energy for his solo turns. Still, giving them both equal standing in a shot made every setup a challenge. Cameraman Joe Valentine was fast but found the forty-seven-year-old actress had a tendency to "flatten out" if not lighted brilliantly. Stepping into a set lit for West, Fields often found himself restricted to her immediate vicinity. After a week, the unit was two days behind on a forty-two-day schedule. The following week, two additional days were lost. West preferred to work afternoons, leaving the mornings to Fields and his scenes. The script was mostly hers, but Fields had inserted scenes of his own and revised others. "I did my very best to make Bill Fields' scenes as funny as possible," she said. "He was pleased with most of them, though he insisted on putting in some of his fine characteristic touches, which was no more than I would have done in his place—and have done in other times and other places."

Margaret Hamilton, as the town busybody, Mrs. Gideon, wasn't used to Fields' working methods when she played her first scene with him aboard a train bound for Greasewood City. He sat down next to her, identified himself as Cuthbert J. Twillie ("novelties and notions") and delivered a fair approximation of the scripted dialogue. Hamilton thought the scene over when he suddenly put his arm around her and said, "Do you live near here, little girl?" Not knowing what to do, she stiffened and waited for Eddie Cline to yell "Cut!" But the camera kept rolling. "Do you live with your parents?" he pressed. Then he began to mug for the camera, the crew started to laugh, and she knew the scene was at last over.

Cline made an annoyance of himself when he tried to hold Fields to the script. Mrs. Gideon asks Twillie if his companion, Milton, is a full-blooded Indian, and the answer, as scripted, is, "On the contrary, he's anemic." In the first take, Fields delivered the line as, "Quite the antithesis, he's anemic." Cline stopped the shot, took Fields aside, and told him the audience would trip over the word "antithesis" and entirely miss the word "anemic," which, after all, was the punch. Fields agreed to do another take, but stubbornly stuck with "antithesis" until the director gave up. Fields, Cline learned, usually tacked his ad-libs onto the ends of his lines so they could easily be removed in the cutting room. In a scene at the Last Gasp saloon, Twillie tells of battling one Chicago Molly by jumping over a bar and gallantly knocking her down. "You knocked

*Playing Edgar Bergen to Eddie Cline's Charlie McCarthy on the set of* My Little Chickadee. *Magda Michael is doing her best to ignore them.*

her down?" colleague Squawk Mulligan erupts. "*I* was the one that knocked her down!" Twillie, recovering quickly, says, "Oh yeah, yes, that's right. He knocked her down. . . . but I was the one that started kicking her."

"Did she ever come back again?" asks a listener.

"I'll say she came back," Mulligan interjects. "She came back a week later and beat the both of us up!"

"Yeah," says Twillie, his ego bruised, "but she had another woman with her." End of scene, but Cline left the camera rolling, "—an elderly lady with gray hair."

The problem with Fields' ad libs was that they usually made the crew laugh, spoiling the take. In this case, it was Cline himself who laughed. Trying again, Fields could never quite get the amendment exactly right, and Cline had to cut hard against the word "hair" in order to use the first take. (Forgetting this, Fields later complained that the line was too harshly cut and not properly protected—". . . just two or three frames more would make the difference between a yell and a titter," he said.) Fields' scenes with West were usually made after lunch. Examining her suite at the Greasewood Hotel, he noted the period bathtub and worked the pump that supplied the water. "A beautiful bathtub, my dear, but I don't see why you have to milk it." Cut. Cline stifled the crew's laughter and asked Fields to do it again. "A beautiful bathtub, my dear, but I don't see how you will empty it." Cut. More laughter. A third take went pretty much the same as the first, the crew held its composure, and Cline decided to print it.

Perhaps the best example of the give-and-take between West and Fields occurred when a scene required the newly married couple to disembark the train. Fields struggled to the platform, his arms laden with valises, bags, and boxes. "Right this way, my little peach bloom," he called. West, as Flower Belle Lee, emerged with only a small ribboned hatbox in one hand. "I wonder if you could take this, dear?" she asked. Feeling his way down the steps, Fields paused. "Certainly, my love. Certainly." She added the box to his already unmanageable load and he steadied himself before resuming his descent. "Careful, my dear," he said. "May I offer you my arm?"

"At that," said Harry Evans, visiting the set for *Family Circle* magazine, "Mr. Cline laughed, the cameraman laughed, five or six other people on the set laughed, and I almost choked to death trying not to. These noises, of course, ruined the scene. The cause of it all was that last line. The words, 'May I offer you my arm?' were not in the script and had never been rehearsed. Mr. Fields just threw them in when the impulse hit him. So they had to do the bit again." Dick Foran, playing the muckraking Carter, editor of the *Greasewood Gazette,* doubted that Fields' ad-lib was as spontaneous as Evans presumed. "I watched him work," he said. "Every motion, every gesture, every slurred or muttered word was a carefully planned and calculated effect." Topped, West took control of the scene on the second take. Before Fields could clamber down the steps and utter the line again, she took the hatbox and, instead of adding it to the cargo as before, stuck the ribbon between his teeth. Muffled, Fields was denied use of the line, and the laugh rebounded to West.* "I have to dominate the action in my scenes," she said, "or they won't go over."

West and Fields had their battles, but they were relatively minor compared to what had been expected. "There were a few times when Bill wouldn't play a scene the way I thought it should be played," she said. "But I would never stop him. I'd just blow a line myself, or forget one. Then we would give each other a look, have a laugh, and do the scene right." Their most serious conflict took place before shooting ever began. In mid-October, after Cowan had been deposed as producer, Fields informed West that he wanted Jan Duggan and Grady Sutton added to the cast. West had no scenes with Duggan, so she didn't care about her, but Sutton was set to play Flower Belle's cousin Zeb, and that was another matter entirely. West was much smaller than she appeared onscreen, and she didn't want to share the frame with such a big man. "Makes

---

*This scene, unfortunately, was cut from the film, but it can be glimpsed in the trailer.

me feel like I'm being crowded out of the picture." Fuzzy Knight, closer to her own height, got the job instead, and Sutton got a raincheck from Fields, who promised to put him into his next picture. Then, without consulting with West, Fields gave Fay Adler a showy bit in the saloon, her first speaking part in a picture.

A second unit, directed by Ray Taylor, was sent to Sonora to film the stage-coach holdup and an Indian attack on the train, but the company remained five days behind schedule. "While this unit is not meeting the demands of our original seven weeks shooting schedule," Martin Murphy reported, "progress has been actually better than our secret expectations." Weather problems cost two days, and Fields lost an entire week to grippe. "Although running a full eight days behind our optimistic seven-weeks schedule," Murphy wrote on December 16, "this picture is steadily moving along toward completion." West seemed genuinely surprised that anyone would expect otherwise. "We were determined to do everything possible to make the picture a financial success," she said. "Both of us can use a big hit, you know."

Exteriors were finished by Christmas, and the last shots to be made were the process shots aboard the train. According to Murphy, temperament crept into these final days, Fields and West doubtless reacting to both the fatigue of a long shoot and the sheer tedium of process work. "Considering the outlook on

*Fields and Mae West were wary of each other, and with good reason.*

this situation before starting, we were most fortunate throughout the entire production in the almost accurate execution of all our plans, and were particularly lucky in defeating weather conditions which might have proven a very costly item. Eddie Cline proved very helpful in his cooperation, reasonable in his demands, and quite conservative on negative." Production finally came to a conclusion on Friday, January 5, after fifty-six days of work, fourteen over schedule. Remarkably, the cost was $628,000, just $8,000 over the original estimate and more than $100,000 under *Destry Rides Again,* which was filmed on many of the same sets.

Cline went off almost immediately to prepare a film version of *The Drunkard* that would briefly reunite him with Buster Keaton. The completion of the West-Fields picture was left in the hands of the editors, a new line producer, Jack J. Gross, and its stars (though Mae West seemed content to let Fields manage the process). Fields began tinkering with the gags, suggesting new footage where appropriate, and was able to view a rough cut only days after filming wrapped. "I was in a screening room one time when Fields came in with his chauffeur," consulting editor Paul Landres recalled. "The chauffeur had a leather case that contained a portable bar. Fields was sipping a drink through the entire show." Landres and associate Ed Curtiss were put on the film after Fields complained so vociferously about Otto Ludwig's handling of *You Can't Cheat an Honest Man.* When the film fell behind, Curtiss went down on the set to work directly with Cline, while Landres remained in the cutting room assembling the footage. "The trick in cutting comedy," said Landres, "is to know where the laughs are going to come. You've got to hold on the laugh or you'll stifle your audience."

As might be expected for a Mae West picture, there were numerous problems with the PCA over script. An incomplete draft authored by West had gone to the Breen Office on October 23, and while Breen conceded the material was "basically satisfactory from the standpoint of the Production Code and of political censorship," he met with Eddie Cline all the same to underscore his concerns over the way West could read even the most innocuous of lines. The final white script came back with three and a half pages of cautions and eliminations; most of Breen's comments centered on West and her material, but the original ending, a sight gag suggesting that Fields had sired a family of five big-nosed half-breeds, was forbidden as well. Jack Gross, new to production after years in exhibition, tried saving the gag, but to no avail.

The fade-out became the weakest part of the script, and nobody seemed to know how to end the thing. Plans to shoot alternates were scrubbed to keep the film within budget. Personally, Fields thought the climax should leave the two of them alone "with no attempts at comedy or wisecracks from either of us," and they did indeed end on a warm exchange of catchphrases, Fields inviting

West to come up and see him sometime, and West responding with, "Yas, yas . . . I'll do that, my little chickadee." The subject of a title caused almost as much consternation as the ending, and a studio-wide contest was held to come up with ideas. Obviously, the intent was to balance it between the two stars, and neither could play the title role unless the other was suitably referenced. Hundreds of suggestions came in a memo to Lester Cowan, among them *Frontier Belle, He Was Her Man, Six-Gun Romeo,* and *How to Win Lands and Influence Indians.* No one, however, came up with the seemingly obvious title that was eventually used—*My Little Chickadee.*

The completed film was shown to Breen and Geoffrey Shurlock of the PCA on January 17, 1940, but a certificate was withheld until January 26, when it was agreed that Fields' curtain line be deleted. The offending words came in reply to West's asking him what he would do upon leaving Greasewood City. "I'll go to India and become a missionary," he says. "I hear there's good money in it, too." Fields flew into a blind rage over the cut, and dispatched Charlie Beyer to Breen's office to plead for reinstatement. After the meeting, he acknowledged defeat in a quick note to the morality czar: "I'm still prepared to sacrifice a valuable part of my anatomy to keep the line in, but if the short-haired women and the long-haired men are back in the driver's seat again, I guess there's nothing to be done." Breen responded with a conciliatory letter assuring Fields that he had a great picture on his hands without the line. "I hate like blazes to seem to trouble you about what must appear to you to be a mere detail," Breen wrote, "but when I next see you, we may be able to have a little chat, and I will then try to let you know something of the difficulties we have in this attempt, by way of the movies, 'to be all things to all men.' "

The missionary line was in for the first preview on January 21, and the film reportedly played to good effect. After Fields' exchange with Breen, a second preview took place in Pasadena, and Fields, afterward, innocently suggested "pepping up" the picture by cutting three of West's biggest scenes: a school routine in which she took command of a roomful of rowdy boys, a love scene with Dick Foran, and the song, "Willie of the Valley." For her part, West suggested cutting Fields' scene at the bar and the tale of Chicago Molly.

Fields was right in that the slow spots in *My Little Chickadee* belonged mostly to West. To be fair, she had to carry the plot while Fields, with no such responsibilities, didn't even make his first appearance until the second reel. When the film was shown to the trade press on February 6 at the Pantages in Hollywood, it was previewed, in the words of the *Motion Picture Herald,* "to an audience that laughed at some sequences so loudly and long as to drown out whole sections of dialogue, toned down to a passive acceptance at times, and then rebounded, finishing on a note of general satisfaction." The reviews were mostly favorable, though some critics noticed the film's similarity to *Destry*

*Rides Again,* which had been released by Universal just two months earlier. Fields smelled a rat in Joe Pasternak's idea of putting Marlene Dietrich in a comedy Western after she had, like West, been dropped by Paramount, and characterized the release of *Destry* ahead of *Chickadee* as "the worst showmanship I have ever heard of in all my experience." (The fact that the competing film had been directed by George Marshall may also have contributed to his ire.)

While everyone thought *Chickadee* would do business—the *Reporter* called it a "box office natural"—it had its share of detractors, and Frank Nugent was downright hostile in his assessment. "Miss West's humor, like Miss West herself, appears to be growing broader with the years, and begins to turn upon the lady; it's one thing to burlesque sex and quite another to be burlesqued by it. Mr. Fields, largely the innocent victim of someone else's bad taste, inevitably is tempted to juggle a few mud pies himself. It puts a heavy strain on an old admiration to endure the old boy's keyhole-peeping and door champing at Flower Belle's boudoir, to see him become just another member of the adulant entourage Miss West thoughtfully creates for all her pictures."

West, her time past, fared worse in the notices than did Fields, and the option Universal held on a second picture with her was never exercised. Embittered, perhaps, she soon came to disparage *My Little Chickadee* and Fields in particular, though he was never less than thoughtful and attentive in return. She claimed, well after his death, that she once had him put off the set due to drunkenness (unlikely) and that the studio had suggested inserting him into a film she already had cooking (rather than the other way around). Her main complaint, however, was that Fields took co-screenplay credit. "I let Bill write one little scene himself—he's a bartender and talks to a fly and then to a woman—and he rephrased some of his speeches. It amounted in all to a few pages out of 135. I don't want to be rude about it, but you have to have 25 pages before you put your name on something. But Matty Fox told me that Bill fought them and held them up until they had to put him in as co-author to get the film finished. I never saw the film until a month after it was released and that was the first I knew of it."

West may not have been very happy about sharing the credit for *My Little Chickadee,* but it probably wasn't the real reason she came to despise W. C. Fields. The picture was still in production when she assured the *New York Times* there would be no friction over billing. She had written the script herself, she acknowledged, but Fields had worked on his dialogue and made suggestions. "So I am going to have his name put on the writing credits." West deplored sharing billing with Fields, even though he permitted her name to come first. "The pictures he had made were B pictures," she sniffed, "and in the few big films in which he had appeared he only played cameo roles." Moreover, West's deal called for just $50,000 against Fields' $150,000 (and her percentage came from the net, not the gross). *My Little Chickadee* was a humiliating come-down for her, a gambit to entice the studio into a second picture at more favor-able terms. Worse, in later years, she was asked more about the picture she did with Fields than about any of her other movies. "Some people have gotten the quaint idea that I made more than one film with W. C. Fields," she said in 1970. "No way, baby. Once was enough."

    *Chickadee* was a hit, eventually earning nearly $2 million in gross receipts. It opened strong in most key cities, but failed to surmount the traditional Holy Week lull in New York and Los Angeles. It found its greatest audience on tele-vision. "*My Little Chickadee* was all right," West told Scott Eyman in 1973. "I think it's a good picture. But Bill Fields got co-script credit, which was a farce." Forty-seven years after its release, West's percentage for *My Little Chickadee* finally kicked in, and her estate was awarded $117,600.

Fields was grappling with Lester Cowan over control of *My Little Chickadee* when the Citron case came up for retrial. The appellate court ruled that Judge Morton had erred in excluding testimony as to the doctor's usual and custom-ary fees. "The measure of the value of services is not the value of the patient, but the reasonable value of the services in the community where they are ren-dered by the persons who rendered them. The very large judgment . . . must shock the conscience until supported by more substantial evidence." The tim-ing couldn't have been worse, for the studio was anxious for Fields to start work on the picture and the script was in nowhere near acceptable shape. The $12,000 the doctor was seeking was merely a week's pay under Fields' pact with Universal, but it was a matter of principle, and Millikan carefully sifted the jury for prejudice against "anyone who sometime in his life used intoxicating liquors." Citron took the stand on the first day, his testimony punctuated with snorts and grimaces from the defendant. Fields wasn't questioned until the third day, when he gruffly characterized Citron as "a bore" who "moved in on me." Foggy on his financial worth, Fields was downright evasive on the subject of alcohol. "I did drink a little whiskey," he admitted under oath, "but not in great quantities and only because of the excruciating pain. It was probably as much as six or seven ounces a day, and maybe a little more." Anything more than a quart, he allowed, would be considerable. "People think a lot of things about me. Some say that I'm drunk while making a picture. They even might think I'm drunk now."

    The trial stretched over most of two weeks, Fields making the daily commute from Soboba. The case finally went to the jury on the afternoon of Monday, September 25. Fields was present in the courtroom some six hours later when the panel of ten women and two men returned a verdict that was satisfactory to neither party. He showed no discernable reaction to the $2,000 fee they awarded to Citron, but privately predicted the good doctor would "screw his lawyer out of his dough" unless Wright held it out for him. "However, no matter how small an amount he receives, my wish is that it was less." Citron's request for another trial was denied, and he left the area a short time later. In 1995, his son, Robert L. Citron, pursuing an investment strategy every bit as flawed as his father's Pernoston-laced treatment plan, precipitated, as treasurer/tax collector of Orange County, California, the greatest municipal bankruptcy in American history.

Just days before the trial opened, Carlotta Monti dropped a bombshell of her own. After nine months in New York, she advised Fields in a letter that she was going to be married. The news brought him up short. At first he was cautiously supportive: "You must make up your own mind. If you are assured the man you are going to marry can take care of you in your old age, and that is what you most desire, you should go ahead." Then his concern gave way to confusion: "Why didn't you let me know about him before? I might have been able to give you some advice. This is all so sudden." In the end, the best he could say was to remind her that he would always provide for her. "No matter what you decide to do, I have you all set in my will for about $25,000, one automobile, and a cut of all my belongings, including my writings. Spending about $25 a week, this would keep you for 25 years." Without a trace of self-pity, he went on to detail all the other eruptions in his life. The trial was approaching, and Dr. Shaw, whose hilltop home he was renting in Bel Air, was back from South America and wanting his house back. The government was suing for $56,500 in back taxes. And the Mae West picture was likely to be an unmitigated disaster. "I have what seems like an unsolvable problem at Universal. My friend Mr. Cowan has double-crossed me eight different ways."

Besieged, Fields threw himself into his writing. He offered the studio an entirely new story and then, trumped by West, turned to the vastly different task of writing prose humor for a national magazine. Over the years, he had produced a handful of autobiographical pieces for newspapers and publicists, but he had never taken a serious crack at a humorous essay. In the fall of 1938, Charles Rice, editor of *This Week* magazine, invited him to try. The result, "My Rules of Etiquette," was published in December. Burnishing his reputation for boorish behavior, Fields picked through a litany of social misdemeanors and gave his reasoned assessment of each. "I agree with most other progressive social arbiters that placing the elbows on the dinner table is quite acceptable today. Putting the feet up is an entirely separate matter, however, and cannot be countenanced unless spats are worn." On the question of relinquishing a trolley seat to a lady, he said he always took the weight of her packages into account. "If over 70 pounds, I stand up—if I can stand up. Otherwise, I fall forward."

Rice, an unabashed fan, was delighted with "My Rules of Etiquette" and asked for more, eventually suggesting they collaborate on a book that would come to be known as *Fields for President.* A second piece, "My Views on Marriage," ran in October 1939, and a contract with Dodd, Mead & Company was signed in December of that year. Rice applied a steady editorial hand; but Fields insisted on reviewing all changes prior to publication. "I have every confidence in Mr. Rice's judgement," he said, "but I have had so darn much trouble with the studios taking a story I have written, or a scene, and deleting bits out of it here and there, which takes all the evenness and most of the humor out of the scene."

"Care of Babies" and "How to Figure Income Tax" followed, and the book, with further embellishments, was published in May 1940. The title, *Fields for President,* followed a tradition of comics standing for national office; Will Rogers, Eddie Cantor, and Gracie Allen all produced books on the subject. Fields, however, declined to support the book with radio appearances, and it was not widely reviewed. Those who did notice it found the Fieldsian rhetoric, sans the voice and the visage, labored and unfunny. "There is no evidence in this book of Fields' comic superiority," said Carlton Brown in the *New Republic.* "Its author or authors clings or cling to the undergraduate idea that all names like Schmackenpfeiffer, Hemmendinger, and Thistleberger are funny *per se.*"

The book's failure did not dampen Fields' enthusiasm for public discourse, and he briefly considered writing a column of comment and wordplay for the Bell Syndicate. Largely apolitical, he privately vented his hatred for the president ("Gumlegs") and the first lady ("Tornpocket"), decrying a confiscatory tax system where "one pays from 94 to 99% income tax, I being one of the ones." His samples for the column were more reasoned but no less impassioned. "Instead of a NEW DEAL," he wrote, "we want a NEW DECK. The New Deal has never ripened. It is still a Raw Deal." He wrote of race relations, the Nazis, and the ruinous effects of candy on little teeth. Most strikingly, he revealed a fervid social conscience. "What we need in this country beside a good five-cent cigar is a little less talk about the white or Caucasian Aryan race running the world. We have with us today some 30 million dark loyal Ameri-

*Largely drawn from articles written for* This Week *magazine,*
Fields for President *didn't sell well.*

cans. The Chinese are not Caucasians and Russia, with its semi-Tartar leader, is not one-hundred percent Aryan. We are allies. Let these megalomaniacal politicians pipe down—or enlist." An effort to shop the feature, called "Gentle Reader," turned up little interest on the part of the dailies, and a plan to have it ghosted proved impractical.

Just prior to the release of *My Little Chickadee,* Fields observed his sixtieth birthday. The event was allowed to pass unnoticed in the press, but a stag gala in his honor was held at the Encino ranch of film director Raoul Walsh. The guest list included John Barrymore, William Wellman, Mark Hellinger, Bruce Cabot, Errol Flynn, and Buster Keaton. Fields keynoted the evening with a rambling tale of love in the Tyrolean Alps, then Walsh toasted him as a genius of comedy who might also have been a great tragedian. "He would have been superb in death scenes," Walsh said, "due to his long practice at lying on his back."

Once the release of the picture was behind him, Fields left on a month's holiday, first to the Hotel Del Monte in Monterey, then on by rail to Sun Valley, where he told *Daily Variety* he would do "some whiz-skiing." Charlie Beyer accompanied him, and the two men spent their days admiring both the scenery and the beer at the Sun Valley Lodge. At night, Fields switched to gin and grew reflective, writing long letters to friends and associates and wondering just how much more there could be to his life. His mother had lived to be seventy, but his grandfather had died at the tender age of fifty-five. His thoughts turned naturally to Hattie and Claude and the life they might have made together. In Idaho he witnessed a scene that haunted him, and he described it to Magda one night in a rambling letter: "O! the carnival was on yesterday—improvised floats emulating Pasadena [and the Rose Parade]. A boy with a home-made dog sleigh was leading in the race, his father standing on the side. The dog recognized the pater and ran over to him and wagged his tail. [The] boy cried and said, 'Dad, why did you do it?' He lost. . . . I thought of little Claude in that race. It taught me a lesson. I'll never attend one of those races as long as I live. Go ahead [and] laugh—you have never had a son and can't realize my feelings. . . . OK, I'm drunk. What of it?"

The subject of Claude was a vexing one, and Fields insulated himself by simply avoiding all contact. He turned down an invitation to dinner on Christmas Day, choosing instead to dine with the Fowlers. On one of the rare occasions when he did come to the Gale Drive apartment Claude shared with his mother, he was seated in the absolute center of the room, uncomfortably on display for the other guests. Gazing across at the elderly woman who was still his wife, the years seemed to melt away. "Hattie," he said, "your skin is still as smooth as ever." Claude's intended bride came west for the first time in 1938, and Fields upped Hattie's stipend to $70 a week to help pay for the visit. But he and Claude rarely spoke, and Claude only occasionally came to the house. "He thought Claude was just a pompous ass," said Ginger Michael. "He didn't like him, and that was painful, I think, because he wanted to like him. He really wanted to be a father, but when Claude came to visit, there was no attempt at intimacy. He wasn't friendly; he was always kind of stuffy. He'd say 'Hullo Father' with a kind of icy distance in his voice."

When Claude's marriage to Anne Ruth Stevens was set in 1942, after a courtship that lasted nearly a decade, Claude dutifully sent an invitation to his father. "You are the very first to get one of the enclosed invitations to my wedding," he said in an accompanying note. "It will be celebrated 9:00 high mass and promises to be a beautiful ceremony. Let me know if you wish to attend." It may have been at Hattie's instigation, or merely the lawyer in him, but Claude sent the invitation by registered mail. Two days later, it was refused at Fields' house and returned unopened.


After pictures like *Big Broadcast* and *My Little Chickadee,* Fields longed to do another family comedy on the order of the best of his Paramount features. He urged Matty Fox to see *You're Telling Me!* and *It's a Gift* as examples. "These pictures in all probability prompted such series as The Hardy Family, The Jones Family, etc. ad libitum," he opined. In fact, Fields asked Fox to look into borrowing Mickey Rooney, star of the Hardy series, from MGM for his next production. Fields had a story he called *The Bank Dick* (which he had written in the dark days immediately following *You Can't Cheat an Honest Man*), but it didn't exactly depict the kind of wholesome American family audiences had come to expect of the popular Hardy series. Fields' equivalent of wise old Judge Hardy was, in the words of his mother-in-law, "a drunkard, a ne'er-do-well, a cicatrice, a rakehell," his youngest child an uncontrollable brat, and his teenage daughter engaged to the town idiot. Through a purely accidental chain of events, Egbert Souse ("Sousè—accent grave over the e") is credited with the capture of a bank robber and rewarded with the position of special officer—a bank dick. "I've always had a hankering to find out what a bank guard thinks and feels like," Fields said. "They always give me the fishy eye. They make me feel as if they thought I had come into the bank to steal the pens, blotters, and any other loose-lying knick-knacks."

Fox assured Fields that he would be left to his own devices, and Cliff Work echoed the sentiment to Charley Beyer. Jack Gross, who had proven such an agreeable supervisor on *My Little Chickadee,* assumed the job once again on *The Bank Dick,* and Eddie Cline was approved as director. It looked as if Fields was finally going to have his way from the outset when he was hobbled by the sudden departure of his trusted secretary, Magda Michael. Never an easy man to work for, Fields had docked her on account of sick time, and she had retaliated by giving notice. He responded to her letter of resignation with a shocked three-page note in pencil. "I did 'dock' you for illness," he acknowledged, "but

I thought I had made up for it in other ways. I did not want you to get into the habit of taking several days off for a holiday, a headache, or a peeve, or just 'because' whenever you felt so disposed. Especially when I had the miseries or the studio was applying the heat. You struck once when I was very ill at Soboba. I raised your salary. You struck once at Las Encinas when I was still very ill, and now in the middle of writing what will probably be my last picture you strike again, making it three strikes." Magda found herself another job and Fields got himself another secretary, a pretty blonde from Kansas City named Malinda Boss. Early in May, Universal announced Fields' *Bank Dick* as part of a slate of forty-two feature films for its upcoming season, which also included two Deanna Durbin musicals, two Marlene Dietrich vehicles, two Hugh Herbert comedies, and an original Jerome Kern musical called *Riviera.* Seven Johnny Mack Brown Westerns, four serials, forty-seven one- and two-reel short subjects, and 104 issues of the house newsreel rounded out the program.

The revised fifty-three-page story, incorporating elements of "the theatrical mother and the infant prodigy" plotline Fields had earlier pitched to the studio, was completed on June 12, 1940. The subplot, in which Sousè induces his daughter's fiancée, Og Oggilby, to buy shares in a beefsteak mine by "borrowing" the funds from the bank at which he works, was clearly inspired by *The Potters,* with Egbert Sousè as a kind of pixilated Pa Potter, disparaged by his family and ever on the lookout for an easy buck. To help assemble his scenes into something approaching a viable script, Fields hired Dick Carroll, an ex-newspaperman who wrote tightly plotted thrillers like *Five Came Back,* to work on the screenplay as an uncredited collaborator. Carroll gave *The Bank Dick* structure and integrated the filmmaking gags, but retained the flavorful dialogue from Fields' original story. On June 29, the first seventy-five pages of the Fields-Carroll draft were submitted to the PCA, bringing cautions about slang words like "stinko" and "nuts" and questioning the name of the town saloon, which Fields had christened the Black Pussy in tribute to his friend Leon Errol, who owned a similarly named establishment on Santa Monica Boulevard.

However sound *The Bank Dick* was from a censorship angle, the studio was still "definite concerning the need of a rewrite, changes, and revisions." A lengthy list of suggestions, which Fields found "so banal that it would reduce the picture to a B type," began by suggesting on page one that the film open with Sousè selling snake oil for an occupation. "Every author has me selling something in the beginning of a picture," he complained. "In the last one, Miss West graciously permitted me to switch from snake oil to phoney jewelry. I do not wish all my pictures to look alike. I would like at least one a bit different." He described *The Bank Dick,* which took place in the tiny Kansas town of Lompoc, as "a tempest in a teapot," and expressed bewilderment that anything at all had to be changed. "The story has more originality than most motion picture stories. The love interest I consider unique, original, and interesting. Further, the story is believable and I have every confidence it will prove as good as anything I have ever done. The public will readily recognize the characters, which is the secret of tickling their risibilities." He excused the short length of the script by noting it had been succinctly written "to avoid overhead and allow for by-play, interpolations, and for extemporaneous dialogue," and pleaded to be let alone, promising to deliver a good Fields picture "in a very short space of time, reasonable and tasty."

*The Bank Dick* was officially purchased by the studio on July 29, 1940, enabling a staff writer named Charles Grayson to immediately set to work on a rewrite. Grayson contributed to cheap musicals and was in part responsible for the disastrous *Top of the Town.* Fields picked collaborators who were story specialists with little experience in comedy, while others tended to pick collaborators for him that were precisely the opposite. Grayson didn't collaborate; he went off to his office and composed a version of *The Bank Dick* that had little of the flavor or uniqueness of Fields' original. He changed some of the character names and rewrote the dialogue, providing the slapstick finish Eddie Cline thought was needed but diminishing the overall impact of the story. When Fields saw the first fifty-nine pages of Grayson's revision, he felt himself back at the point where he was arguing against a wholly inappropriate script that everyone else seemed to like. "All the dialogue has been changed so that the character of Sousè is no longer Fields," he charged. "The dialogue of the other characters has been changed so that I do not recognize them." He was cheered only momentarily when Elise Cavanna reported in early August that the Museum of Modern Art had shown *The Barber Shop* in New York. "I wish I could get the Sheenies at Universal to think as you do and they do," he said in a reply. "They have taken my story, the Sheenies, and torn it to ribbons. They put a writer on after I had finished the story, and a lousier, dumber banal bastard never graced a Moxie studio. . . . If I have much more Eskimo trouble at Universal I may not even do the picture."

## Twenty-six

# Museum Piece

The full 106-page screenplay of *The Bank Dick,* delivered August 22, 1940, was satisfactory to no one. Fields made a last-ditch appeal to Nate Blumberg, but he no longer had the fight left in him to sustain a protracted battle. "I am going to live up to my contract to the letter," he vowed. "But I assure you if I am forced to do this picture as it is now written, it will not only be detrimental to me, but to Universal Studio." Blumberg responded with a soothing vote of confidence, and Fields was mollified, if only for the moment. But to Blumberg and the other administrators, Fields was essentially an actor, not a writer or a director, and permitting him much sway on material was like giving story approval to Deanna Durbin or letting Marlene Dietrich write her own dialogue. "I am having costumes tried on, monkeying around with the script, and trying to get my face healed up from the sunburn I got at Catalina Island," Fields told Carlotta in a sunny note on September 7. Within days, however, he had a Cowanesque letter in hand from Edward Muhl, advising him that he was required to render services in accordance with their agreement under any and all circumstances. "I have called Universal all the names I know," Fields wrote Gene Fowler, who was vacationing on Fire Island. "I hope you will arrive soon with a fresh batch."

*The Bank Dick* seemed headed for certain disaster, and Fields resigned himself to making the last picture of his career a dud. No other star in Hollywood had above-the-title billing and carried contractual responsibility for writing and directing as well as performing at the age of sixty. Chaplin was nine years younger, Stan Laurel, Oliver Hardy, Buster Keaton, and Eddie Cantor all younger still. Fields' threat to "repeat the lines of Mr. Charles Grayson verbatim" must have been chilling, though, for when he went before the cameras in early September, the record shows that he and his fellow cast members were speaking the lines as he himself had written them, and that much of Grayson's script was out.* "I was

---

*Ironically, when the "original" *Bank Dick* screenplay was published in 1973, it was not the Fields-Carroll draft at all, but rather Grayson's version erroneously credited to Fields.

going to throw it in their faces," he said. "The director stopped me. 'Shoot your own script,' he said. 'They won't know the difference.' So we did—and they didn't!'"

Though the Grayson script was the one officially shot—it was the script the Breen Office reviewed—*The Bank Dick,* with the exception of its ending, was almost entirely Fields' work. Grayson's scenes were shortened, restaged, or, as in the case of a bizarre six-page opening, eliminated entirely. "Heavens," said actress Una Merkel, who played his daughter, Myrtle, "if he thought a scene was too long, he'd take a couple of pages and tear them off, saying, 'That's enough, I'm not going to remember anymore.' " Fields used slapstick to cover the deletions and returned, by default, to the style of comedy George Marshall had so insistently favored. Three pages of labored dialogue establishing Egbert's relationship with his family were deftly reduced to forty seconds of playing time when Fields jettisoned all the lines Grayson had written for him and relied instead on physical business—swallowing a lighted cigarette, whacking his younger daughter on the head and getting conked in return with a cat-sup bottle. Nine-year-old Evelyn Del Rio, who had played a funny bit in *You Can't Cheat an Honest Man,* proved adept at knockabout in two key scenes, continuing a tradition started in 1921 when Fields had opened "Off to the Country" with the brutalization of Ray Dooley.

According to Una Merkel, the last scene in *The Bank Dick* was the first scene actually committed to film. Egbert and his family are shown amid the trappings of their newfound wealth. "He was due at nine and came in at eleven, and he'd had quite a night the night before, I guess. The first scene was all of us sitting around the table. . . . I was supposed to say, 'Good morning, pater,' and kiss him. So in the rehearsal he apologized, because you could smell the alcohol, and I said, 'Mr. Fields, on you it smells like Chanel No. 5,' and he said, 'Honey, you're in!' From then on, he was just wonderful to me." It was an arduous shoot, almost clandestine by nature, and made only marginally easier by the handpicked cast and a director who could shoot physical comedy as well as anyone. Eddie Cline once quoted Fields as saying that the reason he let Cline direct his pictures was because Cline was the only man in Hollywood who knew "less about making movies" than he did. In reality, Cline was, like Fields, a man who knew how to give a gag its best chance with an audience. "Fields and Cline were basically the same type," said Ed Montagne. "They both had great comedy sense. Eddie was not one who was particular. He'd let [Fields] run. With actors, if he thought they were on the right track, he'd let them go. He had funny ideas."

Cline worked out gags by acting as Fields' stand-in as he blocked a scene, a practice that kept Tony Rice, Fields' official stand-in, on the sidelines. "I just try to imagine I'm Fields," Cline said. Walking through a scene in which Russell Hicks, as J. Frothingham Waterbury, the crooked stock trader, turns the hard sell on Sousè, Cline backed up, lifted his hat to scratch his head, and caught it on a coat hook. "We'll put that in the picture!" he said, and, in fact, they did. Fields, of course, passed on any business Cline developed and contributed much of his own. "I went out to Universal a couple of times to visit and saw him working," said A. C. Lyles. "I used to think about the poor script clerk who had to keep track of every little move. He was great at adding little touches as he went along."

Having been bumped from *My Little Chickadee,* Grady Sutton had the plum role of Oggilby expressly written for him: "I remember when he did *The Bank Dick* they wanted someone else, I don't know who it was, but the powers-that-be wanted this other guy. Fields said, 'No, I want Grady. I like to work with him. I like the way he reacts to me.' And they said, 'No, we want so-and-so.' He said, 'All right then—get yourself another Fields.' They had to hire me, but I didn't work out there again for three years or so, they were so mad at me." Playing Javert to Og's Jean Valjean was Franklin Pangborn, a superb comic foil whose by-the-book bank examiner, Snoopington, is dedicated to sniffing out the funds "borrowed" at Egbert's behest. (Sousè intercedes by slipping him a "Michael Finn," but Snoopington proves heartier than expected and is back on the job the next day.) Cora Witherspoon, Jessie Ralph, Dick Purcell, and Shemp Howard rounded out the principal cast, which was embroidered with the likes of Bill Wolfe, Jan Duggan, George Moran, and Fay Adler. ("Did any-one ever tell you that you were a ringer for the girl who was chosen Miss Punx-atawney last year at Atlantic City?" Fields ad-libbed. "Or maybe it was Miss Passamaquoddy?") Del Rio, a little Puerto Rican dancer who was often billed as the "Latin Shirley Temple," played Elsie Mae Adele Brunch Sousè, a tip of the special officer's cap to Fields's two sisters.

Approaching the age of sixty-one, Fields' energy was flagging, and he gen-erally worked a short day. Milton Krasner, A.S.C., who photographed *The Bank Dick,* could tell when he was winding down. "At four o'clock every day he'd say to his driver, 'Get me my pill, Al.' His 'pill' was orange juice and rum. His nose would get red and I used a filter on his nose to get the color back." Fields was going through a phase where he was drinking mostly rum drinks and beer—Heineken when he could get it—switching to martinis, as usual, around dinnertime. "We finish the picture on Wednesday," he advised Carlotta in a note on October 20. "I am so tired I could cash in right now."

The climax of the movie was a wild five-minute car chase designed by Ralph Ceder in which Sousè, a gun held on him by Mopey Murphy, the bank bandit, frantically attempts to ditch the police. Ceder, who directed comedy

*Petite Fay Adler played a bit role in* The Bank Dick.

shorts and poverty-row features when he wasn't doing second-unit work, went off for nearly two weeks, working exclusively with stunt doubles, and returned with a sequence that not only gave the film the sock finish it needed, but provided Universal with an amazing wealth of stock footage. Fields' involvement in the chase was limited to matching shots against a process screen back at the studio. "One day he took the wheel off the car in process," Krasner remembered, "and when he threw it out, it went through the screen. You could rest assured that when you did a picture with Fields you had a long picture."

Filming wrapped on October 22, 1940, and Fields beat a hasty retreat to Soboba Hot Springs, where he remained through the end of the month. On Halloween, he sent a wire to Jack Gross to remind him to credit the original story and screenplay to Mahatma Kane Jeeves, a Fieldsian nod to his friend Orson Welles, who had just finished directing *Citizen Kane,* and to author P. G. Wodehouse, whose "Jeeves" stories Welles urged him to read. ("My hat, my cane, Jeeves!") He added: "There is not one line to my knowledge of Grayson's used in the script." The first preview was held on November 3, and the audience reaction was thunderous. Fields dashed off four pages of notes the next morning, suggesting a number of minor eliminations and requesting that several scenes be restored or recut to accommodate the laughs.

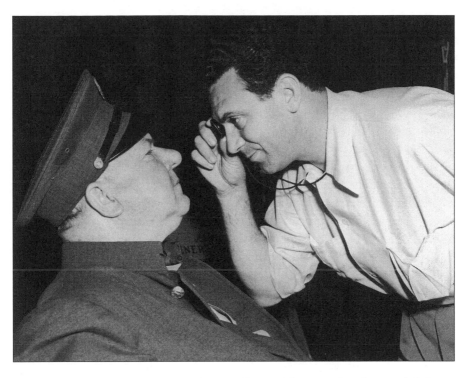

*Cinematographer Milton Krasner had to use a filter to balance out the color in Fields' face.*

The twenty dollar bill gag was cut so short it did not register. . . . Too much of the drunken director. He is very funny but overdone. . . . The two scenes with the girls on the bench and the newspaper routine were omitted. I thought they were to be given a chance at a preview. . . . In the hotel room, one run out of bed to the bathroom for Snoopington is enough; if it can be arranged that he merely covers his head the second time, [it] would be an improvement. . . . In the scene following the last breakfast scene, the business with the straw hat was cut out entirely. It should be retained. As Fields exits from the home the bit of hitting the leaf with the cane should be put back. It will help build up the kicking of the bit of wood. It is his character. . . . The chase I thought the best I have ever seen. But there is one spot where a car knocks a man off a box—looked like the same man to me—three times. This can be easily remedied. The chase was wonderful. Ceder deserved much credit. . . . We have a great comedy if these faults are remedied.

The PCA staff saw the film on November 8 and requested only minor changes. The word "Swissesse" (ass) was removed, as was the tail end of Fields' appreciative comment when awarded a copy of "Spring in Lompoc," the bank's nude calendar: "Looks not unlike the Mona Lisa, *only a little heavier.*" A second viewing on the fourteenth brought forth a caution from Breen about using too much of the drunken movie director, A. Pismo Clam, a point Fields had already made on purely artistic grounds. Ironically, the film's most censorable elements, the star's trademark expletives, sailed past the authorities without any notice whatsoever.

Fields had always been a proponent of swearing onscreen, regarding the practice as fully consistent with a character that would lie, cheat, and boot a small child. As with regular dialogue, however, he found it impossible to embrace the run-of-the-mill vulgarities expressly forbidden under the Production Code. He employed fanciful substitutes instead, delivered with much the same volume and force as the genuine articles. "Mother of Pearl" was a favorite—meaning, of course, "son of a bitch"—and the word "Drat!" is heard at some juncture in most all of his pictures. ("Drat my gullibility!" was one of his favorite expressions.) He reproaches a clumsy carriage driver in *David Copperfield* with "Shades of Nicodemus!" and the once-common expression "nigger in the woodpile" (meaning something's not working) became, in several of his movies, "Ethiopian [or Nubian] in the fuel supply." By far, the most personal and colorful of his exclamations was "Godfrey Daniel!" which stood in for "goddamn" and was also the name of his father's youngest brother, Godfrey Dukenfield (1854–1946). Robert Lewis Taylor, Fields' first biographer, observed, "Just as many comedians have been able, on the legitimate stage, to utter the fiercest oaths and make them sound innocent, Fields could voice tea-party pleasantries and make them sound profane."

Despite the raucous receptions accorded the film at its two preview screenings, Fields' own opinion of *The Bank Dick* curdled with repeated viewings, and he became sure it would fail. Nothing played quite well enough to suit him, and he mistrusted those at the studio who were charged with carrying out his instructions. "The picture gets laughs that are all forced over," he complained in a letter to Matty Fox. "There is no continuity, and that story that they all insisted upon and raved about is, in its present form, unintelligible and will receive a great number of raps from the critics, justly so." With Christmas approaching, he was also worried about competition in the marketplace. Chaplin's first picture in four years, *The Great Dictator,* was playing roadshow at the Carthay Circle, the Marx Brothers were opening at Grauman's Chinese in *Go West,* and Jack Benny and Fred Allen were about to open in Paramount's *Love Thy Neighbor.* Fields observed that moviegoers who wanted to laugh had a lot of options. "I hope Chaplin's picture is as bad as the critics say it is," he said.

Unfortunately, his bad-mouthing of *The Bank Dick* got around, and by the time of the official press preview at the RKO Hillstreet, there wasn't much anticipation. The film's first big laugh came just two minutes into the action, when Sousè does battle with his little daughter over a copy of *Detective* magazine. Beaned with the catsup bottle, he staggers out the front door, only to reappear moments later, poised to clobber the child with a concrete urn. Another thirty seconds pass, and he ingratiates himself with an old lady whose limousine has broken down at the side of the road. Despite the chauffeur's best attempts to wave him off, Sousè helpfully loosens a nut under the hood and watches as the entire engine drops to the ground.

"The rumors that circulated before it was shown indicated that this would not be much of a picture," said Edwin Schallert of the *Los Angeles Times,* "but it is undoubtedly one of the best in which Fields has acted, and this was due to the fact that he himself wrote the screenplay, evolving that special brand of fun for which he is noted." Schallert took the extraordinary step of reviewing the preview some two weeks before the film actually opened in Los Angeles. "W. C. Fields hits his old-time comedy stride in *The Bank Dick,*" he wrote. "In fact, this is probably his top-notch comedy starring vehicle. He had the house both in stitches and an uproar last night at the preview." The trades were all equally impressed; the *Reporter* called it "the funniest picture Fields has made in some

*Producer Jack Gross held the press preview of* The Bank Dick
*at the RKO Hillstreet. Just three years earlier,*
*Gross had been manager of the 2,900-seat house.*

years," and *Daily Variety,* usually a tough judge of Fields' work, said the film was "completely delightful." The subhead in *Film Daily* heralded a rave: "Here's a wow that will bring 'em in and satisfy 'em. Fields is great and Cline's direction corking."

Buoyed by the response of the critics, Fields conceded *The Bank Dick* wasn't so bad after all. A two-page photo layout, "Danger . . . The Great Man is at Work," timed to the film's November 29 release, appeared in *Look* magazine, but Fields was still off radio, and his refusal to do promotional appearances may have doomed the picture. In LA, where it graced the lower half of a double bill with Columbia's *Escape to Glory,* business was so brutally bad that it was pulled after just six days. In New York, where it was universally praised in the dailies, it opened at the RKO Palace in the No. 2 spot, supporting *Seven Sinners* on a second run, and did, in the wan judgment of *Variety,* just an "oke" week. Bosley Crowther wrote,

> No reflection is intended on the appearance of W. C. Fields when we say that the great man has mellowed considerably, and for the best, since he was last among us in *My Little Chickadee* and, before that, in *You Can't Cheat an Honest Man.* Then he gave signs of degenerating into a pesky, cantankerous old fluff with a disposition as vile as that of a wolverine. But now . . . we welcome our old friend Bill back, as magnificently expansive as ever. True, he is herein supported (technically speaking, of course) by an excellent cast of comics. . . . But the gratifying thing is that Bill is at last given his muffin head again, and is not compelled to tag along with such excess baggage as Mae West or even Charlie McCarthy. The picture belongs to him, and his name—or nom de plume—is stamped all over it.

In Philadelphia, *The Bank Dick* had a good opening day at the 2,700-seat Earle Theatre, supported as it was by Vincent Lopez and His Orchestra, but attendance fell off so rapidly it was startling, and the week ended up a pallid $17,000. It was the same story in San Francisco, Providence, Seattle, and Portland, where the film was embraced by the critics but failed to attract an audience. Before long, the pre-Christmas lull had set in and there was no hope of salvaging it in playoff. For the year-end number of *Variety,* William Saroyan penned a deeply felt tribute to the film, but it came too late to do any good. "The Modern Museum in New York might just as well take it right out of the first-run picture houses and show it to the serious-minded people who study motion picture art without waiting for 20 years to go by first," he said. "It's just as funny now as it will be 20 years from now, and there's no need to wait. The world may change, but not this comedy. *Time* magazine will go on picking The

Man of the Year every year, but the guy who will make you laugh just to remember him will be W. C. Fields any year."

Fields was chased from his hilltop home in Bel Air at a most inopportune time. The picture that would become *My Little Chickadee* was in trouble, the second Citron trial was on, the government was after him for back taxes, and his friends, an ever-narrowing circle of cronies, were all concentrated in the nearby hills and canyons along Sunset as it wound its way toward Malibu and the Pacific Ocean. Chasen's Southern Pit at Beverly and Doheny was like a second home to him, with its eight-stool counter and its Ping-Pong tables on the terrace, and Campbell's Book Store, across the street from the UCLA campus in Westwood Village, was a regular stop on his weekly itinerary. Bob Campbell, in fact, remembered Fields as "all business" when he came into the store. "He usually had a list of items to purchase, most of them gifts for friends or neighbors. In spite of Fields' reputation, he was always cold sober, although had the lights gone out we could have seen pretty well by the glow of his nose. When Fields had completed the list he would say, 'That's all, add 'em up.' While we were 'adding 'em up' he would wander around the store and see other things he wanted and add these to his purchase. Usually we had three charges for him before he finally got out of the store, with the record being five separate charges, four being made after his declaration, 'That's all, add 'em up.' "

Sent scrambling for a new place to live, Fields quickly settled on a house in Laughlin Park, in the tony Los Feliz district of Los Angeles where, removed from the West Side, he could still enjoy an arresting view of the city. The home, a two-story Italian villa that sat like a white palace atop three acres of manicured lawn, was built in 1917 by a California oilman named Frank Wood. In the 1920s, the neighborhood was populated by the likes of Jack Dempsey and Cecil B. DeMille, who lived directly across a gravel road known as DeMille Drive. After Wood's death, it was rented to a succession of Hollywood notables, among them Maurice Chevalier and William Le Baron. It was during Le Baron's residency that Fields got his first look at the place, and its subsequent availability coincided neatly with his having to quit the property on Funchal Road. "I like this place because of the lawn," he said. "I think looking at cut grass is the most soothing thing in the world."

With a multiyear lease in hand, Fields set about to make the house his own. There was a dramatic entrance arcade, red tiled and trellised with bougainvillea, that ran the length of the walk from the street to the door, and Fields had it lined with speakers so that he could make announcements from his office on the second story. Inside, he placed speakers in every room, drilling holes through the hand-rubbed mahogany paneling in order to run wires. "If he heard any noise," said Ginger Michael, "he'd get on the system and do his best to ward off the intruders: 'Okay, Bill, go get the gun!' and 'Okay, Joe, what else do you need?' " The living room, to the left of the entry, had a bar at one end, a grand piano shoved off to one corner, and a Ping-Pong table as its centerpiece. The formal dining room contained little more than a pool table. A library on the mezzanine level housed his books behind glass doors, but the cellar in the windowed basement wasn't practical for the storage of wine and spirits because the furnace was there. During the day, the serenity was broken only by Fields' devoted housekeeper, Adele Clines, his secretary, Melinda Boss, and a Japanese gardener who mowed the lawn twice a week. Alone at night—Dell caught the 7:30 bus back to South Central—Fields confined himself to the three rooms on the upper level, reading, listening to the radio, scribbling notes for the next day.

Chasen's was now thirty minutes away by car, but he still managed to get there at least once a week. He liked other restaurants as well (Cafe LaMaize, the Brown Derby, and the House of Murphy were particular favorites, and he actually had money in Joe Leone's Sunset Strip bistro), but Chasen's was comfortable and casual and relatively cheap. Chili cost a quarter a bowl, drinks were thirty-five cents. Dave Chasen had been stooge to Joe Cook, one of the best of the latter-day nut comics in vaudeville, and he knew how to treat his

*Fields' office in Laughlin Park was typically strewn with magazines, newspapers, manuscripts, and books on all manner of subjects.*

celebrity guests. The place was off-limits to photographers, and characters like John Barrymore and Dorothy Parker were indulged and fed regardless of their ability to pay. On a single night in May 1940, the diners, beside Fields, included Robert Benchley, Charlie Chaplin, Sonja Henie, Jack Benny, and Hedda Hopper. "Most successful restaurant owners make me feel like a worm with their superiority, and accents, and ropes," Frank Capra said. "But Chasen says, 'Welcome, brother worm.'" Fields liked the Ping-Pong tables as much as the food and played a devastating game. One night, lacking a partner, he invited Ann Ronell to join him after a CBS broadcast. "I used to stand by just dying to play with him," she said, "but I didn't think I was good enough. This particular evening he was feeling very high indeed, and very happy, and he played a terrific game. It was in the fog. I couldn't see a thing it was so foggy, but he beat everybody around."

Gene Fowler, who returned to California in 1940 to write a book, was also a regular at Chasen's. Fishing around for work more satisfying than scriptwriting (for which he was paid $2,000 a week), Fowler undertook a biography of the bohemian poet and art critic Sadakichi Hartmann, a process that would eventually result in his masterful *Minutes of the Last Meeting*. Fowler took a house on North Barrington Avenue in Brentwood Heights, put Hartmann up at the Hotel Gilbert in the middle of Hollywood, and appropriated artist John Decker's nearby studio on Bundy Drive as a base of operations. Said his son, Gene Fowler Jr., "My father would start working at three o'clock in the morning, and by nine o'clock he was finished writing. He would leave it for his secretary to type up and he'd go to bed. Then when he'd get up, he would correct the stuff and have the rest of the afternoon to himself. So he'd wander down to my house or Decker's house. There was no set routine, no set time. It was just that everyone knew Decker was a focal point."

A gifted art forger, Decker became host to a group of eccentrics comprised of John Barrymore, Errol Flynn, Vincent Price, Anthony Quinn, Roland Young, Thomas Mitchell, Alan Mowbray, Ben Hecht, John Carradine, and, more often than not, Fields. "Barrymore was the center," said Quinn. "He would suddenly start spouting Shakespeare and everybody would quit talking. There was something in his recitation; it wasn't reciting, it was talking. The respect that everyone in that room had for his acting. . . . [Fields] would come in and actually would be very respectful of Barrymore, so much so that he seemed like a shy man. Except now and then he would let a barb go and it was marvelous. It was extraordinary to see him." Fields didn't much like the wheezing, cadaverous Hartmann, whom he referred to variously as Hoochie-Kootchie and Catch-a-Crotchie, but that didn't stop him from giving the old man money whenever he took the trouble to visit. "Sadakichi Hartmann had contracted TB," Steve Fairfield said, "and he was living out at the Morongo

Indian Reservation with an Indian woman. He had no money at all, and he used to hitchhike into Beaumont and walk through Lamb's Canyon, and probably walked from the mouth of Lamb's Canyon over to Soboba Hot Springs to see his friend Bill and come back with a few bucks. And I imagine it was quite a few. Bill never seemed to turn him away."

Fields was still a regular at Soboba, where he could be seen ambling the property with putter in hand—he called it his "snake killer"—and enjoying the solitude of the Pima, the only cottage in the Indian Village that contained a full kitchen. In the spring of 1938 he bought two sixteen-cylinder Cadillacs, a two-door coupe and a seven-passenger sedan, breaking a run of Lincolns that dated back to the 1920s. Owing to the ordeal his bad back made of long car trips, he had the coup outfitted with a barber's chair so that he could sleep through the long drive to San Jacinto.* (Despite repeated paeans to firm mattresses and fine linens, he often found a barber's chair delivered the best night's rest.) Soboba's owner, John Althouse, augmented the recreational facilities on the property with a shuffleboard court poured especially in Fields' honor. "Herr Althouse and the beautiful Frau Althouse were in their usual good health," he reported to Carlotta after one brief sojourn. "At dinner Sunday evening, Mr. Althouse wore a salt-and-pepper suit with a red double-breasted vest, a Piccadilly collar, and red tie. Mrs. Althouse looked ravishing in her new knee-length baby blue chiffon creation which revealed intriguing glimpses of her lace-edged undies."

Sometimes Fields attended the Soboba Theatre on Main Street in San Jacinto, a seven hundred–seat auditorium of faux adobe where, on Friday and Saturday nights, five acts of vaudeville still accompanied the movie. His maroon limousine, which had a bar built into the backseat, was a familiar sight around town. "Quite an automobile," said Fairfield admiringly, "and during my tenure running the Standard Oil gas station in San Jacinto, I washed and polished it a couple of times. Some days, he would take more gasoline than we would sell to all the other customers combined. It seemed that car was always on the go, always busy." Fields' fondness for direct sun and hot food—he loved *menudo* and *huevos rancheros*—aggravated a chronic skin condition known as rosacea, a form of adult acne that also afflicted other members of the Dukenfield family. (Both Adele and Leroy Dukenfield had bad skin like their father.) At first, it appeared to Fields like a stubborn case of sunburn, then a rash broke out and the great face got red and blotchy. In the spring of 1941, he suffered an eruption as the result of an X-ray treatment that got infected, and it kept him out of the public eye for nearly a month. The famous nose got swollen

---

*A third car, a station wagon, was a gift from Philip K. Wrigley for appearing on the *Gateway to Hollywood* broadcast.

and distorted and took on the texture of an old sponge. He put it off to drinking, but that actually had little to do with it. It did, however, raise concerns about his health, and the management at Universal had him scrutinized before approving another picture.


At the completion of *The Bank Dick,* Jules Levey of Mayfair Productions (which had a distribution deal with Universal) tried interesting Fields in *Butch Minds the Baby,* a Damon Runyon story in which he would play an old safecracker charged with caring for an infant. Fields allowed as how "with certain changes" he could do it, but warned that it would delay a new picture he had written called *The Great Man.* As the studio had no enthusiasm for *The Great Man,* which was even more convoluted than *The Bank Dick,* this was not regarded as a bad thing. Edward Muhl, acting on Universal's behalf, rejected Fields' first draft of *The Great Man* as "too sketchy," and a second, more detailed version of the story met with a similar fate.

At age sixty-one, Fields knew his time as a picture star was coming to an end. He abandoned all pretense of playing a character part in *The Great Man* and wrote the lead instead for one Bill Fields—battered, ridiculous, a faded symbol of another generation. (His housekeeper Dell always referred to him as "the Great Man," hence the title.) His idea was to parody his past experiences at Universal, where he was regarded with suspicion and his scripts were invariably "improved" by others. In the case of *The Great Man,* the pompously ungifted writer would be played by Franklin Pangborn (standing in for the aforementioned Charles Grayson), and Fields would be called upon to save the day by trashing the Pangborn rewrite and reverting back to his original script. The film-within-a-film would be a veritable catalog of scenes he had been forced to cut from earlier pictures, beginning with the death of Mlle. Gorgeous from *You Can't Cheat an Honest Man.* For the last picture on Fields' Universal contract—and possibly the last picture of his career—he would settle all scores.

The critical success of *The Bank Dick* had put him in a stronger position with the studio, but its failure at the box office showed that his audience was dwindling. In an agreement dated January 9, 1941, management insisted that he broaden the commercial appeal of his new picture by using Gloria Jean Schoonover, a twelve-year-old contract player being groomed as the next Deanna Durbin, and a pair of rambunctious little boys known professionally as Butch and Buddy. Frustrated, Fields ignored the demand and sent three different synopses of *The Great Man* to Charley Beyer "which I wish you would send to the assistant secretary [Edward Muhl] with the hope that he will understand one of them." Over the phone, Muhl asked that Fields tell the story to

Eddie Cline, who would then put it down in synopsis form "as he is on salary." Muhl further asked that a motion-picture story conference—the frame for the entire picture—be eliminated and, again, that material be specifically created "to utilize the services of Gloria Jean and Butch and Buddy in accordance with the understanding reached during the discussions leading to the present existing agreement between us."

In principle, Fields had no objection to Gloria Jean. Her spirited 1939 debut in *The Underpup* had so impressed the old warrior that he promptly wrote her into one of his stories. (Based on the "Little Lulu" comic panel in the *Saturday Evening Post,* aspects of this idea were subsequently incorporated into *The Bank Dick.*) Butch and Buddy were another matter entirely, but if the intent was to broaden Fields' appeal to women and youngsters, he responded with alacrity and produced a twenty-nine-page epitome that made liberal use of all three. "There is nothing in my contract which says I shall use these children," he noted. "The story was not written with them in mind. But to keep peace in the family I have written them in." He added, "I have engaged two competent and experienced writers, Prescott Chaplin and John Neville, to work on one synopsis."

Neither Chaplin nor Neville were comedy writers, although Neville, like Richard Carroll, had considerable experience writing thrillers and adventure dramas. The two men worked with Fields in the office of his Los Feliz home, where Miss Boss was available for dictation and a sizable reference library was close at hand. "He works in fits and starts," Chaplin observed of Fields at the time. "In the middle of a gag routine, he'll jump up and yell, 'I got it, boys. We'll give the pineapple and banana routine to Mrs. Hemagloben instead of to Ouliotta.' Bill hates to work out the mechanics. . . . As he says, 'All I do is to come up with the ideas.' "

The writers weren't working the day Fields next made the papers. It was a Saturday afternoon, the Ides of March, and the Master was away on errands. From across the road, two-and-a-half-year-old Christopher Quinn toddled over to a shallow fish pond at the lower end of the Fields estate and began playing with a toy sailboat bobbing on the water. (Magda had given Fields the boat when he first took possession of the Wood property, and he liked to sit at the top of the steps and watch the breezes blow it around.) A nurse noticed the baby was missing and called the police. An hour's search of the neighborhood failed to turn up any sign of him, then a gardener saw the boy's white shirt floating on the surface of the pond and the fire department was summoned. The rescue squad worked for over two hours trying to revive the boy. The father, reached at the Fox studios where he was shooting *Blood and Sand,* was present when the child was pronounced dead. "Everything stopped moving," said Anthony Quinn. "My entire world was frozen. All around me was commotion, and grieving, but I could not notice."

Fields arrived home to a grotesque spectacle on the periphery of his grounds, police and fire personnel and the press swarming. If there was any comfort he could offer C. B. DeMille, the boy's grandfather, who stood to one side, tears streaming down his face, it went unrecorded. "The worst thing in my life was losing the child," Quinn said fifty-six years later. "The worst. . . . People who say they can deal with the death of a child are wrong. Nothing else can come near it." Fields' name was prominent in the press accounts the next morning, and the *Times* carried a photo of his concrete pond, the little sailboat floating listlessly on its side. "He was quietly shocked," said Will Fowler, Gene Fowler's younger son. "He was not a demonstrative man. He had a line he would not go over emotionally, and he stayed below that line. But he went into a retreat for three or four days. He wouldn't talk to anybody. It hurt him immensely."

Fields didn't shake it quickly. Like the scene of the boy and the father in Sun Valley, the image of the boy's lifeless body haunted him. Not long after the tragedy, Eddie Dowling and Ray Dooley came through town touring Saroyan's *The Time of Your Life.* "He was still pretty broken up about it," Dowling recounted.

> You know, all this talk about hating children. When we arrived, he insisted we live there in that big house with him, which we wouldn't do, of course, but he was so happy to see us and so happy about our success. He took us to that Russian prince's restaurant one night—that restaurant of Mike Romanoff's. The place was crowded and he was drinking very badly. Ray said to him, "Oh, Mr. Fields, I hate to see you drink so much." He said, "Raysie, what else can I do? Imagine, a little kid. Imagine him drowning in my pool . . ." She said, "You weren't to blame for that. Why do you take it so?" He said, "I don't know. I kind of feel it's because of some of the things I've done."
>
> She said, "Oh, now, that isn't like you at all." He said, "I want out of this cesspool." This was in the place. And he gets up and he screeches and yells and carries on like mad, calling everybody names. It was not like Fields at all. She said, "Well, W. C., we've got to get home now." We had our little girl with us, who was quite small at the time. She was only two years old, in fact. He said, "I'll drive you home. You should be [at my house with me]. But I'm glad you're not because

you've got a kid, too. It would be just my luck . . ." And he went into this other thing again. . . . When he dropped us at the place, Mrs. Dowling said, "You know, Eddie, I feel so bad. I don't think I ever want to see W. C. again. That isn't the W. C. I knew. Whatever has happened to that wonderful, wonderful man?" He was terribly bitter.

# Twenty-seven

# Never Give a Sucker an Even Break

Fields had endured unwelcome publicity a month prior to the Quinn incident when he went before a federal tax court seeking a refund and was grilled over his $6,300 payoff to Carlotta Monti—an amount he had deducted from his 1937 taxes as a business expense. "The government makes you pay twice," he told reporters before entering the courtroom, "and then at the end of maybe 40 years, if they get around to it, they may hold a hearing and you may get some of it back." He ditched a toothpick before going inside. "I was sued up in Riverside some time ago," he explained. "Lost the case because I kept chewing a toothpick all the time."

Inside, the ladies and gentlemen of the fourth estate learned that Fields had earned well over $200,000 in the year 1937—$15,000 for writing, $121,333 for acting, and $95,000 for his radio work. From the aggregate he deducted $9,000 for advertising and publicity, including flowers and perfume for lady writers and photographs for his fans. "If I don't get my big nose in a publicity picture once in a while, people will forget me." Another $5,000 went to his brother Walter and his sister Adele, both of whom he identified as writers. "My brother and sister sent me gags and newspaper clippings. If I didn't send 'em enough money, they wouldn't send me any more gags—and I have to have gags." He also characterized Carlotta as a writer, but her threatened lawsuit was, by now, a matter of public record due to the Rohe disbarment hearing, and the claim met with considerable skepticism. "Well," he allowed, "the nature of the suit was, the girl went haywire, I guess, and she claimed I struck her with a rubber hammer—I hate to bring all this stuff up again—which she later denied."

He prevailed on appeal and, practically on cue, Carlotta returned from her two-year sojourn in New York City. Unmarried and no closer to a singing career than when she had left, she promptly resumed her place in Fields' daily life. "I did all the shopping," she said. "I worked 24 hours a day. I gave him his medicines, his sunlamp treatments, and his vitamins." He paid her a stipend of $25 a week and made her occasional gifts of money. His friends—La Cava, in

*With secretary Malinda Boss during a break in federal tax court,*
*February 1941*

particular—thought her a gold digger, but Gene Fowler knew she was good for the old man. "She was a very sweet and wonderful person," said his son, Gene Jr. "All of Fields' friends figured that she was just some little tramp, but my father didn't. He liked her and was very kind to her. I think he was the only friend of Fields that liked her."

Carlotta energized the house on DeMille Drive while keeping a place of her own on Eighty-second Street. "I'm sure she slept over," said Ginger Michael, "but I don't think she had a room. Most of the time he was throwing her out. He did holler at her a lot. She was just a devil. She was funny, a very nice gal, and she just loved egging him on. It was a fun relationship. She had a boyfriend, and he had people on the side, too, but Carlotta was the main one. I think he really did have affection for her. It gave him some life. It gave him something to think about, and aggravate himself. It kept him on his toes."


Fields spent eight weeks writing *The Great Man,* meeting with his two writers every morning at ten. "Bill has an odd way of getting into the day's work," Prescott Chaplin said. "I recall one morning when Eddie Cline, Fields' director, was discussing the [Rudolf] Hess incident. Bill didn't seem to be listening, but suddenly he said, 'Why not put Mrs. Hemagloben up on a mountain and have her chase me up and down in a bucket? I may not make as good a landing as Hess did, but I'll look funny when she cuts the rope at the top."

In the full version of the story, Fields storms off the Esoteric Pictures lot after his conference with Franklin Pangborn (now a producer), responding to the studio's demands, as he usually did in real life, by muttering, "I've got to have a drink!" In a bar, he tells the story of Old Tom, the fly, a bit he lifted from Eddie Cline that he previously had tried to insert into both *My Little Chick-adee* and *The Bank Dick.* As in the famous snake story, Old Tom becomes a hero to Fields when he dips his hind leg in the governor's inkwell, drags it across the dotted line, and forges a pardon, thereby releasing Fields from "durance vile."

"I love that fly," he says.

"I don't care what he done," Bill Wolfe growls. "I'll kill him if he gets in my ear again!"

"It's people like you that give the West a bad name. You killer!"

The pink script of *The Great Man* went to the PCA on April 16, 1941, where it inspired eight single-spaced pages of objections. It was, said Breen, filled with "vulgar and suggestive scenes and dialogue" and contained "innumerable jocular references to drinking and liquor." By Breen's reckoning, sixty scenes were laid in a cocktail lounge and numerous other shots were set in bars and saloons. All would have to be deleted or changed "since this violates the present policy of the Association re: drinking and drunkenness in pictures." Fields' choice of the prissy Pangborn for the part of the producer came up for scrutiny as well. "If Pangborn plays his role in any way suggestive of a 'pansy,' " Breen warned, "we cannot approve any scenes in which this flavor is present." Universal weighed in, declaring the script "greatly over length" and that, with the addition of musical numbers, it needed to be cut by thirty to forty pages. A closer relationship was needed between Fields and Gloria Jean, a café scene with an insulting waitress was to be cut, and the story of Old Tom was definitely out. "You will recall that this has been done in the last two pictures and it has been found desirable to cut it out both times." All scenes set at a backlot circus were deleted due to cost. "We will require the elimination of the 'motion picture' within the story. We will also require an action sequence in order to build a climax to the picture."

Fields agreed the script was too long and spent another two months revising it. He did away with the unique film-within-a-film framework, making the story a lot more linear but also far more improbable. A leap from the observation deck of a gigantic plane lands him on a mountaintop inhabited by a lovely girl who's never seen a man before. He teaches the girl a kissing game called Squidgilum, a bizarre scene that first appeared in his notes for *The Wizard of Oz.*

OULIOTTA

Have you ever played this game with any other woman before?

FIELDS

Once, with my grandmother.

Stubbornly, Fields clung to the café scene and the bit about Old Tom and the circus sequence that included the death of Mlle. Gorgeous. A car chase originally conceived for *It's a Gift* was added, but it came at the end of the second act instead of the third. One happy result of Breen's tirade was the resetting of the initial bar scene in a soda fountain. "This should have been played in a saloon," Fields says confidentially to the camera, "but the censor objected." When he orders a jumbo chocolate ice cream soda, the soda jerk asks if he wants anything in it. "Yes," he replies, "two straws."

On May 13, Universal announced the film as part of its program for the 1941–42 season under the title *Never Give a Sucker an Even Break.* Fields shrugged off the change, noting it would scarcely fit on a marquee. "It will probably boil down to 'Fields—Sucker,' " he said. The new script, still carrying the title *The Great Man,* was delivered to the studio on June 3 with an accompanying note to Ed Muhl. "There are extra nicknacks which I have prepared to brighten up some of the scenes," Fields wrote, "but I thought it best not to send too much script. These are all the scenes which will enable you to budget the picture." It went to the PCA on June 12 and came back with three additional pages of cautions. One line that was lost to the censors referred to a character who had consumed too much goat's milk: "He's tighter than a dick's hatband." Fields tried saving the line, but to no avail. "Those fellows find double meanings in commas and semicolons," he said.

He alluded to Gloria Jean's numbers in the script, but left the details to Jack Gross and Eddie Cline and Charles Previn, the studio's musical director. As the picture was being budgeted and readied for production, a labored comedy sequence with Franklin Pangborn was added. The business with Old Tom was removed once again, as was the death of Mlle. Gorgeous. Gross, an honorable and down-to-earth man who was now responsible for an entire slate of pictures (including the all-star *Badlands of Dakota* and *The Wolf Man*) was less collaborative than he had been on *The Bank Dick*. He assured Fields that all the changes were due solely to cost, but the explanation didn't wash. "My script has been changed much to its detriment," Fields complained in a letter to Nate Blumberg. "Scenes have been added and others deleted in spite of your assurances that I would be left alone on this one."

Filming began on July 7 with Fields admiring a billboard of *The Bank Dick*. "Was that a Buptkie!" Buddy says to Butch. A vegetable vendor rolls his cart by, a defective tire blowing a flatulent salute with every rotation. "Raspberries!" the man calls between blows. "Raspberries!" The studio was in the midst of a herculean effort to finish fully half the new season's pictures over the summer, when weather conditions were the most favorable and routine economies could be maximized. Every stage on the lot was in use, and pictures underway included *Appointment for Love, Hellzapoppin'*, Deanna Durbin's *Almost an Angel* (released as *It Started with Eve*), and the fourth Abbott and Costello comedy of the year, *Ride 'Em Cowboy*. Distractions from all the activity were so profound that the front office left the Cline unit pretty much alone, and Fields was able to quietly reinstate most all the cuts that had been made in his script. Still, there was so much in the production of the new picture that had nothing to do with its star—three numbers from Gloria Jean and a swing rendition of "Comin' Thro' the Rye" by Susan Miller—that he seemed oddly removed from the process.

"There was something sad about the man," said Gloria Jean. "I can't explain it. I felt a little . . . sorry for him. He was very quiet. He didn't talk to too many people. He never seemed to have any energy. He would sit down and they would have to help him up." Warned that Fields didn't like children, she found him avuncular, even solicitous at times. "We'd be sitting during rehearsal. They'd have to light the set, and they'd just leave us there. And he'd come out with things because he'd have to stay on the set and couldn't escape to his dressing room. One time he said, 'I hope you don't go around with polish on your nails. Just keep your nails natural. Don't have red nails—I don't like that.' Another time, he grew very serious and reflective and said, 'Always keep your family, because they're going to try to take them away from you. Don't listen to them.' I said, 'I don't think they—' but he cut me off. 'No, honey,' he said, 'they'll try it. You've got to always keep with your family.' He was almost stern in the way he said it, as if it had happened to him."

Cline shot the picture in sequence, with Fields doing his best work in the morning hours when he was freshest. Like his friend Barrymore, Fields was now using cue cards—"Notes and big lettering, almost on top of him so he could see it," said Gloria Jean—and yet he still finished most of his scenes in a single take. In the café sequence, he fed lines to actress Jody Gilbert, trying variants and ad-libs and printing most of them. "Do you think it's too hot for pork chops?" he asks. Scratch. "Give me a cup of mocha java." Another scratch. "That only leaves whiskey—roast beef with gin—cherry cordial . . ." Once the scene was in the can, Fields and Cline improvised a poignant speech for the twenty-five-year-old Gilbert, who eked out a living playing waitresses and fat girlfriends. "I'm married to a lug for 25 years," she tells a guy at the counter. "He falls in love for a paloma and gives me the breeze. Then my son gets drafted in the Army. I can't get a good job because I'm past 45 and I can't get a pension because I ain't 65. So I opens a chicken shack and have to stand for lugs like that to come in and bust my ears drums with idle chatter."

Said Gloria Jean, "He would never really follow the script like he was supposed to. He ad-libbed a lot, and that impressed me. As a child, I had to learn every bit of dialogue, just exactly as written. Not him. He threw it away a lot of times." Early on in the schedule, Fields shot the six-page death scene he had long wanted to play. Gorgeous is on the trapeze when the rope breaks and she falls out of frame. In her tent, Fields attempts to comfort her. "Bill, if anything

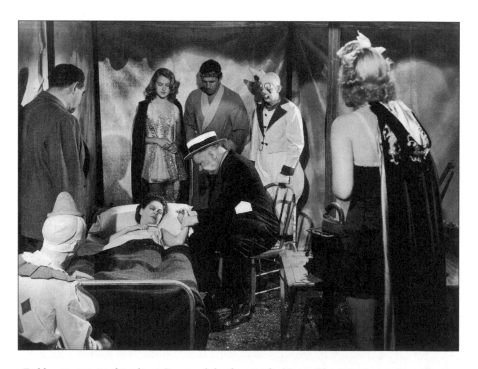

*Fields was permitted to shoot Gorgeous' death scene for* Never Give a Sucker an Even Break.

happens to me," she says, "I know you'll see that everything will be all right for Gloria Jean." He pats her hand. "Sure I will. Before Tom died, you know I wanted to adopt you two kids."* Outside, he tells Leon Errol, who plays Schlepperman, the shooting-gallery proprietor, that he will fold his tent "like the Arab" if Gorgeous dies and go to Mexico to sell wooden nutmegs to a colony of Russians. "They love grated nutmegs on their caviar," he says.

The use of Gloria Jean was limited to five hours a day, with three of them devoted to schoolwork. Apart from the scenes in which she actually appeared with Fields, she was off in a tent that served as her classroom. The teacher, required by the Industrial Welfare Commission, disapproved of Fields' working with children and was sure he was drinking. "She was watching him, and she was going to catch him," she said. Fields had a screen set up in a corner of the stage and, with a white-jacketed assistant, would frequently step behind it for a mysterious ritual. Once, he was tagged by the woman when he emerged cup in hand. "Relax," he said. "It's Listerine." And it was.

"He happened to love my mother," said Gloria Jean. "When you were young on the set, you had to have your mother with you. My mother tried to stay out of the limelight; she wasn't a stage mother at all." Eleanor Schoonover was from Scranton, a Pennsylvania coal mining town a hundred or so miles north of Philadelphia. She was a plain-spoken woman with a show business background, having once worked as a bareback rider in the Ringling Bros. circus. "He laughed at everything my mother said. She really seemed to get him out of the moods he was in. They'd say, 'You better get your mother in there, he's not in a very good mood today.' She'd snap him out of it every time."

Moody and unusually subdued during the making of the film, Fields rarely worked a full day. He never ate lunch ("there are better things to do") and chose instead to remain in his dressing room, conserving his strength. "A lot of people would say, 'Good-bye!' or 'That's it for today!' but he would just disappear. He was always there at nine, but he would be gone by two or two-thirty." More than once, Charlie Beyer was summoned to the studio and warned about his client's lapses, but Fields was invariably able to point out that the picture was ahead of schedule. Finally, on August 31, Muhl fired off a written warning, instructing Fields to keep himself in "proper physical condition" to render services under the terms of his contract. The reply he received the next day was signed by Fields' housekeeper, Adele Clines: "Mr. Fields wishes me to acknowledge receipt of your telegram and to tell you we all got a good laugh out of it."

---

*Gorgeous is clearly identified as Gloria Jean's older sister in the screenplay, but someone in the studio hierarchy evidently felt that Gorgeous should be the girl's mother instead. Alternate takes were made with actress Anne Nagel to cover this point, and these are the shots that were ultimately used in the film.

Filming wound down with process work for another car chase conceived and shot by Ralph Ceder. Thinking he's got a pregnant woman in the backseat, Fields races to the maternity hospital across town with all deliberate speed. Working on Ventura Boulevard, Ceder had Fields' car hooked to the back of a fire engine, but during a run up the street—a stunt double behind the wheel—the coupe came unhitched and slammed into a lamppost, which in turn went crashing through the front window of a drugstore. The event caused United Press' Fred Othman, who observed the crash, to expect the chase to play well onscreen. "The wreck will look real," he said. "It *was*." *Never Give a Sucker an Even Break* wrapped on August 16, 1941, with Fields back in Pangborn's office for an alternate ending: "And that my friends is the finish of the story—the end of the script. Thanks for your kind attention." Miraculously, he had finished the film in just thirty-six days. Said Gloria Jean, "I remember saying, 'It was fun working with you.' I kissed him, and he just stared at me. That gave me the chills. Then they had a little get-together after the last shot with Eddie Cline and the crew, but Fields wasn't there. He was gone."

Fields saw the assembled picture for the first time on September 3. Since his contract gave him control over the initial cut, he submitted an eighteen-point memo detailing additions and trims he would require for the preview.

Fields' entrance into the soda parlor through the door has been omit-ted and I wish and ask that it shall be put back in the picture. . . . Soda jerker should be standing still on cuts. The end where he bangs himself over the head with a bottle to kill a fly is about the worst Mack Sennett comedy I have ever seen. . . . The entire scene of Pangborn's entrance and all the confusion on the sound stage set should be omitted. The whistle, the goose step while little Gloria Jean is singing, and the spit-ting of the cherry stones in each other's face, dancers going by, etc., is not the type of comedy I represent. These were all shot by Mr. Cline unbeknownst to me. There is too much interference with Gloria Jean's songs—unnecessary, unfunny, and cheap comedy. . . . Please put back dialogue where Gloria Jean hits Mr. Pangborn and where he asks her why she did that and she says that's what her Uncle Bill would have done. . . . The chase is far too long and overdone. Policeman on fender losing his pants and finally getting caught on bus is not funny. The shoes on the street is cheap and unfunny, and the man getting knocked first one way and then the other and waving his arms and legs is anti-quated comedy. . . . In hospital, the fat lady should not shove the interns as they did when Mr. Cline was a Keystone Cop. In fact, there is too much Keystone Cop in all the scenes where I am not present. . . . On the mountain top, the game of Squidgilum was ruined. It should

*To Gloria Jean, Fields never seemed to have any energy.*

not be cut; should be played intact as shot and show Ouliotta's reaction to the game. . . . The climb of Leon Errol to the top should be shortened. . . . All the gorilla scenes eliminated. Not funny.

An out-of-town preview took place on an off night—a Wednesday—and the crowd found the film only mildly amusing. The car chase went over big, but the picture itself was judged a disaster. The next day, Fields was at a loss to explain the reaction: "When the audience does not respond, it makes the actors look as though they are not working, or working very slowly, or even carelessly. I think the reaction of the audience in the larger cities will be much more favorable—at least I hope so." After acknowledging that he had no further right to ask or expect anything more in the way of cutting, he thanked Universal for "all their courtesies and every cooperation" and offered some final suggestions.

> In the restaurant, use the straight shot of tossing hat on hatrack instead of curved. . . . In the drugstore, use no shot cutting away from Fields while he is telling the story, except one to show the soda jerker is listening. . . . Cut out the horseshoe throwing over the shoulder breaking the bottles with Gloria Jean and her mother. . . . In Pangborn's office, cut out golf bit with Pangborn. Also the part where we listen to radio. Likewise, where I hit myself on head with club. . . . The chase can be cut to [the] advantage of the film. It is hilarious but a bit too long. . . . Take the whole shooting gallery out, except the part where the attendant informs Fields that Gorgeous has met with an accident. . . . The bouncing on couch after the fall from plane is too much and the cutting too jerky. . . . Cut down quite a lot of the engineer's climb up mountain. . . . Put back Susan Miller's song on mountain, but omit part where she jazzes it up and dances. . . . Throughout the entire picture use as many long or medium shots of Fields as possible in lieu of close-ups. . . . I suggest we try the ending of the picture as it was shown last night, but I think if you add to it the scene where I return to the studio and do the scene with Pangborn where I say, 'That is the end of the story,' we can see which makes the better ending of the picture.

Pangborn and Gloria Jean were called back for two days of retakes. Some of Fields' suggestions were taken, and nearly a full reel of footage was removed from the film. Gone, once again, were the Old Tom story and Gorgeous' death, along with any hint of the circus setting on which Fields had insisted. Pangborn's new shots were made with lines like, "Just a minute, Mr. Fields! There's a limit to everything. This script is an insult to a man's intelligence! Even mine!" and "Marvelous! Wonderful! Amazing! The girl has been living up a mountain top since she was three months old, and for no reason at all, suddenly blossoms out with jumpin' jive! Do you actually think I'm a dope? Now don't you answer that." In trying to fix the film, the studio actually returned it to Fields' original concept of a movie within a movie. Shortened to seventy-one minutes, it still didn't play very smoothly or make a lot of sense, but a second preview in Glendale elicited more laughs than the first audience had been willing to accord it. For once, Fields couldn't kick; Universal had let him make a wildly unconventional comedy in the manner in which he had envisioned it and then had put it before a paying audience virtually intact. Moreover, its release was supported with a full-page ad in *Variety* and all the ballyhoo the studio could muster: "Behold, America! The Lord High Elocutioner, His Nibs, the Prince of Ad Libs, comes to you in all his bold, old-time, pre-sold greatness!"

It was an unfortunate choice of words. With war in the air, comedies were suddenly clicking again, but the hot comedians were mostly all radio stars, a full generation younger than Fields. *The Road to Zanzibar, Charley's Aunt, Love Crazy,* and *The Devil and Miss Jones* were all hits, and exhibitors were petitioning the studios for "more new stars like Abbott and Costello." The world's most popular comedy team was under contract to Universal, where a new Abbott and Costello picture was completed every three months. *Buck Privates, In the Navy,* and *Hold That Ghost* were among the top-grossing films of the year, taking in a combined domestic total of more than $6 million. "The exhibitors realize that a certain amount of risk is involved in the creation of new stars and the use of fresh faces," *Variety* noted, "but, they argue, a meritorious picture, sans established names, has a much greater chance to click than a mediocre film boasting tried-and-true luminaries."

Due to the summer production push, Universal had eighteen completed features in the vaults, amounting to some $3.5 million in unreleased negative, when *Sucker* had its official press preview on October 5, 1941. "This is a Fieldsian silly-dilly that often is more silly than dilly," said *Daily Variety.* "A number of sequences display W. C. Fields at his best, but there are too many dull in-betweens to class it entirely as top-notch entertainment. Its preview reception was evidence that Fields can still make 'em laugh even with sub-standard material, meaning average grosses should be registered in many of its playdates." On the question of commercial merit, the *Motion Picture Daily* hedged in branding it "a W. C. Fields picture by, of, and with W. C. Fields, and for the Fields trade. How good or bad it is for a given theatre's box office requirements depends, more implicitly and completely than may be said of any feature in ready memory, upon the value of its star to the patronage of the theatre concerned."

But where the other trade reviews were merely reserved, the notice in the *Hollywood Reporter* was downright cruel: "It begins to look as if the parade has passed W. C. Fields by, and if Friday night's preview reaction was any indication, the actor will be just the last toot on the calliope unless he gets a script before he makes another film appearance. . . . Those of Friday's audience who are on the 'inside' of this business got a few chuckles now and then at some of the business; the general audience took most of it in unresponsive silence." Wounded by the *Reporter* notice, Fields privately wrote the publisher, W. R. "Billy" Wilkerson, and complained: "First, 'The audience was not responsive' is a fib. Secondly, the screenplay was not a rehash of old business I have been doing these many years.* In fact, there isn't even a semblance of any gags or business I have ever done. . . . The fellow didn't write a true criticism of the picture, but a personal thrust at me."

Having learned from the failure of *The Bank Dick,* Fields went back on the air with Edgar Bergen to support the release of the film. The appearance, his first for Chase & Sanborn in more than three years, was a howling success, but it didn't translate into a renewed demand for Fields at the box office. When *Never Give a Sucker an Even Break* went into general release on October 10, bookings were scant and business in most major markets was brutally bad. In Portland, one of the few bright spots, the manager of the Mayfair Theatre reported that *Sucker* had drawn the longest Sunday lines in two years. The reception at New York's tiny Rialto was equally heartening, with the film finishing its first seven days with a trim $8,500 in the till and holding a second week. In most other cities, though, the results were deadly. *Sucker* didn't make it to Los Angeles until January 1942, when it played a dismal week in support of Hitchcock's *Suspicion* at the RKO Hillstreet. Replacing a *Mexican Spitfire* comedy on the bill, it arrived with virtually no promotion and was consequently ignored in the dailies. The *Los Angeles Times,* which had accorded *The Bank Dick* two rave notices, didn't even bother to review it.

*Never Give a Sucker an Even Break* was an unmitigated commercial flop, virtually the only standout failure in an overcrowded field. Predictably, Universal passed on the chance to make yet another picture with Fields. "He was cranky and old," Edward Muhl reasoned. "After you've paired him with Mae West, what more can you do with him?" Carlotta left for El Paso to play a commercial singing engagement on November 16, and Fields withdrew into his Laughlin Park estate to contemplate his future. "Dell is cooking my Thanksgiving dinner downtown," he reported to Carlotta a few days later, "and Lawrence [his driver] will bring it out to me, and I will listen to the radio, drink my quota of beer, and eat my dinner in divine solitude."


There was a sense among the critics that *Never Give a Sucker an Even Break* would be Fields' last picture, and, as with *Poppy* five years earlier, their notices took on a valedictory tone. Theodore Strauss wrote of Fields' pickled pomposity, his flyblown grandeur. "Squinting at the world over that colossus of a nose, he is, for all his profligacies, the most innocent thing in it." The great James Agee called him one of the funniest men on earth, detailing "a beautifully-

---

*This, of course, wasn't entirely true, as Fields recycled material in nearly all his films. The sleeping-berth scene with the Turk was first used in *The Old Fashioned Way,* and the business of bumping the police car came from *Man on the Flying Trapeze.*

timed exhibit of mock pomposity, puzzled ineffectualness, subtle understatement, and true-blue nonchalance." The most eloquent and heartfelt of these tributes came from Otis Ferguson, who hailed Fields as "one of the natural funny men" battling an impossible tide of change.

> Once again disaster is his friend, once again the forces of gravity and public opinion are against him. . . . His nose is still red but unbloody, he still finds the rich and awful widow by the middle of the picture, he has still about him that majesty of place and breeding which turns the point of any blade save his own; he is still the gay dog with the old tricks—the business with the feet, the stick, the plug hat, the reflective but sonorous aside, the topper, nasal and triumphant, with which the entire architecture of the forces for order is toppled at least once in every picture. . . . If there was ever a great clown in this time of changeover from the beer and music hall to the universal distribution of radio and films, I would say it was in the person and the character and the undying if corny gusto of Bill Fields, who moved mountains until they fell on him, and then brushed himself off and looked around for more.

Nothing, however, was to be drawn from these relatively few lines of appreciation, for Fields was again without a home studio. Everyone knew he was aging and slowing down and that his pictures weren't making any money. He was no longer one of the top stars of the year—as delineated in *Variety*—and he contributed nothing to the $2 million profit miraculously posted by Universal Pictures. Worse, the papers seized on the fact that he was the highest-paid movie star in the country, reporting more than $250,000 in earnings for the year 1940. Fields himself was mortified by the exposure, clinging to his belief that wealthy men weren't funny, and he fretted the news reports would only hurt his chances for work.

Fortunately, there was a job on the horizon, a week's work in an episodic extravaganza known as *Tales of Manhattan*. The producer was Boris Morros, a moon-faced Russian émigré who, back in the mid-1930s, had been the managing director of the New York Paramount. A fine cellist, a fair pianist, and an accomplished orchestra conductor, Morros was put in charge of Paramount's Hollywood music department by Ernst Lubitsch, a position he held for nearly three years. In 1939, Morros left to become a producer, first with Laurel and Hardy, then with Fred Astaire. From his tenure at the Paramount Theatre, Morros held an abiding affection for Fields as both an artist and as a commercial draw, and when he set up his all-star conceit in June 1941, Fields was, according to the production records, the first player signed for the film. Riding a momentary wave of goodwill, the Great Man drove a hard bargain. His fee would be $25,000 a week with a one-week guarantee. He would also insist upon contributing to the film's script. He could not, however, begin work until he was finished with his fourth picture at Universal, delaying the shooting of his segment until October 1941 at the earliest.

The idea for *Tales of Manhattan,* which follows a formal tailcoat through six otherwise unrelated stories, apparently came from an old German picture called *Der Frack.* Billy Wilder and Walter Reisch knew of the film and suggested it, perhaps as a joke, to the perennially penniless Sam Spiegel.* Despite the fact that it required the services of twelve to fifteen principals, Spiegel instantly embraced the idea and eventually recruited Morros, who had a two-picture deal with Paramount, as a partner. Over the summer of 1941, Morros engaged Fields, Joel McCrea, Edward G. Robinson, Charles Boyer, and Paul Robeson for principal parts in the film. But apart from McCrea, he was hiring freelancers, not contract players, and spiraling cost projections soon scuttled the project. Morros and Spiegel shopped it around, quickly selling the package for $40,000 to Twentieth Century–Fox, where it found a champion in William Goetz, executive assistant to Darryl F. Zanuck.

At Fox, *Tales of Manhattan* gathered momentum. Ethel Waters, Bill Robinson, and Duke Ellington were added to the Robeson sequence, Buster Keaton was set to play Hiawatha, and Elsa Lanchester was once again teamed with her husband, Charles Laughton. On the first of October, Henry Fonda, Ginger Rogers, and Rita Hayworth completed the cast. Julien Duvivier, the renowned director of *Pépé le Moko,* became attached to the project when Morros abandoned his original plan to have seven top directors make the various segments. Duvivier's *Un carnet de bal* (1937) had a similar structure and demonstrated the value of stylistic consistency. A total of forty original stories and ideas were purchased for the film, and twenty different writers worked on its segments at various stages. The proposed episodes ranged from tragic to comic, as the tailcoat made its way from a Park Avenue penthouse to Skid Row and, ultimately, to a group of sharecroppers. The last shot fades on the coat adorning a scarecrow.

A seriocomic vaudeville script had been written for Fields by Hungarian playwright Laslo Vadnai, and it went through several hands before it was finally abandoned as unworkable. Filming got underway with the Laughton sequence on October 22, 1941, but it wasn't until mid-December that Morros threw in the towel on the Fields segment and hired Bill Morrow and Ed Beloin

---

*Spiegel, who had produced a number of films in Europe, later claimed the film was based on a book of German stories by Max Nosseck, although none of the Nosseck stories was used.

to craft an entirely new screenplay. Unabashed in his admiration for Jack Benny, Fields had pressed for the hiring of the two men who were responsible for the weekly Benny radio program. Morrow, a quick-witted Irishman in his early thirties, was especially eager to work with his idol. "They spent a lot of time together," recalled Hal Kanter. "Bill was a grand drinker; I assume Fields and he had that in common."

Morrow and Beloin took an entirely different tack with the Fields segment, casting him as a phony temperance lecturer working the gullible society circuit. The idea of pairing Fields with actress Frances Dee was abandoned, and the stately Margaret Dumont was injected as Mrs. Clyborn Langahankie, Fields' mark for the evening. Morrow was a notorious procrastinator, and it took three weeks, working nights, to produce the twenty-page script that constituted Sequence E of the film. Tinkering continued until the morning of January 28, 1942, when filming began at the Twentieth Century–Fox studios in West Los Angeles. Fields had lost weight, primarily through the use of a steam cabinet invented by his personal trainer, a former Harvard professor named Bob Howard. He had also given up bourbon and milk, switching to a steady diet of martinis instead. Trimmer than for *Never Give a Sucker an Even Break,* he was more energetic and worked a longer day, but without makeup he looked drawn and unwell and his hair was now almost completely white. Long before the sequence began, Julien Duvivier was deemed unsuited to directing a low comedian by himself, and the affable and prolific Mal St. Clair was brought in to collaborate. "I can't imagine Duvivier directing Fields," said Gloria Jean, who was herself directed by Duvivier for Universal's *Flesh and Fantasy.* "He was a humorless man, very serious. Good director, but he wouldn't have been suited for comedy."

Officially a consultant, St. Clair directed Fields and the other actors while Duvivier stood to one side and fussed with the camera work. (Surviving outtakes show Duvivier's name on the slates, but St. Clair's voice can be heard yelling, "Action!") The verve St. Clair brought to elegant comedies like *Breakfast at Sunrise* (1927) and the original *Gentlemen Prefer Blondes* had dissipated by the early 1940s, but Fields presented a fresh challenge, and he somehow managed to rise to the occasion. Although glued to the blackboard on which his lines were chalked, Fields was a lively figure throughout, fully in command of the scene and seemingly letter-perfect within it. "He was very disciplined," said Gene Fowler Jr., who edited the sequence and observed on the set. "All Mal had to do was say 'action' and 'cut.' It was a very close collaboration."

Fields worked a full day on his sixty-second birthday, both in the interior of the Santelli Bros. Second-Hand Clothing Store, where the pocket of the coat is primed with a wallet stuffed with newspaper, and in the backseat of Mrs. Langahankie's chauffeured limousine, where, as Professor Diogenes Pothlewhistle, he seduces her with bloodcurdling tales of the savages of Kadoola-Kadoola "guzzling the fermented juice of the Black Papaya." Morrow's dialogue is ornate and self-referential, and when Mrs. Langahankie reacts in horror, he has her exclaim, "Godfrey Daniel!" Fields, as usual, ad-libbed and embellished, and Duvivier was thrown when scripted lines like "Come, my lifeless companion" and "Get this moth incubator off me" became "Come, my anemic bloodbank" and "Get me out of this winter quarters for bees and insects!" Conferring with St. Clair in an entirely unofficial capacity was the estimable Buster Keaton. In the early 1920s, the two men had collaborated on a pair of top-notch comedies, *The Goat* and *The Blacksmith.* Now, some twenty years later, they were reunited at Fox, St. Clair as a contract director under producer Sol Wurtzel and Keaton as a journeyman writer and gag man.

Neither Keaton nor St. Clair had much influence on Fields, who was determinedly putting his dialogue across at the expense of physical business. Duvivier fared even worse. During the shooting of the limousine scene with Margaret Dumont, the director gently suggested at one point that Fields laugh after delivering a particular line. "I have never laughed in a picture," Fields responded. "I will give a cynical smile." The next day, back in the ill-fitting tailcoat on the Santelli set, Fields was scripted to gaze into a trick mirror and do a take-um as the coat suddenly appeared to fit perfectly. Film previously shot of him was rear-projected onto the surface of the mirror. Duvivier expected him to match his movements to the image before him, but gave up on the effect after five takes. "This was a very difficult bit of business, even if you were cold sober," said Phil Silvers, who played the scene with him. "Fields' valet encouraged him every day with a thermos bottle of lemonade." The lemonade, of course, was a mixture of gin and vermouth, exceptionally dry, as confirmed by Silvers when proffered a taste. "He always claimed he could control [his drinking]," said Fowler, "but on the set he had a martini in an outsized glass." Fields worked a total of six days on the picture, much of the time devoted to a lecture the professor delivers to a group of Mrs. Langahankie's wealthy friends. "Let us survey the evil consequences when one imbibes of the noxious corn juice," he intones, solemnly tapping a chart of the human body. "This is the esophagus of which I spoke—the first part of the anatomy to feel the shock of the concoction of Lucifer . . . Beezlebub." As he speaks, glasses of coconut milk are distributed to the people, generously spiked, unbeknownst to the professor, with gin. "Note the bracing results of this harmless, yet exotic, liquid. Note the tingle as it tiptoes through the body, tripling o'er the tongue through the esophagus."

Between shots Fields was a lifeless figure, mustering his energy for those few precious moments when film was rolling. At the call of "Action," it was as if a switch had been flipped inside of him, and up came the smile, the voice, the demeanor, and the lines flowed from him in musical waves. The ending of the sequence was a problem for the writers, and a revision had the professor discovering a revolving bar secreted behind a wall of the Langahankie mansion. "Ah, my car!" he says, stepping aboard and riding it out of sight. The timing of the revolution and the delivery of the line had to be precise, and when it went awry, Fields leaned into his host. "Are Bing Crosby's horses what they're cracked up to be?" he asked. "Or are they cracked?"

The Fields set attracted a lot of visitors, and journalists were encouraged to come watch him work. "As [Hedda] Hopper's leg man, I must have seen every major actor in Hollywood at work over the past 14 years," Spec McClure wrote in 1954.

> Fields was the only man or woman I ever saw who stopped the whole set when he went into a scene. I remember one scene—a rather long shot—at 20th in which the idiot board could not be used, nor could Fields remember his lines. So on each take he simply improvised, making each one vastly different. The usually bored crew, technicians, and everybody else on the stage crowded close to observe the maestro as he went into action. I have also seen him so drunk that two men were required to get him into position on the set, but when "action" was called he marvelously came to life and went through the scene without a hitch. An assistant stood on the sidelines with a quart malted-milk glass filled with martini in case Fields got thirsty. This was no gag, as

*Filming the lecture sequence for* Tales of Manhattan, *1942*

everyone had great respect for the old trouper and nobody thought his leaning on gin funny. Of course, I never wrote up such things as I could feel the life weariness in the man—and I'd never been let back on the stage if I had.

Fields felt good about the picture and was pleased to be part of such a stellar cast. He exchanged cordial letters with Morros and Spiegel, made sure Morrow and Beloin got the credit they deserved, and consented to an afternoon of retakes at no charge to the studio. In its completed form, *Tales of Manhattan* was approved by the PCA at a length of 137 minutes, but there were problems with the film from the very first preview. Duvivier's style was smooth but ponderous, and his comedy staging, on display in the Ginger Rogers–Henry Fonda episode, was leaden. By the time Fields made his appearance, approximately ninety minutes into the action, the audience was primed for his entrance. "W. C. Fields' sequence stole the show at the sneak preview," columnist Paul Harrison reported, "and the agents of the other stars are raising Cain." Erskine Johnson said that Fields rated more applause from the preview audience than did Boyer, Fonda, Laughton, Robinson, Rogers, Robeson, or Hayworth. The sequence was sent back to the editing room, where the introductory scene in the limousine was completely removed. Additional cuts whittled away at its effectiveness until, after two additional showings, there was talk of dropping it from the picture entirely.

Harrison Carroll, in the *Los Angeles Herald and Express,* said there was "a possibility" that Fox might not use the Fields sequence, and Charley Beyer, at his client's direction, promptly dashed off a letter to Zanuck suggesting that, with the addition of another scene, the footage could be released as a two-reeler. William Goetz asked Lew Schreiber of the casting department to discuss the matter with Beyer, but when Schreiber reported back that Fields wanted $25,000 to write and perform another week's worth of material, nothing further was done about it. The news that the sequence had been "definitely snipped" appeared in the *Reporter* on April 2, 1942, along with the intimation that Jack Benny might star in a substitute. This was followed by an erroneous report in *Daily Variety* that Fields had "insisted upon $50,000 for little more than a week's work" when, in fact, he received only $25,000 for his appearance—the same exact rate paid Boyer, Robinson, Laughton, and Rogers. "Pardon this long silence on my part," Fields wrote Elise Cavanna on April 7. "It is not due to remissness, but I have been busy writing and performing on a sequence in *Tales of Manhattan.* Then I got an infected great toe which the doctor says was due to kicking those Jews in the can over at Fox."

The studio announced on April 10 that *Tales* would be held until August 1, the beginning of the company's new fiscal year, and that, as yet, there was no final decision on the fate of the Fields sequence. This prompted Jimmie Fidler, on his Monday-night broadcast over NBC's Blue Network, to suggest that Fields had threatened to sue if the sequence were indeed dropped from the film. Fields, who had tried his best to foster a positive relationship with Zanuck and Fox, was outraged at the report: "Fidler, the man who sneezes misinformation through one nostril over the radio, said I was suing 20th Century–Fox for 50 G's. An untruth if ever I heard one." He shot a letter off to Zanuck, again over the signature of Charlie Beyer, in which he denounced the report as "a creation of Mr. Fidler's for something to say." He had no quarrel whatsoever with Fox, he said, which was, in his opinion, the "best run and equipped studio in the world." In his long career, he truthfully noted, he had never found it necessary to sue anyone. Enclosed, he sent a copy of a letter he wrote to Don Gilman, head of the Blue Network, in which he demanded a retraction "on the same program on which the charge was originally made" unless Fidler could some-how furnish proof of his statement. On May 3, the *New York Times* (possibly in answer to the Fidler controversy) reported that the Fields sequence had been cut "because the producers, having shown it at sneak previews, feel that it is not in keeping with the other five sections." Sam Rheiner, associate producer of the film, estimated the cost of the deleted episode at $70,000.

Fields retained attorney Martin Gang to advise him on proceeding with a lawsuit against Fidler, "an alleged reporter on a radio program selling armpit and body deodorant," as he put it. He took out a full-page ad in the May 8 edition of the *Hollywood Reporter* to assert that Fidler "should have his ears boxed" for glutting up the airways with loose, unsubstantiated gossip. "Can you imagine anyone calling himself a 'he' making a living with untruthful comments about men, women, and children alike? And can you imagine any firm trying to sell a product by engaging one of those—you name it—to ruin some-one willfully and untruthfully who is making an honest living? I suppose the next thing he'll tell people I drink."

Fields didn't sue Fidler, but neither did he get his sequence restored to *Tales of Manhattan.* The film had its world premiere on August 5, 1942, at Grauman's Chinese Theatre, where, according to the army's new dim-out edict, there were no sky-piercing arcs, and even the lights in the famous forecourt and lobby were way below their usual brilliance. Enthusiastically received, *Tales* went on to return more than $3 million in rentals on a relatively modest invest-ment of $1,050,100. Meanwhile, the Fields sequence remained locked in the Fox vault, unseen but never entirely forgotten. In 1946, Morros and Spiegel, having had little luck in capitalizing on the success of their movie, approached Fox about releasing the Fields episode as a short, offering to clear the matter directly with Fields for a nominal amount. In 1951, Spiegel himself tried to buy the film and the Fields segment for distribution to television, and in 1960 he pursued it yet again, this time asking that the film and any outtakes be sent directly to him as one of the participants in the film's profits. The studio's refusal to turn over the elements, on the grounds that Fields' contract was specifically for a feature appearance, sparked a lawsuit, and the footage remained in a kind of limbo until the rights were acquired by Raymond Rohauer, who registered the episode as an unpublished work in 1974. It wasn't until 1996, however, fifty years after Fields' death, that it was finally rejoined with the other five segments of *Tales of Manhattan* for the film's home video release.

# Twenty-eight

# *Little Boys' Parts*

Claude's marriage to Anne Ruth Stevens, on August 4, 1942, was a turning point in his relationship with his father. A pretty brunette, Ruth was bright and well read, and, suddenly, Fields had the daughter he was forever writing into his pictures, the one who could see past Hattie's self-serving sob story and understand his wreck of a family, his loss of a son. "Perhaps the bond he and Ruth had," her daughter Harriet suggested, "was that they shared a common hurt—the inability of a lovely and elegant man to stand up to a woman who wielded too much power." Ruth made the drive to California—the wedding took place in Rhode Island—with Hattie seated firmly between her and her new husband. Once back in LA, she lived under the same roof as the manipulative old woman, who soon set about to undermine the relationship between her son and his wife. As a wedding present, Hattie gave them twin beds.

A taciturn New Englander, Ruth's native sweetness cloaked an iron will. She crossed swords with her mother-in-law from the very beginning, and to her great and everlasting disappointment, her husband never backed her. The Stevens family got a taste of things to come when Hattie came east for the wedding and Sister Mary Oswald, an old family friend, regarded her with alarm. "Don't let Ruthie get married," she warned Ruth's German-born mother after meeting Hattie for the first time. "That woman's a devil!" Sensing Hattie's ire, Fields embraced Ruth instantly, attempting to buy her a "puddle-jumper" as a gift and, failing that in wartime Los Angeles, giving her a $1,500 check so Claude could carry on the search. Father and son took up an exchange of letters, and, for the first time in decades, Fields began signing off again with love.

When Claude entered the aviation branch of the U.S. Navy in October 1942, Fields gave his son a St. Raphael medal. With the patron saint of flyers engraved on one side and a patriotic inscription on the other, it represented a real and heartfelt gesture, the closest he would ever come to acknowledging the faith of his son. While Claude was away at war, his wife was forbidden to speak to his father, prompting Fields to adopt a conspiratorial tone whenever he

*The wedding of Claude Fields and Anne Ruth Stevens,*
*Rhode Island, August 4, 1942*

phoned the house. "Is the coast clear?" he'd ask, making sure Hattie was out somewhere before settling in for a talk. Ruthie came on the scene at just the right time for him, after a dispiriting year that saw the failure of *Never Give a Sucker an Even Break,* the junking of his *Tales of Manhattan* sequence, and the death of his friend John Barrymore.

Two years younger than Fields, Barrymore was a physical wreck of a man whose fortune had been squandered on ex-wives and high living and who had, by necessity, sunk to self-parody in pictures and on radio. Yet there were still flashes of the genius at Barrymore's core, long Shakespearean recitations that poured from him at Decker's modest studio, glimpses into the art and the spirit of perhaps the greatest actor of modern times. Fields often sat spellbound in his presence. "He took all criticism, true or false, on the chin and never complained once," he once said of Barrymore admiringly. "He was the only ham I ever knew that never had a swelled head."

When John Barrymore died on May 29, 1942, felled by a witches' brew of ailments that included nephritis, gastric ulcers, cirrhosis, and, ultimately, myocarditis, Fields was asked by his friend Gene Fowler to be one of the pall-bearers. "The time to carry a pal is when he's still alive," Fields grunted, resisting the overture. He had never performed such a duty for any man and worried his presence would make a spectacle of the event. Fowler persisted, recruiting John Decker and MGM studio executive Eddie Mannix for the procession, and eventually Fields relented. "I'll be a pallbearer," he said, "if I can stand on the back end and be the tail light."

The funeral was every bit the circus he had feared. Just seventy friends were invited, but there were more than one thousand onlookers outside the Catholic cemetery in the heavily Hispanic section of East Los Angeles. Clark Gable, Spencer Tracy, Norma Shearer, and Errol Flynn were among the mourners. "The cholos at the funeral applauded the stars," Fields noted. Taking the right front position at the orchid-covered casket, he solemnly rolled it into the mausoleum, Fowler, Mannix, and Decker shuffling along behind him, white marble crypts lining the walls on either side. The service was mercifully brief, not the requiem mass but a simple twelve-minute committal ceremony conducted in Latin. After the funeral, Fields persuaded Fowler to join him on the return home. Under a lap blanket in the rear of his Cadillac limousine was a cooler holding a supply of beer and a thermos flask of martinis. "This is my last trip to a cemetery," he said.

Barrymore's death marked the gradual dispersal of the Bundy Drive group, and Decker moved to a new studio on Alta Loma, just below the Sunset Strip. For Fields, the most lasting remnant of his time on Bundy was a portrait Decker painted of him in the guise of Victoria Regina. Fields had impersonated the queen one night at Fowler's home—a bunched-up napkin on his head, topped with a salt cellar to simulate a tiara—and his host, struck with the image, had asked his friend Decker to reproduce it in oils. The result followed in the style of other paintings the artist had done in which his friends and patrons were inserted into deft renderings of the old masters—Fannie Brice as Pinky, for example, or Harpo Marx as Blue Boy. The Fields portrait became the most famous of these, primarily because Fowler used it to decorate his office at RKO. Though Fields himself was unimpressed with the portrait ("Decker has kicked history in the groin!"), a steady stream of visitors came to admire the imperious figure in the fancy gilt frame, and the artist was soon filling orders for copies, painting eight-by-tens and even a few miniatures. One, a full-sized version, went to Dave Chasen, who hung it in his restaurant and let Decker take it out in trade. Soon, Fowler's original came to be regarded as a copy. "So I took the thing that was the original," he said, "and gave it to Bill Fields on one Valentine's Day, and he, in turn, gave it back to Decker later." The painting at

*The body of John Barrymore arrives at Calvary Cemetery, June 2, 1942. Among the
pallbearers (left, front to rear): Fields, MGM studio manager Eddie Mannix, and
author Gene Fowler. Artist John Decker can be seen directly opposite Fields.*

Chasen's remained in the entryway, greeting illustrious diners for more than
half a century, until the closure of the restaurant in 1995. The whereabouts of
the true original are today unknown.

The war put a strain on the family in ways other than just Claude's absence.
Rationing limited gasoline to four gallons a week, taxes shot up, and the city
was placed under dim-out restrictions, enforced in the Laughlin Park district
by Cecil B. De Mille. On one of the last outings Fields had with his friend Barrymore, the two men registered for the draft. Responding to the nation's fourth

*John Decker's famous portrait of Fields as Queen Victoria was inspired by
Fields' own impromptu imitation of the British monarch one night at Gene Fowler's house.*

mobilization of manpower, thousands of men between the ages of forty-five
and sixty-four descended on posts within the city of Los Angeles in compliance
with the Selective Service Act. Fields appeared at a station in the Pantages
building on Hollywood Boulevard wearing bunny slippers ("I'm saving my feet
for the Army") and accompanied by Fowler, Barrymore, his brother Lionel,
Sadakichi Hartmann, and John Decker, the latter seriously hungover. "As we
came in," said Fowler, "the lady in charge, rather a school-teacherish fine lady,
looked up at all these cripples and drunks and said, 'Who sent you? The
enemy?' We had no comeback for it, all these so-called wits."

Fields tried interesting one of the studios in *Pickwick,* but no one was taking the bait. "The more I think of Pickwick," he said, "the more intrigued I
become with playing the character." His health was now a major concern, and
the scuttlebutt surrounding *Tales of Manhattan* prompted rumors that he was
ill. In public, his face was mottled and drawn and he no longer made any
attempt to mitigate his reputation for drinking. When asked to contribute a
statement for a book on the subject, he issued the following through a Universal publicist: "He has been drinking for 40 years as a stimulant, drinking eight
or ten cocktails, possibly a bottle of champagne, and a half-dozen or more bot-

tles of beer and ale per day; he has never been drunk in his life, and he has only missed two performances in that long period and that was due to influenza when his fever rose to 105. Contrary to all precepts, when he gets a bad cold he abstains from alcoholic stimulants."

In September 1942, an attack of grippe turned to pneumonia, and he was whisked back to Las Encinas. While under treatment at the hospital, he was diagnosed with chronic liver disease and ordered to stop drinking. He did so furtively, but with time on his hands and his mobility limited by rationing, his resolve didn't last very long. "I think he drank because people had come to expect it of him," Dick Foran suggested. "And he didn't want to let them down." Due to arthritis, Fields lost the dexterity in his fingers and was no longer able to juggle. "I remember one time we were having dinner at Chasen's after he had been told he had to stop drinking," said Gene Fowler Jr. "Chasen's had a ping-pong table out back, and Fields and my sister Jane got into a ping-pong match. He started juggling the paddles and kept dropping them. It was such an embarrassment to him. . . . I felt sorry for the guy."

With no film roles in the offing, Fields made his annual appearance on *The Chase & Sanborn Program* on November 8, 1942. Other than ambling up onstage one night during a performance of *Ken Murray's Blackouts* at the El Capitan, it was his only appearance before the public that year. Standard Brands had switched agencies, Kenyon and Eckhardt having replaced J. Walter Thompson, and Edgar Bergen had hit on a way of working with Fields that kept him feeling he was in control of the material.

> We would have a meeting and discuss what the situation would be. Charlie puts a skunk trap in his garden as a practical joke, and he trips over it. He not only sprains his ankle, but he fractures his flask. So then we would talk about that, and he would write some jokes, and we would write jokes. I would have the notes with the shorthand girl, and we would take these notes, and with another fellow [Zeno Klinker], we would put the jokes in, and then Bill would send his jokes in, and we'd put it all together. Bill would forget which jokes he wrote and which he didn't write, so sometimes he'd get in the habit of saying, "The first joke isn't very good, so let's get rid of that one and just go on to the others." Well, everything depended on the first joke. It's like not doing the straight line. . . . Anytime we wanted to keep a joke in, and his memory was bad, all we had to do was say, "Oh no, Bill, that's one of your own jokes." He'd say, "Oh it is? Well . . ." And I'd say, "It sets off the other jokes." I wanted to keep it fair, I wanted to keep him happy. I didn't want him to play second fiddle to Charlie, because that would be an insult."

In February 1943, there was talk of Fields doing one of his old specialties for *Ziegfeld Follies,* an all-star musical in development at Metro. Then Miss Boss left to get married, and the house assumed a threadbare emptiness that was relieved only by the occasional visitor. When Ruthie's brother Ray, an army doctor, came to visit, he saw that Fields was being bird-dogged by his housekeeper Dell, who put vials of pills before him on a tray. "Well, I guess I should take my pills," Fields said with a note of resignation, "and keep myself together for another 24 hours." On a tour of the upstairs living quarters, Fields threw open a closet stacked from floor to ceiling with canned and bottled goods. "Let the Japs come," he said. "I can hole up for a month."

The isolation of Laughlin Park wasn't good for him, and he became subject to black states of melancholia. "I was talking to W. C. Fields yesterday," Gene Fowler revealed in a letter to Ben Hecht, "and he informs me that it has taken 63 years to come to the blessed point where he hates everyone and does not care a damn what happens. He assures me that this is a very comfortable state of mind." Fortunately, Magda Michael became available again on a part-time basis, and she returned to his employ after an absence of three years. The condition of the house was shocking; it was difficult to maintain eleven rooms under wartime conditions. "The place was falling down," Ginger Michael recalled. "The paper was coming off the walls, and he always had a big thing going with the landlord to fix the walls. But he rented the place for a fixed price and wouldn't pay any more than that, so the place was kind of ramshackle." Outside, the lawn, which he used to keep meticulously trimmed, was overgrown—the result of his Japanese gardener having been sent to an internment camp—and Dell was afraid to go after the evening paper.

When Fields learned that Ruthie was pregnant, he became even more solicitous, staying in relatively close contact with both her and his son, who was stationed in northern California at the time. "I am looking forward to the arrival of the Nipper," he wrote expectantly to Claude on August 26, 1943. The baby, born nine days later, was christened William Claude Fields III. Fields collected Ruth and the baby and her mother, Anna, at the hospital and chauffeured them home, where he posed for snapshots proudly holding his first grandchild.

He tried setting up a feature film at Fox, but with Laurel and Hardy already on the payroll, there didn't seem to be much interest in adding another low comic to the roster. Then Fred Allen made an inquiry concerning a picture he was planning to make, and Fields sent a copy of his old dentist scene from the 1928 *Vanities.* "It is old-fashioned," he cautioned, "but I think it can be brought up to date; however, I have many more to choose from, or you can look over the various versions of the dentist scene, in case that is the one you prefer, or if you find the Chinese people decide against having me in the picture, you are welcome to any parts, or the scene in toto, free, gratis, and with my compli-

*With Ruthie and grandson Bill, September 1943*

ments." Eager to work again, he made it known around town that he was cutting back on the booze. "I am slowly but consistently getting off 'Demon
Rum,'" he told his brother Walter, "and am chomping at the bit to get back
into harness again. I have written quite a bit lately, and must admit egotistically
I am very satisfied with my efforts." In rapid succession, Charlie Beyer lined up

guest appearances in three musicals. The work wasn't much—in each case a week or so at $25,000 per—but the exposure was important, as Fields had now been offscreen for more than two years.

The first of these pictures was also the best, an all-star salute to the Hollywood Victory Committee called *Three Cheers for the Boys.* Eddie Sutherland was set as the director, and he proposed that Fields reprise his famous pool table routine, dusting off an act he had been performing on and off for forty years. "I remember that I rehearsed it at Fields' house and timed a routine I'd done before with him, the billiard act, and Fields had personally slowed down one-fourth, so I undercranked a lot of the scenes silently to make up for his having slowed up, turned the camera slower so he'd seem to work faster."*

Fields appeared for work on the morning of December 2, 1943, and was ready for the first shot promptly at nine o'clock. The set, the post exchange hut of an army camp, had been constructed on Universal's process stage, where Fields had filmed his chase scenes for *The Bank Dick* and *Never Give a Sucker an Even Break.* "That's a wooden door, isn't it?" he said as Sutherland described his entrance. "I've got a piece of business for a glass door without any glass in it. I enter, stepping through the door panel, then turn and see what I've done, step back again, open the door and enter."

"Yeah, very funny," said Sutherland, "but you did that in another picture, remember?"

"You don't say?" said Fields. "I never saw it on screen. I'll have to go and see one of my pictures sometime."

As film began to roll, the crew could hear Fields from the other side of the door singing, "Sunday, Monday, and Always." When the director called for action, he entered, as he did on *Chase & Sanborn,* singing, "Give me my book and bottle . . ." One take. "Cut! Print that!" said Sutherland. "That's our scene—although I'd never recognize it. Let's try the next." With cameras again turning, Fields ambled toward the pool table, then permitted himself to be distracted by a pianist playing incidental music off to one side. It was comedian Clyde Cook, who, like Fields, had been in vaudeville and the *Follies* and silent pictures, but who had never quite caught on with the public. Noticing a dish full of coins on the top of Cook's piano, Fields fished around in his pocket for a fifty-cent piece, applied the tip, then took all the other coins in the dish as change. "Cut!" said Sutherland. "We'll use it."

Fields worked until four o'clock that day, completing eleven camera setups, an impressive total given the extra attention accorded him by the makeup and camera crews. "[He] had this terrible skin condition," Sutherland

---

*This may have been for a master shot, as there is no undercranked footage in the final film, apart from the pocketing of the balls, which appears to be a process shot.

explained, "and we had to use pink filters to neutralize this color." The second day of the shoot, Fields worked from 9:00 to 3:30, with an hour off for lunch, and finished the balance of the segment, a total of seventeen setups. The schedule had allotted ten days for his segment, and Fields was pleased to have finished in so exemplary a manner. "I gave them a 1943 edition of the old billiard table act," he told Maude Fendick in a letter afterward.

The second assignment was not so great a challenge, and even though he was briefly reunited with Edgar Bergen and Charlie McCarthy, there were none of the old fireworks. *Song of the Open Road* was a dreadfully written bit of claptrap, the story of a group of kids cycling around the state harvesting war crops and singing as they went. An independent feature designed to introduce fourteen-year-old Jane Powell to the world, it is arguably the worst film in which Fields ever appeared. He arrived on the set in Azusa with a full bar in the back of his station wagon and, according to Powell, was "boozing it up all the time." The script called for him to be part of a Hollywood contingent recruited to get a thousand acres of oranges picked before a squall hits a Pomona citrus ranch. Briefly, he juggles three oranges for a small group of volunteers. "This used to be my racket," he says without irony, managing an over-the-shoulder fake, "but it isn't anymore."

By now there was a great weariness about the man, like an old prizefighter who had taken too many punches but lacked the sense to quit. "I have slipped from one-hundred fifty-thousand with most everything to say about the picture to 25 G's with nothing to say and playing little boys' parts," he said. Powell, who had exactly one scene with him, wasn't particularly aware of who he was at the time. "I wish I had had more knowledge of him," she said in retrospect. "He was drinking on the set, but nobody raised an eyebrow. To me, he was non compos mentis, an older man in his cups. Basically, the alcohol had taken its toll."

Fields seemed much happier with the third picture, a musical revue for Andrew L. Stone called *Sensations of 1944.* Stone had slightly less than sensational plans for the film, choosing to shoot it in the two-color Cinecolor process rather than full Technicolor and picking up dancer Eleanor Powell, recently dropped by MGM, as its top-billed attraction. "We couldn't get anybody who was on the way up," he admitted. The screenplay set the action in and around a club called the Gay Nineties, at which old vaudevillians such as Fields and Sophie Tucker would perform. Stone planned to lard his picture with circus acts, swing bands, an aquacade finale, and a dozen songs, Fields' principal contribution being "The Caledonian Express," from the *Vanities.* The idea to shoot in color was dropped about a month before production began, and Stone discovered, once he got Fields before the cameras, that he would not be able to carry the full burden of his part. An introduction to Woody Herman's band, with Fields jostling a pinball machine that suddenly comes to life, was given to somebody else to do, and a brief exchange in Eleanor Powell's dressing room had to be laboriously printed out on blackboards and shot several times. Fields passed his sixty-fourth birthday on the set of the film, performing the sketch with other actors in the multiple parts he had once played himself onstage.

The process of filming the sequence at Hollywood's General Service Studio was slow and painful to watch, and it took nearly two weeks for the director to get the footage he needed. "He'd come on at nine o'clock and he'd be all right for an hour," said Stone, "and then he couldn't remember anything." Actress Louise Currie, hired to play the scene with Fields, thought it would take a few days at the most. "He had these little bottles tucked into his coat and his pants, and between each take he would have a little swig and say confidentially, 'This is my cough syrup, you know.' He'd have his little drink, and then he'd forget his lines. We'd need maybe twenty takes to say two lines, and I'd always have mine right, but he'd forget. Then they'd get a blackboard. Well, by the time he finally got it right, I was so undone that I'd blow it. It was a chore for everybody on the set, particularly the director." Doing take after take effectively bled all the spontaneity from the scene, and with it went all the comedy as well. "They'd have to hold the blackboard out of camera range and right where he was going to be looking, and still he couldn't see it. Right in the middle of a take he'd say, 'I can't see the damn thing!' Nobody thought we would ever get it."

The picture finished on March 1, 1944, but when Stone put it before a preview audience in Pomona, "The Caledonian Express" fell horribly flat. "It was so bad," said Stone, "that I had to go to his agent, who was a friend of mine, and say, 'I've got bad news for W. C. Fields. I've got to cut him out of the picture.'" Charley Beyer conveyed the humiliating message to Fields, who sent back word that he would do whatever it took to stay in the movie. Wary of attempting to shoot more dialogue, Stone concocted instead a scene of purely physical comedy in which Fields found himself sharing a tiny compartment with a huge marine. The bit looked too similar to the washroom scene in *Never Give a Sucker an Even Break,* and while Fields thought it might work well for a younger man, it was not the sort of thing he could do anymore. "I'm willing to cooperate, Andy, in any way within my power," he said.

In the end, Stone's solution was to cut the unfunny guts out of "The Caledonian Express" and insert snappier business in its place. "I saw an act up in San Francisco, a nightclub act that was funny. And I thought: Why don't I put them in and have him just stooge with the act? Let the act carry it. Would he be willing to do that? And, by God, he was." Fields dutifully returned to the General Service lot on the morning of April 28, 1944, for his final day before the cameras, stooging for Fritz and Jean Hubert, an elastic pair of knockabout

*With actress Louise Currie in* Sensations of 1945

comics. They stagger on, listing and weaving drunkenly, while he stands behind them and ad-libs his remarks. As a scene, it was impromptu and unworthy of him, but, mercifully, it kept him in the picture, and for that he was grateful. Considering the memory of the experience some fifty years later, Stone characterized Fields as "a very honest man and very nice guy" who had simply come to the end of his days. "He'd lost all his timing," Stone said sadly. "He just wasn't funny anymore."

He could still be funny on radio, where he could hold the script in his hand, his reading glasses perched precariously on the bridge of his nose, and let the audience show him the pauses. He went on with Frank Sinatra in February 1944, then with Bergen and McCarthy, not once but twice. Then came the films—*Follow the Boys* (as *Three Cheers* came to be known) in May, *Song of the Open Road* in June. Andy Stone changed the title of his picture to *Sensations of 1945* to give it more time in release. An MGM cartoon, *Batty Baseball,* opened on a stadium called W. C. FIELD. All of a sudden, he was everywhere.

The movies, unfortunately, showed him to be a dwindling commodity, going as he did from his magnificent old pool routine in *Follow the Boys* to stooging for a pair of second-rate acrobats in *Sensations*. James Agee described him as "looking worn and torn but noble as Stone Mountain" in an all-too-brief sampling of what was once his stock-in-trade. "The producers have cut me down in these pictures to practically nil," Fields lamented in a letter to his sister Dell. "They're new types of pictures taking some little starlet and surrounding her with names and, in their effort to make the little girls stars, they ruin the picture, as the little girls haven't had the experience to carry the load. But when they are willing to pay me twenty-five grand for a day and a half or at the most five days, I go after it like a trout for a worm and then, in turn, our dear Uncle in Washington takes about 90% of it."

That spring, Magda went to New York for a short while to help a friend stage an opera, and Fields, requiring little in the way of secretarial support, took her twenty-year-old daughter Ginger in her place. "I didn't type," said Ginger. "I never even knew how to type. When he dictated a letter, he was very patient with me. . . . Then he used to exercise the cars. He had three cars. They were on DeMille Drive right across from Deanna Durbin, and it was very hard to get them out. The only one I would drive was that sixteen-cylinder Cadillac [limousine] that Carlotta finally got. It was maroon and very pretty. So I would get it out of this horrible driveway—I weighed eighty-seven pounds—and he'd sit up front with me and tell me where to go." Usually, it was up to the Griffith Observatory, around and back down again. Occasionally, he'd ask her to stop so that he could get out and pick some flowers. "Oh, Mr. Fields, I don't think you're supposed to pick those," she'd fret. "Oh, that's all right, dear," he'd tell her. "It's okay." And he'd slowly lower himself down to the pavement, a bit uncertain on his feet, and get himself some flowers. Time weighed heavily on him, and even with the radio appearances and the pictures in release, he still wasn't much in demand after a long dry spell. "One time, we drove down Hollywood Boulevard, and these people were sitting at a bus stop. Naturally, they looked at the car, and then they noticed who was riding in it. He glanced over to see if they knew who he was, and when he was satisfied, he said, 'Yas sir, it's W. C. Fields. Yas it is.' It was the only time I really heard him use his stage voice."

While Magda was away, Fields kept in touch with her, sending newsy little notes and letters from home. "Harriet and Claude [home on leave] dropped in for a spot of tea, toast, and Hartley's jam," he reported one day. "Ruth brought little Bill over. How his lungs have improved. . . . Carlotta's voice improves in volume by the minute. She has a big offer from a cafe in Hemet." Up the coast in Santa Barbara, Carlotta was secretly living with a man and working in a dress shop. "The Santa Barbara thrush paid her respects for a few days, which ended up in a yelling contest. Dell, from her nest on the west side, said she could hear my voice above the Spaniards. [Carlotta] is going to reduce, run, and rest on the beach alternately, and she is going on a diet."

Hattie was up north with Claude, and Ruthie briefly had the run of the place in Beverly Hills, where she collected her own mail and spoke freely to her father-in-law whenever she pleased. Then, without warning, they reappeared, swooped down and snatched her away. "Hattie [and] Claude returned to our fair city unexpectedly [and] told Ruth to prepare the nipper pronto as they were leaving for Santa Rosa. I had a Sunday visit with Claude in which he extolled the virtues of his mater—most interesting. I had Ruth loaded to the scuppers on what not and what to do. She went with them without telephoning me. Nice happy family."

When Magda returned that summer, she found a lonely man in an empty house, a victim of growing infirmities and changing tastes and a life that, perhaps, had continued on too long. It was a dangerous job being W. C. Fields, and now it was slowly killing him. She set about to keep him active, to engage him in some sort of useful activity. A story, "Caviar for the Clown," was submitted to Leo McCarey (who had just directed *Going My Way*) and Eddie Sutherland, but neither could get him insured. "They would take him as sort of a separate character in the picture," Magda said, "but they wouldn't build a picture around him as a star, and that was the only reason." Stories of the *Sensations* fiasco couldn't have helped.

There were occasional appearances on Armed Forces Radio, where he was always warmly received, and he busied himself with benevolent plottings and schemes. "He would do anything in the world for a friend," said Magda. "He loved hearing about something which gave him the opportunity to do a kindness." Fields planned a birthday dinner for his housekeeper Dell, choosing the menu, selecting the wine, having her invite whomever she wished, and then footing the bill. "He could hardly wait until the next morning to find out how they all enjoyed the dinner." Another time, he learned of a boy in the neighborhood who was ill and lacked the money for ice cream. He had Magda fetch $10 in rolled nickels from the bank, went to the boy's house while the parents were away, and helped him find a hiding place for the money. He told the child to buy a cone every day when the Good Humor truck came around, and advised him to keep some change handy because "nothing else gives a boy the kick that jingling coins in his pocket do."

It was Fields' habit to give "unbirthday" gifts to his friends, and the list of women who received floral tributes on Mother's Day was thoughtfully maintained. One year, he was in a quandary over a particular lady whose son was in jail. "How can I send her a Mother's Day gift?" he asked. "She has nothing to celebrate. It will only make her hurt more." He fumed and fussed and reflected until he eventually solved the problem by moving her to his Easter list. The Christmas list was huge, and every gift was the result of serious reflection. He often bought things in bulk, as was his habit with foodstuffs, but rarely just to save money. "He was always afraid of running out," Magda said. He sent her to Magnin's one year to pick out three dozen handbags. "He spent days selecting just the right purse for the right lady. He would mentally review their wardrobes and say, for instance, 'This will go well with that navy blue suit Bess wore last winter.' I was always surprised at his powers of observation in matters of this kind because nothing seemed to escape him."

When a couple he knew got married and moved to a new house, Fields had Magda drive him over; in their absence, he painstakingly measured the backyard and drew up a plan. Then he called up Germain's, a local nursery, and ordered a complete landscaping job. "The contemplation of this gift gave him much pleasure, and he spent many hours deciding when the suggested flowers would bloom and whether there would be too much shade for some of the plants before placing the final order. Needless to say, his friends were overjoyed and had a constant reminder of his affection for them."

There were occasional forays into Mexico with Fowler and Dave Chasen, to Caliente and the races, but mostly Fields remained close to home. Hollywood's lack of interest puzzled him—he wasn't told of the insurance problem—and he continually petitioned Charley Beyer for work. "I have been trying to get into the movies these many months," he said to his friend Roy McCardle. "I've cut the bite almost in half, but still I have no takers." In October 1944, he participated in an all-star Christmas broadcast recorded for Armed Forces Radio, performing a routine Bill Morrow had written for him called "The Temperance Lecture." Also on the show were Bob Hope, Jack Benny, Fred Allen, Danny Kaye, Spencer Tracy, and Judy Garland. Largely unheard stateside, it did little to enhance his standing with the public, and, like all AFRS broadcasts, it paid nothing. Soon he was fretting about money, even though he collected $40.83 in Social Security every month and had more than $800,000 in banks. "I'll have to tighten up a bit," he said ominously, "because I'm scraping the bottom of the barrel." He refused to finance any more of Carlotta's trips— she sang in Mexico City in September—and required her presence at the house in exchange for the $25 salary he paid her each week. Magda, who usually worked three days a week, got $12.42 a day, which worked out to $10 net.

There was no work into 1945, and Fields reluctantly began jotting notes for an autobiography. He had always talked of writing a memoir, but he regarded the job as something one did at the end of one's days. Long plagued by people putting imaginary words in his mouth, he intended to write a relatively serious and reflective book, distancing himself from the character he played onscreen. One surviving page contains the following: "I have always had a fondness for nippers or children as we say. I have always wanted to help the little mites. Mr. Gregory La Cava . . . once claimed I said to his charming wife, in answer to her query, 'Do you like children, Mr. Fields?' (she referred to

*With Fred Allen and Spencer Tracy for the recording of the*
Command Performance *Christmas program, October 1944*

Gilbert, six and a half, and Bilbert, four and five-eighths) . . . 'I do if they're properly cooked.' I seldom, if ever, use the word 'cooked.' I probably said, '. . . prepared, or very good with mustard.' This was several years ago, and if it is my good fortune to meet Mrs. La Cava when she is calm and is willing to listen, [I will advise her of this]."*

The war ended with the Japanese surrender on August 14, 1945, just as southern California was sweltering through a heat wave of near-record intensity. The thermometer was inching toward 100 degrees when Gene Fowler drew

---

*Actually, the "properly cooked" line comes from *Tillie and Gus.* Some of the quips attributed to Fields are best regarded as urban legends. I could not, for example, find a credible source for his oft-quoted remark about water: "Never drink the stuff—fish fuck in it." Likewise, Eddie Sutherland once told me that he doubted that Fields actually said "looking for loopholes" when caught reading a Bible. Fields was the proud owner of one of the most extensive libraries in Hollywood, and it would have come as no surprise to any of his friends that a Bible was among his many volumes. When Claude Fields suggested toward the end of his father's life that he talk to a priest or a minister, Fields simply shook his head and pointed to the books on theology he had already consumed—including one by a famous Jesuit.

up to the house for an unannounced visit, knowing he was always welcome when accompanied by his twenty-four-year-old daughter, Jane. (Fields was an unabashed flirt around Jane, writing coy little notes and signing them "Fieldsie Pie" and "Your Own Willie.") In the party that day as well was clarinetist Artie Shaw, who had asked to meet the legendary comic. "Fields was seated at a table in what appeared to be the living room," Shaw remembered, "going over some household reports. He was wearing a straw hat—a boater—and it appeared as if he was wearing shorts but no shirt. When he saw Jane, he immediately stood—he was a very courtly man—and it was then that we realized he was absolutely stark naked. Fields acted as if it was perfectly natural to receive friends that way. Jane burst out laughing, and the conversation ensued as if nothing happened."

In October, Orson Welles told the *New York Times* that his greatest ambition was to direct W. C. Fields in a screen version of *Pickwick Papers,* a generous thing to say considering that Fields, in reality, was much too ill to ever make another picture. In fact, that same month, Fields made the decision to leave the house on DeMille when the lease was up, though he took the opportunity to squeeze some publicity out of his impending departure. He had read about a stray dog named Pepe, who had been packed off to the animal shelter after getting drunk on wine. "I understand this dog needs a good home," he said. "Well, I do too. If this canine will meet me halfway, we can make a deal." He told the Associated Press he would go to Las Encinas "for a short cure" and that the dog might as well come along. *Life* magazine sent a photographer, but the dog lapped only fitfully at a dish of Dry Sack and Fields' skin condition had worsened to the point where the photos couldn't be used. Shortly thereafter, the house on DeMille was cleared and the furnishings sent to storage.

At Las Encinas, he settled into a modest room with a small alcove and a private bath in the shadow of the old water tower. Now in the advanced stages of cirrhosis, he was regarded by the staff as a dying man, and although he was not placed under a formal program of treatment, the doctors did their best to make him comfortable. His skin had taken on a yellow pallor, and the whites of his eyes were flaxen and dull. The abdomen was distended, but an effort to tap his stomach—a common treatment for patients with liver complaints—was rebuffed. "How do they know they'll get any fluid out of me?" he said. "They'll probably get nothing but denatured alcohol."

Despite Fields' decidedly frail condition, Magda didn't think Charley Beyer was doing enough to find work for him and scared up an appearance on *Request Performance*—the civilian version of *Command Performance*—on her own. Again he performed "The Temperance Lecture" and, in another bit conceived for him by Bill Morrow, drank a glass of water. He was so pleased to be back before an audience that he paid Magda the customary agent's commission, amounting to several hundred dollars. Christmas came and went that year with his usual fuss over gifts, but he genuinely disliked the season for myriad reasons tracing back to his childhood and his father's theft of his money. "I think he also hated Christmas because it meant the passage of time," Gene Fowler Jr. suggested, "and he was very conscious of growing old." One of the ways he marked Christmas was by cutting back Hattie's allowance to $40 a week. "Claude can probably contribute to your support, as you know I contributed to my parents' support all my mother and father's life from the time I was 11 years of age," he wrote.

Fields took early-morning walks around the grounds of the sanitarium but otherwise kept to himself. Occasionally, friends would come to see him—Fowler, La Cava, Dave Chasen, Franklin Pangborn—but Pasadena was a considerable drive from Brentwood and Beverly Hills, and their visits were infrequent. Severely arthritic, Fields had trouble getting around, and working now seemed completely out of the question. Still Magda persisted, arranging yet another appearance with Bergen in March 1946, Bergen obligingly relocating his show to the stage of the Pasadena Playhouse for the occasion. Having learned that Fields' lease has expired, Edgar and Charlie visit him at the Creeking Springs Sanitarium, where he is the occupant of Room $H_2O$. "You know, Bill, two things improve with age," says Edgar. "Old friends and old wine." And Fields replies, "Don't mind if I do!"

Fields had trouble seeing the script, and the rehearsal didn't go well. "They were having problems with him," said Jack Harris, who was on staff at the Playhouse and observed the event firsthand. "He read his lines terribly in rehearsal. His dressing room was downstairs and the door was open. A butler came down the elevator with the most elaborate silver serving cart I have ever seen, and it was stocked with gin, vodka, beer—every kind of drink imaginable. He pushed it into the dressing room and closed the door. When it came time for the broadcast, Fields staggered out of there and up to the microphone, where he gave an absolutely wonderful performance." He was slow in delivery and kept hard to the script, but he was still there in voice and in spirit, and Bergen placed second in the Hooper ratings for the week, just behind Fibber McGee and Molly and far ahead of Jack Benny, Fred Allen, Walter Winchell, and Bing Crosby.

The broadcast took a lot out of Fields, and he stayed in his bed for several days thereafter. Magda delighted in how the challenge of a performance brought him to life once again. "I urged him to write his autobiography many times," she said, "but he never got around to it. Finally I suggested, 'Let me ask you some questions, and I'll jot down what you tell me without striving for literary achievement. And when we have all the facts down, then we can get to work seriously.'" Determined and methodical, the first question she asked him was, "What's your first memory?" And with that they began.

Mickey Mouse wasn't a member of the press, and because she was collecting thoughts to be organized and later massaged into a memoir, he gave her the unvarnished truth. He spoke of his parents, his grandmother, and his school days in Philadelphia. His memory for ancient detail was startling; only dates and some names eluded him, and those would come from the scrapbooks he kept. Eddie Sutherland visited one day and found him in an uncharacteristically nostalgic mood. Fields said to him, "Eddie, you like to drink, don't you?" And Sutherland, who was known around Paramount as the Little Iron Man, said, "Sure. I love it. Why? Don't you?" Fields shook his head sadly. "Booze tastes like medicine to me now." If Fields no longer enjoyed the taste of liquor, he fed his addiction like a methadone addict, stepping up his consumption to the point where it doubtless hastened his death. He had sent his liquor stores to Charley Beyer's house in Whitley Heights—whole cases of bourbon, French cognac, sparkling burgundy, rum, Benedictine, Chartreuse wine. Now he gradually retrieved them in a losing battle with depression. "Almost every time that I called on him at the sanitarium," Magda recounted, "he would request that I bring him some of his liquor. Sometimes I would bring him as much as a case of gin, half a case of vermouth, and a case of beer about every week."

Claude returned to Los Angeles in July 1946, bringing his family, which now included another son, Everett, and Ruthie, pregnant with their third child. He visited his father at Las Encinas, but a tense relationship with Magda—they could scarcely tolerate one another—discouraged him from coming too often. Claude asked one time if he could bring his friend Father Whelan, who was president of Loyola University. "No," said Fields. "After all these years, I'd feel like a hypocrite." On the subject of religion, Fields remained an unrepentant atheist to the bitter last. "Where was God when my father was beating me?" he once demanded of Eddie Cantor when the subject was raised. Carlotta was also unwelcome after a noisy argument in which she called the old man a "stingy bastard" for not raising her salary. "It is very nerve-wracking to have someone snooping around, going through your pockets and stealing money, reading your private mail, going through canceled checks, etc.," he lectured her. "What you hope to gain is an enigma to me." She returned to Santa Barbara, leaving only a trickle of visitors to the room in Pasadena. And of them, only Bill Morrow seemed capable of keeping him active.

Morrow had emerged from the army with the dream of releasing "The Temperance Lecture" and "The Day I Drank a Glass of Water" as commercial recordings, but Fields' condition in Pasadena was worsening. "We've got to get Fields into the studio right away," he told guitarist Les Paul, one of his army buddies and a recording engineer. "He's very ill, and we don't know how long he's going to last. Could we do it at your house in your studio?" Paul had a small house above the Sunset Strip where he had turned the garage into an experimental recording studio. On July 15, 1946, Fields wrote to Elise Cavanna, "I am pleased to report that I will be out of here some day this week, probably tomorrow, as I have some recordings to make and as I have never made records in my life before, it will be something new and interesting, not to mention lucrative (I hope)." He sawed off, as usual, with an old-fashioned hug.

Les Paul remembered,

I was making my first multiple recording. Mary [Ford, his wife and partner] hadn't heard it; no one had heard it. I was expecting Fields, but I was busy recording in my garage. All of a sudden from behind me he says, "That sounds great, Les." I said, "Bill, you're not supposed to hear this." And he said, "You sound like an octopus." So when I invented the multitrack tape recorder, I called it "the Octopus." On the console it says OCT, which bewilders everybody, but it means one octopus, two tentacles.

Anyway, he sat out on the swing [in the backyard] and we talked about it. He said, "What in the world are you doing?" I said, "We're making something new, and you're the first person to hear it. It's a multitrack recording." So he says to me, "It reminds me of when I was in vaudeville. I used to play the banjo." I never knew he played the banjo.

They put a table up in the garage and brought a chair out from the kitchen. Fields, Paul observed, was in pretty rickety shape, leaning heavily on a cane as he walked and wearing shoes slit up the sides so that he could fit his bloated feet into them. "He was pretty sick. It was an effort for him to get around." The old man sat down at the table and immediately asked if he could have his "Listerine." Bill Morrow said, "Better be sure to cool that down first," knowing there'd be no performance if Fields had too much to drink. The flask was stored in the refrigerator, and Magda took her place on the backyard swing as the session began. "I went into the control room," said Paul, "set the level, dropped the needle down, ran back into the studio, and we started to record. Nobody else was engineering that day." Morrow had the script typed up on cards; Fields began to read, but he didn't get very far. "He said, 'And . . . well . . .' and the record's half gone. He couldn't see the next line. The type was too small. So we had to stop recording and get the cards printed up much bigger. Then he said, 'And . . . well . . . what's the next card?' We had about forty cards to get him through it."

Once he got his bearings, Fields went straight through without a hitch, Paul strumming the guitar behind him, and both routines, a total of six sides, were finished in the space of three hours. Fields got his Listerine, Morrow got his recording, and Paul got $36 for the session. When Fields exited the garage studio at 1444 Curzon that day, after witnessing the birth of multitrack recording, a career spanning forty-eight years in most every facet of show business was over. He had given his final performance.

Bill Morrow went on to become head writer and coproducer of Bing Crosby's new series for the American Broadcasting Company. Chafing at the restrictions imposed by live broadcasts, Crosby had been lured to the fledgling network with a promise that he could prerecord his shows, making him the first major star permitted to do so. The quality of sixteen-inch disk transcriptions had always been regarded as inferior to the real thing, but Crosby was a major investor in Ampex, a company that had developed a technique for recording high-fidelity sound on magnetic tape. The technology wasn't ready when *Philco Radio Time* hit the air in October 1946, but Crosby held the new agency, Hutchins, and the network to the deal, recording his shows on disk at the rate of two per week.

An old friend, Crosby was, like Bergen, willing to nurse Fields through one more performance when Morrow proposed the idea. ("Next to Phil Harris," said Hal Kanter, who cowrote the show, "I think Bill Morrow was closest to Bing.") In November, Fay Adler sent Fields a biography of Oscar Wilde. "You

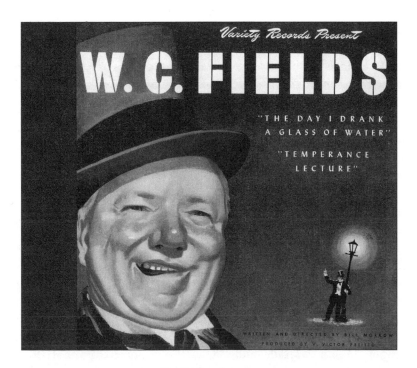

*The final performance*

will think it strange that I haven't called or written you for some months," he said in a note thanking her, "but my gams have gone back on me and I did not wish you to see me hobbling about on canes. . . . If I do get to feeling any better, I will clean up this hospital staff and skip over the border. I may just ride over it."

Around Thanksgiving, he took to his bed, but plans for the Crosby program went forth unabated, both Magda and Morrow hopeful that he somehow would rally. On December 9, Crosby's Christmas show was recorded at the NBC studios in Hollywood, and announcer Ken Carpenter reminded listeners at its conclusion that Bing's guest the following week would be W. C. Fields. Two shows were scheduled to be cut on Sunday, December 22, and Fields was set to appear on both of them. He was failing rapidly, however, and Magda reluctantly came to the conclusion that he wasn't up to it. Jim Tully was a patient at Las Encinas, the victim of multiple strokes, and one afternoon his nurse wheeled him over to Fields' room for a short visit. Neither man had the strength to sustain a conversation. Said Magda, "It was a pathetic sight to view these two formerly virile, strong, vivacious men sitting there in their respective wheelchairs while Tully's nurse and I carried on the conversation in their stead, recounting events and experiences they had shared in the past, and which we both knew about, while the two of them sat silently nodding their heads in acquiescence. I truly believe this was one of the saddest afternoons I ever lived through."

Morrow "postponed" the Crosby appearances, refusing to believe that Fields would not somehow get better again, and the shows went off as planned with Joe Frisco subbing for Fields on the first show and Mickey Rooney on the second. The following day, a wistful Christmas greeting on holiday notepaper arrived at the sanitarium:

Dear Little Woody

My outside men tell me your [*sic*] the same as ever. And I am always the same as ever—

Truly yours,
Carlotta

Eddie Cantor came by to visit the man who had been his mentor, his taskmaster, and his friend over the momentous tour of the 1917 *Follies*. Fields had always addressed him as Rabbi or "Christ Killer," but the old spirit had all but left him. "Eddie," he said weakly, "I've often wondered how far I could have gone had I laid off the booze." The following day, he fell into a coma. Magda stayed with him through Christmas Eve, maintaining a vigil at his bedside. Denied all powers of communication and the singular wit that had sustained him for nearly sixty-seven years, this most independent of men was now unable to perform even the simplest of tasks for himself, and it must have come as a relief when, at 12:03 on a rainy Christmas afternoon, Death gave him an old-fashioned hug.

# Twenty-nine

# Undue Inconvenience

Magda phoned Walter, Adele, and Carlotta, but left it to the sanitarium to notify the family. Claude Fields learned what had happened when an attorney for Forest Lawn called the house. "We've got your father's body here," he was told, "and we've been ordered to cremate it." Claude flew out the door without a word to his wife, and Ruth didn't see him again for three days. Later that evening, she heard the news over the radio.

Gene Fowler hadn't suspected the gravity of his friend's condition until he called the sanitarium on Christmas Eve to arrange a visit. Someone, whose voice he did not recognize, told him that Mr. Fields could not answer the phone, nor could he receive any callers until after the first of the year. Like Cantor, Fowler would have fared better had he simply showed up. Dave Chasen and Billy Grady did so, arriving in Pasadena a little before one with a hamper of food and bottles secreted of both scotch and bourbon. When advised of Fields' death, the two men found a sheltered spot on the grounds, broke one of the bottles open, and passed it between them. "Dave and I sat on the grass," Grady remembered, "and blubbered like children."

Claude, Hattie, and Carlotta converged on Las Encinas at approximately the same time. In later testimony, it was alleged that Claude actually struck Carlotta, a charge he vehemently denied. "I did not strike Miss Monti," he said. "I merely pushed her to keep her from striking my mother." Carlotta accused Claude and Hattie of impounding some of her own property along with the deceased's personal effects. "Mrs. Fields called me a lot of names," she said, "and everything she called me I called her twice back." After being pushed, Carlotta came back with: "You should love me, Claude, because I gave your father love and care." Claude's reaction, when he heard this repeated in court, was to snort, shake his head violently, and pound the arm of his chair.

Bob Hope's quip about Fields ("I . . . waved, and he weaved back") prompted the Associated Press to ask for a statement. Hope hadn't yet heard the news, and was caught in an unguarded moment when advised that the subject of his joke had died shortly before he delivered it. "I feel terrible about that," he said quietly, explaining that he had always included Fields in his routines because the old man "got such a big kick" out of it. "He was one of the world's greatest comedians. The world is certainly going to lose a lot of laughs."

Gene Fowler dashed off an obituary for the *Herald-Express* and signed his son Will's name to it. Will Fowler was a twenty-four-year-old cub reporter for the Hearst paper, and the Fields piece became his first page one story. Fowler's command of the details was a bit shaky: he wrote that Fields had been christened Claude William, which is quite possible, but also said that Fields was born in the Germantown section of Philadelphia of English and Dutch parentage and that he was sixty-eight years of age. Fowler's assertion that Fields died winking at the nurses with a finger to his lips is unlikely as well, and the *Pasadena Star-News,* with sources inside the hospital, reported only that Fields had been lucid up to a few hours before his death. There were no last words. All accounts reported the immediate cause of death to be a "dropsical condition" that would today be known as congestive heart failure. The attending physician, Douglas R. Dodge, minced no words in completing the death certificate. Fields, he wrote, had succumbed to cirrhosis of the liver due to "chronic alcoholism" of an unknown duration.

Magda, as executrix to the estate, lost no time in carrying out her employer's express wishes. In his 1943 will, Fields had directed that, immediately upon his death, his body be placed in an "inexpensive coffin" and cremated. "Since I do not wish to cause my friends undue inconvenience or expense, I direct my executors not to have any funeral or other ceremony or to permit anyone to view my remains, except as is necessary to furnish satisfactory proof of my death." Cremation, however, was in conflict with Claude's Catholic faith, and Fields was, even by Magda's admission, too important a man not to have a memorial service of some kind. A negotiation ensued, with Claude, acting on his mother's behalf, determined to gain control of the estate, and Magda loyally insisting that the directives of the will be carried out to the letter. The cremation was stopped, at least temporarily, but Magda won out in having the body placed in a crypt instead of buried in the ground, as Hattie and Claude wanted. As part of the "compromise agreement" there would be two funerals: a public memorial for which Magda would select the speaker and the pallbearers, and a private committal ceremony, similar to Barrymore's, for the immediate family.

Originally, there was to have been no public ceremony whatsoever, but Gene Fowler, who, along with a group of friends, placed a memorial page in *Daily Variety,* warned Claude that his father's pals would likely show up regardless. The event took place on Thursday, January 2, 1947, in the Church of the

Recessional at Forest Lawn, Glendale. About fifty mourners attended the brief ceremony, among them Fowler, Chasen, Grady, Jack Dempsey, Leo McCarey, John Decker, Earl Carroll, Gregory La Cava, Eddie Sutherland, George Moran, and William Le Baron. Eddie Cline was there with Kilroy peeking over his tweed vest pocket. Carlotta Monti, dressed in black and described in the press as "gravely quiet," took a front-row seat. A heart of white chrysanthemums and scarlet roses sent by her stood on an easel next to the metal casket that contained Fields' body.

Edgar Bergen's eulogy, in which he referred to Fields as "one of America's best-loved men," took just four minutes to deliver. "Let his faults be buried with him," he said, "and let us keep the memories of the happy moments he brought us. . . . Few can boast of such talent as his, and few can boast of having given so much happiness to the world. His request was that we do not go into deep mourning or pray for his departed soul. It seems wrong not to pray for a man who gave such happiness to the world, but it was the way he wanted it. Bill knew life, and knew that laughter was the way to live it. He knew that happiness depended on disposition, not position. We simply say farewell."

After the memorial, Fields' cronies adjourned to the Los Feliz home of Jack Dempsey, who was an honorary pallbearer. The committal ceremony at

*Hattie, Adele, Walter, and Claude at the funeral, January 2, 1947*

the Sanctuary of Ascension was attended only by Claude, Hattie, Walter, and Adele. Carlotta, accompanied by her father, sister, nieces, and a Hollywood spiritualist named Mae Taylor, was stopped from entering the mausoleum until the crypt was sealed. Waiting for the family to leave the premises, she told reporters that she had messages from Fields "every night at the church I have been attending." The family, she said, was opposed to her presence at the funeral, but she decided to come anyway. "I'm certainly not intruding on the grief of his family because they have seen nothing of him for years and years."

The will, which had been filed for probate on December 31, was a model of simplicity and evenhandedness. Fields remembered Walter, Adele, Maude Fendick, Ruthie, and Charley Beyer with gifts of $5,000 each. In addition, he established trust funds for both Walter and Adele. Carlotta received no lump sum, given her witless ways with money, but was instead given $25 a week until a total of $25,000 was paid out. Fields' faithful housekeeper, Adele Clines, received $2,500. Mabel Roach, a cousin, got $2,000, as did Mabel Clapsadle, Fields' personal banker at the Hollywood and Cahuenga branch of Security First National Bank. Leroy Dukenfield and Elise May Cunningham, neither of whom had seen their brother in years, were left $500 apiece.

The matter of the residual and its disposition was always perplexing to Fields. "He debated with himself out loud," said Magda. "He said, 'I don't know what to do about Harriet. She isn't entitled to a penny. I think I'll give her 10 Gs and Claude 10 Gs so they won't give us any trouble later on.'" He then added a provision specifically disinheriting anyone who "tries to confuse or break this will or who contributes in any way to break this will." He told Magda, with some degree of satisfaction, "Harriet won't get anything if she fights it." He dedicated the balance of his estate to the establishment of the W. C. Fields College for orphan white boys and girls "where no religion of any sort is to be preached."

This last clause was the subject of considerable discussion when it first came out in the press, and Fields was characterized in some corners as a racist. Clearly, he wanted to put the money where neither Hattie nor Claude could get their hands on it, and the inspiration for a school most likely came from the example of Philadelphia's Girard College, which occupies forty-two acres in South Penn and was established by a local shipbuilder for the rearing and education of orphan boys. According to Magda, the college in the draft will was at first for both white and colored children, and he was genuine in his affection for people of African descent. His friendship and work on behalf of Bert Williams was well known among his contemporaries, and he regarded Adele and Frank Clines as members of the family. (He paid for their house on West Twenty-sixth Place in Los Angeles, and when they would not accept it as an outright gift, he let them pay for it as they pleased, charging a nominal rate of 1 percent interest on the loan.) Dell interested him in the *Los Angeles Sentinel,* a black-owned paper he read every day, and when he wrote an open letter to William Randolph Hearst in 1940 on the subject of the Negro's plight, it was front-page news in the *Sentinel.*

"They were brought here under duress," he said, "but have accepted the vile treatment we have meted out to them uncomplainingly and are loyal and dependable. There are some 16 million of them, I believe, in the United States, and there are few of them in high positions in our government. They are just as intelligent as the Litvoks, the Germans, the Russians, the Galicians, or the Balkans that migrate to our country. Japanese, Chinese, in fact, Mongolians are treated with much more respect and are rented houses where the colored folks are denied rentals. The housing propositions with these unfortunate loyal people is deplorable, and their rents in the colored districts are very much higher than in the white districts of homes of similar construction and age."*

He could be quite impulsive, however, and when he read in the *Sentinel* that the Pullman Porters Union had formally voted to exclude Caucasians from their ranks, he was so incensed over the action that he canceled his subscription to the paper and struck the word "colored" from his will. "If they're going to discriminate against us," he stormed, "I'm going to discriminate against them!" Magda said, "This was typical of his reaction to one single act—however insignificant—that would change his entire thinking or belief in a subject or person. Often the offending person never really knew what precipitated his change of heart and the fact that he 'played them for a chill.' "

Once the will was filed, Hattie entered a petition for support of $500 a month, almost tripling the amount Fields was paying her at the time of his death. Magda was sent scrambling to inventory the estate, not completing a formal appraisal until May 26. There was cash in the amount of $400,000 and bonds worth another $70,000. In 1940, with the establishment of the FDIC, which insured deposits up to $5,000, Fields had Magda compile a list of the top banks in fifteen principal cities and sent each of them a deposit of exactly $5,000. Other accounts already in existence held deposits of as much as $26,000, giving rise to the legend that Fields had money secreted under fanciful names in banks all over the world. There were, in reality, only twenty-four accounts, and they were all in his own name. The value of the estate eventually established was in excess of $750,000.

Fields' personal effects were divvied up in a two-page amendment to the

---

*Fields held similar thoughts for the American Indians whose living conditions he had observed firsthand on the Soboba reservation. "All we ever gave the Indians were our choice diseases and a lot of broken treaties," he said. "Isn't it wonderful what we're doing *to* the Indians?"

will. "He spent days and hours thinking up this long list and arranging it," Gene Fowler said. "In fact, he used up more time on this phase of his bequests than he did on the will itself." Furniture and knickknacks were left to Charlie Beyer, books and kitchenware to Carlotta. Walter got his trunks, liquor, and first pick of his neckties. Magda got the secretarial stuff, La Cava revolvers and pictures, Chasen one half his collection of Decker paintings.

Claude Fields sprang into action. On July 23, 1947, Hattie entered a creditor's claim and disaffirmation detailing Fields' estimated gifts to other women and claiming 50 percent of his earnings dating from 1927 under California's community property laws. On August 6, Magda formally denied the claim, a move that effectively tied the estate up in litigation for seven long years, a total of 291 days in trial. Under a veritable scorched-earth strategy, Hattie even sought the proceeds of a $25,000 life insurance policy that named Walter Fields as the beneficiary on the grounds that the premiums had been paid with community funds. Whatever civility that existed between the two factions of the family in the days immediately following Fields' death was completely lost in the rancorous dispute that followed. Neither Adele nor Walter would ever speak to their brother's widow or his son again.

The battle hinged on exactly when Fields became a legal resident of California. Hattie, through her attorney Ernest A. Tolin (to whom Claude Fields was a consulting attorney), contended that Fields had established residency when he came to California at the behest of Paramount Pictures in 1927. Walter, Adele, and the estate maintained that Fields was a legal resident of New Jersey until 1937, when he had his books and trunks shipped out, and that none of his earnings prior to that date qualified as community property. The proceedings continued for more than a year, with testimony elicited from Charley Beyer, Chester Conklin, and others with whom Fields came in day-to-day contact. Carlotta, through her attorney, Arthur E. T. Chapman, fought tenaciously for her share of the estate, while Magda, through her own attorney, sought to administer the will as it was written. On a gray day in November 1948, Tolin was pressing the widow's claims when suddenly Chapman leapt to his feet to suggest that Mrs. Fields was not only fully aware of at least one of her husband's extramarital relationships, but that he had actually acknowledged paternity of an illegitimate son and made payments accordingly. Within weeks, William R. F. Morris had joined the fight, acting through yet another Los Angeles attorney in seeking a share of the estate.

Carlotta took the stand on May 12, 1949, and leveled a withering blast at Hattie and Claude. "When his widow was on the stand here, she said she didn't know about his earnings. She did; she knew all about them. She accepted $60 a week, though, and when I asked Woody why she didn't holler for more, he told me he had an agreement with her. I asked him why he didn't divorce her, and he

*Claude comforts his mother during a court appearance.*

told me, 'I never married her.' " The result of Carlotta's testimony was to call
the legitimacy of Hattie's marriage into question, and since civil records of the
union were destroyed in the 1906 San Francisco earthquake, evidence had to be
amassed from other sources to overcome the implication of a fraudulent claim.
"They are trying to make this thing a beautiful sanctimonious marriage," said
Carlotta, "and it wasn't. What he thought of it was unprintable."

While Hattie and Carlotta (whom Hattie referred to as "the Monti
woman") exchanged poisonous glares from across the courtroom, Magda quietly pressed for authorization to proceed with the cremation. Originally, she
had wanted to dispose of the body on January 29, 1948, the sixty-eighth
anniversary of Fields' birth, but was unable to obtain a court order to do so
until May 1949—a full two and a half years after his death. The event finally
occurred on June 2 under Claude's reluctant supervision. Carlotta, who was
present for the disinterment, was barred from the final services but allowed to
place a single rose on the casket as it was wheeled away. A month later, Judge
William R. McKay handed Hattie the victory she sought in finding that Fields
had become a legal resident of California on November 12, 1927, the day he
leased the house in Whitley Heights and became a member of the Automobile
Club of Southern California. In the same decision, McKay found that William
Morris, a Dallas airline clerk, had no claim to a share of the estate. Now all
that remained was to decide what part of the estate was earned prior to 1927.

The disputes in court managed to keep Fields' name in the papers for years, creating a ready market for an unauthorized biography that appeared in 1949. Fields had always considered Gene Fowler to be his official biographer, and he bequeathed Fowler numerous letters and manuscript items contained in a small leather trunk. (Fields' scrapbooks, which eventually were returned to the family, were willed to Charlie Beyer.) In 1948, however, Fowler was approached by Robert Lewis Taylor, a writer for the *New Yorker,* who asked his blessing and cooperation in doing a biography of his own, and Fowler, deep in the writing of Jimmy Walker's story, acceded to the request. "Pop said he'd never write a biography of Fields," Gene Jr. recalled, "because he was such a mean bastard—unsympathetic. So one day Taylor contacted him and he turned over all the stuff on him. Fields *was* a nasty old son of a bitch, but we loved him."

Fields, it seems, tended to show a resolutely gruff exterior to his drinking buddies, and, lacking Claude Fields' cooperation, that was the side Taylor chose to detail in his book. Fowler gave him notes and an interview, and arranged access to people like Grady, La Cava, Sutherland, and others. Taylor went to particularly extreme lengths to locate Kitty Hughes, Hattie's sister, who was married to a Japanese American and living on Long Island. He placed an ad in a New York paper for "the woman living in Jackson Heights who has a cat named Mickey and is the sister-in-law of the late W. C. Fields" and, with the help of radio personality Pegeen Fitzgerald, finally made contact with Kitty. She proved not to be a particularly accurate resource—she told Taylor her mother was a French Creole, when she was in fact born in Pennsylvania of British ancestry—but he was warmed by her general attitude toward the Fields family and her apparent loathing for her sister Hattie. Claude warned Taylor that he could not quote from any of Fields' unpublished letters, further limiting him to old interviews and other public sources. Taylor retaliated by portraying Claude in the book as a silly oaf on the order of Grady Sutton and ascribing the Encino encounter between Fields and William Morris to him.

An eight-part serialization began in the May 21, 1949, issue of the *Saturday Evening Post,* and was followed in October with the book's publication by Doubleday. It became an immediate best-seller, prompting reissues of Fields' films by both Paramount and Realart (distributing the Universal product). Coming as it did while the trial was still in full swing, Taylor's book did much to reinforce the impression that Fields was largely the same character he portrayed onscreen. Denied access to his subject's scrapbooks and correspondence, Taylor also made some horrendous blunders with regard to the historic record. Nevertheless, *W. C. Fields: His Follies and Fortunes* was a swift and amusing read by a talented portraitist, and it remained in print, in one form or another, for more than half a century.

The success of Taylor's book began an inevitable move to adapt Fields' story to the screen. In 1951, Twentieth Century–Fox commissioned an original treatment from Herman Mankiewicz based on Fields' life. A second treatment was written by I. A. L. Diamond and developed into a screenplay by Lynn Root, author of *Green Grow the Lilacs,* the basis for *Oklahoma!* Root's script was embraced by producer Sol C. Siegel, who said he'd start shooting "without a moment's delay" if he could find a suitable actor to play Fields. The project went cold after Claude Fields threatened a lawsuit, and a plan to base a film on Gene Fowler's *Minutes of the Last Meeting* two years later met with a similar fate. Red Skelton was set to play Fields in that one, with Frank Borzage directing in Technicolor. "Bill often said before he died that no one else but Red could play Fields," Fowler said.*

All the while, the court battle dragged on. On December 14, 1949, Judge McKay threw out the provision of the will that established a college for orphans. "Mr. Fields, in his lifetime, could have discriminated against other races," he said, "but he cannot in death call upon the state to undertake the administration of his affairs and supervise a corporation which overrides the constitutionality of equality of rights common to all races." Six months later, over the objections of Magda's attorney, the judge ordered $100,000 paid to Hattie, $3,850 to Carlotta, $11,550 to Walter, and $9,240 to Adele. Federal taxes of $186,000 were paid by the estate, as were approximately $20,000 in California inheritance taxes. In June, the court ordered the estate to pay each of the legatees one half the amount bequeathed them. The remainder was held back in anticipation of Hattie's suit, which was scheduled to go to trial on October 9, 1950. On December 29, 1950, a compromise agreement was announced in which William Morris received a $15,000 distribution, and the clause establishing the orphans' college was reinstated but limited to $25,000 to go directly to the support of orphan white boys and girls "in some college in Los Angeles County" upon the deaths of Walter, Adele, and Carlotta.

At a time when all other issues had been settled and the estate seemed ready for the final distributions, along came a Mrs. Edith Williams, a seventy-year-old crackpot from Chicago who was convinced that she had married Fields in St. Louis in 1893, when the historic record shows that he was just thirteen years of age. Mrs. Williams claimed that he was thirty-four at the time (making him eighty-seven when he died) and had a history of hectoring him even during his lifetime. "Three sets of lawyers . . . are after me on that old Mrs. Edith Williams case again," Fields had informed Magda back in 1944. "I quit her holding the bag with a mess of kids, one letter seven, another eleven, and if I do not make some settlement immediately, my fair name will adorn the

---

*As unlikely as this sounds, Skelton actually did play Fields once on his CBS variety series, and he gave a surprisingly good account of himself.

front pages of the world's newspapers showing me up in my true character. The idea, of course, being to give some lawyers employment."

Mrs. Williams filed a claim in superior court on January 25, 1951, knocking the compromise into a cocked hat and extending the tussle well into the summer. Ed Wynn was called upon to testify, as were other ex-vaudevillians who squinted at old photographs of one "Billy Williams" and wondered whether the man pictured could really have been Bill Fields. As ridiculous as the claim was on its face, the judgment denying family allowance to Mrs. Williams was not handed down until January 1952, a full year almost to the day from the filing of the original claim. The distribution of Fields' personal effects began in May, and Magda set about to settle all costs and legal fees before wrapping things up. Hattie's allowance was stopped on the grounds that it was depleting the estate for the other beneficiaries.

Judge McKay ordered distribution of the $84,401 remaining in the executor's hands on March 4, 1954. In the end, Hattie was paid the $10,000 left to her in the will. She also won a $65,000 settlement from the estate on her community property claim, and received approximately $55,800 in allowance over the length of the trial. With one half the residual of the estate also due her, she ended up with $330,000. With what was left, trust funds were established for Walter, Adele, and Carlotta, but all three outlived the solvency of the trust. Magda resigned as trustee to the estate in 1956, when the amount left in the trust was about $23,000, and by 1959 the funds were completely exhausted. A final payment of $59.65 was made to Carlotta Monti on June 26, 1962, and on January 16, 1963, the estate of W. C. Fields was officially closed—sixteen years after his death.

May Cunningham died in 1962, Walter Fields in 1967, Adele Smith in 1973. Leroy Dukenfield, the youngest of Fields' siblings, died in Philadelphia on November 18, 1974, after a career as a landscape gardener. Although he disparaged the memory of his eldest brother, whom he always referred to as "Big Nose," the Felton countenance overtook him, and toward the end of his life, Roy both looked and sounded like Fields.

Claude and Ann Ruth Fields had a total of five children, Harriet, Allen, and Ronald coming in the years immediately following their grandfather's death. They established a home in Westchester, from which Claude commuted daily to his downtown office at Eighth and Spring. He was a member of Delta Kappa Epsilon, Phi Delta Phi, the Columbia University Club, the Newman Club, the Serra Club, and the Holy Name Society. In 1955, he established a family corporation, Harcourt Enterprises, as custodian for the rights and materials of W. C. Fields.

Throughout his life as an attorney, Claude Fields was indelibly linked to his mother. Into her eighties, Hattie would accompany him to dinners and functions as if he had no other family in the world. Ruth remained at home with the children, and Hattie and she never spoke. On Sunday afternoons, when the family made their requisite visit to the apartment house that Hattie built with the money from the Fields estate, Ruth always stayed behind. Upstairs, Hattie put the children through recitations, dressing them alike and sometimes dragging them along on individual outings. "Hattie would trip people with her cane on the bus or in the downtown department stores where she used to take me shopping," said Harriet Fields, recalling her grandmother. "I thought at the time it was a terrible thing to do to other people, especially in front of a child."

Harriet would remember her grandmother as poised, affected, dramatic. "She was proud of being Mrs. W. C. Fields. She played it to the hilt. I think that was her identity." In 1961, Hattie consented to a series of interviews with playwright Emmet Lavery, author of *The Magnificent Yankee,* whom Claude knew from the Newman Club. Lavery and Claude formed a partnership to develop a movie based on the life of W. C. Fields, with Claude playing his late father. There was no interest in the idea, however, especially with the restrictions Claude and Hattie imposed on such a project.* It eventually became "a play with music," Claude coming to terms with his father and, in the end, forgiving him. "A son emerges who is able to take the true measure of his father; he can meet the father on his own terms, talk to him without bitterness, and feel certain in the end that his values will prevail. The clown was a cynic, the son is a believer—and, in spite of himself, the older man has a grudging respect for the younger man. Even when he realizes that the boy may very well outsmart him in the end. And all because of a mother's faith."

There was no such reconciliation in real life, and the kids were never allowed to speak the name of their grandfather around the house. "Hattie kept all of the scrapbooks and the papers in one of the bedrooms, which was used as a storeroom," said Everett Fields. "We called it the Inner Sanctum. If any of us went in there and were caught, we were punished." Hattie's hold on Claude was broken only by her death, on November 7, 1963. Claude wore a black tie for over a year, but three weeks after her funeral, he moved his family to a larger house with a swimming pool and had an addition built on. Without his mother standing between them, Claude and Ann Ruth finally began enjoying the marriage that had been, in so many ways, on hold for twenty-one years. Claude started going around with his wife and kids, and friends, in some cases, were surprised to find that he was married at all. Ruthie began assisting him in his

---

*Bandleader Spike Jones discovered this the previous year when he tried to interest Claude in authorizing a film biography. Jones had Eddie Cline on his payroll, which he apparently thought was an advantage.

law practice, riding to work with him every morning, dining out with him, shopping, and going for long walks amid the construction at Marina del Rey.

Ironically, Hattie's death came just as a revival of interest in W. C. Fields was beginning to grow. In 1966, Donald Deschner's *The Films of W. C. Fields* became the first modern book on Fields, followed in 1967 by William K. Everson's *The Art of W. C. Fields.* Late that year, Universal put their four starring Fields vehicles back into service in glistening new 35mm prints. Grouped into two double features, they outgrossed most modern films at the Fairfax Theatre in Los Angeles and the 72nd Street Playhouse in New York City, prompting a national release in 1968. Next came the distribution of his Paramount features in 16mm, and sales of a photo poster skyrocketed. Johnny Wayne and Frank Shuster hosted a one-hour CBS tribute in his honor, in which they affectionately described him as "a combination of Mr. Pickwick and Frank Nitti." Wedged between Karlheinz Stockhausen and Carl Gustav Jung, he was also one of the cultural icons surrounding the Beatles on the cover of *Sgt. Pepper's Lonely Hearts Club Band.* With the Vietnam War at full throttle, W. C. Fields, along with Humphrey Bogart, became a potent symbol of cynicism and rebellion to the generation of his grandchildren.

For Claude Fields, the renaissance lasted barely eight years. He took advantage of his father's newfound popularity—arguably greater than at any time in Fields' natural life—by affiliating himself with Raymond Rohauer on the distribution of his father's shorts, appearing on the *Tonight Show* with Johnny Carson, and even playing his father once for a show called *Curtain Call.* Back in his beloved New York, he took his teenage kids through Central Park, up to Columbia University at 116th Street, and on to Baker Field at 216th and back, joyously straphanging on the subway, his cherubic face reflecting a delight he rarely exuded in earlier days. "I must have spent a year of my life here," he said nostalgically. In 1970, he was diagnosed with pancreatic cancer, and he died on February 16, 1971—like his father, at the age of sixty-six.

More books followed, including the groundbreaking *W. C. Fields by Himself,* compiled by Ronald J. Fields from his grandfather's papers and scrapbooks, and a heavily ghosted and self-serving memoir from Carlotta, *W. C. Fields and Me.* Throughout the decade of the 1970s, Fields' image was licensed to sell scores of products, ranging from aftershave and neckwear to battery testers. To market corn chips in the days following the demise of the Frito Bandito, a cartoon character named W. C. Fritos was invented. ("Greetings my little chip-a-dee," he'd drawl in animated commercials.) In 1976, a movie was finally made of Fields' life, but it was a sorry affair starring the singularly unfunny Rod Steiger, and it flopped deservedly.

All that remained left to do was to put him on a postage stamp, which was done in a ceremony at the Academy of Motion Picture Arts and Sciences on

January 29, 1980, the true centenary of his birth. A parade of costars, Mary Brian, Buddy Rogers, Constance Moore, and Grady Sutton among them, advanced to the podium, relating tab versions of their favorite anecdotes. The image on the stamp itself was somewhat sanitized for mass consumption—no bottle being anywhere in sight—but, happily, he was pictured juggling, tossing balls in the air between takes on the set of *Poppy,* thoroughly engrossed in the exercise and oblivious to all else around him. In attaining philatelic immortality, Fields followed his old friend Will Rogers, as he so often had on the bill of the *Ziegfeld Follies.* That the two men were now coupled in centennials and dual commemorations would have pleased and amused them both, and no one thought to mention that, on the whole, Fields would rather, as he had once suggested for an epitaph, be living in Philadelphia.

On a cloudy Christmas Day in 1965, Claude Fields, in tie and sport coat, placed flowers on Hattie's crypt at Holy Cross Cemetery in Culver City, as had been his habit every Christmas since her passing. His twenty-year-old son Everett accompanied him and, not entirely sure of the reaction he'd get, waited until the task was finished before broaching the subject. "Pa," he said, "do you think we should put flowers on your father's grave?" And without hesitation, Claude Fields replied, "Yes, I think we should."

They drove to Glendale, stopping to buy flowers at a florist's shop on Los Feliz Avenue. Then they drove around the corner onto Glendale Boulevard and through the five-ton iron gates of the venerable cemetery where Fields and so many of his contemporaries had been laid to rest, past the Tudor administration building and up the winding road to the Great Mausoleum, its gothic facade and marble statuary as much a part of the tourist landscape of southern California as Disneyland. Entering through a side door, Claude was at first unsure as to where exactly the grave was located. They made their way up a marble staircase, the weak December light filtering through walls of stained glass, and at last found the niche in the Columbarium of the Nativity.

Claude Fields was a stoic man, his dignity one of the signal traits he inherited from his famous father. This was as emotional an experience as Everett had ever witnessed with him, and he stood to one side so as not to intrude on his father's thoughts. Claude paused at first, as if transfixed by the sight of the name on the gold-plated tablet, and then, for the first time in fifteen years, positioned himself directly in front of the niche that held his father's ashes, crossed himself, and bowed his head in prayer.

# Appendix I

## Stage Chronology

### The Monte Carlo Girls

(Star Theatre, Troy, New York, September 19, 1898.) Manager: James C. Fulton. Company: Eva Swinburne, Fulton Bros., William T. Bryant, W. C. Fields, Rose Lewis, Harry S. Marion, Kluteldi and Larein, Marie Rogers. Closed in Kent, Ohio, December 16, 1898.

### The Monte Carlo Girls

(Miner's Bowery Theatre, January 23, 1899.) Manager: James C. Fulton. Company: Eva Swinburne, Fulton Bros., Hi Tom Ward, W. C. Fields, Byron G. Harlan, Billy Cross, Mable Holden, Ramza and Arno, Glissando Trio, Marie Rogers. Closed in Philadelphia, May 29, 1899.

### Murphy and Gibson's Minstrels

(Steel Pier, Atlantic City, June 26, 1899.) Managers: John E. Murphy, Alf S. Gibson. Company: Bogert and O'Brien, W. C. Fields, Lew Mettier, Old Homested Quartet, J. B. Bradley, Fred Clare, J. B. Rogers, T. Vale Wood, Murphy and Gibson. Fields left the show on July 22, 1899.

### Irwin's Burlesquers

(People's Theatre, Cincinnati, August 12, 1899.) Manager: Fred Irwin. Company: W. C. Fields, Fred Bailey and Harry Madison, Baroness Viola Von Waldenburg, Silver and Sparks, Sisters Tedwyn, Minerva Lee and Belle Travers, Mlle. Marie, Louise Carver, Genie Pollard. Fields left the show in Buffalo, New York, on March 12, 1900.

### The Ham Tree

By George V. Hobart. Music and lyrics by William Jerome, Jean Schwartz. (New York Theatre, August 28, 1905.) Cast: James McIntyre, Thomas K. Heath, W. C. Fields (Sherlock Baffles), Forrest Huff, David Torrance, Alfred Fisher, Jobyna Howland, Carolyn Gordon, Belle Gold, John Dobson, Otto F. Johnson. Staged by Herbert Gresham, Ned Wayburn. Ninety performances. Also toured.

## Watch Your Step

By Harry B. Smith. Music and lyrics by Irving Berlin. (Empire Theatre, Syracuse, New York, November 25, 1914.) Cast: Vernon Castle, Irene Castle, Frank Tinney, Harry Kelly, Elizabeth Brice, Charles King, W. C. Fields, Dama Sykes, Renee Gratz, William J. Halligan. Produced by Charles Dillingham. Staged by R. H. Burnside. One performance.

## Ziegfeld Follies of 1915

By Channing Pollock, Rennold Wolf, Gene Buck. Music by Louis Hirsch, Dave Stamper. (New Amsterdam, June 21, 1915.) Cast: Ina Claire, Bert Williams, Ann Pennington, Bernard Granville, Carl Randall, Kay Laurell, Leon Errol, Ed Wynn, W. C. Fields, George White, Mae Murray, Olive Thomas, Justine Johnstone. Produced by Florenz Ziegfeld Jr. Staged by Julian Mitchell, Leon Errol. 104 performances. Also toured.

## Ziegfeld Follies of 1916

By George V. Hobart, Gene Buck. Music by Louis Hirsch, Jerome Kern, Dave Stamper. (New Amsterdam, June 12, 1916.) Cast: Ina Claire, Bert Williams, Ann Pennington, Sam Hardy, Fannie Brice, W. C. Fields, Will Rogers, Don Barclay, William Rock. Produced by Florenz Ziegfeld Jr. Staged by Ned Wayburn. 112 performances. Also toured.

## Ziegfeld Follies of 1917

By George V. Hobart, Gene Buck. Music by Raymond Hubbell, Dave Stamper, Victor Herbert. (New Amsterdam, June 12, 1917.) Cast: Bert Williams, Fannie Brice, Will Rogers, Walter Catlett, W. C. Fields, Tom Richards, Irving Fisher, Eddie Cantor, Allyn King, Russell Vokes, Peggy Hopkins. Produced by Florenz Ziegfeld Jr. Staged by Ned Wayburn. 111 performances. Also toured.

## Ziegfeld Follies of 1918

By Rennold Wolf, Gene Buck. Music by Louis Hirsch, Dave Stamper. Interpolations by Irving Berlin, Victor Jacobi. (New Amsterdam, June 18, 1918.) Cast: Will Rogers, Fannie Brice, Lillian Lorraine, Eddie Cantor, W. C. Fields, Harry Kelly, Joe Frisco, Frank Carter, Marilyn Miller, Ann Pennington, Savoy and Brennan, the Fairbanks Twins. Produced by Florenz Ziegfeld Jr. Staged by Ned Wayburn. 151 performances. Also toured.

## Ziegfeld Midnight Frolic

Lyrics by Gene Buck. Music by Dave Stamper. (New Amsterdam Roof, October 2, 1919.) Cast: Fannie Brice, W. C. Fields, Savoy and Brennan, Chic Sale, Ted Lewis, Keegan and Edwards, Allyn King, Martha Mansfield, Frances White. Produced by Florenz Ziegfeld Jr. Staged by Ned Wayburn. 126 performances.

### Ziegfeld Nine O'Clock Revue

Lyrics by Gene Buck. Music by Dave Stamper. (New Amsterdam Roof, March 8, 1920.) Cast: Lillian Lorraine, Fannie Brice, W. C. Fields, John Price Jones, Allyn King, Kathlene Martyn, Sybil Carmen, Mlle. Spinelly, Carl Randall, Jessie Reed. Produced by Florenz Ziegfeld Jr. Staged by Ned Wayburn. Seventy-eight performances.

### Ziegfeld Midnight Frolic

Lyrics by Gene Buck. Music by Dave Stamper. (New Amsterdam Roof, March 15, 1920.) Cast: Lillian Lorraine, Fannie Brice, W. C. Fields, Joe Frisco, John Price Jones, Allyn King, Mlle. Spinelly, Carl Randall, Sam Moore. Produced by Florenz Ziegfeld Jr. Staged by Ned Wayburn. Seventy-two performances.

### Ziegfeld Follies of 1920

By Gene Buck, Irving Berlin. Music by Dave Stamper, Irving Berlin, Victor Herbert. (New Amsterdam, June 22, 1920.) Cast: Fannie Brice, W. C. Fields, Charles Winninger, Mary Eaton, Ray Dooley, Van and Schenck, Moran and Mack, Bernard Granville, Carl Randall, Doris Eaton, John Steel, Jack Donahue, Margaret Irving, Jessie Reed. Produced by Florenz Ziegfeld Jr. Staged by Edward Royce. 123 performances. Also toured.

### Ziegfeld Follies of 1921

By Channing Pollock, Gene Buck, George Marion, Willard Mack, Ralph Spence. Music by Dave Stamper, Rudolf Friml, B. G. De Sylva, Victor Herbert. (New Amsterdam, June 21, 1921.) Cast: Fannie Brice, Raymond Hitchcock, W. C. Fields, Mary Eaton, Ray Dooley, Van and Schenck, Doris Eaton, John Steel, Charlie Eaton, Charles O'Donnell, Jessie Reed. Produced by Florenz Ziegfeld Jr. Staged by Edward Royce. 119 performances. Also toured.

### George White's Scandals

Fourth annual edition by Andy Rice, George White, W. C. Fields. Music by George Gershwin. Lyrics by Buddy De Sylva, E. Ray Goetz. (Globe, August 28, 1922.) Cast: W. C. Fields, Winnie Lightner, George White, Pearl Regay, Franklyn Ardell, Lester Allen, Newton Alexander, Jack McGowan, Olive Vaughn, Paul Whiteman's Palais Royal Orchestra. Produced and staged by George White. Ninety-seven performances. Also toured.

### Poppy

By Dorothy Donnelly. Music by Stephen Jones, Arthur Samuels, John Egan. Lyrics by Dorothy Donnelly, Howard Dietz. (Apollo, September 3, 1923.) Cast: Madge Kennedy, W. C. Fields (Prof. Eustace McGargle), Robert

Woolsey, John Cherry, Alan Edwards, Emma Janvier, Luella Gear, Hugh Chilvers, William Blanche. Produced by Philip Goodman. Staged by Dorothy Donnelly, Philip Goodman, Julian Alfred. 336 performances. Also toured.

### The Comic Supplement ( of American Life )

By J. P. McEvoy. (Uncredited: W. C. Fields.) Music by Con Conrad, Henry Souvaine. Lyrics by J. P. McEvoy. (National Theatre, January 20, 1925.) Cast: W. C. Fields (Pa Jones), Ray Dooley, Martha-Byron Allen, Clarence Nordstrom, Brooke Johns, Joyce White, Mansford Wilson. Produced by Florenz Ziegfeld Jr. Dances staged by Julian Mitchell. Book staged by Augustin Duncan. Closed out of town.

### Ziegfeld Follies of 1925 ( Spring Edition )

By J. P. McEvoy, Will Rogers, W. C. Fields. Lyrics by Gene Buck. Music by Raymond Hubbell, Dave Stamper, Werner Janssen. (New Amsterdam, March 10, 1925.) Cast: Will Rogers, W. C. Fields, Ray Dooley, Ann Pennington, Vivienne Segal, Irving Fisher, Martha Lorber, Clarence Nordstrom, Naomi Johnson, Dorothy Knapp. Produced by Florenz Ziegfeld Jr. Staged by Julian Mitchell. 136 performances.

### Ziegfeld Follies of 1925 ( Summer Edition )

By J. P. McEvoy, Will Rogers, W. C. Fields, Gus Weinberg. Lyrics by Gene Buck. Music by Raymond Hubbell, Dave Stamper, Werner Janssen. (New Amsterdam, July 6, 1925.) Cast: Will Rogers, W. C. Fields, Ray Dooley, Ann Pennington, Vivienne Segal, Irving Fisher, Bertha Belmore, Clarence Nordstrom, Cricket Wooten, Dorothy Knapp. Produced by Florenz Ziegfeld Jr. Staged by Julian Mitchell. Eighty-eight performances. Also toured.

### Earl Carroll's Vanities

Seventh edition by W. C. Fields, Joe Frisco, Thomas R. Tarrant, Herman Meyer. Music and lyrics by Grace Henry, Morris Hamilton. Additional music by George Bagby, G. Romilli. (Earl Carroll, August 6, 1928.) Cast: W. C. Fields, Joe Frisco, Ray Dooley, Gordon Dooley, Dorothy Knapp, Lillian Roth, Fay Adler, Ted Bradford, Dorothy Lull, Joey Ray, Naomi Johnson, Vincent Lopez and His Band. Produced by Earl Carroll. Dances staged by Busby Berkeley. Dialogue staged by Edgar MacGregor. 203 performances. Also toured.

### Show Boat

By Oscar Hammerstein II. Music by Jerome Kern. Lyrics by Oscar Hammerstein II. (St. Louis Municipal Opera, August 11, 1930.) Cast: W. C. Fields (Cap'n Andy), Charlotte Lansing, Guy Robertson, Maude Ream Stover,

Sammy White, Eva Puck, Louis B. Deppe, William Blanche. Staged by Lew Morton. Fourteen performances.

## *Ballyhoo*

By Harry Ruskin, Leighton K. Brill. (Uncredited: Oscar Hammerstein II, W. C. Fields.) Music by Louis Alter. (Hammerstein's, December 22, 1930.) Cast: W. C. Fields (Q. Q. Quale), Janet Reade, Grace Hayes, Jeanie Lang, Don Tomkins, Andy Rice Jr., Floria Vestoff, William Blanche. Produced by Arthur Hammerstein. Dances staged by Earl Lindsay. Dialogue staged by Reginald Hammerstein. Sixty-eight performances.

## *W. C.*

By Milton Sperling, Sam Locke. Music and lyrics: Al Carmines. (Westbury Music Fair, July, 1971.) Cast: Mickey Rooney (W. C. Fields), Bernadette Peters, Virginia Martin, Gary Oakes, Rudy Tronto, Jack Bittner, David Vaughan, Sam Stoneburner, Martin J. Cassidy, Freddie James Ebert, Pip Sarser. Dances staged by Bob Herget. Dialogue staged by Richard Altman. Closed out of town.

# Appendix II

## Film Chronology

### Pool Sharks

Director: Edwin Middleton. Production: Gaumont Company. Distribution: Mutual Film Corporation. Release Date: September 19, 1915. Home Video Release: Home Vision Cinema (Video Tape), Voyager (Laserdisc, DVD). Length: One Reel. Cast: W. C. Fields (a pool shark), Bud Ross.

### His Lordship's Dilemma

Director: William F. Haddock. Production: Gaumont Company. Distribution: Mutual Film Corporation. Release Date: October 3, 1915. Length: One Reel. Cast: W. C. Fields (a remittance man), Bud Ross, Walter Fields.

### Janice Meredith

Producer: William Randolph Hearst. Associate Producer: William Le Baron. Director: E. Mason Hopper. Based upon the novel by Paul Leicester Ford. Screenplay: Lillie Hayward. Photography: Ira H. Morgan, George Barnes. Editor: Walter Futter. Production: Cosmopolitan Corporation. Distribution: Metro-Goldwyn. Release Date: December 8, 1924. Running Time: 153 minutes. Cast: Marion Davies, Holbrook Blinn, Harrison Ford, Maclyn Arbuckle, Hattie Delaro, Olin Howard, Spencer Charters, Mae Vokes, Mildred Arden, Joseph Kilgour, Douglas Stevenson, George Nash, W. C. Fields (a British sergeant), George Siegmann, Helen Lee Worthing, Tyrone Power, Princess De Bourbon, Wilfred Noy, Ken Maynard.

### Sally of the Sawdust

Director: D. W. Griffith. Based upon the play *Poppy* by Dorothy Donnelly. Adaptation: Forrest Halsey. Photography: Harry Fishbeck, Hal Sintzenich. Editor: James Smith. Production: D. W. Griffith, Inc./Famous Players–Lasky. Distribution: United Artists. Release Date: August 2, 1925. Home Video Release: Kino Video (Video Tape), Image Entertainment (Laserdisc and DVD). Running Time: 118 minutes. Cast: Carol Dempster, W. C. Fields (Prof. Eustace McGargle), Alfred Lunt, Effie Shannon, Erville Alderson, Glenn Anders, Charles Hammond, Roy Applegate, Florence Fair, Marie Shotwell.

## That Royle Girl

Director: D. W. Griffith. Based upon the novel by Edwin Balmer. Screenplay: Paul Schofield. Photography: Harry Fishbeck, Hal Sintzenich. Editor: James Smith. Production: Famous Players–Lasky. Distribution: Paramount. Release Date: December 7, 1925. Running Time: 114 minutes. Cast: Carol Dempster, W. C. Fields (Joan Daisy Royle's father), James Kirkwood, Harrison Ford, Marie Chambers, Paul Everton, George Rigas, Florence Auer, Ida Waterman, Alice Laidley, Dorothea Love, William Blanche.

## It's the Old Army Game

Associate Producer: William Le Baron. Director: A. Edward Sutherland. Supervising Editor: Tom J. Geraghty. Based upon *The Comic Supplement* by J. P. McEvoy. Screenplay: Tom J. Geraghty. Titles: Ralph Spence. Photography: Alvin Wyckoff. Production: Famous Players–Lasky. Distribution: Paramount. Release Date: May 24, 1926. Running Time: 70 minutes. Cast: W. C. Fields (Elmer Prettywillie), Louise Brookes, Blanche Ring, William Gaxton, Mary Foy, Mickey Bennett, Josephine Dunn, Jack Luden, George Currie, Elise Cavanna.

## So's Your Old Man

Associate Producer: William Le Baron. Director: Gregory La Cava. Production Editor: Ralph Block. Based upon the story "Mr. Bisbee's Princess" by Julian Street. Adaptation: Howard Emmett Rogers, Tom J. Geraghty. Screenplay: J. Clarkson Miller. Titles: Julian Johnson. Photography: George Webber. Editor: Julian Johnson. Production: Famous Players–Lasky. Distribution: Paramount. Release Date: October 25, 1926. Running Time: 67 minutes. Cast: W. C. Fields (Samuel Bisbee), Alice Joyce, Charles Rogers, Kittens Reichert, Marcia Harris, Julia Ralph, Frank Montgomery, Jerry Sinclair, William Blanche.

## The Potters

Associate Producer: William Le Baron. Director: Fred Newmeyer. Based upon the play by J. P. McEvoy. Adaptation: Sam Mintz, Ray Harris. Screenplay: J. Clarkson Miller. Photography: Paul Vogel. Production: Famous Players–Lasky. Distribution: Paramount. Release Date: January 29, 1927. Running Time: 71 minutes. Cast: W. C. Fields (Pa Potter), Mary Alden, Ivy Harris, Jack Egan, Richard "Skeets" Gallagher, Joseph Smiley, Bradley Barker.

## Running Wild

Associate Producer: William Le Baron. Director: Gregory La Cava. Based upon the story "Fearless Finch" by Roy Briant. Adaptation: Roy Briant,

Gregory La Cava. Titles: Roy Briant. Photography: Paul Vogel. Production and Distribution: Paramount. Release Date: August 20, 1927. Home Video Release: Paramount (Video Tape). Running Time: 60 minutes. Cast: W. C. Fields (Elmer Finch), Mary Brian, Marie Shotwell, Claude Buchanan, Frederick Burton, Barnet Raskin, Frank Evans, Edward Roseman.

### A Trip through the Paramount Studio

Promotional short made in cooperation with West Coast Theatres, Inc. Release: August 1927. Running Time: 9 minutes. Featuring Esther Ralston, Fay Wray, Clarence Badger, Fred Kohler, Mary Brian, Richard Arlen, Arlette Marchal, Fanchon & Marco, Betty Bronson, George Bancroft, Clara Bow, W. C. Fields (himself), Chester Conklin, Sally Blane, Blanche Le Claire, Shirley Dorman, Gene Morgan, Dolores Costello, Mervyn Le Roy, Mary Astor, Lloyd Hughes, Milton Sills, Doris Kenyon, Dorothy Mackaill.

### Two Flaming Youths

Associate Producer: Louis D. Lighton. Director: John Waters. Based upon the story "The Side Show" by Percy Heath. Screenplay: Percy Heath, Donald Davis. (Uncredited: Eddie Moran, Julian Josephson, Gil Pratt, Norman McLeod, Grover Jones.) Titles: Jack Conway, Herman J. Mankiewicz. Photography: H. Kinley Martin. Editor: Rose Loewinger. Production and Distribution: Paramount. Release Date: December 17, 1927. Running Time: 55 minutes. Cast: W. C. Fields (Gabby Gilfoil), Chester Conklin, Mary Brian, Jack Luden, George Irving, Cissy Fitzgerald, Jimmie Quinn.

### Tillie's Punctured Romance

Producer: Al Christie. Director: A. Edward Sutherland. Screenplay: Monte Brice, Keene Thompson. Photography: Charles Boyle, William Wheeler. Editor: Arthur Huffsmith. Production: Christie Film Co. Distribution: Paramount. Release Date: March 3, 1928. Running Time: 70 minutes. Cast: W. C. Fields (Ringmaster), Chester Conklin, Louise Fazenda, Mack Swain, Doris Hill, Grant Withers, Tom Kennedy, Babe London, Kalla Pasha, William Platt, Mickey Bennett, Mike Rafetto.

### Fools for Luck

Associate Producer: Louis D. Lighton. Director: Charles F. Reisner. Based upon the story "Men About Town" by Harry Fried. Screenplay: Sam Mintz, J. Walter Ruben. (Uncredited: Hank Mann, Grover Jones.) Titles: George Marion Jr. Photography: William Marshall. Editor: George Nichols Jr. Production and Distribution: Paramount. Release Date: May 5, 1928. Running Time: 60 minutes. Cast: W. C. Fields (Richard Whitehead), Chester Conklin, Sally Blane, Jack Luden, Mary Alden, Arthur Houseman, Robert Dudley, Martha Mattox, Eugene Pallett.

## The Family Ford

Vitaphone Release #790. Director: Bryan Foy. A comedy in three scenes from the sketch by W. C. Fields. Release: July 1930. Cast: Jim Harkins, Marion Harkins, Marie Dolan, Hope Eden, Harry Lauter, Joe Kavanaugh.

## The Golf Specialist

Producer: Louis Brock. Director: Monte Brice. Screenplay: W. C. Fields. Photography: Frank Zucker. Editor: Russell G. Shields. Production: Radio Pictures. Distribution: RKO. Release Date: July 24, 1930. Rereleased: 1975 (Janus Films). Home Video Release: Home Vision Cinema (Video Tape), Voyager (Laserdisc, DVD). Running Time: 21 minutes. Cast: W. C. Fields (J. Eppington Bellweather), Shirley Grey, Johnnie Kane, Allan Bennett, John Dunsmuir, Naomi Casey, Bill Black.

## Her Majesty, Love

Executive Producer: Hal B. Wallis. Associate Producer: Henry Blanke. Director: Wilhelm Dieterle. Based upon the screenplay *Ihre Majestät die Liebe* by Rudolf Bernauer, Rudolf Österreicher. Screenplay: Robert Lord, Arthur Caesar. (Uncredited: Henry Blanke, Joseph Jackson.) Music: Walter Jurrmann. English Lyrics: Al Dubin. Photography: Robert Kurrle. Editor: Ralph Dawson. Production and Distribution: First National. Release Date: December 26, 1931. Running Time: 78 minutes. Cast: Marilyn Miller, Ben Lyon, W. C. Fields (Dad Torreck), Leon Errol, Ford Sterling, Chester Conklin, Harry Stubbs, Clarence Wilson, Harry Holman, Ruth Hall, Mae Madison, Maude Eburne, Guy Kibbee, Donald Novis, Gus Arnheim's Coconut Grove Orchestra.

## Million Dollar Legs

Executive Producer: B. P. Schulberg. Associate Producer: Herman J. Mankiewicz. Director: Edward F. Cline. Story: Joseph L. Mankiewicz. Screenplay: Joseph L. Mankiewicz, Henry Myers. (Uncredited: Nick Barrows, Herman J. Mankiewicz, Sam Mintz.) Photography: Arthur Todd. Production and Distribution: Paramount. Release Date: July 8, 1932. Rereleased: 1949 (Paramount). Home Video Release: MCA Home Video (Video Tape). Running Time: 64 minutes. Cast: Jack Oakie, W. C. Fields (the President of Klopstokia), Andy Clyde, Lyda Roberti, Susan Fleming, Ben Turpin, Hugh Herbert, George Barbier, Dickie Moore, Hank Mann, Billy Gilbert, Vernon Dent, Teddy Hart.

## If I Had a Million

Executive Producer: Emanuel L. Cohen. Associate Producer: Louis D. Lighton. Director: Norman Taurog. Based upon the novel *Windfall* by Robert

Andrews. Adaptation: Grover Jones, William Slavens McNutt. Screenplay: Robert Sparks. Cast: Richard Bennett, Frederick Santley, John St. Polis.

*"Henry Peabody and the China Shop"*
Director: Norman Z. McLeod. Story: Joseph L. Mankiewicz. Screenplay: Lawton Mackall, Robert Sparks. Photography: Gilbert Warrenton. Cast: Charles Ruggles, Mary Boland, Reginald Barlow.

*"Violet"*
Director: Stephen Roberts. Story and screenplay: Joseph L. Mankiewicz. Cast: Wynne Gibson, Jack Pennick, Hooper Aatchley.

*"The Bank Forger"*
Director: H. Bruce Humberstone. Story: John Bright. Screenplay: Oliver H. P. Garrett. Cast: George Raft, Kent Taylor, Wallis Clark.

*"Emily, Rollo and the Road Hogs"*
Director: Norman Z. McLeod. Story and screenplay: Joseph L. Mankiewicz. Photography: Alvin Wyckoff. Cast: Alison Skipworth, W. C. Fields (Rollo), Cecil Cunningham, Harrison Greene, Rolfe Sedan.

*"Death Cell"*
Director: James Cruze. Story and screenplay: Lester Cole. Photography: C. Edgar Schoenbaum. Cast: Gene Raymond, Frances Dee, Berton Churchill, Clarence Muse, Grant Mitchell.

*"The Clerk"*
Director: Ernst Lubitsch. Photography: Harry Fischbeck. Cast: Charles Laughton, Edward J. LeSaint.

*"The Three Marines"*
Director: William A. Seiter. Story: Claude Binyon, Joseph L. Mankiewicz. Screenplay: Harvey Gates, Malcolm Stuart Boylan. Photography: C. Edgar Schoenbaum. Cast: Gary Cooper, Jack Oakie, Roscoe Karns, Joyce Compton, Lucian Littlefield.

*"Grandma Walker"*
Director: Stephen Roberts. Story: Grover Jones, William Slavens McNutt. Screenplay: Whitney Bolton. Cast: May Robson, Blanche Friderici, Dewey Robinson, Margaret Seddon, Gail Patrick.

Production and distribution: Paramount. Release Date: November 16, 1932. Rereleased: 1949 (Paramount). Home Video Release: DiscoVision Associates (Laserdisc). Running Time: 87 minutes.

Note: A one-reel condensation of the Fields sequence, also titled *If I Had a Million,* was released to the home market in 8mm and 16mm by Castle Films in 1971.

## The Dentist

Producer: Mack Sennett. Director: Leslie Pearce. Screenplay: W. C. Fields. Photography: John Boyle. Production: Mack Sennett. Distribution: Paramount. Release Date: December 9, 1932. Rereleased: 1975 (Janus). Home Video Release: Home Vision Cinema (Video Tape), Voyager (Laserdisc, DVD). Running Time: 21 minutes. Cast: W. C. Fields (Dr. Pain), Babe Kane, Arnold Gray, Dorothy Granger, Elise Cavanna, Zedna Farley, Bud Jamison, Billy Bletcher.

## Too Many Highballs

Producer: Mack Sennett. Director: Clyde Bruckman. Story: Clyde Bruckman. Screenplay: Clyde Bruckman, W. C. Fields, Mack Sennett. Photography: George Unholz. Production: Mack Sennett. Distribution: Paramount. Release Date: February 9, 1933. Running Time: 18 minutes. Cast: Lloyd Hamilton, Marjorie Beebe, Tom Dugan, Aggie Herring.

Note: David Turconi, in the 1966 edition of his book *Mack Sennett il 're delle comiche',* asserts that Fields also contributed to the writing of the 1932 Donald Novis short *The Singing Boxer.* There is, however, no indication in the Sennett production records that Fields had any involvement with that film.

## The Fatal Glass of Beer

Producer: Mack Sennett. Director: Clyde Bruckman. Screenplay: W. C. Fields. Production: Mack Sennett. Distribution: Paramount. Release Date: March 3, 1933. Rereleased: 1975 (Janus). Home Video Release: Home Vision Cinema (Video Tape), Voyager (Laserdisc, DVD). Running Time: 18 minutes. Cast: W. C. Fields (Mr. Snavely), Rosemary Theby, George Chandler, Rychard Cramer, George Moran.

## Hip Action (How to Break 90 #3)

Vitaphone Release #5821. Director: George Marshall. Screenplay: Andrew Bennison. Photography: Arthur Todd. Editor: Al Clark. Release Date: June 24, 1933. Running Time: 10 minutes. Cast: Bobby Jones, W. C. Fields (himself), Warner Oland, William B. Davidson.

Note: *Hip Action* was released to the home market in 8mm and 16mm by Associated Artists Productions.

## The Pharmacist

Producer: Mack Sennett. Director: Arthur Ripley. Screenplay: W. C. Fields. Photography: George Unholz, Frank Good. Production: Mack Sennett. Distribution: Paramount. Release Date: April 21, 1933. Rereleased: 1975 (Janus Films). Home Video Release: Home Vision Cinema (Video Tape), Voyager

(Laserdisc, DVD). Running Time: 19 minutes. Cast: W. C. Fields (Dilweg), Babe Kane, Elise Cavanna, Grady Sutton, Lorena Carr.

### International House

Executive Producer: Emanuel L. Cohen. Associate Producer: Albert Lewis. Director: A. Edward Sutherland. Story: Neil Brandt, Louis E. Heifetz. Screenplay: Francis Martin, Walter DeLeon. Music: Ralph Ringer. Lyrics: Leo Robin, Ralph Ringer. Photography: Ernest Haller. Production and distribution: Paramount. Release Date: June 2, 1933. Home Video Release: MCA Home Video (Video Tape, Laserdisc). Running Time: 70 minutes. Cast: Peggy Hopkins Joyce, W. C. Fields (Professor Henry Quail), Rudy Vallée, Stuart Erwin, George Burns, Gracie Allen, Sari Maritza, Colonel Stoopnagle and Budd, Cab Calloway and His Orchestra, Bela Lugosi, Baby Rose Marie, Franklin Pangborn, Edmund Breese, Lumsden Hare, Sterling Holloway, Lona Andre, Harrison Greene.

### The Barber Shop

Producer: Mack Sennett. Director: Arthur Ripley. Screenplay: W. C. Fields. Photography: Johnny Boyle. Production: Mack Sennett. Distribution: Paramount. Release Date: July 28, 1933. Rereleased: 1975 (Janus Films). Home Video Release: Home Vision Cinema (Video Tape), Voyager (Laserdisc, DVD). Running Time: 20 minutes. Cast: W. C. Fields (Cornelius O'Hare), Elise Cavanna, Harry Watson, Dagmar Oakland, John St. Clair, Cyril Ring, George Humbert, Frank Alexander.

### Tillie and Gus

Executive Producer: Emanuel L. Cohen. Associate Producer: Douglas MacLean. Director: Francis Martin. Story: Rupert Hughes. Screenplay: Francis Martin, Walter DeLeon. Photography: Ben Reynolds. Editor: James Smith. Production and Distribution: Paramount. Release Date: October 13, 1933. Rereleased: 1949 (Paramount). Running Time: 59 minutes. Cast: W. C. Fields (Agustus Q. Winterbottom), Alison Skipworth, Baby LeRoy, Jacqueline Wells, Clifford Jones, Clarence Wilson, George Barbier, Barton MacLane, Edgar Kennedy, Robert McKenzie, Ivan Linow.

### Screen Snapshots (Series 13, No. 7)

Producer: Harriet Parsons. Director and Narrator: Ralph Staub. Production and Distribution: Columbia. Release Date: April 24, 1934. Running Time: 18 minutes. Cast: Guy Kibbee, W. C. Fields (himself), Wallace Ford, Randolph Scott, James Dunn, Andy Clyde, Elissa Landi, Jeanette MacDonald, Al Jolson, Ruby Keeler, Barbara Stanwyck, Frederic March, Florence Eldridge, Hoot Gibson, Lois Wilson, Leslie Howard, Jimmy Durante, Constance Bennett, Marie Dressler, Polly Moran, Ann Sothern, Fay Wray, Carole Lombard,

John Barrymore, Walter Connolly, Johnny Weissmuller, Lupe Velez, Marion Davies, Charles Farrell.

### Alice in Wonderland

Executive Producer: Emanuel L. Cohen. Associate Producer: Benjamin Glazer. Director: Norman Z. McLeod. (Uncredited: William Cameron Menzies.) Based upon the books *Alice's Adventures in Wonderland* and *Through the Looking Glass* by Lewis Carroll. Screenplay: Joseph L. Mankiewicz, William Cameron Menzies. Music: Dimitri Tiomkin. Photography: Harry Sharp, Bert Glennon. Editor: Ellsworth Hoagland. Production and Distribution: Paramount. Release Date: December 22, 1933. Running Time: 76 minutes. Cast: Charlotte Henry, Leon Erroll, Louise Fazenda, Ford Sterling, Skeets Gallagher, Raymond Hatton, Polly Moran, Ned Sparks, Sterling Holloway, Roscoe Ates, Alison Skipworth, Lillian Harmer, Richard Arlen, Edward Everett Horton, Jackie Searl, Charlie Ruggles, Baby LeRoy, May Robson, Alec B. Francis, William Austin, Cary Grant, Edna May Oliver, Jack Oakie, Roscoe Karns, Mae Marsh, W. C. Fields (Humpty-Dumpty), Gary Cooper, Billy Bevan, Jacqueline Wells.

### Six of a Kind

Executive Producer: Emanuel L. Cohen. Associate Producer: Douglas MacLean. Director: Leo McCarey. Story: Keene Thompson, Douglas MacLean. Screenplay: Walter DeLeon, Harry Ruskin. Photography: Henry Sharp. Editor: LeRoy Stone. Production and Distribution: Paramount. Rereleased: 1938 (Paramount). Home Video Release: MCA Home Video (Video Tape). Release Date: February 9, 1934. Running Time: 62 minutes. Cast: Charlie Ruggles, Mary Boland, W. C. Fields (Honest John Hoxley), George Burns, Gracie Allen, Alison Skipworth, Bradley Page, Grace Bradley, William J. Kelly, Phil Tead, Walter Long, Tammany Young.

### You're Telling Me!

Executive Producer: Emanuel L. Cohen. Associate Producer: William Le Baron. Director: Erle C. Kenton. Based upon the story "Mr. Bisbee's Princess" by Julian Street. Screenplay: Walter DeLeon, Paul Jones. Dialogue: J. P. McEvoy. Photography: Alfred Gilks. Editor: Otho Lovering. Production and Distribution: Paramount. Release Date: April 6, 1934. Home Video Release: MCA Home Video (Video Tape). Running Time: 66 minutes. Cast: W. C. Fields (Samuel Bisbee), Joan Marsh, Larry "Buster" Crabbe, Adrienne Ames, Louise Carter, Kathleen Howard, Tammany Young, Del Henderson, James B. "Pop" Kenton, Robert McKenzie, Nora Cecil, George Irving, Elise Cavanna.

Note: A one-reel condensation, titled *Much Ado About Golf,* was released to the home market in 8mm and 16mm by Castle Films in 1976.

### Hollywood on Parade (B-10)

Director: Louis Lewyn. Production and Distribution: Paramount. Release Date: April 27, 1934. Running Time: 10 minutes. Cast: Jack Oakie, Chico Marx, W. C. Fields (himself), Larry "Buster" Crabbe, Jack LaRue, Richard Arlen, Mitchell Leisen, Duke Ellington, Claudette Colbert, George Raft, Groucho Marx, Mary Pickford, Dick Powell, Mae West, Jimmy Durante, Clark Gable.

Note: Fields is seen in a brief clip with Chico Marx. When asked for his autograph by some girls from the Earl Carroll *Vanities,* he asks them to sign his book instead.

### Hollywood on Parade (B-12)

Director: Louis Lewyn. Production and Distribution: Paramount. Release Date: June 22, 1934. Running Time: 9 minutes. Cast: Larry "Buster" Crabbe, Jack Haley, George Burns, Gracie Allen, Bing Crosby, Mary Brian, Cecil B. De Mille, Henry Wilcoxon, Tammany Young, W. C. Fields (himself).

Note: For a gathering of exhibitors at the Paramount studios, Fields performs the checkers routine from *The Pharmacist* with Tammany Young.

### The Old Fashioned Way

Producer: William Le Baron. Director: William Beaudine. Story: W. C. Fields (as Charles Bogle). (Uncredited: Tom J. Geraghty.) Screenplay: Garnett Weston, Jack Cunningham. (Uncredited: J. P. McEvoy, Lex Neal, Walter DeLeon, Paul Jones, Ralph Ceder.) Music and Lyrics: Mack Gordon, Harry Revel. Photography: Benjamin Reynolds. Production and Distribution: Paramount. Release Date: July 13, 1934. Running Time: 70 minutes. Cast: W. C. Fields (the Great McGonigle), Joe Morrison, Baby LeRoy, Judith Allen, Jan Duggan, Tammany Young, Nora Cecil, Jack Mulhall, Samuel Ethridge, Ruth Marion, Richard Carle, Dell Henderson, Clarence Wilson, Otis Harlan.

Note: A one-reel condensation, titled *The Great McGonigle,* was released to the home market in 8mm and 16mm by Castle Films in 1966.

### Mrs. Wiggs of the Cabbage Patch

Producer: Douglas MacLean. Director: Norman Taurog. Based upon the play by Alice Hegan Rice and Anne Crawford Flexner. Screenplay: William Slavens McNutt, Jane Storm. Photography: Charles Lang. Editor: Hugh Bennett. Production and Distribution: Paramount. Release Date: October 19, 1934. Running Time: 73 minutes. Cast: Pauline Lord, W. C. Fields (C. Ellsworth Stubbins), ZaSu Pitts, Evelyn Venable, Kent Taylor, Donald Meek, Jimmy Butler, George Breakston, Virginia Weidler, Carmencita Johnson, Edith Fellows, Charles Middleton, George Reed, Mildred Gover, Arthur Housman, Walter Walker.

## It's a Gift

Producer: William Le Baron. Director: Norman Z. McLeod. Based upon the play *The Comic Supplement* by J. P. McEvoy. Adaptation: W. C. Fields (as Charles Bogle). Screenplay: Jack Cunningham. (Uncredited: Garnett Weston, Claude Binyon, Paul Gerard Smith, Howard J. Green.) Photography: Henry Sharp. Production and Distribution: Paramount. Release Date: November 30, 1934. Home Video Release: MCA Home Video (Video Tape, Laserdisc). Running Time: 67 minutes. Cast: W. C. Fields (Harold Bissonette), Kathleen Howard, Jean Rouverol, Julian Madison, Tommy Bupp, Baby LeRoy, Tammany Young, Morgan Wallace, Charles Sellon, Josephine Whittell, T. Roy Barnes, Diana Lewis, Spencer Charters, Guy Usher, Del Henderson.

Note: Two one-reel condensations, titled *The Big Thumb* and *California Bound,* were released to the home market in 8mm and 16mm by Castle Films in 1967 and 1968, respectively.

## David Copperfield

Producer: David O. Selznick. Director: George Cukor. Based upon the novel *The Personal History, Adventures, Experience, and Observation of David Copperfield, the Younger* by Charles Dickens. Adaptation: Hugh Walpole. Screenplay: Howard Estabrook. Music: Herbert Stothart. Photography: Oliver T. Marsh. Editor: Robert J. Kern. Production and Distribution: Metro-Goldwyn-Mayer. Release Date: January 18, 1935. Rereleased: 1939, 1962 (MGM). Home Video Release: MGM/UA Home Video (Video Tape, Laserdisc). Running Time: 133 minutes. Cast: W. C. Fields (Wilkins Micawber), Lionel Barrymore, Maureen O'Sullivan, Madge Evans, Edna May Oliver, Lewis Stone, Frank Lawton, Freddie Bartholomew, Elizabeth Allan, Roland Young, Basil Rathbone, Elsa Lanchester, Jean Cadell, Jessie Ralph, Lennox Pawle, Violet Kemble Cooper, Una O'Connor, John Buckler, Hugh Williams, Ivan Simpson, Herbert Mundin, Ray Chaldecott, Marilyn Knowlden.

## Mississippi

Producer: Arthur Hornblow Jr. Director: A. Edward Sutherland. Based upon the play *Magnolia* by Booth Tarkington. Adaptation: Herbert Fields, Claude Binyon. Screenplay: Francis Martin, Jack Cunningham. (Uncredited: Lou Breslow, Grant Garrett, Franz Schulz.) Music: Richard Rodgers. Lyrics: Lorenz Hart. Photography: Charles Lang. Editor: Chandler House. Production and Distribution: Paramount. Release Date: March 22, 1935. Rereleased: 1949 (Paramount). Running Time: 75 minutes. Cast: Bing Crosby, W. C. Fields (Commodore Orlando Jackson), Joan Bennett, Gail Patrick, Queenie Smith, Claude Gillingwater, John Miljan, Fred Kohler Sr., Edward Pawley, Theresa Maxwell Conover, Paul Hurst, John Larkin, Libby Taylor, Jan Duggan, the Cabin Kids.

## Man on the Flying Trapeze

Producer: William Le Baron. Director: Clyde Bruckman. Story: W. C. Fields (as Charles Bogle). (Uncredited: Clyde Bruckman, Roy Briant.) Screenplay: Ray Harris, Sam Hardy. (Uncredited: Jack Cunningham, Frank Griffin.) Photography: Alfred Gilks. Editor: Richard Currier. Production and Distribution: Paramount. Release Date: July 26, 1935. Running Time: 65 minutes. Cast: W. C. Fields (Ambrose Wolfinger), Mary Brian, Kathleen Howard, Grady Sutton, Vera Lewis, Lucien Littlefield, Oscar Apfel, Lew Kelly, Tammany Young, Walter Brennan, Edward Gargan, James Burke, Carlotta Monti.

## Hollywood Capers

Fields is caricatured in this one-reel Looney Tune, produced by Leon Schlesinger and released by Warner Bros. on October 19, 1935.

Note: This is apparently the first animated cartoon to include a character patterned after W. C. Fields. Some references list an earlier Walter Lantz production, *Toyland Premiere,* as containing a Fields caricature, but a viewing of that film confirmed he is not in it.

## Broken Toys

Fields is caricatured in this one-reel Silly Symphony, produced in color by Walt Disney and released by United Artists on December 19, 1935.

## Mickey's Polo Team

Fields is caricatured in this one-reel Mickey Mouse cartoon, produced in color by Walt Disney and released by United Artists on January 4, 1936.

## Poppy

Executive Producer: William Le Baron. Associate Producer: Paul Jones. Director: A. Edward Sutherland. Based upon the play *Poppy* by Dorothy Donnelly. Screenplay: Waldemar Young, Virginia Van Upp. (Uncredited: Jack Cunningham, Frederick Hazlitt Brennan, Bobby Vernon.) Music: Ralph Ringer, Frederick Hollander. Lyrics: Leo Robin, Sam Coslow. Photography: William C. Mellor. Editor: Stuart Heisler. Production and Distribution: Paramount. Release Date: June 19, 1936. Rereleased: 1949 (Paramount). Running Time: 73 minutes. Cast: W. C. Fields (Prof. Eustace McGargle), Rochelle Hudson, Richard Cromwell, Catharine Doucet, Lynne Overman, Granville Bates, Maude Eburne, Bill Wolfe, Adrian Morris, Rosalind Keith, Ralph Remley, Cyril Ring, Tammany Young, Tom Kennedy, Jan Duggan.

## At Your Service Madam

Fields is caricatured in this one-reel Merrie Melodie, produced in color by Leon Schlesinger and released by the Vitaphone Corporation on August 29, 1936.

## The Coocoonut Grove

Fields is caricatured in this one-reel Merrie Melodie, produced in color by Leon Schlesinger and released by the Vitaphone Corporation on November 29, 1936.

## Porky's Road Race

Fields is caricatured in this one-reel Looney Tune, produced by Leon Schlesinger and released by the Vitaphone Corporation on February 6, 1937.

## It Happened in Hollywood

Executive Producer: William Perlberg. Associate Producer: Myles Connolly. Director: Harry Lachman. Story: Myles Connolly. Screenplay: Ethel Hill, Harvey Fergusson, Samuel Fuller. Photography: Joseph Walker. Editors: Al Clark, Otto Meyer. Production and Distribution: Columbia. Release Date: September 7, 1937. Running Time: 70 minutes. Cast: Richard Dix, Fay Wray, Victor Kilian, Franklin Pangborn, Charlie Arnt, Granville Bates, William B. Davidson.

Note: A party sequence in this film features the "doubles" of a number of Hollywood stars, including Myrna Loy, Charlie Chaplin, Marlene Dietrich, John Barrymore, and Mae West. Actor James May appeared as Fields in this scene.

## The Woods Are Full of Cuckoos

Fields is caricatured in this one-reel Merrie Melodie, produced in color by Leon Schlesinger and released by the Vitaphone Corporation on December 4, 1937.

## Hollywood Picnic

Fields is caricatured in this one-reel Color Rhapsody, produced by Charles Mintz and released by Columbia Pictures on December 18, 1937.

## The Big Broadcast of 1938

Producer: Harlan Thompson. Director: Mitchell Leisen. (Uncredited: Ted Reed.) Story: Frederick Hazlitt Brennan. (Uncredited: J. P. McEvoy.) Adaptation: Howard Lindsay, Russell Crouse. Screenplay: Walter DeLeon, Francis Martin, Ken Englund. (Uncredited: W. C. Fields, Patterson McNutt.) Music: Ralph Rainger. Lyrics: Leo Robin. Photography: Harry Fischbeck. Editors: Eda Warren, Chandler House. Production and Distribution: Paramount. Release Date: February 18, 1938. Home Video Release: MCA Home Video (Video Tape, DVD). Running Time: 97 minutes. Cast: W. C. Fields (T. Frothingill Bellows/S. B. Bellows), Martha Raye, Dorothy Lamour, Shirley Ross, Lynne Overman, Bob Hope, Ben Blue, Leif Erikson, Patricia Wilder, Grace

Bradley, Rufe Davis, Lionel Pape, Dorothy Howe, Russell Hicks. Specialties: Shep Fields and His Rippling Rhythm Orchestra, Kirsten Flagstad, Tito Guizar and Company.

### A Star Is Hatched
Fields is caricatured in this one-reel Merrie Melodie, produced in color by Leon Schlesinger and released by the Vitaphone Corporation on April 2, 1938.

### Screen Snapshots (Series 17, No. 9)
Producer and Narrator: Harriet Parsons. Production and Distribution: Columbia. Release Date: April 29, 1938. Running Time: 18 minutes. Cast: Tommy Kelly, Ann Gillis, Margaret Tallichet, Victor Jory, Stu Erwin, June Collier, Ann Miller, Lon Chaney Jr., Edith Fellows, Leo Carrillo, Margaret Irving, Alice Brady, Charles Winninger, Luise Rainer, Edgar Bergen, Frank Capra, W. C. Fields (himself), Mack Sennett, Louis B. Mayer, Mrs. Spencer Tracy.

Note: Fields is shown posing for pictures with Mack Sennett and Frank Capra prior to the tenth Academy Awards ceremony at the Biltmore Bowl.

### Have You Got Any Castles?
Fields is caricatured in this one-reel Merrie Melodie, produced in color by Leon Schlesinger and released by the Vitaphone Corporation on June 25, 1938.

### Milk for Baby
Fields is caricatured in this one-reel Terry-Toon, produced by Paul Terry for Educational Pictures and released by Twentieth Century–Fox on July 8, 1938.

### String Bean Jack
Fields is caricatured in this one-reel Terry-Toon, produced in color by Paul Terry and released by Twentieth Century–Fox on August 29, 1938.

### Cracked Ice
Fields is caricatured in this one-reel Merrie Melodie, produced in color by Leon Schlesinger and registered for copyright by the Vitaphone Corporation on December 16, 1938.

### Mother Goose Goes Hollywood
Fields is caricatured in this one-reel Silly Symphony, produced in color by Walt Disney and released by RKO–Radio Pictures on December 23, 1938.

### You Can't Cheat an Honest Man
Producer: Lester Cowan. Director: George Marshall. (Uncredited: Edward Sedgwick, Edward F. Cline.) Story: W. C. Fields (as Charles Bogle). Screen-

play: George Marion Jr., Richard Mack, Everett Freeman. (Uncredited: Manuel Seff, Lew Lipton, James Seymour, James Mulhauser, Henry Johnson.) Photography: Milton Krasner. Editor: Otto Ludwig. Production and Distribution: Universal. Release Date: February 17, 1939. Rereleased: 1949 (Realart). Home Video Release: MCA Home Video (Video Tape). Running Time: 79 minutes. Cast: W. C. Fields (Larson E. Whipsnade), Edgar Bergen, Constance Moore, John Arledge, James Bush, Thurston Hall, Mary Forbes, Edward Brophy, Arthur Hohl, Princess Baba, Blacaman, Eddie Anderson, Charles Coleman, Grady Sutton, Jan Duggan, Bill Wolfe.

Note: A one-reel condensation, titled *Circus Slicker,* was released to the home market in 8mm and 16mm by Castle Films in 1958.

### My Little Chickadee

Producer: Lester Cowan. (Uncredited: Jack J. Gross.) Director: Edward F. Cline. Screenplay: Mae West, W. C. Fields. Music: Frank Skinner. Photography: Joseph Valentine. Editor: Edward Curtiss. (Uncredited: Paul Landres.) Production and Distribution: Universal. Release Date: February 9, 1940. Rereleased: 1948 (Realart). Home Video Release: MCA Home Video (Video Tape). Running Time: 84 minutes. Cast: Mae West, W. C. Fields (Cuthbert J. Twillie), Joseph Calleia, Dick Foran, Ruth Donnelly, Margaret Hamilton, Donald Meek, Fuzzy Knight, Willard Robertson, George Moran, Jackie Searl, Fay Adler, Gene Austin (and "Candy" and "Coco"), Bill Wolfe, Jan Duggan.

### Little Blabbermouse

Fields is caricatured in this one-reel Merrie Melodie, produced in color by Leon Schlesinger and released by the Vitaphone Corporation on July 6, 1940.

### Picture People (No. 3)

Production and Distribution: RKO–Radio Pictures. Release Date: November 8, 1940. Running Time: 10 minutes. Cast: Dorothy Lamour, Gary Cooper, Ken Murray, Ralph Bellamy, Rudy Vallée, W. C. Fields (himself).

Note: Fields is shown at the opening of Don Dickerman's Pirates' Den in Hollywood.

### The Bank Dick

Executive Producer: Cliff Work. Associate Producer: Jack J. Gross. Director: Edward F. Cline. Collaborating Director: Ralph Ceder. Screenplay: W. C. Fields (as Mahatma Kane Jeeves). (Uncredited: Richard Carroll.) Music: Frank Skinner. Photography: Milton Krasner. Editor: Arthur Hilton. Production and Distribution: Universal. Release Date: November 29, 1940. Rereleased: 1949 (Realart). Home Video Release: MCA Home Video (Video Tape, Laserdisc), Voyager (DVD). Running Time: 72 minutes. Cast: W. C. Fields (Egbert Souse), Cora Witherspoon, Una Merkel, Evelyn Del Rio, Jessie Ralph, Franklin Pangborn, Shemp Howard, Richard Purcell, Grady Sutton,

Russell Hicks, Pierre Watkin, Al Hill, George Moran, Bill Wolfe, Jack Norton, Pat West, Reed Hadley, Heather Wilde, Harlan Briggs, Bill Alston, Fay Adler, Jan Duggan.

Note: A one-reel condensation, titled *The Great Chase,* was released to the home market in 8mm and 16mm by Castle Films in 1949.

*Added to the National Film Registry of the Library of Congress, 1992.*

### Shop, Look and Listen

Fields is caricatured in this one-reel Merrie Melodie, produced in color by Leon Schlesinger and released by the Vitaphone Corporation on December 21, 1940.

### Never Give a Sucker an Even Break

Executive Producer: Cliff Work. Associate Producer: Jack J. Gross. Director: Edward F. Cline. Associate Director: Ralph Ceder. Story: W. C. Fields (as Otis Criblecoblis). Screenplay: John T. Neville, Prescott Chaplin. Music: Frank Skinner. Photography: Charles Van Enger, Jerome Ash. Editor: Arthur Hilton. Production and Distribution: Universal. Release Date: October 10, 1941. Rereleased: 1949 (Realart). Home Video Release: MCA Home Video (Laserdisc). Running Time: 71 minutes. Cast: W. C. Fields (the Great Man), Gloria Jean, Leon Errol, Butch and Buddy (Billy Lenhart and Kenneth Brown), Margaret Dumont, Susan Miller, Franklin Pangborn, Mona Barrie, Charles Lang, Anne Nagel, Nell O'Day, Irving Bacon, Jody Gilbert, Minerva Urecal, Emmett Vogan, Carlotta Monti, Claud Allister, Bill Wolfe.

Note: A one-reel condensation, titled *Hurry! Hurry!,* was released to the home market in 8mm and 16mm by Castle Films in 1950.

### A Hollywood Detour

Fields is caricatured in this one-reel Color Rhapsody, produced by Frank Tashlin and released by Columbia Pictures on January 23, 1942.

### Tales of Manhattan

Producers: Boris Morros, Sam Spiegel (as S. P. Eagle). Associate Producer: Samuel Rheiner. Director: Julian Duvivier. Original Stories and Screenplays: Ben Hecht, Ferenc Molnar, Donald Ogden Stewart, Samuel Hoffenstein, Alan Campbell, Ladislas Fodor, Laslo Vadnai, Ladislas Gorog, Lamar Trotti, Henry Blankfort. Music: Sol Kaplan. Photography: Joseph Walker. Editor: Robert Bischoff. Cast: Charles Boyer, Rita Hayworth, Ginger Rogers, Henry Fonda, Charles Laughton, Edward G. Robinson, Paul Robeson, Ethel Waters, Eddie (Rochester) Anderson, Thomas Mitchell, Eugene Pallette, Cesar Romero, Gail Patrick, Roland Young, Marion Martin, Elsa Lanchester, Victor Francen, George Sanders, James Gleason. Production and Distribution: Twentieth Century–Fox. Release Date: October 30, 1942. Home Video Release: Fox Home Video (Video Tape). Running Time: 118 minutes.

### *"Sequence E"*

Director: Malcolm St. Clair. Screenplay: William Morrow, Edmund Beloin. Editor: Gene Fowler Jr. Cast: W. C. Fields (Prof. Diogenes Pothlewhistle), Margaret Dumont, Phil Silvers, Marcel Dalio, Jerry Bergen, Chester Clute, E. E. Clive. Running Time: 9 minutes.

Note: The Fields sequence was deleted from the film prior to its theatrical release. It was restored in May 1996 for the film's home video release.

### *Follow the Boys*

Producer: Charles K. Feldman. Associate Producer: Albert L. Rockett. Director: A. Edward Sutherland. (Uncredited: John Rawlins, Lou Breslow.) Story: William Anthony McGuire. Screenplay: Lou Breslow, Gertrude Purcell. (Uncredited: A. Edward Sutherland, Stephen Longstreet.) Photography: David Abel. Editor: Fred R. Feitshans Jr. Studio: Universal. Production: Charles K. Feldman Group Productions. Distribution: Universal. Release Date: May 5, 1944. Rereleased: 1949 (Realart). Home Video Release: MCA Home Video (Video Tape). Running Time: 122 minutes. Cast: George Raft, Vera Zorina, Charley Grapewin, Grace McDonald, Charles Butterworth, George Macready, Elizabeth Patterson, Theodore von Eltz, Regis Toomey, Ramsay Ames, Martha O'Driscoll, Maxie Rosenbloom. Specialties: Jeanette MacDonald, Orson Welles, Marlene Dietrich, Dinah Shore, Donald O'Connor, Peggy Ryan, W. C. Fields (himself), the Andrews Sisters, Artur Rubinstein, Carmen Amaya and Her Company, Sophie Tucker, Delta Rhythm Boys, Leonard Gautier's Bricklayers, Ted Lewis and His Band, Freddie Slack and His Orchestra, Charlie Spivak and His Orchestra, Louis Jordan and His Orchestra.

### *Song of the Open Road*

Producer: Charles R. Rogers. Director: S. Sylvan Simon. Story: Irving Phillips, Edward Verdier. Screenplay: Albert Mannheimer. Music: Walter Kent. Lyrics: Kim Gannon. Photography: John W. Boyle. Editor: Truman K. Wood. Studio: General Service. Production: Charles R. Rogers Talking Pictures Corp. Distribution: United Artists. Release Date: June 2, 1944. Running Time: 93 minutes. Cast: Edgar Bergen, Bonita Granville, W. C. Fields (himself), Sammy Kaye and His Orchestra, Jane Powell, Peggy O'Neill, Jackie Moran, Bill Christy, Reginald Denny, Regis Toomey, Rose Hobart. Specialties: Condos Brothers, Lipham Four, Catron & Popp, Hollywood Canteen Kids.

### *Sensations of 1945*

Producer: Andrew L. Stone. Associate Producer: James Nasser. Director: Andrew L. Stone. Story: Frederick Jackson. (Uncredited: Andrew L. Stone.) Screenplay: Dorothy Bennett. (Uncredited: W. C. Fields.) Music: Al Sherman.

Lyrics: Harry Tobias. Photography: Peverell Marley, John J. Mescall. Editor: James E. Smith. Studio: General Service. Production: Andrew Stone Pictures Corp. Distribution: United Artists. Release Date: June 30, 1944. Rereleased: 1950 as *Sensations* (Astor). Running Time: 86 minutes. Cast: Eleanor Powell, Dennis O'Keefe, C. Aubrey Smith, Eugene Pallette, Mimi Forsaythe, Lyle Talbot, Hubert Castle, W. C. Fields (himself), Sophie Tucker, Dorothy Donegan, the Christianis, the Pallenberg Bears, Cab Calloway and His Band, Woody Herman and His Band.

Note: A one-reel condensation, titled *One Too Many*, was released to the home market in 8mm and 16mm by Manbeck Pictures.

## Screen Snapshots (Series 24, No. 9)
Production and Distribution: Columbia. Release Date: May 17, 1945. Running Time: 10 minutes. Pays tribute to comedians of the silent and talking screens. Among those glimpsed are: Harold Lloyd, Charlie Chaplin, Roscoe "Fatty" Arbuckle, Ben Turpin, Lloyd Hamilton, Buster Keaton, Chester Conklin, Charlie Chase, Harry Langdon, Laurel and Hardy, Eddie Cantor, W. C. Fields, the Marx Brothers, Jimmy Durante, and Bob Hope.

## The Baby Sitter
Fields is caricatured in this one-reel Little Lulu cartoon, produced in color by Famous Studios and released by Paramount on November 28, 1947.

## Down Memory Lane
Producer: Aubrey Schenck. Director: Phil Karlson. Photography: Walter Strenge. Production and Distribution: Eagle-Lion Films. Release Date: September 27, 1949. Rereleased: 1964 (Medallion). Running Time: 73 minutes. Cast: Mack Sennett, Steve Allen. Incorporating scenes from "Sing, Bing, Sing" (Bing Crosby), "The Dentist" (W. C. Fields), "Blues of the Night" (Bing Crosby), and "The Singing Boxer" (Donald Novis).

## Memories of Famous Hollywood Comedians
### (Screen Snapshots, Series 31, No. 5)
Production and Distribution: Columbia. Release Date: January 24, 1952. Running Time: 10 minutes.

Note: This is a reworking of the 1945 *Screen Snapshots,* narrated by Joe E. Brown.

## Featherweight Champ
Fields is caricatured in this one-reel Terry-Toon, produced in color by Paul Terry and registered for copyright on February 6, 1953.

## The Big Parade of Comedy

Producer: Robert Youngson. Production and Distribution: Metro-Goldwyn-Mayer. Release Date: September 1964. Running Time: 109 minutes.

Note: Fields appears in a scene from *David Copperfield.*

## Merlin, the Magic Mouse

Fields was the inspiration for the title character in this one-reel Merrie Melodie, directed by Alex Lovy and released by Warner Bros. in November 1967. The character subsequently appeared in four additional Warner cartoons: *Hocus Pocus Powwow* (1968), *A Feud with a Dude* (1968), *Fistic Mystic* (1969), and *Shamrock and Roll* (1969).

## W. C. Fields and Me

Producer: Jay Weston. Director: Arthur Hiller. Based upon the book by Carlotta Monti. Screenplay: Bob Merrill. Music: Henry Mancini. Photography: David M. Walsh. Editor: John C. Howard. Production and Distribution: Universal. Release Date: April 1976. Running Time: 112 minutes. Cast: Rod Steiger (W. C. Fields), Valerie Perrine, John Marley, Jack Cassidy, Bernadette Peters, Dana Elcar, Paul Stewart, Billy Barty.

## That's Entertainment! Part Two

Producer: Saul Chaplin. Director: Gene Kelly. Production: Metro-Goldwyn-Mayer. Distribution: United Artists. Release Date: May 1976. Running Time: 133 minutes.

Note: Fields appears in a scene from *David Copperfield.*

## Mae West

Producer: Terry Morse Jr. Director: Lee Philips. Screenplay: E. Arthur Kean. Photography: Matthew F. Leonetti. Produced by Hill-Mandelker for ABC. Broadcast Date: May 2, 1982. Cast: Ann Jillian, James Brolin, Piper Laurie, Roddy McDowall, Louis Giambalvo, Chuck McCann (W. C. Fields), Lee de Broux, Donald Hotton, Ian Wolfe.

## W. C. Fields Straight Up

Producer: Robert B. Weide. Coproducer: Ronald J. Fields. Director: Joe Adamson. Written by Joe Adamson, Ronald J. Fields. Narrated by Dudley Moore. Made for PBS, 1986. Running Time: 94 minutes.

Note: Fields has been the subject of several other documentaries for television, most notably *Wayne and Schuster Take an Affectionate Look at W. C. Fields* (1966). *W. C. Fields Rediscovered* (1967) features a studio interview with Claude Fields and clips from his father's Mack Sennett shorts. In 1996, an episode of A&E's *Biography* was devoted to Fields as well.

# Appendix III

## Radio Chronology

### Ballyhoo

Week of January 19, 1931. Special promotional broadcast.

### D. W. Griffith's Hollywood

April 2, 1933 (NBC Blue, New York). Cast: D. W. Griffith. Announcer: Kelvin Keech. Music: William Artzt. Sponsor: Hinds Honey and Almond Cream. Length: 15 minutes. This episode of highly romanticized reminiscences by the great director concerned the making of *Sally of the Sawdust*. An unidentified actor played Fields.

### California Melodies

May 30, 1933 (CBS, Los Angeles). Cast: Raymond Paige and His Orchestra. Guest: W. C. Fields. Length: 30 minutes.

### Paramount Movie Parade #16

February 4, 1934 (syndicated). Fields was heard in audio excerpts from *Six of a Kind*. Length: 15 minutes.

### Forty-Five Minutes from Hollywood

March 17, 1934 (CBS, Los Angeles). Cast: Cal York, Mark Warnow. Guest: W. C. Fields. Announcer: Bert Parks. Director: Tom Harrington. Sponsor: Borden's. Length: 45 minutes.

### Paramount Movie Parade #24

April 1, 1934 (syndicated). Fields was heard in audio excerpts from *You're Telling Me!* Length: 15 minutes.

### Paramount Silver Jubilee

January 7, 1937 (NBC Blue, Los Angeles). Cast: Jack Benny (host), Cecil B. DeMille, Leopold Stokowski, Frank Forest, Jack Oakie, Charles Butterworth, Dorothy Lamour, Shirley Ross, W. C. Fields, Bob Burns, Martha Raye, Carole Lombard, Gladys Swarthout, Lloyd Nolan, Wallace Beery, Raymond Hatton,

Victor Moore, Edward Arnold, Adolphe Menjou. Announcer: Ken Carpenter. Music: Boris Morros. Director: Herb Polesie. Length: 75 minutes. A special broadcast honoring Adolph Zukor.

### The Chase & Sanborn Hour

May 9–September 12, 1937 (NBC Red, Los Angeles). Cast: Don Ameche (host), W. C. Fields, Edgar Bergen, Dorothy Lamour, Ray Middleton. (Nelson Eddy joined the cast on August 8, 1937.) Guests: Ann Harding, Carole Lombard, Mary Boland, Jose Iturbe, Constance Bennett, Flora Robson, Sonja Henie, ZaSu Pitts, Gladys George, Ann Sothern, Mary Pickford, Alice Brady, Glenda Farrell, Ida Lupino, Bette Davis. Announcer: Don Briggs. Music: Werner Janssen. Producer: Dwight Cooke. Director: Earl Ebi. Sponsor: Standard Brands. Agency: J. Walter Thompson. Length: 60 minutes.

### Lux Radio Theatre

"Poppy," March 7, 1938 (CBS, Los Angeles). Cast: Cecil B. De Mille (host), W. C. Fields (Prof. Eustace McGargle), John Payne, Anne Shirley, Skeets Gallagher, Helena Grant, Lou Merrill, Gretchen Thomas, W. L. Thorn, Frank Nelson. Announcer: Melville Ruick. Music: Louis Silvers. Director: Frank Woodruff. Sponsor: Lever Brothers. Agency: J. Walter Thompson. Length: 60 minutes.

### Hollywood Is On the Air

Spring, 1938 (syndicated). Fields was heard in audio excerpts from *The Big Broadcast of 1938*. Length: 15 minutes.

### The Chase & Sanborn Hour

June 5, 1938 (NBC Red, Los Angeles). Cast: Don Ameche (host), Edgar Bergen, Dorothy Lamour, Ray Middleton. Guests: W. C. Fields, Nelson Eddy. Announcer: Wendell Niles. Music: Robert Armbruster. Sponsor: Standard Brands. Agency: J. Walter Thompson. Length: 60 minutes.

### Your Hit Parade

October 15–November 5, 1938 (CBS, New York/Los Angeles). Cast: W. C. Fields, Hanley Stafford, Elvia Allman, Jack Smart, Walter Tetley. Announcers: Andre Baruch (New York), Harlow Wilcox (Hollywood). Music: Al Goodman. Producer (New York): Karl W. Schullinger. Segment Producer (Hollywood): George McGarett. Sponsor: American Tobacco. Agency: Lord & Thomas. Length: 45 minutes.

### Tuesday Night Party

March 21, 1939 (CBS, Los Angeles). Cast: Dick Powell (host), Martha Raye, Harry Einstein. Guest: W. C. Fields. Announcer: Tiny Ruffner. Music: Lud

Gluskin. Sponsor: Lever Brothers. Agency: Ruthrauff & Ryan. Length: 30 minutes.

### Gateway to Hollywood

April 23, 1939 (CBS, Los Angeles). Cast: Jesse L. Lasky (host). Guest: W. C. Fields. Announcer: Ken Niles. Music: Wilber Hatch. Director: Charles Vanda. Sponsor: Wrigley's Gum. Agency: J. Walter Thompson. Length: 30 minutes.

### The Chase & Sanborn Program

September 21, 1941 (NBC Red, Los Angeles). Cast: Edgar Bergen, Bud Abbott, Lou Costello, Guest: W. C. Fields. Announcer: Buddy Twiss. Music: Ray Noble. Sponsor: Standard Brands. Agency: J. Walter Thompson. Length: 30 minutes.

### The Chase & Sanborn Program

November 8, 1942 (NBC Red, Los Angeles). Cast: Don Ameche (host), Edgar Bergen, Dale Evans. Guest: W. C. Fields. Announcer: Bill Goodwin. Music: Ray Noble. Sponsor: Standard Brands. Agency: Kenyon and Eckhardt. Length: 30 minutes.

### The Chase & Sanborn Program

September 19, 1943 (NBC Red, Los Angeles). Cast: Edgar Bergen, William Gaxton, Victor Moore, Dale Evans, the Sportsmen. Guest: W. C. Fields. Announcer: Bill Goodwin. Music: Ray Noble. Sponsor: Standard Brands. Agency: Kenyon and Eckhardt. Length: 30 minutes.

### The Frank Sinatra Show

February 4, 1944 (CBS, Los Angeles). Cast: Frank Sinatra, Bert Wheeler. Guest: W. C. Fields. Announcer: Truman Bradley. Music: Axel Stordahl. Director: Bob Brewster. Sponsor: Lever Brothers. Agency: J. Walter Thompson. Length: 30 minutes.

### The Chase & Sanborn Program

February 20, 1944 (NBC Red, Los Angeles). Cast: Edgar Bergen, Jane Powell. Guest: W. C. Fields. Announcer: Ken Carpenter. Music: Ray Noble. Sponsor: Standard Brands. Agency: Kenyon and Eckhardt. Length: 30 minutes.

### The Chase & Sanborn Program

March 26, 1944 (NBC Red, Los Angeles). Cast: Edgar Bergen, Jane Powell. Guest: W. C. Fields. Announcer: Ken Carpenter. Music: Ray Noble. Sponsor: Standard Brands. Agency: Kenyon and Eckhardt. Length: 30 minutes.

### Command Performance

October 14, 1944 (AFRS, Los Angeles). Cast: Bob Hope, Jack Benny, W. C. Fields, Fred Allen, Danny Kaye, Spencer Tracy, Judy Garland, Jimmy Durante, Dorothy Lamour, Johnny Mercer, Xavier Cugat, Jerry Colonna, Spike Jones, Virginia O'Brien, Dinah Shore. Announcer: Ken Carpenter. Producer: Vick Knight. Length: 120 minutes. A special Christmas show recorded for the Armed Forces Radio Service and broadcast via short wave.

### Request Performance

October 28, 1945 (CBS, Los Angeles). Cast: Ida Lupino, Reginald Gardiner, W. C. Fields, Agnes Moorehead. Music: Leith Stevens. Produced by the Masquers Club of Hollywood. Director: William N. Robson. Sponsor: Campbell's Soups. Agency: Ward Wheelock. Length: 30 minutes.

### The Charlie McCarthy Show

March 24, 1946 (NBC, Pasadena). Cast: Edgar Bergen, Verna Felton, Anita Gordon. Guest: W. C. Fields. Announcer: Ken Carpenter. Music: Ray Noble. Sponsor: Standard Brands. Agency: Kenyon and Eckhardt. Length: 30 minutes.

### Biography in Sound

"Magnificent Rogue," February 28, 1956 (NBC, New York). Cast: Fred Allen (host), Edgar Bergen, Maurice Chevalier, Lester Cowan, Ray Dooley, Errol Flynn, Jim Harkins, Kitty Hughes, William Le Baron, Leo McCarey, Ronald Overacker (Baby LeRoy), Mack Sennett, Norman Taurog, Robert Lewis Taylor, Ed Wynn. Producer: Joseph T. Dembo. Length: 60 minutes. A radio biography of Fields, featuring the recollections of friends and coworkers.

# Notes and Sources

| | |
|---|---|
| AMPAS | Margaret Harrick Library, Academy of Motion Picture Arts and Sciences, Los Angeles |
| AE | Actors' Equity Files, New York University |
| CD | Charles B. Dillingham Papers, Manuscripts and Archives Division, New York Public Library, Astor, Lenox, and Tilden Foundations |
| EL | Emmet Lavery Papers, Theatre Arts Library, Special Collections, University of California, Los Angeles |
| GF | Gene Fowler Papers, University of Colorado, Boulder |
| GH | Houle Rare Books and Autographs, Los Angeles |
| IAM | Institute of the American Musical, Los Angeles |
| JS | James Smart, Philadelphia |
| JIS | Juggling Information Service, World Wide Web |
| KA | Keith/Albee Collection, Special Collections Department, University of Iowa Libraries, Iowa City, Iowa |
| MGM | Metro-Goldwyn-Mayer Script Collection at the Cinema-TV Library, University of Southern California, Los Angeles |
| MM | Magda Michael Papers, Los Angeles |
| MOMA | Museum of Modern Art, New York |
| NA | National Archives, Washington, D.C. |
| PFL | Philadelphia Free Library |
| TW | Tim Walker Collection, Los Angeles |
| UCLA | Film and Television Archives, University of California, Los Angeles |
| USC | Universal Pictures Collection at the Cinema-TV Library, University of Southern California, Los Angeles |
| WB | Warner Bros. Collection, University of Southern California, Los Angeles |
| WCF | W. C. Fields Papers, Los Angeles |
| WHS | Philip Goodman Papers, Wisconsin State Historical Society, Madison |
| WFG | Waiting for Godot Books, Hadley, Massachusetts |

## Chapter One

3  "The fact": *New York Times,* 1/5/35.

"You've heard": James Reid, "Nobody's Dummy," *Motion Picture,* October 1937.

4  "I never saw": Max Eastman, *Enjoyment of Laughter* (New York: Simon and Schuster, 1936), p. 336.

"I was the first": Reid, "Nobody's Dummy."

Lloyd and Keaton: Press release, *The Comic Supplement,* Philadelphia, January 1925 (PFL).

Keaton considered him: Buster Keaton Oral History, Columbia University, November 1958.

5  "The first thing": Maude Cheatham, "Juggler of Laughs," *Silver Screen,* April 1935.

"the funniest thing": Eastman, *Enjoyment of Laughter,* p. 92.

6  Darby: My knowledge of Darby comes primarily from conversations with local historians Tom DiFilippo and Harold Finigan, whose 1953 booklet *Darby Centennial Celebration* was also helpful.

Arlington House: Jim Dukenfield leased the building from Dwight B. Fuller, a Philadelphia baker who had acquired the land in 1869. The hotel's name may have derived from the fact that Fuller also owned property in Arlington, New Jersey.

7  Fire Zouaves: Details of James L. Dukenfield's Civil War service are from Pension File #761364, National Archives. A history of the Seventy-second Regiment Infantry can be found in Frank H. Taylor, *Philadelphia in the Civil War* (Philadelphia: City of Philadelphia, 1913).

Lord Dukinfield: Details of John Dukinfield's life in England and the United States are contained in research compiled in the 1930s by George E. Stevenson, cousin to W. C. Fields (WCF).

"above the mouth": George E. Stevenson to WCF, 3/7/35 (WCF).

8  The older boys: Names, addresses, and occupations for various members of the Dukenfield and Felton families are from Philadelphia City Directories, 1855–1925 (PFL). Names, ages, and birthplaces are from Philadelphia census records, 1870 and 1880 (NA).

"intemperate habits": Ann Dukenfield, Mother's Pension File #44846 (NA).

Marriage: Details of the marriage of Kate Spangler Felton and James Lyden Dukenfield are contained in notes made by Milton Kenin in the library of Old St. George's Methodist Church, Philadelphia.

Butcher shop: In testimony before the Superior Court of the State of California in 1951, Walter Fields gave his understanding of how his parents met (WCF). According to the 1860 and 1870 Philadelphia census records, as well as city directories of the time, Tom Felton worked as a butcher and victualer. (Butchers were often referred to as "licensed victualers.") Later, in the 1880s, his son, William C. Felton, also worked as a butcher. In the 1870 census, Jim Dukenfield was identified as a huckster (NA/PFL).

9   Birthplace: There is no birth record for W. C. Fields on file in either Philadelphia or Delaware County. Will Fowler recalled Fields telling his father, author Gene Fowler, that he was "born in Darby," in his book, *The Second Handshake* (New York: Lyle Stuart, 1980), p. 107. Fields' sister, Adele C. Smith, identified the Arlington House as the birthplace in an interview with William C. Fields III, New Jersey, 9/10/72 (WCF).

Birthdate: On June 5, 1880, John A. Brown, enumerator for the U.S. Census, visited the Dukenfield household on Woodland Avenue, east of Sixty-fourth Street, in West Philadelphia. There he found J. L. Dukenfield, a hotelkeeper, age forty, Katie S. Dukenfield, his wife, a housekeeper, age twenty-five, and Claude W. Dukenfield, their son, age "4/12." To clarify, Brown added "Jan" to the notation to indicate that the child had been born in January, not February, of that year.

Fields always observed his birthday on January 29, and his death certificate confirms this. Certificate of Death #46-089728, State of California.

When Fields married Harriet Veronica Hughes in San Francisco, on April 8, 1900, he was twenty years old and, under California law, could not enter into a marriage without parental consent. He therefore gave his birthdate as April 9, 1879, and often used this date thereafter. However, when he applied for a passport later that same year, he swore under oath that his correct birthdate was January 29, 1880. Fields, Passport Application for a Native Citizen, Chicago, 11/5/1900 (NA).

Colored woman: James Smart, "The Difficulty of Being Leroy Dukenfield," *Sunday Bulletin Magazine,* 3/23/69.

Name: According to Adele C. Smith, Fields was named after his uncle, William Claude Felton, but the 1880 census record clearly identifies him as "Claude W.," not "William C." Therefore, it is conceivable that he was actually born Claude William Dukenfield and not William Claude. Fields himself indicated that he was born Claude William in several interviews, most notably for Alva Johnston's "Legitimate Nonchalance," *New Yorker,* 2/2, 2/9, and 2/16/35, which he later described as "the best and more authentic" of his biographies.

"Claude William Dukenfield was my real name. I changed it to W. C. Fields for the juggling act." Dee Lowrance, "Bogeyman's Bluff," *Washington Post,* 10/26/41.

A certificate commending him as one of the Cambria School's "distinguished scholars of the week" in 1889 identifies him as Claude Dukenfield. His name was also given as Claude by his family in the Philadelphia census records, 1900 and 1910, and in the Philadelphia City Directories, 1902–1913, where he was generally listed as "Claude W. Dukenfield, actor."

It must be noted, however, that on his 1900 passport application, he swore under oath that his correct name was William Claude Dukenfield.

9     Claude Duval: Fields told Magda Michael, his secretary, that he was named after highwayman Claude Duval while dictating notes for his autobiography in 1946. Magda Michael, undated manuscript, p. 93 (MM).

"My first memory": W. C. Fields, "The Story of My Life," Variety Records, 1947.

10     "low cunning": Details of Fields' early life are contained in "Notes for Life Story," which he dictated to Magda Michael in 1946 (MM).

Oakdale School: *Ibid.*

Stuttered: Fields admitted in a 1901 interview with the *Chicago Tribune* "that I stutter badly when I talk, and I therefore concluded that I would go through my act without saying a word." He is widely thought to have been left-handed, but according to his widow in sworn testimony, he was actually right-handed. He may well have been one of those natural lefties who was taught as a child to write and perform other critical tasks with his right hand. The practice was common in public schools of the day and was thought to result in stuttering.

"lazy boy": Interview, 1914, as quoted in Ronald J. Fields, *W. C. Fields by Himself* (Englewood Cliffs, N.J.: Prentice-Hall, 1973), p. 6.

11     Maternal grandmother: Fields, "Notes for Life Story."

"My duties": John C. Moffett, "The Saga of Wild Willie Fields," *Kansas City Star,* 1/27/35.

12     "besotted with gin": Fields described his mother's behavior to author Corey Ford, who reported his comments in *A Time of Laughter* (Boston: Little, Brown & Co., 1967), p. 173. Alva Johnston's account in "Legitimate Nonchalance," also provided by Fields, is similar.

"old-fashioned homebody": Smart, "The Difficulty of Being Leroy Dukenfield."

"snowballs": WCF to Gene Fowler, via phone, as quoted in Robert Lewis Taylor, *W. C. Fields: His Follies and Fortunes* (Garden City, N.Y.: Doubleday, 1949), p. 14.

That spring: Details of Jim Dukenfield's produce business are from
William C. Fields III's conversations with Adele C. Smith (WCF).
Details of the Philadelphia marketplace are from Frank H. Taylor,
ed., *The City of Philadelphia as It Appears in the Year 1893* (Philadelphia: Trade League of Philadelphia, 1893). Also consulted: Robert
Shackleton, *The Book of Philadelphia* (Philadelphia: Penn Publishing, 1918); Cornelius Weygandt, *Philadelphia Folks* (New York: D.
Appleton-Century, 1938); and Frank Brookhouser, *Our Philadelphia*
(Garden City, N.Y.: Doubleday, 1957).

13    Northern Liberties: Information on the geographical and political divisions of Philadelphia County comes from William Bucke Campbell,
*Old Towns and Districts of Philadelphia* (Philadelphia: City History
Society, 1942).

Kate was selling: Fields, "Notes for Life Story."

"Dad": Smart, "The Difficulty of Being Leroy Dukenfield."

"door bells": Charles H. Van Tagen's memories of W. C. Fields and the
Dukenfield family are contained in a 1934 letter to Elsie Finn of the
*Philadelphia Record* (WCF).

"My father": WCF to Richard Crandall, 10/27/42 (MM).

Big-busted: Roy R. Smith (son of Adele C. Smith) to William C. Fields
III, September 1973 (WCF).

14    "I felt bad": John Chapman, "The Beloved Mountebank," *New York
Daily News,* 10/16 and 10/23/38.

"run away": "Lacking Good Clothes, Became Tramp Juggler," *Comic
Supplement* press release, February 1925 (PFL).

"Some of the fellows": Chapman, "The Beloved Mountebank."

"I'm no chump": Lowrance, "Bogeyman's Bluff."

"It was so short": Mary B. Mullett, "Bill Fields Disliked His Label, So
He Laughed It Off," *American Magazine,* January 1926.

"bad beatings": Chapman, "The Beloved Mountebank."

"No one": Handwritten note, circa 1945 (MM).

"Every kid": Clara Beranger, "The Most Melancholy Funny Man on
the Screen," *Liberty,* 2/15/36.

15    "most vivid": WCF to Joe Mackey, 7/18/39 (MM).

"Any kid": Ida Zeitlin, "W. C. Fields' Real Life Story," *Screenland,* June
1935.

"I slept": WCF to Thomas A. Hunt, 6/23/38 (WCF).

"wonderful ideas": Marion Bussang, "An Actor Can Only Relax After
He's 60," *New York Post,* 11/22/40.

"We'd sneak": John P. Carmichael, "W. C. Fields—Who Wouldn't Play
Stooge to a Dummy," *Chicago Daily News,* 5/21/38.

16    "It was only": Michael, undated manuscript, p. 77 (MM).

Queue of boys: W. Claude Fields Jr., as quoted in *W. C. Fields by Himself,* p. 10.

17    "I realized": Moffett, "The Saga of Wild Willie Fields."
       "emulate": Michael, undated manuscript, p. 75 (MM).
       Drive home: Roy R. Smith to William C. Fields III, 12/11/72 (WCF).
       Vaudeville: For the history of vaudeville, I relied on two books in par-
          ticular: Douglas Gilbert, *American Vaudeville, Its Life and Times*
          (New York: Whittlesey House, 1940), and Joe Laurie Jr., *Vaudeville*
          (New York: Henry Holt and Co., 1953). For specific information on
          Philadelphia theaters of the nineteenth century, I referred to Irvin R.
          Glazer, *Philadelphia Theatres* (Mineola, N.Y.: Dover, 1994), and to
          various issues of the *Philadelphia Inquirer.*
18    "sideshow": W. C. Fields, resume of early appearances, 1939 (MM).
       "I had to be up": Mullett, "Bill Fields Disliked His Label."
19    "tumor": Smart, "The Difficulty of Being Leroy Dukenfield."
       *Eight Bells:* Details of the Byrne Brothers' Philadelphia engagement are
          from the *Philadelphia Inquirer,* 9/15 and 9/17/1895. Fields usually
          misidentified the Byrne Brothers as the "Burns" Brothers—most
          notably in "Legitimate Nonchalance" and "W. C. Fields—Who
          Wouldn't Play Stooge to a Dummy." Similarly, he referred to
          Matthew "Matt" Byrne as "Nat" Burns in "The Beloved Mounte-
          bank." Matt was indeed the juggler of the troupe, but he reportedly
          withdrew from *Eight Bells* a few weeks prior to its Philadelphia
          opening. James A. Byrne (1868–1927) took over the part originally
          played by his younger brother, and it is likely that it was his jug-
          gling—and not Matt's—that made such an impression on young
          Whitey Dukenfield.
       The setting: The script of *Eight Bells,* dated May 14, 1891, is in the Rare
          Books Department at the Library of Congress.
20    "With pleasure": Jim Tully, "Let's Laugh at Life with W. C. Fields,"
          *Screen Play,* June 1935.
       "taking tomatoes": Moffett, "The Saga of Wild Willie Fields."
       Harrigan: Details of Harrigan's Philadelphia engagement are from the
          *Philadelphia Inquirer,* 9/22 and 9/24/1895.
       "we played theatre": Van Tagen letter, *Philadelphia Record* (WCF).
       "running wild": Mullett, "Bill Fields Disliked His Label."
21    "foolish juggling notion": Fields, "Notes for Life Story" (MM).


## Chapter Two

22    "she thought": Michael, undated manuscript, p. 76 (MM).
23    "let the chump": Joseph L. Mankiewicz to Joe Adamson, 1/8/86, in
          unused interview footage shot for the documentary *W. C. Fields
          Straight Up* (UCLA).
       "An unharnessed": W. C. Fields, "Alcohol and Me," *Pic,* 10/13/42.

24    "given me money": Interview, 1914.

"particularly funny": Adele C. Smith to Ronald Fields, 12/8/72 (WCF).

"I hastily": As quoted by H. M. Lorette in "About Tramp Jugglers,"
*Juggler's Bulletin*, March 1948 (JIS).

"Hallo": Details of James Harrigan's act are from a written description
he filed with the U.S. Copyright Office in 1898 (LOC).

25    "If a juggler": Fred Allen, *Much Ado About Me* (Boston: Atlantic/
Little, Brown & Co., 1956), p. 101.

"keep it up": Harold Cary, "The Loneliest Man in the Movies," *Collier's*, 11/28/25.

"kept at it": "Simple Juggling Tricks Take Where Difficult Stunts Fail,"
*Portland Evening Express*, 4/23/08.

"I'd balance": Pressbook, *The Big Broadcast of 1938*, Paramount Pictures, 1938.

"a nondescript character": H. M. Lorette, "W. C. Fields Gets Help from
His Friends," *IJA Newsletter*, May 1957 (JIS).

26    "little concert halls": Transcript, *Penn Mutual Life Insurance Co. v. Walter Fields, et al.,* U.S. District Court, Central Division, Los Angeles,
9/22/48 (WCF).

"I could juggle": "Lacking Good Clothes, Became Tramp Juggler."

"clipped": WCF to Joe Mackey, 7/18/39 (MM).

27    "We waited": WCF to William T. Dailey, 10/18/25 (JS).

"Everyone worked": "Let's Laugh at Life with W. C. Fields."

"We had some tickets": WCF to William T. Dailey, 2/16/43 (JS).

28    "my first real money": WCF to William T. Dailey, undated (JS).

Sandwiches: Adele C. Smith to William C. Fields III, 9/10/72 (WCF).

Blind baggage: The front platform of a railway baggage car, referred to
as "blind" because it had no door and was therefore a favorite place
for tramps to ride undetected.

Union Square: Bernard Sobel, *Burleycue* (New York: Farrar & Rinehart, 1931), p. 119.

29    "go to Europe": W. C. Fields, "Symposium," undated manuscript
(MM).

30    "I was nervous": Taylor, *W. C. Fields: His Follies and Fortunes,* p. 37.

"small approval": Tully, "Let's Laugh at Life with W. C. Fields."

"I was booked": Lorette, "W. C. Fields Gets Help from His Friends."

31    "It broke my heart": Chapman, "The Beloved Mountebank."

32    "I would swim": Sobel, *Burleycue,* p. 116.

"If it was a woman": W. C. Fields, "From Boy Juggler to Star Comedian," *Theatre*, October 1928.

33    "I juggled": Fields, "From Boy Juggler to Star Comedian."

"*Monte Carlo Girls:*" *New York Clipper*, 9/3/1898.

"Sometimes": Sobel, *Burleycue,* p. 117.

"bothered": Fields, "From Boy Juggler to Star Comedian."

34   "no routine": Interview, quoted in *W. C. Fields by Himself,* p. 15.
     "laundry": Fields, undated notes for autobiography, circa 1946 (MM).
     "The first week": Sobel, *Burleycue,* p. 117.

35   Skip: According to the *New York Clipper, The Monte Carlo Girls* played
         Kent, Ohio, on December 16, 1898.
     "It is strange": Mullett, "Bill Fields Disliked His Label."
     "two silver dollars": Tully, "Let's Laugh at Life with W. C. Fields."
     "theatrical business": W. C. Fields, undated career notes, circa 1939
         (MM).

## Chapter Three

36   "clubs": Transcript, "In the Matter of the Estate of William C. Fields,
         Deceased," Superior Court of the State of California in and for the
         County of Los Angeles, Department No. 12, 8/2/51 (WCF).
37   "young and green": Transcript, "In the Matter of William C. Fields,
         Deceased," 8/1/51.
     "musical comedy": Transcript, "In the Matter of William C. Fields,
         Deceased," 8/3/51.
     "sketching": Sobel, *Burleycue,* p. 91.
     "Notch" joints: WCF to Fowler, 9/1/42 (MM).
38   "Elsie received": Kate Dukenfield to WCF, 1/12/1899 (WCF).
     serge suit: Mullett, "Bill Fields Disliked His Label."
     "clubs and entertainments": Transcript, "In the Matter of William C.
         Fields, Deceased," 8/1/51.
     "High Mass": Transcript, "In the Matter of William C. Fields,
         Deceased," 8/3/51.
39   "Boys went around hawking popcorn": Fred Stone, *Rolling Stone* (New
         York: Whittlesey House, 1945), p. 109.
     "pleasing tramp juggler": *New York Dramatic Mirror,* 2/4/1899.
     "We are all well": *New York Clipper,* 2/18/1899.
     "great big hit": *Philadelphia Inquirer,* 5/23/1899.
41   "Irwin was so amazed": Mullett, "Bill Fields Disliked His Label."
     "The newspaper critics": Fields, "From Boy Juggler to Star Comedian."
42   "His pride": Tully, "Let's Laugh at Life with W. C. Fields."
     $100: Jim Tully, "The Clown Who Juggled Apples," *Photoplay,* January
         1934.
     "one of the best": *New York Clipper,* 11/18/1899.
     "improved his act": Lorette, "W. C. Fields Gets Help from His Friends."
     "Juggling is difficult": Sobel, *Burleycue,* p. 118.
     "This incident": Moffett, "The Saga of Wild Willie Fields."
43   "To conceal my youth": Tully, "Let's Laugh at Life with W. C. Fields."
     "no contract": Mullett, "Bill Fields Disliked His Label."

Frank James: W. C. Fields, "It's a Tough Spot," feature press release, St. Louis Municipal Opera, August 1930 (IAM).

"The artists": Undated news clipping, circa 1901 (WCF).

45    "a noble and superb": Elizabeth Hughes to WCF, 8/22/1899 (WCF).

"play four weeks": Epes W. Sargent, "Those Good Orpheum Days," *Variety*, 1/5/38.

"packed": *San Francisco Chronicle*, 3/19/1900.

"clung": Undated news clipping, circa 1901 (WCF).

46    "in case": Hattie Fields to Emmet Lavery, Los Angeles, 6/12/61 (EL).

Marriage: "Dukenfield-Hughes," *San Francisco Chronicle*, 4/13/1900.

47    "Hebraic": *Los Angeles Times*, 4/10/1900.

Pasadena: *Los Angeles Times*, 5/5/49, and "Summary of Testimony," undated, files of W. Claude Fields Jr. (WCF).

"his father": Hattie Fields to Lavery, 6/28/61 (EL).

"get his goat": Fields, *W. C. Fields by Himself*, p. 12.

"Dinner was served": W. C. Fields, "Over a Barrel," *Esquire*, October 1934.

48    "simplest juggling trick": "Magnificent Rogue," *Biography in Sound*, NBC Radio, 2/28/56.

"pick up your vaudeville dates": Fields, resume of early appearances (MM).

50    "wonderful hands": Hattie Fields to Lavery, 8/12/61 (EL).

"don't hang on": Elizabeth Borton, "I Take a Juggling Lesson from W. C. Fields," *Hollywood*, September 1935.

"When you juggle": James Reid, "Nobody's Dummy."

"The opening night": Pressbook, *Six of a Kind*, Paramount Pictures, 1934.

"encores": *New York Clipper*, 3/2/1901.

"Sometimes he would drink": Transcript, "In the Matter of William C. Fields, Deceased," 8/1/51.

51    "always the same": H. L. Adams, "A Tramp Juggler," *Black and White Budget*, 3/16/1901.

"drop anything": *Showman*, 3/1/1901.

52    "a new idea": *Blackpool Times and Fylde Observer*, 7/6/1901.

"no fun": *Kansas City Journal*, 2/7/1902.

53    "tremendous success": *New York Clipper*, 5/25/1901.

"he liked class": Joe Laurie Jr., *Vaudeville* (New York: Henry Holt and Co., 1953), p. 362.

"practicing": *Nottingham Football Post*, 9/10/04.

55    "I waited": J. P. McEvoy, "Go On, Make Me Laugh," *Saturday Evening Post*, 12/24/32.

"same the world over": *Nottingham Football Post*, 9/10/04.

"hell of a time": Grant Felton to WCF, 1/27/02 (WCF).

56  "individuality": *New York Morning Telegraph,* 5/28/02.

"Being young": Tully, "Let's Laugh at Life with W. C. Fields."

"five balls": Paul Cinquevalli, "How to Succeed as a Juggler," *Cassell's Magazine,* March 1909 (JIS).

"It's all rhythm": Borton, "I Take a Juggling Lesson from W. C. Fields."

57  "This time": Ida Zeitlin, "W. C. Fields' Real Life Story."

## *Chapter Four*

58  "Even acrobats": Pressbook, *Six of a Kind.*

"seeing the world": Mullett, "Bill Fields Disliked His Label."

"hanging around": Cheatham, "Juggler of Laughs."

"copied": Pressbook, *It's a Gift,* Paramount Pictures, 1934.

59  The new Fields act: The pool act evolved over the years. My description is an amalgam drawn from contemporary accounts and filmed reenactments.

60  "most value": Charles Lovenberg, Manager's Report, Keith's Providence, 2/9/03 (KA).

"big laughing hit": J. Keating, Manager's Report, Keith's Boston, 2/16/03 (KA).

61  "good enough": H. A. Daniels, Manager's Report, Keith's Philadelphia, 3/3/03 (KA).

"take a trip": Transcript, "In the Matter of William C. Fields, Deceased," 8/1/51.

"He begged": Transcript, "In the Matter of William C. Fields, Deceased," 8/2/51.

"I stood": Transcript, "In the Matter of William C. Fields, Deceased," 8/3/51.

62  "artist's dream": *The Truth,* 10/17/03.

"biggest draw": C. H. W., "W. C. Fields: An Appreciation," *Theatre,* March 1904.

63  "coward": Hattie Fields' memories of the violent incidents involving her husband in Australia are from a conversation with Emmet Lavery, 6/12/61 (EL), and the recollections of Everett F. Fields, to whom she recounted the incident with the Cockneys in the late 1950s.

64  "The Redfern Railway": *Music Hall and Theatre Review,* 12/11/03.

"Zulus": W. C. Fields, "A Ham's Soliloquy," undated manuscript (WCF).

65  "dead of summer": WCF to James McIntyre, 1/28/04.

67  "suggestion": Transcript, "In the Matter of William C. Fields, Deceased," 8/2/51.

Birth: Details of the birth of William Claude Dukenfield are from birth certificate #33961, City of New York, and a baby book kept by Hattie Fields (WCF). He automatically became William Claude Fields Jr. in 1908 when his father legally changed his name to Fields.

"worst thing": WCF to Hattie Fields, 7/30/04 (WCF).

68   "baptized": Transcript, "In the Matter of William C. Fields, Deceased," 8/3/51.

"creditable letters": WCF to Hattie Fields, 9/14/04 (WCF).

"Walter must have been": WCF to Hattie Fields, 5/21/03 (WCF).

69   "first letter": Fields, "Notes for Life Story" (MM).

"There's no place": *Nottingham Football Post,* 9/10/04.

"Papa's departure": WCF to Hattie Fields, 9/14/04 (WCF).

70   "When our father": Fields, *W. C. Fields by Himself,* p. 23.

"I couldn't walk": Transcript, "In the Matter of William C. Fields, Deceased," 8/1/51.

71   "running comedy gag": Cheatham, "Juggler of Laughs."

Moscow: Pressbook, *Six of a Kind,* and *New York Dramatic Mirror,* 5/27/05.

"nigger singers": Details of McIntyre and Heath's working relationship are from *Variety,* 12/20/12 and 10/13/19.

72   "He would reprimand": W. Buchanan-Taylor, *Shake the Bottle* (London: Heath Cranton, 1942), p. 216.

73   "I came on": "Star Entertains in Private," *Saturday Evening Post,* 6/21/24.

"John W. Gates": George V. Hobart, *The Ham Tree,* unpublished playscript, 8/15/05 (LOC).

"more to do": *Rochester Evening Times,* 8/18/05.

"some fine place": WCF to Hattie Fields, 8/23/05 (WCF).

"light and whimsical": *New York News,* 8/29/05.

"far surpassed": *Globe and Commercial Advertiser,* 8/29/05.

"Clever work": *New York Clipper,* 9/2/05.

74   "so familiar": *Everybody's Magazine,* August 1905.

## Chapter Five

75   "Wired": WCF to W. C. Fields Jr., 12/22/05 (WCF).

"I loved children": Transcript, "In the Matter of William C. Fields, Deceased," 8/3/51.

76   "certain person": WCF to James L. Dukenfield, 4/22/06 (WCF).

77   "more than pleased": WCF to W. C. Fields Jr., 5/25/07 (WCF).

79   "misses more": *Variety,* 6/1/07.

"I didn't know": Transcript, "In the Matter of William C. Fields, Deceased," 8/3/51.

79 "This woman": Belle Gold to Hattie Fields, 8/16/07 (WCF).

"Perhaps if you ask": Belle Gold to Hattie Fields, 9/29/07 (WCF).

80 Lavine and Leonard: *New York Clipper,* 9/2/05.

"filching": WCF to Billy Grady, 6/3/43 (MM).

81 "most copied man": Buchanan-Taylor, *Shake the Bottle,* p. 216.

"doesn't make any difference": *Variety,* 1/4/08.

"very funny": J. B. Priestley, "W. C. Fields," *Atlantic Monthly,* March 1947.

82 "In the three decades": Buchanan-Taylor, *Shake the Bottle,* p. 217.

"No one ever knew him": Taylor, *W. C. Fields: His Follies and Fortunes,* p. 108.

"An actor": *New York Masonic Outlook,* July 1932.

83 "the first town": WCF to Gene Fowler, 9/1/42 (MM).

"I never vote": Taylor, *W. C. Fields: His Follies and Fortunes,* p. 275.

84 "rather naive": Transcript, "In the Matter of William C. Fields, Deceased," 8/3/51.

"three women": Maude Fendick to WCF, undated (WCF).

"Isn't there a school": WCF to Hattie Fields, undated, circa 1910 (WCF).

85 "never raced": Smart, "The Difficulty of Being Leroy Dukenfield."

French girl: William Dukenfield (son of Arthur Dukenfield) to William C. Fields III, 4/27/75 (WCF).

"Mrs. W. C. Fields": "Sailings," *Variety,* 5/31/13.

"real comedian": Mullett, "Bill Fields Disliked His Label."

"He is a juggler": *San Francisco Chronicle,* 8/26/12.

87 "such an artiste": *Manchester Guardian,* 10/12/13.

"fitted the Palace": *Variety,* 5/23/13.

"greatest entertainment": *Variety,* 8/1/13.

88 Fragson: Details of the murder of Harry Fragson are from *Times* (London), 1/1/14, *Variety,* 1/2/14, and Fields, undated notes for autobiography, circa 1946 (MM).

"Aren't you afraid": WCF to Hattie Fields, 12/22/13 (WCF).

"Please drop": WCF to Hattie Fields, 2/5/14 (WCF).

"grim-faced Boers": Taylor, *W. C. Fields: His Follies and Fortunes,* p. 104.

"would not tempt": WCF to Hattie Fields, 2/5/14 (WCF).

89 "European war": WCF to Hattie Fields, 8/10/14 (WCF).

"a contented mind": WCF to Hattie Fields, 12/23/14 (WCF).

90 "church": Harry Bache Smith, *First Nights and First Editions* (Boston: Little, Brown, 1931), p. 282.

"sure thing": Irene Castle, *Castles in the Air* (Garden City, N.Y.: Doubleday, 1958), p. 133.

91 "the individual hit": *Variety,* 11/28/14.

## Chapter Six

92    "Ran into Irving Berlin": Carmichael, "W. C. Fields—Who Wouldn't Play Stooge to a Dummy."

Dillingham: Zeitlin, "W. C. Fields' Real Life Story."

"partial route": WCF to Hattie Fields, 12/12/14 (WCF).

93    "I do not wish": WCF to Bruce Edwards, 12/12/14 (CD).

94    "greatly pleased": WCF to Charles Dillingham, 12/12/14 (CD).

"New York": Bruce Edwards to WCF, 12/23/14 (CD).

"bad season": WCF to Hattie Fields, 12/23/14 (WCF).

96    "tough, bitter": Gene Buck in a letter to Gene Fowler, as quoted in Taylor, *W. C. Fields: His Follies and Fortunes*, p. 3.

"mistaken judgement": *Syracuse Standard*, 12/21/14.

"The comedy": *Columbus Journal*, 1/12/15.

"Most of the time": Richard J. Anobile, *The Marx Brothers Scrapbook* (New York: Crown, 1973), p. 17.

"He injured his hand": *Columbus Journal*, 1/14/15.

98    "Ziegfeld telephoned": Channing Pollock, "Building the Follies," *Green Book*, September 1915.

"was not tied": "Ed Wynn is Court Host in Fields Estate Fight," *Los Angeles Times*, 8/17/51.

"will close": *Duluth Herald*, 4/22/15.

101    "The makers": Pressbook, *Six of a Kind*.

102    "Everybody is": *Variety*, 6/25/15.

103    A deal: Stage stars were paid a lot more than film actors, which was a source of considerable resentment at the time. A popular film personality might get $125 a week, while a prominent stage figure could command $1,000 or more. Fields' fee, which he may have had to share with Ziegfeld, probably fell somewhere in between.

"exclusive services": *Clipper*, 9/11/15.

"less than four hours": Pressbook, *The Bank Dick*, Universal Pictures, 1940.

"one camera": Sara Redway, "W. C. Fields Pleads for Rough Humor," *Motion Picture Classic*, September 1925.

104    Intricate breaks: Gaumont's chief cameraman, Walter Pritchard, considered himself a specialist in trick photography. He may well have been responsible for the crude animation of the balls in *Pool Sharks*.

"Admirers of Fields": *Motion Picture News*, 10/2/15.

"an eccentric comedy": *Moving Picture World*, 10/30/15.

Girl: The lead actress in *His Lordship's Dilemma* is uncredited, but she bears a striking resemblance to Marion Sunshine (1897–1963), who, with her sister Florenze Tempest, made her feature debut for Gaumont in *Sunshine and Tempest*. Also directed by William F. "Silent Bill" Haddock, *Sunshine and Tempest* was released the same week as the Fields short.

106    "Gaumont quit": Bernard Rosenberg and Harry Silverstein, *The Real Tinsel* (New York: Macmillan, 1970), p. 331. The Casino Star Comedies continued at the rate of approximately one per week through the end of the year and into January 1916. Cissy Fitzgerald, a star for the late Charles Frohman, appeared in several, as did Eddie Boulden, Harry Vokes (of Ward and Vokes, a tramp comedy team), and Oliver "Babe" Hardy. Many of the shorts were directed by Edwin Middleton, and most all of them featured Bud Ross.

## Chapter Seven

107    "up-to-date houses": WCF to Hattie Fields, 9/17/12 (WCF).
"never wanted it": Transcript, *Penn Mutual v. Walter Fields,* 9/22/48.
"lonely": Hattie Fields to Emmet Lavery, Los Angeles, 6/28/61 (EL).
"Your mother's methods": WCF to Hattie Fields, 5/10/15 (WCF).

108    "devoted mother": W. Claude Fields Jr., "Fields on Fields," undated manuscript (WCF).
"I am pleased": WCF to Claude Fields, 9/2/13 (WCF).

109    "Europe": WCF to Claude Fields, 2/4/15 (WCF).
"I agree": WCF to Claude Fields, 4/5/15 (WCF).
"everything a boy": WCF to Hattie Fields, 11/23/15 (WCF).
"stupid people": WCF to Hattie Fields, 5/13/15 (WCF).
"Your low cunning": WCF to Hattie Fields, 5/10/15 (WCF).
"not feel offended": WCF to Hattie Fields, 5/13/15 (WCF).

110    "Let him prospect": WCF to Hattie Fields, 11/23/15 (WCF).
"Sure enough": *Detroit News,* 11/16/15.
"Ziegfeld": Tully, "Let's Laugh at Life with W. C. Fields."

111    "Ziggy hired": J. P. McEvoy, "W. C. Fields' Best Friend," *This Week,* 7/26/42.
"Mr. Ziegfeld did not": "Magnificent Rogue."
"I had seen him": *Los Angeles Times,* 8/17/51.
A history of stealing: Gene Buck's account of the Ed Wynn incident is from Alva Johnston, "Czar of Song," *New Yorker,* 12/17/32.

113    "losing some laughs": *Detroit News,* 11/16/15.
"curtain of secrecy": Mankiewicz to Adamson, *W. C. Fields Straight Up.*
"I sincerely hope": WCF to Ed Wynn, 10/21/38 (WCF).

114    Brice: Fannie Brice signed her checks "Fanny" but always billed herself

as "Fannie." For the sake of clarity, I have chosen to stick with the latter spelling throughout.

"looking shocked": *Variety,* 6/16/16.

115    "funny in English": McEvoy, "Go On, Make Me Laugh."

"given up": *New York Times,* 6/13/16.

"He offered": W. C. Fields, Recollection of Will Rogers for the Memorial Fund Drive, August 1935, Will Rogers Memorial, Claremore, Oklahoma.

116    "Certain scenes": Betty Rogers, *Will Rogers: His Wife's Story* (Indianapolis: Bobbs-Merrill, 1941), p. 131.

"Can't predict": Richard and Paulette Ziegfeld, *The Ziegfeld Touch* (New York: Abrams, 1993), p. 78.

"After a tough performance": Taylor, *W. C. Fields: His Follies and Fortunes,* p. 96.

117    "biggest drinker": George Burns, *All My Best Friends* (New York: Putnam, 1989), p. 81.

"best dancer": *Los Angeles Examiner,* 5/2/49.

118    "weight conscious": Transcript, "In the Matter of William C. Fields, Deceased," 8/1/51.

"one-gal guy": Billy Grady, *The Irish Peacock* (New Rochelle: Arlington House, 1972), p. 21.

"scallop dinners": *Los Angeles Examiner,* 4/29/49.

"my daughter loved him": *Los Angeles Examiner,* 4/28/49.

Costs: *Variety,* 3/9/17.


# Chapter Eight

119    "We minced": Taylor, *W. C. Fields: His Follies and Fortunes,* p. 155.

"Mr. Fields plays": *Green Book,* September 1917.

120    Enter Fields: Director Ned Wayburn's script for the *Ziegfeld Follies of 1917* is in the Ole Olsen Collection at the Cinema-TV Library, University of Southern California, Los Angeles. Playwright Marc Connelly described the way Fields performed the scene in his memoir *Voices Offstage* (New York: Holt, Rinehart & Winston, 1968), p. 67.

"The birds are singing": Screenplay, *The Man With a Grouch* (TW).

121    "Who's pregnant": Grady, *The Irish Peacock,* p. 20.

"Bessie and I": *Los Angeles Examiner,* 5/2/49.

"a lot off our minds": Transcript, "In the Matter of William C. Fields, Deceased," 4/15/49.

122    "good enough": Eddie Cantor, *Take My Life* (Garden City, N.Y.: Doubleday, 1957), p. 139.

124    "I haven't played": Typescript, "An Episode on the Links," 8/30/18 (LOC).

124   "Use a girl": Pressbook, *Her Majesty, Love,* Warner Bros., 1931.

125   "dropped the paper": W. C. Fields, "Anything for a Laugh," *American Magazine,* September 1934.

126   "Ziegfeld spent": Fields, "Over a Barrel."
        "Cut Fields' number": WCF telegram to William Anthony McGuire, 3/23/36 (MGM legal files, courtesy Fred Santon).
        "had a mood": Fields, "Over a Barrel."
        "When we play Columbus": Cantor, *Take My Life,* p. 140.

127   "stage clearer": *New York World,* 1/27/24. William Blanche was a Philadelphian who had come to New York City during the construction of Pennsylvania Station to be with his father, a workman on the project.
        "looked as though": Grady, *The Irish Peacock,* p. 31.
        "a lot of noise": "Magnificent Rogue."

128   "Bessie": Doris Eaton Travis to the author, via telephone, 1/11/98.
        "wonderful opportunities": "Bill Fields Disliked His Label."

## Chapter Nine

130   "an excessive charge": *Variety,* 9/5/19.

131   "a rather big task": *Variety Daily Bulletin,* 8/9/19.
        "several desertions": Alfred Harding, *The Revolt of the Actors* (New York: William Morrow, 1929), p. 127.

134   "golf scene": *Variety,* 6/18/20.
        "slows up the show": J. P. McEvoy, "He Knew What They Wanted," *Saturday Evening Post,* 9/10/32.
        "Stories wafted": *Variety,* 6/25/20.
        "many little incidents": *New York Sun/New York Herald,* 7/18/20.

135   "torrid legislation": *Variety,* 8/1/19.
        "Newspapermen and others": Connelly, *Voices Offstage,* p. 64.

136   "Fields' money": Cantor, *Take My Life,* p. 147.
        "Spring": Fields' handwritten manuscript for "Spring" is in the author's collection.
        "Mr. Fields juggles": *New York Times,* 6/22/21.

138   "guzzled the gravy": *Variety,* 6/24/21.
        "these thugs": W. C. Fields, "Down Memory Lane," newspaper clipping, 1936, New York Public Library.
        "From your attitude": Florenz Ziegfeld Jr. to WCF, 10/28/21 (WCF).

139   "a flop": WCF to Hattie Fields, 11/28/21 (WCF).
        War on Ziegfeld: See *Variety,* 12/30/21, 1/6/22, and 4/7/22. See also Harding, *The Revolt of the Actors,* pp. 330–2.

## Chapter Ten

142    "I realized": Mullett, "Bill Fields Disliked His Label."

"smell your cellar": Typescript, "What A Night!" 5/25/21 (LOC).

144    "nothing but wires": Typescript, "Ten Thousand People Killed," 5/29/22 (LOC).

146    "didn't know anything": *Variety,* 9/7/23.

147    "make money": Charles Angoff, *H. L. Mencken: A Portrait from Memory* (New York: Thomas Yoseloff, 1956), p. 73.

"marvelously funny": Philip Hamburger, "On the Whole," *New Yorker,* 3/8/93.

149    "Miss Donnelly": Howard Dietz, *Dancing in the Dark* (New York: Quadrangle, 1974), p. 66.

Fields removed: Fields' annotated sides for *Poppy* are in the John McLaughlin Collection.

150    "This woman": Bert Wheeler Oral History, Columbia University, 9/5/58.

"stolen a horse": Eastman, *Enjoyment of Laughter,* pp. 296–7.

151    "When he did *Poppy*": Madge Kennedy to Joe Adamson, 5/3/85, *W. C. Fields Straight Up.*

"Purple Bark Sarsaparilla": Dorothy Donnelly, *Poppy Comes to Town,* unpublished playscript, 6/9/23 (LOC).

152    "quite so amusing": *New York Times,* 9/4/23.

"gorgeously funny": *New York Evening World,* 9/4/23.

"gorgeous scaramouch": *The Smart Set,* 11/23/23.

"Put his name up": Madge Kennedy to Anthony Slide, Astoria Studio Oral History Program, 6/26/79.

153    "incredible things": *Ibid.*

"one night": Kennedy to Adamson.

"dark library": Fields, "Anything for a Laugh."

"He had a scene": Jane Wyatt to the author, 6/13/98.

"Halfway": James M. Cain, "The Gentle Side of W. C. Fields," *Washington Post,* 9/26/76.

155    "squeeze his nose": Transcript, "In the Matter of William C. Fields, Deceased," 8/1/51.

"The moustache": *Sunday Telegraph,* 1/13/24.

Business: Details of the week-to-week box office performance for *Poppy* are summarized in *Variety,* 1/3/24.

156    "kindest personal regards": H. L. Mencken to Philip Goodman, 2/19/32 (WCF).

156    "I was warned": Grady, *The Irish Peacock,* p. 21.

157    "plump blonde": Louise Brooks, *Lulu in Hollywood* (New York: Alfred
          A. Knopf, 1982), p. 84.
          "And darling": *Los Angeles Examiner,* 5/5/49.
          "average speech": Undated clipping, J. P. McEvoy file (PFL).
          "When people come away": J. P. McEvoy, *The Potters* (New York: Reilly
          & Lee, 1924), p. IX.

158    "not making any efforts": Press release, *The Comic Supplement* (PFL).
          "Listen": McEvoy, "He Knew What They Wanted."
          "Here is a theme": *New York Times,* 12/7/24.

159    "terrible little male offspring": In quoting lines and content from *The
          Comic Supplement,* I have referenced several different sources. J. P.
          McEvoy's original version, registered with the Copyright Office on
          2/23/24, is at the Library of Congress. An undated revision, includ-
          ing Fields' initial contributions, is at the New York Public Library.
          Fields' handwritten drafts are in the Tim Walker Collection. Fields'
          "sides" for the show are in the John McLaughlin Collection at the
          Book Sail.

161    "Off the stage": McEvoy, "He Knew What They Wanted."
          "almost impossible": Norman Bel Geddes, *Miracle in the Evening* (New
          York: Doubleday, 1960), p. 311.

162    "greatest extravaganza": *Washington Post,* 1/25/25.
          "sparkled": *Washington Star,* 1/25/25.
          "complete flop": *Variety,* 1/28/25.

163    "unending conflict": *New York Times,* 2/1/25.

164    "the show was good": Nona Otero Friedman to the author, via tele-
          phone, 2/5/99.
          "a damn thing": Zeitlin, "W. C. Fields' Real Life Story."
          "great possibilities": *Variety,* 2/11/5.

# Chapter Eleven

165    "staircase": Marion Davies, *The Times We Had* (Indianapolis: Bobbs-
          Merrill, 1975), p. 8.

167    "momentary hit": *Variety,* 8/13/24.
          "comic scenes": Contract, *The Showman,* 6/3/24 (WCF).
          "Watch W. C. Fields": WCF, undated statement, Loyd Wright files
          (AMPAS).

168    "He introduced himself": *Ibid.*
          "much to do": D. W. Griffith, deposition, 4/18/28 (AMPAS).
          "finest men": *Boston Herald,* 10/4/25.
          Artist: *New York Times,* 1/27/29.

169 "She ruined him": Rudy Koubek to Richard Kozarski, Astoria Studio Oral History Program, undated.

"She had nothing": Ed Flaherty to Sam Robert, 10/26/63.

everything planned: Frank Nelson to Judd Tully, Astoria Studio Oral History Program, 6/28/79.

"eliminated": Helen Hanemann, "He Hated Alarm Clocks," *Motion Picture,* August 1926.

170 "charming trait": *Life,* 7/17/24.

171 "Here, at last": *Variety,* 3/18/25.

"physical accuracy": Stark Young, "In Praise of Four," *New York Times,* 7/28/25.

"His ad libbing": Alfred Lunt to Kevin Brownlow, London, 1965 (courtesy of Kevin Brownlow).

"Scenario": Barnet George Bravermann, *Sally of the Sawdust* diary, 3/13–6/10/25 (MOMA). See also J. B. Kaufman, "It Was Always Funny Working with Fields," *Griffithiana,* May 1998.

173 "Every memory": Bernard Sobel, *Ziegfeld and Me,* unpublished manuscript, New York Public Library.

Chaplin: Bernard Sobel, *Broadway Heartbeat* (New York: Hermitage House, 1953), p. 141.

174 "I said yes": Transcript, *Penn Mutual v. Walter Fields,* 9/22/48.

"perfection itself": Adolph Zukor to D. W. Griffith, 7/1/25 (MOMA).

"common picture making": *Variety,* 8/5/25.

175 "featured player": Ruth Biery, "I Don't Care If I Ever Make Another Picture," *Photoplay,* July 1928.

176 "vain effort": *Variety,* 1/13/26.

"comical conduct": *New York Times,* 1/11/26.

"racket": W. Adolphe Roberts, "Confidences Off Screen," *Motion Picture,* December 1925.

177 "crowned with laurel": Redway, "W. C. Fields Pleads for Rough Humor."

"land Bill Fields": As quoted in Donald Elder, *Ring Lardner: A Biography* (Garden City, N.Y.: Doubleday, 1956), p. 263.

178 "spirit of Christmas": WCF to Philip Goodman, 12/25/25 (WHS).

"I was surprised": Barbara Hunter (Billee Blanchard) to the author, via telephone, 2/10/99.

179 "not worked": *Los Angeles Examiner,* 5/6/49.

"Your monologue": WCF to Hattie Fields, 8/20/17 (WCF).

"Know positively": WCF to Hattie Fields, 9/24/19 (WCF).

"You have been a lazy": WCF to Hattie Fields, 2/4/20 (WCF).

180 "long time": Redway, "W. C. Fields Pleads for Rough Humor."

"best sort of humor": Roberts, "Confidences Off Screen."

"I have talked": Redway, "W. C. Fields Pleads for Rough Humor."

"What is there of art": *Boston Herald,* 10/4/25.

## Chapter Twelve

183    "He said": Sheila Gladys Geraghty, undated manuscript, Thomas J. Geraghty Papers (LOC).

184    "ugly man": A. Edward Sutherland Oral History, Columbia University, February 1959.

"occasional suggestion": Hanemann, "He Hated Alarm Clocks."

185    "never really left": Louise Brooks, "The Other Face of W. C. Fields," *Sight and Sound,* Spring 1971.

"great enough comedian": Joe Pasternak, *Easy the Hard Way* (New York: G. P. Putnam's Sons, 1956), p. 81.

"a scene in Florida": Sutherland Oral History.

186    "Queen Victoria": Grady, *The Irish Peacock,* p. 34.

"rushes look so peculiar": Louise Brooks to Richard and Diane Kozarski, Astoria Studio Oral History Program, 6/3/79.

"young comedy directors": Kevin Brownlow, *The Parade's Gone By* (New York: Alfred A. Knopf, 1968), p. 361.

187    "The trouble": *Motion Picture News,* 7/24/26.

"back to the stage": Hanemann, "He Hated Alarm Clocks."

188    "skeleton framework": Dunham Thorp, "The Up-to-Date Old Timer," *Motion Picture Classic,* September 1926.

"instant success": *Ibid.*

189    "The peculiar thing": Taylor, *W. C. Fields: His Follies and Fortunes,* p. 199.

"wonderful about Bill": Brooks Oral History.

"testing": Charles "Buddy" Rogers to Anthony Slide, Astoria Studio Oral History Program, undated.

190    "Behind the camera": *New York Times,* 8/15/26.

"amazing set of clubs": Buddy Rogers to Kevin Brownlow, 1978.

191    "stand all the praise": *Moving Picture World,* 3/1/27.

"fathers of this school": Iris Berry, *Let's Go to the Movies* (New York: Payson & Clarke, 1926), p. 138.

"played on the stage": Pressbook, *The Potters,* Paramount Pictures, 1927.

Rights: Details of the purchase and subsequent performance of *The Potters* are from the Paramount Pictures collection at the Academy of Motion Picture Arts and Sciences, as well as various issues of *Variety.*

193    "not so dependent": *Motion Picture News,* 2/4/27.

"enough slapstick": *Variety,* 1/19/27.

"struck his stride": *New York Times,* 1/18/27.

"such a strain": Elizabeth Fontron, "W. C. Fields Hated to Get Up Early in the Morning, and So—," *Cinema Art,* August 1927.

194    Purchase: Details of the purchase and subsequent performance of *Running Wild* are from the Paramount Collection (AMPAS).

"research work": *Variety,* 3/9/27.

"I play the part": Fontron, "W. C. Fields Hated to Get Up."

"great stage comic": Mary Brian to the author, Studio City, 5/25/97.

195    "There he was": Fontron, "W. C. Fields Hated to Get Up."

"quite some forward": *Variety,* 6/15/27.

196    "piggy": WCF to Philip Goodman, 6/4/27.


## Chapter Thirteen

199    "play golf": *Los Angeles Times,* 12/4/34.

201    "Conklin was rather in awe": Mary Brian to the author.

"menagerie": Pressbook, *Two Flaming Youths,* Paramount Pictures, 1927.

"complete freedom": Brooks Oral History.

"very funny": Jim Rogers to the author, via telephone, 2/17/98.

202    "That day": Cecil "Teet" Carle, "Beating the Drums for Another Comic of the Silents," *Los Angeles Times,* 12/19/71.

"Fields was very easy": Cecil "Teet" Carle to Joe Adamson, 12/23/85, *W. C. Fields Straight Up.*

$13,000 under budget: Cost and scheduling details for *Two Flaming Youths* are from the Paramount Collection (AMPAS).

The driver: Details of Fields' accident are from *New York Times,* 10/4/27, *Los Angeles Times,* 10/5/27, and *Moving Picture World,* 10/8/27.

"I should": Fields, "Down Memory Lane."

203    "I heard it snap": Fields, "Over a Barrel."

204    "the gags": *Variety,* 1/11/28. (Incidentally, *Variety* staffer Jack Conway is not to be confused with the Jack Conway who directed features at MGM.)

"The public didn't want": *Variety,* 3/1/28.

Christie: Although Sennett registered *Tillie's Punctured Romance* with the Copyright Office as an unpublished work in December 1914, the Christie Film Company claimed ownership of the film upon its publication the following year.

205    "got up promptly": Sutherland Oral History.

"I remember Bill": Brooks, "The Other Face of W. C. Fields."

208    "God help": Jack Regan, "The Two Sides of W. C. Fields," *Movie Mirror,* April 1935.

208 "fed up": Fields, undated career notes (MM).

"option not renewed": *Los Angeles Times,* 12/4/34.

209 "violent dislike": As quoted in Ken Murray, *The Body Merchant* (Pasadena: Ward Richie Press, 1976), p. 136.

210 "I took the offer": McEvoy, "W. C. Fields' Best Friend."

"How I miss California": WCF to Loyd Wright, 5/4/28 (AMPAS).

211 "nicked Earl Carroll": WCF to Tom Geraghty, 5/27/28 (LOC).

212 "Carroll is standing": Undated manuscript fragment (TW).

213 "cast size": *New York Telegraph,* 8/7/28.

"You know": Press release, *Earl Carroll's Vanities* (PFL).

215 "the proper apples": Transcript, *People v. William C. Fields,* 9/14/28 (WCF).

Bessie Poole's death: *New York Times,* 10/9, 10/14, 10/16/28; *Evening Graphic,* 10/10, 10/11/28; *New York Daily News,* 10/10, 10/11, 10/12/28; *New York American,* 10/10, 10/12/28; *Variety,* 10/10, 10/17/28.

"Persons who patronize": *New York Times,* 10/12/28.

216 "A romance": *Philadelphia Evening Bulletin,* 11/20/28.

## Chapter Fourteen

217 "ill with grippe": WCF to Hattie Fields, 2/19/29 (WCF).

"one lung": WCF to Walter E. Williams, 6/10/37 (WCF).

"raw wine": Ida Zeitlin, "Life Begins Again at Fifty," *Screenland,* April 1935.

218 "history of your life": WCF to Hattie Fields, 6/2/27 (WCF).

"I have worked": WCF to Hattie Fields, 12/7/28 (WCF).

"house-made dinners": Hattie Fields to Mrs. James McIntyre, 10/11/23.

"several offers": WCF to Tom Geraghty, 4/5/29 (LOC).

219 "pompous": Undated treatment, *The Great McGillicuddy* (TW).

"quickly found out": Cain, "The Gentle Side of W. C. Fields."

220 "so bad": "Allan Wood, On Stage with W. C. Fields," *Witzend,* no. 9, 1973.

221 "In addition": Cain, "The Gentle Side of W. C. Fields."

"stocks": *Variety,* 1/1/47.

"They were terrible": Sworn Testimony, Bill of Exceptions, Superior Court of Riverside County, Case #28734, p. 103.

"He was hysterical": Cantor, *Take My Life,* p. 146.

223 "They belted him": Grady, *The Irish Peacock,* p. 12.

225 "I regret it": "W. C. Fields Gives Expert Opinion on Why People Laugh," *St. Louis Globe Democrat,* 8/10/30.

226 "banal": WCF to Arthur Hammerstein, 1/12/31 (WCF).

227 "isn't altogether fair": *Philadelphia Record,* 12/2/30.

228 "lacked": *Philadelphia Inquirer,* 12/2/30.

"riotous": *Philadelphia Evening Bulletin,* 12/2/30.

"masterly dignity": *New York Times,* 12/23/30.

"Miss Ray Dooley": *New Yorker,* 1/3/31.

"tragic note": *The Nation,* 1/7/31.

229   "process of elimination": WCF to Arthur Hammerstein, 1/1/31 (WCF).

"I have sold": Arthur Hammerstein to WCF, 1/2/31 (AE).

*Ballyhoo: Variety,* 1/21, 1/28, 2/11, 2/5/31.

230   "one matinee": Percy N. Stone, "Cast-Managed Show is Far From Failure," *New York Herald-Tribune,* 3/1/31.

231   Shorty: William Blanche died in New York on August 2, 1931. Contrary to legend, Fields did not pay for his burial nor buy him a suit of clothes for the occasion. His remains were cremated and consigned to a common grave.

232   "the river": Taylor, *W. C. Fields: His Follies and Fortunes,* p. 211.

"hawk my wares": Ida Zeitlin, "Fields in Clover," *Screenland,* August 1935.

"In desperation": Fields, "Over a Barrel."

"All they had to do": Pressbook, *Mississippi,* Paramount Pictures, 1935.

## Chapter Fifteen

235   "If the west": Zeitlin, "Life Begins Again at Fifty."

"Bill changed women": Taylor, *W. C. Fields: His Follies and Fortunes,* p. 174.

"Her composure": Brooks, "The Other Face of W. C. Fields."

238   "The comedy": *Hollywood Reporter,* 6/23/32.

239   Loss: Figures on *Her Majesty, Love* are from the research library of Karl Thiede.

"a hell of a lot": WCF to Elise Cavanna, 12/14/31 (TW).

"picture work": Transcript, *Penn Mutual v. Walter Fields.*

"Health": WCF to Hattie Fields, 3/22/32.

240   "With salaries": Billy Grady to WCF, 2/27/32 (WCF).

"Wiggle and I": Undated telegram (WCF).

"Ben Schulberg": Max Wilk, *The Wit and Wisdom of Hollywood* (New York: Atheneum, 1971), p. 55.

241   "Bill loved it": Mankiewicz to Adamson, *W. C. Fields Straight Up* (UCLA).

"children will like it": Lamar Trotti to Gov. Carl Milliken, 6/25/32 (AMPAS).

"Mankiewicz": *Nation,* 8/3/32.

242   Adequate business: At a cost of $267,000, *Million Dollar Legs* returned a modest profit of $57,000 on worldwide rentals of $470,000.

"I was thinking": WCF to Albert A. Kaufman, 6/9/32 (WCF).

243   "Regarding your letter": Albert A. Kaufman to WCF, 7/6/32 (WCF).

243    "The entire atmosphere": Wilk, *The Wit and Wisdom of Hollywood,*
          p. 54.
       "an idea for you": Zeitlin, "Life Begins Again at Fifty."
244    "adored Fields": Mankiewicz to Adamson, *W. C. Fields Straight Up.*
       "every whim": All quotes for "Episode of Emily, Rollo and the Road
          Hogs" are drawn from the final script, dated 9/8/32.
246    "[Fields] expected": Carle to Adamson, *W. C. Fields Straight Up.*
       "I'll bet": Constance Binney to Richard Kozarski, Astoria Studio Oral
          History Program, 12/6/79.
247    Negative cost: Figures on *If I Had a Million* are from the research
          library of Karl Thiede.
       "one of the best": *Hollywood Reporter,* 11/3/32.
248    "nurtured": *Variety,* 12/6/32.

## Chapter Sixteen

249    "I thought": Mack Sennett, *King of Comedy* (Garden City, N.Y.: Dou-
          bleday, 1954), p. 265.
       "During our games": "Magnificent Rogue."
251    "First picture": WCF to Robert P. Burkhalter, undated (WCF).
       "Sennett shared": Fields, "Over a Barrel."
252    "definitely kill": WCF to Mack Sennett, 12/7/32 (WCF).
       "no real laffs": *Variety,* 6/20/33.
253    "tremendous success": WCF to Mack Sennett, 12/18/32 (WCF).
       "Might consider": WCF to Robert P. Burkhalter, undated (WCF).
254    "Finished two scenes": WCF to Philip Goodman, 1/27/33 (WHS).
255    "It was discovered": *Variety,* 3/18/24.
       "From one end": Ivan St. Johns, "What is that Lure of Peggy Joyce?"
          *Photoplay,* November 1925.
256    "one story": A. Edward Sutherland to the author, 1969.
257    "Gradually": Sutherland Oral History.
258    "last shot": *Los Angeles Herald-Examiner,* 5/11/71.
       "a dilly": *Los Angeles Herald-Examiner,* 5/12/71.
259    "The bank president": Tully, "Clowns Never Laugh."
260    "Prohibition ends": WCF to Philip Goodman, 5/15/33 (WHS).
261    "perturbed": A. M. Botsford to Dr. James Wingate, 5/10/33 (AMPAS).
       "The gags": *Hollywood Reporter,* 5/8/33.
       "regal and somewhat beery manner": *New York Times,* 5/27/33.
262    "various comments": James B. M. Fisher to Dr. James Wingate, 6/23/33
          (AMPAS).
       "He is primarily": Loyd Wright, contract memo, 5/5/33 (AMPAS).
       "gross vulgarities": Joseph I. Breen to John Hammell, 10/8/35
          (AMPAS).

## Chapter Seventeen

264    "nothing funny": Gladys Hall, "Have You Got the Makings of a Comedian?" *Movie Classic,* December 1934.

"hungry": Cheatham, "Juggler of Laughs."

"derogatory rumors": WCF to Hattie Fields, 5/5/32 (WCF).

"swans": Mary Brian to the author.

265    "ten of us": Harry Watson to the author, via telephone, 5/14/98.

"Sits in chair": F. G. Bradford to WCF, 5/2/17 (TW).

268    "When he finished": William Cahn, *Harold Lloyd's World of Comedy* (New York: Duell, Sloan and Pearce, 1964), p. 154.

"long ball": Bing Crosby, *Call Me Lucky* (New York: Simon and Schuster, 1953), p. 155.

"left-footed game": "People in Sports," *Philadelphia Evening Bulletin,* 9/10/42.

Donated: Will Fowler, "W. C. Fields: He Always Called His Own Shots," unedited manuscript for *Golf Digest,* 1983.

269    "fit": Elsie Janis, "I Was That Way About W. C. Fields," *New Movie,* January 1935.

270    "We're expecting": WCF to Philip Goodman, 6/22/33 (WHS).

271    "middle of the lake": Mary Brian to the author.

"little bits": WCF to Douglas McLean, 6/10/33 (WCF).

272    "In the beginning": Julie Bishop Bergin (Jacqueline Wells) in a letter to the author, 7/25/97.

"couldn't stand the kid": Philip Trent (Clifford Jones) to the author, via telephone, 4/28/99.

"carpet slippers": Alva Johnson, "Who Knows What is Funny?" *Saturday Evening Post,* 8/6/38.

273    "the cause": Fields, "Over a Barrel."

"We took": Fields, "Alcohol and Me."

"preview": WCF to Robert P. Burkhalter, 9/30/33.

"All the laughs": *Hollywood Reporter,* 9/29/33.

275    "Unhappy Linelle": Robert P. Burkhalter to WCF, 7/6/34 (WCF).

"Fields went berserk": Frank Westmore and Muriel Davidson, *The Westmores of Hollywood* (New York: Lippincott, 1976), p. 101.

276    "I guess": Suzanne Antles to the author, Thousand Oaks, 9/29/99.

277    "He didn't show up": "Magnificent Rogue."

279    "The hell of it": Peter Bogdanovich, *Who the Devil Made It* (New York: Alfred A. Knopf, 1997), p. 408.

"I meet Fields": Tammany Young, "World's Champion Gate Crasher," press release, Paramount Pictures, 1934 (AMPAS).

280  "I was making a picture": "Magnificent Rogue."
281  "so enthusiastic": *Motion Picture Herald,* 2/27/34.
"One particular scene": *Los Angeles Post-Record,* 2/9/34.

## Chapter Eighteen

282  "no tenderfoot": Zeitlin, "Fields in Clover."
283  "great guy": Erle C. Kenton in a letter to Donald Deschner, 2/7/66.
"people laugh": Eastman, *Enjoyment of Laughter,* p. 94.
"If I sat": Fields, "Anything for a Laugh."
286  "pantomimic talents": *Los Angeles Times,* 4/7/34.
"quietly harassed": *New York Sun,* 4/9/34.
"last appearance": Fields' annotated manuscript for "Playing the Sticks" is in the McLaughlin Collection at the Book Sail.
287  "in a louse": WCF to Philip Goodman, 4/28/34 (WHS).
288  "in an uproar": William Beaudine, "Just a Lovable Old So-and-So," *Film Weekly,* 12/7/34.
289  "Dad went over": Dick Moore, *Twinkle, Twinkle Little Star* (New York: Harper and Row, 1984), p. 153.
290  "kind to Lubo": Steve Fairfield to the author, San Jacinto, 10/16/97.
291  Soboba: For information on Soboba Hot Springs and John and Tillie Althouse, I am grateful to Wolfgang Dietzel, a local historian whose father was a family friend. The local history files at the San Jacinto and Riverside Public Libraries were also helpful.
"She loved attention": Rosita Del Mar to the author, via telephone, 9/27/98.
293  "psychotic": Mankiewicz to Adamson, *W. C. Fields Straight Up* (UCLA).
"most of us": Sutherland Oral History.
"All you had to do": Harry Caplan to Joe Adamson, 9/10/83, *W. C. Fields Straight Up.*
"met him halfway": Michael, undated manuscript, p. 85 (MM).
294  "bunch of fun": WCF to Roger Montandon, 10/16/34 (courtesy of Roger Montandon).
"The great man": *New York Times,* 7/14/34.
"house afire": Will Rogers, weekly article, 6/3/34.
"new deal": WCF to Loyd Wright, 1/9/34 (AMPAS).
"Almost everyone": WCF to Charles Beyer, 7/14/34 (WCF).
295  "newsreel editor": Eugene Zukor to Douglas Bell, oral history, 2/16/93 (AMPAS).
"four feet tall": Sidney Salkow to the author, via telephone, 7/20/97.
"no honey wagons": Edward J. Montagne to the author, via telephone, 8/7/98.

296    "school tent": Edith Fellows in a letter to the author, 7/22/97.

"always fried": William Drew, *At the Center of the Frame: Leading Ladies of the Twenties and Thirties* (New York: Vestal Press, 2000), p. 281.

"box lunches": Carmencita Johnson to the author, via telephone, 12/15/97.

298    "ashamed": WCF to Jim Tully, 11/6/34 (WCF).

## Chapter Nineteen

299    "If I flop": *Los Angeles Times,* 12/4/34.

"I was in love": Eastman, *Enjoyment of Laughter,* p. 336.

"English class": Mankiewicz to Adamson, *W. C. Fields Straight Up.*

300    Philadelphia dialect: Dr. William Lebov rendered his opinion after viewing a tape of *The Bank Dick,* produced in 1940 when Fields was sixty years of age. "There is not enough evidence," he wrote, "to say for sure that Fields has preserved the Philadelphia pattern of tense (raised) short /a/ vowels (in *man, ham, pass, path, laugh, mad, bad, glad*) as against lax vowels (*mat, bang, cap, cash, dad, sad,* etc.), but whatever words there are seem to fit the pattern." Dr. Lebov's comments are contained in an e-mail to the author, 3/23/99.

"Charley Bogle": Fields, "Anything for a Laugh."

"advocate of moderation": Jack Grant, "Proud of His Big Nose," *Movie Classic,* February 1935.

301    "After breakfast": *Los Angeles Daily News,* 4/12/51.

"opening scene": Fields' original outline for *Back Porch,* as well as the resulting treatment, are in the Tim Walker Collection (TW). The 8/20 and 8/30/34 drafts of the screenplay are in the Paramount Collection (AMPAS).

"really was awful": WCF to Billy Grady, 2/4/43 (WCF).

304    Course of the morning: My account of the filming of *It's a Gift* is drawn chiefly from the daily production reports in the Paramount collection (AMPAS).

"improve any gag": Caplan to Adamson, *W. C. Fields Straight Up.*

305    "over one hundred children": Jane Withers to the author, Sherman Oaks, 11/10/98.

307    "going from Shakespeare": Jean Rouverol Butler to the author, Santa Monica, 5/10/97.

"his call": Ed Montagne to the author.

308    "needed a line": Zeitlin, "Life Begins Again at Fifty."

310    "Micawber": *Hollywood Reporter,* 10/12/34.

"most people": Rudy Behlmer, *Memo from David O. Selznick* (New York: Viking Press, 1972), p. 3.

310    Summary: Estabrook's list, along with other documents associated with the film's development, are in the MGM collection at USC (MGM).

311    "Laughton unavailable": Behlmer, *Memo from David O. Selznick,* p. 73.

"didn't like the idea": *Daily Telegraph* (London), 10/30/34.

"like to know": Behlmer, *Memo from David O. Selznick,* p. 75.

"looked wonderful": George Cukor Oral History, Columbia University, 6/22/71.

312    "He was good": Joseph Newman to the author, via telephone, 1/26/2001.

"Charles lost": Elsa Lanchester, *Elsa Lanchester by Herself* (New York: St. Martin's Press, 1983), p. 125.

313    "I've been playing": Pressbook, *David Copperfield,* Metro-Goldwyn-Mayer, 1935.

"always admired": *Los Angeles Times,* 1/20/35.

314    "something snide": Anne Edwards, "W. C. Fields," *Architectural Digest,* April 1994.

"To play Micawber": Maxine Marx, *Growing Up with Chico* (Englewood Cliffs, N.J.: Prentice-Hall, 1980), p. 96.

"charming": Gavin Lambert, *On Cukor* (New York: G. P. Putnam's Sons, 1972), p. 86.

"Fields runs riot": *Daily Variety,* 11/8/34.

315    "Some of the material": *Hollywood Reporter,* 11/8/34.

"mean man": Arthur Hornblow Jr. Oral History, Columbia University, 3/4/59.

"good job": WCF to Elise Cavanna, 12/3/34 (TW).

## Chapter Twenty

317    "a killer": Bert Wheeler Oral History.

"I was awakened": Mankiewicz to Adamson, *W. C. Fields Straight Up.*

319    "my rompers": Janis, "I Was That Way About W. C. Fields."

"quaffing some scotch": Spec McClure to Gene Fowler, 1954 (GF).

320    "extremely well": David O. Selznick to WCF, 1/9/35 (WCF).

"shipwreck scene": WCF to Roland Young, 1/15/35.

"walked away": Roland Young to WCF, 1/19/35 (WCF).

321    "I don't believe": Will Rogers to WCF, 1/7/35 (WCF).

"some wonderful scenes": WCF to Loyd Wright, 2/19/35 (AMPAS).

"confessional": Andre Sennwald, "W. C. Fields, Buffoon," *New York Times,* 1/13/35.

"essence of his comedy": J. C. Furnas, "W. C. Fields, Comic or Phenomenon?" *New York Herald-Tribune,* 1/20/35.

322    "knows his business": WCF to Elise Cavanna, 1/22/35 (TW).

Trouble: Daily production reports for *Mississippi* are in the Paramount Collection (AMPAS).

"Fields was all right": Sutherland Oral History.

"lost time": Carle to Adamson, *W. C. Fields Straight Up.*

323   "rarely know the lines": Hornblow Oral History.

324   "The calliope": Idwal Jones, "Fields (W. C.) and Stream," *New York Times,* 4/14/35.

325   "Please": WCF to Arthur Hornblow Jr., 2/5/35 (WCF).

"fellow who roars": Fields, "Anything for a Laugh."

326   "Before releasing": *Daily Variety,* 2/21/35.

"never had": WCF to Maude Fendick, 1/5/35 (WCF).

327   The solution: The original script for *His Perfect Day* is in the Mack Sennett Collection (AMPAS).

"Sam Hardy": Mary Brian to the author.

"On my arrival": Magda Michael, undated manuscript, p. 83 (MM).

"my pictures": WCF to Philip Goodman, 10/6/34 (WHS).

329   "persuaded": *Hollywood Reporter,* 6/12/35.

"humanness": Cheatham, "Juggler of Laughs."

331   "Bill likes": Alma Whitaker, "Career as Opera Contralto Aids Work with W. C. Fields," *Los Angeles Times,* 6/16/35.

"waiting for script": Daily production reports for *Man on the Flying Trapeze* are in the Paramount Collection (AMPAS).

"played a glutton": Hedda Hopper, "Grady Sutton—Movie Extra with That Extra Something," *Los Angeles Times,* 8/24/65.

332   "His timing": Taylor, *W. C. Fields: His Follies and Fortunes,* p. 247.

333   "very bad": *Daily Variety,* 6/26/35.

"howls are frequent": *Hollywood Reporter,* 6/26/35.

"bad case of nerves": WCF to Elise Cavanna, 6/20/35 (TW).

## Chapter Twenty-one

334   Contract: Fields' new contract with Paramount called for three films over a twelve-month period, beginning 1/1/36, at a rate of $100,000 a picture (payable at $6,000 a week for fifty weeks). He was also to receive 10 percent of the gross receipts in excess of twice the production costs. For purposes of computing the percentage, all three productions were to be grouped together.

"Just when": WCF to Ralph Huston, 12/10/35 (WCF).

"I was with him": Draft manuscript, November 1935 (WCF).

"He'd drive": Sara Hamilton, "That Man's Here Again," *Photoplay,* August 1937.

335   "I couldn't walk": W. C. Fields, "W. C. Fields Comes Back," *Kansas City Star,* 12/12/35.

336   "an honor": WCF to William Anthony McGuire, 1/6/36 (courtesy of Fred Santon).

336    "we get there": Sutherland Oral History.

337    "last two years": Idwal Jones, "Mr. Fields Cultivates Poppy," *New York Times,* 6/14/36.

341    "Frankly": Edward Sutherland, "W. C. Fields Laughed at Death," *Hollywood,* August 1936.

342    "various doctors": Buchanan-Taylor, *Shake the Bottle,* p. 218.
       "ruinous": "Magnificent Rogue."

343    "pull through": Sworn Testimony, Case #28734, p. 6.

344    "nearly died": *The Bystander,* 7/22/36.
       "crisis": Sworn Testimony, Case #28734.

345    "He looked dreadful": Doris Nolan to Anthony Slide, Berwick-upon-Tweed, 10/14/97.

346    "You claim": WCF to Hattie Fields, 7/7/33 (WCF).
       "a shock to me": *Los Angeles Examiner,* 5/5/49.
       "Norwegian butler": Sutherland Oral History.

347    "After much discussion": *Los Angeles Examiner,* 4/30/49.
       "limited this bequest": Fields' 11/36 draft of his will is in the Lloyd Wright file (AMPAS).

348    "very sick man": Julian Street to Waldemar Young, 7/22/36 (courtesy of Scott Eyman).
       "first holiday": Adela Rogers St. Johns, "How W. C. Fields Fought His Way Back to Health," *Physical Culture,* December 1937.
       "old nemesis": WCF to Loyd Wright, 11/5/36 (AMPAS).

349    "evidently fearful": Sobel, *Ziegfeld and Me.*
       "can't accept radio": WCF to Robert Burkhalter, March 1935 (WCF).
       "regular business": Reid, "Nobody's Dummy."

350    "We were out": Philip K. Scheuer, "Town Called Hollywood," *Los Angeles Times,* 4/11/37.

## Chapter Twenty-two

352    "great pleasure": Edgar Bergen's scripts for *The Chase & Sanborn Hour* are at the Cinema-TV Library, USC.

354    "No new show": *Radio Guide,* 6/5/37.

355    "This radio business": WCF to Maude Fendick, undated (WCF).
       "Those who heard": *Variety,* 5/19/37.
       "real person": Don Ameche to Betty Gropley, WRC, Washington, D.C., undated.

356    "Citron ended up": Steve Fairfield to the author.

358    "too cozy": Hamilton, "That Man's Here Again."
       "Heaven": Transcript, *Penn Mutual v. Walter Fields,* 9/22/48.
       "never felt better": WCF to Dr. Steven Smith, 6/29/37 (GH).
       "straighten them out": Michael, undated manuscript, p. 94 (MM).

359   "Every week": Charles Champlin, "Don Ameche—A Life Well Spent in Hollywood," *Los Angeles Times,* 8/4/91.

"shivers": Naomi Lewis to the author, via telephone, 2/17/98.

"nervous": Edgar Bergen to Chuck Schaden, Los Angeles, 2/20/75 (courtesy of John and Larry Gassman).

"I can't work": Dudley Early, "The Gentleman Speaks His Mind," *Family Circle,* 4/8/38.

360   "No matter": "Charlie McCarthy Is the Most Objectionable Young Man in America," *Life,* 6/28/37.

"accused": Early, "The Gentleman Speaks His Mind."

361   "several guests": Magda Michael, undated manuscript, p. 87 (MM).

"very jealous": Earl Wilson, "Fields' Little Chickadee," *Los Angeles Herald-Examiner,* 6/7/71.

362   "ill for months": Early, "The Gentleman Speaks His Mind."

"excessive display": Joseph I. Breen, 8/9/37 (AMPAS).

"The Fields character": Comedy Sequences, 8/18/37 (AMPAS).

363   "shooting": Howard Lindsay, "No Thanks for the Memories," *Saturday Review,* 7/15/67.

"doesn't make sense": "The Beloved Mountebank."

"never slept": Tichi Wilkerson and Marcia Borie, *The Hollywood Reporter: The Golden Years* (New York: Coward-McCann, 1984), p. 103.

364   "very beautiful": Magda Michael, undated manuscript, p. 84 (MM).

"black-and-blue": *Hollywood Citizen News,* 9/24/37.

"Fields said": *Los Angeles Times,* 11/13/40.

"dispensed": WCF, testimony before federal tax court, Los Angeles, 2/19/41 (WCF).

365   "hard stuff": *Los Angeles Times,* 10/17/37.

"obstinate": David Chierichetti, *Hollywood Director* (New York: Curtis Books, 1973), p. 120.

"in the wings": Grace Bradley Boyd to the author, Dana Point, 7/30/97.

"wasn't an easy": Bob Hope, undated interview clip for American Movie Classics.

"One of the crew": A. C. Lyles to the author, Los Angeles, 10/9/97.

"wouldn't direct it": Chierichetti, *Hollywood Director,* p. 122.

"in character": WCF to William Le Baron, 1/19/38 (WCF).

367   "very considerate": Ginger McFarlane (Ginger Michael) to the author, Seal Beach, 3/20/98.

"new element": *Daily Variety,* 2/8/38.

"a pity": *New York Herald-Tribune,* 3/10/38.

"not himself": *New York Times,* 3/10/38.

368   Noble project: At various times, *Things Began to Happen* was also known as *That Man Is Here Again, Behind the Eight Ball,* and *Mr. Bumpus Goes to Town.*

368   Payments: According to his contract for the period commencing 11/22/37, Fields was to write "skits, gags, comedy sequences, and situations" for *Things Began to Happen* and collaborate "with the writers assigned thereto for the writing of the treatment or adaptation and continuity with dialogue therefor" (WCF).

"long absence": *Variety,* 3/2/38.

369   "fought like a fiend": WCF, draft letter, 5/4/38 (WCF).

"downbeat": WCF to Jack Norworth, 5/27/38 (WCF).

370   "enjoyed": WCF to Danny Danker, 3/8/38 (WCF).

"The shorter the time": Reid, "Nobody's Dummy."

"Trolley": Gene Fowler to WCF, undated letter (TW).

371   "Sunday afternoon": Ameche to Gropley.

372   "let out": WCF to Danny Danker, 7/13/43 (WCF).

## *Chapter Twenty-three*

373   "fortune telling": Fields' notes for *The Wizard of Oz* are in the Magda Michael Collection.

374   "never go back": Frederick James Smith, "Is His Nose Red?" *Liberty,* 9/4/37.

375   "The front office": Edward Muhl to the author, via telephone, 7/8/97.

"a yen": *You Can't Cheat an Honest Man,* 8/15/38 (WCF).

376   "all rogue": "W. C. Fields Gives Expert Opinion on Why People Laugh."

"reading the contract": WCF to Lester Cowan, 8/2/38 (WFG).

377   "Fields listened": Hal Kanter to the author, via telephone, 4/27/98.

378   "engaging rascal": *Hollywood Citizen News,* 10/15/38.

"fairly tired": WCF to Ed Wynn, 10/21/38 (WCF).

"In time": *New York World-Telegram,* 11/14/38.

379   Easy decision: Details of Fields' contract amendments with Universal are from the interoffice contract memos in the Universal Collection at USC and the Lester Cowan Papers held by Waiting for Godot Books.

380   "Whatever rights": Lester Cowan to Edgar Bergen, 9/16/38 (WFG).

"best comedy": McEvoy, "W. C. Fields' Best Friend."

"introduction of Bergen": *You Can't Cheat an Honest Man* synopsis, 12/9/38.

381   "exceptionally slow": M. F. Murphy, production report, 12/3/38 (USC).

"leading lady": Constance Moore to the author, Westwood, 8/21/97.

382   "overnight he decided": George E. Marshall, "A Director Looks at W. C. Fields," unpublished introduction to *The Films of W. C. Fields,* 1965 (courtesy of Donald Deschner).

"bilking the gilpins": W. C. Fields, "You Can't Cheat an Honest Man," original story, 8/8/38 (WCF).

384   "a form of script": M. F. Murphy, production report, 12/17/38 (USC).

"Bergen is willing": Lester Cowan to Cliff Work, 1/3/39 (WFG).

"most unfunny": WCF to Cliff Work, 8/30/39 (WCF).

"Spanish things": Irene Kahn Atkins, *David Butler* (Metuchen, N.J.: Scarecrow Press/Directors Guild of America, 1993), p. 158.

385   "definite improvement": M. F. Murphy, production report, 1/14/39 (USC).

"dropped in": *New York Times,* 2/5/39.

386   "write dialogue": *Hollywood Reporter,* 12/18/67.

"He told me": James Bacon, *Hollywood Is a Four-Letter Town* (Chicago: Regnery, 1976), p. 7.

"a telegram": David Lipton to Rae Andre Lindquist, UCLA Oral History, 4/16/69 (UCLA).

"meeting with Marshall": M. F. Murphy, production report, 1/21/39 (USC).

"not the buffoon": Lester Cowan to Cliff Work, 1/24/39 (WFG).

388   "I suggest": WCF to Cliff Work, 1/27/39 (WCF).

"beyond the limits": Cliff Work to Lester Cowan, 2/13/39 (WFG).


## Chapter Twenty-four

389   "big romance": *Los Angeles Times,* 5/21/80.

"help people out": "Fields' Little Chickadee."

390   "voice has improved": WCF to Carlotta Monti, 1/11/39 (GH).

"Enjoy": WCF to Carlotta Monti, 1/6/39 (GH).

"quite a fight": WCF to Carlotta Monti, 1/30/39 (GH).

"told the truth": WCF to Maude Fendick, 10/4/38 (WCF).

391   "on the air": WCF to Lester Cowan, 2/8/39 (WCF).

"just thinking": Associated Press wire story, 2/10/39.

392   "jugular vein": Details of the Masquers dinner are from accounts in *Daily Variety,* 2/17/39, *Hollywood Citizen News,* 2/17/39, *Philadelphia Evening Bulletin,* 2/17/39, and *Variety,* 2/22/39.

Memorable: Of all the press coverage accorded the dinner, only one account actually reported the line. Frederick C. Othman, in the *Hollywood Citizen News,* gave the quote as, "Any man who hates babies and dogs can't be all bad." Leo Rosten, in 1977, remembered it as "dogs and babies," and *Bartlett's* preserved it as "children and dogs." Evidently, the line previously appeared in the November 1937 issue of *Harper's* magazine, credited to one Byron Darnton of the *New York Times.* Whether Rosten ever saw this reference and consciously or unconsciously appropriated it is purely a matter of conjecture. For posterity's sake, it certainly fits Fields better than anyone else.

394   "felt very silly": WCF to Maude Fendick, 2/17/39 (WCF).

395   "roaring comedy": *Motion Picture Herald,* 2/18/39.

"singularly ignorant": *New York Times,* 2/20/39.

"All rested": WCF to Lester Cowan, 3/6/39 (WFG).

396   "every week": WCF to Carlotta Monti, 3/23/39 (GH).

"I object": W. C. Fields, "You Can't Say a Damn Thing on the Air," *Look,* 2/14/39.

"abortion": WCF to Carlotta Monti, 4/13/39 (GH). On 10/10/39, Universal reported rentals of $828,410 for *You Can't Cheat an Honest Man,* making it their second-highest-grossing film of the year. (It was bettered by *When Tomorrow Comes,* which starred Irene Dunne and Charles Boyer, but took in slightly more than either of the year's two Deanna Durbin pictures, *Three Smart Girls Grow Up* and *That Certain Age.* Another high-profile production of the new Work regime, *Son of Frankenstein,* did only average business.)

"I recall": WCF to D. W. Griffith, 3/10/39 (WCF).

"busily engaged": WCF to Carlotta Monti, 5/12/39 (GH).

398   "pedestal": George Eells and Stanley Musgrove, *Mae West* (New York: William Morrow, 1982), p. 194.

"My suggestion": W. C. Fields, "December and Mae," 5/1/39 (WCF).

399   "meticulous": Ginger Michael to the author.

"similar": Lester Cowan, Story Conference Notes, 7/10/39 (AMPAS).

"Fields character": Cowan, Conference Notes, 7/17/39.

400   "card-sharper": "The Jayhawkers," a fifty-one-page treatment by Grover Jones, is in the Lester Cowan Collection (AMPAS).

"had the reputation": *Hollywood Citizen News,* 9/24/40.

"routines": WCF to Lester Cowan, undated memo (WCF).

"little too big": Cowan, Conference Notes, 7/27/39.

"encourage": Transcript, phone conversation between Lester Cowan and Mae West, 7/28/39 (WFG).

401   "absurd": WCF to Nate J. Blumberg, 8/21/39 (WFG).

"Mr. Ripley": W. C. Fields, "Corn With the Wind," undated (WCF).

"[Jones'] script": Cowan, Conference Notes, 8/29/39.

402   "The work I'm doing": WCF to Cliff Work, 8/30/39 (WCF).

"I picked Mr. Cline": WCF to Cliff Work, 9/1/39 (WCF).

"understand each other": WCF to Mae West, 9/11/39 (WCF).

403   "friend of mine": WCF to Gene Fowler, undated (TW).

"I withdrew": Gene Fowler to Ben Hecht, undated, Newberry Library, Chicago.

"situation": Lester Cowan to WCF, 9/23/39 (WFG).

"entire experience": WCF to Cliff Work, 9/28/39 (WCF). An undated outline of Mae West's screenplay in the Lester Cowan Collection follows almost exactly the plot of the finished film.

"young friend": WCF to Lester Cowan, 9/29/39 (WFG).

"best judgment": WCF to Matty Fox, 10/12/39 (WCF).

"asked to leave": David Lipton to Rae Andre Lindquist.

## Chapter Twenty-five

405　"Eddie Sutherland": Caplan to Adamson, *W. C. Fields Straight Up.*

"hell of a job": WCF to Matty Fox, 10/12/39 (WCF).

"unique": A. C. Lyles to the author.

"owl": David N. Bruskin, *The White Brothers* (Metuchen, N.J.: Scarecrow Press/Directors Guild of America, 1990), p. 29.

"waste time": WCF to Lester Cowan, 9/29/39 (WCF).

406　"A director": Angelica Huston and Peter Lester, "Mae West," *Interview,* December 1974.

"my very best": Mae West, *Goodness Had Nothing to Do with It* (Englewood Cliffs, N.J.: Prentice-Hall, 1959), p. 202.

407　"two or three frames": WCF to Jack J. Gross, 1/25/40 (WCF).

408　"Mr. Cline laughed": Harry Evans, "Hollywood Diary," *Family Circle,* 3/22/40.

"I watched him work": Robert Bloch, "The Unexplored Fields," *Gent,* February 1962.

"a few times": Evans, "Hollywood Diary."

409　"this unit": M. F. Murphy, production report, 12/2/39 (USC).

"We were determined": Evans, "Hollywood Diary."

"Considering the outlook": M. F. Murphy, production report, 1/6/40 (USC).

410　"screening room": Paul Landres to the author, Studio City, 6/8/97.

"no attempts": WCF to Mae West, 12/11/39 (WCF).

411　"sacrifice": WCF to Joseph I. Breen, 1/22/40 (WCF).

"hate like blazes": Joseph I. Breen to WCF, 1/23/40 (AMPAS).

"audience that laughed": *Motion Picture Herald,* 2/10/40.

412　"Miss West's humor": *New York Times,* 3/16/40.

"one little scene": Richard Meryman, "Mae West," *Life,* 4/18/69.

"his name": *New York Times,* 11/12/39.

"B pictures": Unedited manuscript page for the 1970 edition of *Goodness Had Nothing to Do with It* (AMPAS).

413　"good picture": Scott Eyman, "Mae West," *Take One,* January 1974.

Estate: Universal Pictures, *My Little Chickadee,* Report to October 3, 1987.

"The measure": Associated Press wire story, 12/21/38.

413    "The $12,000": By way of comparison, Fields' subsequent nine-month
        stay at Las Encinas cost $10,052.33.
        "a bore": Quotes from the second trial are from accounts in the *River-
        side Daily Press* and *Riverside Enterprise,* 9/13–26/39.
414    "screw his lawyer": WCF to Carlotta Monti, undated (GH).
        "make up your own mind": WCF to Carlotta Monti, 9/12/39 (GH).
415    "every confidence": WCF to Paul Hesse, 8/30/39 (WCF).
        "no evidence": *New Republic,* 6/24/40.
        "What we need": Fragments of a column, undated (WCF).
417    "superb": Raoul Walsh, *Each Man in His Own Time* (New York: Farrar,
        Straus & Giroux, 1974), p. 304.
        "the carnival": WCF to Magda Michael, undated handwritten letter,
        incomplete photocopy (TW).
        "pompous ass": Ginger McFarlane to the author.
418    "very first": Claude Fields to WCF, 7/19/42 (WCF).
        "These pictures": WCF to Matty Fox, 1/8/40 (WCF).
        "a drunkard": Fields, *The Bank Dick,* 6/12/40.
        "had a hankering": Pressbook, *The Bank Dick,* Universal Pictures,
        1940.
        "I did 'dock' you": WCF to Magda Michael, 4/20/40 (TW).
419    "so banal": WCF to Eddie Cline and Jack Gross, 7/24/40 (WCF).
420    "All the dialogue": WCF to Edward Muhl, 8/5/40 (WCF).
        "I wish": WCF to Elise Cavanna, 8/12/40 (TW).

## Chapter Twenty-six

421    "live up to my contract": WCF to Nate Blumberg, 8/22/40 (WCF).
        "costumes tried on": WCF to Carlotta Monti, 9/7/40 (GH).
        "Universal": WCF to Gene Fowler, 9/16/40 (TW).
422    "throw it": Lowrance, "Bogeyman's Bluff."
        "too long": Leonard Maltin, "FFM Interviews Una Merkel," *Film Fan
        Monthly,* January 1971.
        "Fields and Cline": Ed Montagne to the author.
423    "imagine": "Cline Doubles as Stand-In," unidentified news clipping
        (AMPAS).
        "visit": A. C. Lyles to the author.
        "they wanted someone else": Leonard Maltin, "FFM Interviews Grady
        Sutton," *Film Fan Monthly,* October 1969.
        "At four o'clock": George Turner, "Milton Krasner, A.S.C.," *American
        Cinematographer,* September 1986.
        "finish the picture on Wednesday": WCF to Carlotta Monti, 10/20/40
        (GH).
424    "not one line": WCF to Jack J. Gross, 10/31/40 (WCF).

425    "twenty dollar bill": Preview notes, *The Bank Dick,* 11/4/40 (WCF).

426    "many comedians": Taylor, *W. C. Fields: His Follies and Fortunes,*
         p. 233.

         "picture gets laughs": WCF to Matty Fox, 11/8/40 (WCF).

         "Chaplin's picture": WCF to Gene Fowler, 11/14/40 (TW).

427    "rumors": *Los Angeles Times,* 12/8/40.

         "old-time comedy stride": *Los Angeles Times,* 11/29/40.

428    "No reflection": *New York Times,* 12/13/40.

         "Modern Museum": *Variety,* 12/25/40.

429    "all business": Bob Campbell, "Busy Fowler Pens Tale of Old N.Y.
         Days," *American Booksellers' Association Bulletin,* 8/6/54.

         "I like this place": Thomas Nord Riley, "Bottle Baby," *Motion Picture,*
         May 1944.

430    "any noise": Ginger McFarlane to the author.

431    "restaurant owners": *Los Angeles Times,* 8/26/73.

         "dying to play": "Magnificent Rogue."

         "My father": Gene Fowler Jr. to the author, Los Angeles, 9/10/97.

         "Barrymore was the center": Anthony Quinn to Scott Eyman, via tele-
         phone, 7/31/97 (courtesy of Scott Eyman).

         "Sadakichi Hartmann": Steve Fairfield to the author.

432    "Herr Althouse": WCF to Carlotta Monti, 5/9/39 (GH).

433    "with certain changes": Charles Beyer to Leo Spitz, 2/24/41 (WCF).

434    "utilize the services": Edward Muhl to WCF, 2/21/41 (WCF).

         "nothing in my contract": WCF to Charles Beyer, 2/26/41 (WCF).

         "fits and starts": Prescott Chaplin, "Hand It to Bill Fields, A Killer-
         Diller on Ideas," undated news clipping (AMPAS).

435    "Everything stopped moving": Anthony Quinn (with Daniel Paisner),
         *One Man Tango* (New York: HarperCollins, 1995), p. 152.

         "The worst thing": Quinn to Eyman.

         "quietly shocked": Will Fowler to Joe Adamson, 2/16/85, *W. C. Fields
         Straight Up.*

         "broken up": Eddie Dowling Oral History, Columbia University,
         10/31/63.

## Chapter Twenty-seven

437    "The government": *Los Angeles Herald Express,* 2/19/41.

         "all the shopping": *Los Angeles Times,* 9/16/49.

438    "very sweet": Gene Fowler Jr. to the author.

         "slept over": Ginger McFarlane to the author.

439    "odd way": Chaplin, "Hand It to Bill Fields."

         "vulgar and suggestive": Joseph I. Breen to Maurice Pivar, 4/16/41.

         "over length": Edward Muhl to WCF, 4/23/41 (WCF).

440  "boil down": *Philadelphia Advertiser,* 11/8/41.

"extra nicknacks": WCF to Edward Muhl, 6/3/41 (WCF).

441  "My script": WCF to Nate Blumberg, 7/5/41 (WCF).

"something sad": Gloria Jean Schoonover to the author, Canoga Park, 9/26/97.

442  Variants and ad-libs: The filming of *Never Give a Sucker an Even Break* is documented in the film's continuity records (USC).

443  "proper physical condition": Edward Muhl to WCF, 7/31/41 (WCF).

"receipt": WCF to Edward Muhl, 8/1/41 (WCF).

444  "The wreck": Frederick C. Othman, "Fields Continues Long Feud with Eddie Cline," *Long Beach Sun,* 8/16/41.

"Fields' entrance": WCF to Edward Muhl, 9/4/41 (WCF).

446  "In the restaurant": WCF to Edward Muhl, 9/18/41 (WCF).

Trying to fix the film: After the studio returned *Never Give a Sucker an Even Break* to its original shape, the Mayfair comedy *Hellzapoppin'* was given the same film-within-a-film structure. Ten days of additional scenes were directed by Eddie Cline, and Shemp Howard, Jody Gilbert, and Hugh Herbert were added to the cast. Long unseen due to rights problems, *Hellzapoppin'* expanded on Fields' original concept, with actors on the screen talking back to the projectionist in the booth. Its influence can be seen in a number of later comedies, most notably in Mel Brooks' *Blazing Saddles* (1974).

447  "The exhibitors": *Variety,* 8/27/41.

"silly-dilly": *Daily Variety,* 10/6/41.

"Fields at his best": *Motion Picture Daily,* 10/7/41.

"the parade": *Hollywood Reporter,* 10/6/41.

"First": WCF to W. R. Wilkerson, 10/7/41 (WCF).

448  "He was cranky": Edward Muhl to the author.

"Dell": WCF to Carlotta Monti, 11/41 (GH).

"Squinting": *New York Times,* 10/27/41.

"beautifully-timed": *Time,* 11/24/41.

449  "tide of change": *New Republic,* 11/10/41.

First player: Production files and script materials for *Tales of Manhattan* are contained in the Twentieth Century–Fox Collection at the Theatre Arts Library, USC, Los Angeles.

451  "time together": Hal Kanter to the author.

"can't imagine": Gloria Jean Schoonover to the author.

Surviving outtakes: Outtakes from Fields' *Tales of Manhattan* sequence, along with an expanded cut of the footage, is contained in Van Ness Films' *Hidden Hollywood III* (2001).

"very disciplined": Gene Fowler Jr. to the author.

452  "never laughed": John Chapman, "W. C. Fields Gives Rules for Love," *Philadelphia Evening Bulletin,* 2/5/42.

"very difficult bit": Phil Silvers, *This Laugh Is On Me* (Englewood Cliffs, N.J.: Prentice-Hall, 1973), p. 116.

453  "every major actor": Spec McClure to Gene Fowler.

"stole the show": *Hollywood Reporter,* 5/8/42.

454  "insisted upon $50,000": *Daily Variety,* 4/6/42.

"long silence": WCF to Elise Cavanna, 4/7/42 (TW).

455  "Fidler": WCF to Gene Fowler, 4/14/42 (TW).

"a creation": Charles Beyer to Darryl F. Zanuck, 4/16/42 (WCF).

Enthusiastically received: Financial data on *Tales of Manhattan* is from the research library of Karl Thiede.

## Chapter Twenty-eight

457  "the bond": Harriet A. Fields to the author, 2/25/2001.

458  "all criticism": W. C. Fields, handwritten notes for *Good Night, Sweet Prince* (GF).

459  "the original": Gene Fowler, transcript of taped notes recorded for *Minutes of the Last Meeting,* 8/4/52 (GF).

461  "As we came in": Fowler transcript, 8/7/52 (GF). See also *Los Angeles Examiner,* 4/26/42.

"Pickwick": Letter, quoted in Fields, *W. C. Fields by Himself,* p. 424.

"drinking": WCF to Dan Thomas, 6/27/40 (WCF).

462  "he drank": Bloch, "The Unexplored Fields."

"have a meeting": Bergen to Schaden.

463  "take my pills": Dr. Raymond Stevens to the author, via telephone, 2/10/99.

"hates everyone": Gene Fowler to Ben Hecht, 4/14/43.

"falling down": Ginger McFarlane to the author.

"old-fashioned": WCF to Fred Allen, 11/3/43 (WCF).

464  "slowly but consistently": WCF to Walter Fields, 9/29/43 (WCF).

465  "rehearsed it": Sutherland Oral History.

"wooden door": *New York Herald-Tribune,* 1/24/44.

466  1943 edition: WCF to Maude Fendick, 12/6/43 (WCF).

"I have slipped": WCF to Magda Michael, undated (MM).

"I wish": Jane Powell to Scott Eyman, via telephone, 5/17/00 (courtesy of Scott Eyman).

467  "little bottles": Louise Currie to the author, via telephone, 10/15/97.

"It was so bad": Andrew L. Stone to Anthony Slide, 7/5/95 (courtesy of Anthony Slide).

"willing to cooperate": WCF to Andrew L. Stone, undated letter in the Andrew L. Stone Collection, USC.

469  "looking worn": *Time,* 4/24/44.

469    "The producers": WCF to Adele C. Smith, 7/10/44 (WCF).

"I didn't type": Ginger McFarlane to the author.

"Harriet and Claude": WCF to Magda Michael, undated (MM).

"Santa Barbara thrush": WCF to Magda Michael, 4/23/44 (MM).

470    "Hattie [and] Claude": *Ibid.*

"They would take him": Transcript, "In the Matter of William C. Fields, Deceased," 9/16/49.

"He would do anything": Michael, undated manuscript, p. 85 (MM).

471    "I have been trying": Taylor, *W. C. Fields: His Follies and Fortunes,* p. 334.

"always had a fondness": Handwritten page, undated (MM).

473    "Fields was seated": Artie Shaw to the author, via telephone, 11/9/98.

"dog needs a good home": *Newsweek,* 11/5/45.

"How do they know": Michael, undated manuscript, p. 12 (MM).

474    "Claude can probably contribute": WCF to Hattie Fields, 12/12/45 (WCF).

"having problems": Jack Harris to the author, 2/9/2000.

"I urged him": Magda Michael, handwritten note, undated (MM).

475    "like to drink": Eddie Sutherland to the author, 1971.

"Almost every time": *Los Angeles Times,* 8/13/52.

"nerve-wracking": WCF to Carlotta Monti, 6/9/46 (WCF).

"He's very ill": Les Paul to the author, via telephone, 1/29/98.

478    "think it strange": WCF to Fay Adler, 11/14/46 (MM).

Crosby's Christmas show: Details of Fields' planned appearances on *Philco Radio Time* are from *Hollywood Reporter,* 12/6, 12/9, 12/18/46, and *Daily Variety,* 12/27/46.

"pathetic sight": Michael, undated manuscript, p. 74 (MM).

"My outside men": Carlotta Monti to WCF, 12/21/46 (WCF).

"I've often wondered": Eddie Cantor, *As I Remember Them* (New York: Duell, Sloan and Pearce, 1963), p. 32. In 1971, Eddie Sutherland told me that Fields had said the same thing to him.

## Chapter Twenty-nine

480    "Dave and I": Grady, *The Irish Peacock,* p. 41.

"did not strike": *Los Angeles Herald-Express,* 5/13/49.

"You should love me": *Los Angeles Times,* 5/13/49.

481    "feel terrible": *Los Angeles Times,* 12/26/46.

"inexpensive coffin": Last Will and Testament of William C. Fields, 4/28/43 (WCF).

482    "Let his faults": Edgar Bergen's remarks are reconstructed from accounts of the funeral in the *Los Angeles Times, Hollywood Citizen News, Los Angeles Herald-Express,* and the Pueblo (Colorado) *Chieftain.*

483    "not intruding": *Los Angeles Herald-Express,* 1/4/47.

      "debated with himself": *Los Angeles Times,* 5/13/49.

484    "under duress": *Los Angeles Sentinel,* 12/12/40.

      "discriminate against us": Michael, undated manuscript, p. 91.

      "gave the Indians": Gene Fowler, *Minutes of the Last Meeting* (New York: Viking Press, 1954), p. 104 (MM).

485    "days and hours": Gene Fowler to Will Fowler, 1/8/47 (TW).

      "on the stand": *Los Angeles Herald-Express,* 5/13/49.

487    "never write": Gene Fowler Jr. to the author.

488    "Bill often said": *Los Angeles Times,* 5/2/54.

      "in his lifetime": *Los Angeles Times,* 12/15/49.

      "Three sets of lawyers": WCF to Magda Michael, 4/23/44.

490    "Hattie would trip": Harriet A. Fields to the author, via e-mail, 2/24/2001.

      "A son emerges": Emmet Lavery, *The World's My Oyster,* proposal for a screen treatment, 8/7/61 (EL).

      "the scrapbooks": Everett F. Fields to the author, Los Angeles, 4/3/98.

492    Epitaph: The famous epitaph, often misquoted, first appeared in *Vanity Fair* in October 1924. In full, it reads:

HERE LIES

W. C. FIELDS

I WOULD RATHER BE LIVING

IN PHILADELPHIA

# Selected Bibliography

## Books and Pamphlets

Anobile, Richard J. (ed.) *Drat!* New York: World Publishing, 1968.

———, (ed.). *A Flask of Fields.* New York: W. W. Norton, 1972.

———, (ed.). *Godfrey Daniels!* [sic]. New York: Crown Publishers, 1975.

Deschner, Donald. *The Films of W. C. Fields.* New York: Citadel Press, 1966.

Everson, William K. *The Art of W. C. Fields.* Indianapolis: Bobbs-Merrill, 1967.

Fields, Ronald J. *W. C. Fields: A Life on Film.* New York: St. Martin's Press, 1984.

———, (ed.). *W. C. Fields by Himself.* Englewood Cliffs, N.J.: Prentice-Hall, 1973.

———, (with Shaun O. L. Higgins). *Never Give a Sucker an Even Break: W. C. Fields on Business.* Paramus, N.J.: Prentice-Hall, 2000.

Fields, W. C. (with Charles Grayson). *The Bank Dick.* New York: Simon and Schuster, 1973. (The August 22, 1940, screenplay.)

———. *Fields' Day.* Kansas City, Missouri: Hallmark Attic Press, 1972.

———. *Fields for President.* New York: Dodd, Mead & Co., 1940.

——— (as Otis Criblecoblis) (with John T. Neville and Prescott Chaplin). *Never Give a Sucker an Even Break.* (Rupert Hughes, Francis Martin, and Walter DeLeon.) *Tillie and Gus.* New York: Simon and Schuster, 1973. (Continuity scripts derived from these two films.)

———. *W. C. Fields Speaks.* Los Angeles: Price/Stern/Sloan, 1981.

Fields, W. Claude Jr. *A Tribute to W. C. Fields.* New York: Gallery of Modern Art, 1967.

Finke, Blythe Foote. *W. C. Fields, Renowned Comedian of the Early Motion Picture Industry.* New York: SamHar Press, 1972.

Fitzgerald, Ed (ed.). *Tales for Males.* New York: Cadillac Publishing, 1945. (Reprints "My Views on Marriage.")

Fowler, Gene. *Minutes of the Last Meeting.* New York: Viking Press, 1954.

Fowler, Will. *The Second Handshake.* New York: Lyle Stuart, 1980.

Garver, Jack, and Dave Stanley. *There's Laughter in the Air.* New York: Greenberg, 1945. (The script for Fields' March 26, 1944, appearance on *The Charlie McCarthy Show,* pp. 77–9.)

Gardner, Gerald (ed.). *The Censorship Papers.* New York: Dodd, Mead & Co., 1987. (Excerpts from Breen Office memos regarding *The Bank Dick* and *Never Give a Sucker an Even Break,* pp. 133–8.)

Gehring, Wes D. *Groucho and W. C. Fields: Huckster Comedians.* Jackson: University Press of Mississippi, 1994.

———. *W. C. Fields: A Bio-Bibliography.* Westport: Greenwood Press, 1984.

Harlan, Kenneth, and Rex Lease. *What Actors Eat When They Eat.* Los Angeles: Lymanhouse, 1939. (Fields contributes Brandied Peaches and Omelet Au Rum to this collection of celebrity recipes.)

Kaminsky, Stuart. *A Fatal Glass of Beer.* New York: Mysterious Press, 1997. (A Toby Peters Mystery in which Fields retains the detective to recover some stolen bank books.)

Levis, Marjorie Rice. *Blackouts.* New York: Samuel French, 1932. ("All Aboard," performed by Fields and Dorothy Knapp in the *Earl Carroll Vanities,* pp. 49–55.)

Lewis, Martin (ed.). *The Quotations of W. C. Fields.* New York: Drake Publishers, 1976.

Louvish, Simon. *It's a Gift.* London: British Film Institute, 1994.

———. *Man on the Flying Trapeze: The Life and Times of W. C. Fields.* London: Faber and Faber, 1997.

Mason, Paul (ed.). *I Never Met a Kid I Liked.* Los Angeles: Stanyan Books, 1970.

———, (ed.). *Never Trust a Man Who Doesn't Drink.* Los Angeles: Stanyan Books, 1971.

Monti, Carlotta (with Cy Rice). *W. C. Fields and Me.* Englewood Cliffs, N.J.: Prentice-Hall, 1971.

Mora, Jo (ill.). *Hotel Del Monte Cocktail Book.* Monterey: Del Monte Properties Co., 1933. (Fields contributes Juggler's Scaffa to this collection of
celebrity cocktail recipes.)

Pearson, Bill. *The W. C. Fields Book.* New York: Wonderful Publishing Co.,
1973.

Rocks, David T. *W. C. Fields—An Annotated Guide.* Jefferson, N.C.: McFar-
land & Co., 1993.

Rowland, Mabel. *Bert Williams: Son of Laughter.* New York: The English
Crafters, 1923. (Fields contributes a remembrance of Bert Williams.)

Scully, Frank (ed.). *Bedside Manna.* New York: Simon and Schuster, 1936.
(Fields contributes "The Art of Breaking a Neck.")

Selbit [Percy T. Tibbles]. *The Magician's Handbook.* London: Dawbarn &
Ward, Ltd., 1901. (Fields contributes "A New Hat and Cigar Effect" and
"The Great Cigar Box Trick" to this "encyclopedia of the magic art.")

Smart, James. *W. C. Fields in Philadelphia.* Philadelphia: The Shackamaxon
Society, 1972.

Taylor, Robert Lewis. *W. C. Fields: His Follies and Fortunes.* Garden City,
N.Y.: Doubleday, 1949.

Volland, Gordon (ed.). *Bottoms Up.* Minneapolis: The Buzza Company, 1928.
(Fields contributes the Clover Club Cocktail to this collection of celebrity
drink recipes.)

Weber, Joan. *Tillie's Punctured Romance.* New York: Jacobsen-Hodgkinson,
1928. (A novelization of the otherwise lost film.)

Yanni, Nicholas. *W. C. Fields.* New York: Pyramid, 1974.

# Periodicals

Beaudine, William. "Just a Lovable Old So-and-So." *Film Weekly,* 12/7/34.
(Beaudine's account of directing Fields in *The Old Fashioned Way.*)

Bloch, Robert. "The Unexplored Fields." *Gent,* February 1962. (Good interview with Dick Foran.)

Borton, Elizabeth. "I Take a Juggling Lesson from W. C. Fields." *Hollywood,*
September 1935. (One of the rare instances in which Fields talked about
juggling.)

Brooks, Louise. "The Other Face of W. C. Fields." *Sight and Sound,* Spring
1971. (Original publication of Brooks' memoir of Fields.)

Cain, James M. "The Gentle Side of W. C. Fields." *Washington Post,* 9/26/76.

Carle, Teet. "The Man Who Was Fascinated by Names." *Hollywood Studio Magazine,* February 1972. (Publicist Teet Carle's memoir of working with Fields.)

Chapman, John. "The Beloved Mountebank." *New York News,* 10/16 and 10/23/38. (A remarkably accurate and detailed interview.)

Evans, Harry. "Hollywood Diary." *Family Circle,* 3/22/40. (Excellent on-the-set account of the filming of *My Little Chickadee.*)

Fields, W. C. "Alcohol and Me." *Pic,* 10/13/42.

———. "Anything for a Laugh." *American Magazine,* September 1934.

——— (with Irving Wallace). "Can-You-Keep-a-Straight-Face Quiz." *Liberty,* 11/29/41.

———. "The Care of Babies." *This Week,* 2/18/40. (Reprinted in *Fields for President.*)

———. "Danger . . . The Great Man is at Work." *Look,* 12/3/40.

———. "Down Memory Lane." 1936.

———. "From Boy Juggler to Star Comedian." *Theatre,* October 1928. (Important autobiographical essay.)

———. "The Good Old Days of Vaudeville." *Coronet,* December 1943.

———. "Here's How to Make Movies." *Screen and Radio Weekly,* 7/22/34.

———. "How to Figure Your Income Tax." *This Week,* 3/10/40. (Reprinted in *Fields for President.*)

———. "How to Make New Year's Resolutions." *This Week,* 12/31/41.

———. "It's a Class Theatre." *Variety,* 12/20/12.

———. "Life Begins at Twenty." *Motion Picture,* 10/26/35.

———. "Little Censor Annie." *Ballyhoo,* October 1934. (Poem in praise of Mae West.)

———. "My Rules of Etiquette." *This Week,* 12/4/38. (Reprinted in *Fields for President.*)

———. "My Views on Marriage." *This Week,* 10/15/39. (Reprinted in *Fields for President.*)

———. "Now I'm a Gentleman Farmer." *Hollywood Reporter,* 12/31/34.

———— (with Jim Tully). "Over a Barrel." *Esquire,* October 1934.

————. "Silent Juggling." *Sunday Chronicle Pantomine Annual,* 1913–14.

————. "Speaking of Benefits." *New York Times,* 11/25/23.

————. "Teetotalling—The National Bottleneck." *1000 Jokes,* October-December 1946.

————. "This Radio Gadget." *Radio Guide,* 11/6/37.

————. "The Trouble with Women Is." *Cosmopolitan,* August 1942.

————. "Traveling in Foreign Lands." *New York Masonic Outlook,* July 1932.

————. "You Can't Say a Damn Thing on the Air." *Look,* 2/14/39.

Fowler, Gene. "The Man Who Hated Christmas." *Chicago Sunday Tribune,* 12/4/49.

Janis, Elsie. "I Was That Way About W. C. Fields." *New Movie,* January 1935.

Johnston, Alva. "Legitimate Nonchalance." *New Yorker,* 2/2, 2/9, and 2/16/35. (Fields considered this three-part biography "the best and more authentic.")

————. "Local Man." *New Yorker,* 1/25/47.

————. "Who Knows What Is Funny?" *Saturday Evening Post,* 8/6/38.

MacArthur, Mildred. "Watch Out for My Putter, Chickadee, or I'll Bury Your Head in a Sandtrap." *Los Angeles,* April 1975. (MacArthur was the widow of Arthur MacArthur, who was the partner of agent Charles Beyer.)

McEvoy, J. P. "W. C. Fields' Best Friend." *This Week,* 7/26/42. (A disappointing profile from the author of *The Comic Supplement.*)

Prelutsky, Bert. "Woody and the Chinaman." *West,* 5/26/68. (A major profile of Carlotta Monti.)

Redway, Sara. "W. C. Fields Pleads for Rough Humor." *Motion Picture Classic,* September 1925. (Fields' first fan magazine profile.)

Smart, James. "The Difficulty of Being Leroy Dukenfield." *Sunday Bulletin Magazine,* 3/23/69. (An interview with Fields' youngest sibling.)

Sutherland, Edward (with Scoop Conlon). "W. C. Fields Laughed at Death." *Hollywood,* August 1936. (Sutherland's account of directing Fields in *Poppy.*)

Tully, Jim. "Clowns Never Laugh." *This Week,* 9/6/36.

————. "The Clown Who Juggled Apples." *Photoplay,* January 1934.

————. "Let's Laugh at Life with W. C. Fields." *Screen Play,* June 1935.

Zeitlin, Ida. "Life Begins Again at Fifty." *Screenland,* April 1935.

———. "W. C. Fields' Real Life Story." *Screenland,* June, July, and August 1935. (An interesting three-part biography, though not as important as Johnston.)

# Recordings

*W. C. Fields Famous Lectures*
Studio recordings of "The Day I Drank a Glass of Water" and "Temperance Lecture" in an album of three disks. Written and directed by Bill Morrow. Produced by V. Victor Petitto. Released by Variety Records, January 1947.

# *Index*

Page numbers in *italics* refer to illustrations.

## A Note on the Type

The text of this book was set in a typeface called Times New Roman, designed by Stanley Morison for *The Times* (London), and introduced by that newspaper in 1932.

Among typographers and designers of the twentieth century, Stanley Morison was a strong forming influence, as typographical adviser to the Monotype Corporation of London, as a director of two distinguished English publishing houses, and as a writer of sensibility, erudition, and keen practical sense.

In 1930 Morison wrote: "Type design moves at the pace of the most conservative reader. The good type-designer therefore realizes that, for a new font to be successful, it has to be so good that only very few recognize its novelty. If readers do not notice the consummate reticence and rare discipline of a new type, it is probably a good letter." It is now generally recognized that in the creation of Times Roman, Morison successfully met the qualifications of his theoretical doctrine.

*Composed by North Market Street Graphics*
*Lancaster, Pennsylvania*
*Printed by Berryville Graphics*
*Berryville, Virginia*
*Designed by Johanna S. Roebas*